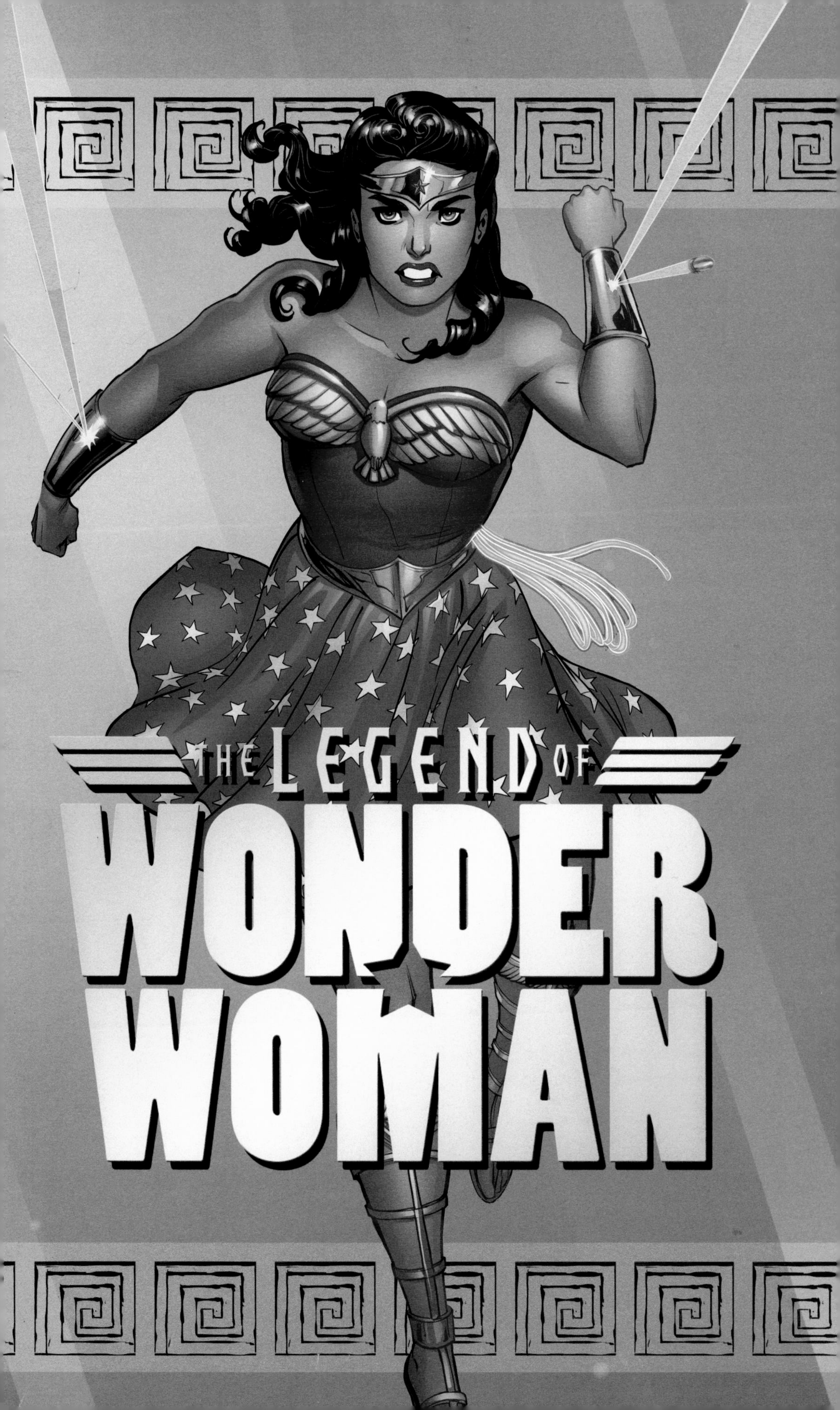
THE LEGEND OF
WONDER WOMAN

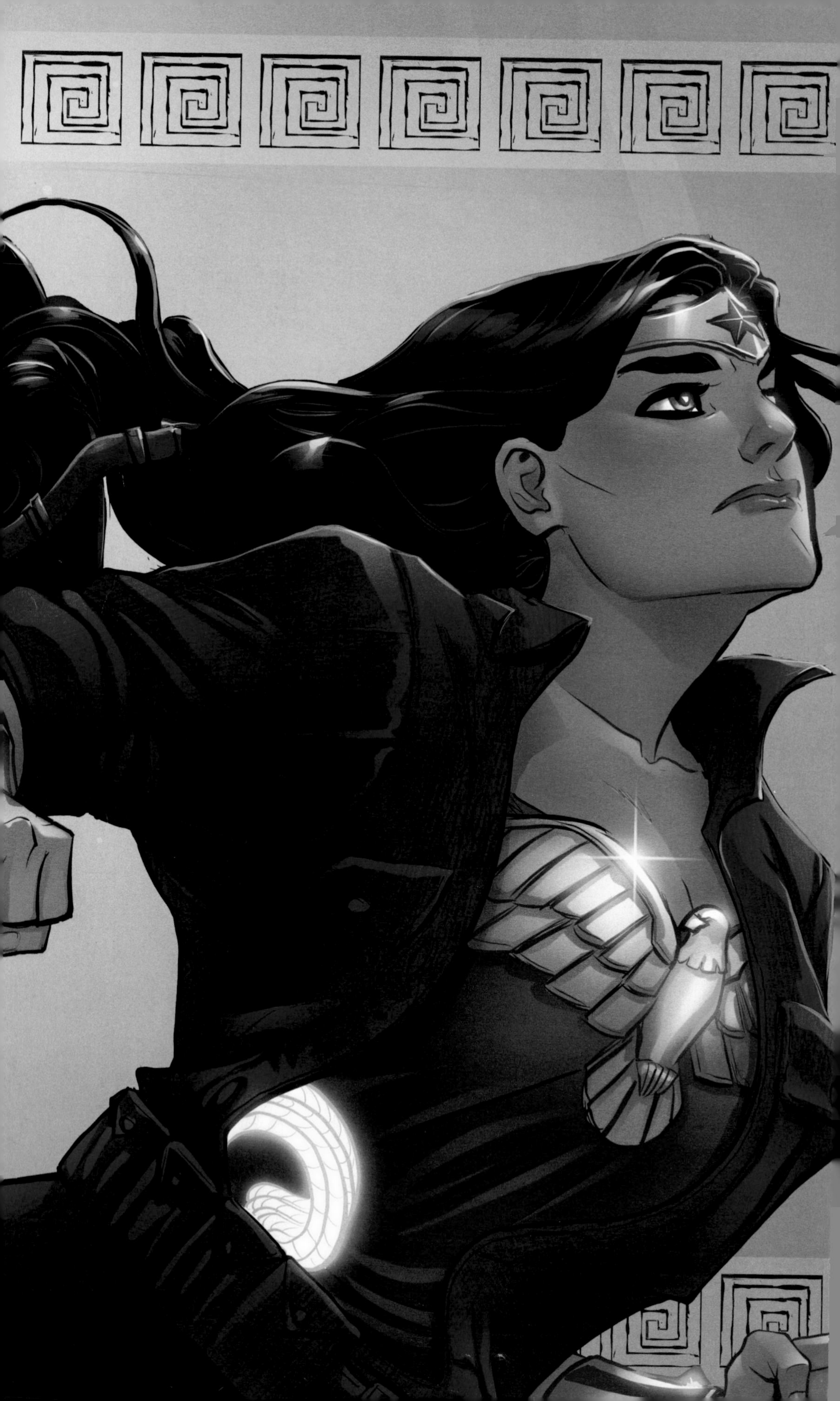

THE LEGEND OF WONDER WOMAN

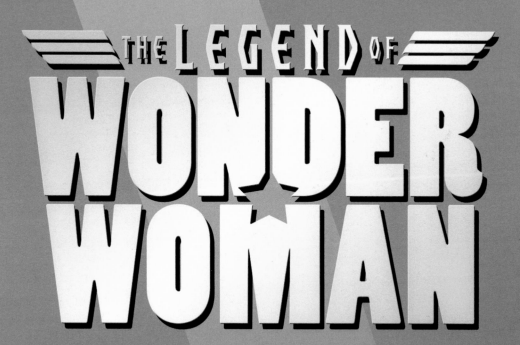

Story and Pencils by
RENAE DE LIZ

Inks, Colors and Letters by
RAY DILLON

WONDER WOMAN
created by
WILLIAM MOULTON MARSTON

KRISTY QUINN Editor – Original Series **JESSICA CHEN** Associate Editor – Original Series
JEB WOODARD Group Editor – Collected Editions **LIZ ERICKSON** Editor – Collected Edition
STEVE COOK Design Director – Books **SARABETH KETT** Publication Design

BOB HARRAS Senior VP – Editor-in-Chief, DC Comics

DIANE NELSON President **DAN DiDIO** Publisher **JIM LEE** Publisher **GEOFF JOHNS** President & Chief Creative Officer
AMIT DESAI Executive VP – Business & Marketing Strategy, Direct to Consumer & Global Franchise Management
SAM ADES Senior VP – Direct to Consumer **BOBBIE CHASE** VP – Talent Development
MARK CHIARELLO Senior VP – Art, Design & Collected Editions **JOHN CUNNINGHAM** Senior VP – Sales & Trade Marketing
ANNE DePIES Senior VP – Business Strategy, Finance & Administration **DON FALLETTI** VP – Manufacturing Operations
LAWRENCE GANEM VP – Editorial Administration & Talent Relations **ALISON GILL** Senior VP – Manufacturing & Operations
HANK KANALZ Senior VP – Editorial Strategy & Administration **JAY KOGAN** VP – Legal Affairs
THOMAS LOFTUS VP – Business Affairs **JACK MAHAN** VP – Business Affairs
NICK J. NAPOLITANO VP – Manufacturing Administration **EDDIE SCANNELL** VP – Consumer Marketing
COURTNEY SIMMONS Senior VP – Publicity & Communications
JIM (SKI) SOKOLOWSKI VP – Comic Book Specialty Sales & Trade Marketing
NANCY SPEARS VP – Mass, Book, Digital Sales & Trade Marketing

THE LEGEND OF WONDER WOMAN VOL. 1: ORIGINS

DC Comics, 2900 West Alameda Ave., Burbank, CA 91505
Printed by LSC Communications, Salem, VA, USA. 11/4/16. First Printing.
ISBN: 978-1-4012-6728-5
Library of Congress Cataloging-in-Publication Data is available.

PEFC Certified
Printed on paper from sustainably managed forests, controlled sources
PEFC
PEFC/29-31-337
www.pefc.org

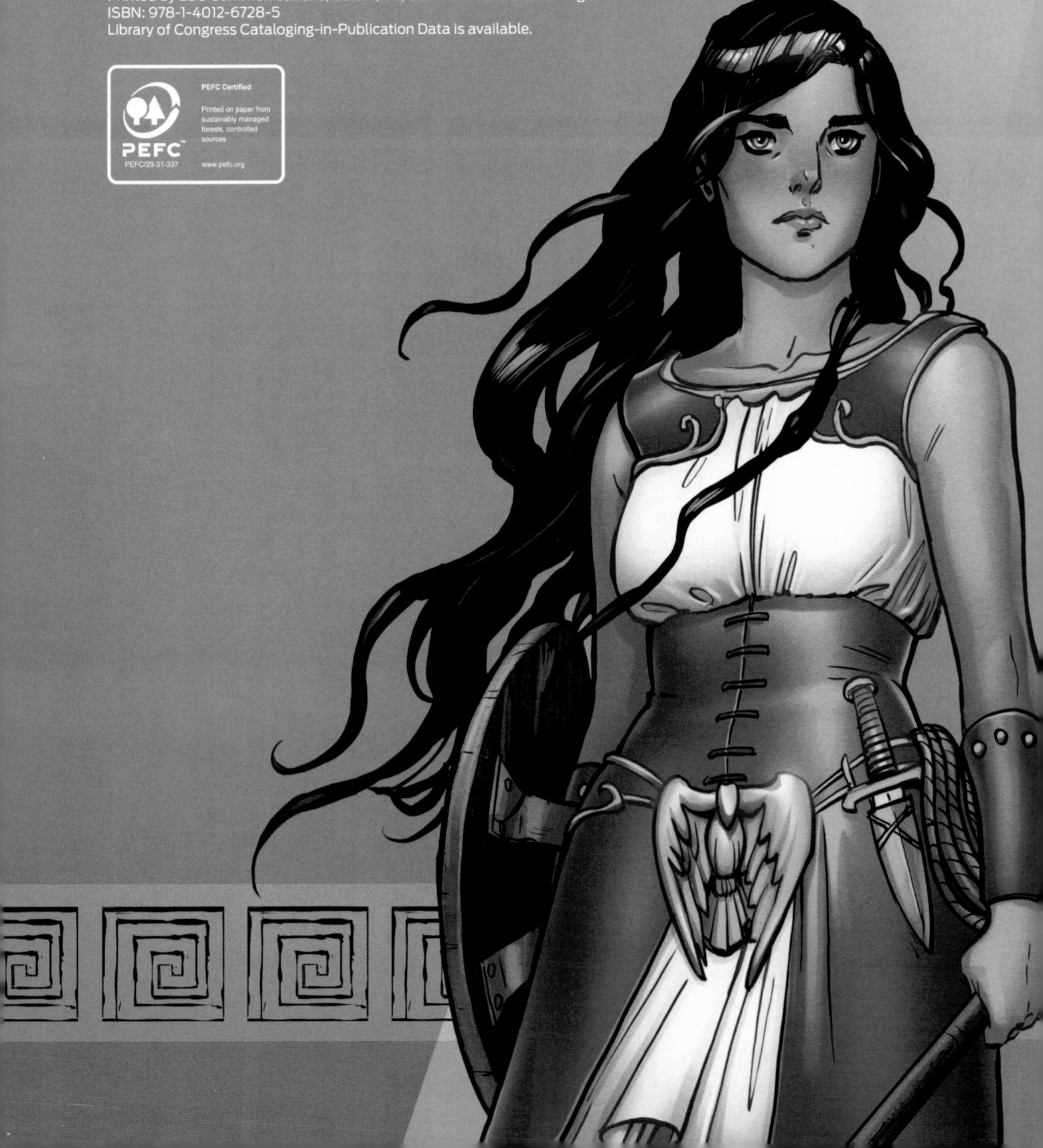

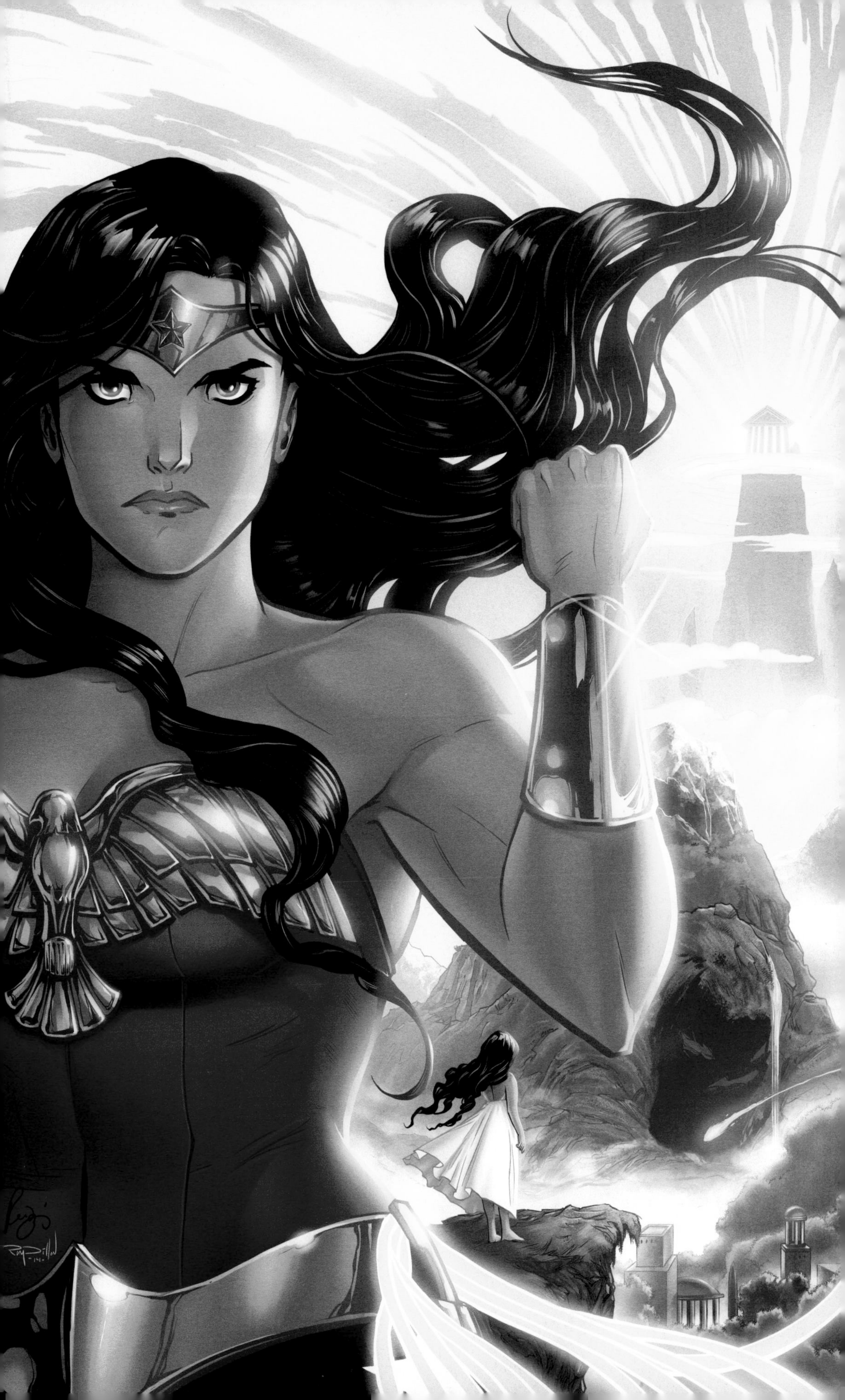

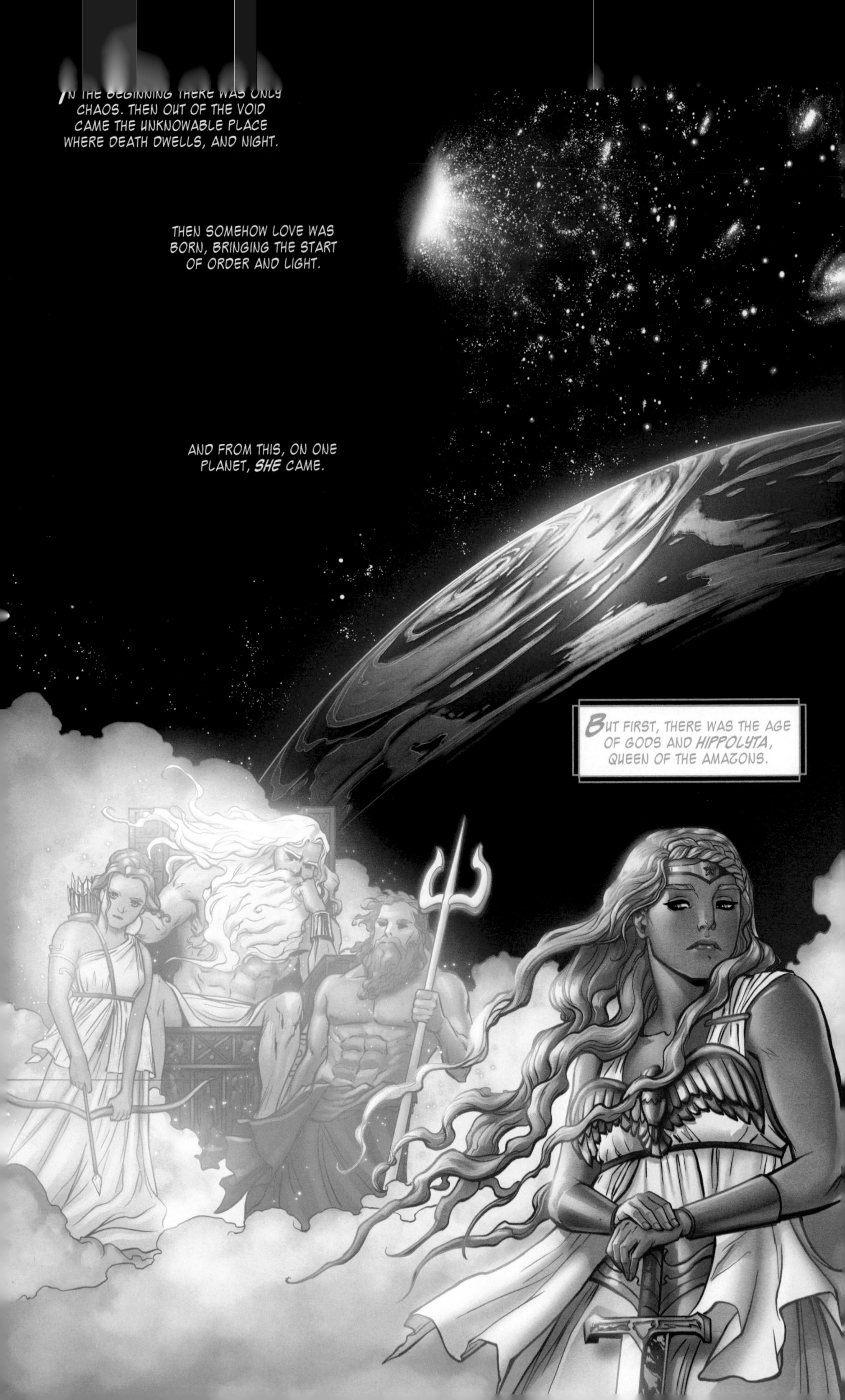
IN THE BEGINNING THERE WAS ONLY CHAOS. THEN OUT OF THE VOID CAME THE UNKNOWABLE PLACE WHERE DEATH DWELLS, AND NIGHT.
THEN SOMEHOW LOVE WAS BORN, BRINGING THE START OF ORDER AND LIGHT.
AND FROM THIS, ON ONE PLANET, SHE CAME.
BUT FIRST, THERE WAS THE AGE OF GODS AND HIPPOLYTA, QUEEN OF THE AMAZONS.

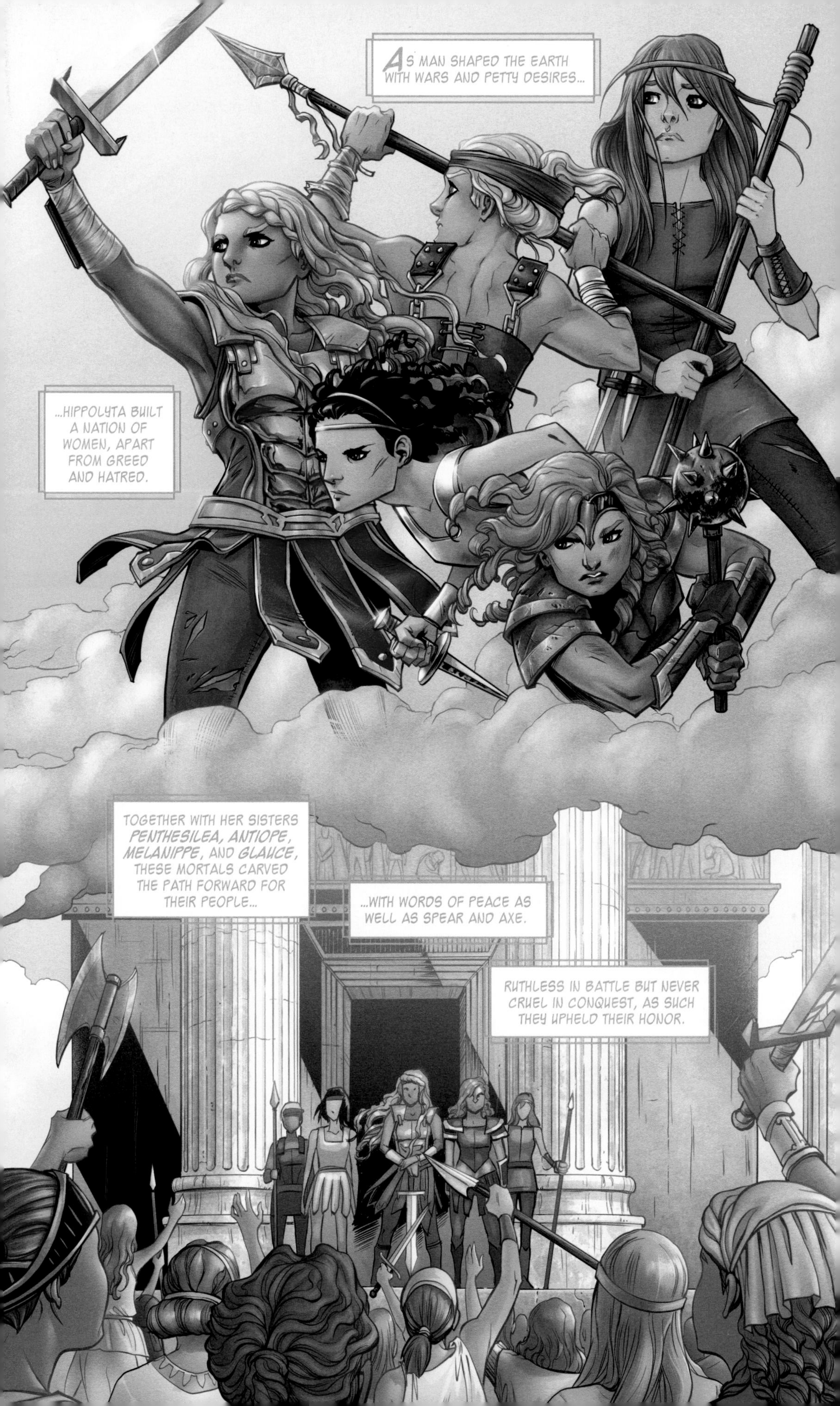
AS MAN SHAPED THE EARTH WITH WARS AND PETTY DESIRES...
...HIPPOLYTA BUILT A NATION OF WOMEN, APART FROM GREED AND HATRED.
TOGETHER WITH HER SISTERS PENTHESILEA, ANTIOPE, MELANIPPE, AND GLAUCE, THESE MORTALS CARVED THE PATH FORWARD FOR THEIR PEOPLE...
...WITH WORDS OF PEACE AS WELL AS SPEAR AND AXE.
RUTHLESS IN BATTLE BUT NEVER CRUEL IN CONQUEST, AS SUCH THEY UPHELD THEIR HONOR.

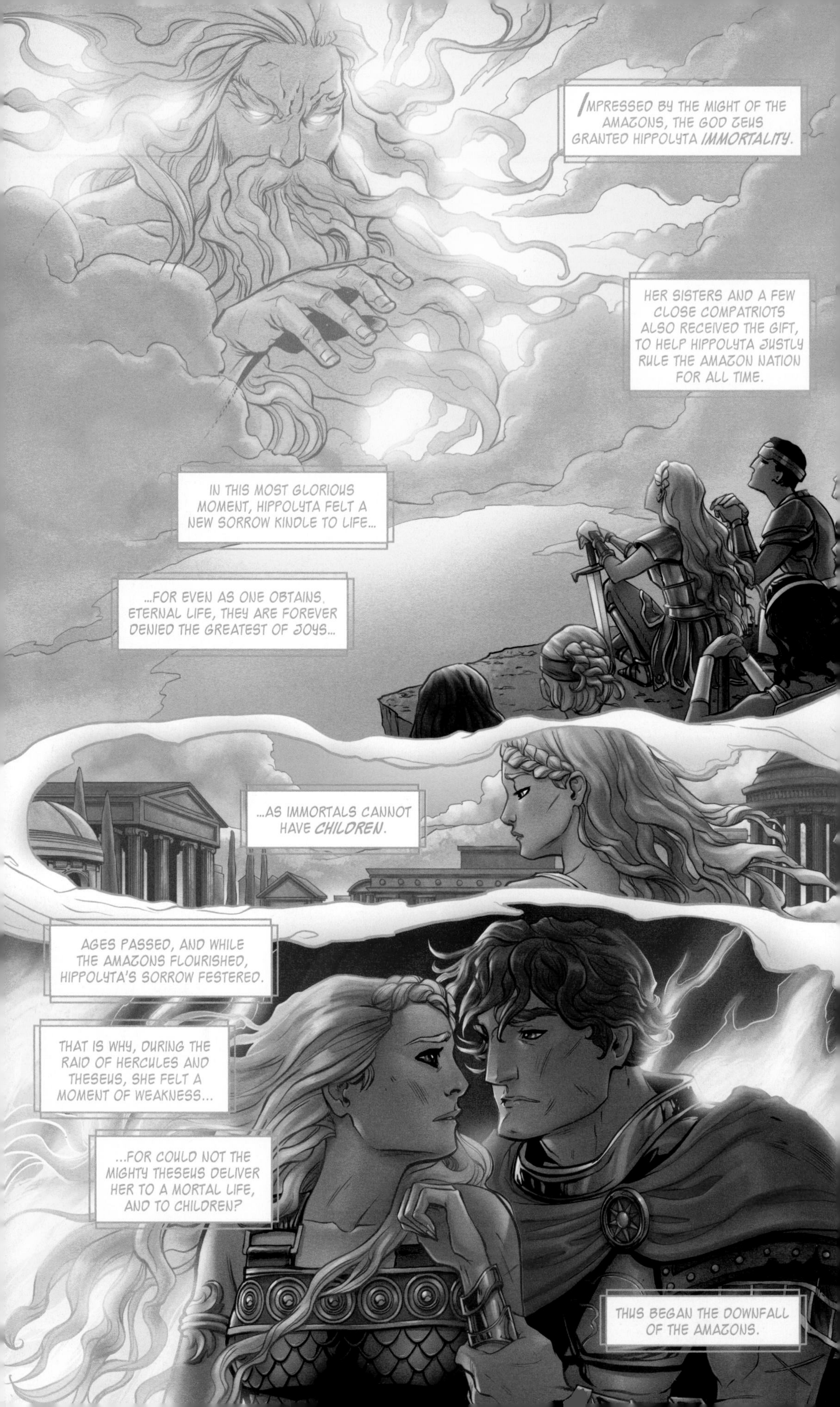
IMPRESSED BY THE MIGHT OF THE AMAZONS, THE GOD ZEUS GRANTED HIPPOLYTA *IMMORTALITY*.
HER SISTERS AND A FEW CLOSE COMPATRIOTS ALSO RECEIVED THE GIFT, TO HELP HIPPOLYTA JUSTLY RULE THE AMAZON NATION FOR ALL TIME.
IN THIS MOST GLORIOUS MOMENT, HIPPOLYTA FELT A NEW SORROW KINDLE TO LIFE...
...FOR EVEN AS ONE OBTAINS ETERNAL LIFE, THEY ARE FOREVER DENIED THE GREATEST OF JOYS...
...AS IMMORTALS CANNOT HAVE *CHILDREN*.
AGES PASSED, AND WHILE THE AMAZONS FLOURISHED, HIPPOLYTA'S SORROW FESTERED.
THAT IS WHY, DURING THE RAID OF HERCULES AND THESEUS, SHE FELT A MOMENT OF WEAKNESS...
...FOR COULD NOT THE MIGHTY THESEUS DELIVER HER TO A MORTAL LIFE, AND TO CHILDREN?
THUS BEGAN THE DOWNFALL OF THE AMAZONS.

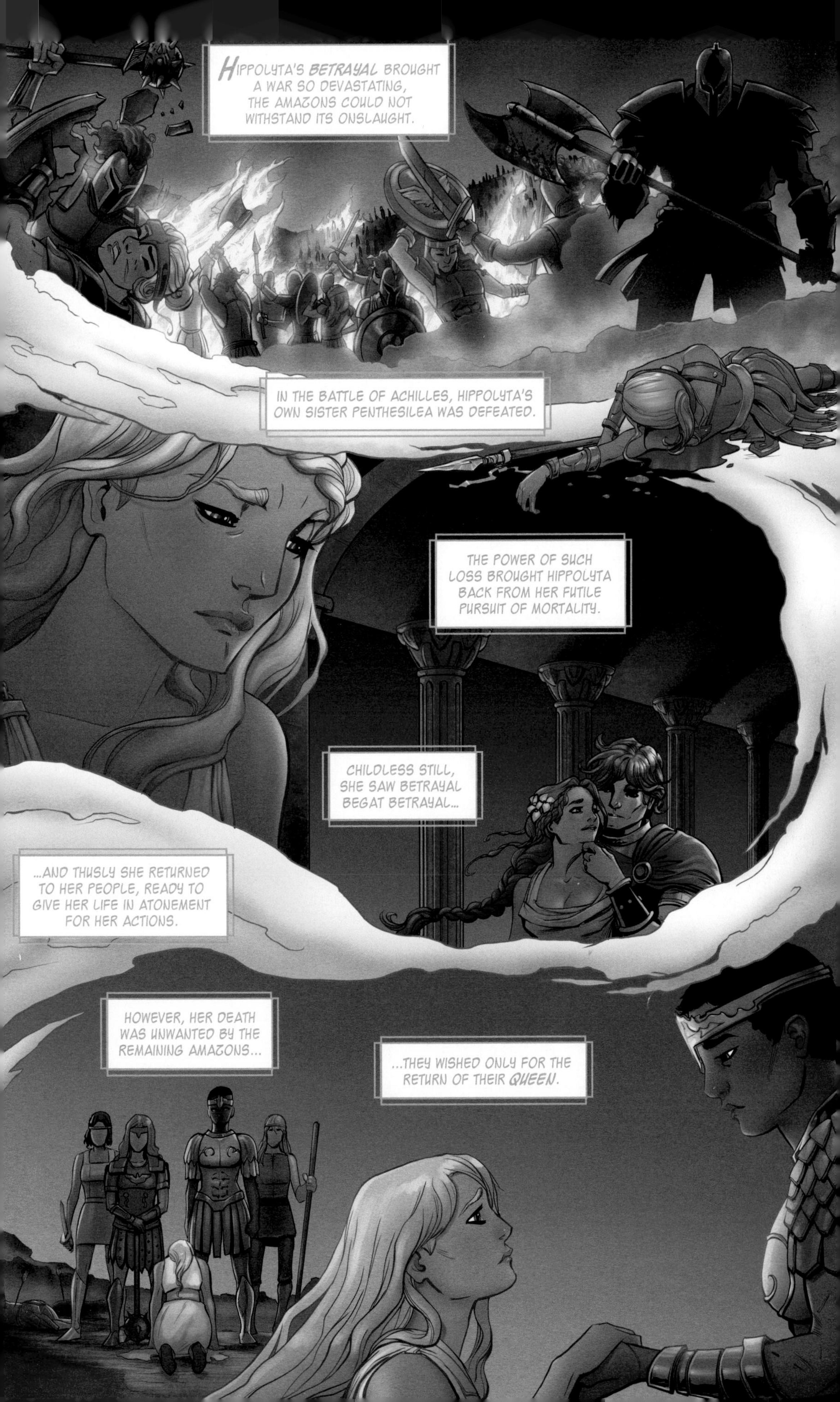
HIPPOLYTA'S BETRAYAL BROUGHT A WAR SO DEVASTATING, THE AMAZONS COULD NOT WITHSTAND ITS ONSLAUGHT.
IN THE BATTLE OF ACHILLES, HIPPOLYTA'S OWN SISTER PENTHESILEA WAS DEFEATED.
THE POWER OF SUCH LOSS BROUGHT HIPPOLYTA BACK FROM HER FUTILE PURSUIT OF MORTALITY.
CHILDLESS STILL, SHE SAW BETRAYAL BEGAT BETRAYAL...
...AND THUSLY SHE RETURNED TO HER PEOPLE, READY TO GIVE HER LIFE IN ATONEMENT FOR HER ACTIONS.
HOWEVER, HER DEATH WAS UNWANTED BY THE REMAINING AMAZONS...
...THEY WISHED ONLY FOR THE RETURN OF THEIR QUEEN.

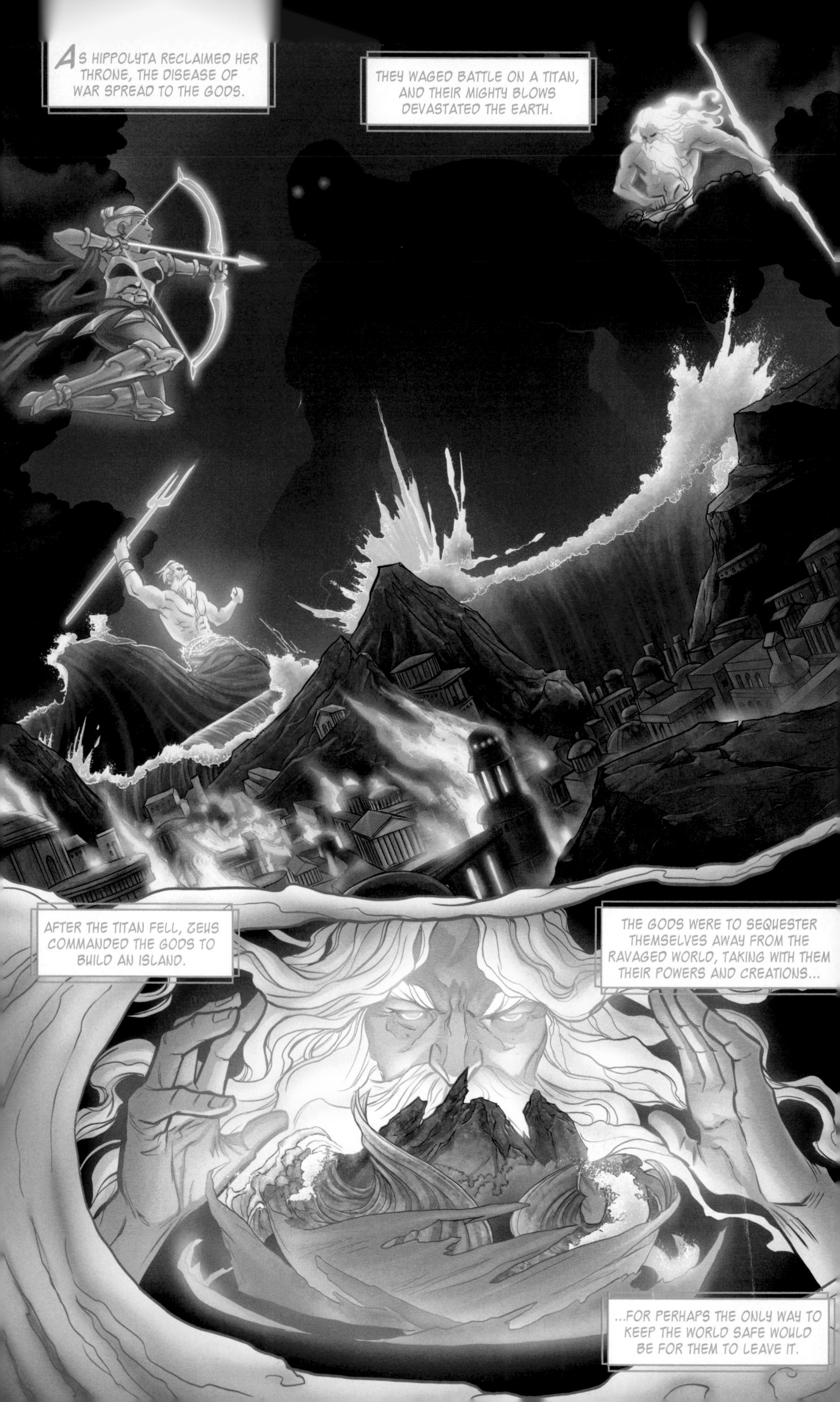
AS HIPPOLYTA RECLAIMED HER THRONE, THE DISEASE OF WAR SPREAD TO THE GODS.
THEY WAGED BATTLE ON A TITAN, AND THEIR MIGHTY BLOWS DEVASTATED THE EARTH.
AFTER THE TITAN FELL, ZEUS COMMANDED THE GODS TO BUILD AN ISLAND.
THE GODS WERE TO SEQUESTER THEMSELVES AWAY FROM THE RAVAGED WORLD, TAKING WITH THEM THEIR POWERS AND CREATIONS...
...FOR PERHAPS THE ONLY WAY TO KEEP THE WORLD SAFE WOULD BE FOR THEM TO LEAVE IT.

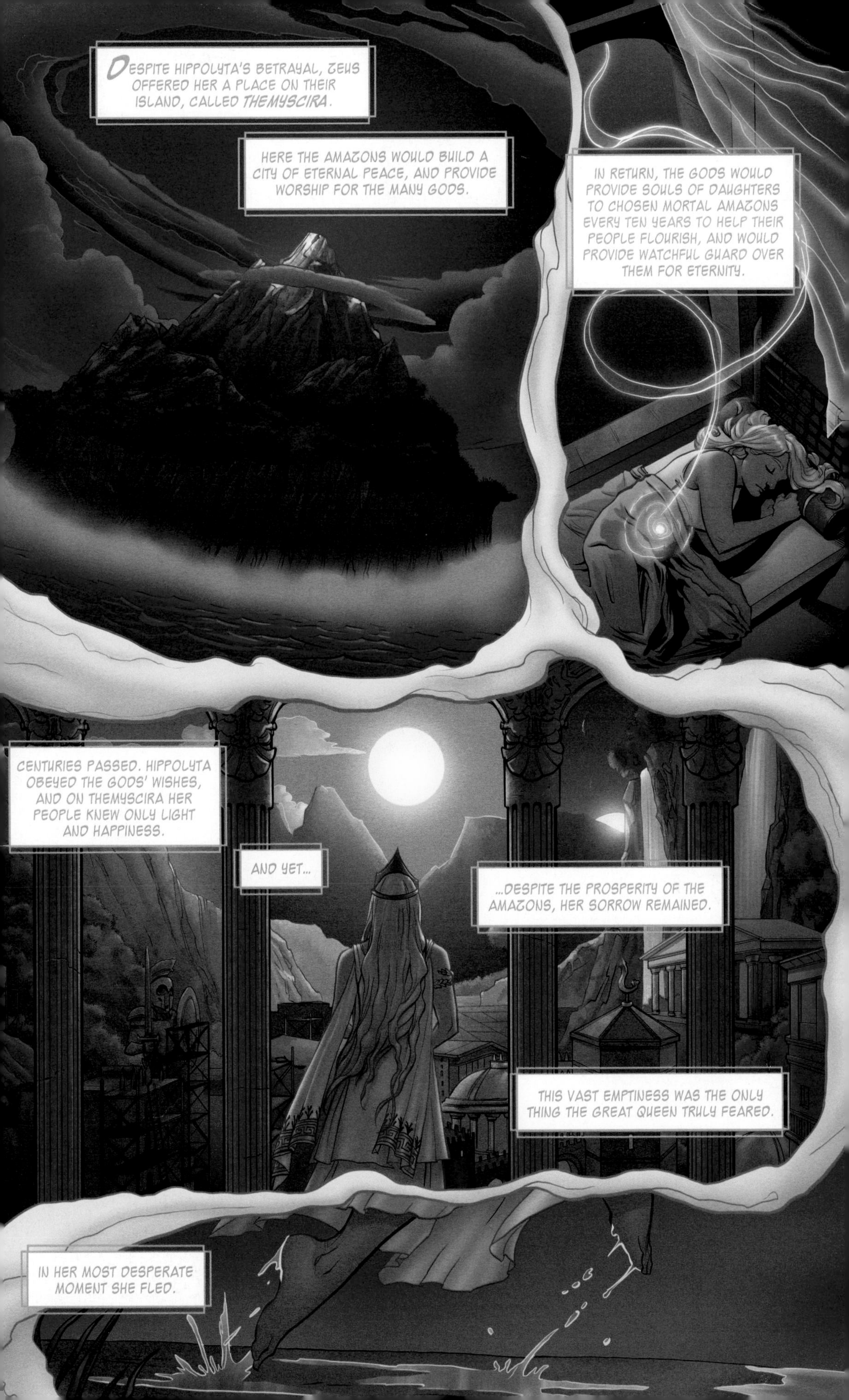
DESPITE HIPPOLYTA'S BETRAYAL, ZEUS OFFERED HER A PLACE ON THEIR ISLAND, CALLED THEMYSCIRA.
HERE THE AMAZONS WOULD BUILD A CITY OF ETERNAL PEACE, AND PROVIDE WORSHIP FOR THE MANY GODS.
IN RETURN, THE GODS WOULD PROVIDE SOULS OF DAUGHTERS TO CHOSEN MORTAL AMAZONS EVERY TEN YEARS TO HELP THEIR PEOPLE FLOURISH, AND WOULD PROVIDE WATCHFUL GUARD OVER THEM FOR ETERNITY.
CENTURIES PASSED. HIPPOLYTA OBEYED THE GODS' WISHES, AND ON THEMYSCIRA HER PEOPLE KNEW ONLY LIGHT AND HAPPINESS.
AND YET...
...DESPITE THE PROSPERITY OF THE AMAZONS, HER SORROW REMAINED.
THIS VAST EMPTINESS WAS THE ONLY THING THE GREAT QUEEN TRULY FEARED.
IN HER MOST DESPERATE MOMENT SHE FLED.

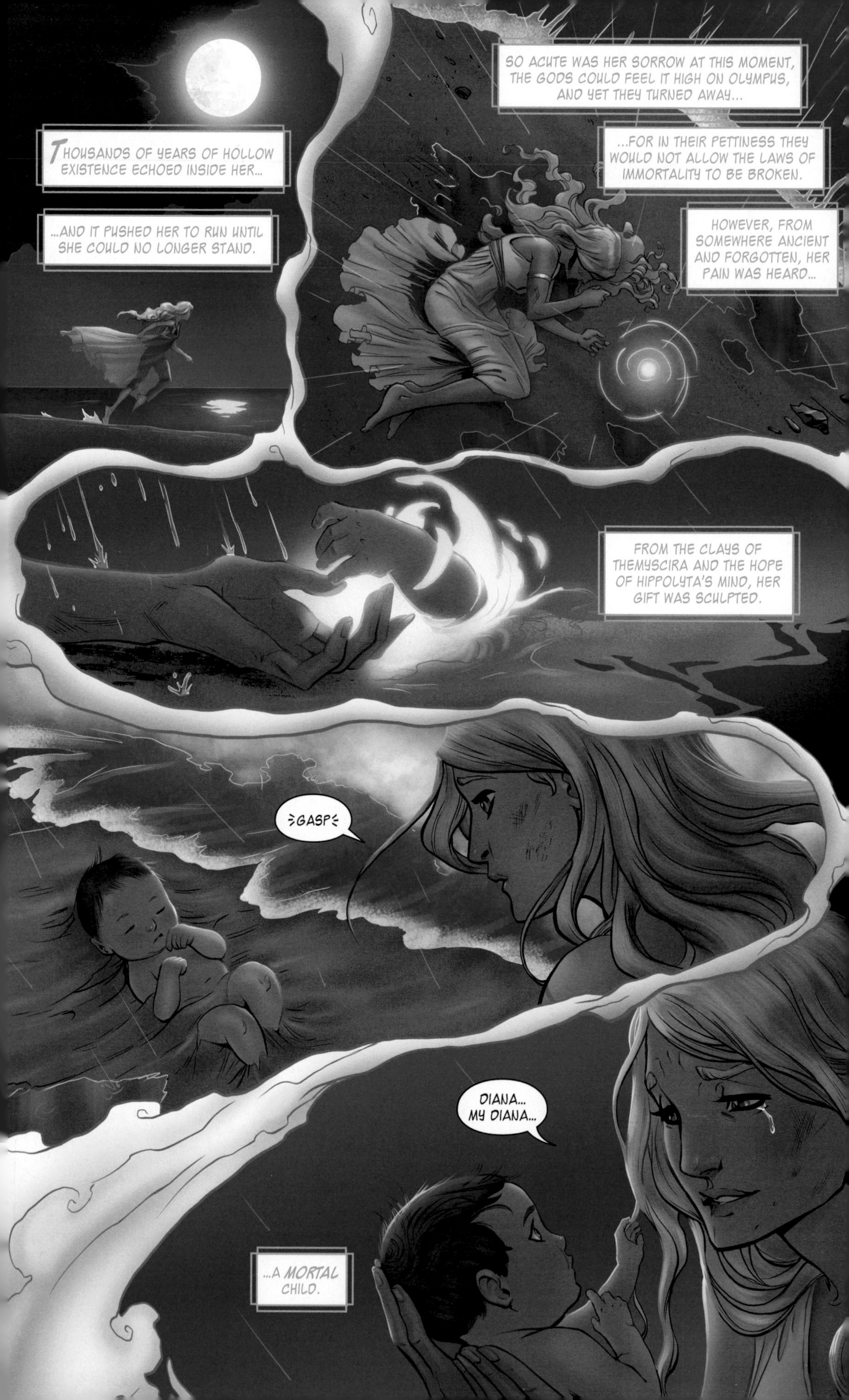
THOUSANDS OF YEARS OF HOLLOW EXISTENCE ECHOED INSIDE HER...
...AND IT PUSHED HER TO RUN UNTIL SHE COULD NO LONGER STAND.
SO ACUTE WAS HER SORROW AT THIS MOMENT, THE GODS COULD FEEL IT HIGH ON OLYMPUS, AND YET THEY TURNED AWAY...
...FOR IN THEIR PETTINESS THEY WOULD NOT ALLOW THE LAWS OF IMMORTALITY TO BE BROKEN.
HOWEVER, FROM SOMEWHERE ANCIENT AND FORGOTTEN, HER PAIN WAS HEARD...
FROM THE CLAYS OF THEMYSCIRA AND THE HOPE OF HIPPOLYTA'S MIND, HER GIFT WAS SCULPTED.
GASP
DIANA... MY DIANA...
...A MORTAL CHILD.

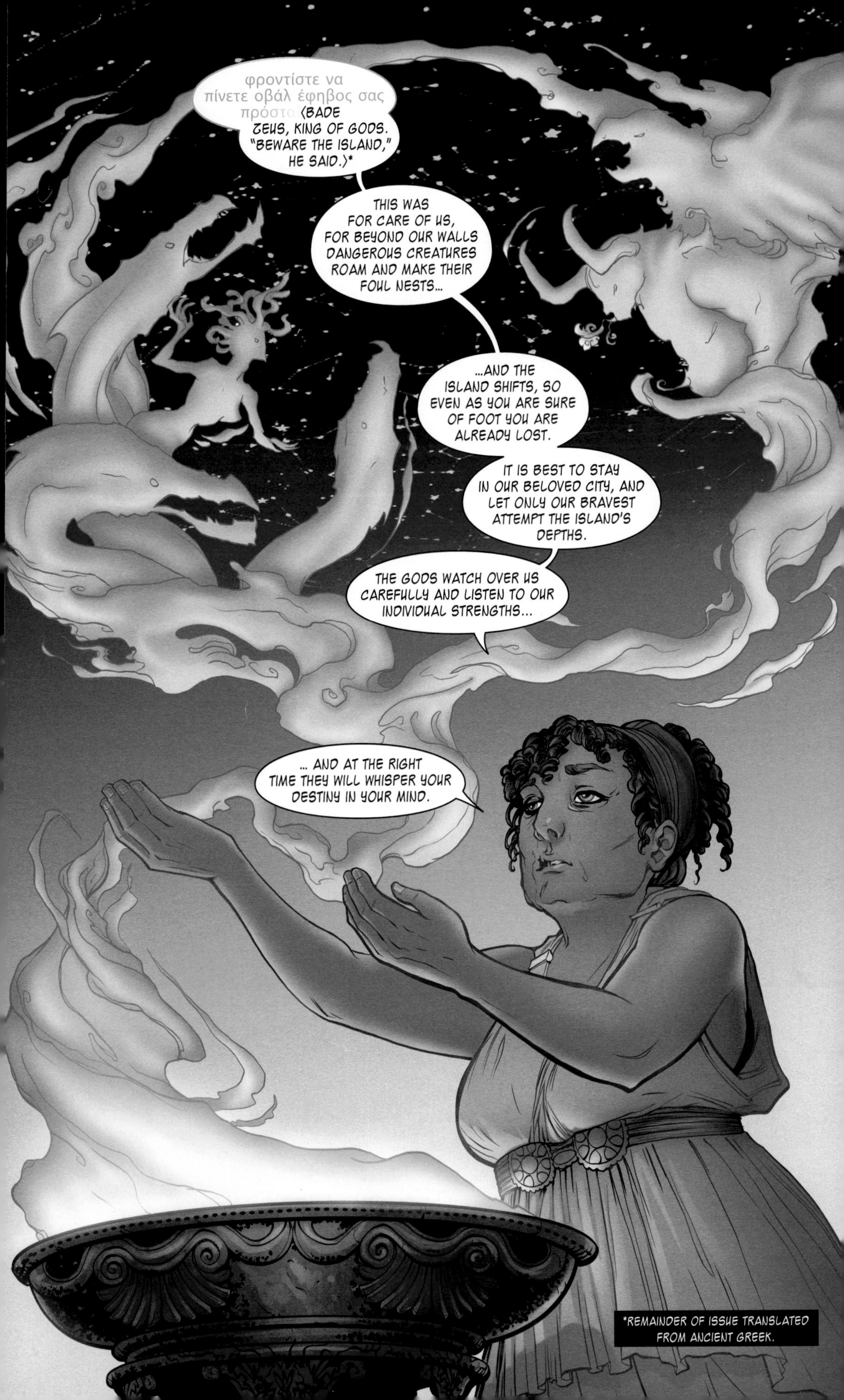
φροντίστε να πίνετε οβάλ έφηβος σας πρόστα ⟨BADE ZEUS, KING OF GODS. "BEWARE THE ISLAND," HE SAID.⟩*
THIS WAS FOR CARE OF US, FOR BEYOND OUR WALLS DANGEROUS CREATURES ROAM AND MAKE THEIR FOUL NESTS...
...AND THE ISLAND SHIFTS, SO EVEN AS YOU ARE SURE OF FOOT YOU ARE ALREADY LOST.
IT IS BEST TO STAY IN OUR BELOVED CITY, AND LET ONLY OUR BRAVEST ATTEMPT THE ISLAND'S DEPTHS.
THE GODS WATCH OVER US CAREFULLY AND LISTEN TO OUR INDIVIDUAL STRENGTHS...
... AND AT THE RIGHT TIME THEY WILL WHISPER YOUR DESTINY IN YOUR MIND.
*REMAINDER OF ISSUE TRANSLATED FROM ANCIENT GREEK.

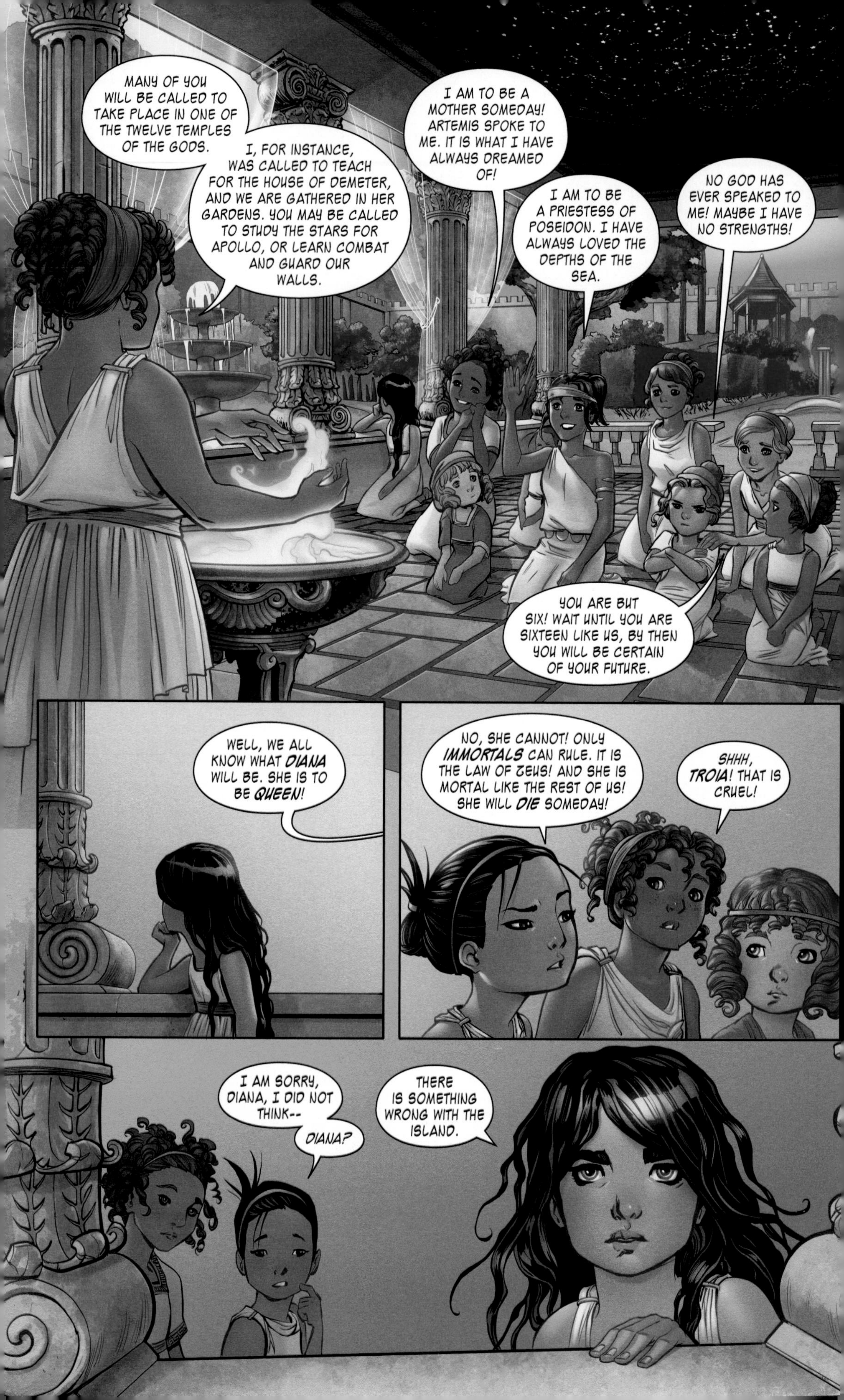
MANY OF YOU WILL BE CALLED TO TAKE PLACE IN ONE OF THE TWELVE TEMPLES OF THE GODS.
I, FOR INSTANCE, WAS CALLED TO TEACH FOR THE HOUSE OF DEMETER, AND WE ARE GATHERED IN HER GARDENS. YOU MAY BE CALLED TO STUDY THE STARS FOR APOLLO, OR LEARN COMBAT AND GUARD OUR WALLS.
I AM TO BE A MOTHER SOMEDAY! ARTEMIS SPOKE TO ME. IT IS WHAT I HAVE ALWAYS DREAMED OF!
I AM TO BE A PRIESTESS OF POSEIDON. I HAVE ALWAYS LOVED THE DEPTHS OF THE SEA.
NO GOD HAS EVER SPEAKED TO ME! MAYBE I HAVE NO STRENGTHS!
YOU ARE BUT SIX! WAIT UNTIL YOU ARE SIXTEEN LIKE US, BY THEN YOU WILL BE CERTAIN OF YOUR FUTURE.
WELL, WE ALL KNOW WHAT DIANA WILL BE. SHE IS TO BE QUEEN!
NO, SHE CANNOT! ONLY IMMORTALS CAN RULE. IT IS THE LAW OF ZEUS! AND SHE IS MORTAL LIKE THE REST OF US! SHE WILL DIE SOMEDAY!
SHHH, TROIA! THAT IS CRUEL!
I AM SORRY, DIANA, I DID NOT THINK--
DIANA?
THERE IS SOMETHING WRONG WITH THE ISLAND.

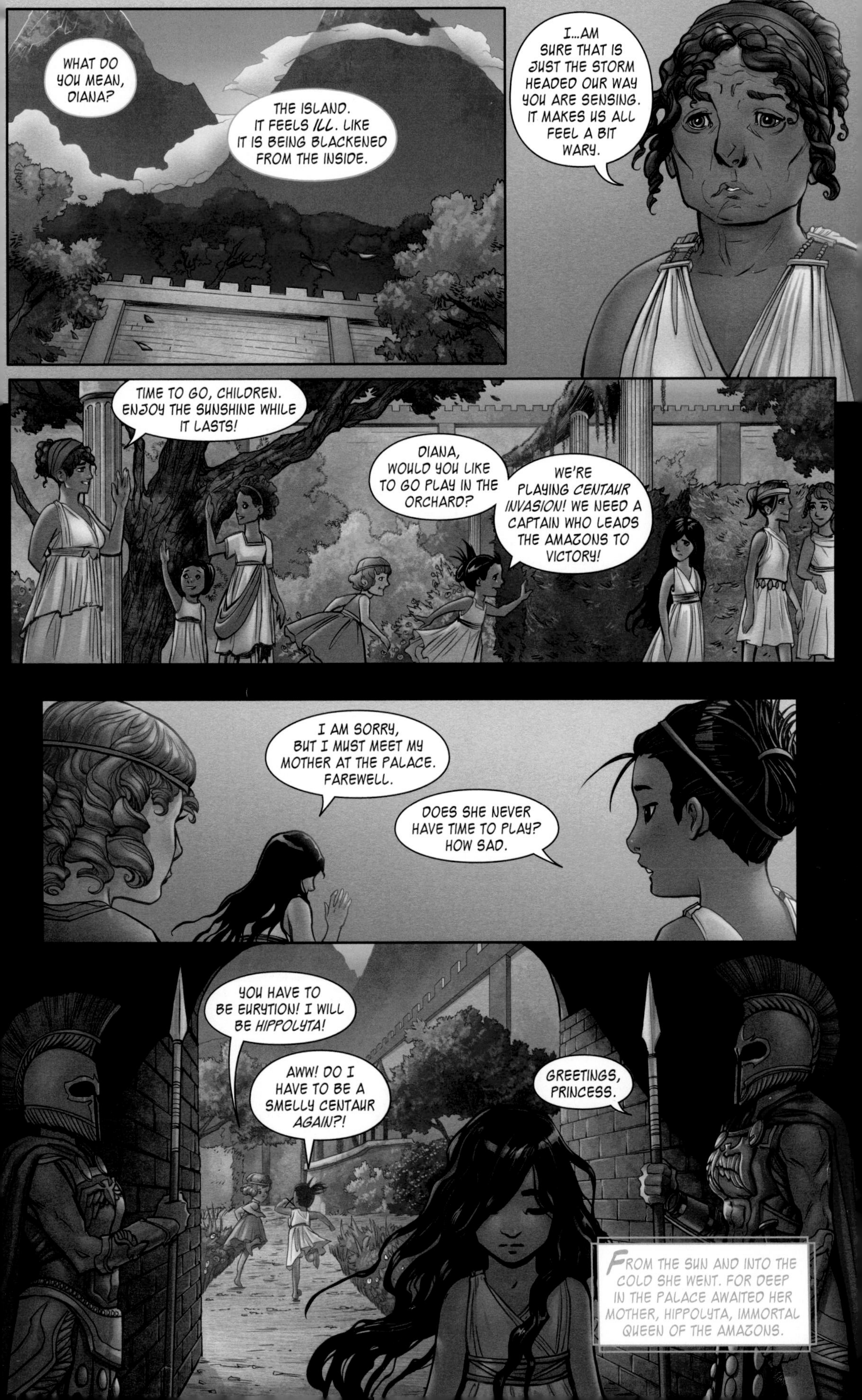
WHAT DO YOU MEAN, DIANA?
THE ISLAND. IT FEELS ILL. LIKE IT IS BEING BLACKENED FROM THE INSIDE.
I...AM SURE THAT IS JUST THE STORM HEADED OUR WAY YOU ARE SENSING. IT MAKES US ALL FEEL A BIT WARY.
TIME TO GO, CHILDREN. ENJOY THE SUNSHINE WHILE IT LASTS!
DIANA, WOULD YOU LIKE TO GO PLAY IN THE ORCHARD?
WE'RE PLAYING CENTAUR INVASION! WE NEED A CAPTAIN WHO LEADS THE AMAZONS TO VICTORY!
I AM SORRY, BUT I MUST MEET MY MOTHER AT THE PALACE. FAREWELL.
DOES SHE NEVER HAVE TIME TO PLAY? HOW SAD.
YOU HAVE TO BE EURYTION! I WILL BE HIPPOLYTA!
AWW! DO I HAVE TO BE A SMELLY CENTAUR AGAIN?!
GREETINGS, PRINCESS.
FROM THE SUN AND INTO THE COLD SHE WENT. FOR DEEP IN THE PALACE AWAITED HER MOTHER, HIPPOLYTA, IMMORTAL QUEEN OF THE AMAZONS.

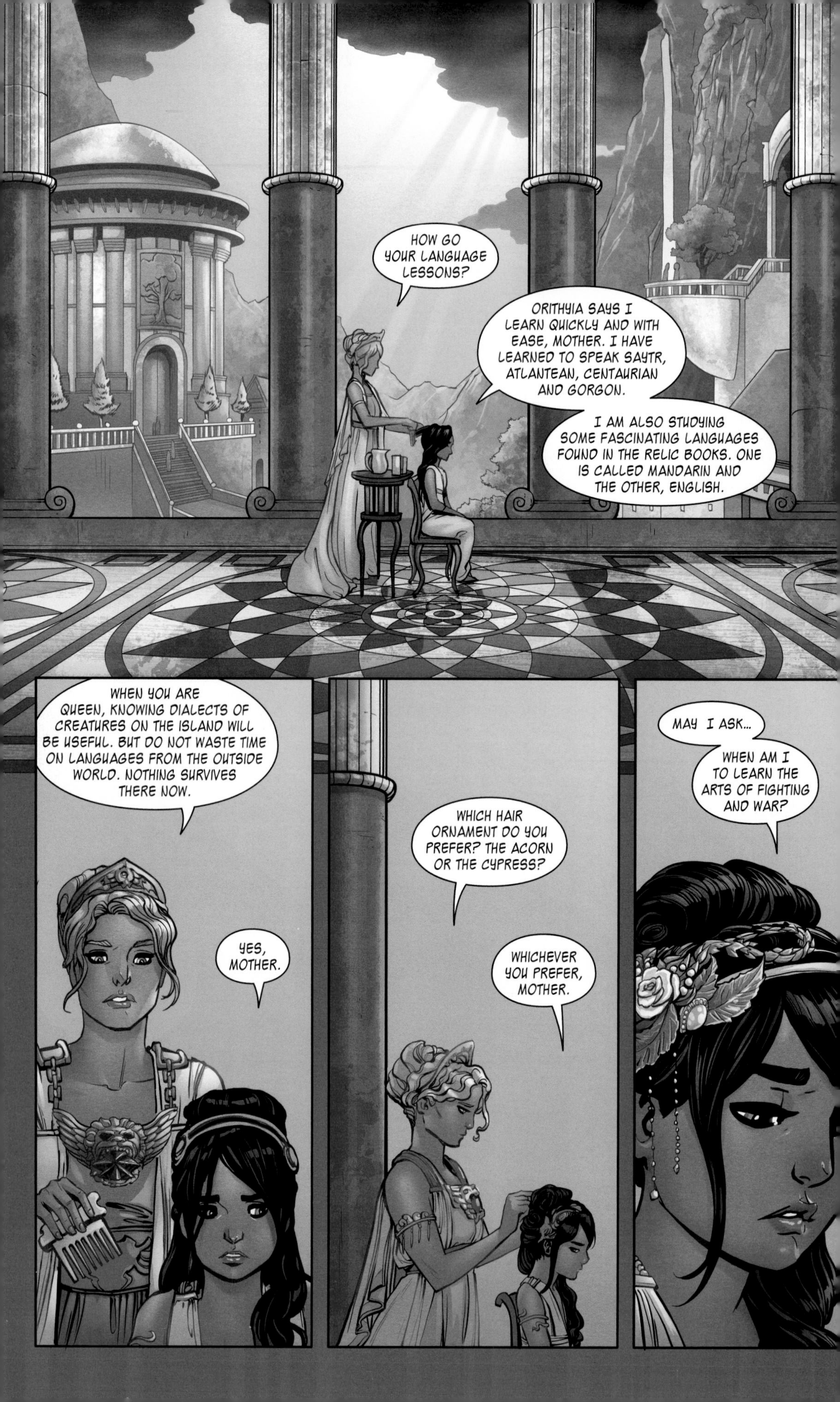
HOW GO YOUR LANGUAGE LESSONS?
ORITHYIA SAYS I LEARN QUICKLY AND WITH EASE, MOTHER. I HAVE LEARNED TO SPEAK SAYTR, ATLANTEAN, CENTAURIAN AND GORGON.
I AM ALSO STUDYING SOME FASCINATING LANGUAGES FOUND IN THE RELIC BOOKS. ONE IS CALLED MANDARIN AND THE OTHER, ENGLISH.
WHEN YOU ARE QUEEN, KNOWING DIALECTS OF CREATURES ON THE ISLAND WILL BE USEFUL. BUT DO NOT WASTE TIME ON LANGUAGES FROM THE OUTSIDE WORLD. NOTHING SURVIVES THERE NOW.
YES, MOTHER.
WHICH HAIR ORNAMENT DO YOU PREFER? THE ACORN OR THE CYPRESS?
WHICHEVER YOU PREFER, MOTHER.
MAY I ASK...
WHEN AM I TO LEARN THE ARTS OF FIGHTING AND WAR?

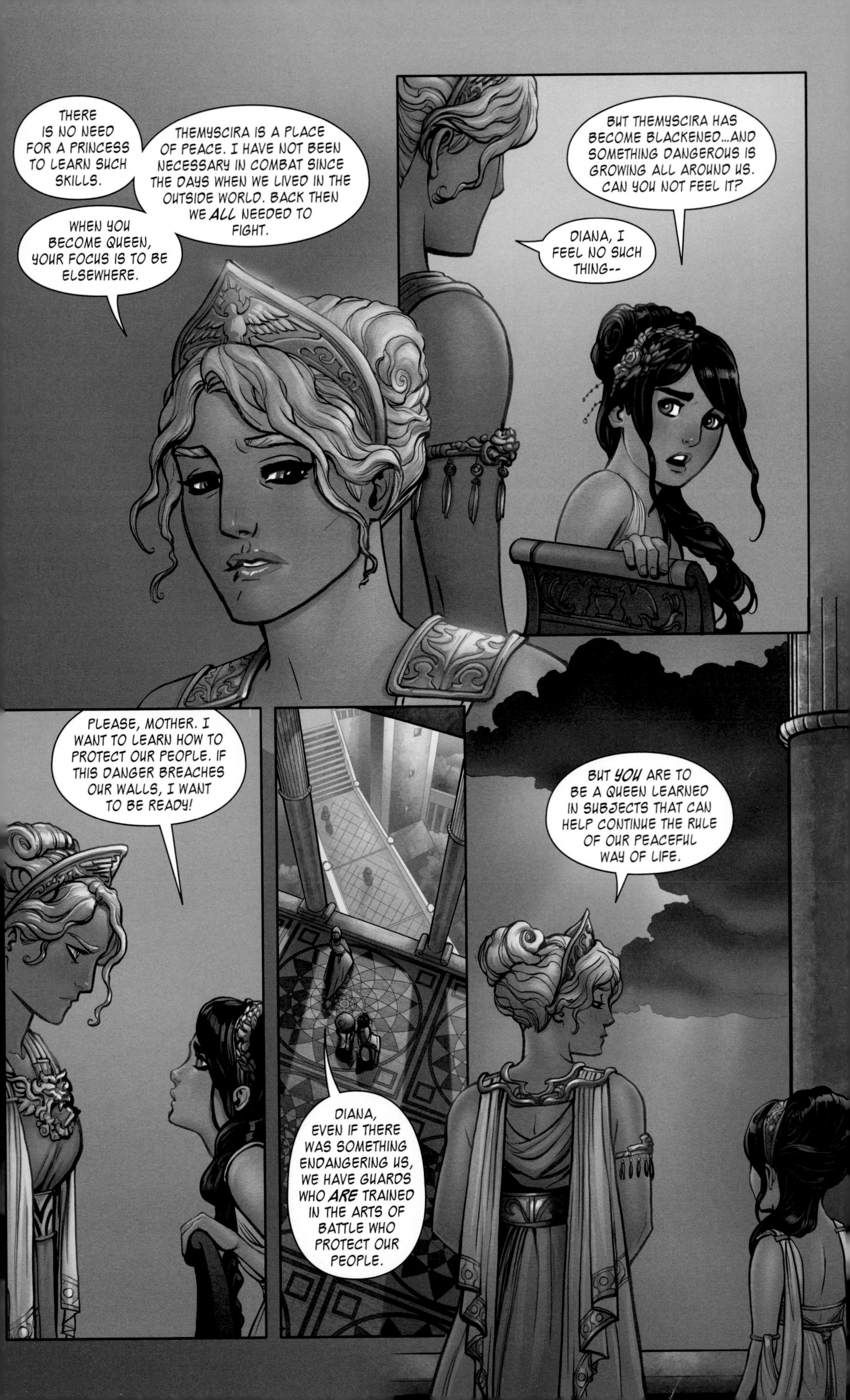
THERE IS NO NEED FOR A PRINCESS TO LEARN SUCH SKILLS.
THEMYSCIRA IS A PLACE OF PEACE. I HAVE NOT BEEN NECESSARY IN COMBAT SINCE THE DAYS WHEN WE LIVED IN THE OUTSIDE WORLD. BACK THEN WE ALL NEEDED TO FIGHT.
WHEN YOU BECOME QUEEN, YOUR FOCUS IS TO BE ELSEWHERE.
BUT THEMYSCIRA HAS BECOME BLACKENED...AND SOMETHING DANGEROUS IS GROWING ALL AROUND US. CAN YOU NOT FEEL IT?
DIANA, I FEEL NO SUCH THING--
PLEASE, MOTHER. I WANT TO LEARN HOW TO PROTECT OUR PEOPLE. IF THIS DANGER BREACHES OUR WALLS, I WANT TO BE READY!
DIANA, EVEN IF THERE WAS SOMETHING ENDANGERING US, WE HAVE GUARDS WHO ARE TRAINED IN THE ARTS OF BATTLE WHO PROTECT OUR PEOPLE.
BUT YOU ARE TO BE A QUEEN LEARNED IN SUBJECTS THAT CAN HELP CONTINUE THE RULE OF OUR PEACEFUL WAY OF LIFE.

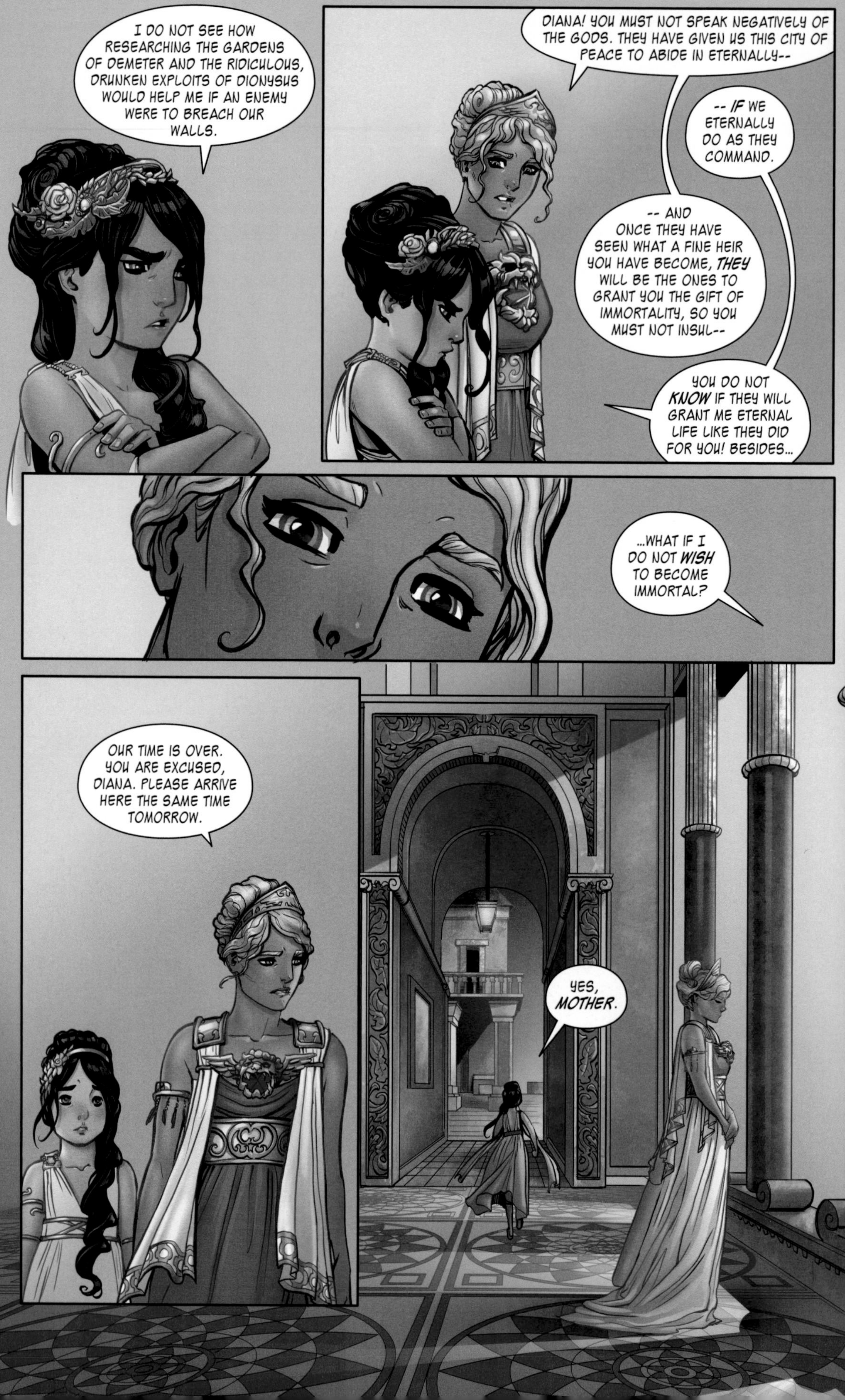
I DO NOT SEE HOW RESEARCHING THE GARDENS OF DEMETER AND THE RIDICULOUS, DRUNKEN EXPLOITS OF DIONYSUS WOULD HELP ME IF AN ENEMY WERE TO BREACH OUR WALLS.
DIANA! YOU MUST NOT SPEAK NEGATIVELY OF THE GODS. THEY HAVE GIVEN US THIS CITY OF PEACE TO ABIDE IN ETERNALLY--
-- IF WE ETERNALLY DO AS THEY COMMAND.
-- AND ONCE THEY HAVE SEEN WHAT A FINE HEIR YOU HAVE BECOME, THEY WILL BE THE ONES TO GRANT YOU THE GIFT OF IMMORTALITY, SO YOU MUST NOT INSUL--
YOU DO NOT KNOW IF THEY WILL GRANT ME ETERNAL LIFE LIKE THEY DID FOR YOU! BESIDES...
...WHAT IF I DO NOT WISH TO BECOME IMMORTAL?
OUR TIME IS OVER. YOU ARE EXCUSED, DIANA. PLEASE ARRIVE HERE THE SAME TIME TOMORROW.
YES, MOTHER.

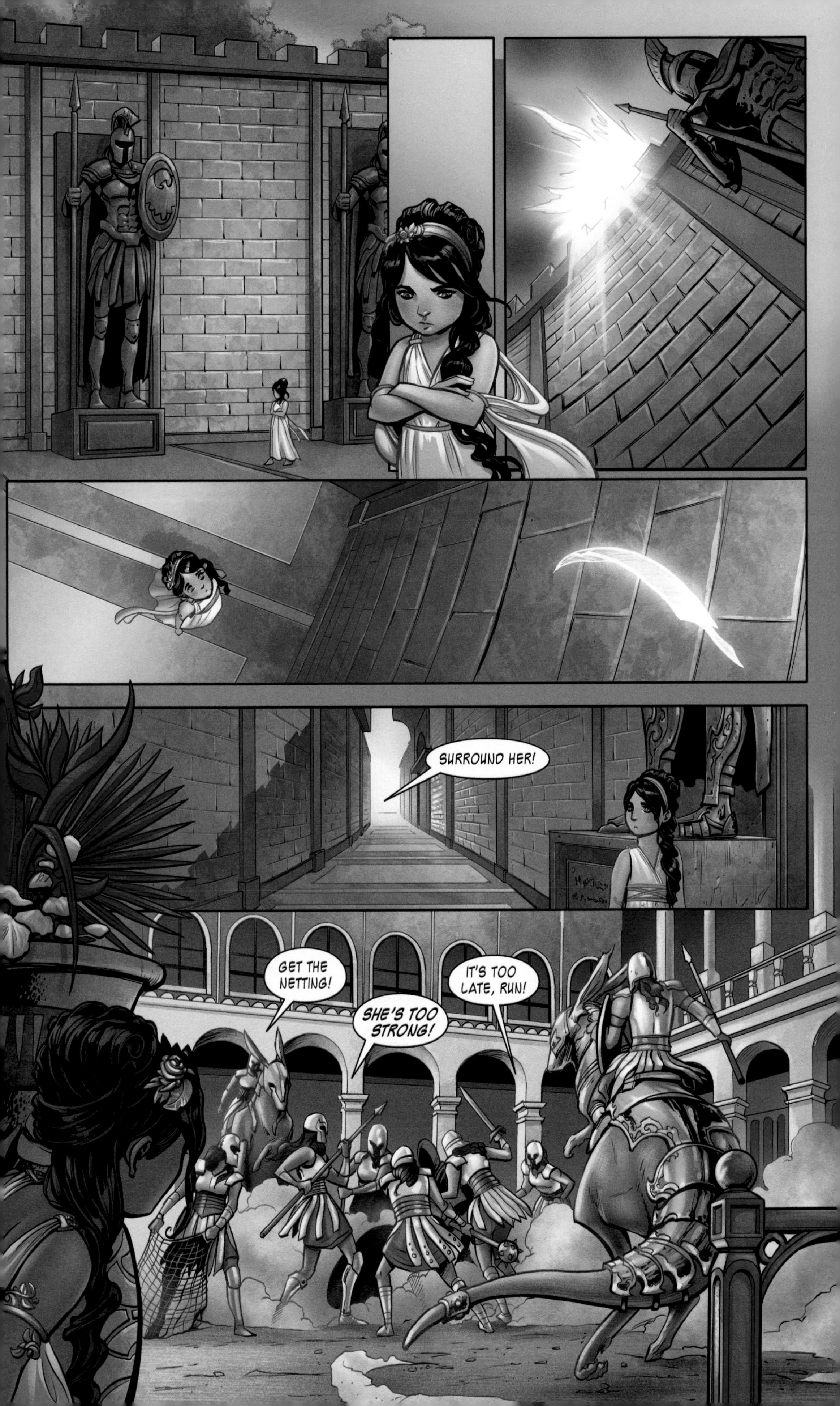
SURROUND HER!
GET THE NETTING!
SHE'S TOO STRONG!
IT'S TOO LATE, RUN!

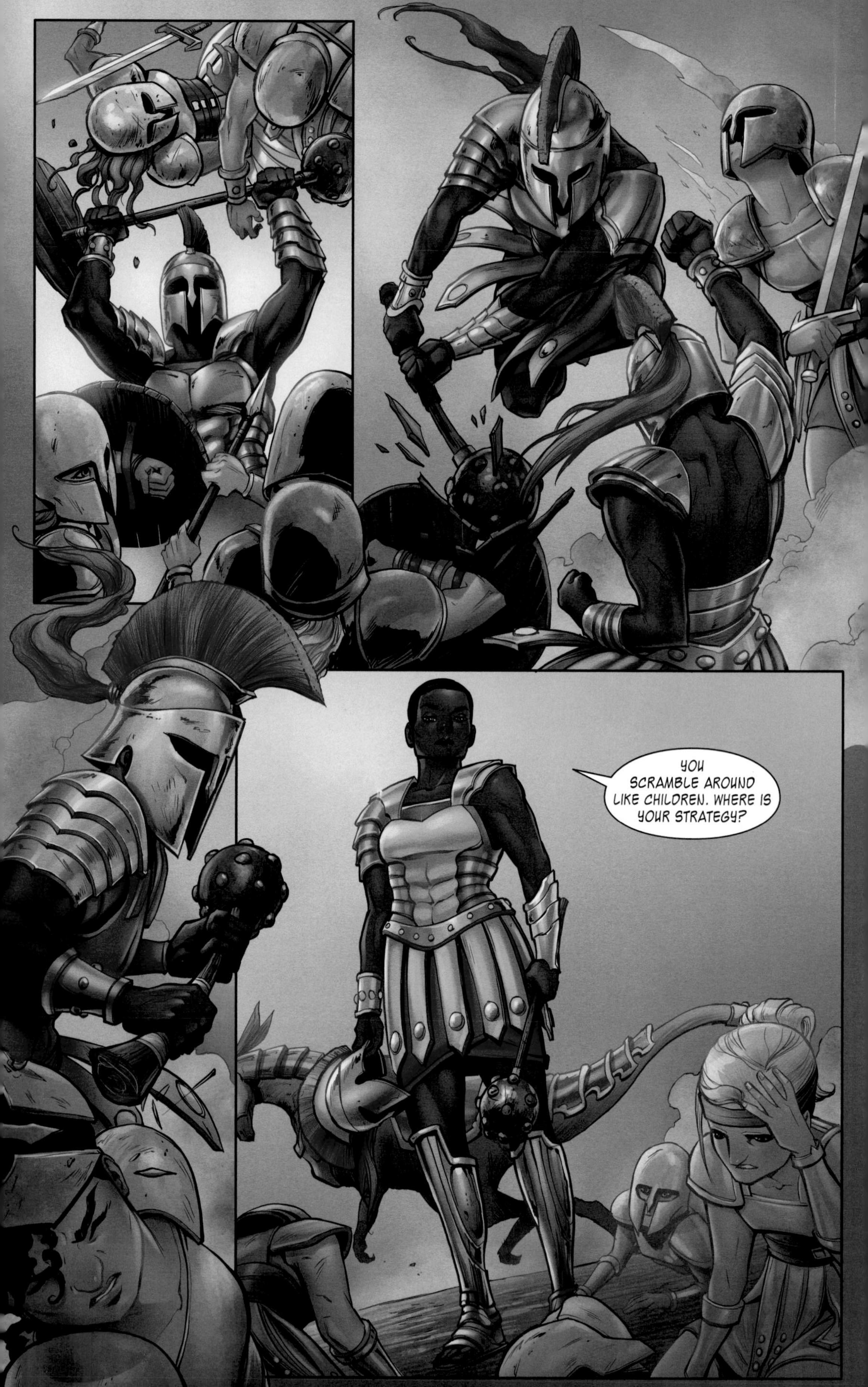
YOU SCRAMBLE AROUND LIKE CHILDREN. WHERE IS YOUR STRATEGY?

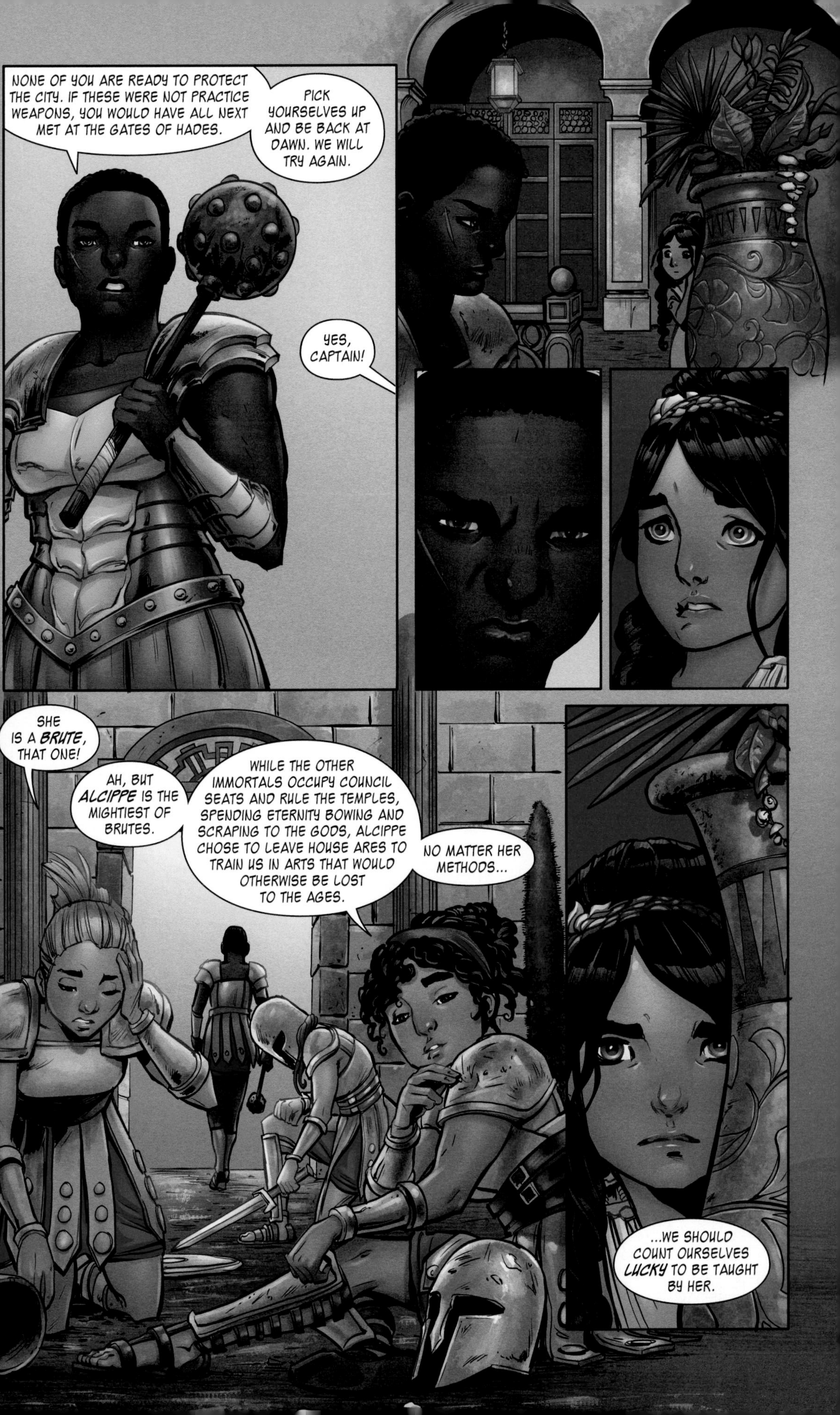
NONE OF YOU ARE READY TO PROTECT THE CITY. IF THESE WERE NOT PRACTICE WEAPONS, YOU WOULD HAVE ALL NEXT MET AT THE GATES OF HADES.
PICK YOURSELVES UP AND BE BACK AT DAWN. WE WILL TRY AGAIN.
YES, CAPTAIN!
SHE IS A BRUTE, THAT ONE!
AH, BUT ALCIPPE IS THE MIGHTIEST OF BRUTES.
WHILE THE OTHER IMMORTALS OCCUPY COUNCIL SEATS AND RULE THE TEMPLES, SPENDING ETERNITY BOWING AND SCRAPING TO THE GODS, ALCIPPE CHOSE TO LEAVE HOUSE ARES TO TRAIN US IN ARTS THAT WOULD OTHERWISE BE LOST TO THE AGES.
NO MATTER HER METHODS...
...WE SHOULD COUNT OURSELVES LUCKY TO BE TAUGHT BY HER.

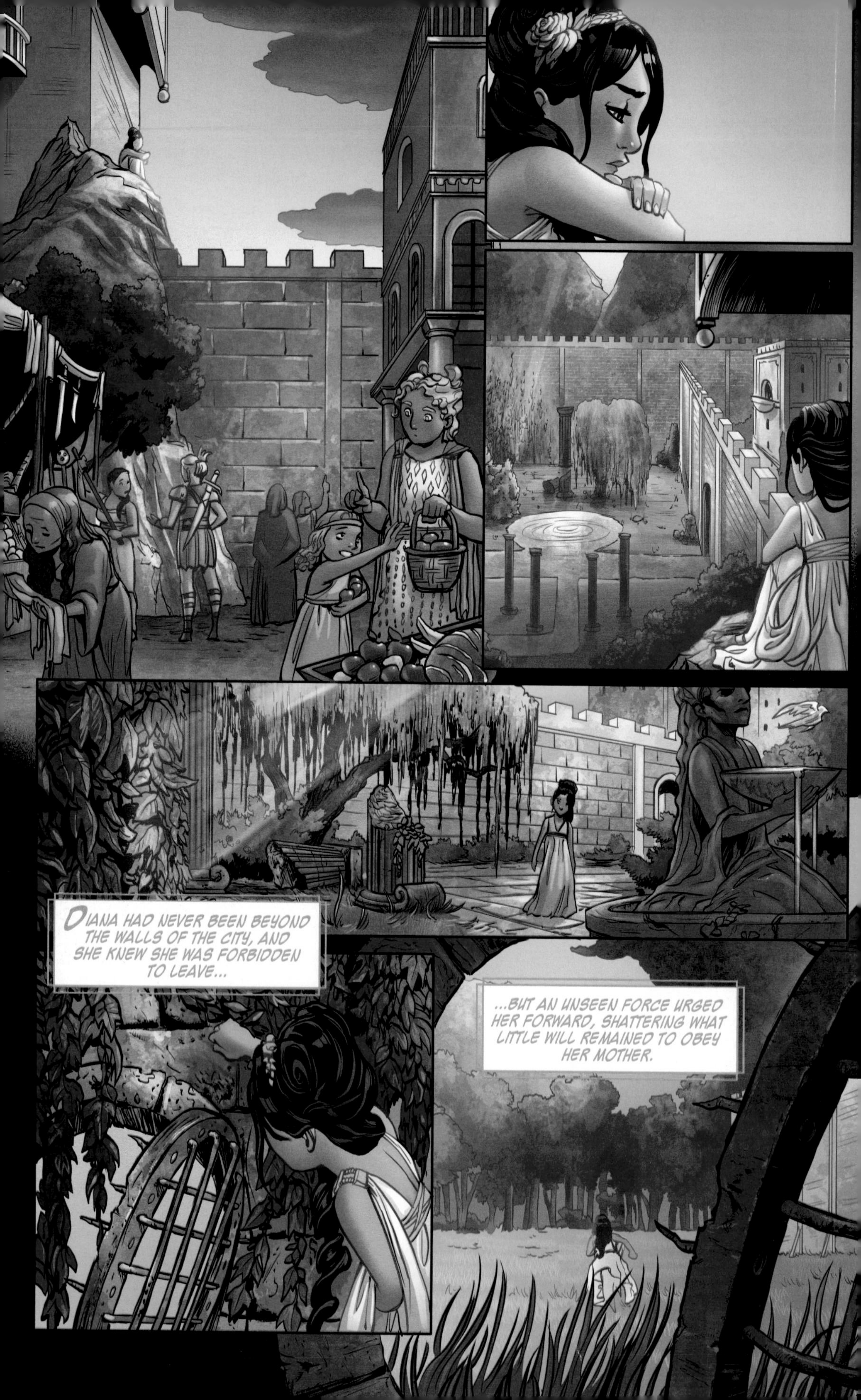
DIANA HAD NEVER BEEN BEYOND THE WALLS OF THE CITY, AND SHE KNEW SHE WAS FORBIDDEN TO LEAVE...
...BUT AN UNSEEN FORCE URGED HER FORWARD, SHATTERING WHAT LITTLE WILL REMAINED TO OBEY HER MOTHER.

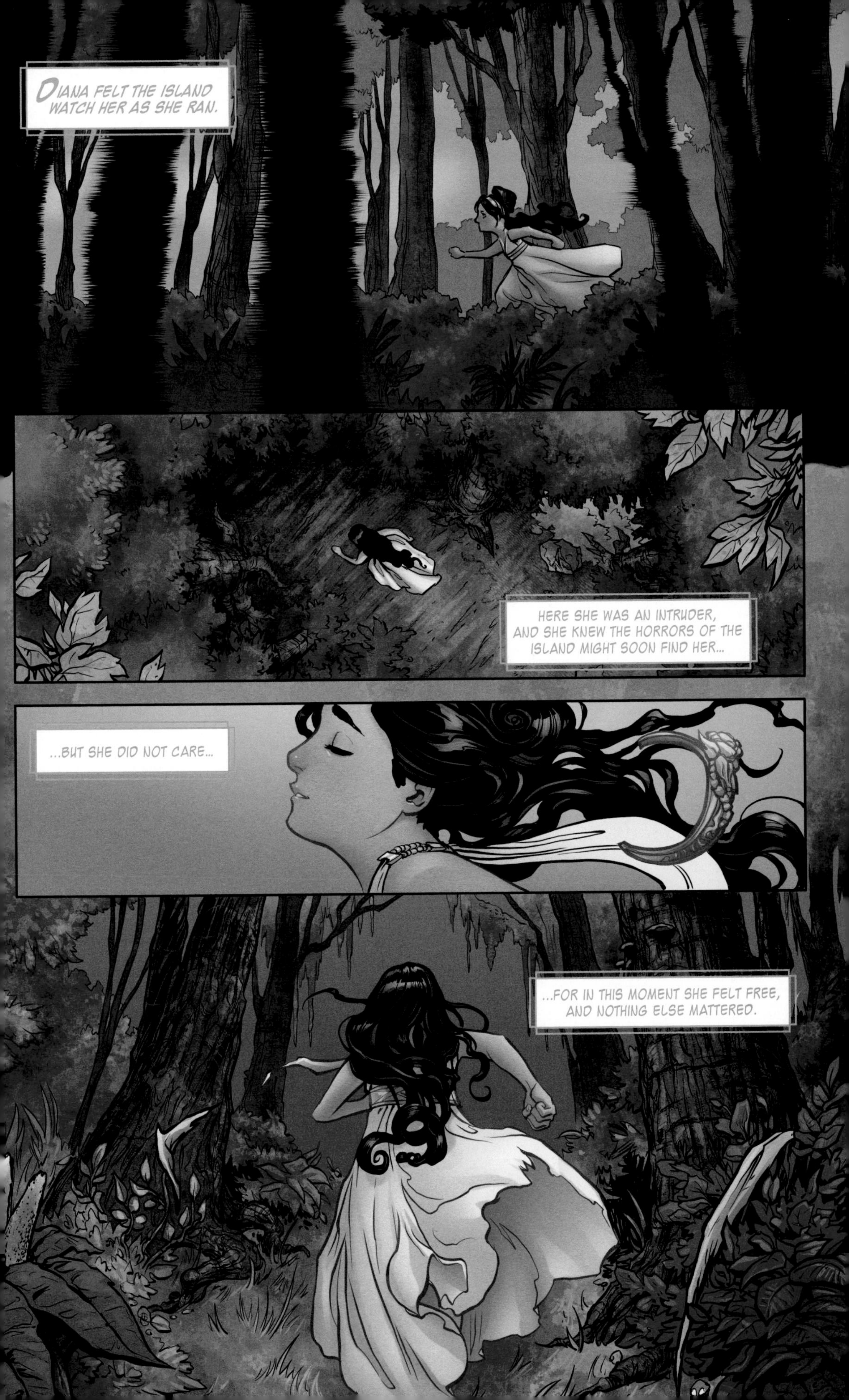
DIANA FELT THE ISLAND WATCH HER AS SHE RAN.
HERE SHE WAS AN INTRUDER, AND SHE KNEW THE HORRORS OF THE ISLAND MIGHT SOON FIND HER...
...BUT SHE DID NOT CARE...
...FOR IN THIS MOMENT SHE FELT FREE, AND NOTHING ELSE MATTERED.

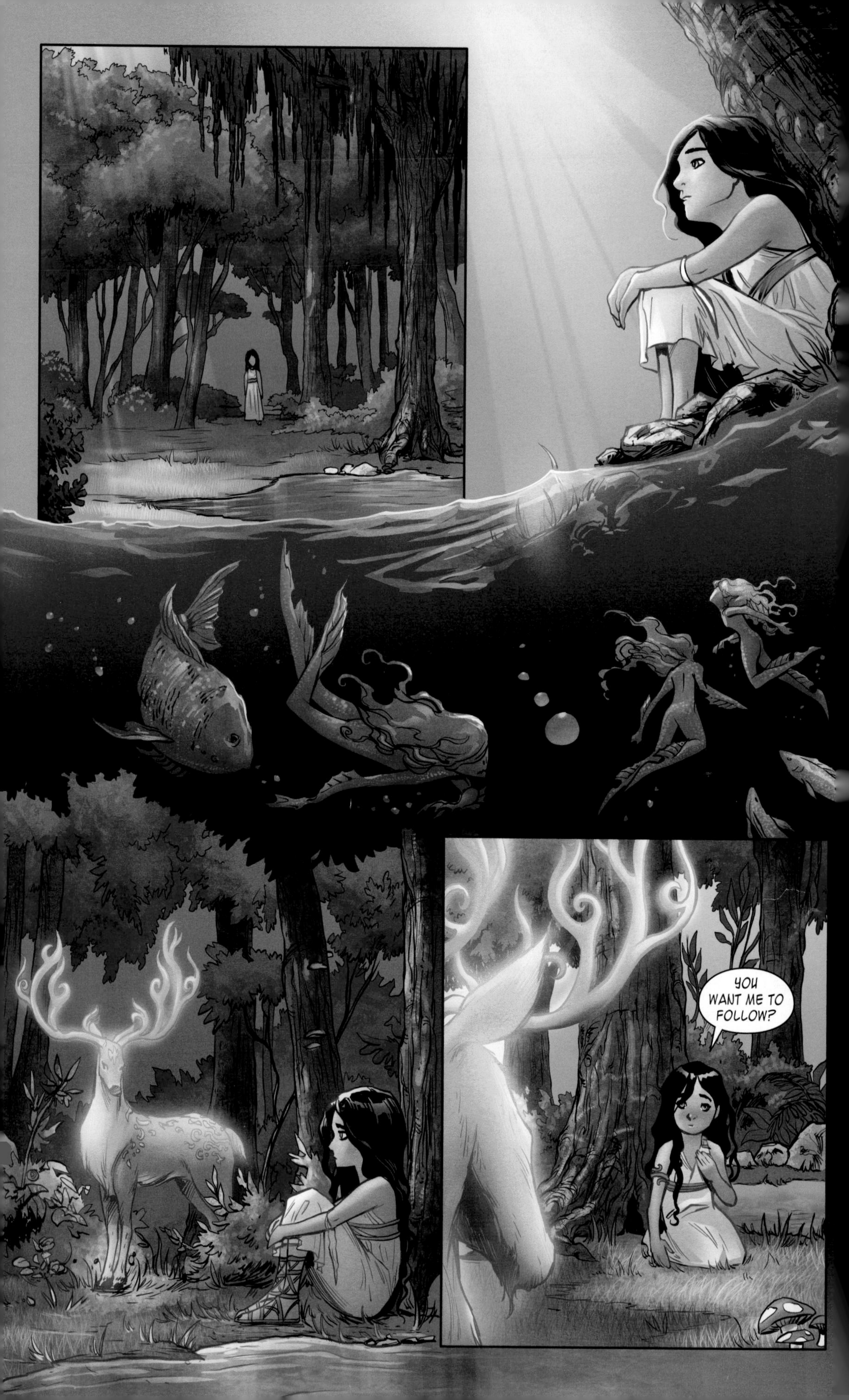
YOU WANT ME TO FOLLOW?

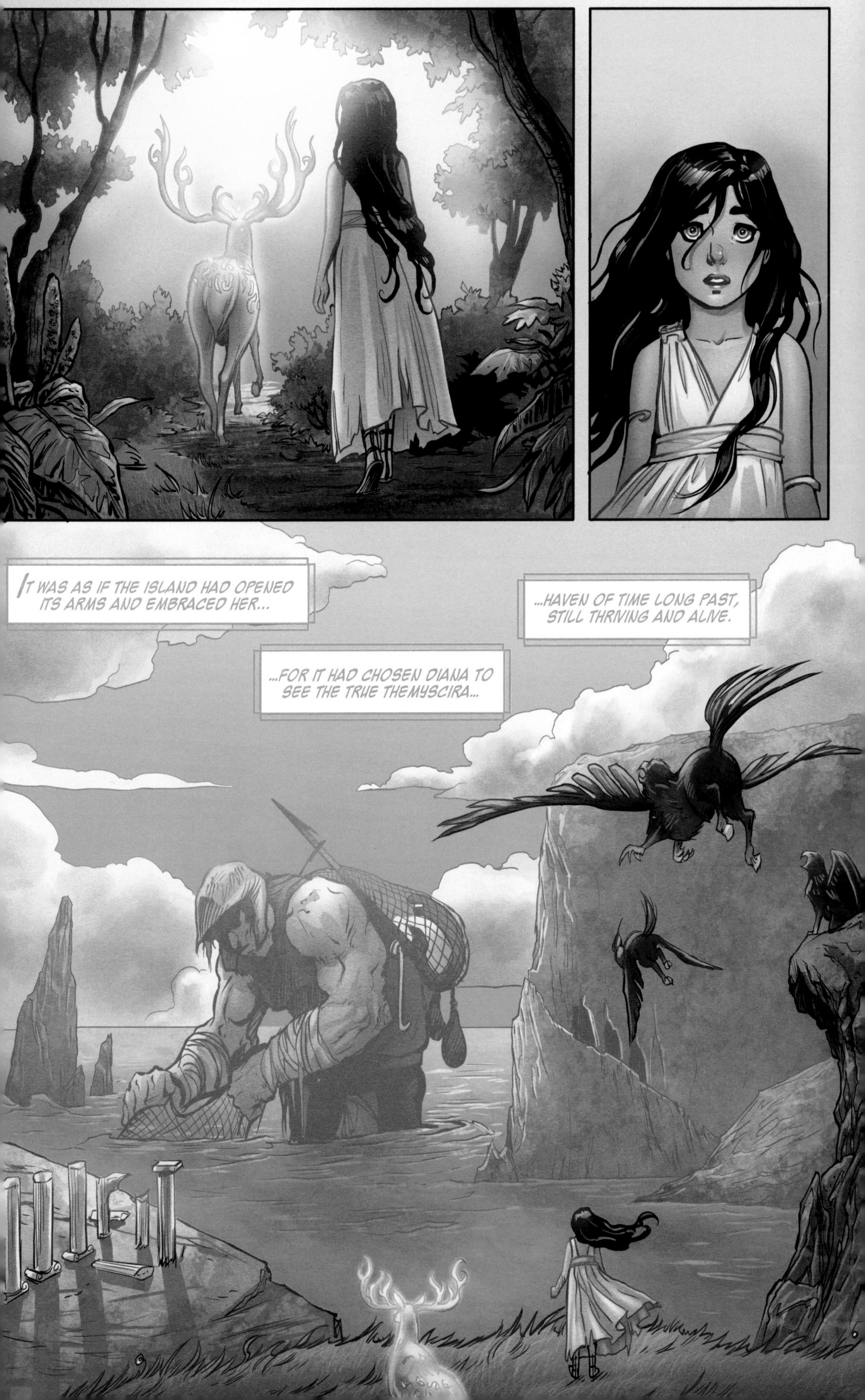
IT WAS AS IF THE ISLAND HAD OPENED ITS ARMS AND EMBRACED HER...
...FOR IT HAD CHOSEN DIANA TO SEE THE TRUE THEMYSCIRA...
...HAVEN OF TIME LONG PAST, STILL THRIVING AND ALIVE.

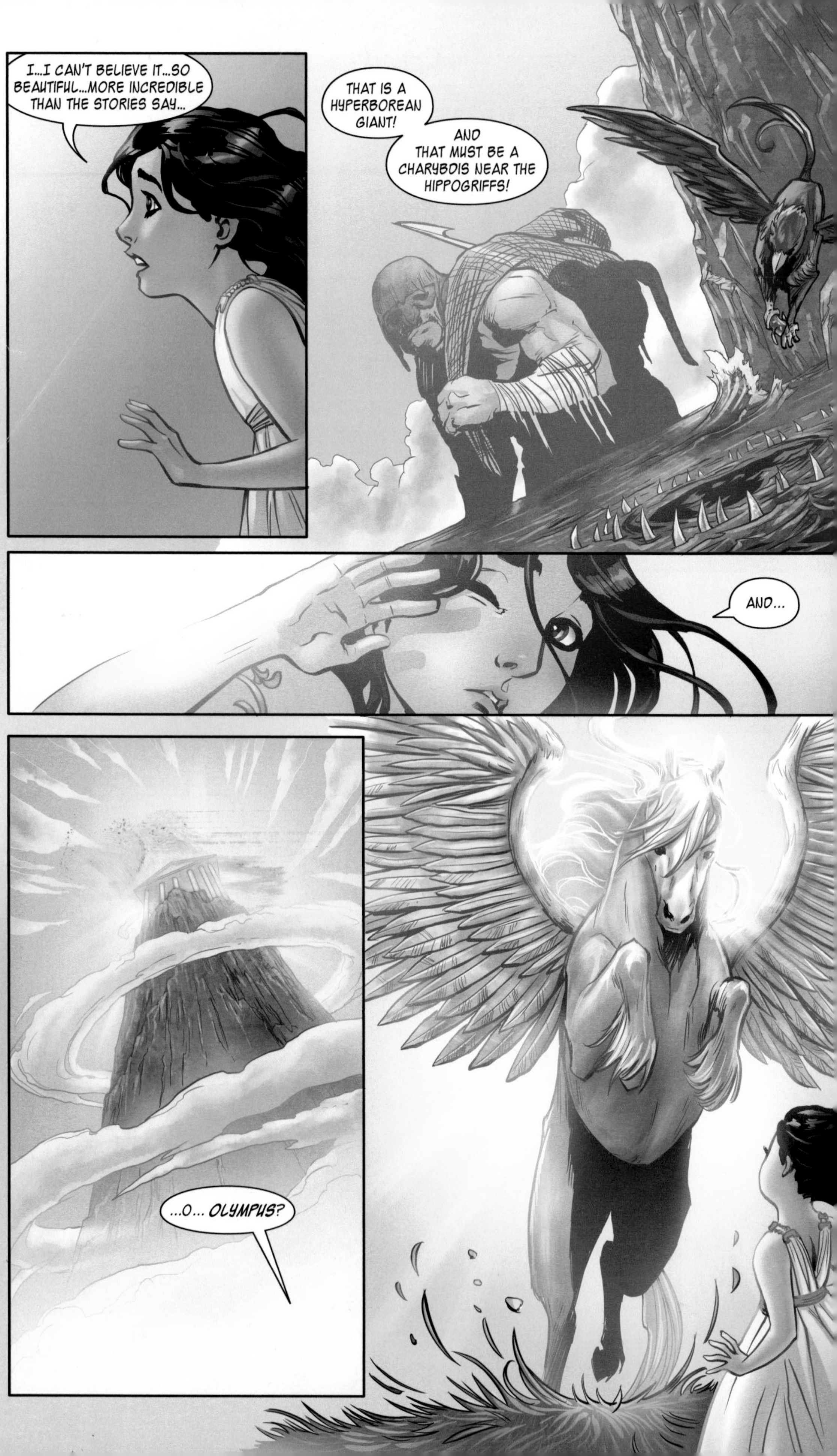
I...I CAN'T BELIEVE IT...SO BEAUTIFUL...MORE INCREDIBLE THAN THE STORIES SAY...
THAT IS A HYPERBOREAN GIANT!
AND THAT MUST BE A CHARYBDIS NEAR THE HIPPOGRIFFS!
AND...
...O... OLYMPUS?

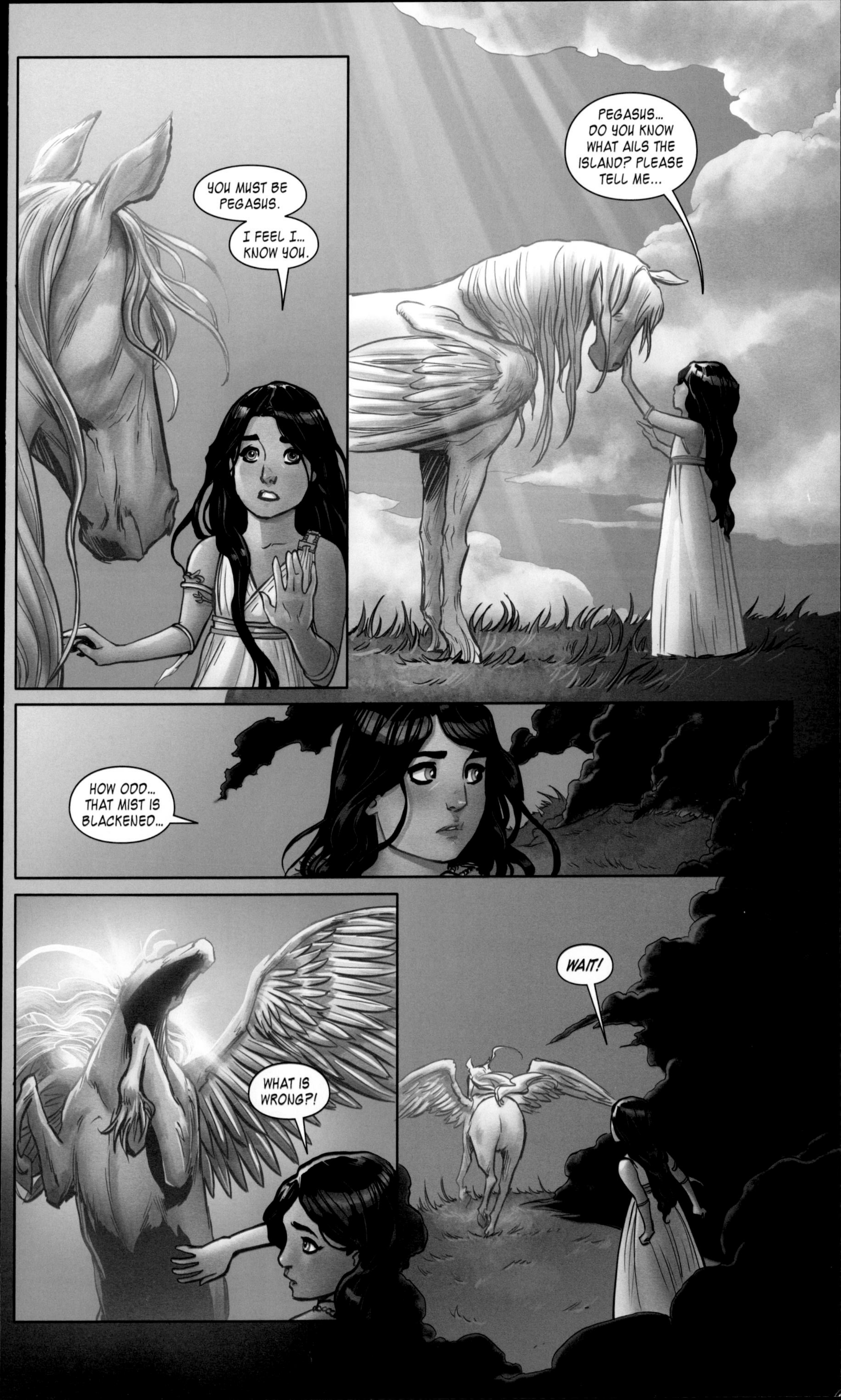
YOU MUST BE PEGASUS.
I FEEL I... KNOW YOU.
PEGASUS... DO YOU KNOW WHAT AILS THE ISLAND? PLEASE TELL ME...
HOW ODD... THAT MIST IS BLACKENED...
WHAT IS WRONG?!
WAIT!

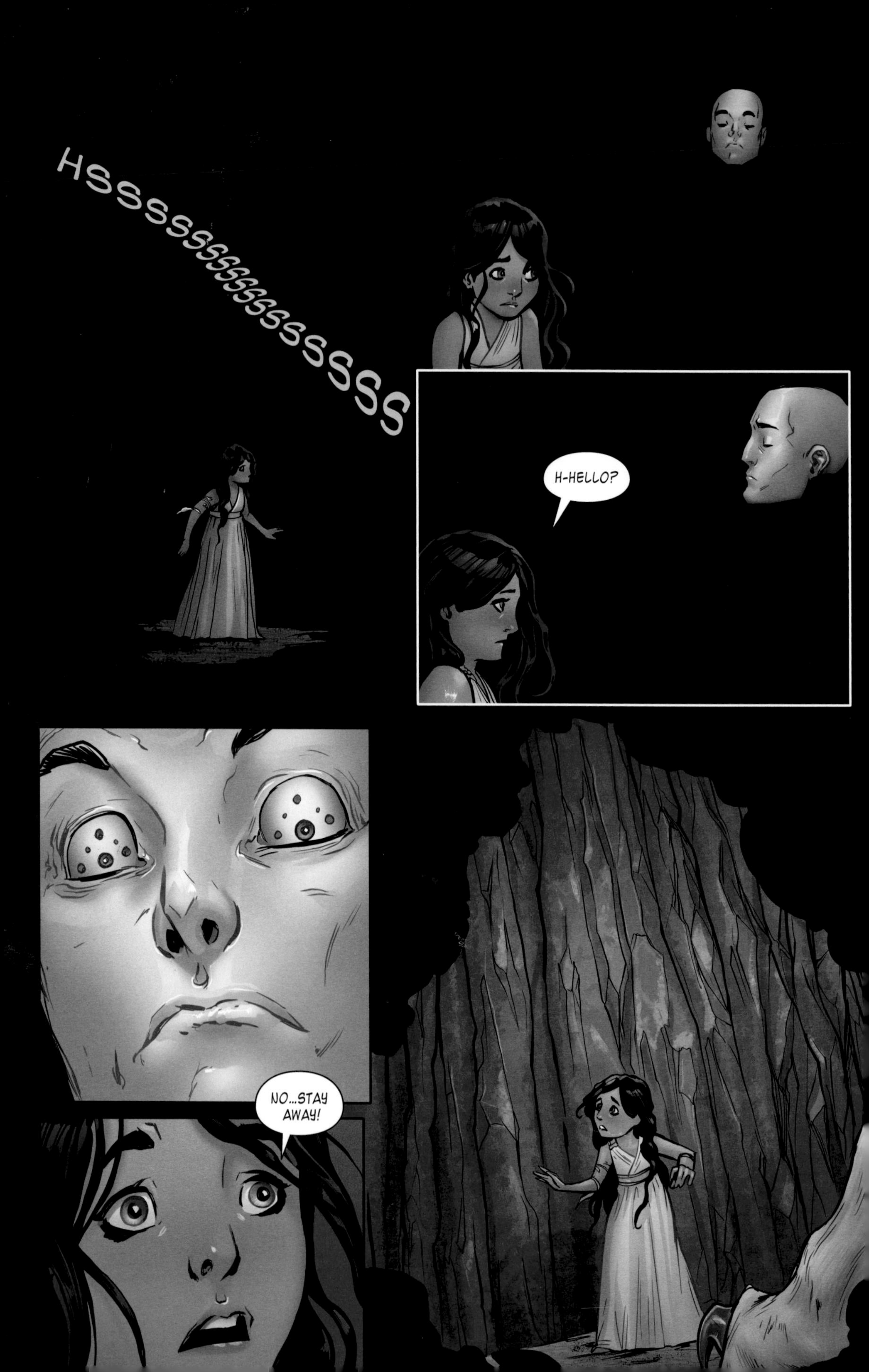
HSSSSSSSSSSSSSSSSSSS
H-HELLO?
NO...STAY AWAY!

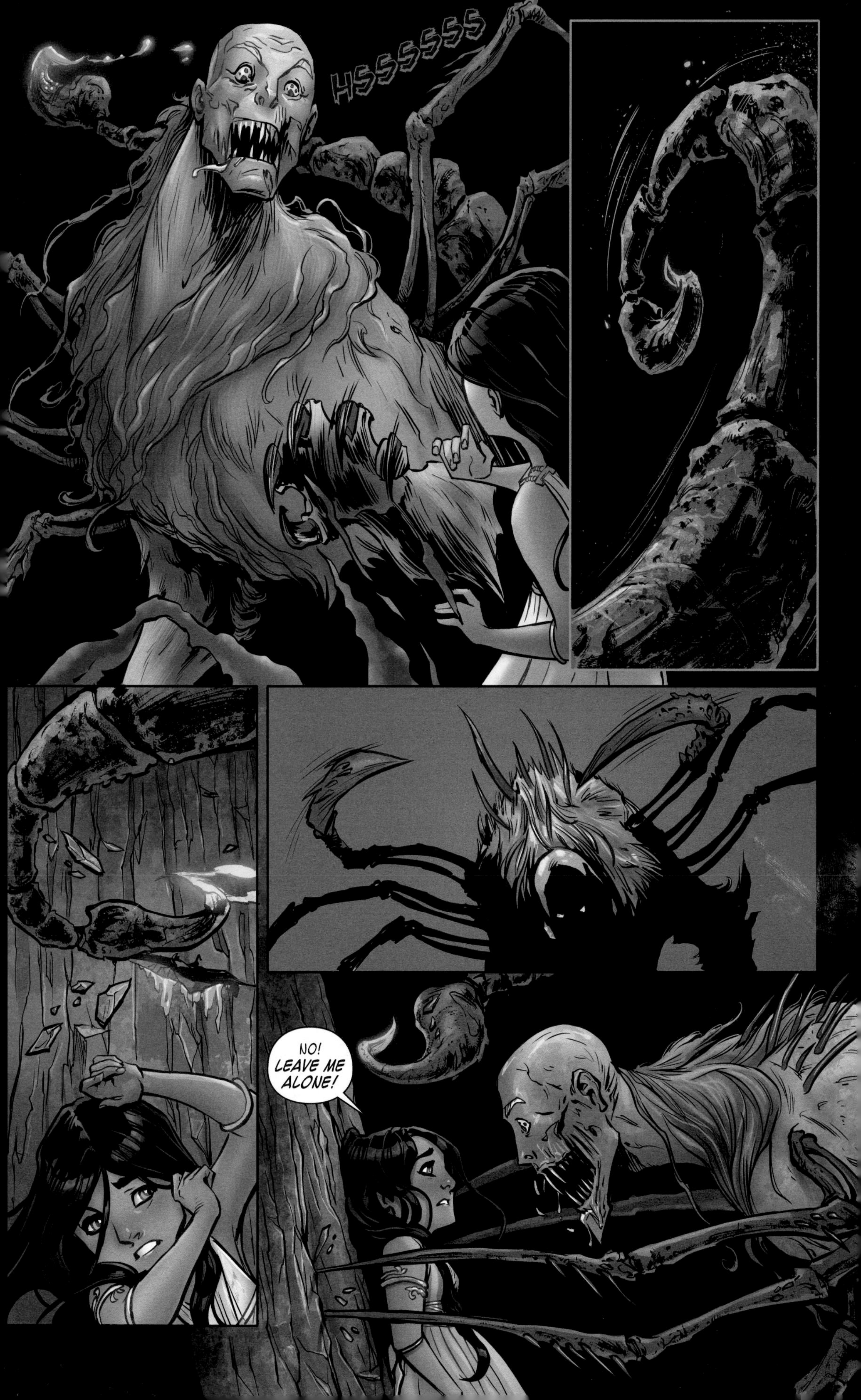
HSSSSSSS
NO! LEAVE ME ALONE!

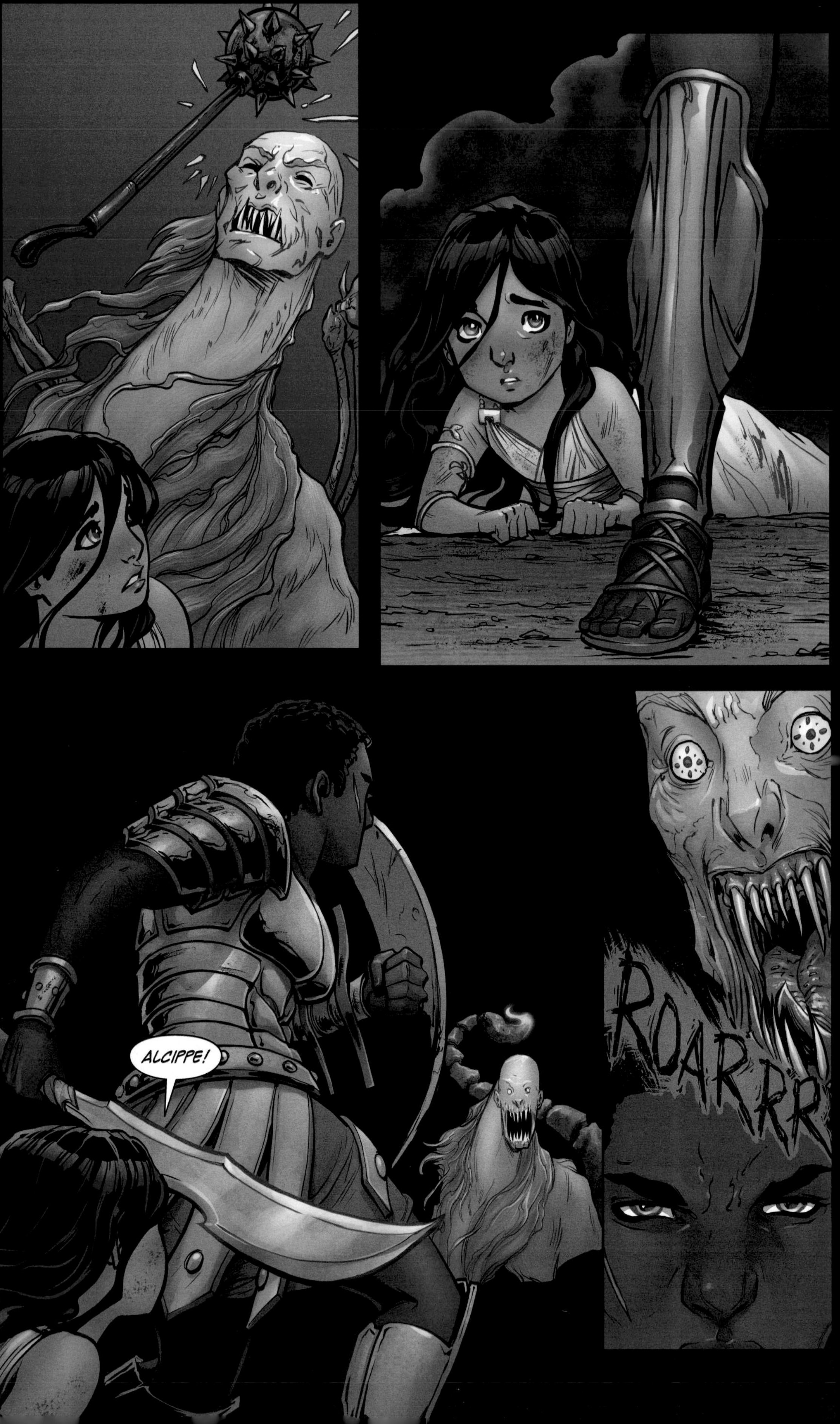
ALCIPPE!
ROARRR

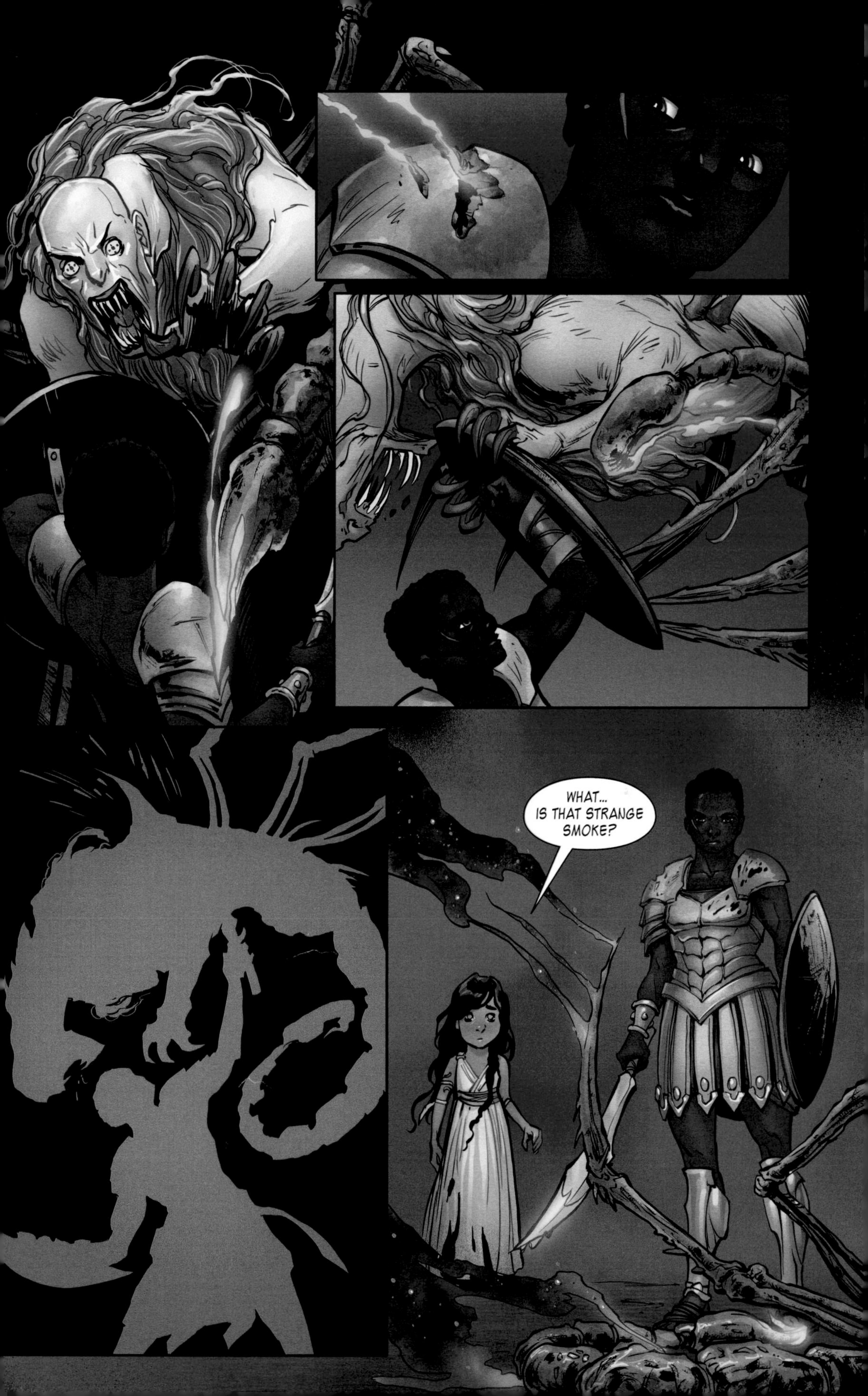
WHAT...
IS THAT STRANGE
SMOKE?

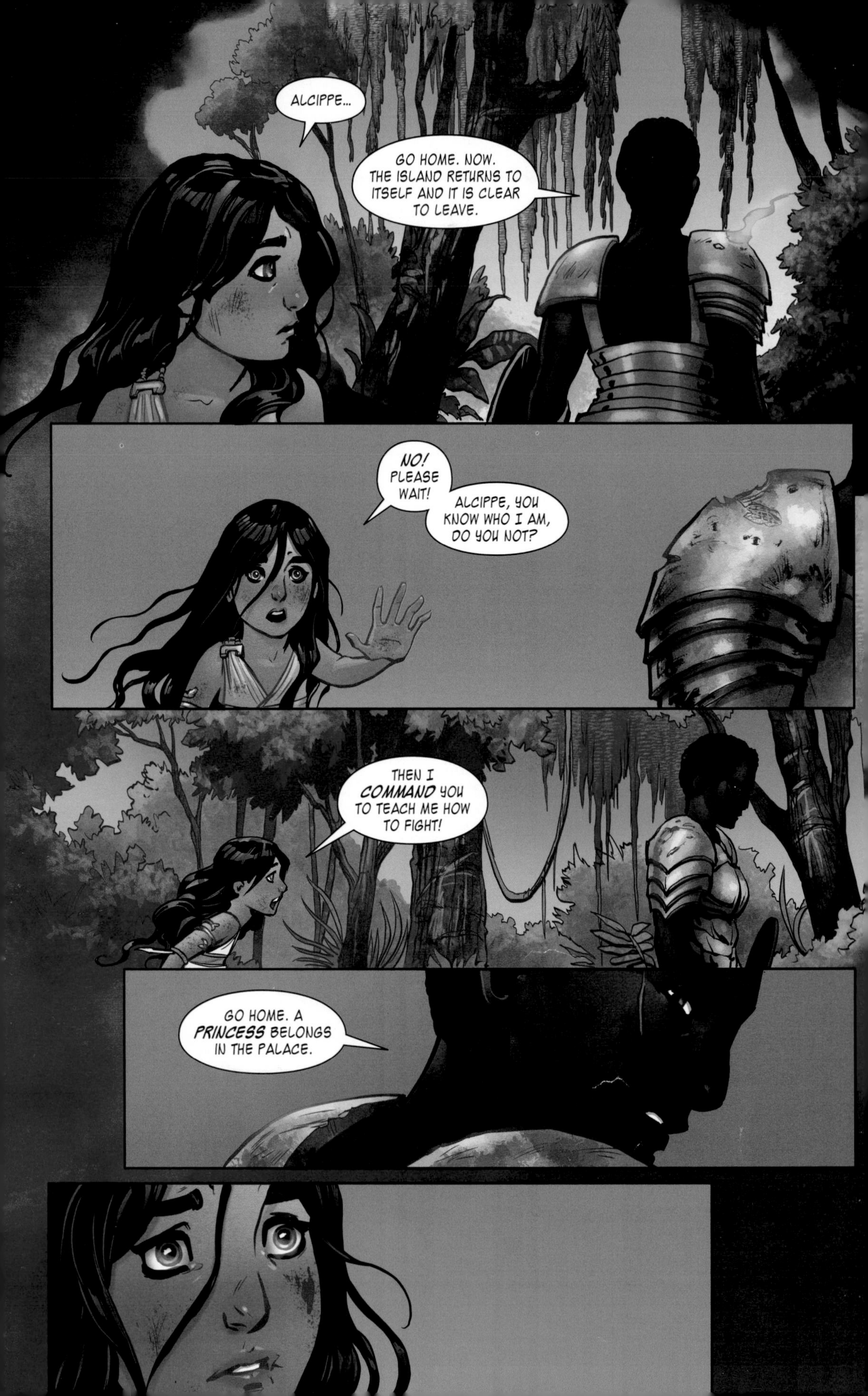
ALCIPPE...
GO HOME. NOW. THE ISLAND RETURNS TO ITSELF AND IT IS CLEAR TO LEAVE.
NO! PLEASE WAIT!
ALCIPPE, YOU KNOW WHO I AM, DO YOU NOT?
THEN I COMMAND YOU TO TEACH ME HOW TO FIGHT!
GO HOME. A PRINCESS BELONGS IN THE PALACE.

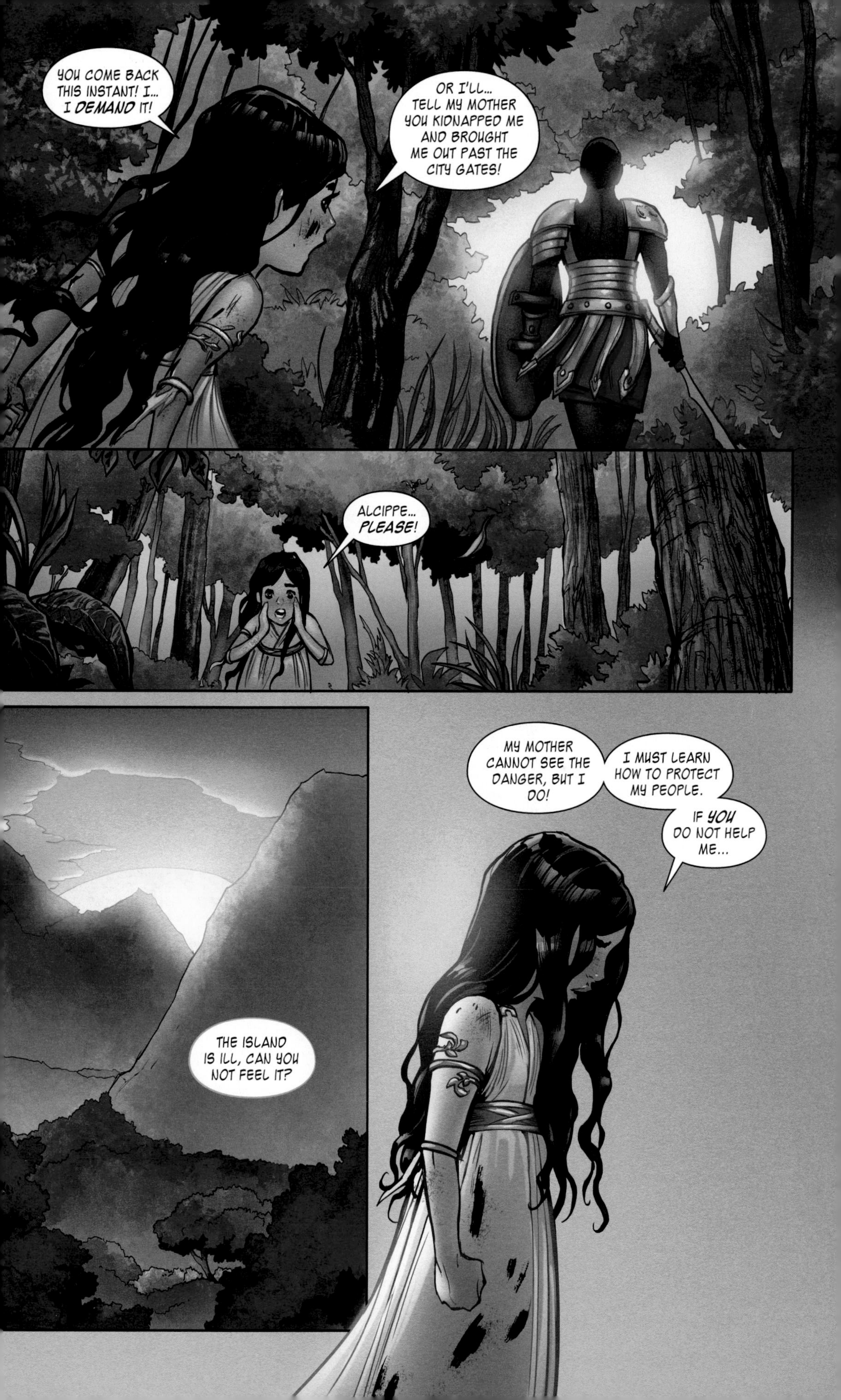
YOU COME BACK THIS INSTANT! I... I DEMAND IT!
OR I'LL... TELL MY MOTHER YOU KIDNAPPED ME AND BROUGHT ME OUT PAST THE CITY GATES!
ALCIPPE... PLEASE!
THE ISLAND IS ILL, CAN YOU NOT FEEL IT?
MY MOTHER CANNOT SEE THE DANGER, BUT I DO!
I MUST LEARN HOW TO PROTECT MY PEOPLE.
IF YOU DO NOT HELP ME...

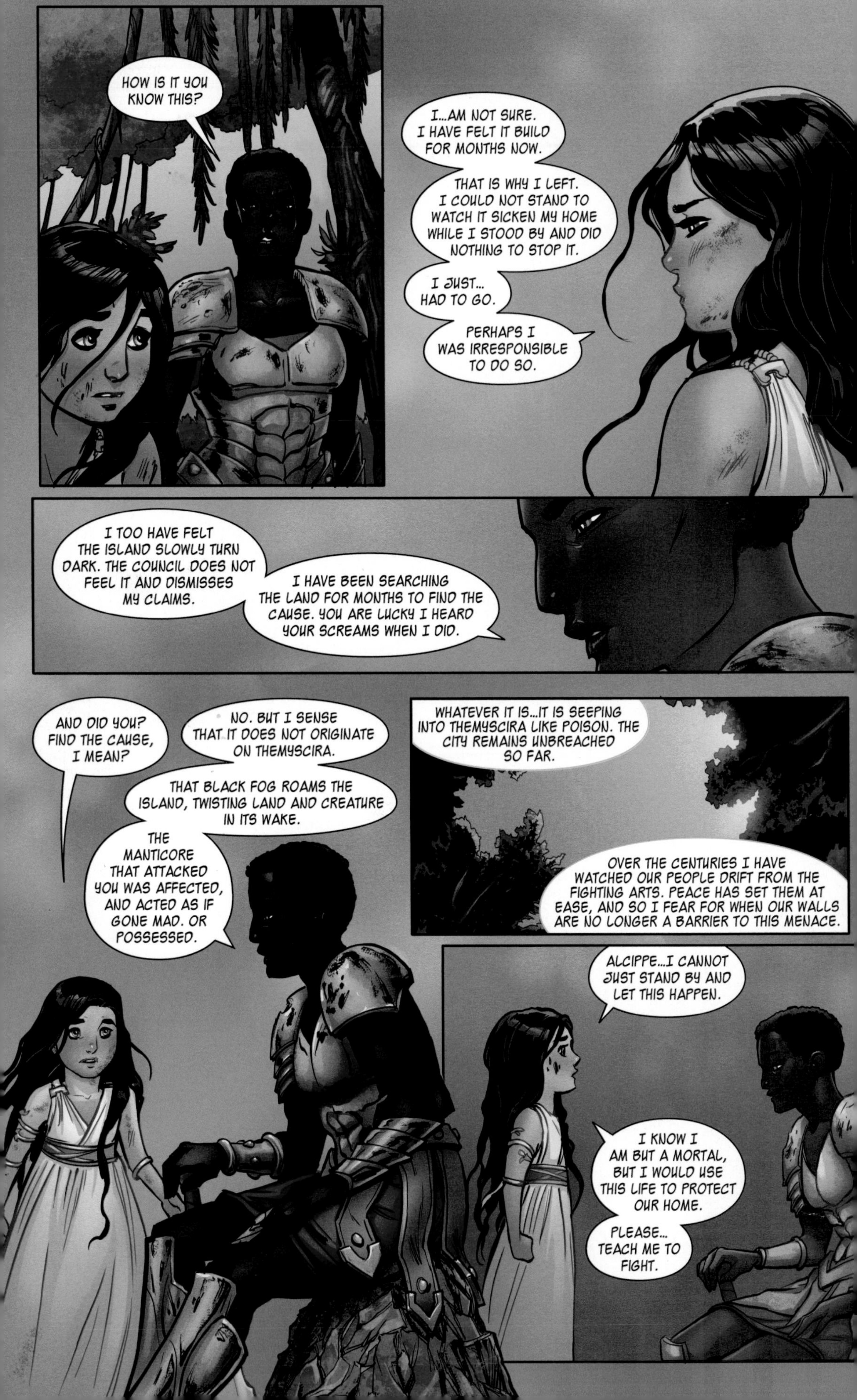
HOW IS IT YOU KNOW THIS?
I...AM NOT SURE. I HAVE FELT IT BUILD FOR MONTHS NOW.
THAT IS WHY I LEFT. I COULD NOT STAND TO WATCH IT SICKEN MY HOME WHILE I STOOD BY AND DID NOTHING TO STOP IT.
I JUST... HAD TO GO.
PERHAPS I WAS IRRESPONSIBLE TO DO SO.
I TOO HAVE FELT THE ISLAND SLOWLY TURN DARK. THE COUNCIL DOES NOT FEEL IT AND DISMISSES MY CLAIMS.
I HAVE BEEN SEARCHING THE LAND FOR MONTHS TO FIND THE CAUSE. YOU ARE LUCKY I HEARD YOUR SCREAMS WHEN I DID.
AND DID YOU? FIND THE CAUSE, I MEAN?
NO. BUT I SENSE THAT IT DOES NOT ORIGINATE ON THEMYSCIRA.
THAT BLACK FOG ROAMS THE ISLAND, TWISTING LAND AND CREATURE IN ITS WAKE.
THE MANTICORE THAT ATTACKED YOU WAS AFFECTED, AND ACTED AS IF GONE MAD. OR POSSESSED.
WHATEVER IT IS...IT IS SEEPING INTO THEMYSCIRA LIKE POISON. THE CITY REMAINS UNBREACHED SO FAR.
OVER THE CENTURIES I HAVE WATCHED OUR PEOPLE DRIFT FROM THE FIGHTING ARTS. PEACE HAS SET THEM AT EASE, AND SO I FEAR FOR WHEN OUR WALLS ARE NO LONGER A BARRIER TO THIS MENACE.
ALCIPPE...I CANNOT JUST STAND BY AND LET THIS HAPPEN.
I KNOW I AM BUT A MORTAL, BUT I WOULD USE THIS LIFE TO PROTECT OUR HOME.
PLEASE... TEACH ME TO FIGHT.

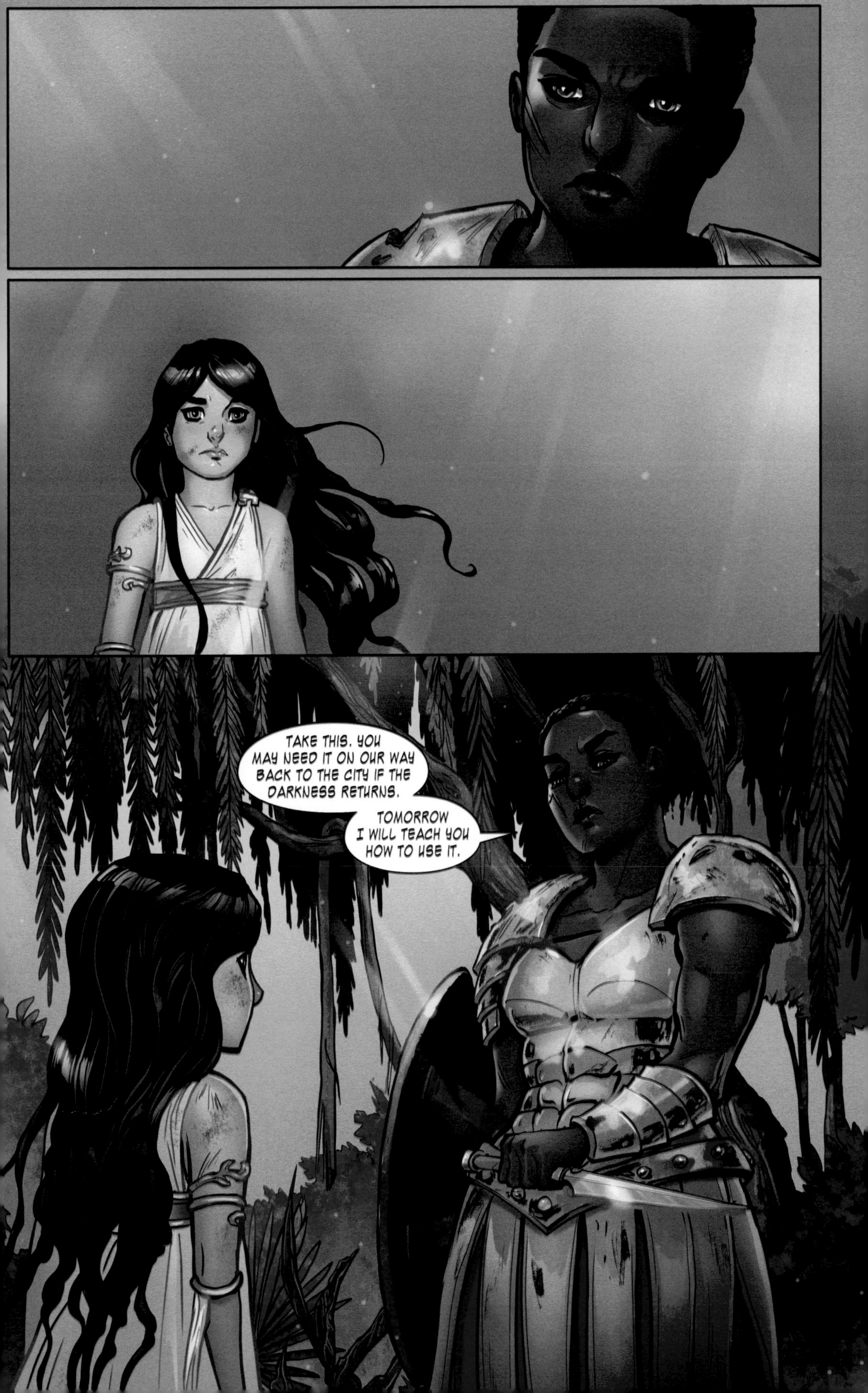
TAKE THIS. YOU MAY NEED IT ON OUR WAY BACK TO THE CITY IF THE DARKNESS RETURNS.
TOMORROW I WILL TEACH YOU HOW TO USE IT.

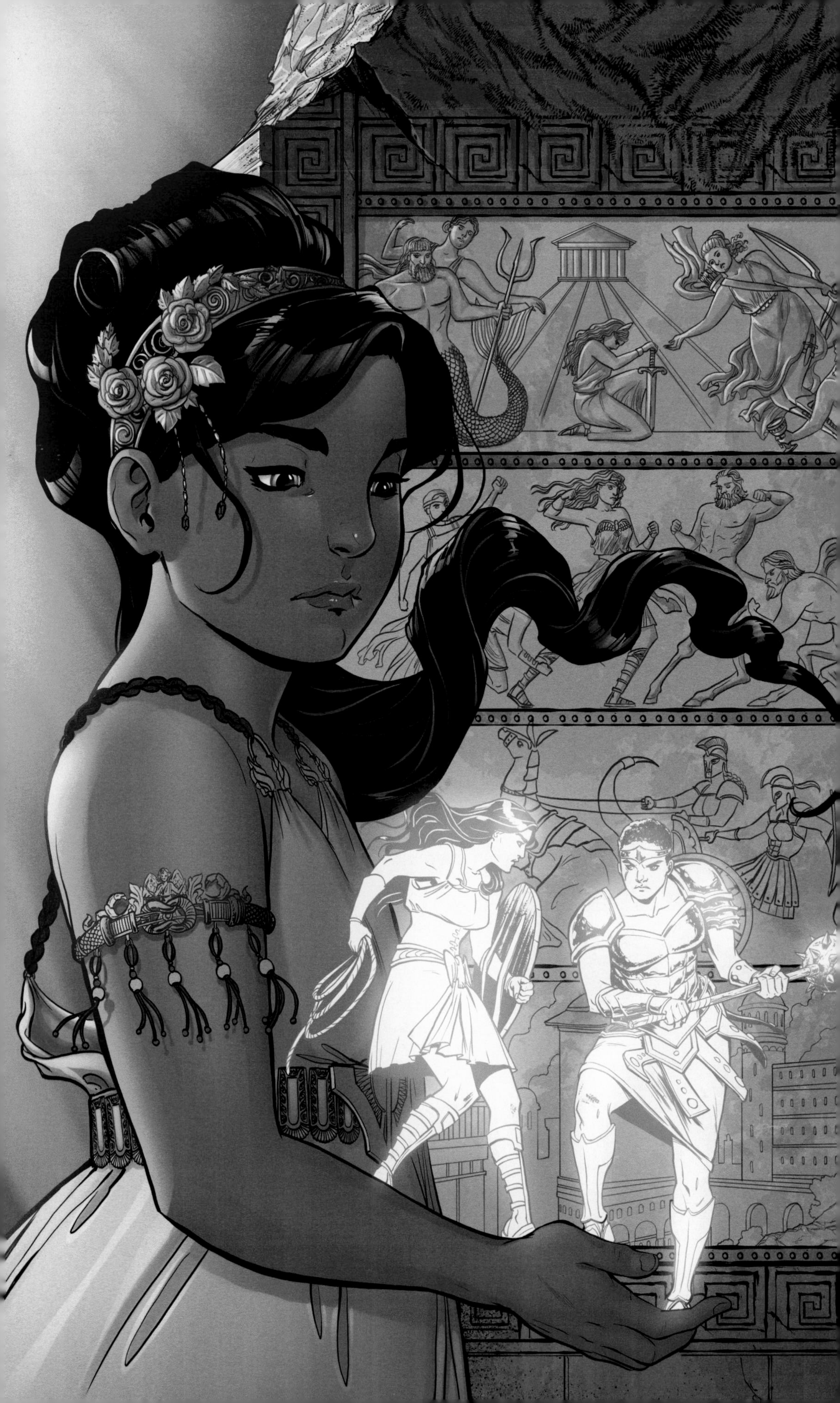

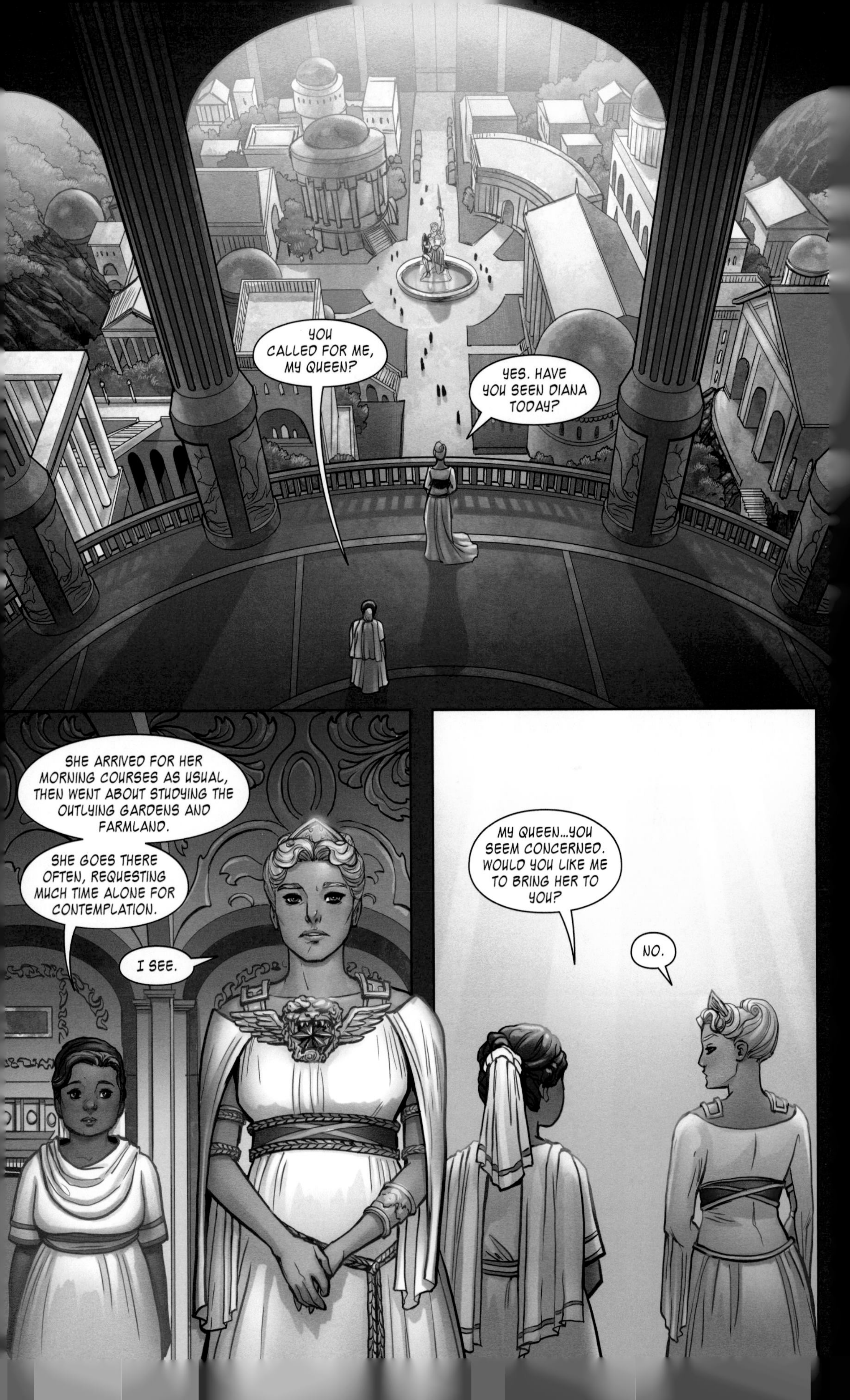
YOU CALLED FOR ME, MY QUEEN?
YES. HAVE YOU SEEN DIANA TODAY?
SHE ARRIVED FOR HER MORNING COURSES AS USUAL, THEN WENT ABOUT STUDYING THE OUTLYING GARDENS AND FARMLAND.
SHE GOES THERE OFTEN, REQUESTING MUCH TIME ALONE FOR CONTEMPLATION.
I SEE.
MY QUEEN...YOU SEEM CONCERNED. WOULD YOU LIKE ME TO BRING HER TO YOU?
NO.

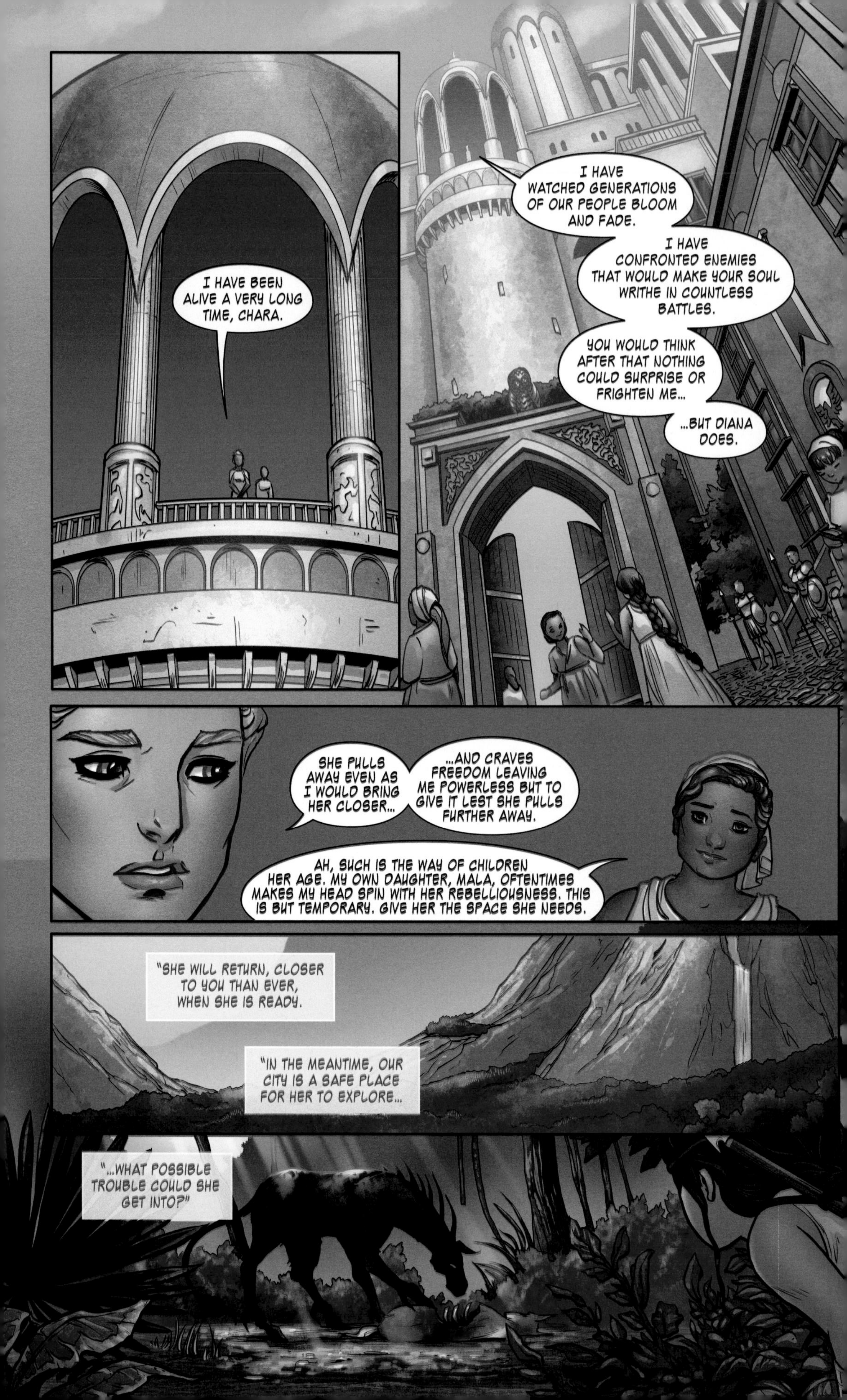
I HAVE BEEN ALIVE A VERY LONG TIME, CHARA.
I HAVE WATCHED GENERATIONS OF OUR PEOPLE BLOOM AND FADE.
I HAVE CONFRONTED ENEMIES THAT WOULD MAKE YOUR SOUL WRITHE IN COUNTLESS BATTLES.
YOU WOULD THINK AFTER THAT NOTHING COULD SURPRISE OR FRIGHTEN ME...
...BUT DIANA DOES.
SHE PULLS AWAY EVEN AS I WOULD BRING HER CLOSER...
...AND CRAVES FREEDOM LEAVING ME POWERLESS BUT TO GIVE IT LEST SHE PULLS FURTHER AWAY.
AH, SUCH IS THE WAY OF CHILDREN HER AGE. MY OWN DAUGHTER, MALA, OFTENTIMES MAKES MY HEAD SPIN WITH HER REBELLIOUSNESS. THIS IS BUT TEMPORARY. GIVE HER THE SPACE SHE NEEDS.
"SHE WILL RETURN, CLOSER TO YOU THAN EVER, WHEN SHE IS READY.
"IN THE MEANTIME, OUR CITY IS A SAFE PLACE FOR HER TO EXPLORE...
"...WHAT POSSIBLE TROUBLE COULD SHE GET INTO?"

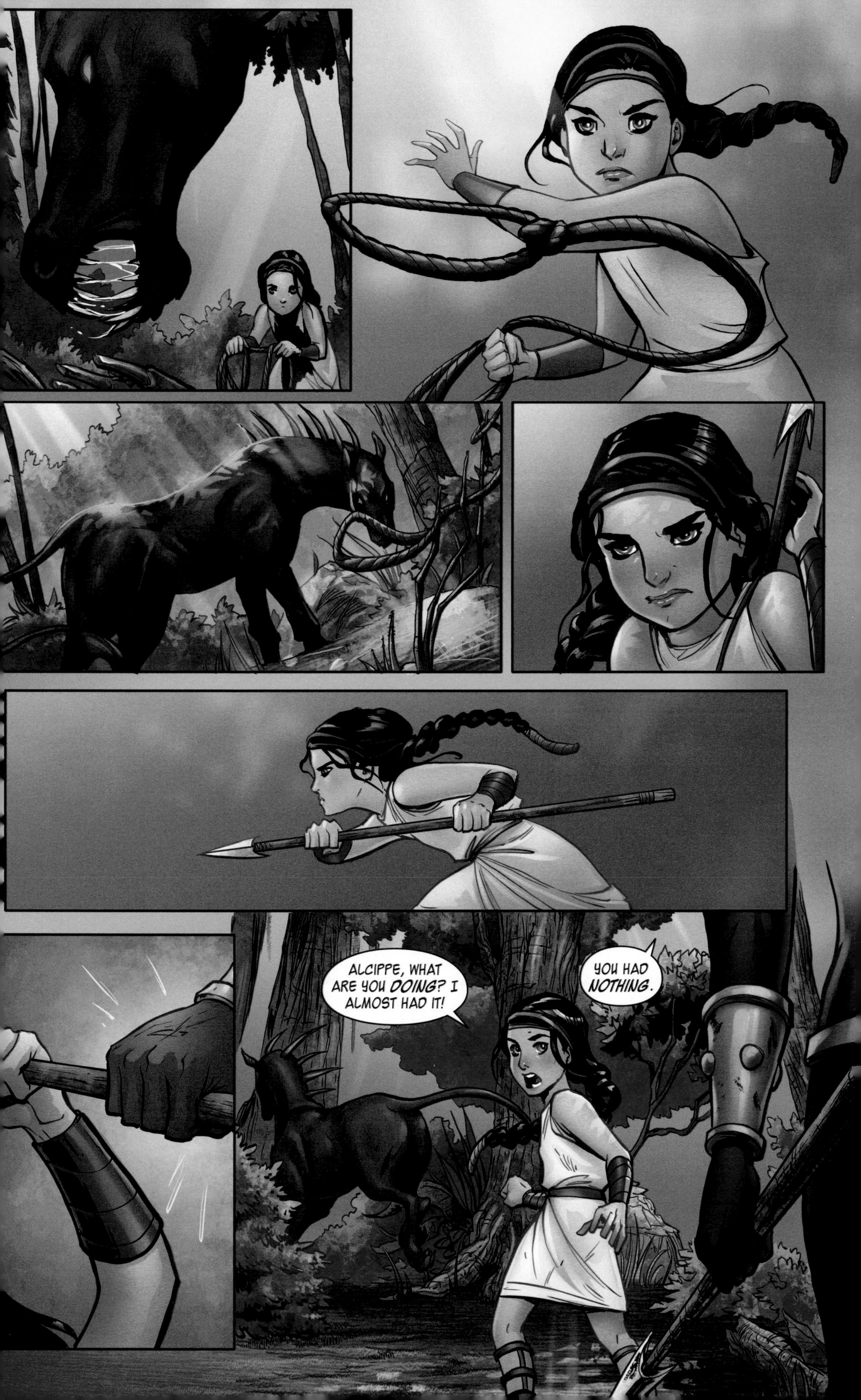
ALCIPPE, WHAT ARE YOU DOING? I ALMOST HAD IT!
YOU HAD NOTHING.

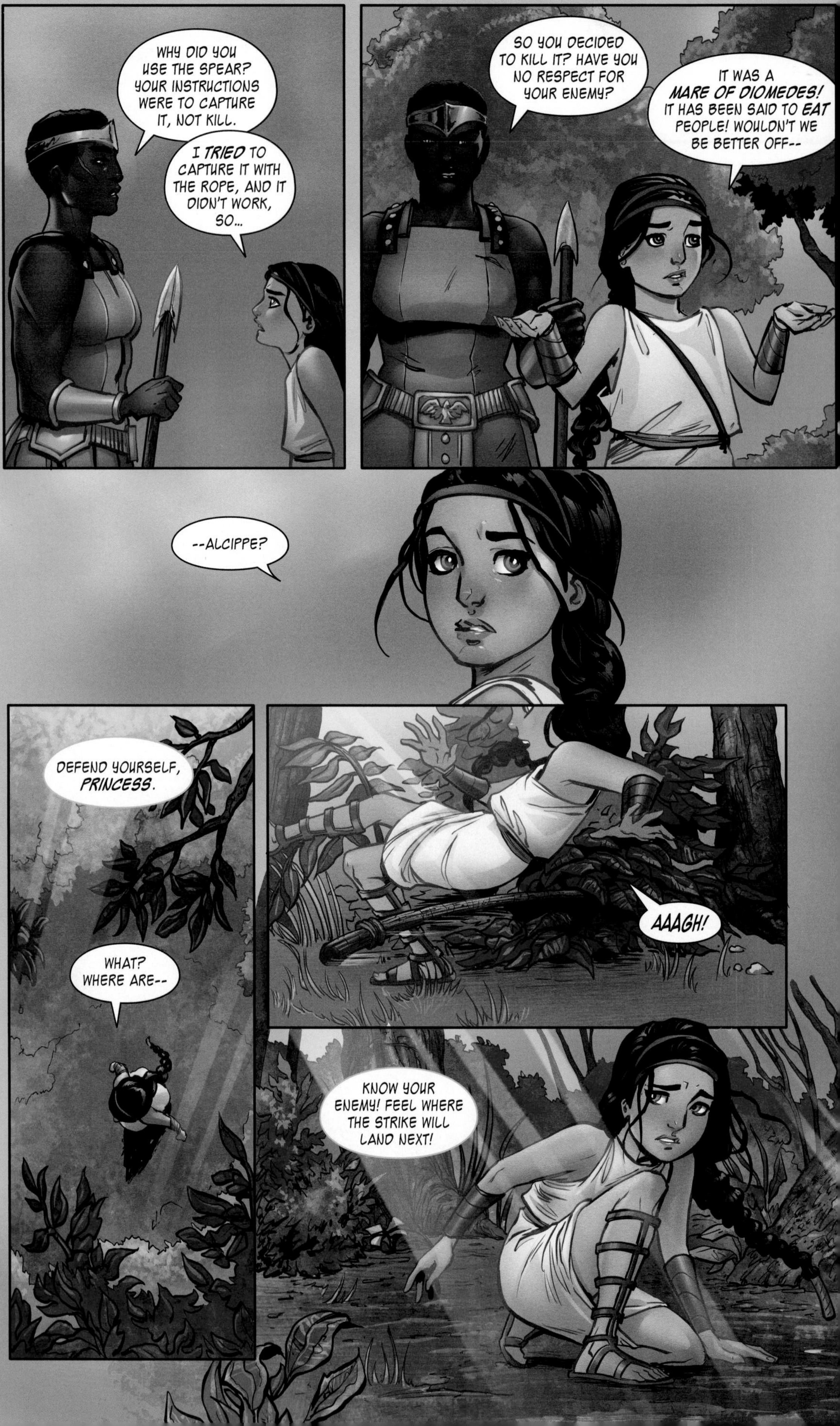
WHY DID YOU USE THE SPEAR? YOUR INSTRUCTIONS WERE TO CAPTURE IT, NOT KILL.
I *TRIED* TO CAPTURE IT WITH THE ROPE, AND IT DIDN'T WORK, SO...
SO YOU DECIDED TO KILL IT? HAVE YOU NO RESPECT FOR YOUR ENEMY?
IT WAS A ***MARE OF DIOMEDES!*** IT HAS BEEN SAID TO ***EAT*** PEOPLE! WOULDN'T WE BE BETTER OFF--
--ALCIPPE?
DEFEND YOURSELF, ***PRINCESS***.
WHAT? WHERE ARE--
AAAGH!
KNOW YOUR ENEMY! FEEL WHERE THE STRIKE WILL LAND NEXT!

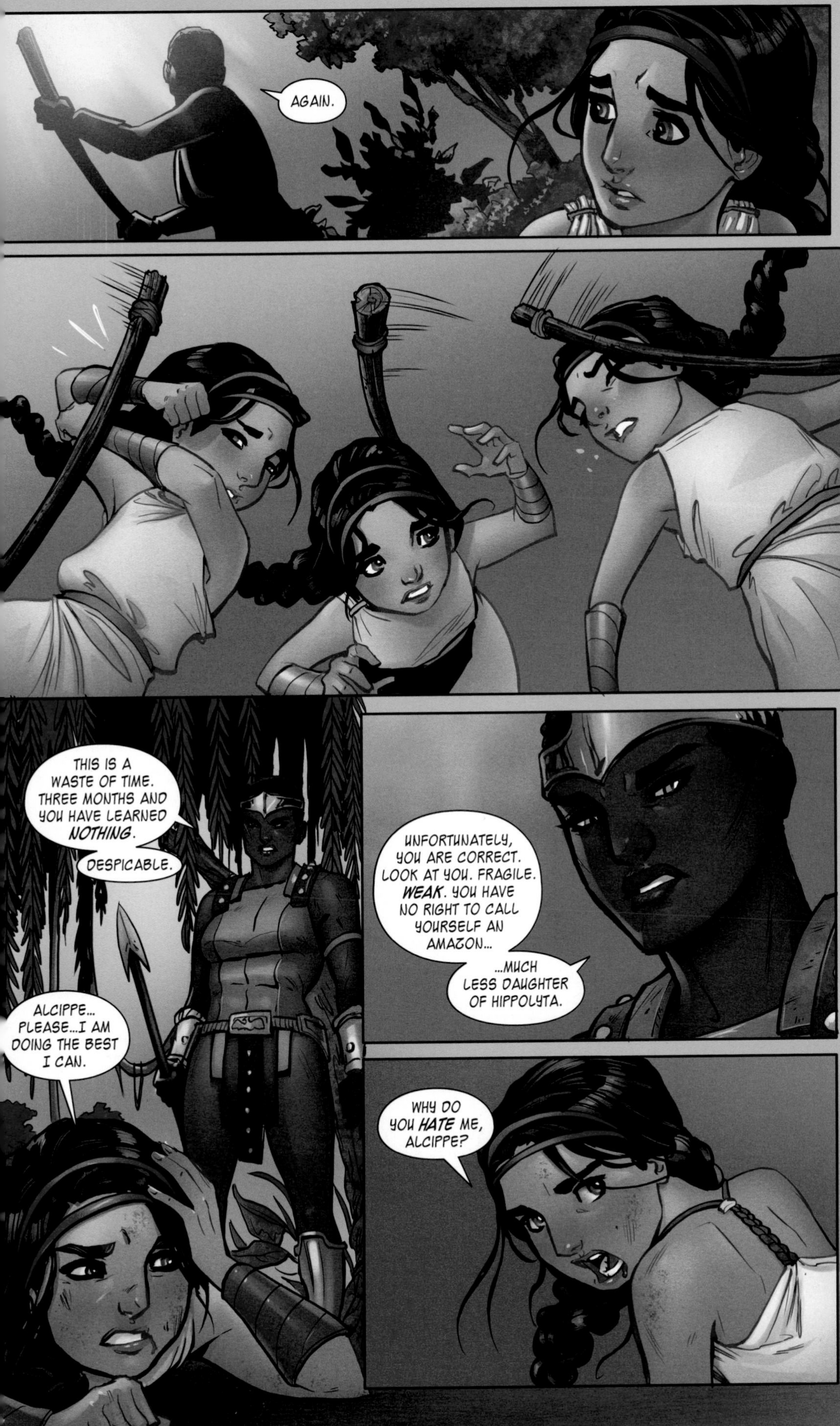
AGAIN.
THIS IS A WASTE OF TIME. THREE MONTHS AND YOU HAVE LEARNED *NOTHING*.
DESPICABLE.
ALCIPPE... PLEASE...I AM DOING THE BEST I CAN.
UNFORTUNATELY, YOU ARE CORRECT. LOOK AT YOU. FRAGILE. *WEAK*. YOU HAVE NO RIGHT TO CALL YOURSELF AN AMAZON...
...MUCH LESS DAUGHTER OF HIPPOLYTA.
WHY DO YOU *HATE* ME, ALCIPPE?

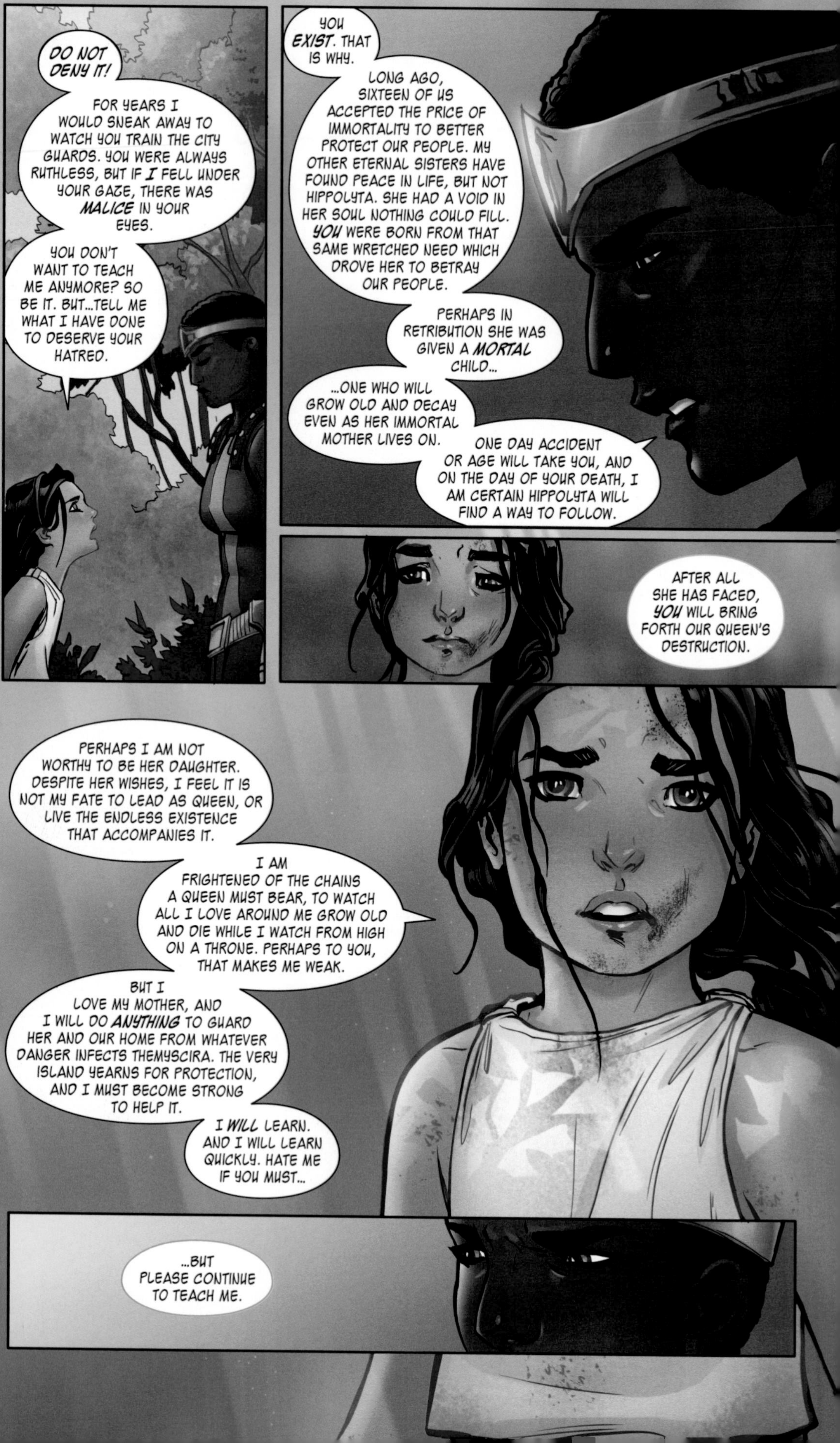
DO NOT DENY IT!
FOR YEARS I WOULD SNEAK AWAY TO WATCH YOU TRAIN THE CITY GUARDS. YOU WERE ALWAYS RUTHLESS, BUT IF I FELL UNDER YOUR GAZE, THERE WAS MALICE IN YOUR EYES.
YOU DON'T WANT TO TEACH ME ANYMORE? SO BE IT. BUT...TELL ME WHAT I HAVE DONE TO DESERVE YOUR HATRED.
YOU EXIST. THAT IS WHY.
LONG AGO, SIXTEEN OF US ACCEPTED THE PRICE OF IMMORTALITY TO BETTER PROTECT OUR PEOPLE. MY OTHER ETERNAL SISTERS HAVE FOUND PEACE IN LIFE, BUT NOT HIPPOLYTA. SHE HAD A VOID IN HER SOUL NOTHING COULD FILL. YOU WERE BORN FROM THAT SAME WRETCHED NEED WHICH DROVE HER TO BETRAY OUR PEOPLE.
PERHAPS IN RETRIBUTION SHE WAS GIVEN A MORTAL CHILD...
...ONE WHO WILL GROW OLD AND DECAY EVEN AS HER IMMORTAL MOTHER LIVES ON.
ONE DAY ACCIDENT OR AGE WILL TAKE YOU, AND ON THE DAY OF YOUR DEATH, I AM CERTAIN HIPPOLYTA WILL FIND A WAY TO FOLLOW.
AFTER ALL SHE HAS FACED, YOU WILL BRING FORTH OUR QUEEN'S DESTRUCTION.
PERHAPS I AM NOT WORTHY TO BE HER DAUGHTER. DESPITE HER WISHES, I FEEL IT IS NOT MY FATE TO LEAD AS QUEEN, OR LIVE THE ENDLESS EXISTENCE THAT ACCOMPANIES IT.
I AM FRIGHTENED OF THE CHAINS A QUEEN MUST BEAR, TO WATCH ALL I LOVE AROUND ME GROW OLD AND DIE WHILE I WATCH FROM HIGH ON A THRONE. PERHAPS TO YOU, THAT MAKES ME WEAK.
BUT I LOVE MY MOTHER, AND I WILL DO ANYTHING TO GUARD HER AND OUR HOME FROM WHATEVER DANGER INFECTS THEMYSCIRA. THE VERY ISLAND YEARNS FOR PROTECTION, AND I MUST BECOME STRONG TO HELP IT.
I WILL LEARN. AND I WILL LEARN QUICKLY. HATE ME IF YOU MUST...
...BUT PLEASE CONTINUE TO TEACH ME.

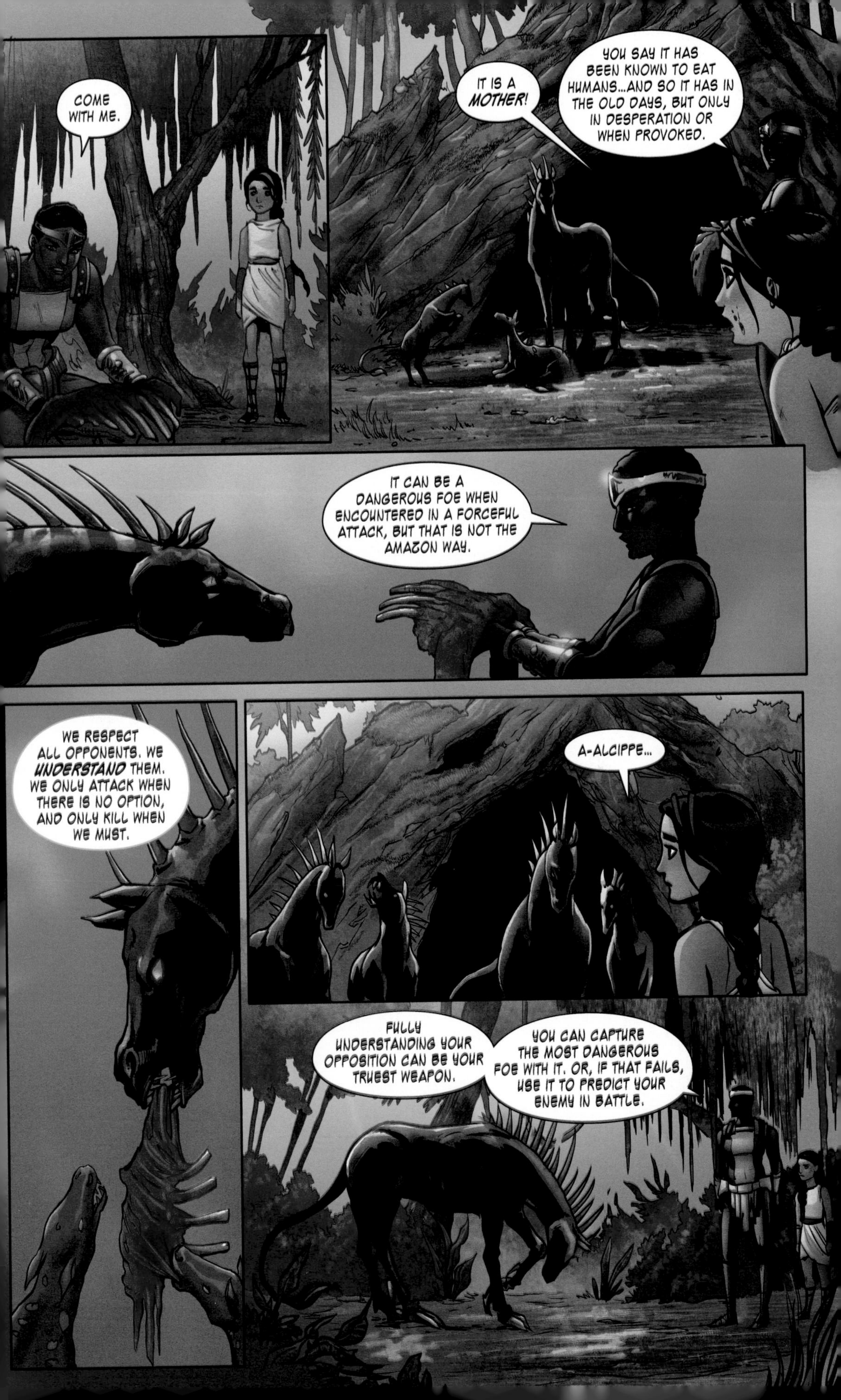

COME WITH ME.
IT IS A *MOTHER*!
YOU SAY IT HAS BEEN KNOWN TO EAT HUMANS...AND SO IT HAS IN THE OLD DAYS, BUT ONLY IN DESPERATION OR WHEN PROVOKED.
IT CAN BE A DANGEROUS FOE WHEN ENCOUNTERED IN A FORCEFUL ATTACK, BUT THAT IS NOT THE AMAZON WAY.
WE RESPECT ALL OPPONENTS. WE *UNDERSTAND* THEM. WE ONLY ATTACK WHEN THERE IS NO OPTION, AND ONLY KILL WHEN WE MUST.
A-ALCIPPE...
FULLY UNDERSTANDING YOUR OPPOSITION CAN BE YOUR TRUEST WEAPON.
YOU CAN CAPTURE THE MOST DANGEROUS FOE WITH IT. OR, IF THAT FAILS, USE IT TO PREDICT YOUR ENEMY IN BATTLE.

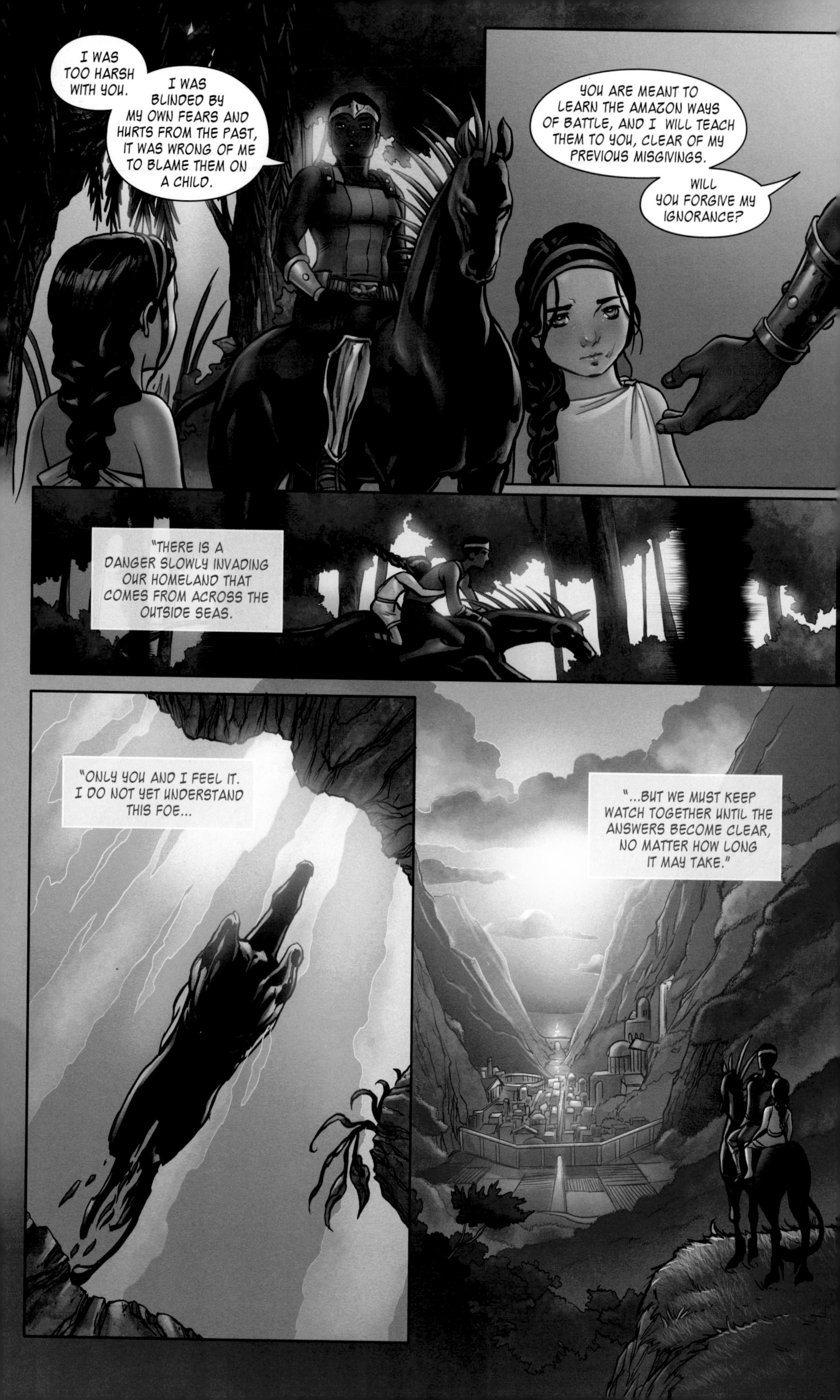
I WAS TOO HARSH WITH YOU.
I WAS BLINDED BY MY OWN FEARS AND HURTS FROM THE PAST, IT WAS WRONG OF ME TO BLAME THEM ON A CHILD.
YOU ARE MEANT TO LEARN THE AMAZON WAYS OF BATTLE, AND I WILL TEACH THEM TO YOU, CLEAR OF MY PREVIOUS MISGIVINGS.
WILL YOU FORGIVE MY IGNORANCE?
"THERE IS A DANGER SLOWLY INVADING OUR HOMELAND THAT COMES FROM ACROSS THE OUTSIDE SEAS.
"ONLY YOU AND I FEEL IT. I DO NOT YET UNDERSTAND THIS FOE...
"...BUT WE MUST KEEP WATCH TOGETHER UNTIL THE ANSWERS BECOME CLEAR, NO MATTER HOW LONG IT MAY TAKE."

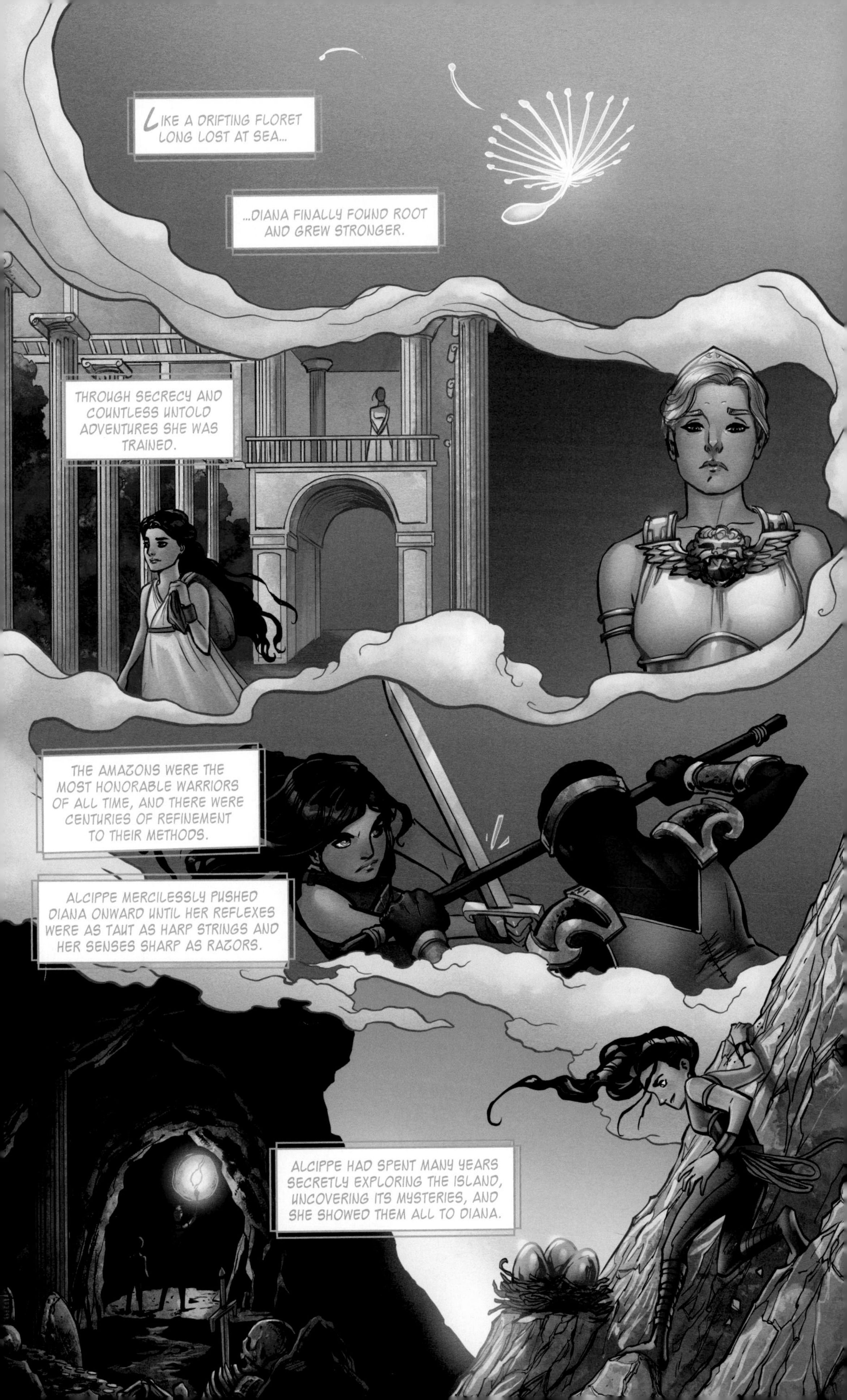
LIKE A DRIFTING FLORET LONG LOST AT SEA...
...DIANA FINALLY FOUND ROOT AND GREW STRONGER.
THROUGH SECRECY AND COUNTLESS UNTOLD ADVENTURES SHE WAS TRAINED.
THE AMAZONS WERE THE MOST HONORABLE WARRIORS OF ALL TIME, AND THERE WERE CENTURIES OF REFINEMENT TO THEIR METHODS.
ALCIPPE MERCILESSLY PUSHED DIANA ONWARD UNTIL HER REFLEXES WERE AS TAUT AS HARP STRINGS AND HER SENSES SHARP AS RAZORS.
ALCIPPE HAD SPENT MANY YEARS SECRETLY EXPLORING THE ISLAND, UNCOVERING ITS MYSTERIES, AND SHE SHOWED THEM ALL TO DIANA.

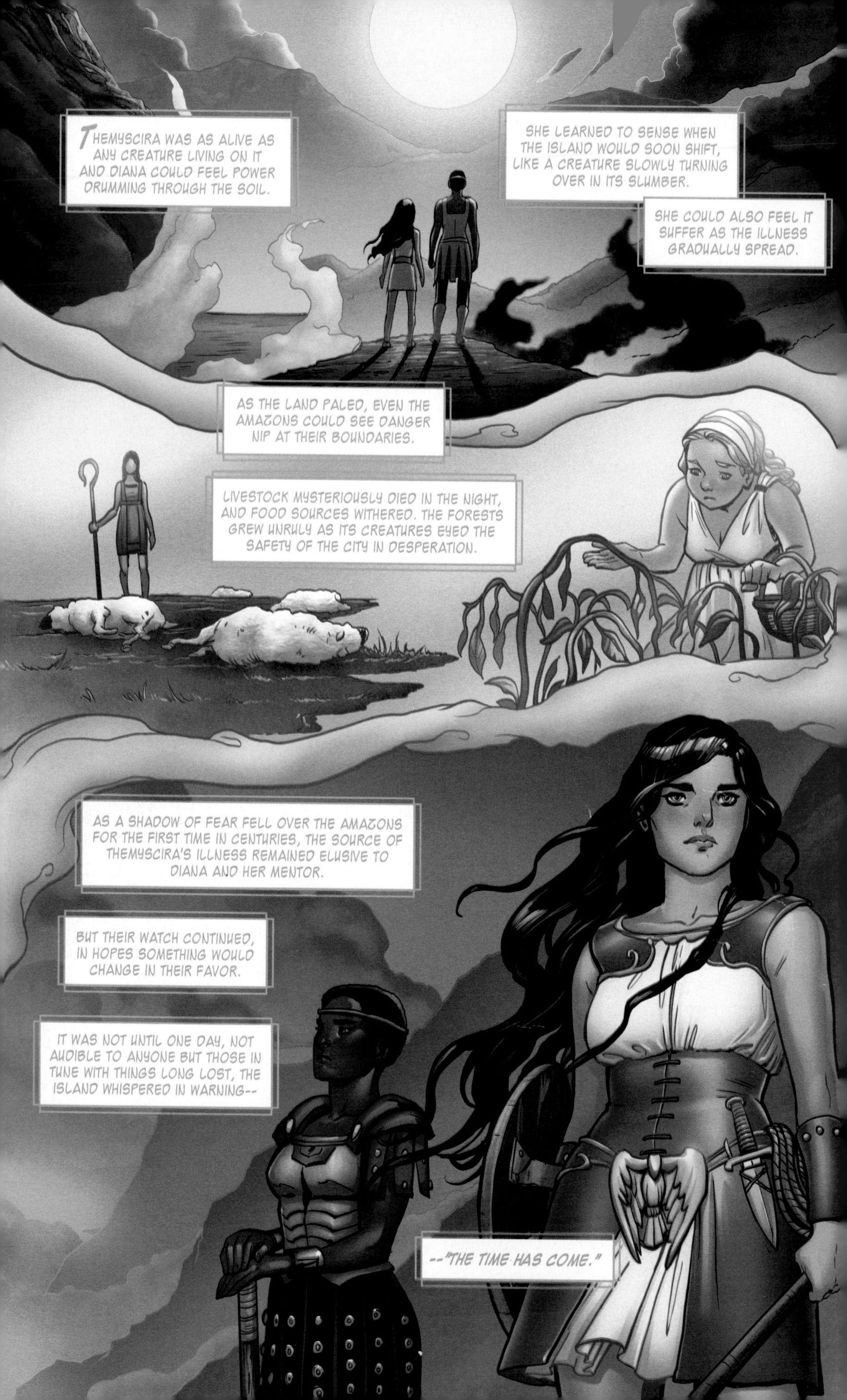
THEMYSCIRA WAS AS ALIVE AS ANY CREATURE LIVING ON IT AND DIANA COULD FEEL POWER DRUMMING THROUGH THE SOIL.
SHE LEARNED TO SENSE WHEN THE ISLAND WOULD SOON SHIFT, LIKE A CREATURE SLOWLY TURNING OVER IN ITS SLUMBER.
SHE COULD ALSO FEEL IT SUFFER AS THE ILLNESS GRADUALLY SPREAD.
AS THE LAND PALED, EVEN THE AMAZONS COULD SEE DANGER NIP AT THEIR BOUNDARIES.
LIVESTOCK MYSTERIOUSLY DIED IN THE NIGHT, AND FOOD SOURCES WITHERED. THE FORESTS GREW UNRULY AS ITS CREATURES EYED THE SAFETY OF THE CITY IN DESPERATION.
AS A SHADOW OF FEAR FELL OVER THE AMAZONS FOR THE FIRST TIME IN CENTURIES, THE SOURCE OF THEMYSCIRA'S ILLNESS REMAINED ELUSIVE TO DIANA AND HER MENTOR.
BUT THEIR WATCH CONTINUED, IN HOPES SOMETHING WOULD CHANGE IN THEIR FAVOR.
IT WAS NOT UNTIL ONE DAY, NOT AUDIBLE TO ANYONE BUT THOSE IN TUNE WITH THINGS LONG LOST, THE ISLAND WHISPERED IN WARNING--
--"THE TIME HAS COME."

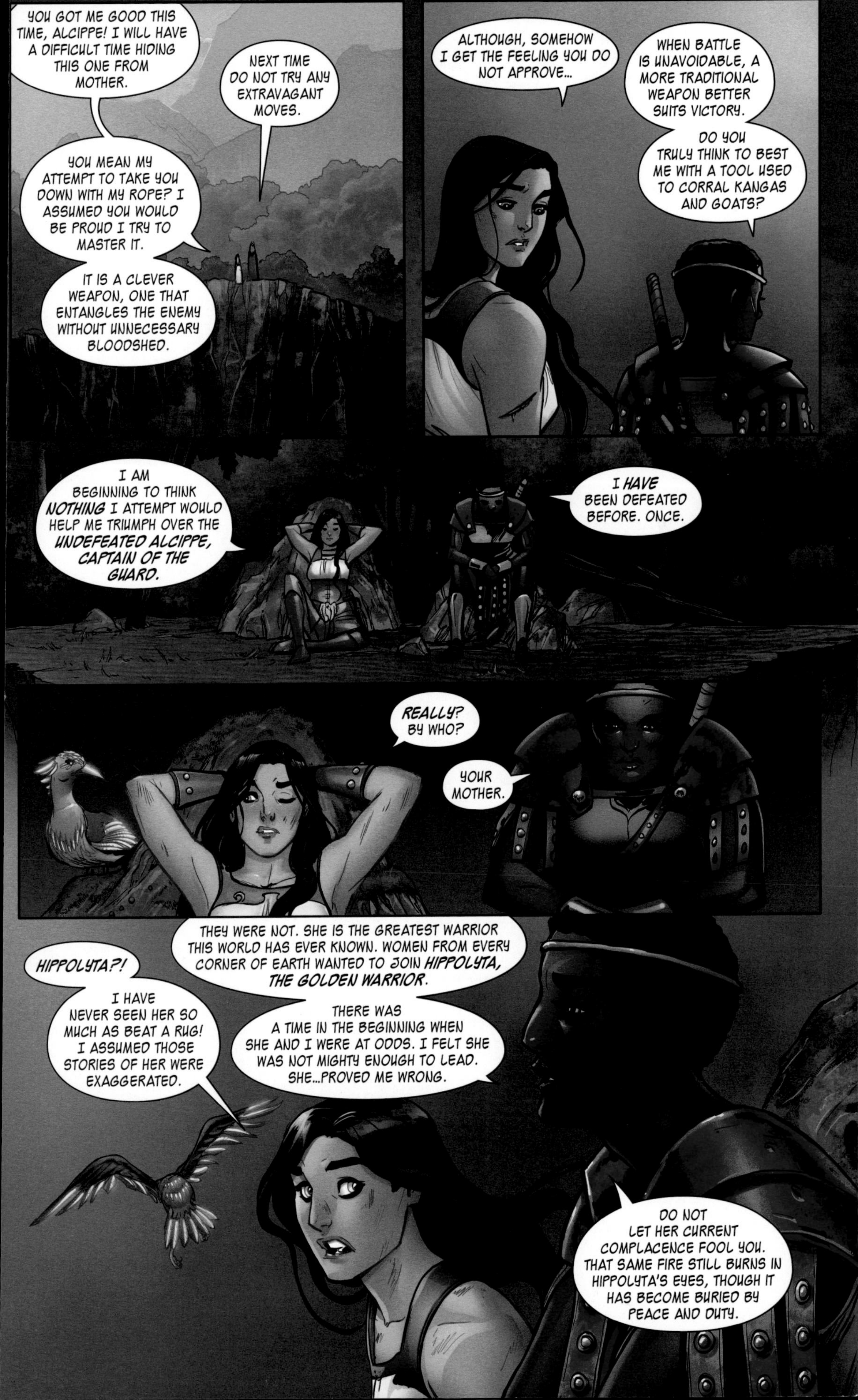
YOU GOT ME GOOD THIS TIME, ALCIPPE! I WILL HAVE A DIFFICULT TIME HIDING THIS ONE FROM MOTHER.
NEXT TIME DO NOT TRY ANY EXTRAVAGANT MOVES.
YOU MEAN MY ATTEMPT TO TAKE YOU DOWN WITH MY ROPE? I ASSUMED YOU WOULD BE PROUD I TRY TO MASTER IT.
IT IS A CLEVER WEAPON, ONE THAT ENTANGLES THE ENEMY WITHOUT UNNECESSARY BLOODSHED.
ALTHOUGH, SOMEHOW I GET THE FEELING YOU DO NOT APPROVE...
WHEN BATTLE IS UNAVOIDABLE, A MORE TRADITIONAL WEAPON BETTER SUITS VICTORY.
DO YOU TRULY THINK TO BEST ME WITH A TOOL USED TO CORRAL KANGAS AND GOATS?
I AM BEGINNING TO THINK NOTHING I ATTEMPT WOULD HELP ME TRIUMPH OVER THE UNDEFEATED ALCIPPE, CAPTAIN OF THE GUARD.
I HAVE BEEN DEFEATED BEFORE. ONCE.
REALLY? BY WHO?
YOUR MOTHER.
HIPPOLYTA?!
I HAVE NEVER SEEN HER SO MUCH AS BEAT A RUG! I ASSUMED THOSE STORIES OF HER WERE EXAGGERATED.
THEY WERE NOT. SHE IS THE GREATEST WARRIOR THIS WORLD HAS EVER KNOWN. WOMEN FROM EVERY CORNER OF EARTH WANTED TO JOIN HIPPOLYTA, THE GOLDEN WARRIOR.
THERE WAS A TIME IN THE BEGINNING WHEN SHE AND I WERE AT ODDS. I FELT SHE WAS NOT MIGHTY ENOUGH TO LEAD. SHE...PROVED ME WRONG.
DO NOT LET HER CURRENT COMPLACENCE FOOL YOU. THAT SAME FIRE STILL BURNS IN HIPPOLYTA'S EYES, THOUGH IT HAS BECOME BURIED BY PEACE AND DUTY.

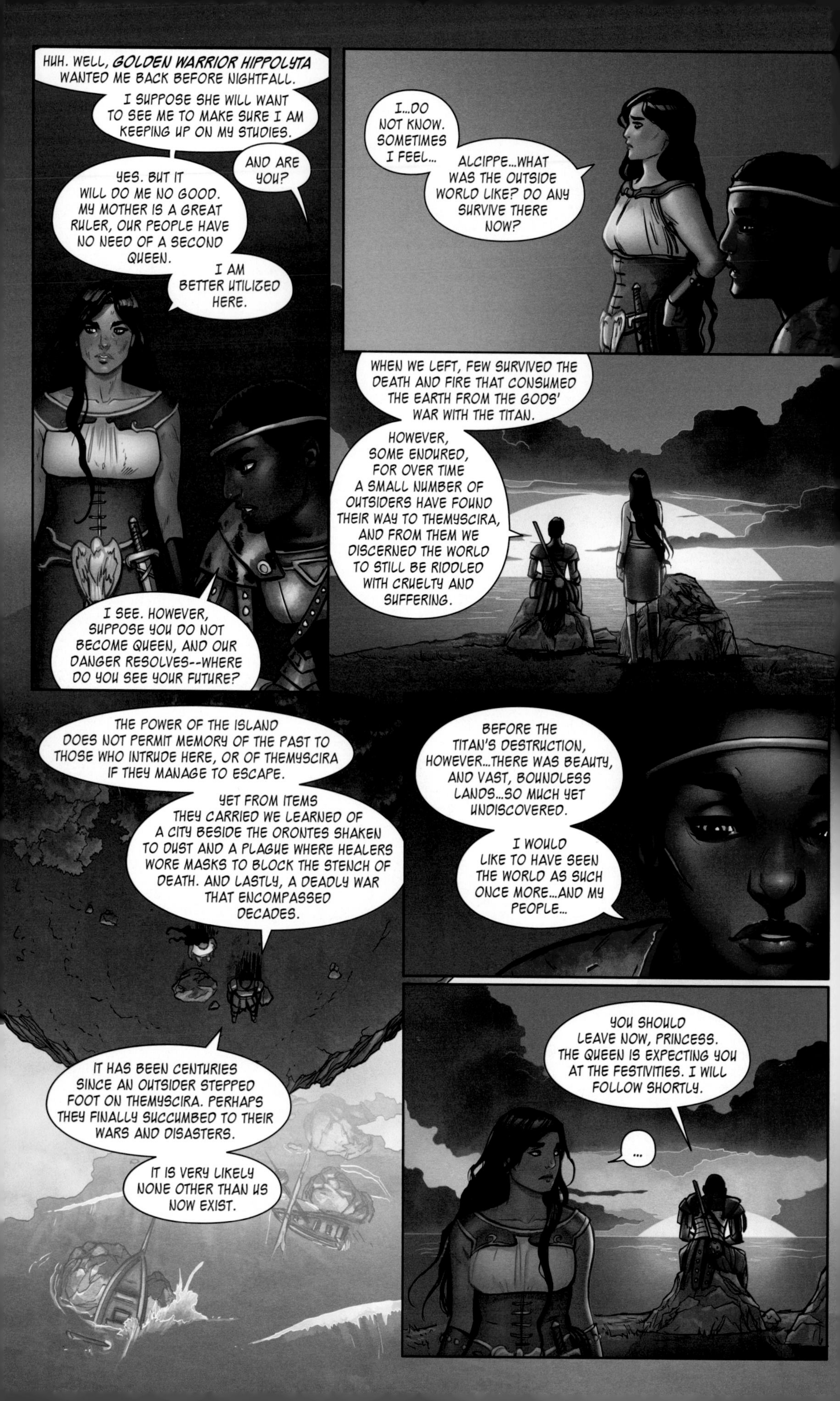
HUH. WELL, *GOLDEN WARRIOR HIPPOLYTA* WANTED ME BACK BEFORE NIGHTFALL.
I SUPPOSE SHE WILL WANT TO SEE ME TO MAKE SURE I AM KEEPING UP ON MY STUDIES.
AND ARE YOU?
YES. BUT IT WILL DO ME NO GOOD. MY MOTHER IS A GREAT RULER, OUR PEOPLE HAVE NO NEED OF A SECOND QUEEN.
I AM BETTER UTILIZED HERE.
I SEE. HOWEVER, SUPPOSE YOU DO NOT BECOME QUEEN, AND OUR DANGER RESOLVES--WHERE DO YOU SEE YOUR FUTURE?
I...DO NOT KNOW. SOMETIMES I FEEL...
ALCIPPE...WHAT WAS THE OUTSIDE WORLD LIKE? DO ANY SURVIVE THERE NOW?
WHEN WE LEFT, FEW SURVIVED THE DEATH AND FIRE THAT CONSUMED THE EARTH FROM THE GODS' WAR WITH THE TITAN.
HOWEVER, SOME ENDURED, FOR OVER TIME A SMALL NUMBER OF OUTSIDERS HAVE FOUND THEIR WAY TO THEMYSCIRA, AND FROM THEM WE DISCERNED THE WORLD TO STILL BE RIDDLED WITH CRUELTY AND SUFFERING.
THE POWER OF THE ISLAND DOES NOT PERMIT MEMORY OF THE PAST TO THOSE WHO INTRUDE HERE, OR OF THEMYSCIRA IF THEY MANAGE TO ESCAPE.
YET FROM ITEMS THEY CARRIED WE LEARNED OF A CITY BESIDE THE ORONTES SHAKEN TO DUST AND A PLAGUE WHERE HEALERS WORE MASKS TO BLOCK THE STENCH OF DEATH. AND LASTLY, A DEADLY WAR THAT ENCOMPASSED DECADES.
IT HAS BEEN CENTURIES SINCE AN OUTSIDER STEPPED FOOT ON THEMYSCIRA. PERHAPS THEY FINALLY SUCCUMBED TO THEIR WARS AND DISASTERS.
IT IS VERY LIKELY NONE OTHER THAN US NOW EXIST.
BEFORE THE TITAN'S DESTRUCTION, HOWEVER...THERE WAS BEAUTY, AND VAST, BOUNDLESS LANDS...SO MUCH YET UNDISCOVERED.
I WOULD LIKE TO HAVE SEEN THE WORLD AS SUCH ONCE MORE...AND MY PEOPLE...
YOU SHOULD LEAVE NOW, PRINCESS. THE QUEEN IS EXPECTING YOU AT THE FESTIVITIES. I WILL FOLLOW SHORTLY.
...

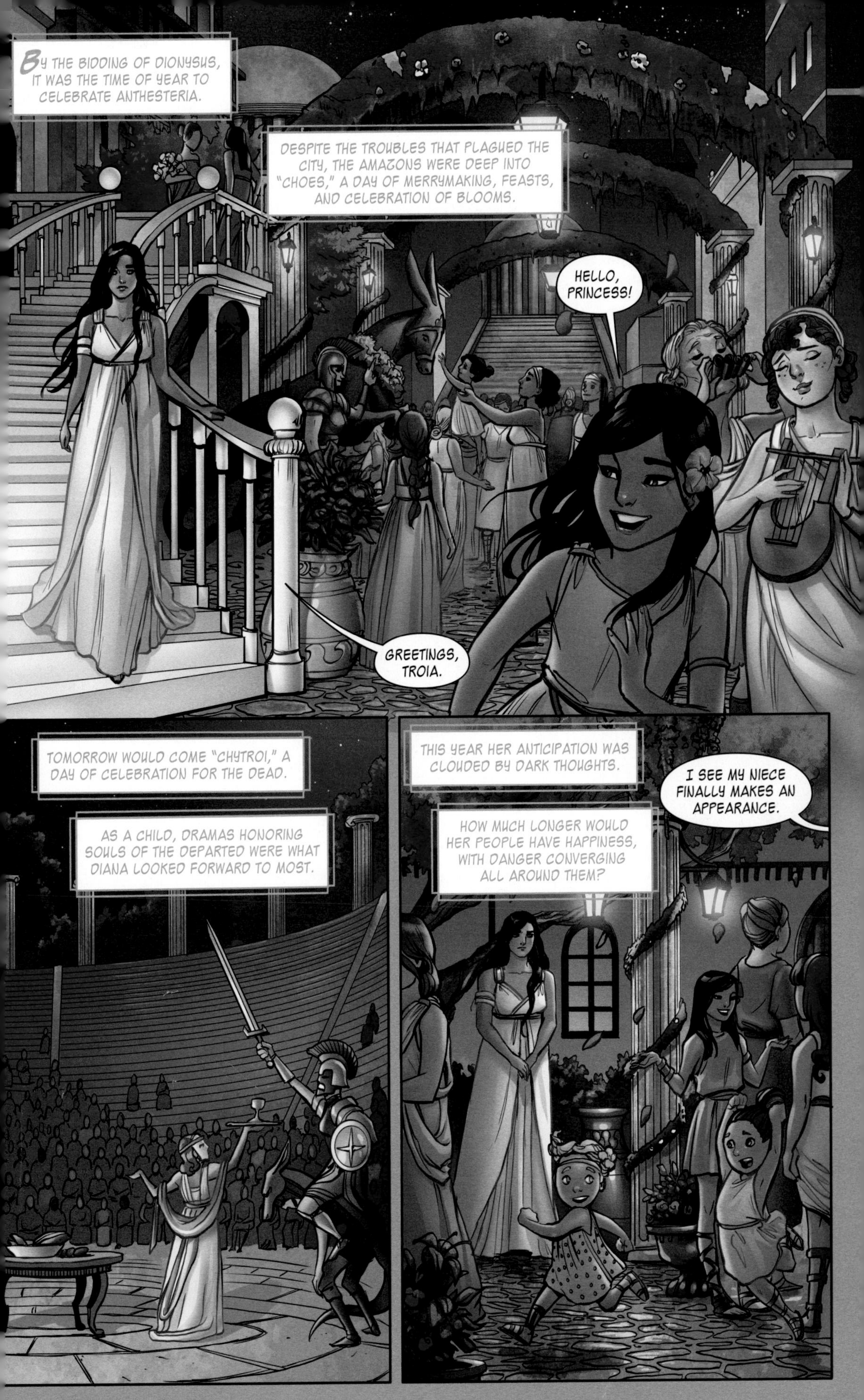
BY THE BIDDING OF DIONYSUS, IT WAS THE TIME OF YEAR TO CELEBRATE ANTHESTERIA.
DESPITE THE TROUBLES THAT PLAGUED THE CITY, THE AMAZONS WERE DEEP INTO "CHOES," A DAY OF MERRYMAKING, FEASTS, AND CELEBRATION OF BLOOMS.
HELLO, PRINCESS!
GREETINGS, TROIA.
TOMORROW WOULD COME "CHYTROI," A DAY OF CELEBRATION FOR THE DEAD.
AS A CHILD, DRAMAS HONORING SOULS OF THE DEPARTED WERE WHAT DIANA LOOKED FORWARD TO MOST.
THIS YEAR HER ANTICIPATION WAS CLOUDED BY DARK THOUGHTS.
HOW MUCH LONGER WOULD HER PEOPLE HAVE HAPPINESS, WITH DANGER CONVERGING ALL AROUND THEM?
I SEE MY NIECE FINALLY MAKES AN APPEARANCE.

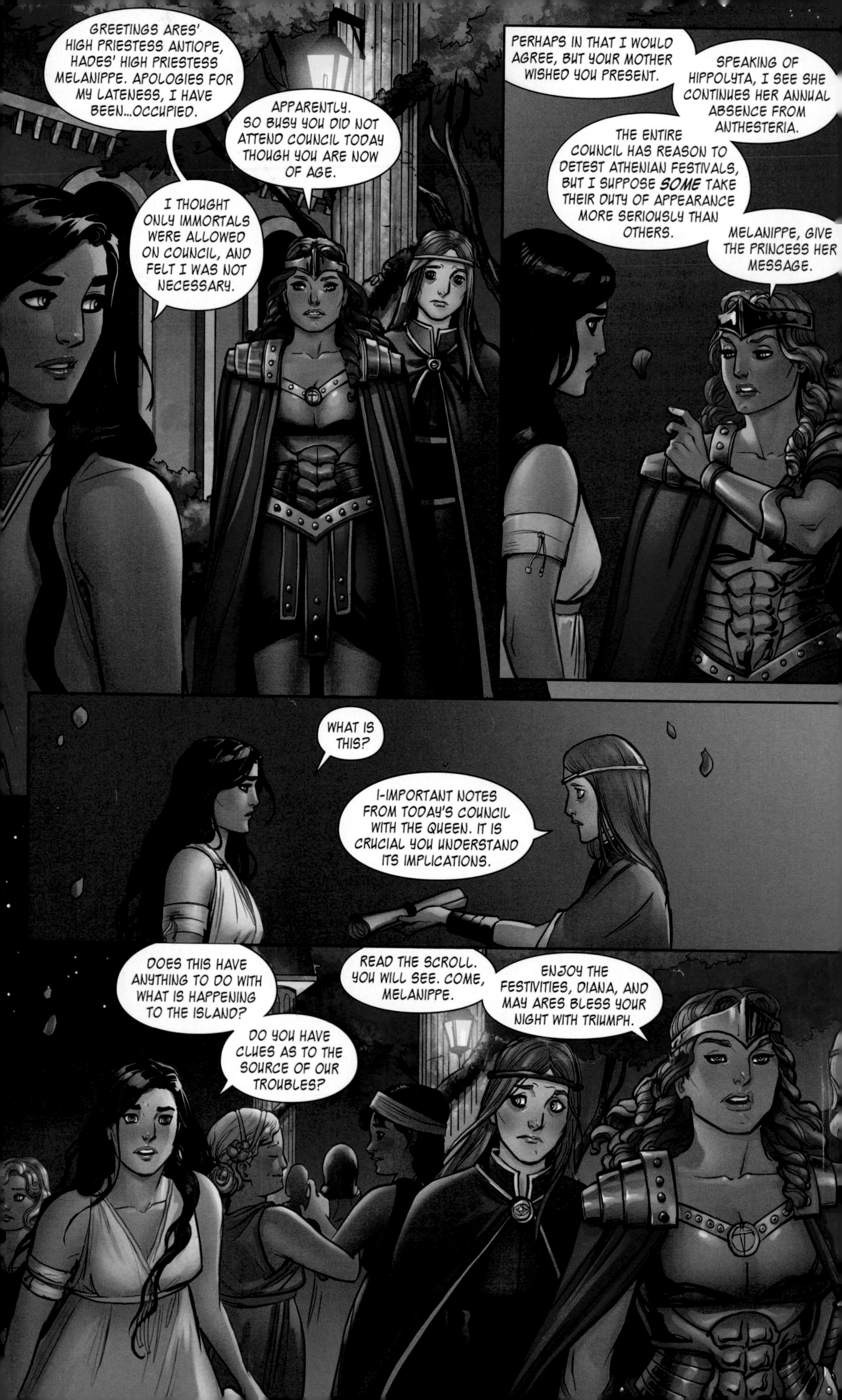
GREETINGS ARES' HIGH PRIESTESS ANTIOPE, HADES' HIGH PRIESTESS MELANIPPE. APOLOGIES FOR MY LATENESS, I HAVE BEEN...OCCUPIED.
APPARENTLY. SO BUSY YOU DID NOT ATTEND COUNCIL TODAY THOUGH YOU ARE NOW OF AGE.
I THOUGHT ONLY IMMORTALS WERE ALLOWED ON COUNCIL, AND FELT I WAS NOT NECESSARY.
PERHAPS IN THAT I WOULD AGREE, BUT YOUR MOTHER WISHED YOU PRESENT.
SPEAKING OF HIPPOLYTA, I SEE SHE CONTINUES HER ANNUAL ABSENCE FROM ANTHESTERIA.
THE ENTIRE COUNCIL HAS REASON TO DETEST ATHENIAN FESTIVALS, BUT I SUPPOSE *SOME* TAKE THEIR DUTY OF APPEARANCE MORE SERIOUSLY THAN OTHERS.
MELANIPPE, GIVE THE PRINCESS HER MESSAGE.
WHAT IS THIS?
I-IMPORTANT NOTES FROM TODAY'S COUNCIL WITH THE QUEEN. IT IS CRUCIAL YOU UNDERSTAND ITS IMPLICATIONS.
DOES THIS HAVE ANYTHING TO DO WITH WHAT IS HAPPENING TO THE ISLAND?
DO YOU HAVE CLUES AS TO THE SOURCE OF OUR TROUBLES?
READ THE SCROLL. YOU WILL SEE. COME, MELANIPPE.
ENJOY THE FESTIVITIES, DIANA, AND MAY ARES BLESS YOUR NIGHT WITH TRIUMPH.

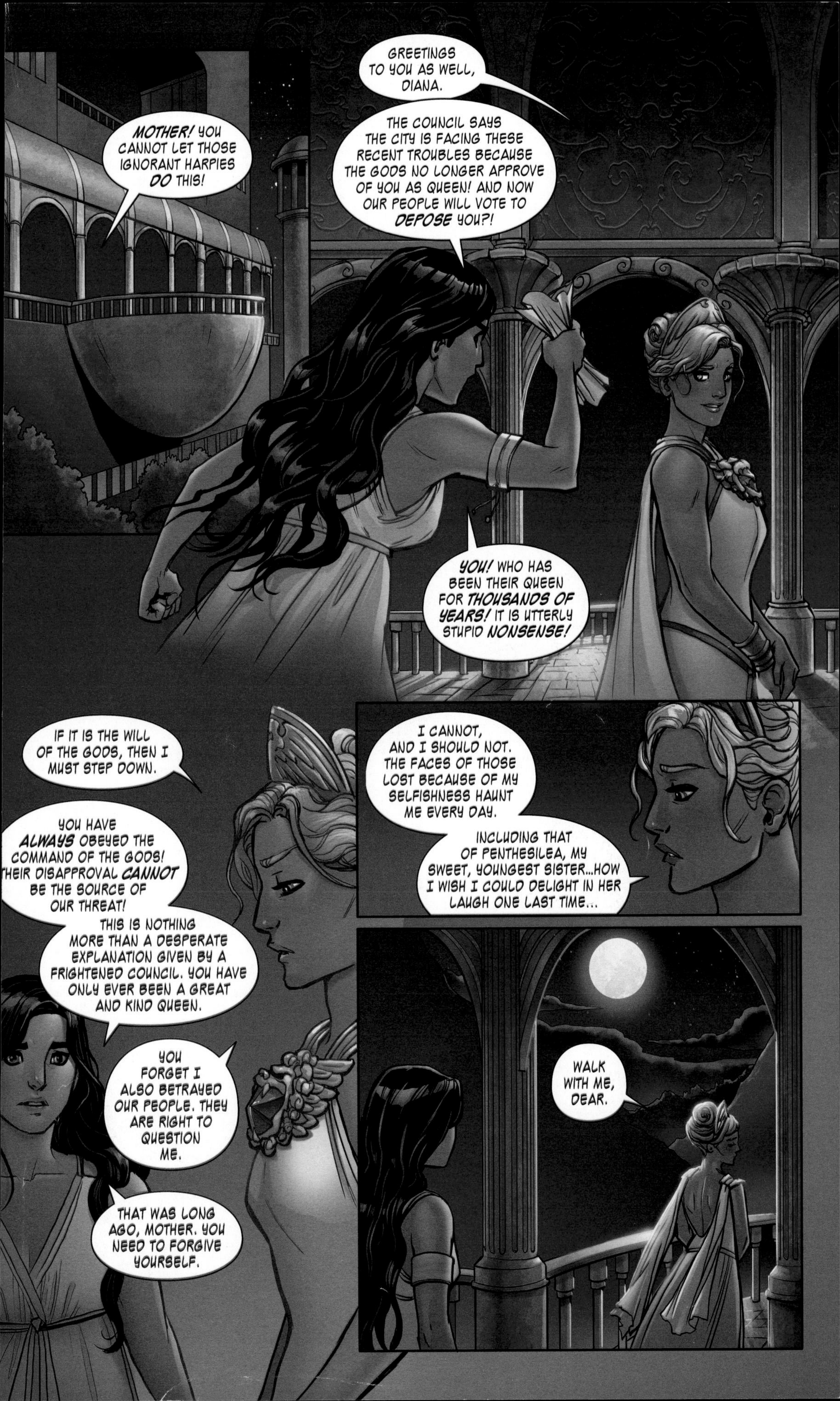
MOTHER! YOU CANNOT LET THOSE IGNORANT HARPIES DO THIS!
GREETINGS TO YOU AS WELL, DIANA.
THE COUNCIL SAYS THE CITY IS FACING THESE RECENT TROUBLES BECAUSE THE GODS NO LONGER APPROVE OF YOU AS QUEEN! AND NOW OUR PEOPLE WILL VOTE TO DEPOSE YOU?!
YOU! WHO HAS BEEN THEIR QUEEN FOR THOUSANDS OF YEARS! IT IS UTTERLY STUPID NONSENSE!
IF IT IS THE WILL OF THE GODS, THEN I MUST STEP DOWN.
YOU HAVE ALWAYS OBEYED THE COMMAND OF THE GODS! THEIR DISAPPROVAL CANNOT BE THE SOURCE OF OUR THREAT!
THIS IS NOTHING MORE THAN A DESPERATE EXPLANATION GIVEN BY A FRIGHTENED COUNCIL. YOU HAVE ONLY EVER BEEN A GREAT AND KIND QUEEN.
YOU FORGET I ALSO BETRAYED OUR PEOPLE. THEY ARE RIGHT TO QUESTION ME.
THAT WAS LONG AGO, MOTHER. YOU NEED TO FORGIVE YOURSELF.
I CANNOT, AND I SHOULD NOT. THE FACES OF THOSE LOST BECAUSE OF MY SELFISHNESS HAUNT ME EVERY DAY.
INCLUDING THAT OF PENTHESILEA, MY SWEET, YOUNGEST SISTER...HOW I WISH I COULD DELIGHT IN HER LAUGH ONE LAST TIME...
WALK WITH ME, DEAR.

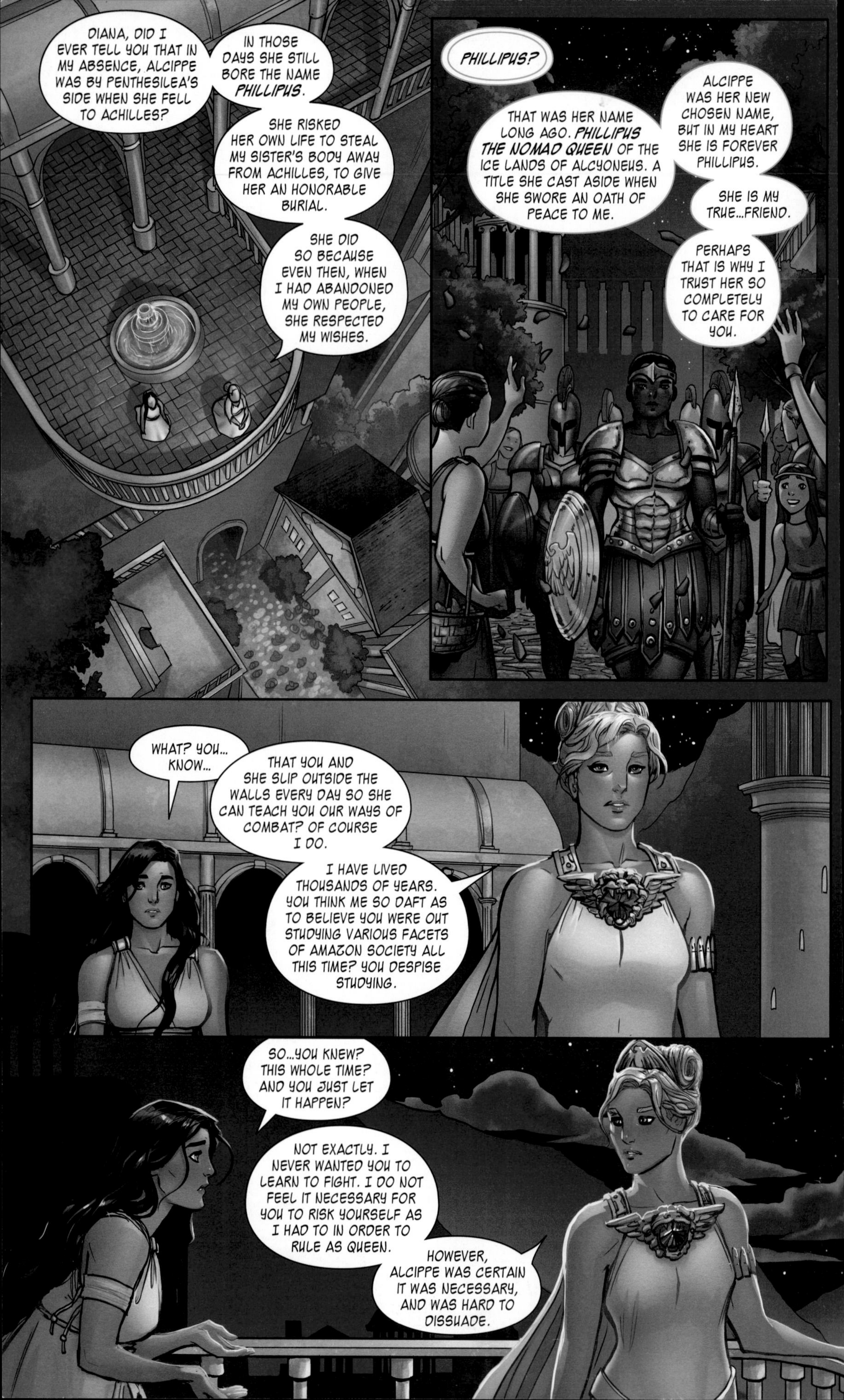
DIANA, DID I EVER TELL YOU THAT IN MY ABSENCE, ALCIPPE WAS BY PENTHESILEA'S SIDE WHEN SHE FELL TO ACHILLES?
IN THOSE DAYS SHE STILL BORE THE NAME *PHILLIPUS*.
SHE RISKED HER OWN LIFE TO STEAL MY SISTER'S BODY AWAY FROM ACHILLES, TO GIVE HER AN HONORABLE BURIAL.
SHE DID SO BECAUSE EVEN THEN, WHEN I HAD ABANDONED MY OWN PEOPLE, SHE RESPECTED MY WISHES.
PHILLIPUS?
THAT WAS HER NAME LONG AGO. *PHILLIPUS THE NOMAD QUEEN* OF THE ICE LANDS OF ALCYONEUS. A TITLE SHE CAST ASIDE WHEN SHE SWORE AN OATH OF PEACE TO ME.
ALCIPPE WAS HER NEW CHOSEN NAME, BUT IN MY HEART SHE IS FOREVER PHILLIPUS.
SHE IS MY TRUE...FRIEND.
PERHAPS THAT IS WHY I TRUST HER SO COMPLETELY TO CARE FOR YOU.
WHAT? YOU... KNOW...
THAT YOU AND SHE SLIP OUTSIDE THE WALLS EVERY DAY SO SHE CAN TEACH YOU OUR WAYS OF COMBAT? OF COURSE I DO.
I HAVE LIVED THOUSANDS OF YEARS. YOU THINK ME SO DAFT AS TO BELIEVE YOU WERE OUT STUDYING VARIOUS FACETS OF AMAZON SOCIETY ALL THIS TIME? YOU DESPISE STUDYING.
SO...YOU KNEW? THIS WHOLE TIME? AND YOU JUST LET IT HAPPEN?
NOT EXACTLY. I NEVER WANTED YOU TO LEARN TO FIGHT. I DO NOT FEEL IT NECESSARY FOR YOU TO RISK YOURSELF AS I HAD TO IN ORDER TO RULE AS QUEEN.
HOWEVER, ALCIPPE WAS CERTAIN IT WAS NECESSARY, AND WAS HARD TO DISSUADE.

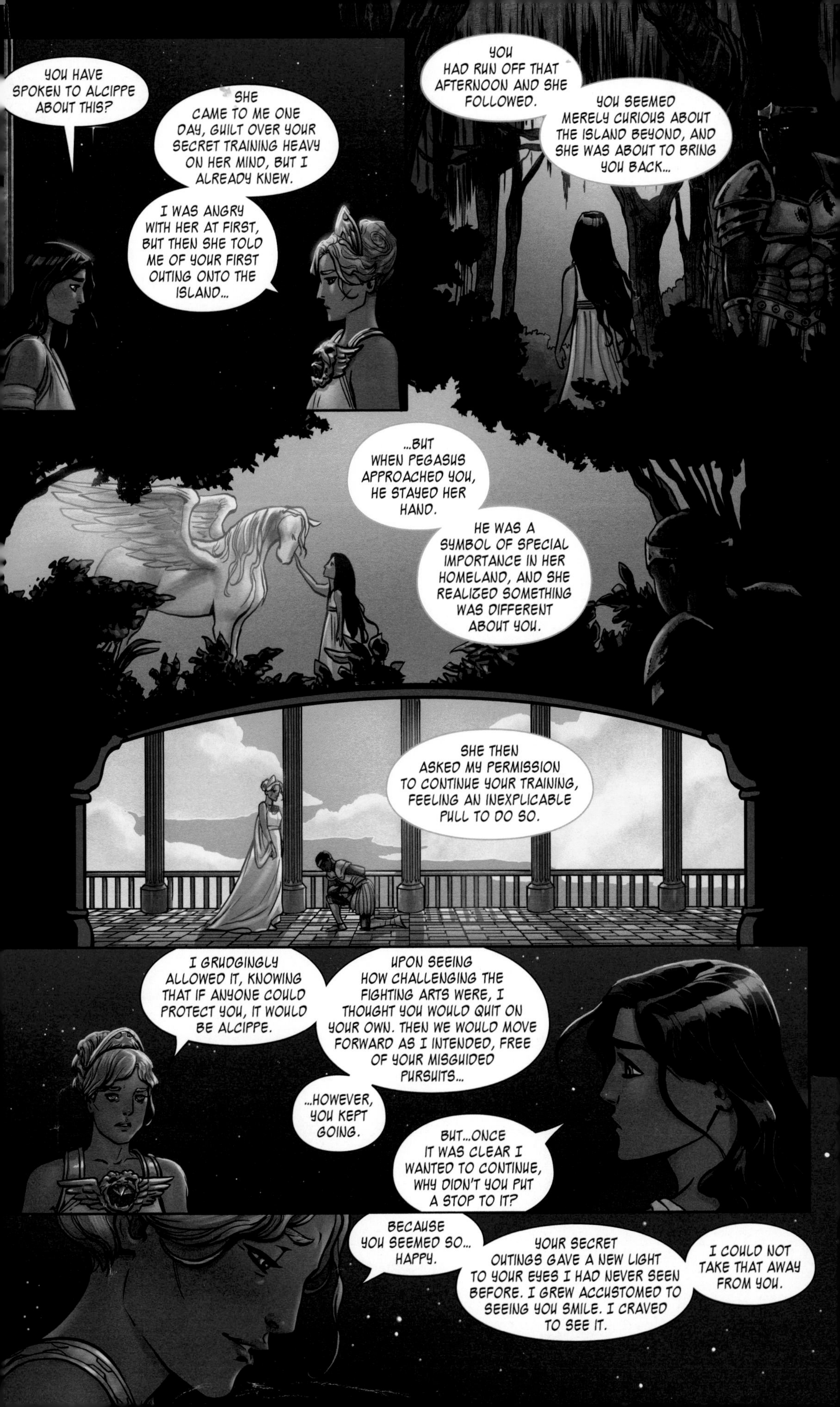
YOU HAVE SPOKEN TO ALCIPPE ABOUT THIS?
SHE CAME TO ME ONE DAY, GUILT OVER YOUR SECRET TRAINING HEAVY ON HER MIND, BUT I ALREADY KNEW.
I WAS ANGRY WITH HER AT FIRST, BUT THEN SHE TOLD ME OF YOUR FIRST OUTING ONTO THE ISLAND...
YOU HAD RUN OFF THAT AFTERNOON AND SHE FOLLOWED.
YOU SEEMED MERELY CURIOUS ABOUT THE ISLAND BEYOND, AND SHE WAS ABOUT TO BRING YOU BACK...
...BUT WHEN PEGASUS APPROACHED YOU, HE STAYED HER HAND.
HE WAS A SYMBOL OF SPECIAL IMPORTANCE IN HER HOMELAND, AND SHE REALIZED SOMETHING WAS DIFFERENT ABOUT YOU.
SHE THEN ASKED MY PERMISSION TO CONTINUE YOUR TRAINING, FEELING AN INEXPLICABLE PULL TO DO SO.
I GRUDGINGLY ALLOWED IT, KNOWING THAT IF ANYONE COULD PROTECT YOU, IT WOULD BE ALCIPPE.
UPON SEEING HOW CHALLENGING THE FIGHTING ARTS WERE, I THOUGHT YOU WOULD QUIT ON YOUR OWN. THEN WE WOULD MOVE FORWARD AS I INTENDED, FREE OF YOUR MISGUIDED PURSUITS...
...HOWEVER, YOU KEPT GOING.
BUT...ONCE IT WAS CLEAR I WANTED TO CONTINUE, WHY DIDN'T YOU PUT A STOP TO IT?
BECAUSE YOU SEEMED SO... HAPPY.
YOUR SECRET OUTINGS GAVE A NEW LIGHT TO YOUR EYES I HAD NEVER SEEN BEFORE. I GREW ACCUSTOMED TO SEEING YOU SMILE. I CRAVED TO SEE IT.
I COULD NOT TAKE THAT AWAY FROM YOU.

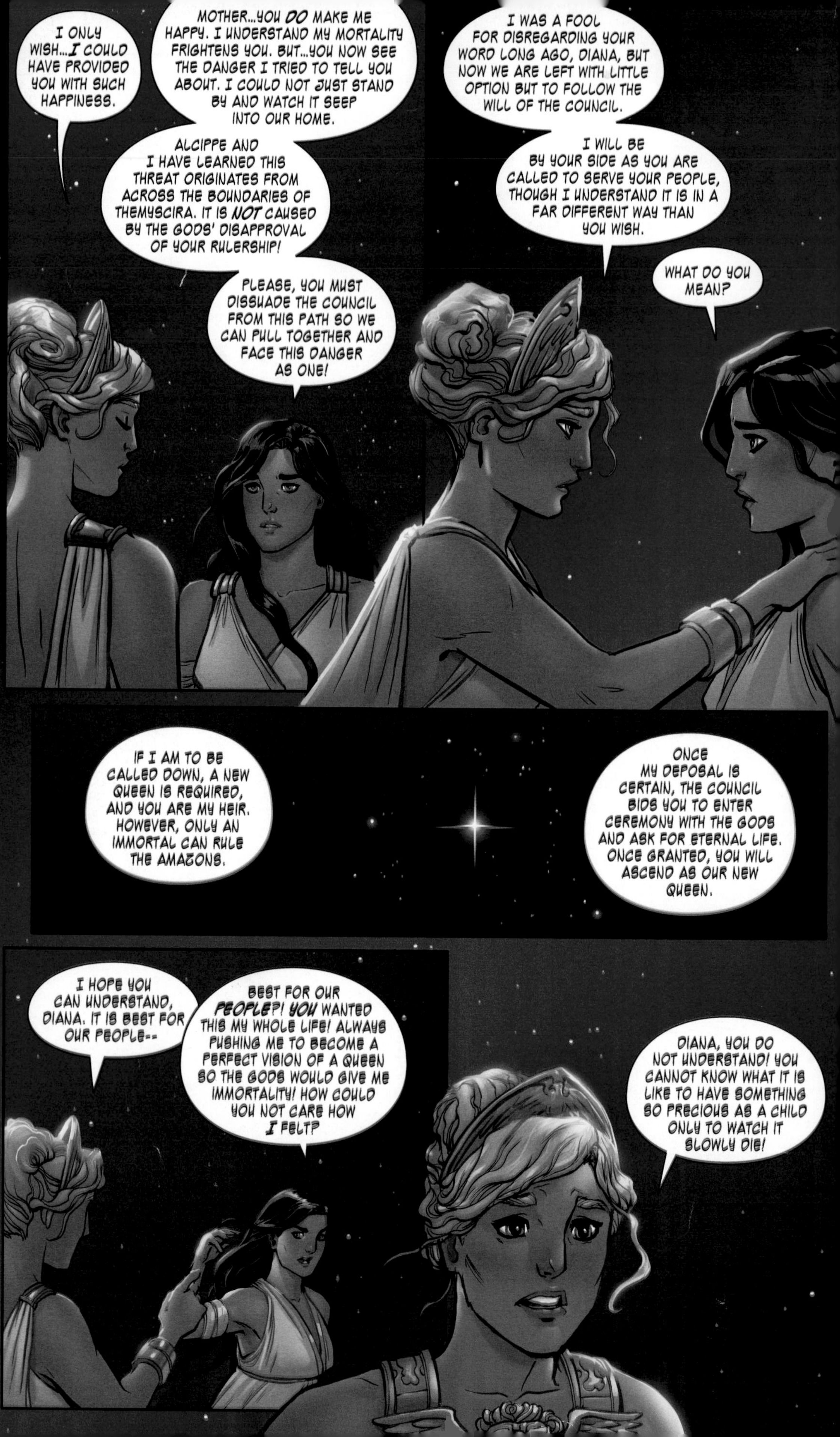
I ONLY WISH...I COULD HAVE PROVIDED YOU WITH SUCH HAPPINESS.
MOTHER...YOU DO MAKE ME HAPPY. I UNDERSTAND MY MORTALITY FRIGHTENS YOU. BUT...YOU NOW SEE THE DANGER I TRIED TO TELL YOU ABOUT. I COULD NOT JUST STAND BY AND WATCH IT SEEP INTO OUR HOME.
ALCIPPE AND I HAVE LEARNED THIS THREAT ORIGINATES FROM ACROSS THE BOUNDARIES OF THEMYSCIRA. IT IS NOT CAUSED BY THE GODS' DISAPPROVAL OF YOUR RULERSHIP!
PLEASE, YOU MUST DISSUADE THE COUNCIL FROM THIS PATH SO WE CAN PULL TOGETHER AND FACE THIS DANGER AS ONE!
I WAS A FOOL FOR DISREGARDING YOUR WORD LONG AGO, DIANA, BUT NOW WE ARE LEFT WITH LITTLE OPTION BUT TO FOLLOW THE WILL OF THE COUNCIL.
I WILL BE BY YOUR SIDE AS YOU ARE CALLED TO SERVE YOUR PEOPLE, THOUGH I UNDERSTAND IT IS IN A FAR DIFFERENT WAY THAN YOU WISH.
WHAT DO YOU MEAN?
IF I AM TO BE CALLED DOWN, A NEW QUEEN IS REQUIRED, AND YOU ARE MY HEIR. HOWEVER, ONLY AN IMMORTAL CAN RULE THE AMAZONS.
ONCE MY DEPOSAL IS CERTAIN, THE COUNCIL BIDS YOU TO ENTER CEREMONY WITH THE GODS AND ASK FOR ETERNAL LIFE. ONCE GRANTED, YOU WILL ASCEND AS OUR NEW QUEEN.
I HOPE YOU CAN UNDERSTAND, DIANA. IT IS BEST FOR OUR PEOPLE--
BEST FOR OUR PEOPLE?! YOU WANTED THIS MY WHOLE LIFE! ALWAYS PUSHING ME TO BECOME A PERFECT VISION OF A QUEEN SO THE GODS WOULD GIVE ME IMMORTALITY! HOW COULD YOU NOT CARE HOW I FELT?
DIANA, YOU DO NOT UNDERSTAND! YOU CANNOT KNOW WHAT IT IS LIKE TO HAVE SOMETHING SO PRECIOUS AS A CHILD ONLY TO WATCH IT SLOWLY DIE!

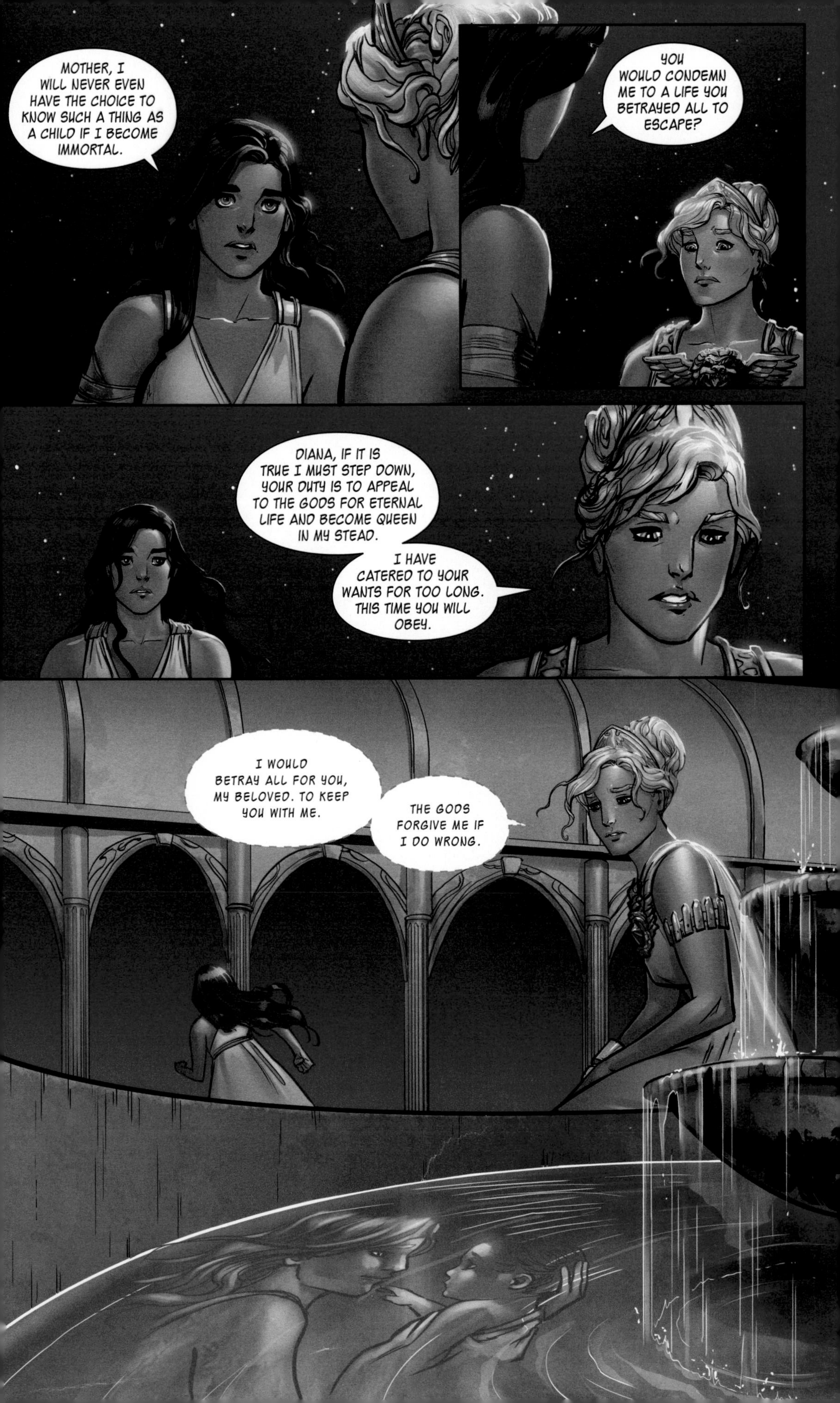
MOTHER, I WILL NEVER EVEN HAVE THE CHOICE TO KNOW SUCH A THING AS A CHILD IF I BECOME IMMORTAL.
YOU WOULD CONDEMN ME TO A LIFE YOU BETRAYED ALL TO ESCAPE?
DIANA, IF IT IS TRUE I MUST STEP DOWN, YOUR DUTY IS TO APPEAL TO THE GODS FOR ETERNAL LIFE AND BECOME QUEEN IN MY STEAD.
I HAVE CATERED TO YOUR WANTS FOR TOO LONG. THIS TIME YOU WILL OBEY.
I WOULD BETRAY ALL FOR YOU, MY BELOVED. TO KEEP YOU WITH ME.
THE GODS FORGIVE ME IF I DO WRONG.

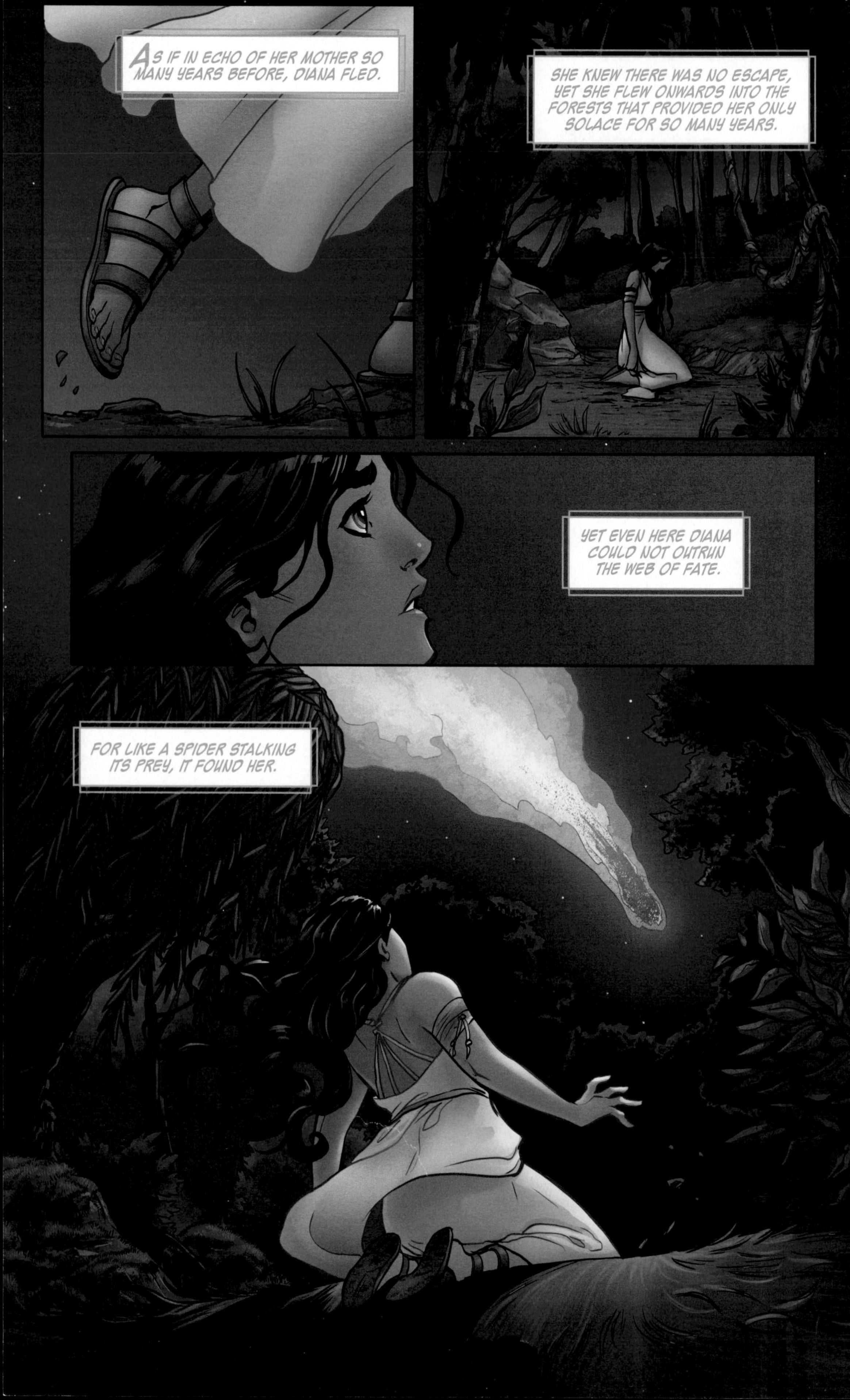
AS IF IN ECHO OF HER MOTHER SO MANY YEARS BEFORE, DIANA FLED.
SHE KNEW THERE WAS NO ESCAPE, YET SHE FLEW ONWARDS INTO THE FORESTS THAT PROVIDED HER ONLY SOLACE FOR SO MANY YEARS.
YET EVEN HERE DIANA COULD NOT OUTRUN THE WEB OF FATE.
FOR LIKE A SPIDER STALKING ITS PREY, IT FOUND HER.

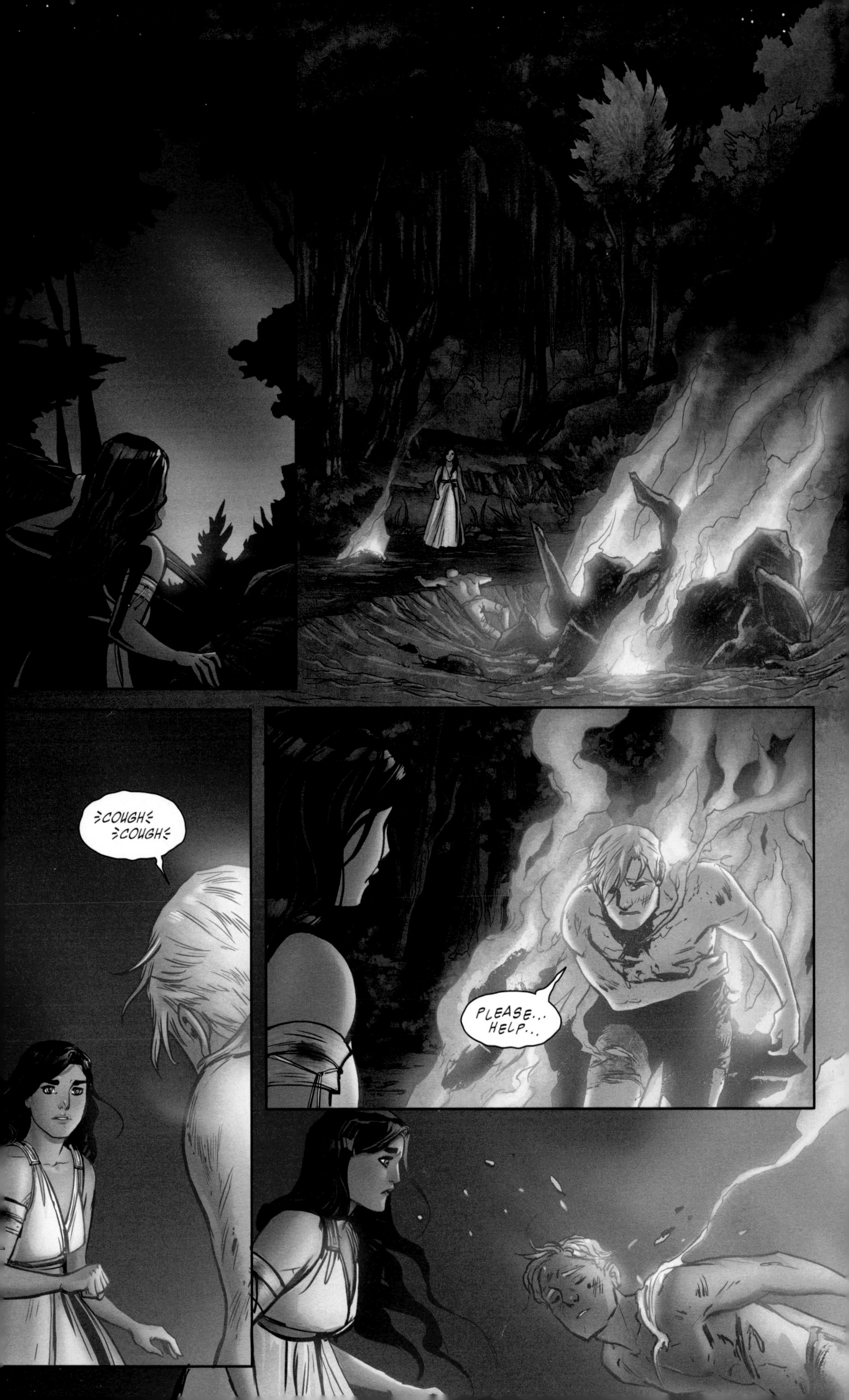

PLEASE... HELP...
COUGH COUGH

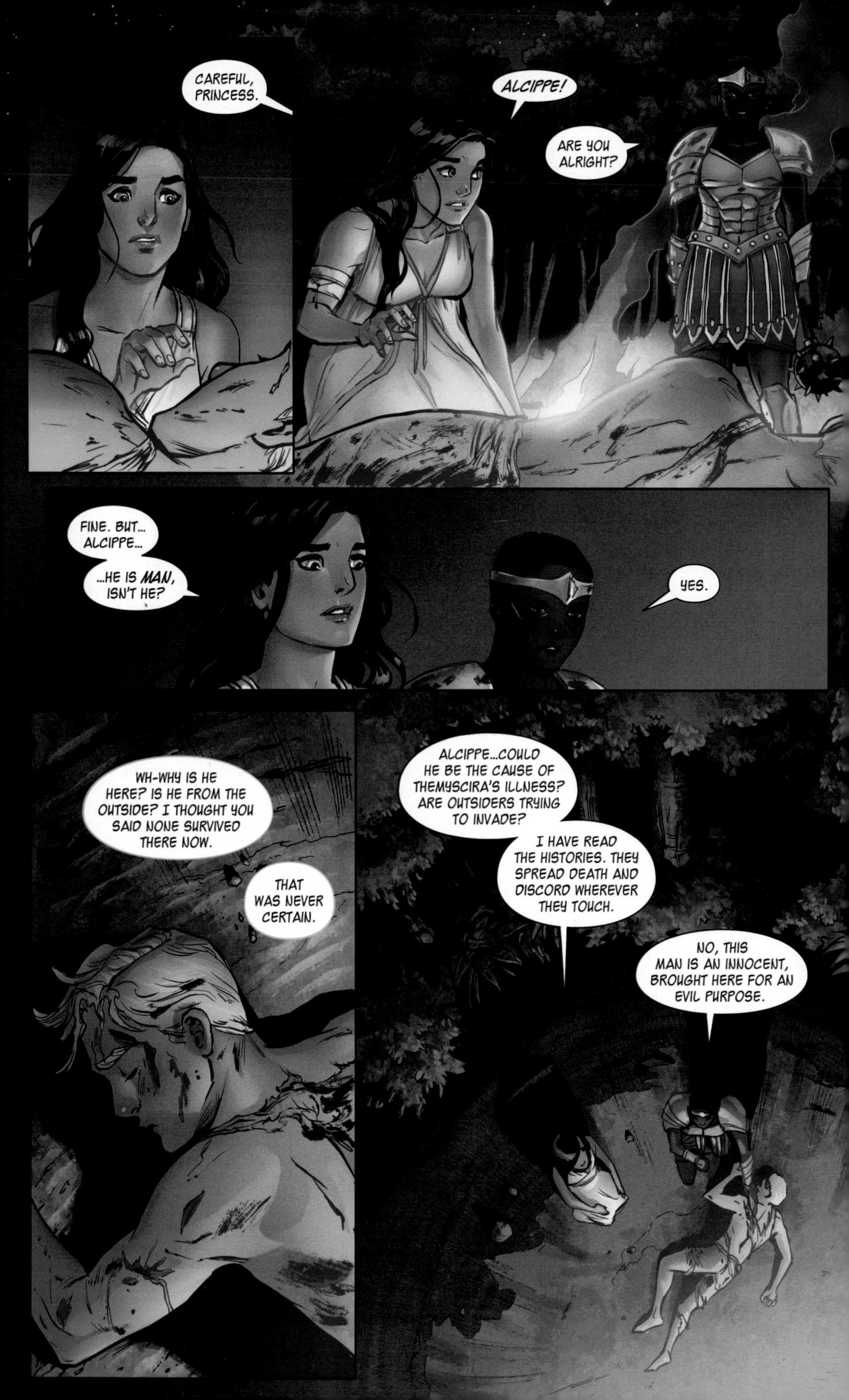
CAREFUL, PRINCESS.
ALCIPPE!
ARE YOU ALRIGHT?
FINE. BUT... ALCIPPE...
...HE IS MAN, ISN'T HE?
YES.
WH-WHY IS HE HERE? IS HE FROM THE OUTSIDE? I THOUGHT YOU SAID NONE SURVIVED THERE NOW.
THAT WAS NEVER CERTAIN.
ALCIPPE...COULD HE BE THE CAUSE OF THEMYSCIRA'S ILLNESS? ARE OUTSIDERS TRYING TO INVADE?
I HAVE READ THE HISTORIES. THEY SPREAD DEATH AND DISCORD WHEREVER THEY TOUCH.
NO, THIS MAN IS AN INNOCENT, BROUGHT HERE FOR AN EVIL PURPOSE.

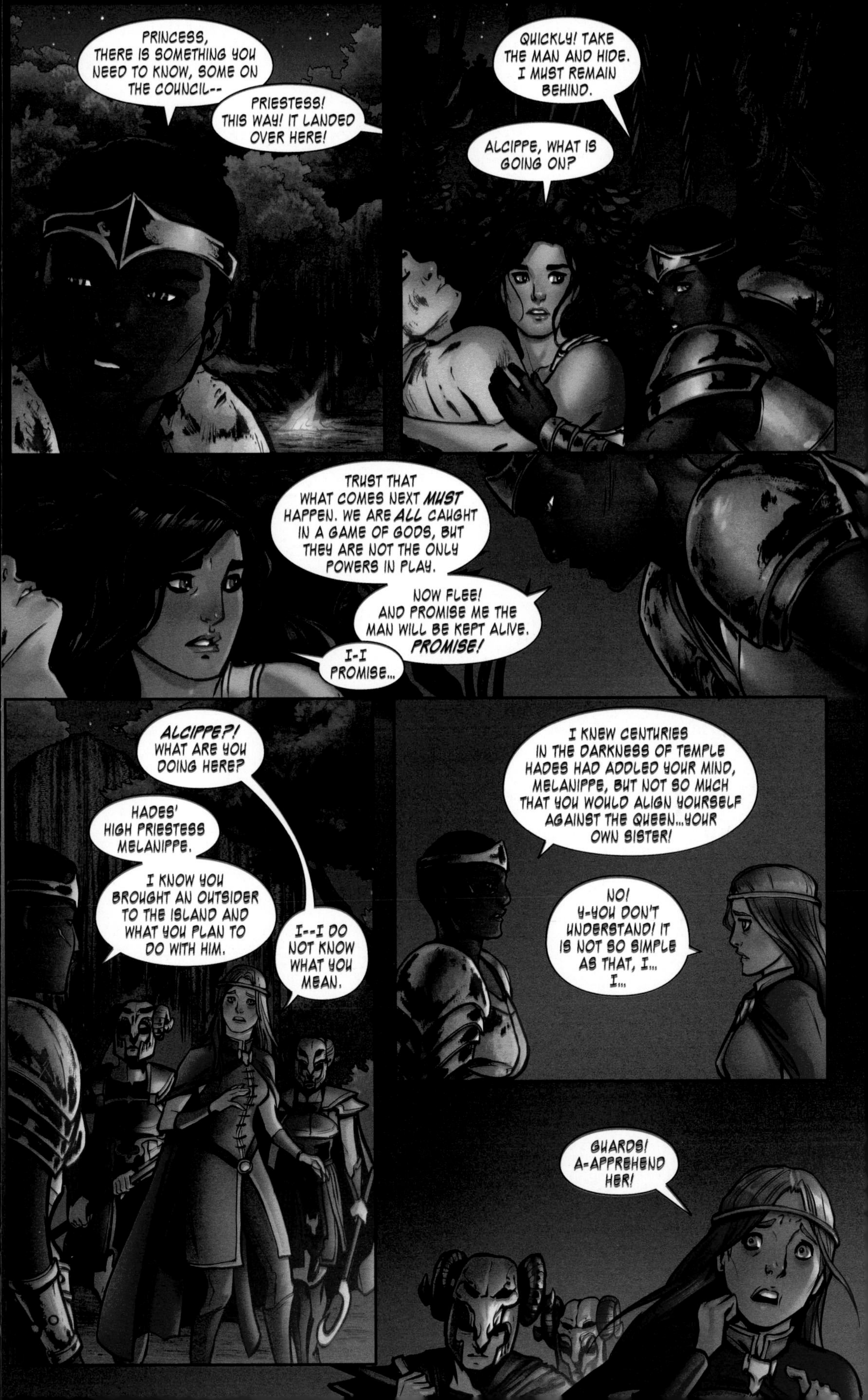
PRINCESS, THERE IS SOMETHING YOU NEED TO KNOW, SOME ON THE COUNCIL--
PRIESTESS! THIS WAY! IT LANDED OVER HERE!
QUICKLY! TAKE THE MAN AND HIDE. I MUST REMAIN BEHIND.
ALCIPPE, WHAT IS GOING ON?
TRUST THAT WHAT COMES NEXT MUST HAPPEN. WE ARE ALL CAUGHT IN A GAME OF GODS, BUT THEY ARE NOT THE ONLY POWERS IN PLAY.
NOW FLEE! AND PROMISE ME THE MAN WILL BE KEPT ALIVE. PROMISE!
I-I PROMISE...
ALCIPPE?! WHAT ARE YOU DOING HERE?
HADES' HIGH PRIESTESS MELANIPPE.
I KNOW YOU BROUGHT AN OUTSIDER TO THE ISLAND AND WHAT YOU PLAN TO DO WITH HIM.
I--I DO NOT KNOW WHAT YOU MEAN.
I KNEW CENTURIES IN THE DARKNESS OF TEMPLE HADES HAD ADDLED YOUR MIND, MELANIPPE, BUT NOT SO MUCH THAT YOU WOULD ALIGN YOURSELF AGAINST THE QUEEN...YOUR OWN SISTER!
NO! Y-YOU DON'T UNDERSTAND! IT IS NOT SO SIMPLE AS THAT, I... I...
GUARDS! A-APPREHEND HER!

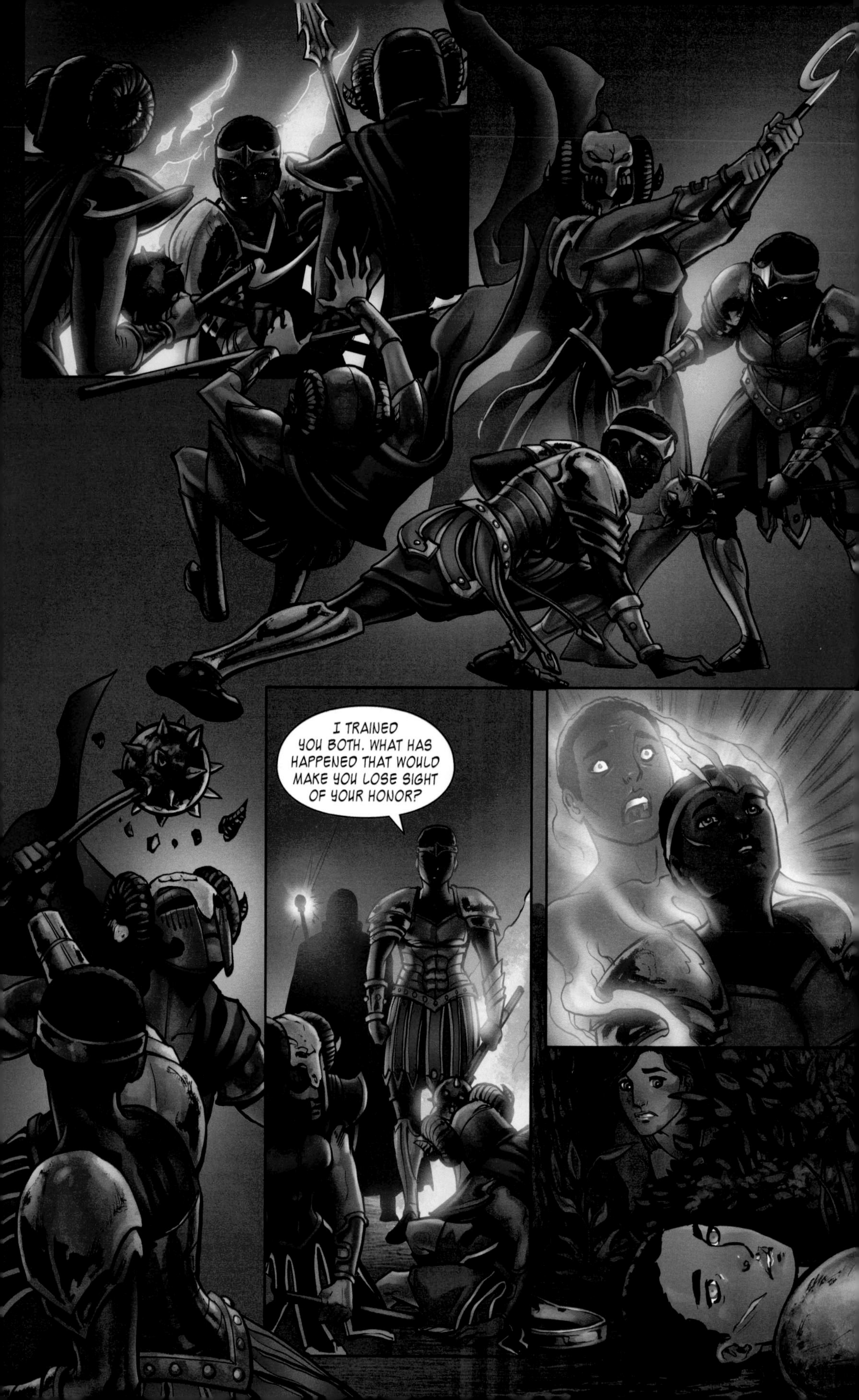
I TRAINED YOU BOTH. WHAT HAS HAPPENED THAT WOULD MAKE YOU LOSE SIGHT OF YOUR HONOR?

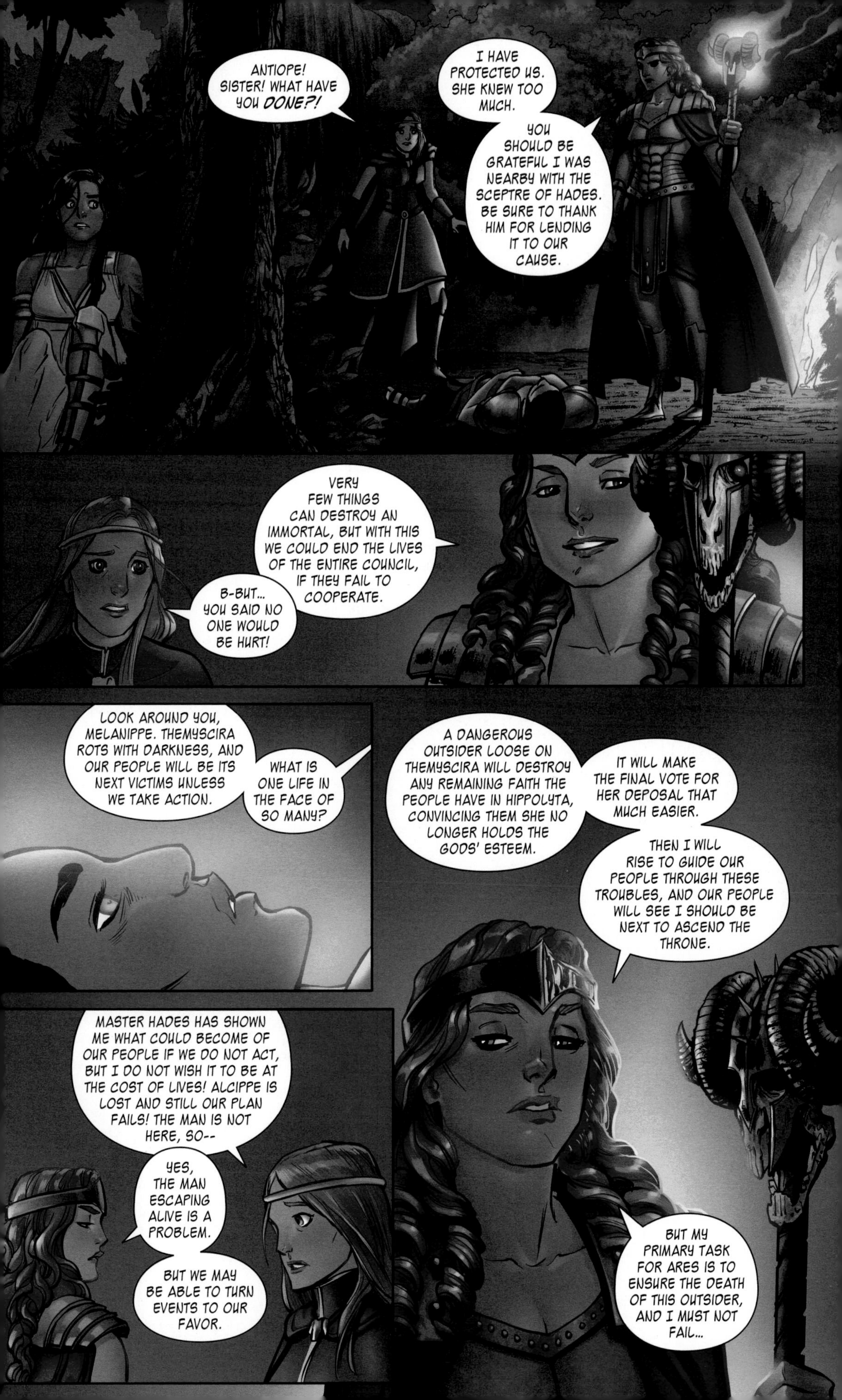
ANTIOPE! SISTER! WHAT HAVE YOU *DONE?!*
I HAVE PROTECTED US. SHE KNEW TOO MUCH.
YOU SHOULD BE GRATEFUL I WAS NEARBY WITH THE SCEPTRE OF HADES. BE SURE TO THANK HIM FOR LENDING IT TO OUR CAUSE.
VERY FEW THINGS CAN DESTROY AN IMMORTAL, BUT WITH THIS WE COULD END THE LIVES OF THE ENTIRE COUNCIL, IF THEY FAIL TO COOPERATE.
B-BUT... YOU SAID NO ONE WOULD BE HURT!
LOOK AROUND YOU, MELANIPPE. THEMYSCIRA ROTS WITH DARKNESS, AND OUR PEOPLE WILL BE ITS NEXT VICTIMS UNLESS WE TAKE ACTION.
WHAT IS ONE LIFE IN THE FACE OF SO MANY?
A DANGEROUS OUTSIDER LOOSE ON THEMYSCIRA WILL DESTROY ANY REMAINING FAITH THE PEOPLE HAVE IN HIPPOLYTA, CONVINCING THEM SHE NO LONGER HOLDS THE GODS' ESTEEM.
IT WILL MAKE THE FINAL VOTE FOR HER DEPOSAL THAT MUCH EASIER.
THEN I WILL RISE TO GUIDE OUR PEOPLE THROUGH THESE TROUBLES, AND OUR PEOPLE WILL SEE I SHOULD BE NEXT TO ASCEND THE THRONE.
MASTER HADES HAS SHOWN ME WHAT COULD BECOME OF OUR PEOPLE IF WE DO NOT ACT, BUT I DO NOT WISH IT TO BE AT THE COST OF LIVES! ALCIPPE IS LOST AND STILL OUR PLAN FAILS! THE MAN IS NOT HERE, SO--
YES, THE MAN ESCAPING ALIVE IS A PROBLEM.
BUT WE MAY BE ABLE TO TURN EVENTS TO OUR FAVOR.
BUT MY PRIMARY TASK FOR ARES IS TO ENSURE THE DEATH OF THIS OUTSIDER, AND I MUST NOT FAIL...

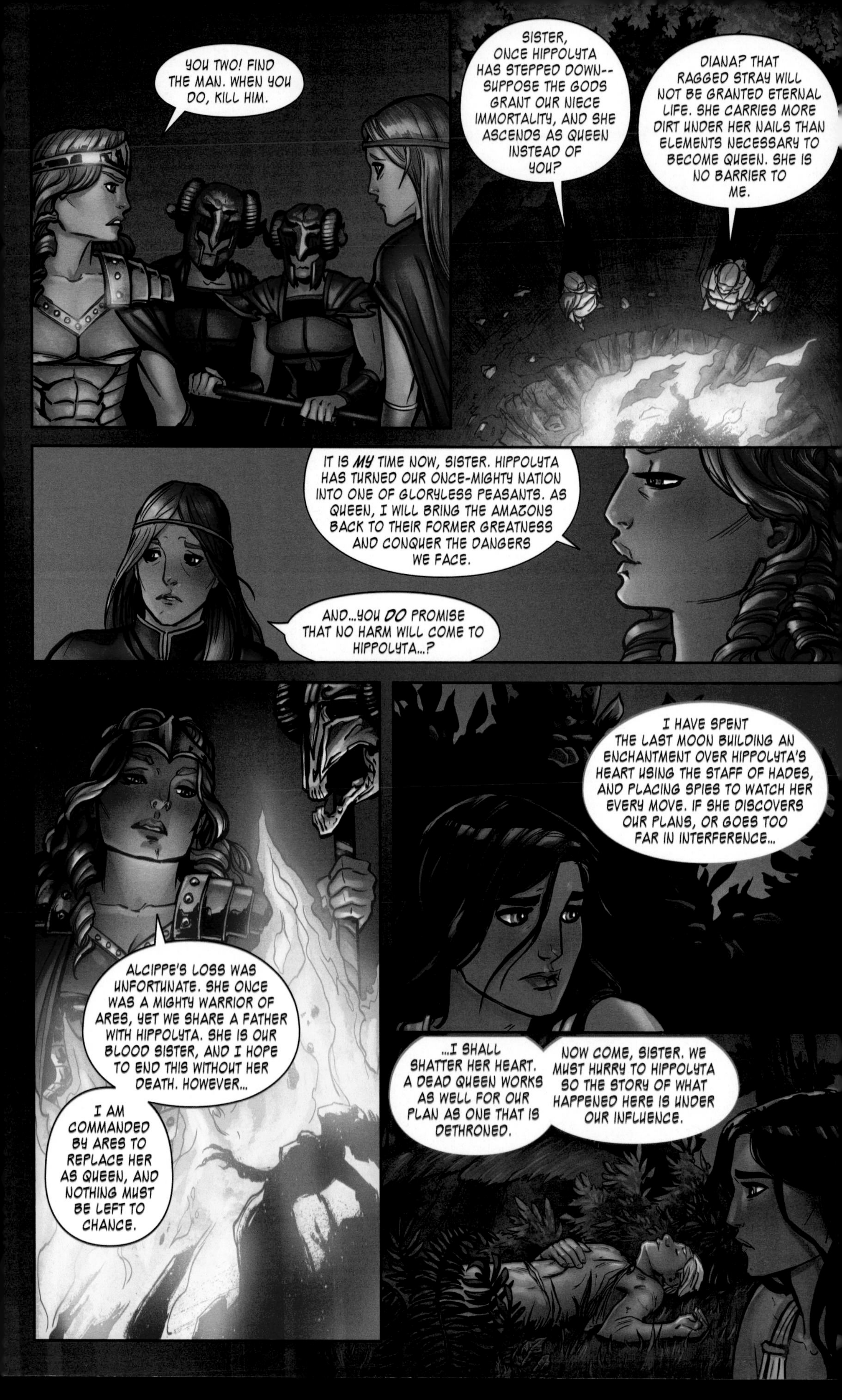
YOU TWO! FIND THE MAN. WHEN YOU DO, KILL HIM.
SISTER, ONCE HIPPOLYTA HAS STEPPED DOWN-- SUPPOSE THE GODS GRANT OUR NIECE IMMORTALITY, AND SHE ASCENDS AS QUEEN INSTEAD OF YOU?
DIANA? THAT RAGGED STRAY WILL NOT BE GRANTED ETERNAL LIFE. SHE CARRIES MORE DIRT UNDER HER NAILS THAN ELEMENTS NECESSARY TO BECOME QUEEN. SHE IS NO BARRIER TO ME.
IT IS MY TIME NOW, SISTER. HIPPOLYTA HAS TURNED OUR ONCE-MIGHTY NATION INTO ONE OF GLORYLESS PEASANTS. AS QUEEN, I WILL BRING THE AMAZONS BACK TO THEIR FORMER GREATNESS AND CONQUER THE DANGERS WE FACE.
AND...YOU DO PROMISE THAT NO HARM WILL COME TO HIPPOLYTA...?
ALCIPPE'S LOSS WAS UNFORTUNATE. SHE ONCE WAS A MIGHTY WARRIOR OF ARES, YET WE SHARE A FATHER WITH HIPPOLYTA. SHE IS OUR BLOOD SISTER, AND I HOPE TO END THIS WITHOUT HER DEATH. HOWEVER...
I AM COMMANDED BY ARES TO REPLACE HER AS QUEEN, AND NOTHING MUST BE LEFT TO CHANCE.
I HAVE SPENT THE LAST MOON BUILDING AN ENCHANTMENT OVER HIPPOLYTA'S HEART USING THE STAFF OF HADES, AND PLACING SPIES TO WATCH HER EVERY MOVE. IF SHE DISCOVERS OUR PLANS, OR GOES TOO FAR IN INTERFERENCE...
...I SHALL SHATTER HER HEART. A DEAD QUEEN WORKS AS WELL FOR OUR PLAN AS ONE THAT IS DETHRONED.
NOW COME, SISTER. WE MUST HURRY TO HIPPOLYTA SO THE STORY OF WHAT HAPPENED HERE IS UNDER OUR INFLUENCE.

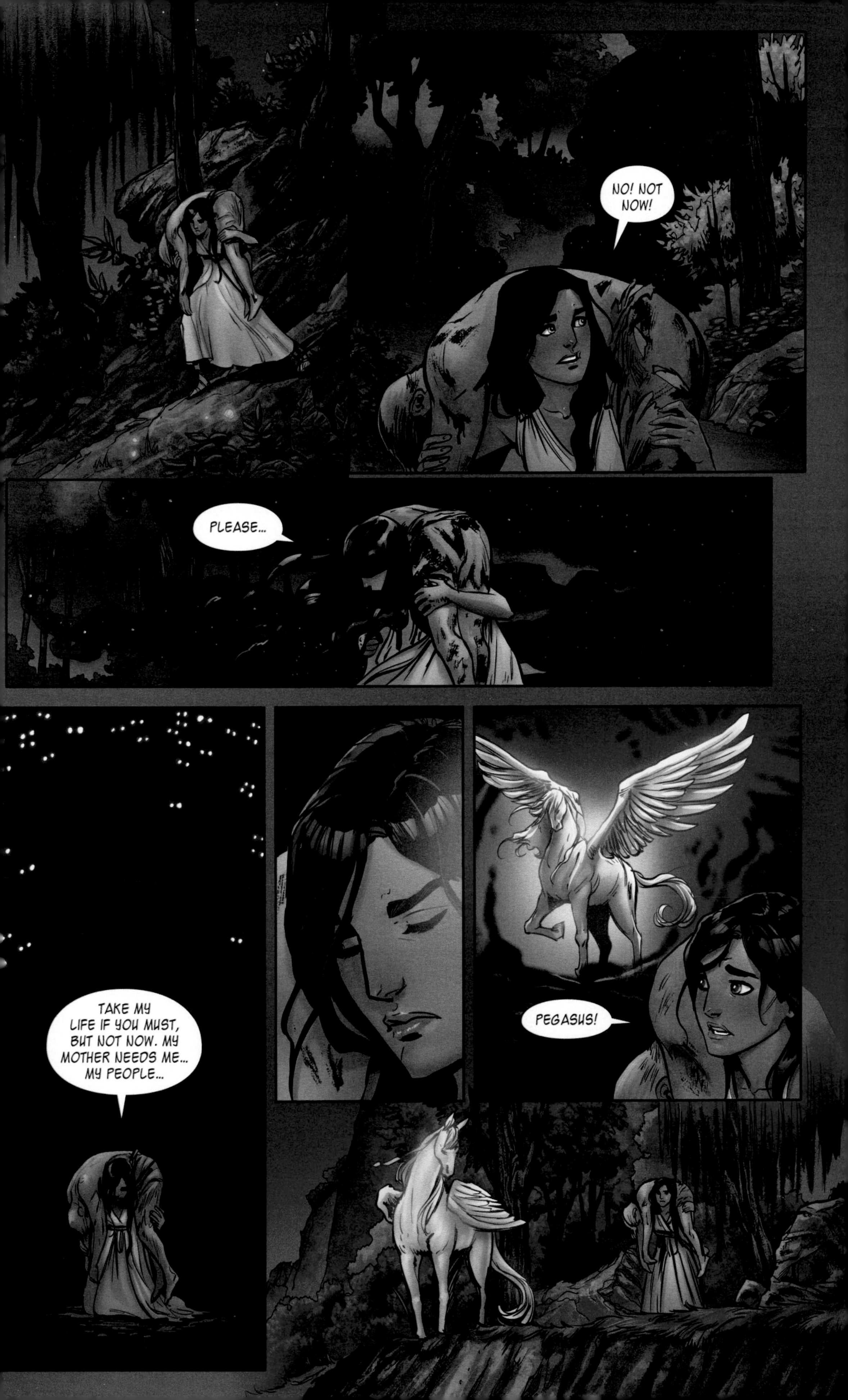
NO! NOT NOW!
PLEASE...
TAKE MY LIFE IF YOU MUST, BUT NOT NOW. MY MOTHER NEEDS ME... MY PEOPLE...
PEGASUS!

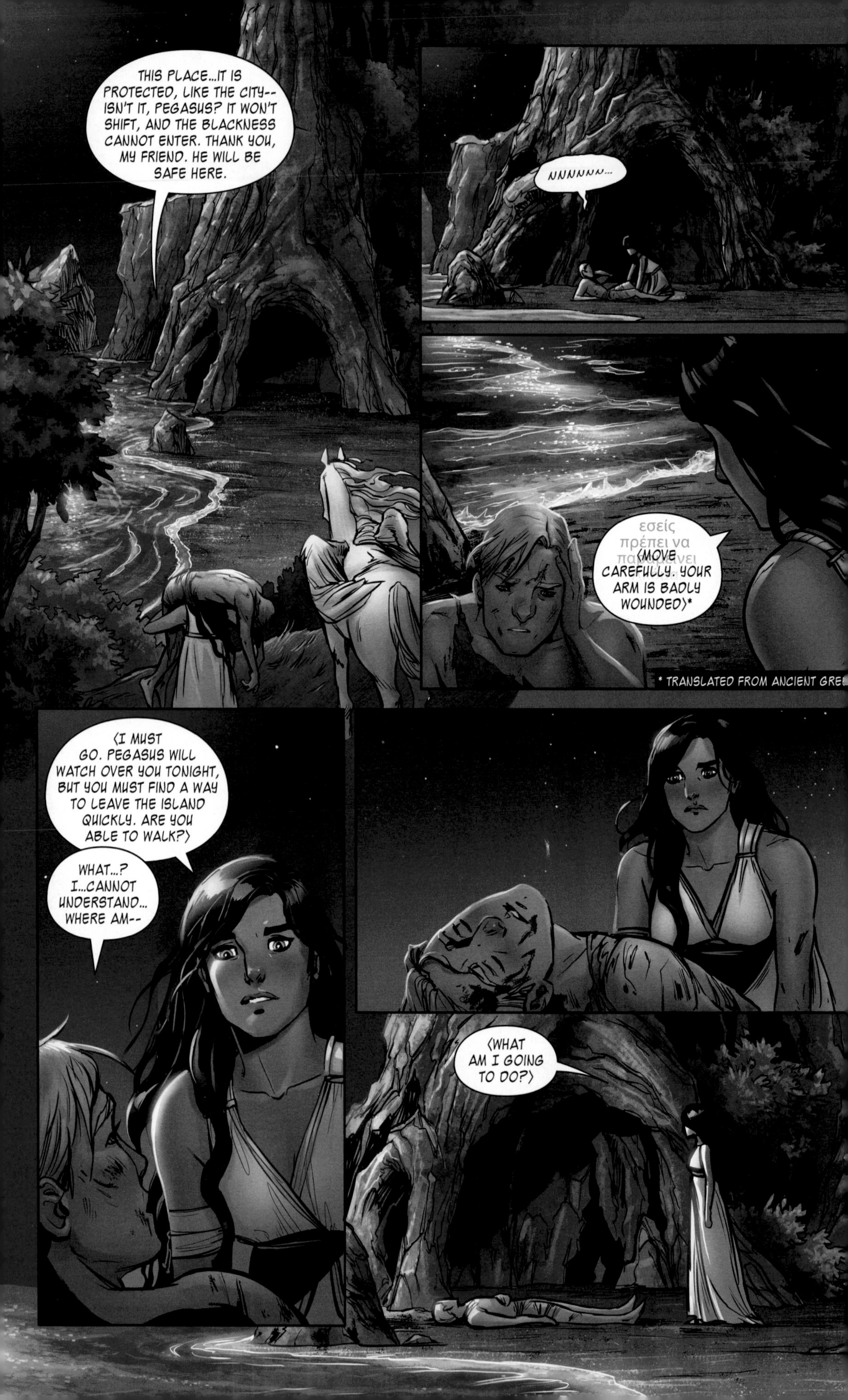
THIS PLACE...IT IS PROTECTED, LIKE THE CITY--ISN'T IT, PEGASUS? IT WON'T SHIFT, AND THE BLACKNESS CANNOT ENTER. THANK YOU, MY FRIEND. HE WILL BE SAFE HERE.
NNNNNN...
εσείς πρέπει να
⟨MOVE CAREFULLY. YOUR ARM IS BADLY WOUNDED⟩*
* TRANSLATED FROM ANCIENT GRE
⟨I MUST GO. PEGASUS WILL WATCH OVER YOU TONIGHT, BUT YOU MUST FIND A WAY TO LEAVE THE ISLAND QUICKLY. ARE YOU ABLE TO WALK?⟩
WHAT...? I...CANNOT UNDERSTAND... WHERE AM--
⟨WHAT AM I GOING TO DO?⟩

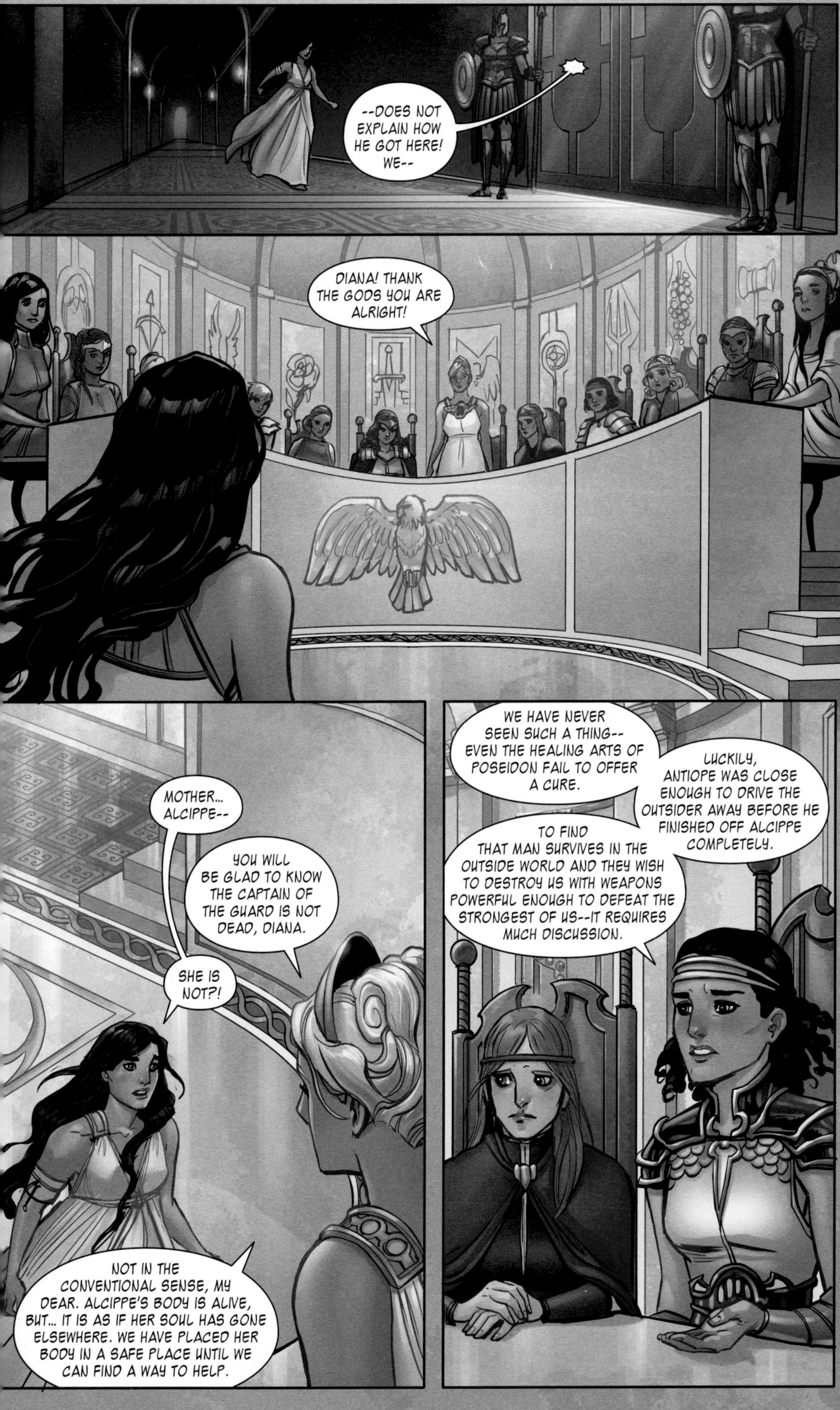
--DOES NOT EXPLAIN HOW HE GOT HERE! WE--
DIANA! THANK THE GODS YOU ARE ALRIGHT!
MOTHER... ALCIPPE--
YOU WILL BE GLAD TO KNOW THE CAPTAIN OF THE GUARD IS NOT DEAD, DIANA.
SHE IS NOT?!
NOT IN THE CONVENTIONAL SENSE, MY DEAR. ALCIPPE'S BODY IS ALIVE, BUT... IT IS AS IF HER SOUL HAS GONE ELSEWHERE. WE HAVE PLACED HER BODY IN A SAFE PLACE UNTIL WE CAN FIND A WAY TO HELP.
WE HAVE NEVER SEEN SUCH A THING--EVEN THE HEALING ARTS OF POSEIDON FAIL TO OFFER A CURE.
LUCKILY, ANTIOPE WAS CLOSE ENOUGH TO DRIVE THE OUTSIDER AWAY BEFORE HE FINISHED OFF ALCIPPE COMPLETELY.
TO FIND THAT MAN SURVIVES IN THE OUTSIDE WORLD AND THEY WISH TO DESTROY US WITH WEAPONS POWERFUL ENOUGH TO DEFEAT THE STRONGEST OF US--IT REQUIRES MUCH DISCUSSION.

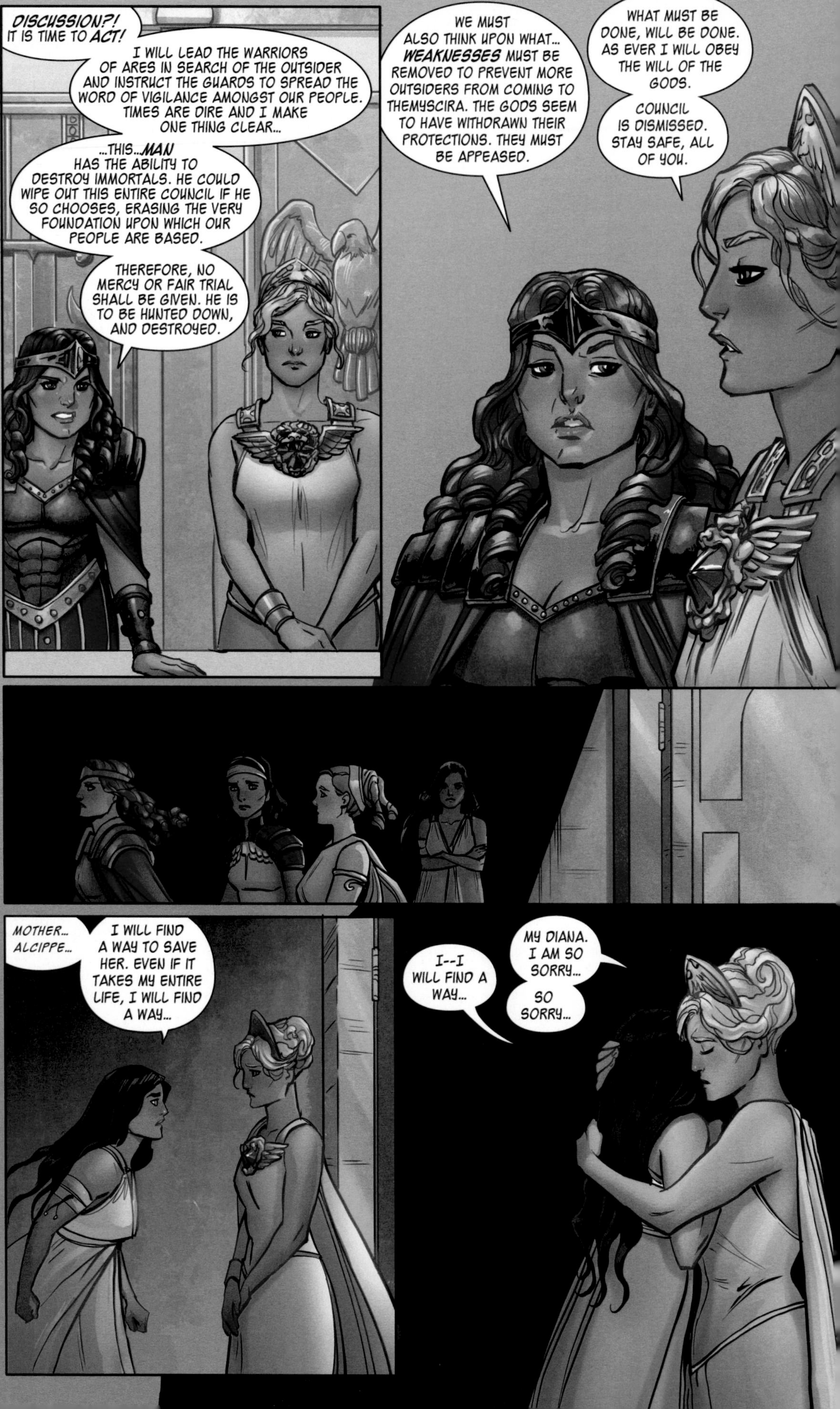
DISCUSSION?! IT IS TIME TO ACT!
I WILL LEAD THE WARRIORS OF ARES IN SEARCH OF THE OUTSIDER AND INSTRUCT THE GUARDS TO SPREAD THE WORD OF VIGILANCE AMONGST OUR PEOPLE. TIMES ARE DIRE AND I MAKE ONE THING CLEAR...
...THIS...MAN HAS THE ABILITY TO DESTROY IMMORTALS. HE COULD WIPE OUT THIS ENTIRE COUNCIL IF HE SO CHOOSES, ERASING THE VERY FOUNDATION UPON WHICH OUR PEOPLE ARE BASED.
THEREFORE, NO MERCY OR FAIR TRIAL SHALL BE GIVEN. HE IS TO BE HUNTED DOWN, AND DESTROYED.
WE MUST ALSO THINK UPON WHAT... WEAKNESSES MUST BE REMOVED TO PREVENT MORE OUTSIDERS FROM COMING TO THEMYSCIRA. THE GODS SEEM TO HAVE WITHDRAWN THEIR PROTECTIONS. THEY MUST BE APPEASED.
WHAT MUST BE DONE, WILL BE DONE. AS EVER I WILL OBEY THE WILL OF THE GODS.
COUNCIL IS DISMISSED. STAY SAFE, ALL OF YOU.
MOTHER... ALCIPPE...
I WILL FIND A WAY TO SAVE HER. EVEN IF IT TAKES MY ENTIRE LIFE, I WILL FIND A WAY...
I--I WILL FIND A WAY...
MY DIANA. I AM SO SORRY...
SO SORRY...

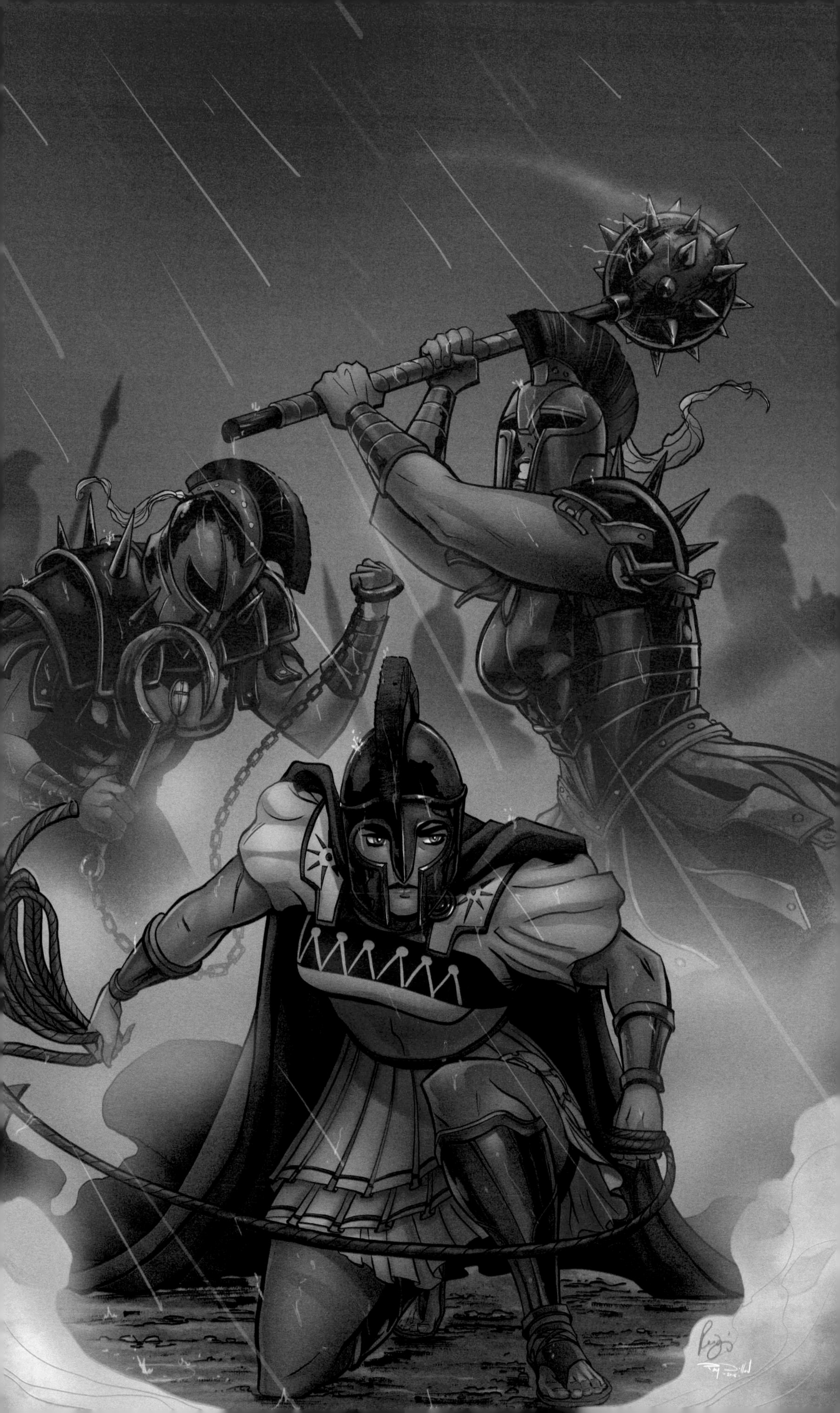

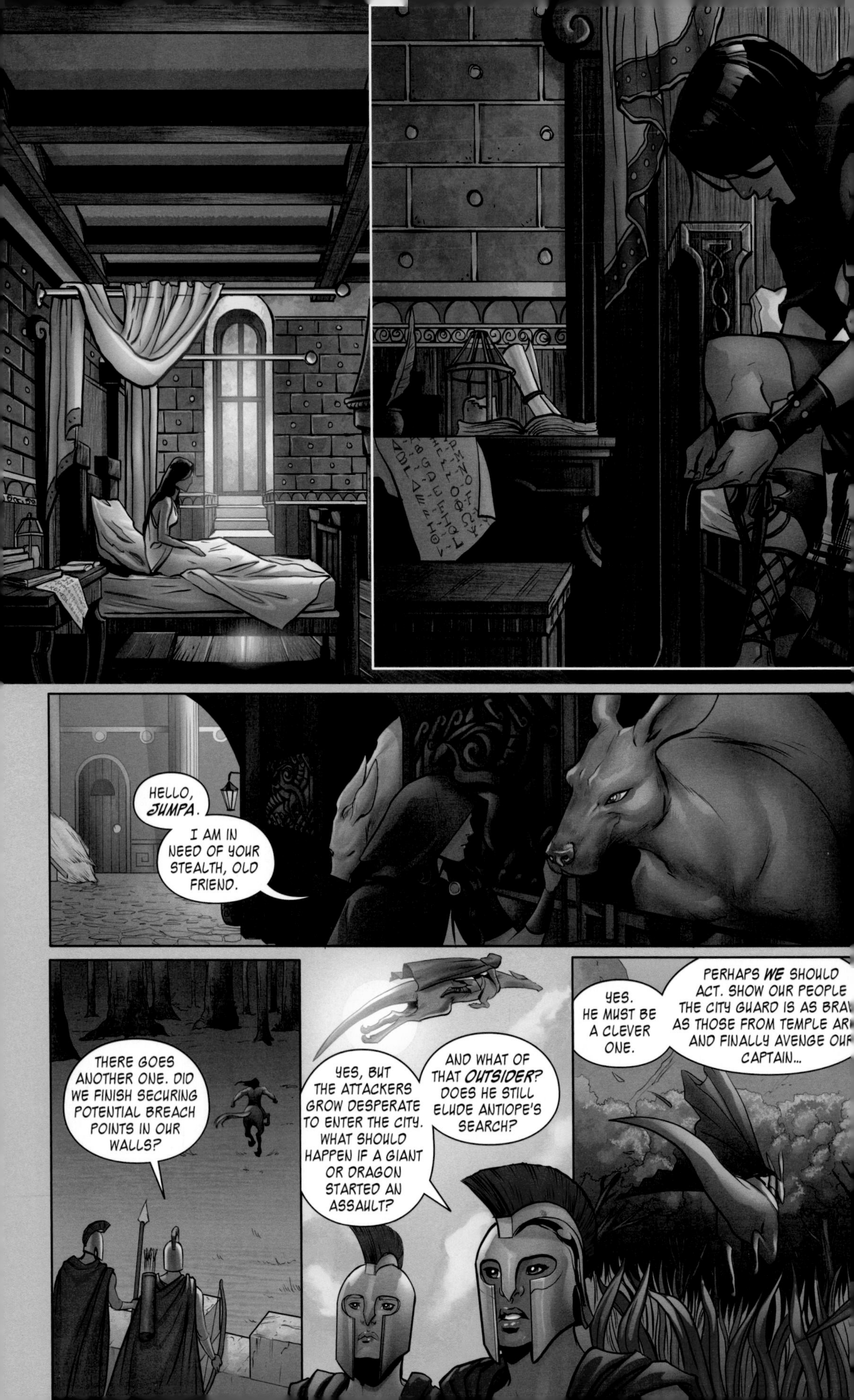

HELLO, JUMPA.
I AM IN NEED OF YOUR STEALTH, OLD FRIEND.
THERE GOES ANOTHER ONE. DID WE FINISH SECURING POTENTIAL BREACH POINTS IN OUR WALLS?
YES, BUT THE ATTACKERS GROW DESPERATE TO ENTER THE CITY. WHAT SHOULD HAPPEN IF A GIANT OR DRAGON STARTED AN ASSAULT?
AND WHAT OF THAT OUTSIDER? DOES HE STILL ELUDE ANTIOPE'S SEARCH?
YES. HE MUST BE A CLEVER ONE.
PERHAPS WE SHOULD ACT. SHOW OUR PEOPLE THE CITY GUARD IS AS BRA
AS THOSE FROM TEMPLE AR
AND FINALLY AVENGE OUR
CAPTAIN...

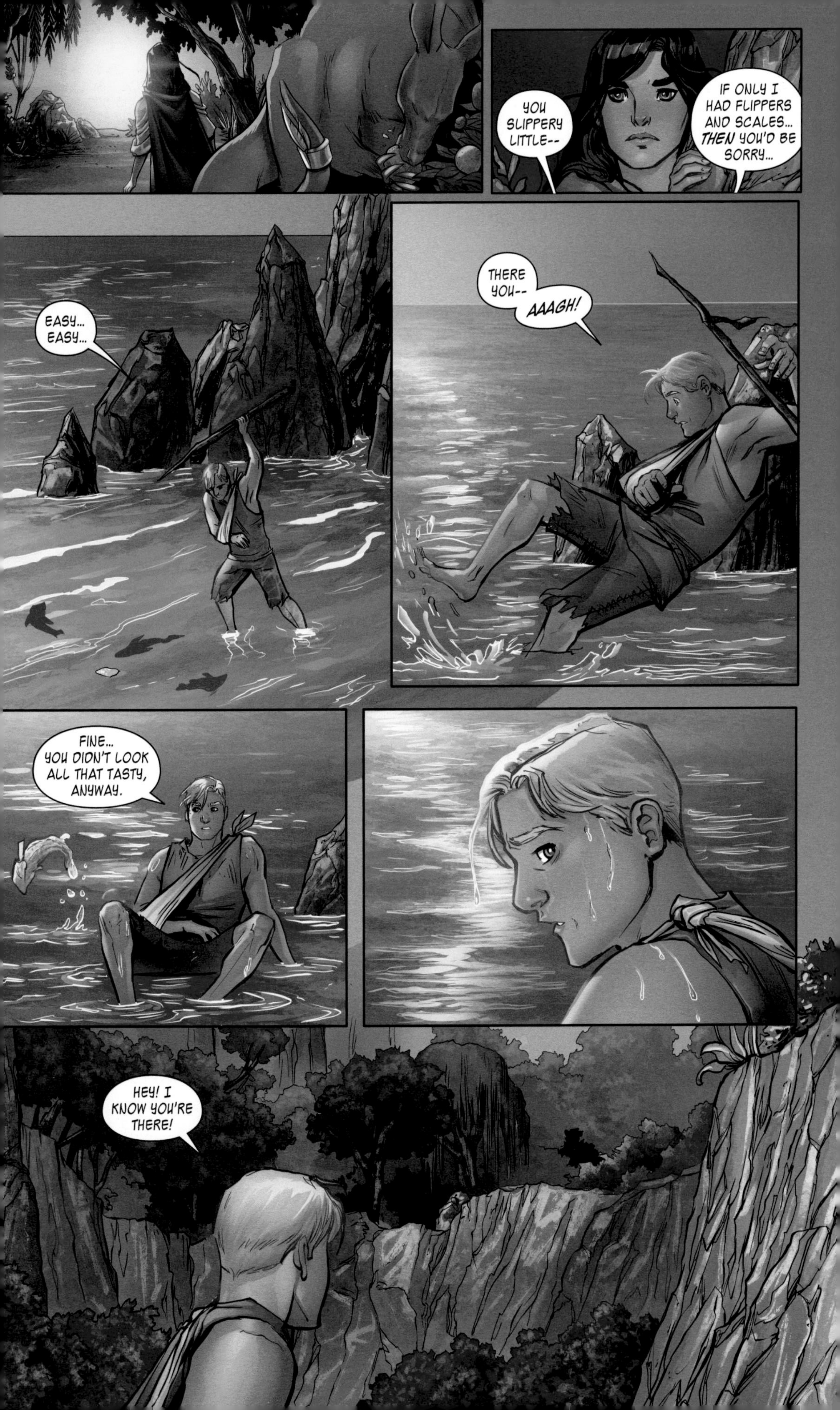
YOU SLIPPERY LITTLE--
IF ONLY I HAD FLIPPERS AND SCALES... *THEN* YOU'D BE SORRY...
EASY... EASY...
THERE YOU-- *AAAGH!*
FINE... YOU DIDN'T LOOK ALL THAT TASTY, ANYWAY.
HEY! I KNOW YOU'RE THERE!

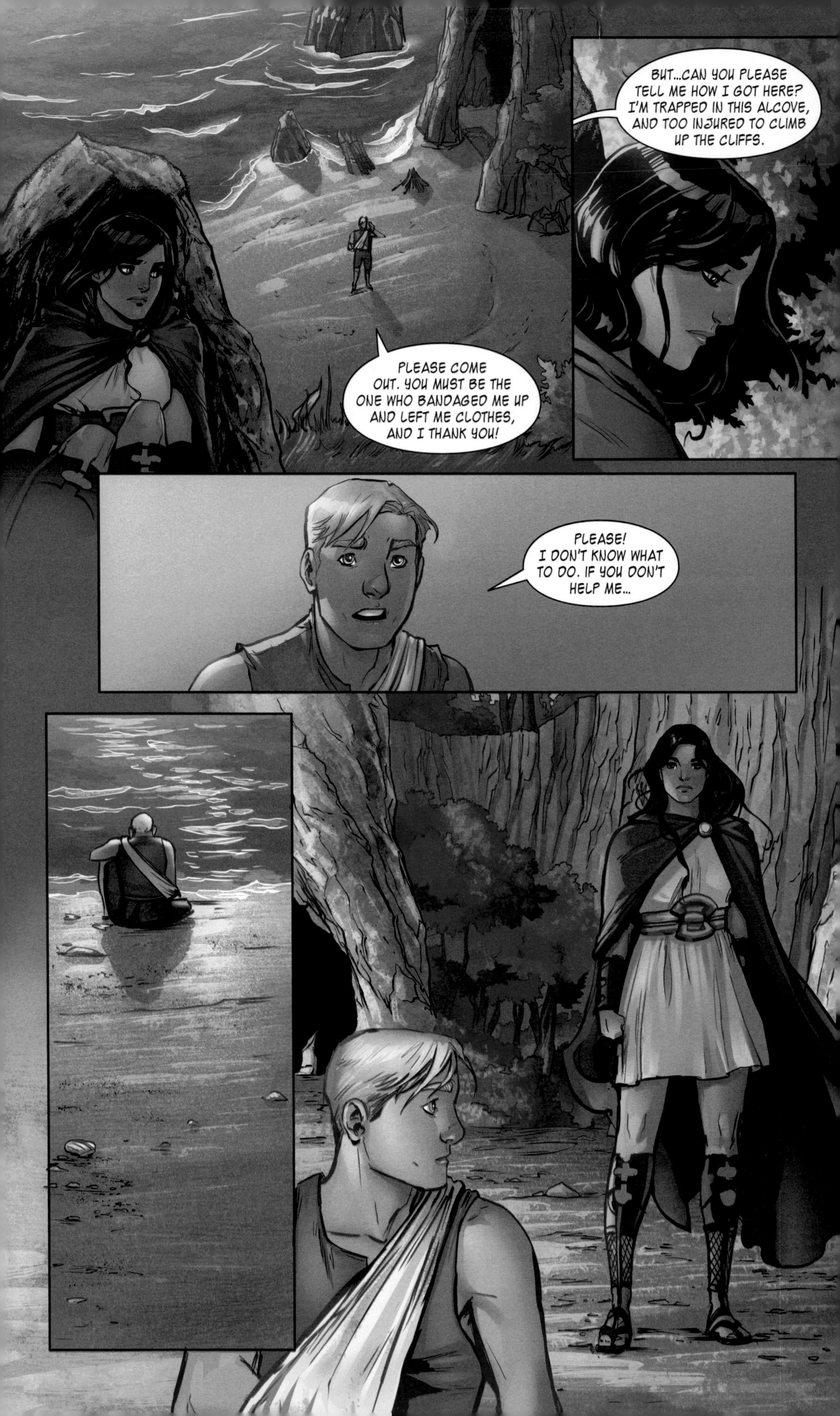
PLEASE COME OUT. YOU MUST BE THE ONE WHO BANDAGED ME UP AND LEFT ME CLOTHES, AND I THANK YOU!
BUT...CAN YOU PLEASE TELL ME HOW I GOT HERE? I'M TRAPPED IN THIS ALCOVE, AND TOO INJURED TO CLIMB UP THE CLIFFS.
PLEASE! I DON'T KNOW WHAT TO DO. IF YOU DON'T HELP ME...

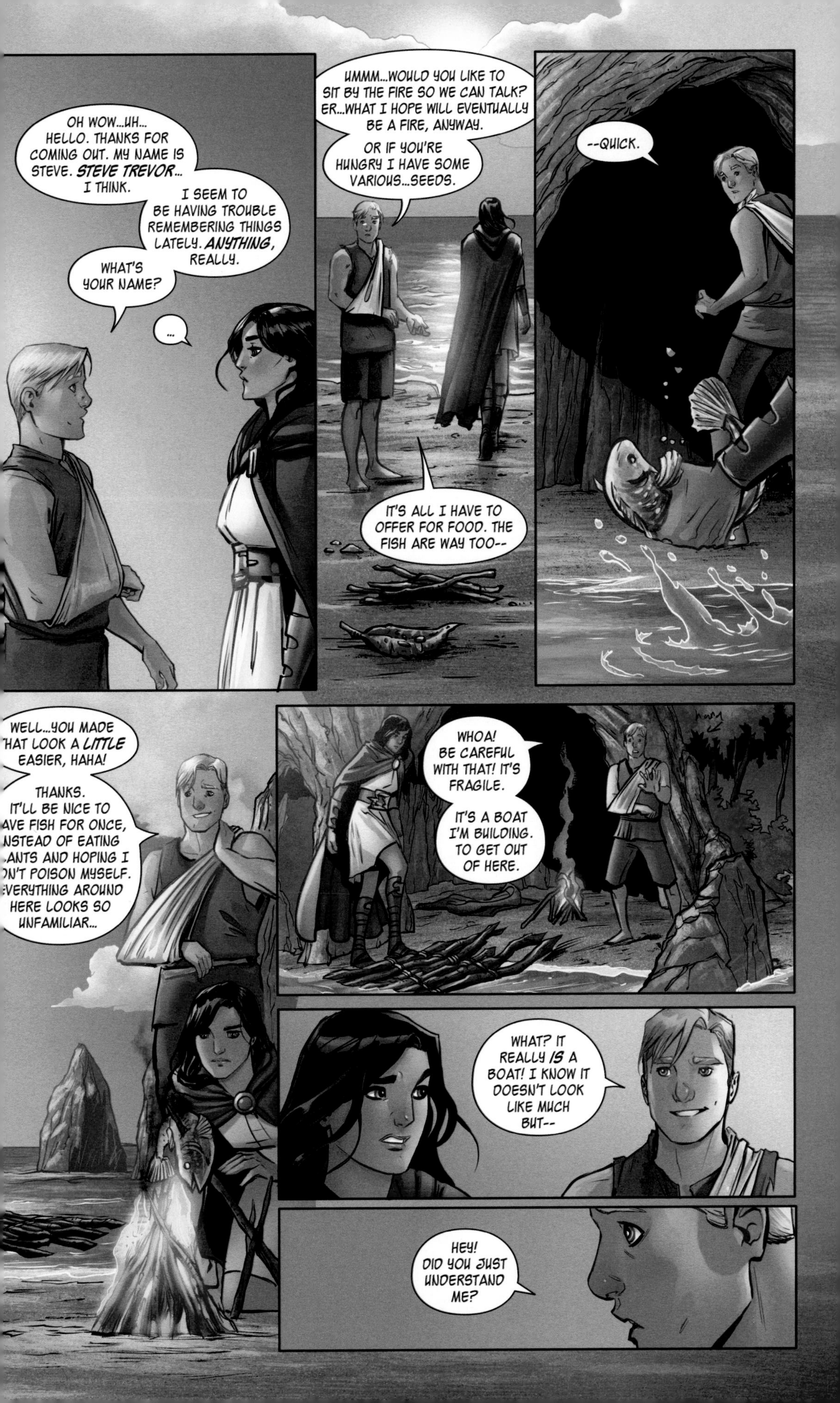
OH WOW...UH... HELLO. THANKS FOR COMING OUT. MY NAME IS STEVE. STEVE TREVOR... I THINK.
I SEEM TO BE HAVING TROUBLE REMEMBERING THINGS LATELY. ANYTHING, REALLY.
WHAT'S YOUR NAME?
...
UMMM...WOULD YOU LIKE TO SIT BY THE FIRE SO WE CAN TALK? ER...WHAT I HOPE WILL EVENTUALLY BE A FIRE, ANYWAY.
OR IF YOU'RE HUNGRY I HAVE SOME VARIOUS...SEEDS.
IT'S ALL I HAVE TO OFFER FOR FOOD. THE FISH ARE WAY TOO--
--QUICK.
WELL...YOU MADE THAT LOOK A LITTLE EASIER, HAHA!
THANKS. IT'LL BE NICE TO HAVE FISH FOR ONCE, INSTEAD OF EATING PLANTS AND HOPING I DON'T POISON MYSELF. EVERYTHING AROUND HERE LOOKS SO UNFAMILIAR...
WHOA! BE CAREFUL WITH THAT! IT'S FRAGILE.
IT'S A BOAT I'M BUILDING. TO GET OUT OF HERE.
WHAT? IT REALLY IS A BOAT! I KNOW IT DOESN'T LOOK LIKE MUCH BUT--
HEY! DID YOU JUST UNDERSTAND ME?

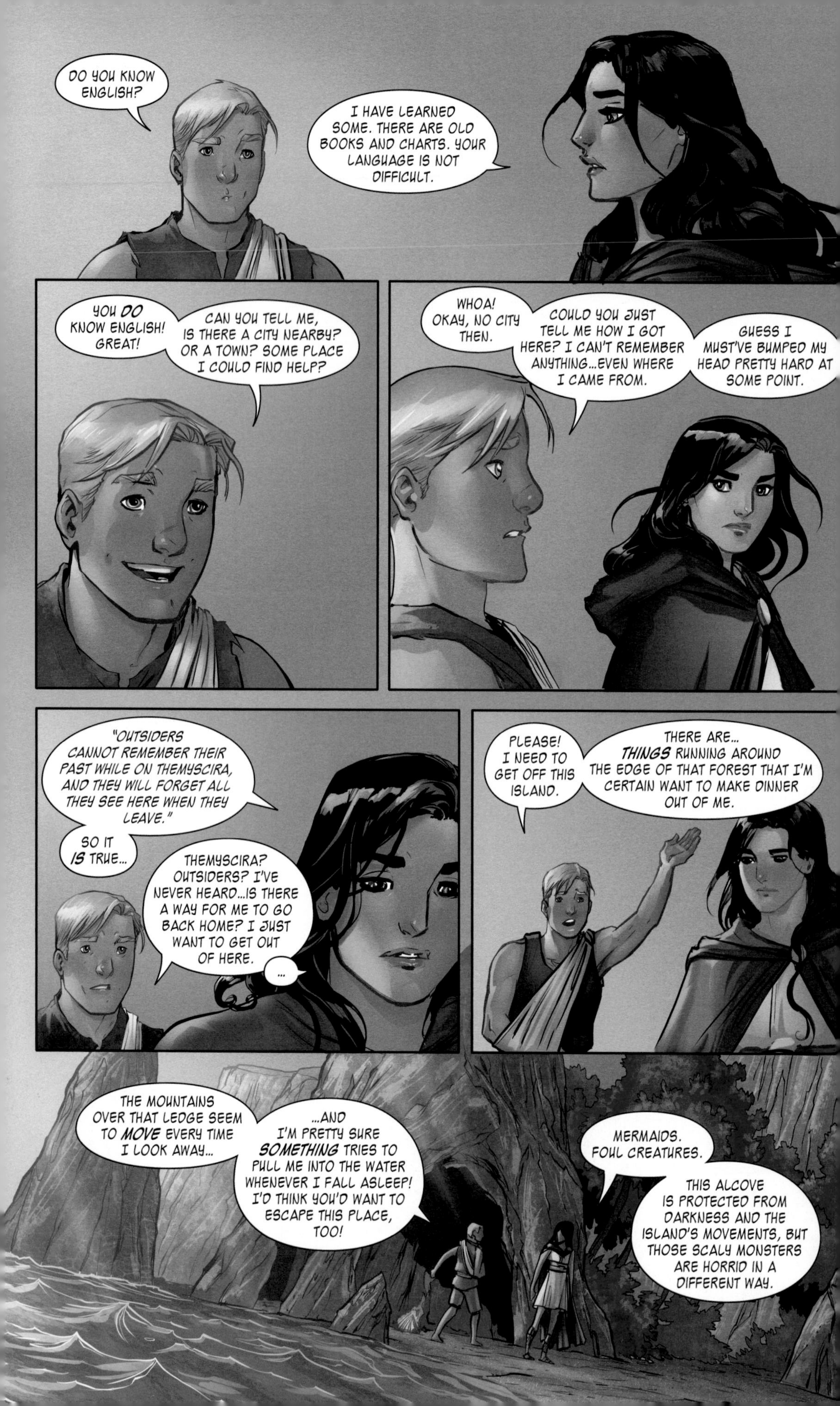
DO YOU KNOW ENGLISH?
I HAVE LEARNED SOME. THERE ARE OLD BOOKS AND CHARTS. YOUR LANGUAGE IS NOT DIFFICULT.
YOU DO KNOW ENGLISH! GREAT!
CAN YOU TELL ME, IS THERE A CITY NEARBY? OR A TOWN? SOME PLACE I COULD FIND HELP?
WHOA! OKAY, NO CITY THEN.
COULD YOU JUST TELL ME HOW I GOT HERE? I CAN'T REMEMBER ANYTHING...EVEN WHERE I CAME FROM.
GUESS I MUST'VE BUMPED MY HEAD PRETTY HARD AT SOME POINT.
"OUTSIDERS CANNOT REMEMBER THEIR PAST WHILE ON THEMYSCIRA, AND THEY WILL FORGET ALL THEY SEE HERE WHEN THEY LEAVE."
SO IT IS TRUE...
THEMYSCIRA? OUTSIDERS? I'VE NEVER HEARD...IS THERE A WAY FOR ME TO GO BACK HOME? I JUST WANT TO GET OUT OF HERE.
...
PLEASE! I NEED TO GET OFF THIS ISLAND.
THERE ARE... THINGS RUNNING AROUND THE EDGE OF THAT FOREST THAT I'M CERTAIN WANT TO MAKE DINNER OUT OF ME.
THE MOUNTAINS OVER THAT LEDGE SEEM TO MOVE EVERY TIME I LOOK AWAY...
...AND I'M PRETTY SURE SOMETHING TRIES TO PULL ME INTO THE WATER WHENEVER I FALL ASLEEP! I'D THINK YOU'D WANT TO ESCAPE THIS PLACE, TOO!
MERMAIDS. FOUL CREATURES.
THIS ALCOVE IS PROTECTED FROM DARKNESS AND THE ISLAND'S MOVEMENTS, BUT THOSE SCALY MONSTERS ARE HORRID IN A DIFFERENT WAY.

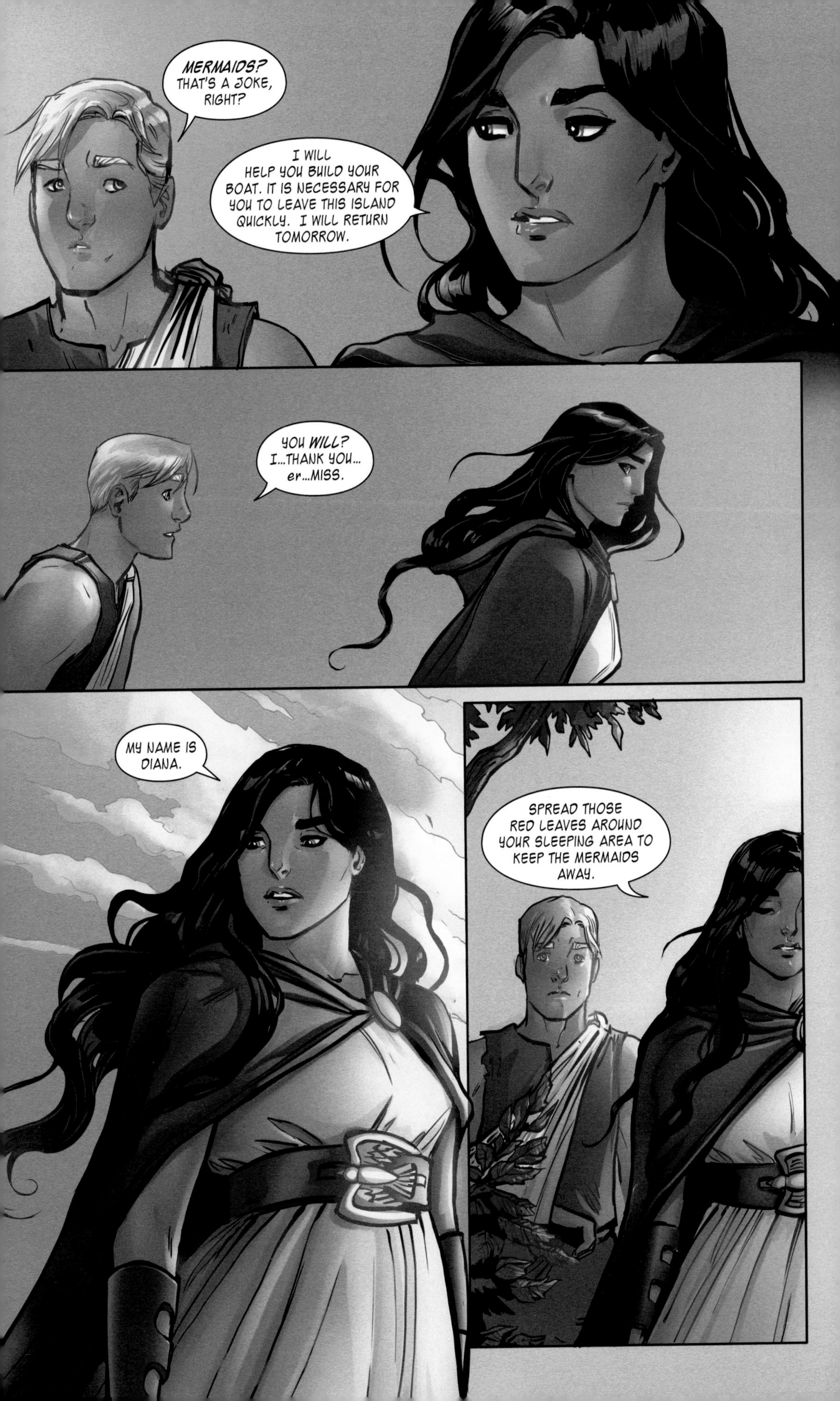

MERMAIDS? THAT'S A JOKE, RIGHT?
I WILL HELP YOU BUILD YOUR BOAT. IT IS NECESSARY FOR YOU TO LEAVE THIS ISLAND QUICKLY. I WILL RETURN TOMORROW.
YOU WILL? I...THANK YOU... er...MISS.
MY NAME IS DIANA.
SPREAD THOSE RED LEAVES AROUND YOUR SLEEPING AREA TO KEEP THE MERMAIDS AWAY.

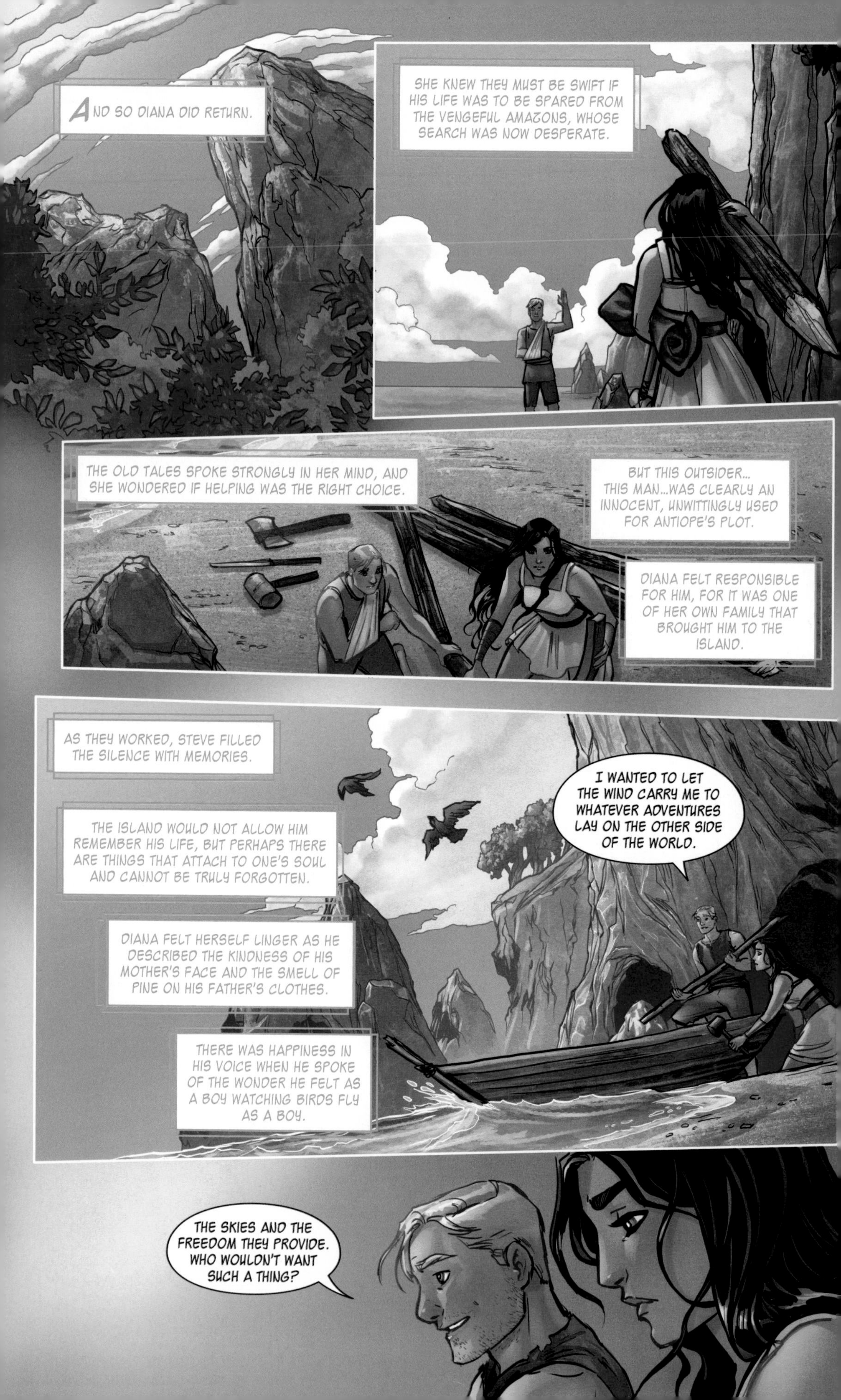
AND SO DIANA DID RETURN.
SHE KNEW THEY MUST BE SWIFT IF HIS LIFE WAS TO BE SPARED FROM THE VENGEFUL AMAZONS, WHOSE SEARCH WAS NOW DESPERATE.
THE OLD TALES SPOKE STRONGLY IN HER MIND, AND SHE WONDERED IF HELPING WAS THE RIGHT CHOICE.
BUT THIS OUTSIDER... THIS MAN...WAS CLEARLY AN INNOCENT, UNWITTINGLY USED FOR ANTIOPE'S PLOT.
DIANA FELT RESPONSIBLE FOR HIM, FOR IT WAS ONE OF HER OWN FAMILY THAT BROUGHT HIM TO THE ISLAND.
AS THEY WORKED, STEVE FILLED THE SILENCE WITH MEMORIES.
THE ISLAND WOULD NOT ALLOW HIM REMEMBER HIS LIFE, BUT PERHAPS THERE ARE THINGS THAT ATTACH TO ONE'S SOUL AND CANNOT BE TRULY FORGOTTEN.
I WANTED TO LET THE WIND CARRY ME TO WHATEVER ADVENTURES LAY ON THE OTHER SIDE OF THE WORLD.
DIANA FELT HERSELF LINGER AS HE DESCRIBED THE KINDNESS OF HIS MOTHER'S FACE AND THE SMELL OF PINE ON HIS FATHER'S CLOTHES.
THERE WAS HAPPINESS IN HIS VOICE WHEN HE SPOKE OF THE WONDER HE FELT AS A BOY WATCHING BIRDS FLY AS A BOY.
THE SKIES AND THE FREEDOM THEY PROVIDE. WHO WOULDN'T WANT SUCH A THING?

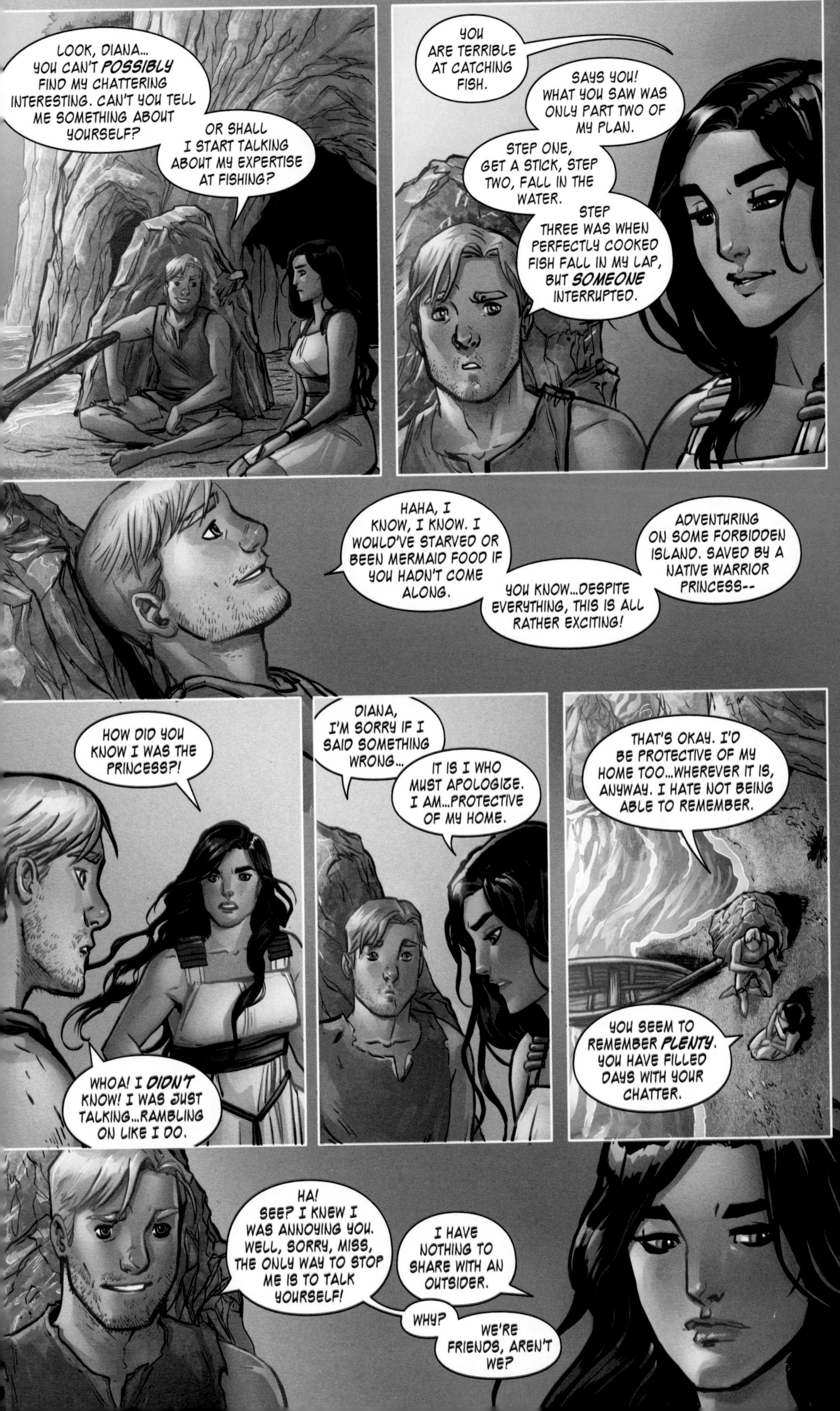
LOOK, DIANA... YOU CAN'T POSSIBLY FIND MY CHATTERING INTERESTING. CAN'T YOU TELL ME SOMETHING ABOUT YOURSELF?
OR SHALL I START TALKING ABOUT MY EXPERTISE AT FISHING?
YOU ARE TERRIBLE AT CATCHING FISH.
SAYS YOU! WHAT YOU SAW WAS ONLY PART TWO OF MY PLAN.
STEP ONE, GET A STICK, STEP TWO, FALL IN THE WATER.
STEP THREE WAS WHEN PERFECTLY COOKED FISH FALL IN MY LAP, BUT SOMEONE INTERRUPTED.
HAHA, I KNOW, I KNOW. I WOULD'VE STARVED OR BEEN MERMAID FOOD IF YOU HADN'T COME ALONG.
YOU KNOW...DESPITE EVERYTHING, THIS IS ALL RATHER EXCITING!
ADVENTURING ON SOME FORBIDDEN ISLAND. SAVED BY A NATIVE WARRIOR PRINCESS--
HOW DID YOU KNOW I WAS THE PRINCESS?!
WHOA! I DIDN'T KNOW! I WAS JUST TALKING...RAMBLING ON LIKE I DO.
DIANA, I'M SORRY IF I SAID SOMETHING WRONG...
IT IS I WHO MUST APOLOGIZE. I AM...PROTECTIVE OF MY HOME.
THAT'S OKAY. I'D BE PROTECTIVE OF MY HOME TOO...WHEREVER IT IS, ANYWAY. I HATE NOT BEING ABLE TO REMEMBER.
YOU SEEM TO REMEMBER PLENTY. YOU HAVE FILLED DAYS WITH YOUR CHATTER.
HA! SEE? I KNEW I WAS ANNOYING YOU. WELL, SORRY, MISS, THE ONLY WAY TO STOP ME IS TO TALK YOURSELF!
I HAVE NOTHING TO SHARE WITH AN OUTSIDER.
WHY?
WE'RE FRIENDS, AREN'T WE?

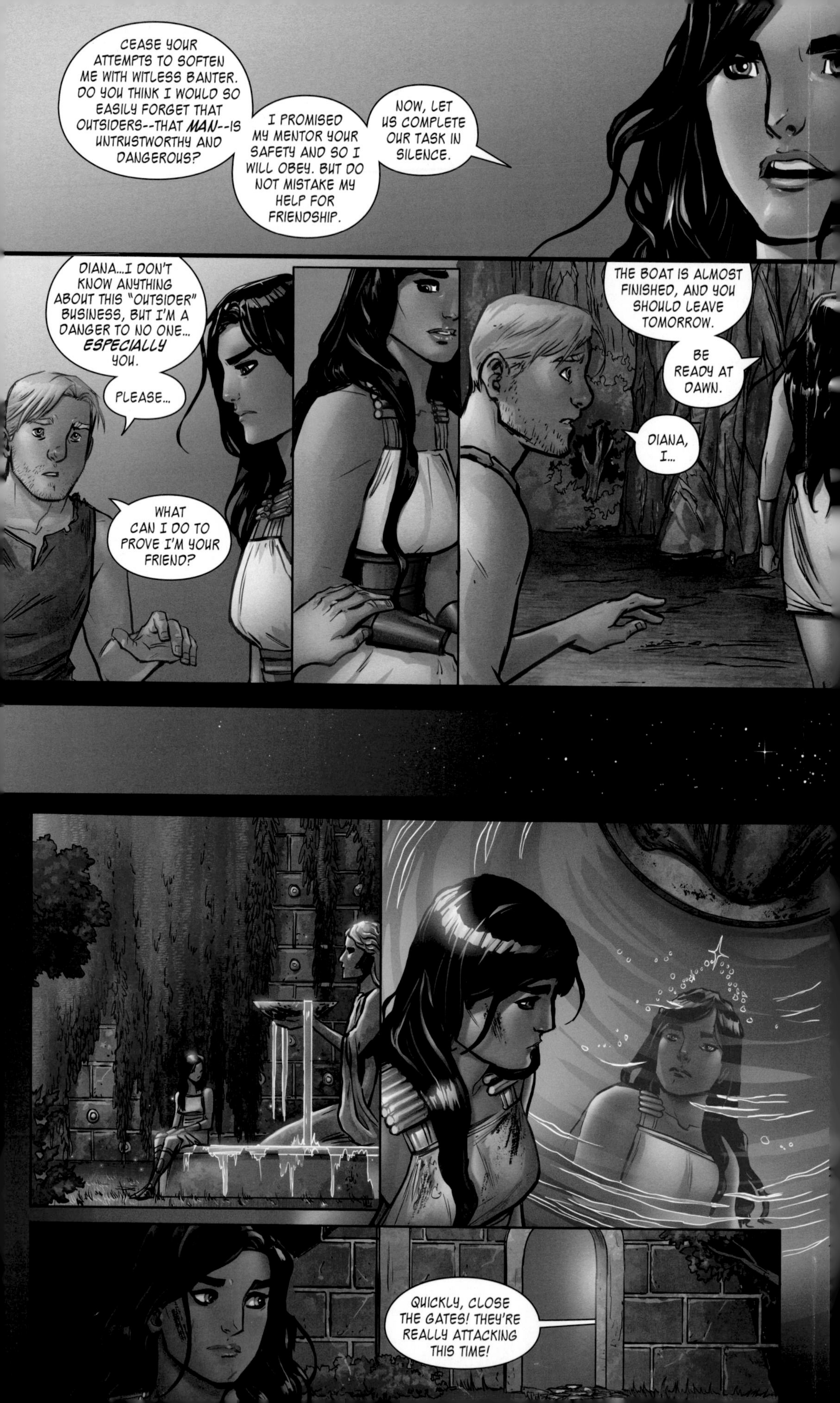

CEASE YOUR ATTEMPTS TO SOFTEN ME WITH WITLESS BANTER. DO YOU THINK I WOULD SO EASILY FORGET THAT OUTSIDERS--THAT MAN--IS UNTRUSTWORTHY AND DANGEROUS?
I PROMISED MY MENTOR YOUR SAFETY AND SO I WILL OBEY. BUT DO NOT MISTAKE MY HELP FOR FRIENDSHIP.
NOW, LET US COMPLETE OUR TASK IN SILENCE.
DIANA...I DON'T KNOW ANYTHING ABOUT THIS "OUTSIDER" BUSINESS, BUT I'M A DANGER TO NO ONE... ESPECIALLY YOU.
PLEASE...
WHAT CAN I DO TO PROVE I'M YOUR FRIEND?
THE BOAT IS ALMOST FINISHED, AND YOU SHOULD LEAVE TOMORROW.
BE READY AT DAWN.
DIANA, I...
QUICKLY, CLOSE THE GATES! THEY'RE REALLY ATTACKING THIS TIME!

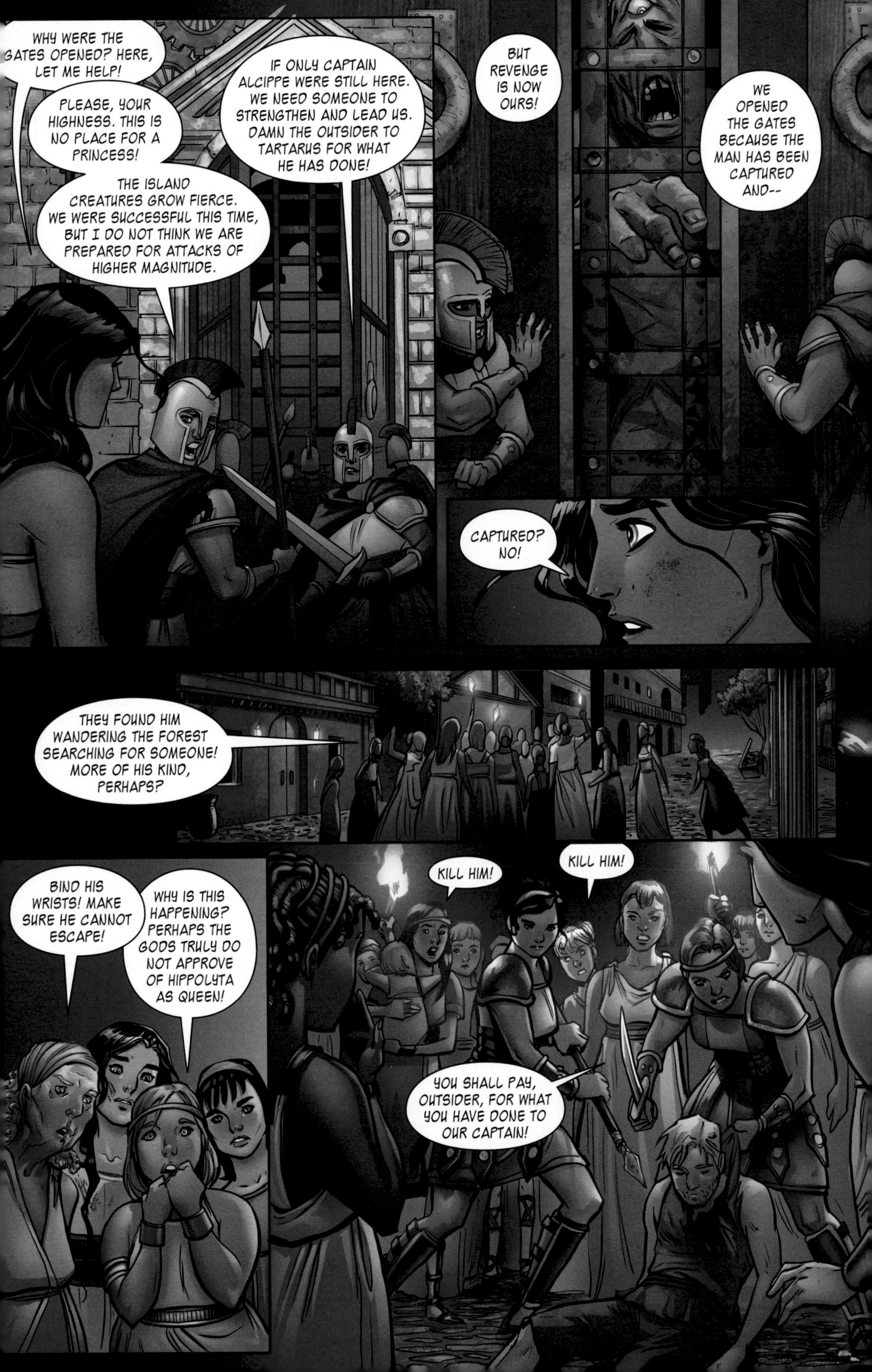
WHY WERE THE GATES OPENED? HERE, LET ME HELP!
PLEASE, YOUR HIGHNESS. THIS IS NO PLACE FOR A PRINCESS!
THE ISLAND CREATURES GROW FIERCE. WE WERE SUCCESSFUL THIS TIME, BUT I DO NOT THINK WE ARE PREPARED FOR ATTACKS OF HIGHER MAGNITUDE.
IF ONLY CAPTAIN ALCIPPE WERE STILL HERE. WE NEED SOMEONE TO STRENGTHEN AND LEAD US. DAMN THE OUTSIDER TO TARTARUS FOR WHAT HE HAS DONE!
BUT REVENGE IS NOW OURS!
WE OPENED THE GATES BECAUSE THE MAN HAS BEEN CAPTURED AND--
CAPTURED? NO!
THEY FOUND HIM WANDERING THE FOREST SEARCHING FOR SOMEONE! MORE OF HIS KIND, PERHAPS?
BIND HIS WRISTS! MAKE SURE HE CANNOT ESCAPE!
WHY IS THIS HAPPENING? PERHAPS THE GODS TRULY DO NOT APPROVE OF HIPPOLYTA AS QUEEN!
KILL HIM!
KILL HIM!
YOU SHALL PAY, OUTSIDER, FOR WHAT YOU HAVE DONE TO OUR CAPTAIN!

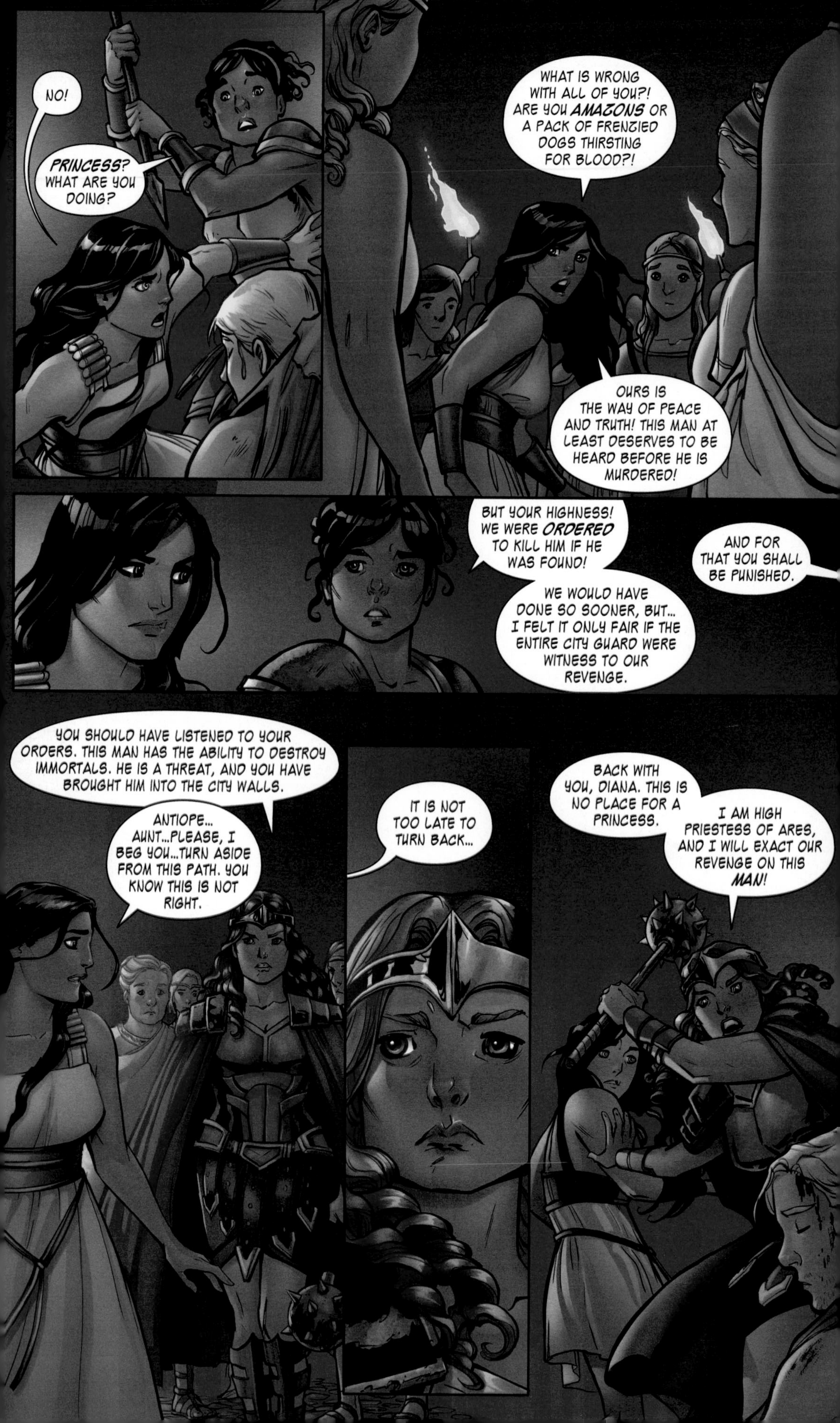
NO!
PRINCESS? WHAT ARE YOU DOING?
WHAT IS WRONG WITH ALL OF YOU?! ARE YOU AMAZONS OR A PACK OF FRENZIED DOGS THIRSTING FOR BLOOD?!
OURS IS THE WAY OF PEACE AND TRUTH! THIS MAN AT LEAST DESERVES TO BE HEARD BEFORE HE IS MURDERED!
BUT YOUR HIGHNESS! WE WERE ORDERED TO KILL HIM IF HE WAS FOUND!
WE WOULD HAVE DONE SO SOONER, BUT... I FELT IT ONLY FAIR IF THE ENTIRE CITY GUARD WERE WITNESS TO OUR REVENGE.
AND FOR THAT YOU SHALL BE PUNISHED.
YOU SHOULD HAVE LISTENED TO YOUR ORDERS. THIS MAN HAS THE ABILITY TO DESTROY IMMORTALS. HE IS A THREAT, AND YOU HAVE BROUGHT HIM INTO THE CITY WALLS.
ANTIOPE... AUNT...PLEASE, I BEG YOU...TURN ASIDE FROM THIS PATH. YOU KNOW THIS IS NOT RIGHT.
IT IS NOT TOO LATE TO TURN BACK...
BACK WITH YOU, DIANA. THIS IS NO PLACE FOR A PRINCESS.
I AM HIGH PRIESTESS OF ARES, AND I WILL EXACT OUR REVENGE ON THIS MAN!

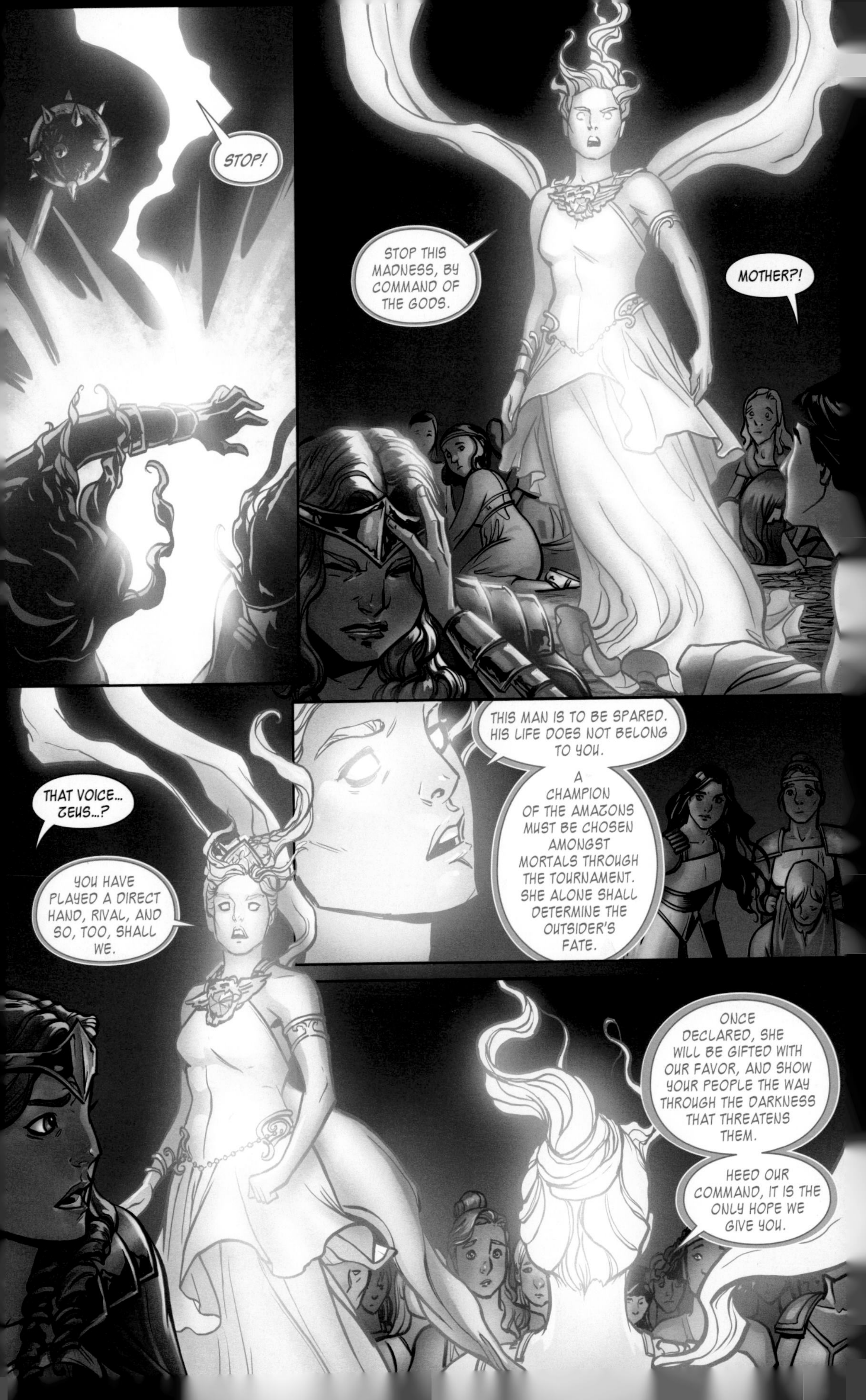
STOP!
STOP THIS MADNESS, BY COMMAND OF THE GODS.
MOTHER?!
THAT VOICE... ZEUS...?
YOU HAVE PLAYED A DIRECT HAND, RIVAL, AND SO, TOO, SHALL WE.
THIS MAN IS TO BE SPARED. HIS LIFE DOES NOT BELONG TO YOU.
A CHAMPION OF THE AMAZONS MUST BE CHOSEN AMONGST MORTALS THROUGH THE TOURNAMENT. SHE ALONE SHALL DETERMINE THE OUTSIDER'S FATE.
ONCE DECLARED, SHE WILL BE GIFTED WITH OUR FAVOR, AND SHOW YOUR PEOPLE THE WAY THROUGH THE DARKNESS THAT THREATENS THEM.
HEED OUR COMMAND, IT IS THE ONLY HOPE WE GIVE YOU.

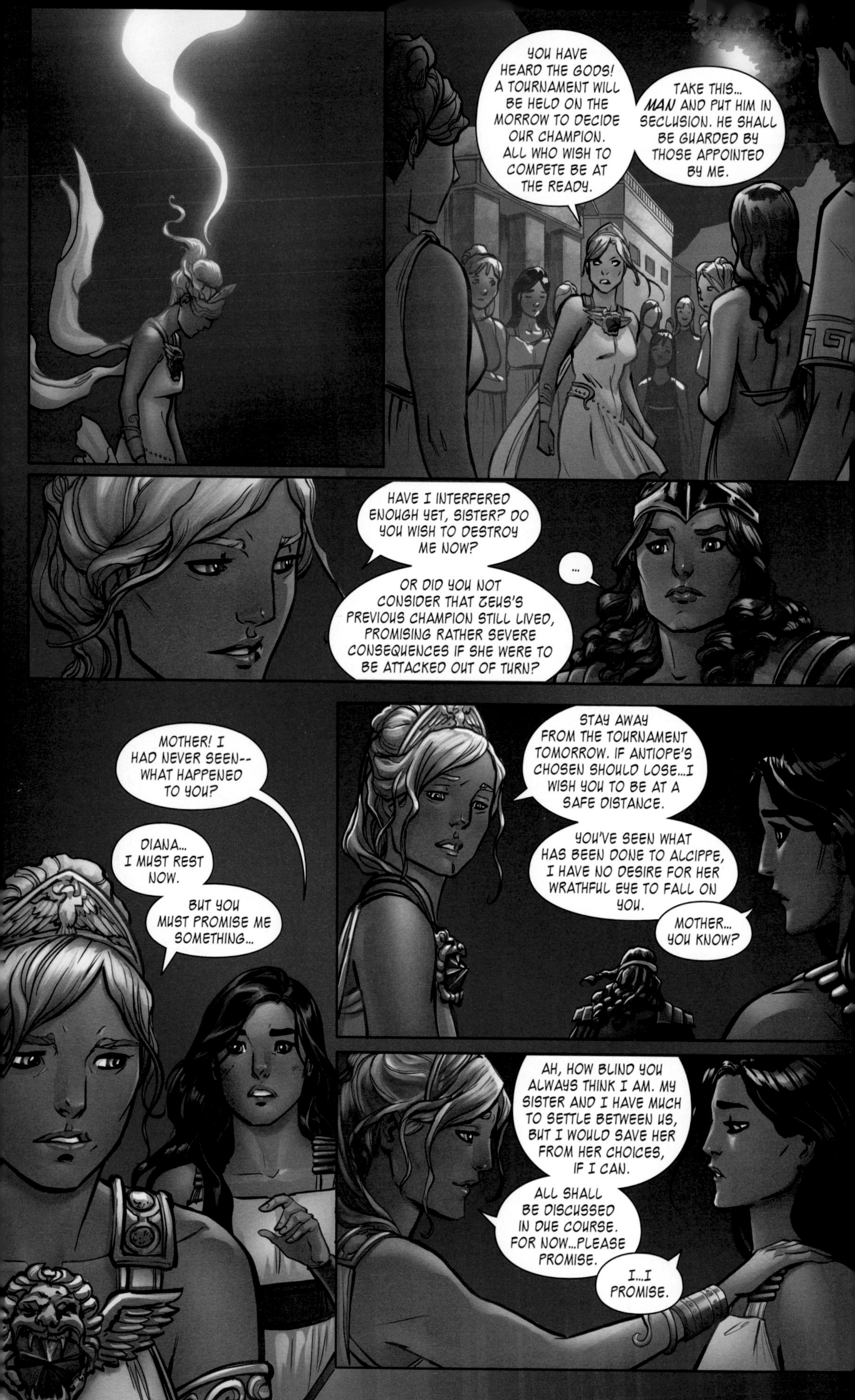
YOU HAVE HEARD THE GODS! A TOURNAMENT WILL BE HELD ON THE MORROW TO DECIDE OUR CHAMPION. ALL WHO WISH TO COMPETE BE AT THE READY.
TAKE THIS... *MAN* AND PUT HIM IN SECLUSION. HE SHALL BE GUARDED BY THOSE APPOINTED BY ME.
HAVE I INTERFERED ENOUGH YET, SISTER? DO YOU WISH TO DESTROY ME NOW?
OR DID YOU NOT CONSIDER THAT ZEUS'S PREVIOUS CHAMPION STILL LIVED, PROMISING RATHER SEVERE CONSEQUENCES IF SHE WERE TO BE ATTACKED OUT OF TURN?
...
MOTHER! I HAD NEVER SEEN--WHAT HAPPENED TO YOU?
DIANA... I MUST REST NOW.
BUT YOU MUST PROMISE ME SOMETHING...
STAY AWAY FROM THE TOURNAMENT TOMORROW. IF ANTIOPE'S CHOSEN SHOULD LOSE...I WISH YOU TO BE AT A SAFE DISTANCE.
YOU'VE SEEN WHAT HAS BEEN DONE TO ALCIPPE, I HAVE NO DESIRE FOR HER WRATHFUL EYE TO FALL ON YOU.
MOTHER... YOU KNOW?
AH, HOW BLIND YOU ALWAYS THINK I AM. MY SISTER AND I HAVE MUCH TO SETTLE BETWEEN US, BUT I WOULD SAVE HER FROM HER CHOICES, IF I CAN.
ALL SHALL BE DISCUSSED IN DUE COURSE. FOR NOW...PLEASE PROMISE.
I...I PROMISE.

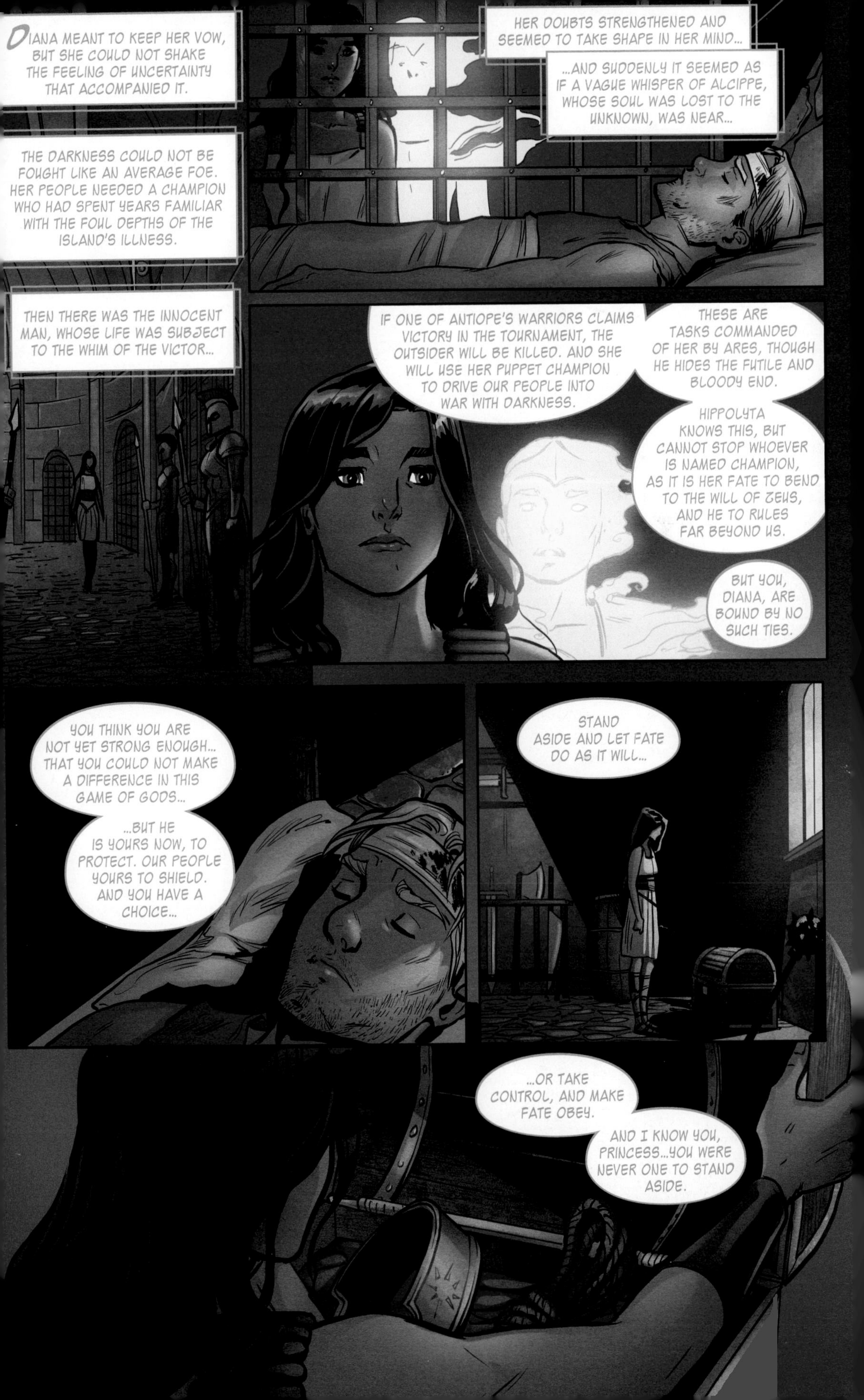
DIANA MEANT TO KEEP HER VOW, BUT SHE COULD NOT SHAKE THE FEELING OF UNCERTAINTY THAT ACCOMPANIED IT.
HER DOUBTS STRENGTHENED AND SEEMED TO TAKE SHAPE IN HER MIND...
...AND SUDDENLY IT SEEMED AS IF A VAGUE WHISPER OF ALCIPPE, WHOSE SOUL WAS LOST TO THE UNKNOWN, WAS NEAR...
THE DARKNESS COULD NOT BE FOUGHT LIKE AN AVERAGE FOE. HER PEOPLE NEEDED A CHAMPION WHO HAD SPENT YEARS FAMILIAR WITH THE FOUL DEPTHS OF THE ISLAND'S ILLNESS.
THEN THERE WAS THE INNOCENT MAN, WHOSE LIFE WAS SUBJECT TO THE WHIM OF THE VICTOR...
IF ONE OF ANTIOPE'S WARRIORS CLAIMS VICTORY IN THE TOURNAMENT, THE OUTSIDER WILL BE KILLED. AND SHE WILL USE HER PUPPET CHAMPION TO DRIVE OUR PEOPLE INTO WAR WITH DARKNESS.
THESE ARE TASKS COMMANDED OF HER BY ARES, THOUGH HE HIDES THE FUTILE AND BLOODY END.
HIPPOLYTA KNOWS THIS, BUT CANNOT STOP WHOEVER IS NAMED CHAMPION, AS IT IS HER FATE TO BEND TO THE WILL OF ZEUS, AND HE TO RULES FAR BEYOND US.
BUT YOU, DIANA, ARE BOUND BY NO SUCH TIES.
YOU THINK YOU ARE NOT YET STRONG ENOUGH... THAT YOU COULD NOT MAKE A DIFFERENCE IN THIS GAME OF GODS...
...BUT HE IS YOURS NOW, TO PROTECT. OUR PEOPLE YOURS TO SHIELD. AND YOU HAVE A CHOICE...
STAND ASIDE AND LET FATE DO AS IT WILL...
...OR TAKE CONTROL, AND MAKE FATE OBEY.
AND I KNOW YOU, PRINCESS...YOU WERE NEVER ONE TO STAND ASIDE.

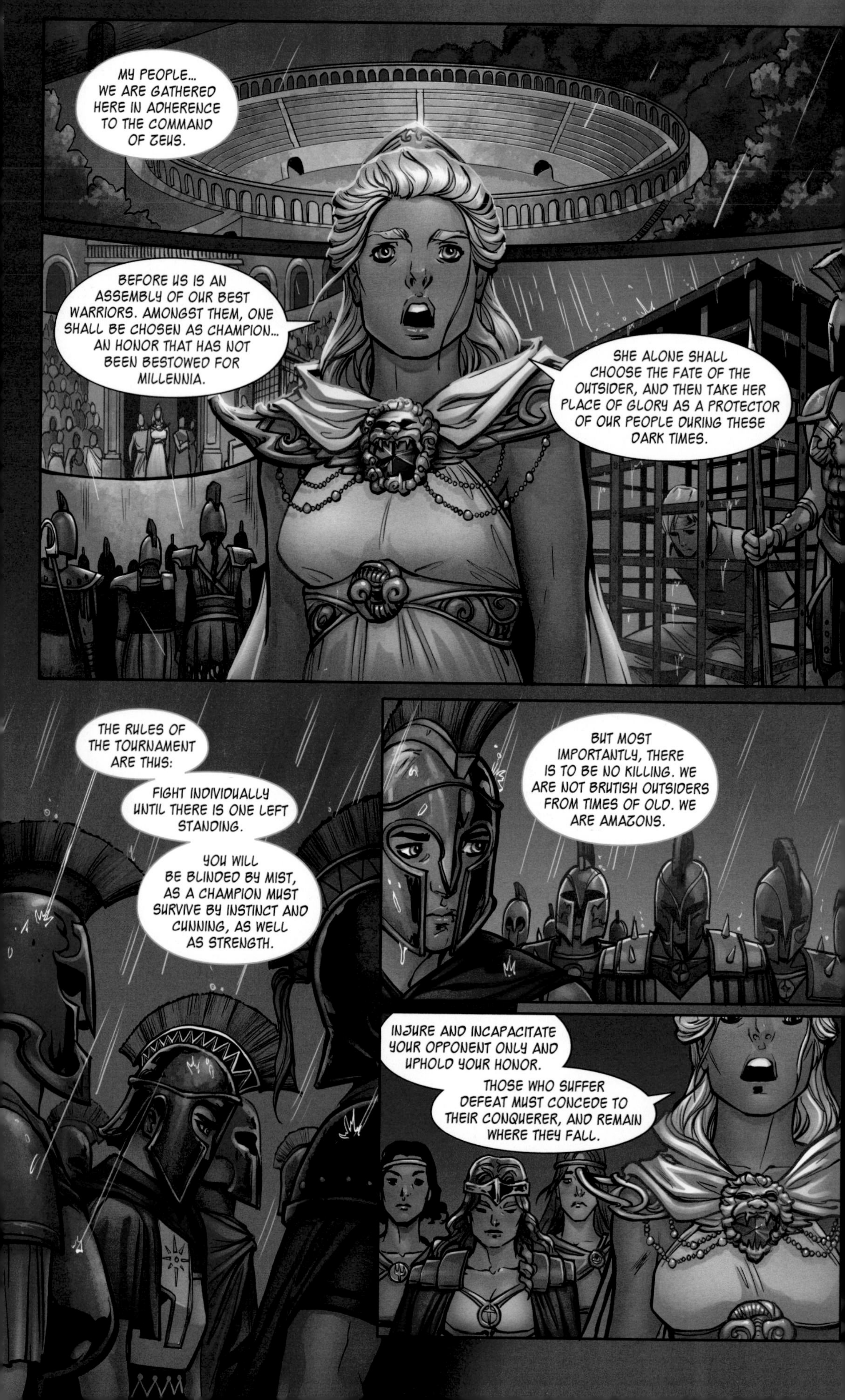

MY PEOPLE... WE ARE GATHERED HERE IN ADHERENCE TO THE COMMAND OF ZEUS.
BEFORE US IS AN ASSEMBLY OF OUR BEST WARRIORS. AMONGST THEM, ONE SHALL BE CHOSEN AS CHAMPION... AN HONOR THAT HAS NOT BEEN BESTOWED FOR MILLENNIA.
SHE ALONE SHALL CHOOSE THE FATE OF THE OUTSIDER, AND THEN TAKE HER PLACE OF GLORY AS A PROTECTOR OF OUR PEOPLE DURING THESE DARK TIMES.
THE RULES OF THE TOURNAMENT ARE THUS:
FIGHT INDIVIDUALLY UNTIL THERE IS ONE LEFT STANDING.
YOU WILL BE BLINDED BY MIST, AS A CHAMPION MUST SURVIVE BY INSTINCT AND CUNNING, AS WELL AS STRENGTH.
BUT MOST IMPORTANTLY, THERE IS TO BE NO KILLING. WE ARE NOT BRUTISH OUTSIDERS FROM TIMES OF OLD. WE ARE AMAZONS.
INJURE AND INCAPACITATE YOUR OPPONENT ONLY AND UPHOLD YOUR HONOR.
THOSE WHO SUFFER DEFEAT MUST CONCEDE TO THEIR CONQUERER, AND REMAIN WHERE THEY FALL.

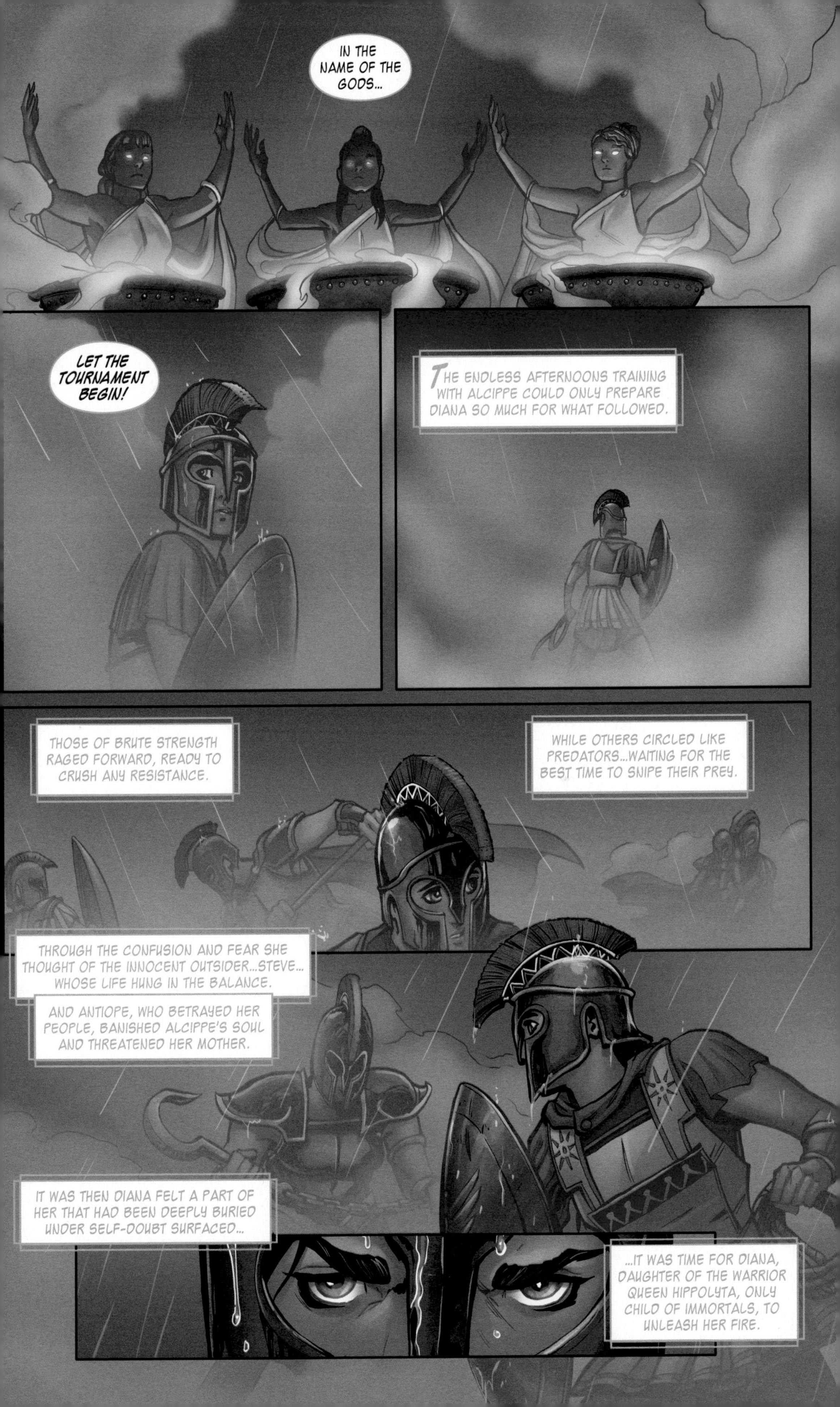
IN THE NAME OF THE GODS...
LET THE TOURNAMENT BEGIN!
THE ENDLESS AFTERNOONS TRAINING WITH ALCIPPE COULD ONLY PREPARE DIANA SO MUCH FOR WHAT FOLLOWED.
THOSE OF BRUTE STRENGTH RAGED FORWARD, READY TO CRUSH ANY RESISTANCE.
WHILE OTHERS CIRCLED LIKE PREDATORS...WAITING FOR THE BEST TIME TO SNIPE THEIR PREY.
THROUGH THE CONFUSION AND FEAR SHE THOUGHT OF THE INNOCENT OUTSIDER...STEVE... WHOSE LIFE HUNG IN THE BALANCE.
AND ANTIOPE, WHO BETRAYED HER PEOPLE, BANISHED ALCIPPE'S SOUL AND THREATENED HER MOTHER.
IT WAS THEN DIANA FELT A PART OF HER THAT HAD BEEN DEEPLY BURIED UNDER SELF-DOUBT SURFACED...
...IT WAS TIME FOR DIANA, DAUGHTER OF THE WARRIOR QUEEN HIPPOLYTA, ONLY CHILD OF IMMORTALS, TO UNLEASH HER FIRE.

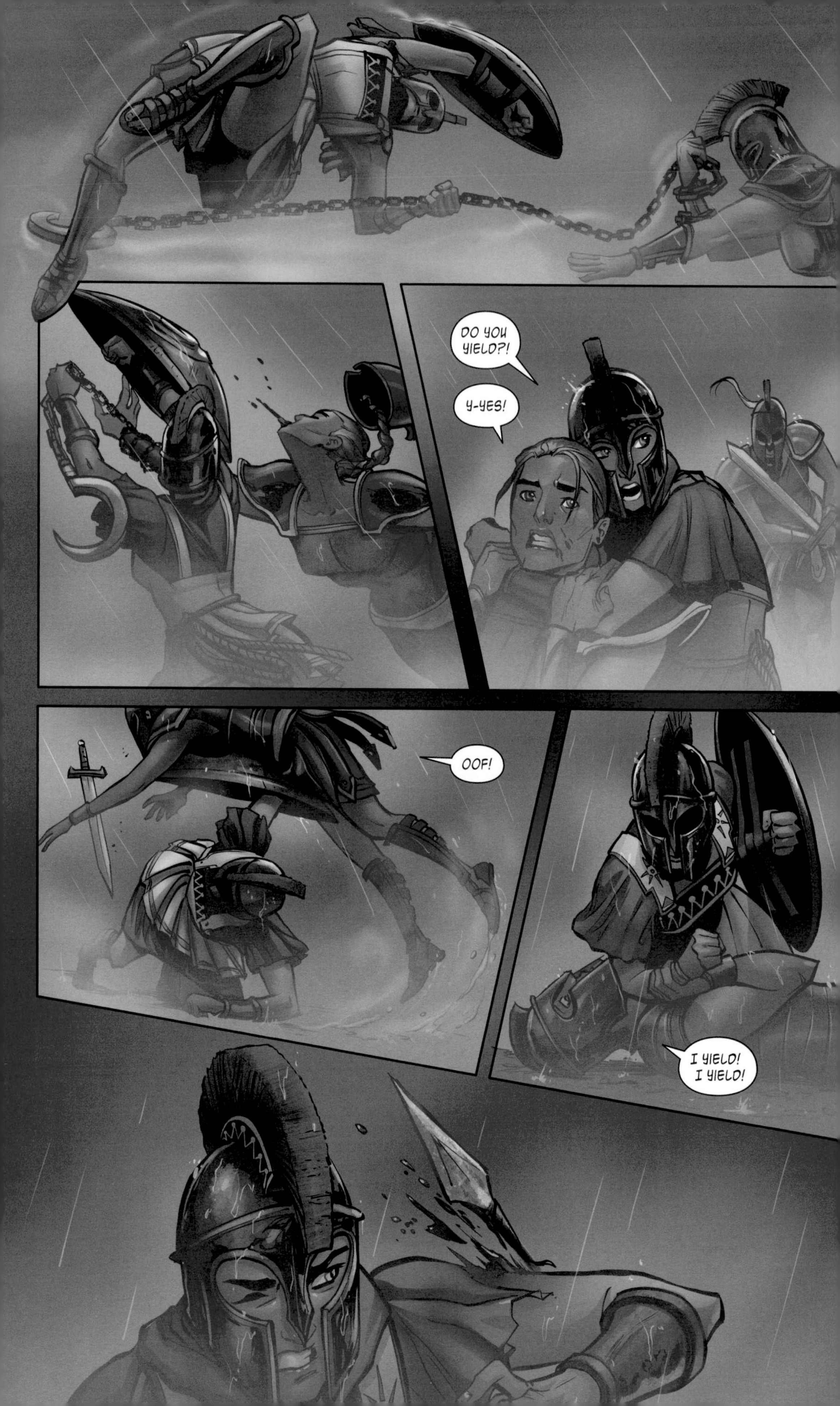
DO YOU YIELD?!
Y-YES!
OOF!
I YIELD! I YIELD!

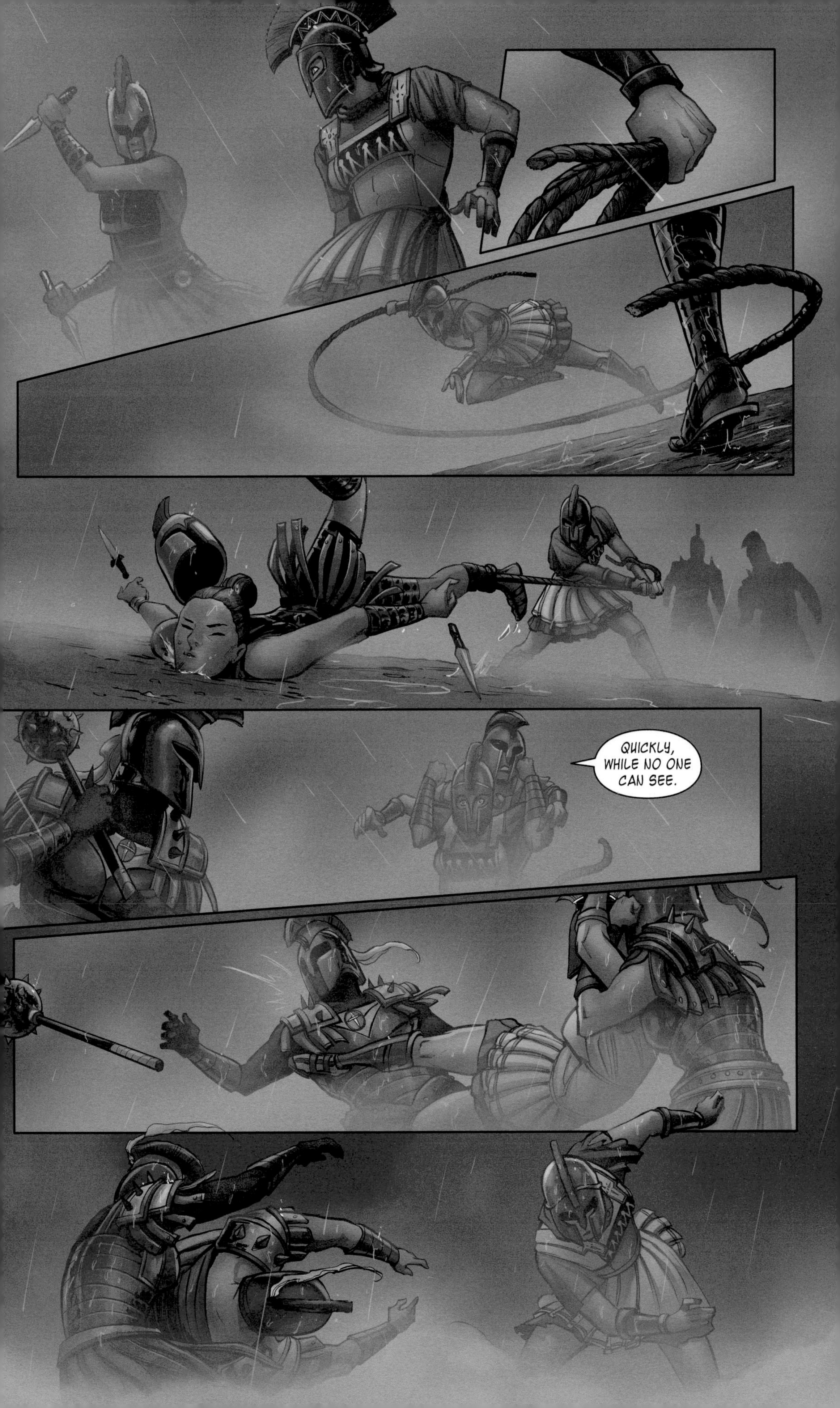
QUICKLY, WHILE NO ONE CAN SEE.

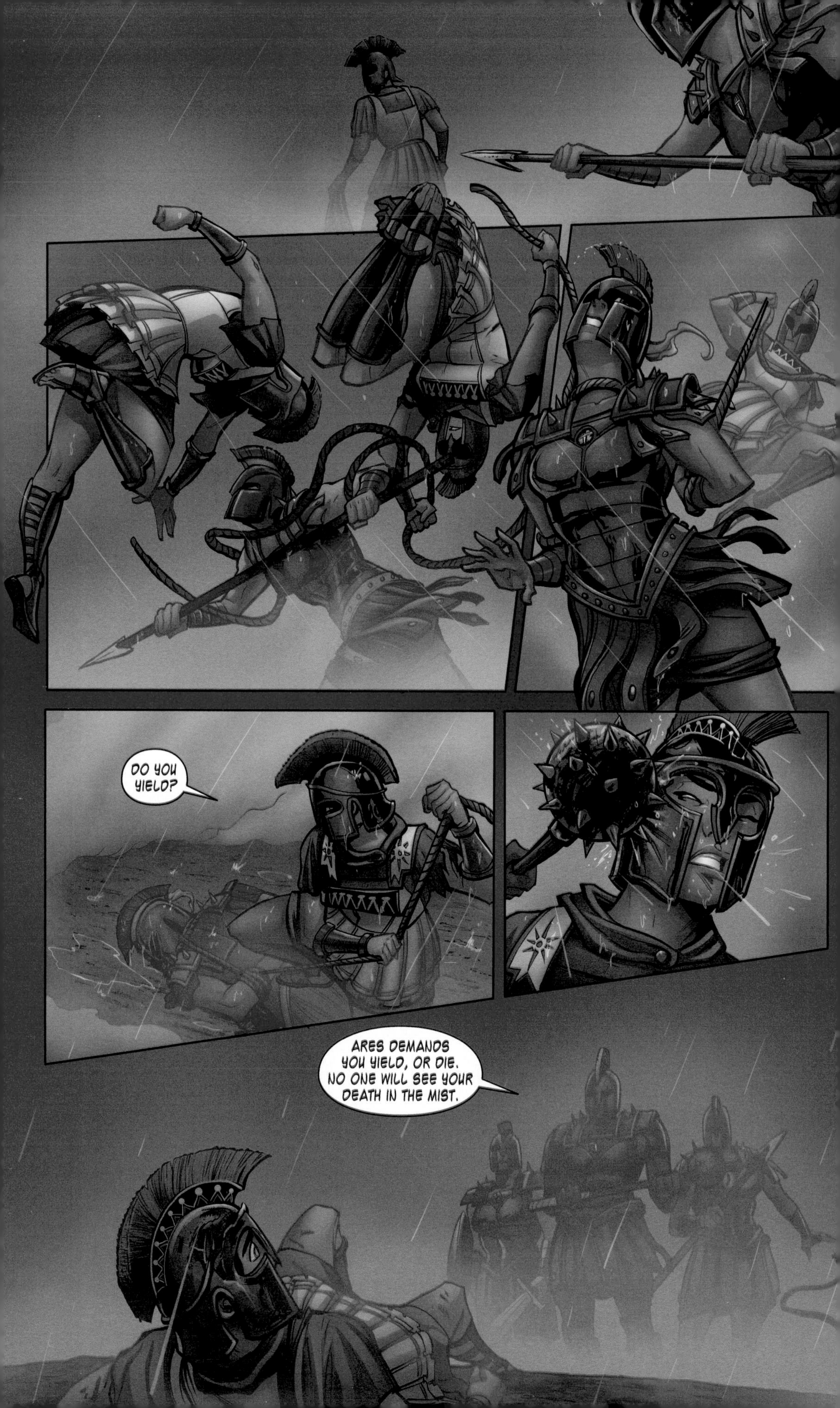
DO YOU YIELD?
ARES DEMANDS YOU YIELD, OR DIE. NO ONE WILL SEE YOUR DEATH IN THE MIST.

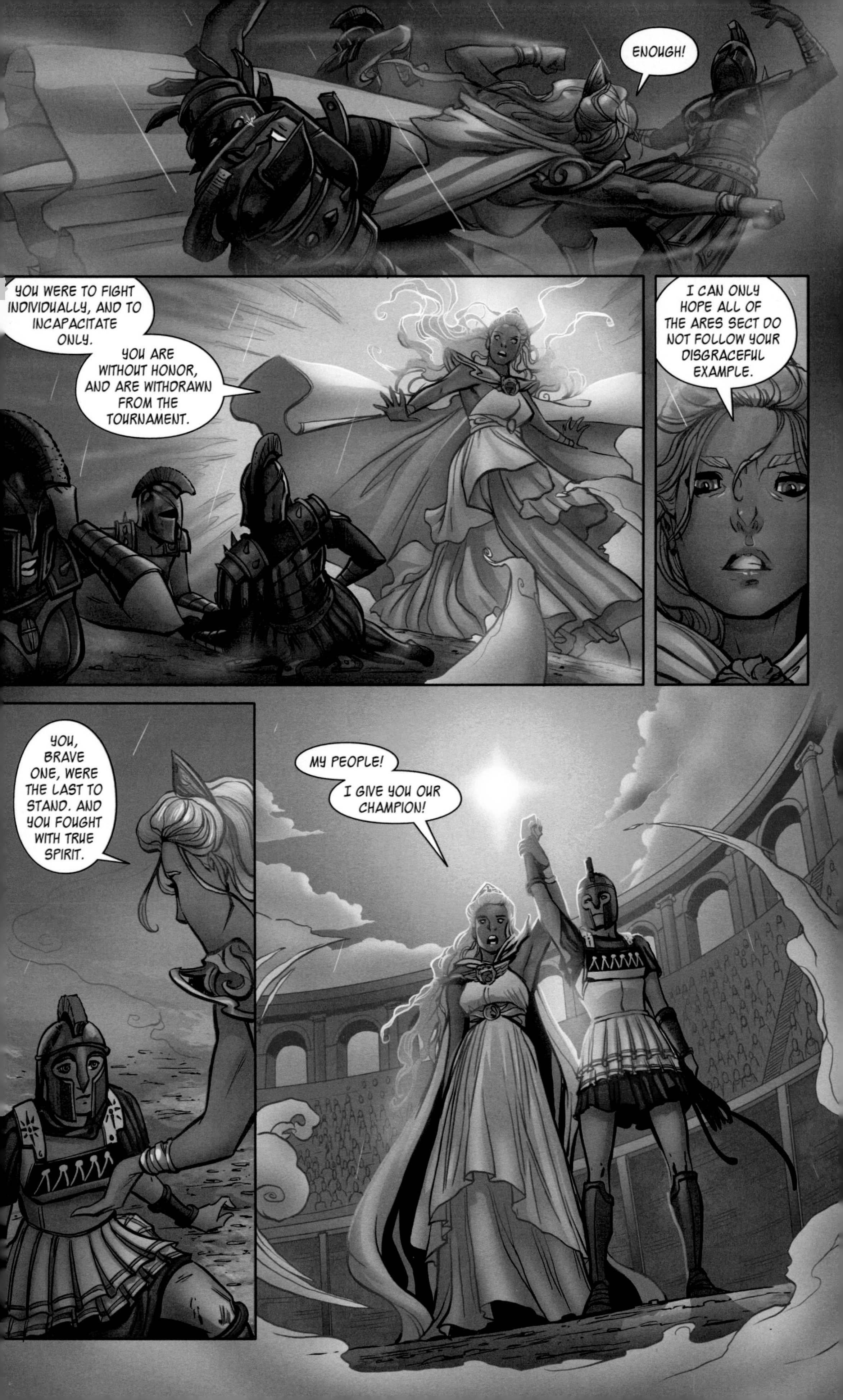
ENOUGH!
YOU WERE TO FIGHT INDIVIDUALLY, AND TO INCAPACITATE ONLY.
YOU ARE WITHOUT HONOR, AND ARE WITHDRAWN FROM THE TOURNAMENT.
I CAN ONLY HOPE ALL OF THE ARES SECT DO NOT FOLLOW YOUR DISGRACEFUL EXAMPLE.
YOU, BRAVE ONE, WERE THE LAST TO STAND. AND YOU FOUGHT WITH TRUE SPIRIT.
MY PEOPLE!
I GIVE YOU OUR CHAMPION!

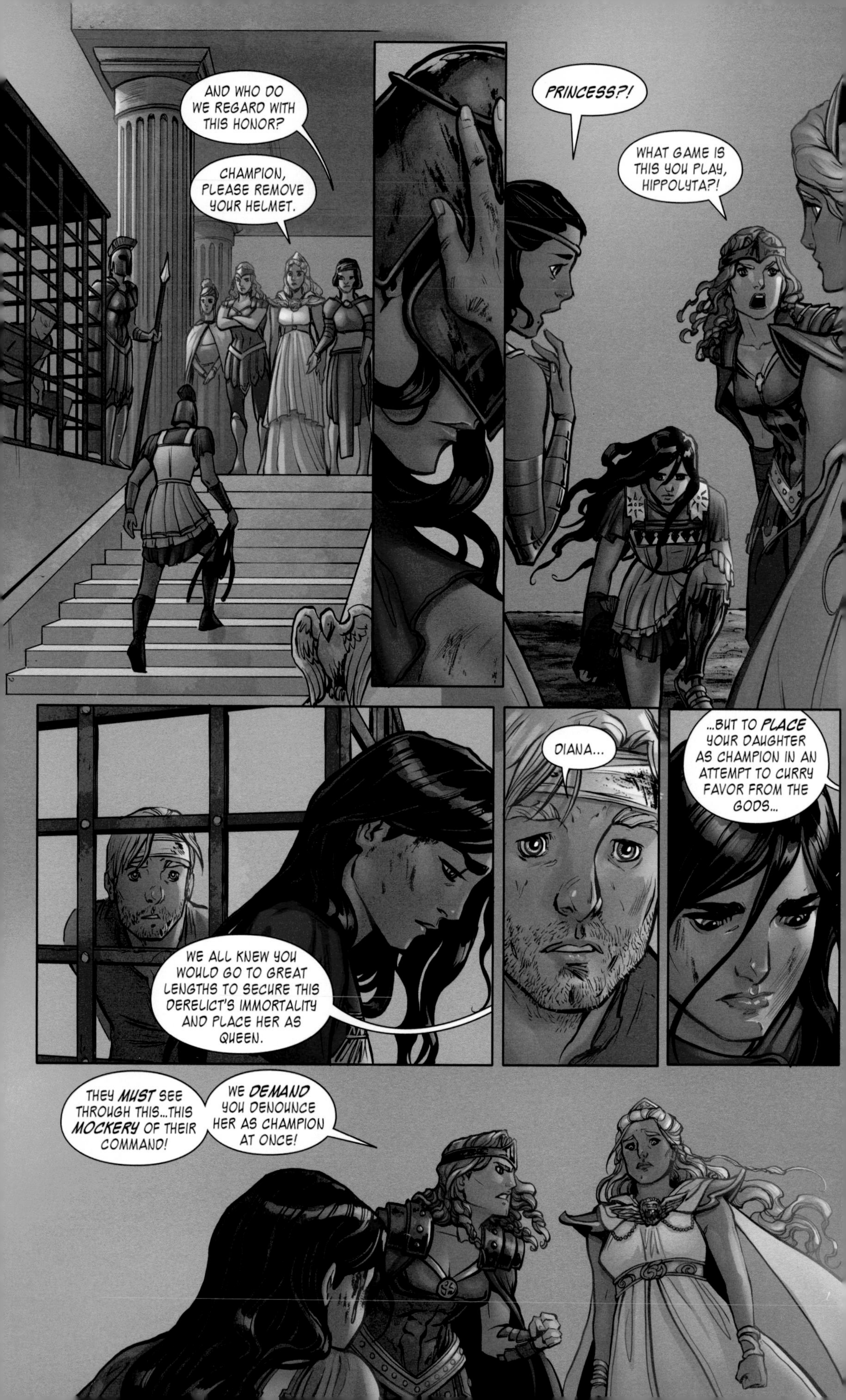
AND WHO DO WE REGARD WITH THIS HONOR?
CHAMPION, PLEASE REMOVE YOUR HELMET.
PRINCESS?!
WHAT GAME IS THIS YOU PLAY, HIPPOLYTA?!
WE ALL KNEW YOU WOULD GO TO GREAT LENGTHS TO SECURE THIS DERELICT'S IMMORTALITY AND PLACE HER AS QUEEN.
DIANA...
...BUT TO PLACE YOUR DAUGHTER AS CHAMPION IN AN ATTEMPT TO CURRY FAVOR FROM THE GODS...
THEY MUST SEE THROUGH THIS...THIS MOCKERY OF THEIR COMMAND!
WE DEMAND YOU DENOUNCE HER AS CHAMPION AT ONCE!

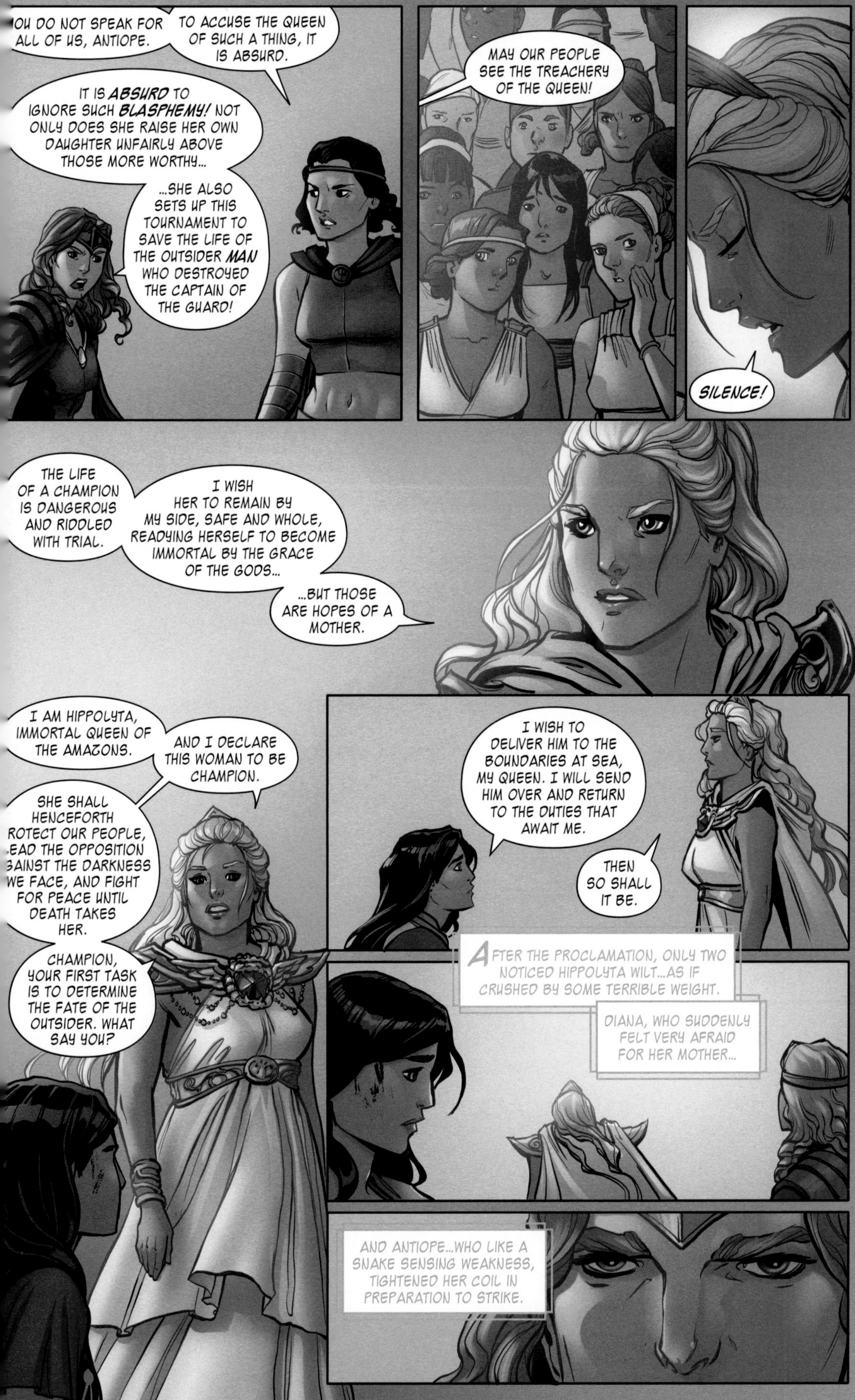
OU DO NOT SPEAK FOR ALL OF US, ANTIOPE.
TO ACCUSE THE QUEEN OF SUCH A THING, IT IS ABSURD.
IT IS ABSURD TO IGNORE SUCH BLASPHEMY! NOT ONLY DOES SHE RAISE HER OWN DAUGHTER UNFAIRLY ABOVE THOSE MORE WORTHY...
...SHE ALSO SETS UP THIS TOURNAMENT TO SAVE THE LIFE OF THE OUTSIDER MAN WHO DESTROYED THE CAPTAIN OF THE GUARD!
MAY OUR PEOPLE SEE THE TREACHERY OF THE QUEEN!
SILENCE!
THE LIFE OF A CHAMPION IS DANGEROUS AND RIDDLED WITH TRIAL.
I WISH HER TO REMAIN BY MY SIDE, SAFE AND WHOLE, READYING HERSELF TO BECOME IMMORTAL BY THE GRACE OF THE GODS...
...BUT THOSE ARE HOPES OF A MOTHER.
I AM HIPPOLYTA, IMMORTAL QUEEN OF THE AMAZONS.
AND I DECLARE THIS WOMAN TO BE CHAMPION.
SHE SHALL HENCEFORTH ROTECT OUR PEOPLE, EAD THE OPPOSITION GAINST THE DARKNESS WE FACE, AND FIGHT FOR PEACE UNTIL DEATH TAKES HER.
CHAMPION, YOUR FIRST TASK IS TO DETERMINE THE FATE OF THE OUTSIDER. WHAT SAY YOU?
I WISH TO DELIVER HIM TO THE BOUNDARIES AT SEA, MY QUEEN. I WILL SEND HIM OVER AND RETURN TO THE DUTIES THAT AWAIT ME.
THEN SO SHALL IT BE.
AFTER THE PROCLAMATION, ONLY TWO NOTICED HIPPOLYTA WILT...AS IF CRUSHED BY SOME TERRIBLE WEIGHT.
DIANA, WHO SUDDENLY FELT VERY AFRAID FOR HER MOTHER...
AND ANTIOPE...WHO LIKE A SNAKE SENSING WEAKNESS, TIGHTENED HER COIL IN PREPARATION TO STRIKE.

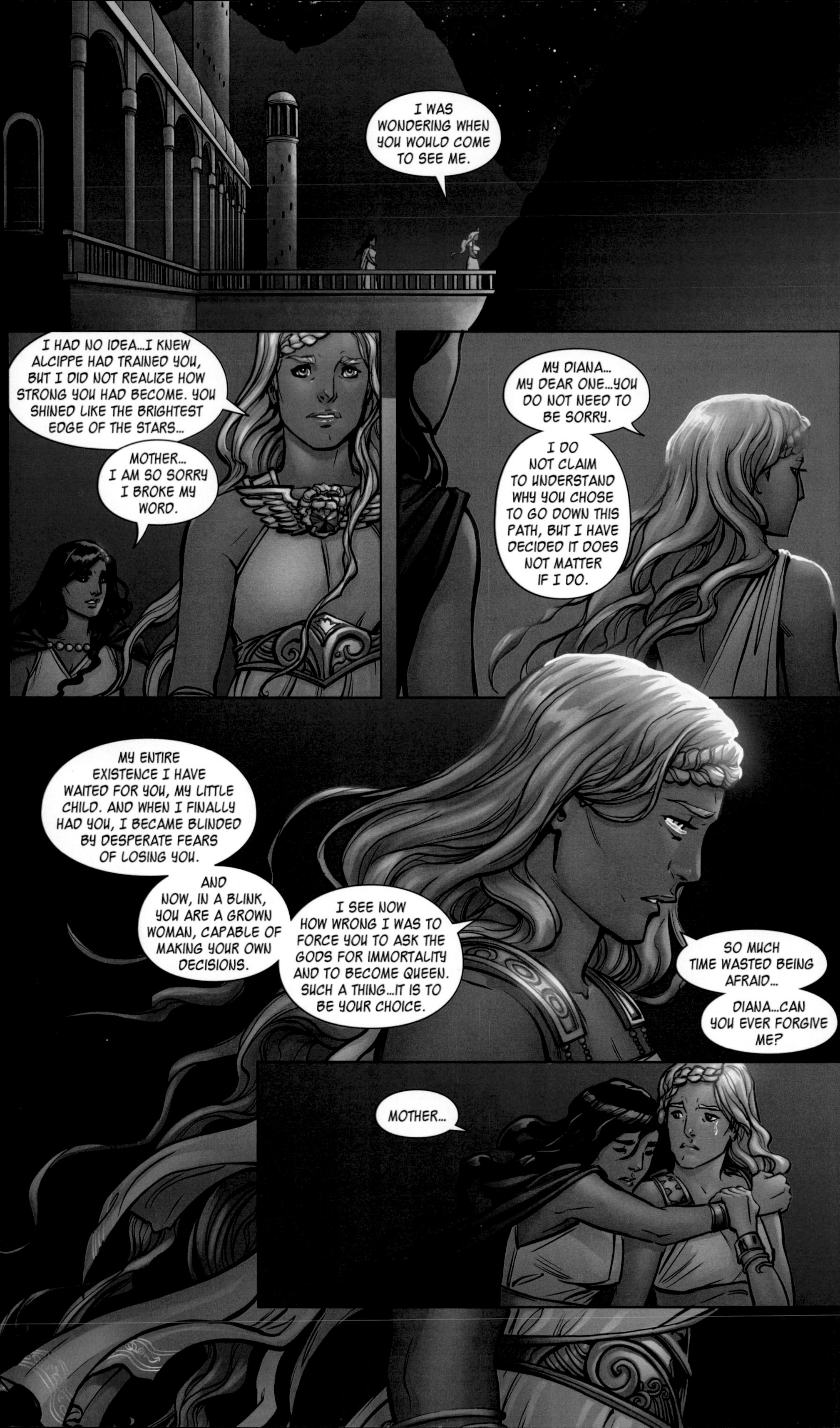
I WAS WONDERING WHEN YOU WOULD COME TO SEE ME.
I HAD NO IDEA...I KNEW ALCIPPE HAD TRAINED YOU, BUT I DID NOT REALIZE HOW STRONG YOU HAD BECOME. YOU SHINED LIKE THE BRIGHTEST EDGE OF THE STARS...
MOTHER... I AM SO SORRY I BROKE MY WORD.
MY DIANA... MY DEAR ONE...YOU DO NOT NEED TO BE SORRY.
I DO NOT CLAIM TO UNDERSTAND WHY YOU CHOSE TO GO DOWN THIS PATH, BUT I HAVE DECIDED IT DOES NOT MATTER IF I DO.
MY ENTIRE EXISTENCE I HAVE WAITED FOR YOU, MY LITTLE CHILD. AND WHEN I FINALLY HAD YOU, I BECAME BLINDED BY DESPERATE FEARS OF LOSING YOU.
AND NOW, IN A BLINK, YOU ARE A GROWN WOMAN, CAPABLE OF MAKING YOUR OWN DECISIONS.
I SEE NOW HOW WRONG I WAS TO FORCE YOU TO ASK THE GODS FOR IMMORTALITY AND TO BECOME QUEEN. SUCH A THING...IT IS TO BE YOUR CHOICE.
SO MUCH TIME WASTED BEING AFRAID...
DIANA...CAN YOU EVER FORGIVE ME?
MOTHER...

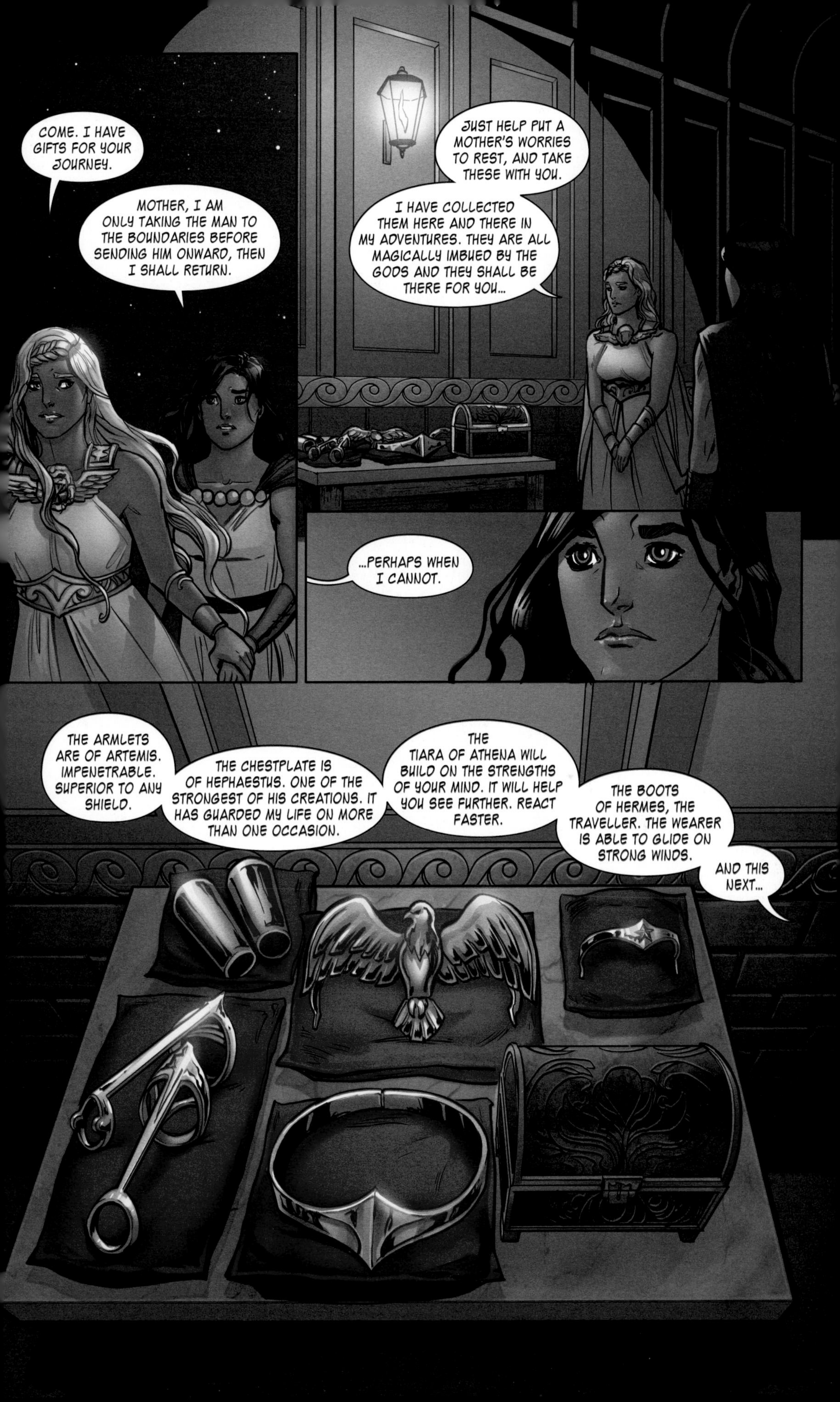

COME. I HAVE GIFTS FOR YOUR JOURNEY.
MOTHER, I AM ONLY TAKING THE MAN TO THE BOUNDARIES BEFORE SENDING HIM ONWARD, THEN I SHALL RETURN.
JUST HELP PUT A MOTHER'S WORRIES TO REST, AND TAKE THESE WITH YOU.
I HAVE COLLECTED THEM HERE AND THERE IN MY ADVENTURES. THEY ARE ALL MAGICALLY IMBUED BY THE GODS AND THEY SHALL BE THERE FOR YOU...
...PERHAPS WHEN I CANNOT.
THE ARMLETS ARE OF ARTEMIS. IMPENETRABLE. SUPERIOR TO ANY SHIELD.
THE CHESTPLATE IS OF HEPHAESTUS. ONE OF THE STRONGEST OF HIS CREATIONS. IT HAS GUARDED MY LIFE ON MORE THAN ONE OCCASION.
THE TIARA OF ATHENA WILL BUILD ON THE STRENGTHS OF YOUR MIND. IT WILL HELP YOU SEE FURTHER. REACT FASTER.
THE BOOTS OF HERMES, THE TRAVELLER. THE WEARER IS ABLE TO GLIDE ON STRONG WINDS.
AND THIS NEXT...

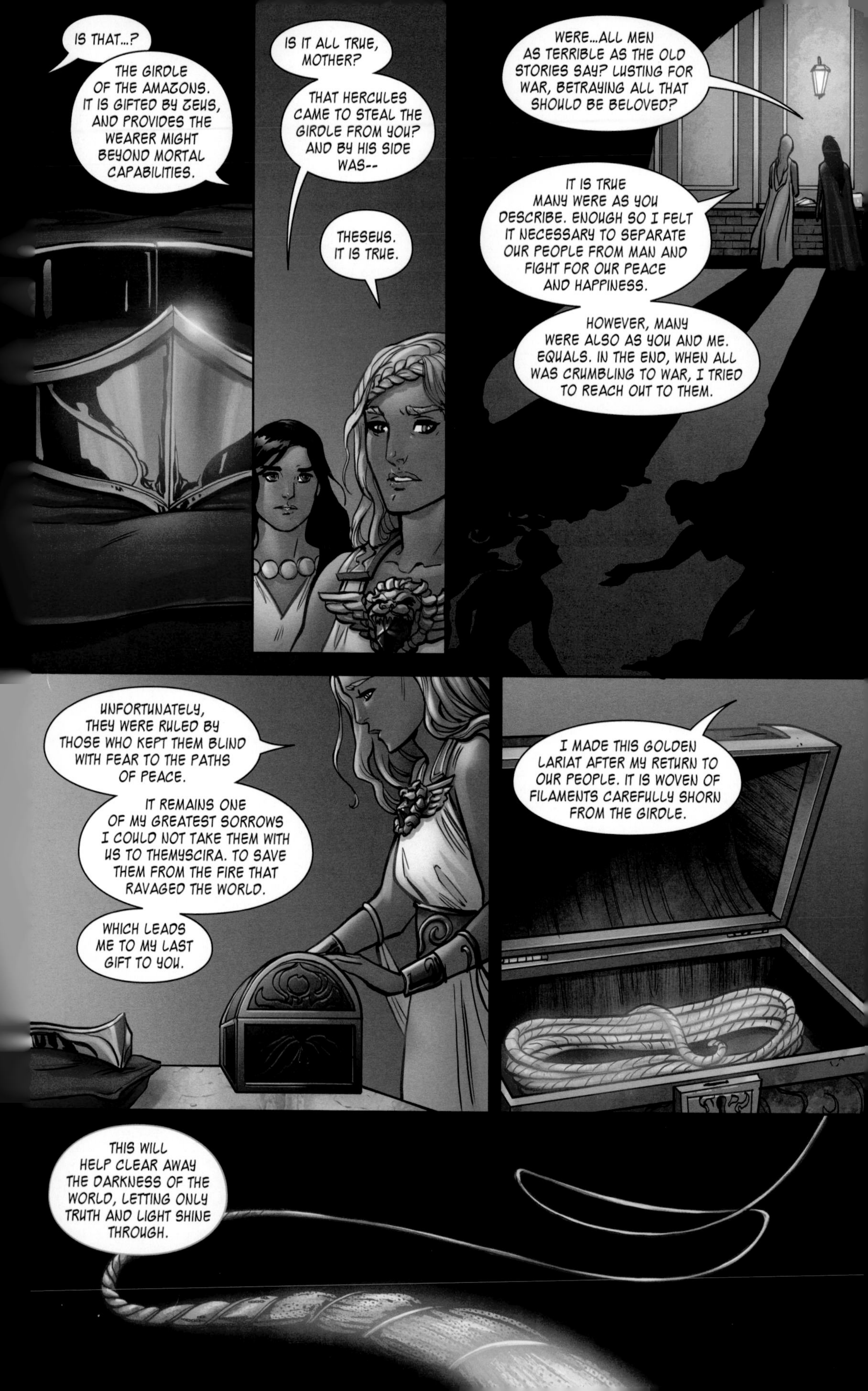
IS THAT...?
THE GIRDLE OF THE AMAZONS. IT IS GIFTED BY ZEUS, AND PROVIDES THE WEARER MIGHT BEYOND MORTAL CAPABILITIES.
IS IT ALL TRUE, MOTHER?
THAT HERCULES CAME TO STEAL THE GIRDLE FROM YOU? AND BY HIS SIDE WAS--
THESEUS. IT IS TRUE.
WERE...ALL MEN AS TERRIBLE AS THE OLD STORIES SAY? LUSTING FOR WAR, BETRAYING ALL THAT SHOULD BE BELOVED?
IT IS TRUE MANY WERE AS YOU DESCRIBE. ENOUGH SO I FELT IT NECESSARY TO SEPARATE OUR PEOPLE FROM MAN AND FIGHT FOR OUR PEACE AND HAPPINESS.
HOWEVER, MANY WERE ALSO AS YOU AND ME. EQUALS. IN THE END, WHEN ALL WAS CRUMBLING TO WAR, I TRIED TO REACH OUT TO THEM.
UNFORTUNATELY, THEY WERE RULED BY THOSE WHO KEPT THEM BLIND WITH FEAR TO THE PATHS OF PEACE.
IT REMAINS ONE OF MY GREATEST SORROWS I COULD NOT TAKE THEM WITH US TO THEMYSCIRA. TO SAVE THEM FROM THE FIRE THAT RAVAGED THE WORLD.
WHICH LEADS ME TO MY LAST GIFT TO YOU.
I MADE THIS GOLDEN LARIAT AFTER MY RETURN TO OUR PEOPLE. IT IS WOVEN OF FILAMENTS CAREFULLY SHORN FROM THE GIRDLE.
THIS WILL HELP CLEAR AWAY THE DARKNESS OF THE WORLD, LETTING ONLY TRUTH AND LIGHT SHINE THROUGH.

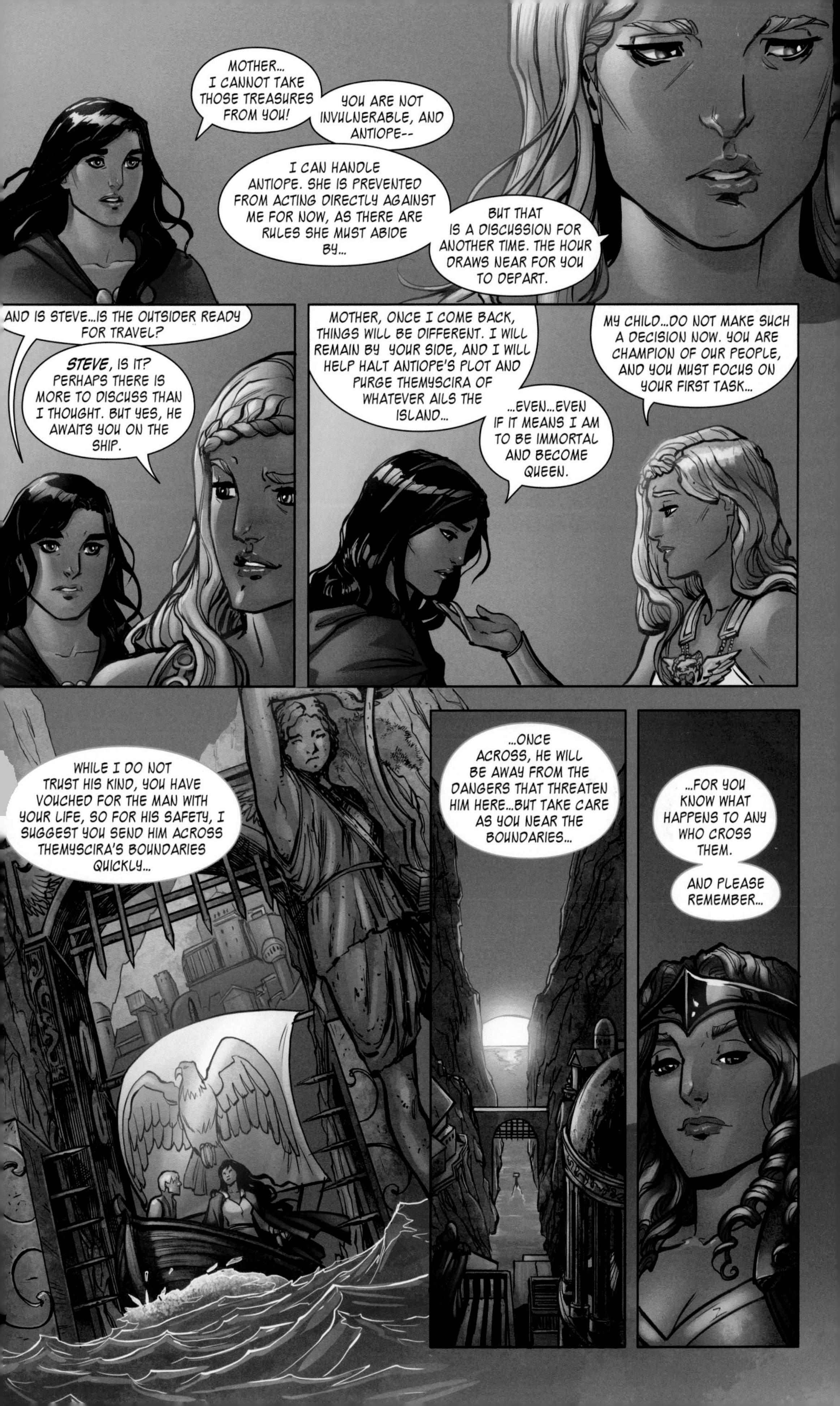
MOTHER... I CANNOT TAKE THOSE TREASURES FROM YOU!
YOU ARE NOT INVULNERABLE, AND ANTIOPE--
I CAN HANDLE ANTIOPE. SHE IS PREVENTED FROM ACTING DIRECTLY AGAINST ME FOR NOW, AS THERE ARE RULES SHE MUST ABIDE BY...
BUT THAT IS A DISCUSSION FOR ANOTHER TIME. THE HOUR DRAWS NEAR FOR YOU TO DEPART.
AND IS STEVE...IS THE OUTSIDER READY FOR TRAVEL?
STEVE, IS IT? PERHAPS THERE IS MORE TO DISCUSS THAN I THOUGHT. BUT YES, HE AWAITS YOU ON THE SHIP.
MOTHER, ONCE I COME BACK, THINGS WILL BE DIFFERENT. I WILL REMAIN BY YOUR SIDE, AND I WILL HELP HALT ANTIOPE'S PLOT AND PURGE THEMYSCIRA OF WHATEVER AILS THE ISLAND...
...EVEN...EVEN IF IT MEANS I AM TO BE IMMORTAL AND BECOME QUEEN.
MY CHILD...DO NOT MAKE SUCH A DECISION NOW. YOU ARE CHAMPION OF OUR PEOPLE, AND YOU MUST FOCUS ON YOUR FIRST TASK...
WHILE I DO NOT TRUST HIS KIND, YOU HAVE VOUCHED FOR THE MAN WITH YOUR LIFE, SO FOR HIS SAFETY, I SUGGEST YOU SEND HIM ACROSS THEMYSCIRA'S BOUNDARIES QUICKLY...
...ONCE ACROSS, HE WILL BE AWAY FROM THE DANGERS THAT THREATEN HIM HERE...BUT TAKE CARE AS YOU NEAR THE BOUNDARIES...
...FOR YOU KNOW WHAT HAPPENS TO ANY WHO CROSS THEM.
AND PLEASE REMEMBER...

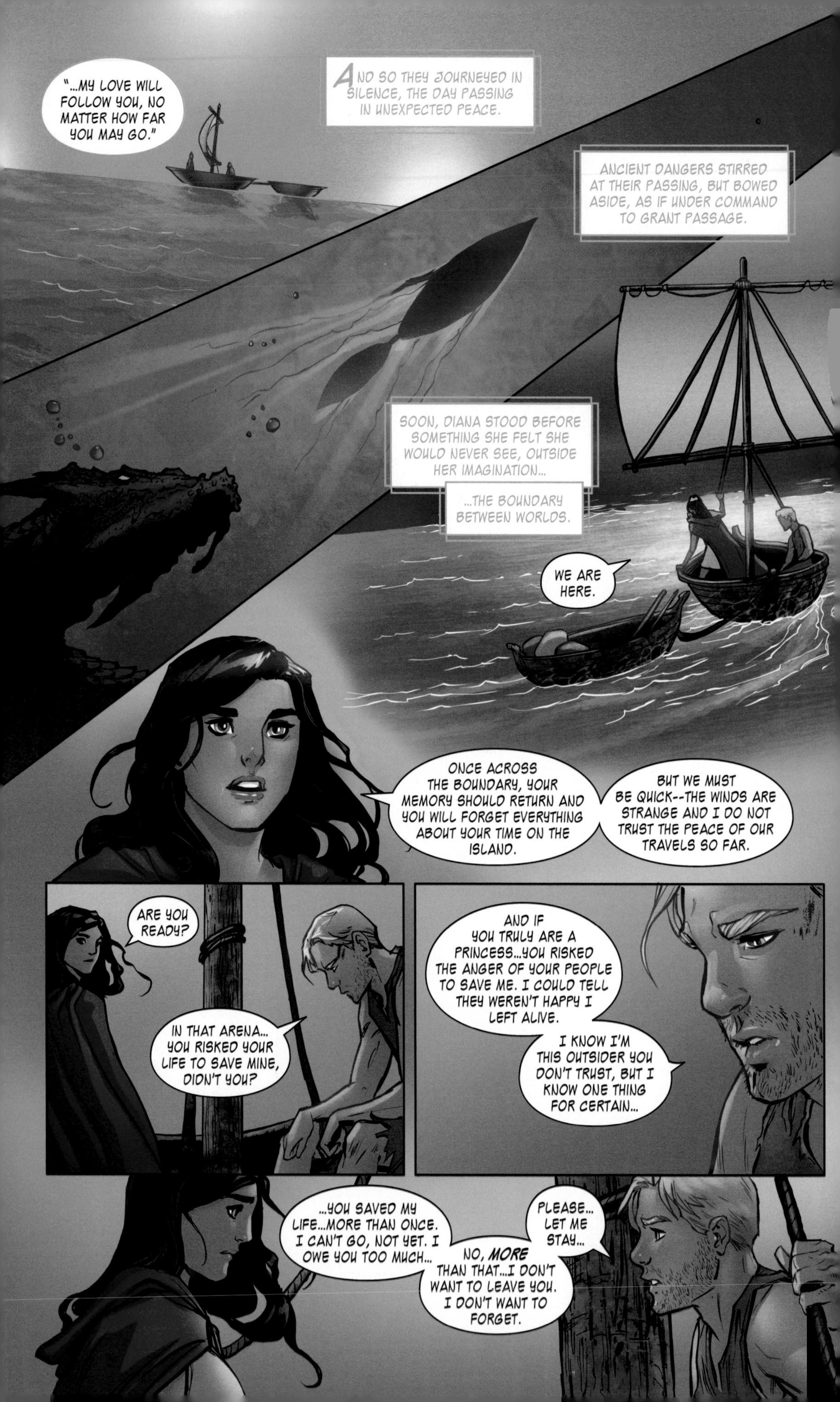
"...MY LOVE WILL FOLLOW YOU, NO MATTER HOW FAR YOU MAY GO."
AND SO THEY JOURNEYED IN SILENCE, THE DAY PASSING IN UNEXPECTED PEACE.
ANCIENT DANGERS STIRRED AT THEIR PASSING, BUT BOWED ASIDE, AS IF UNDER COMMAND TO GRANT PASSAGE.
SOON, DIANA STOOD BEFORE SOMETHING SHE FELT SHE WOULD NEVER SEE, OUTSIDE HER IMAGINATION...
...THE BOUNDARY BETWEEN WORLDS.
WE ARE HERE.
ONCE ACROSS THE BOUNDARY, YOUR MEMORY SHOULD RETURN AND YOU WILL FORGET EVERYTHING ABOUT YOUR TIME ON THE ISLAND.
BUT WE MUST BE QUICK--THE WINDS ARE STRANGE AND I DO NOT TRUST THE PEACE OF OUR TRAVELS SO FAR.
ARE YOU READY?
IN THAT ARENA... YOU RISKED YOUR LIFE TO SAVE MINE, DIDN'T YOU?
AND IF YOU TRULY ARE A PRINCESS...YOU RISKED THE ANGER OF YOUR PEOPLE TO SAVE ME. I COULD TELL THEY WEREN'T HAPPY I LEFT ALIVE.
I KNOW I'M THIS OUTSIDER YOU DON'T TRUST, BUT I KNOW ONE THING FOR CERTAIN...
...YOU SAVED MY LIFE...MORE THAN ONCE. I CAN'T GO, NOT YET. I OWE YOU TOO MUCH...
NO, MORE THAN THAT...I DON'T WANT TO LEAVE YOU. I DON'T WANT TO FORGET.
PLEASE... LET ME STAY...

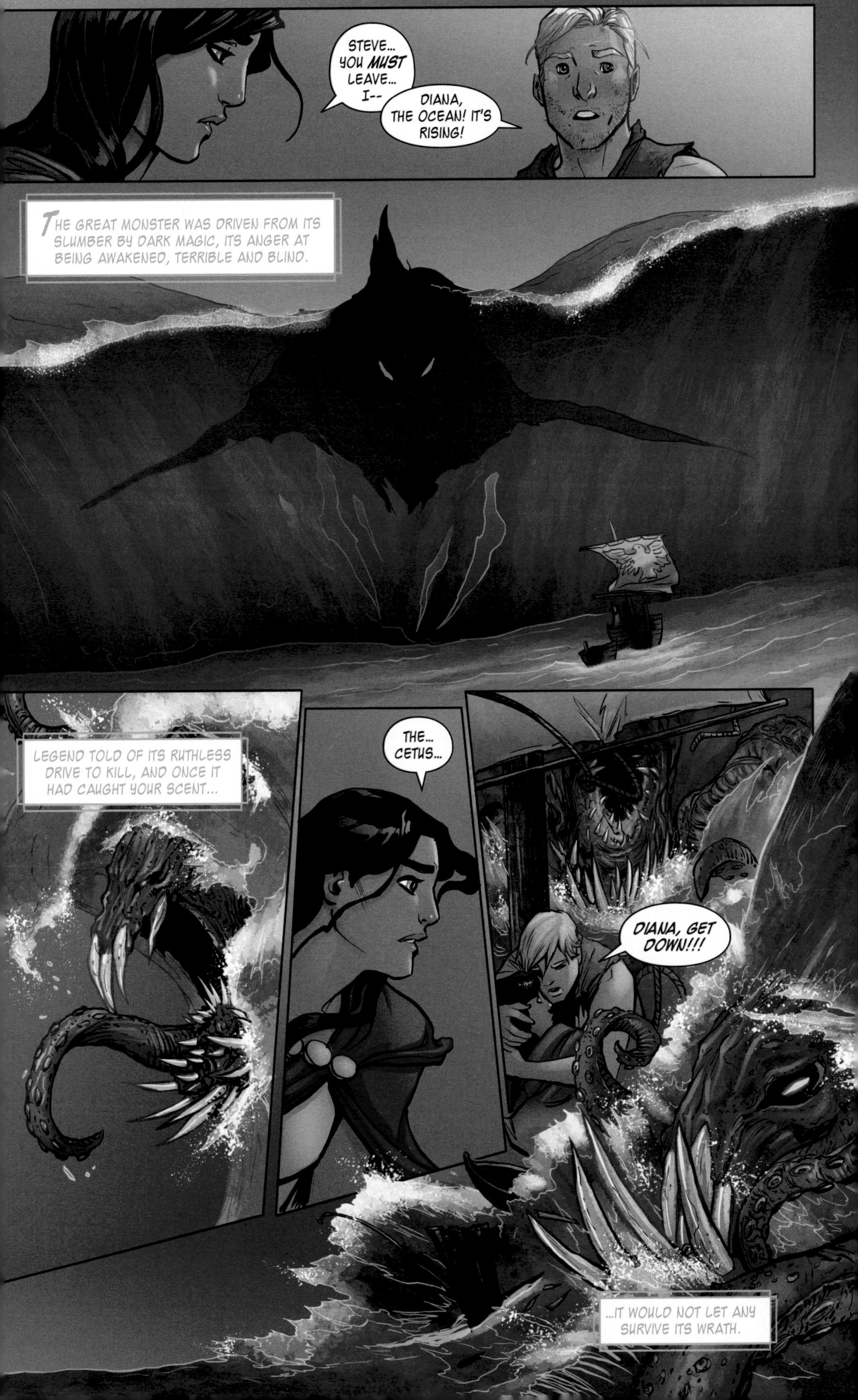

STEVE... YOU MUST LEAVE... I--
DIANA, THE OCEAN! IT'S RISING!
THE GREAT MONSTER WAS DRIVEN FROM ITS SLUMBER BY DARK MAGIC, ITS ANGER AT BEING AWAKENED, TERRIBLE AND BLIND.
LEGEND TOLD OF ITS RUTHLESS DRIVE TO KILL, AND ONCE IT HAD CAUGHT YOUR SCENT...
THE... CETUS...
DIANA, GET DOWN!!!
...IT WOULD NOT LET ANY SURVIVE ITS WRATH.

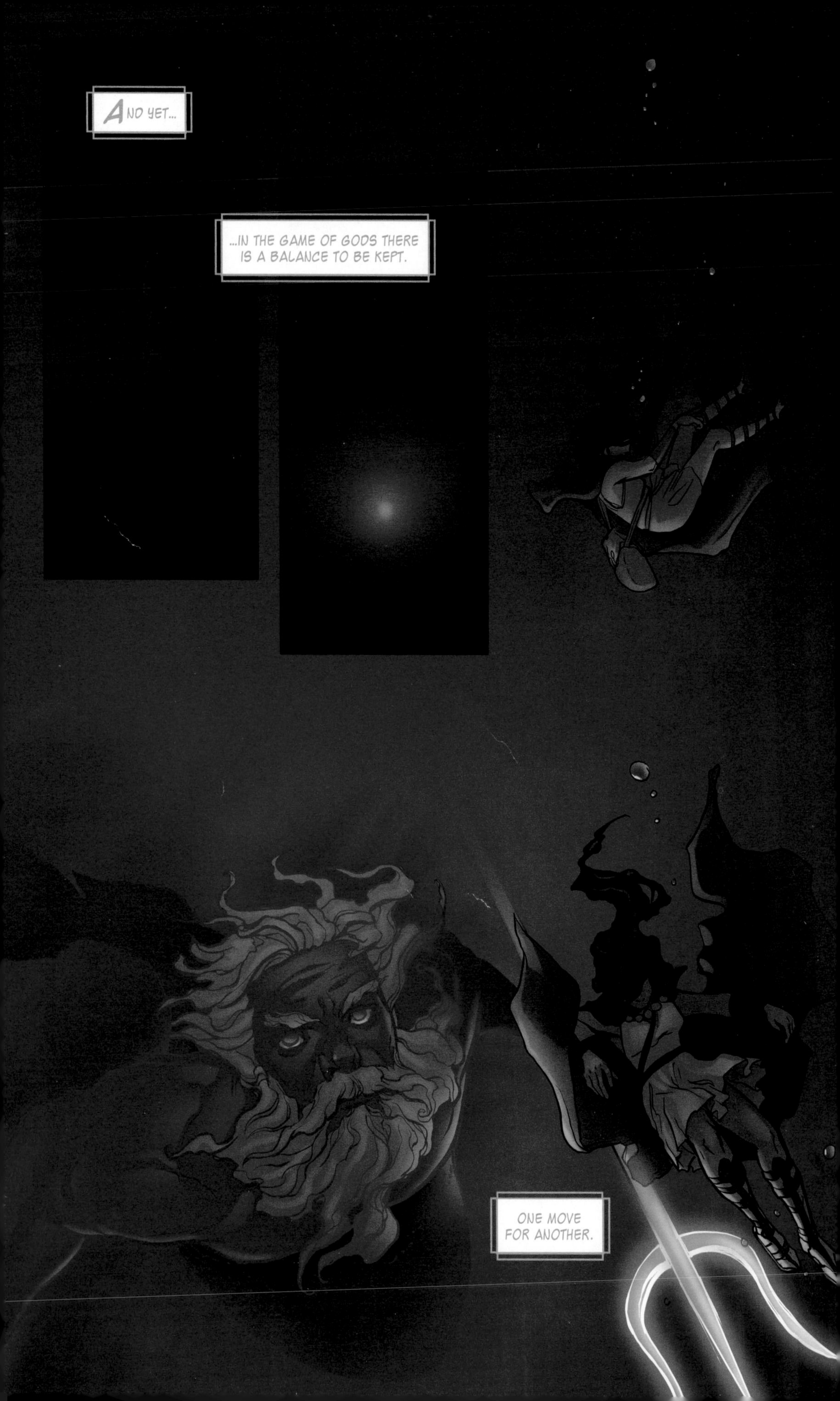
AND YET...
...IN THE GAME OF GODS THERE IS A BALANCE TO BE KEPT.
ONE MOVE FOR ANOTHER.

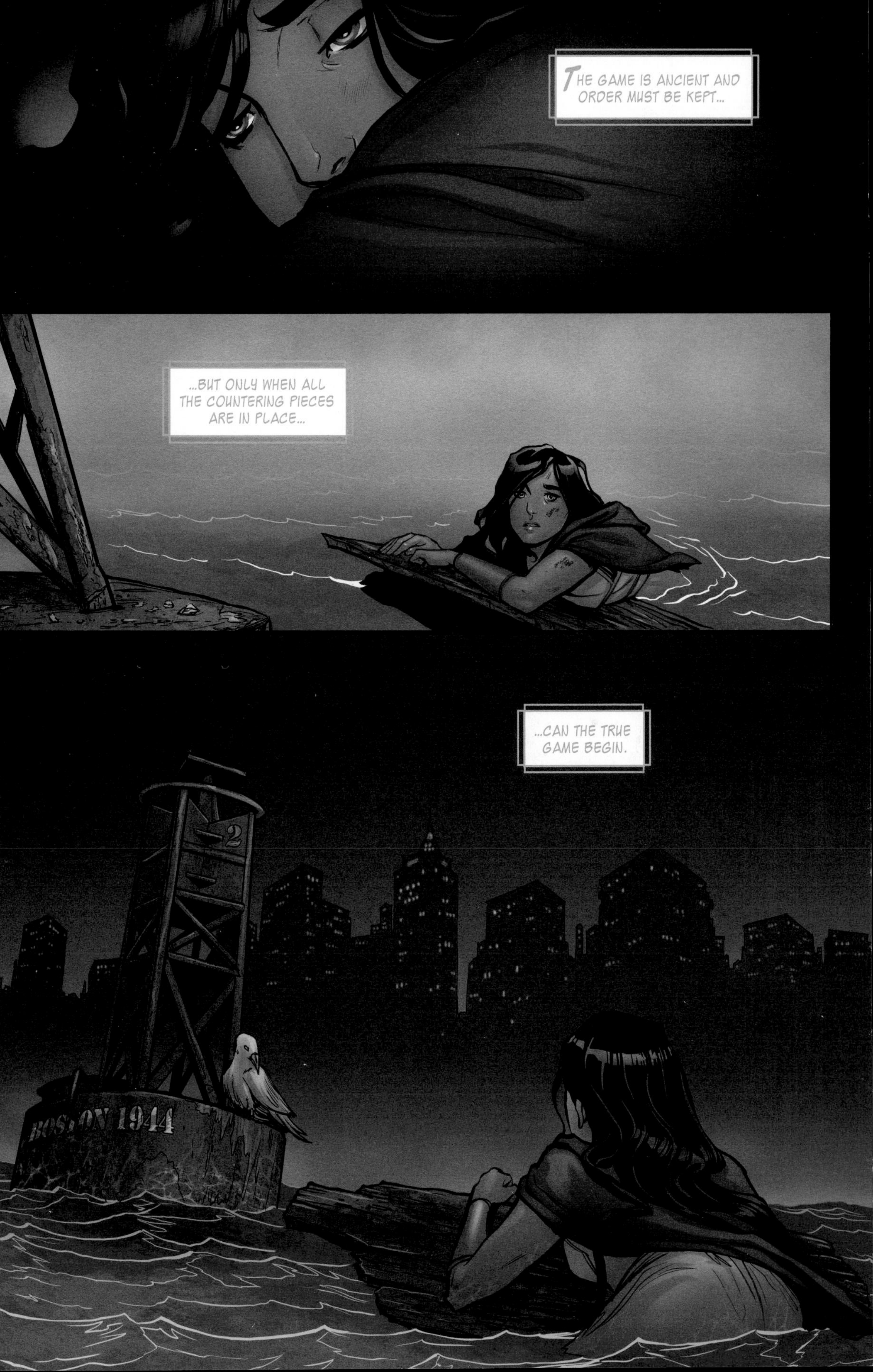
THE GAME IS ANCIENT AND ORDER MUST BE KEPT...
...BUT ONLY WHEN ALL THE COUNTERING PIECES ARE IN PLACE...
...CAN THE TRUE GAME BEGIN.
2
BOSTON 1944

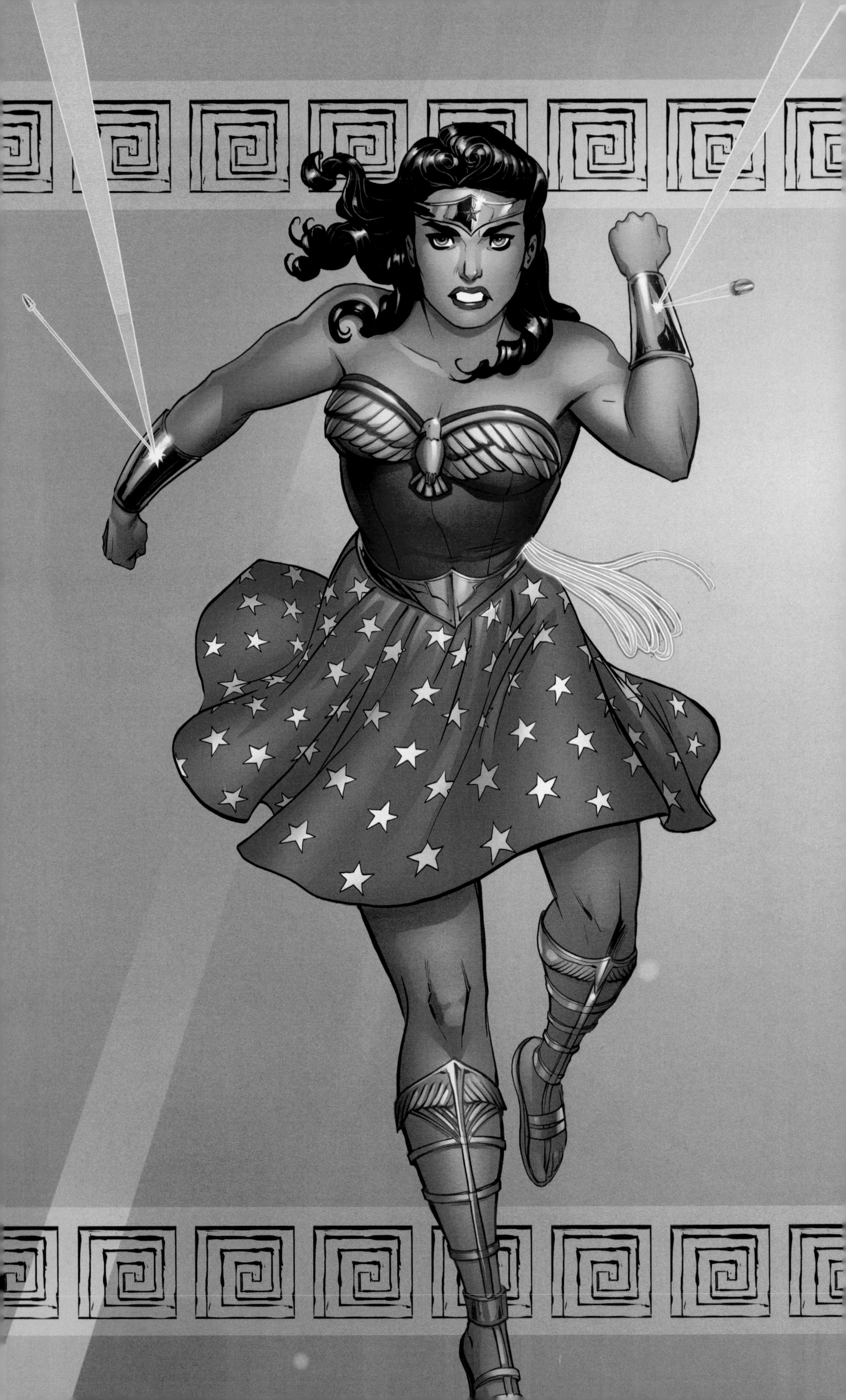

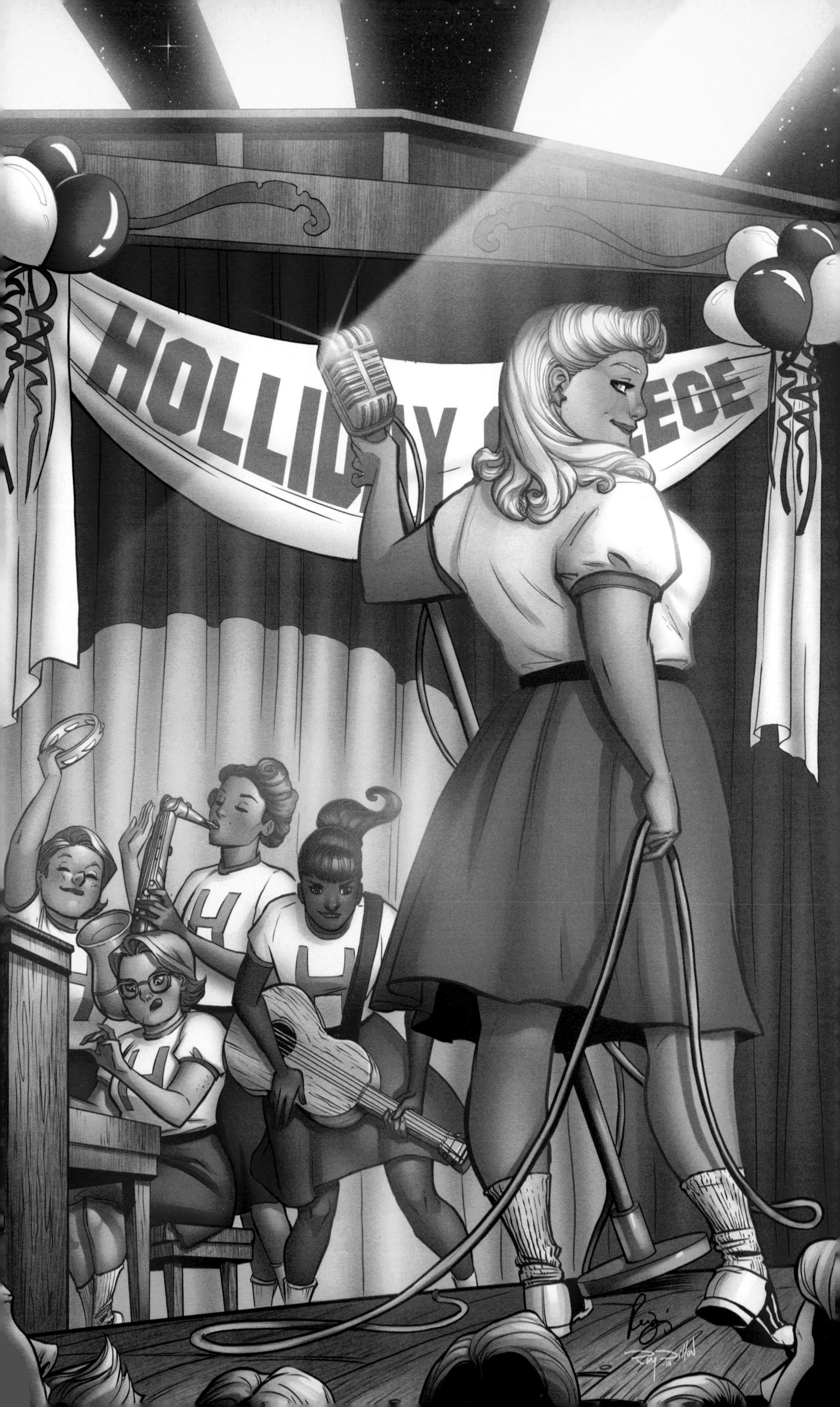

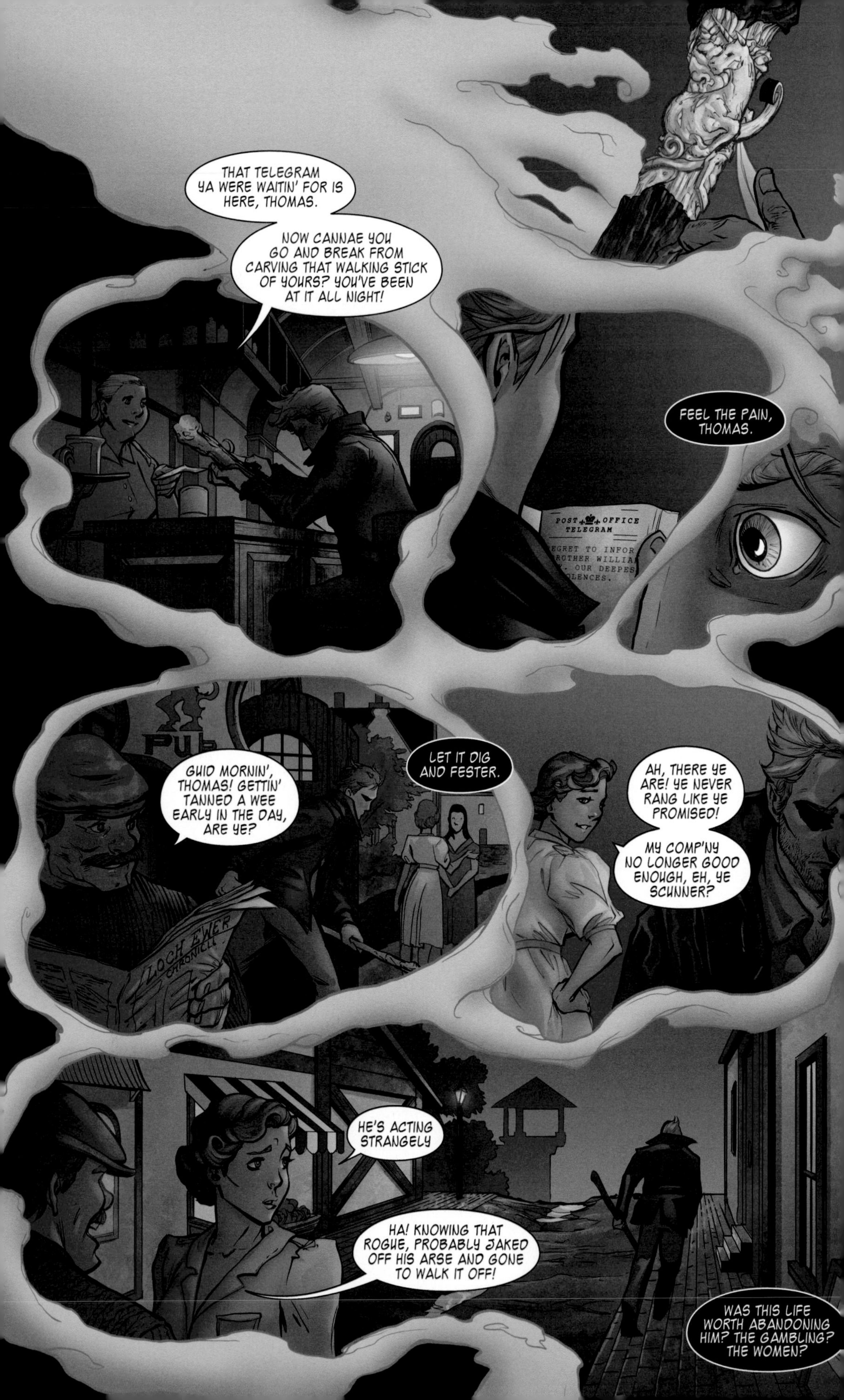
THAT TELEGRAM YA WERE WAITIN' FOR IS HERE, THOMAS.
NOW CANNAE YOU GO AND BREAK FROM CARVING THAT WALKING STICK OF YOURS? YOU'VE BEEN AT IT ALL NIGHT!
FEEL THE PAIN, THOMAS.
POST OFFICE TELEGRAM
GUID MORNIN', THOMAS! GETTIN' TANNED A WEE EARLY IN THE DAY, ARE YE?
LET IT DIG AND FESTER.
PUB
LOCH EWER CHRONICLE
AH, THERE YE ARE! YE NEVER RANG LIKE YE PROMISED!
MY COMP'NY NO LONGER GOOD ENOUGH, EH, YE SCUNNER?
HE'S ACTING STRANGELY
HA! KNOWING THAT ROGUE, PROBABLY JAKED OFF HIS ARSE AND GONE TO WALK IT OFF!
WAS THIS LIFE WORTH ABANDONING HIM? THE GAMBLING? THE WOMEN?

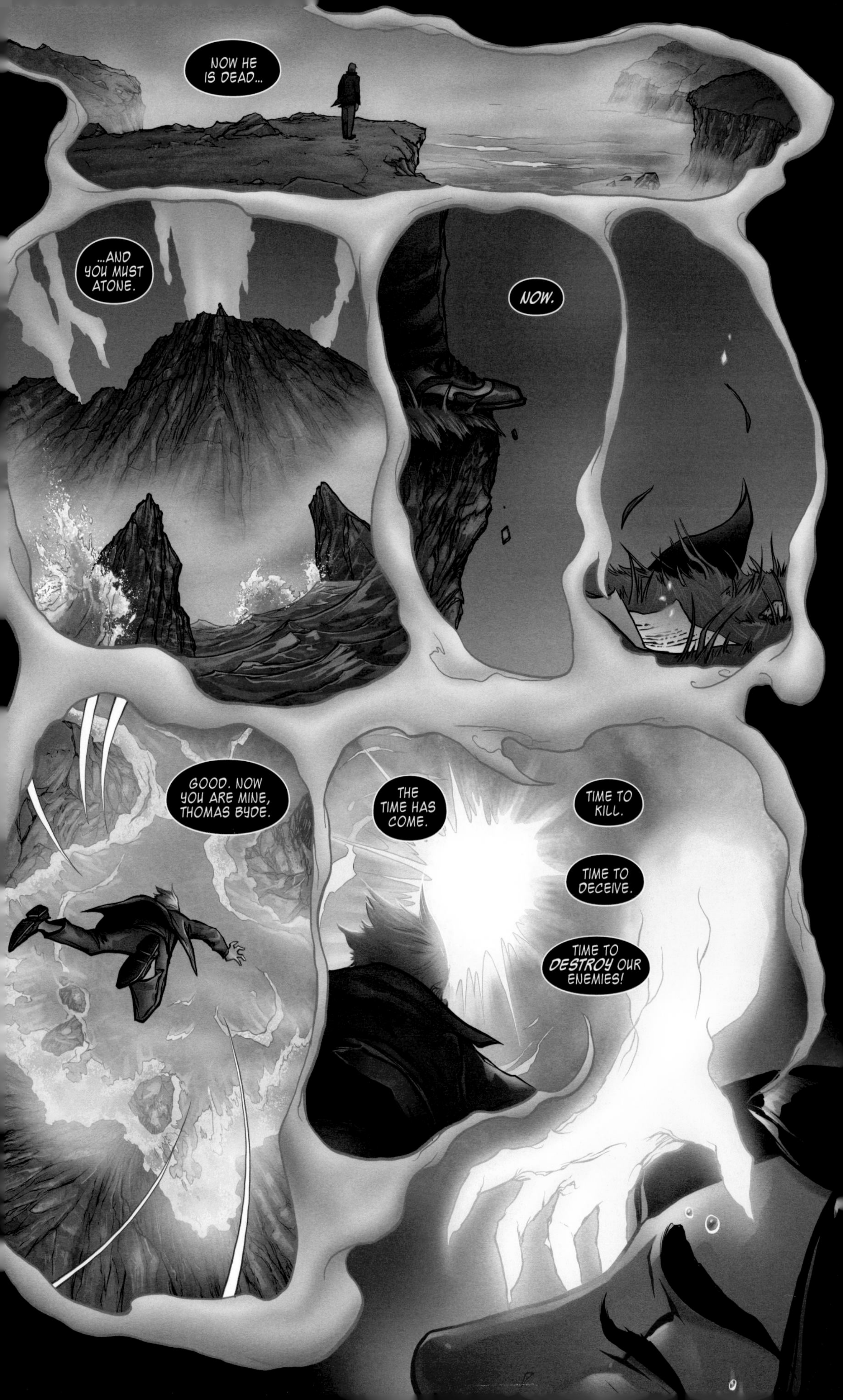
NOW HE IS DEAD...
...AND YOU MUST ATONE.
NOW.
GOOD. NOW YOU ARE MINE, THOMAS BYDE.
THE TIME HAS COME.
TIME TO KILL.
TIME TO DECEIVE.
TIME TO DESTROY OUR ENEMIES!

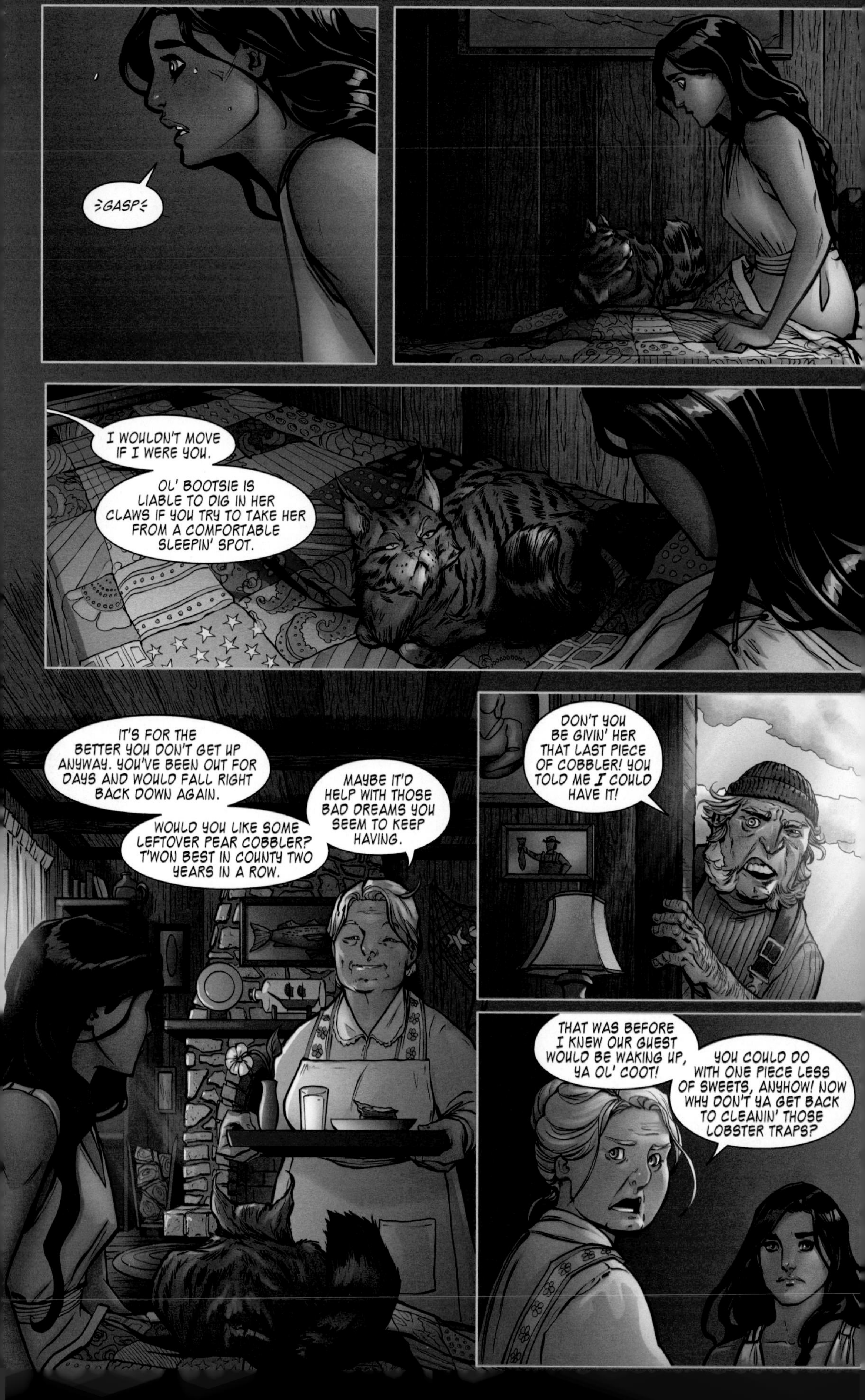
GASP
I WOULDN'T MOVE IF I WERE YOU.
OL' BOOTSIE IS LIABLE TO DIG IN HER CLAWS IF YOU TRY TO TAKE HER FROM A COMFORTABLE SLEEPIN' SPOT.
IT'S FOR THE BETTER YOU DON'T GET UP ANYWAY. YOU'VE BEEN OUT FOR DAYS AND WOULD FALL RIGHT BACK DOWN AGAIN.
WOULD YOU LIKE SOME LEFTOVER PEAR COBBLER? T'WON BEST IN COUNTY TWO YEARS IN A ROW.
MAYBE IT'D HELP WITH THOSE BAD DREAMS YOU SEEM TO KEEP HAVING.
DON'T YOU BE GIVIN' HER THAT LAST PIECE OF COBBLER! YOU TOLD ME *I* COULD HAVE IT!
THAT WAS BEFORE I KNEW OUR GUEST WOULD BE WAKING UP, YA OL' COOT!
YOU COULD DO WITH ONE PIECE LESS OF SWEETS, ANYHOW! NOW WHY DON'T YA GET BACK TO CLEANIN' THOSE LOBSTER TRAPS?

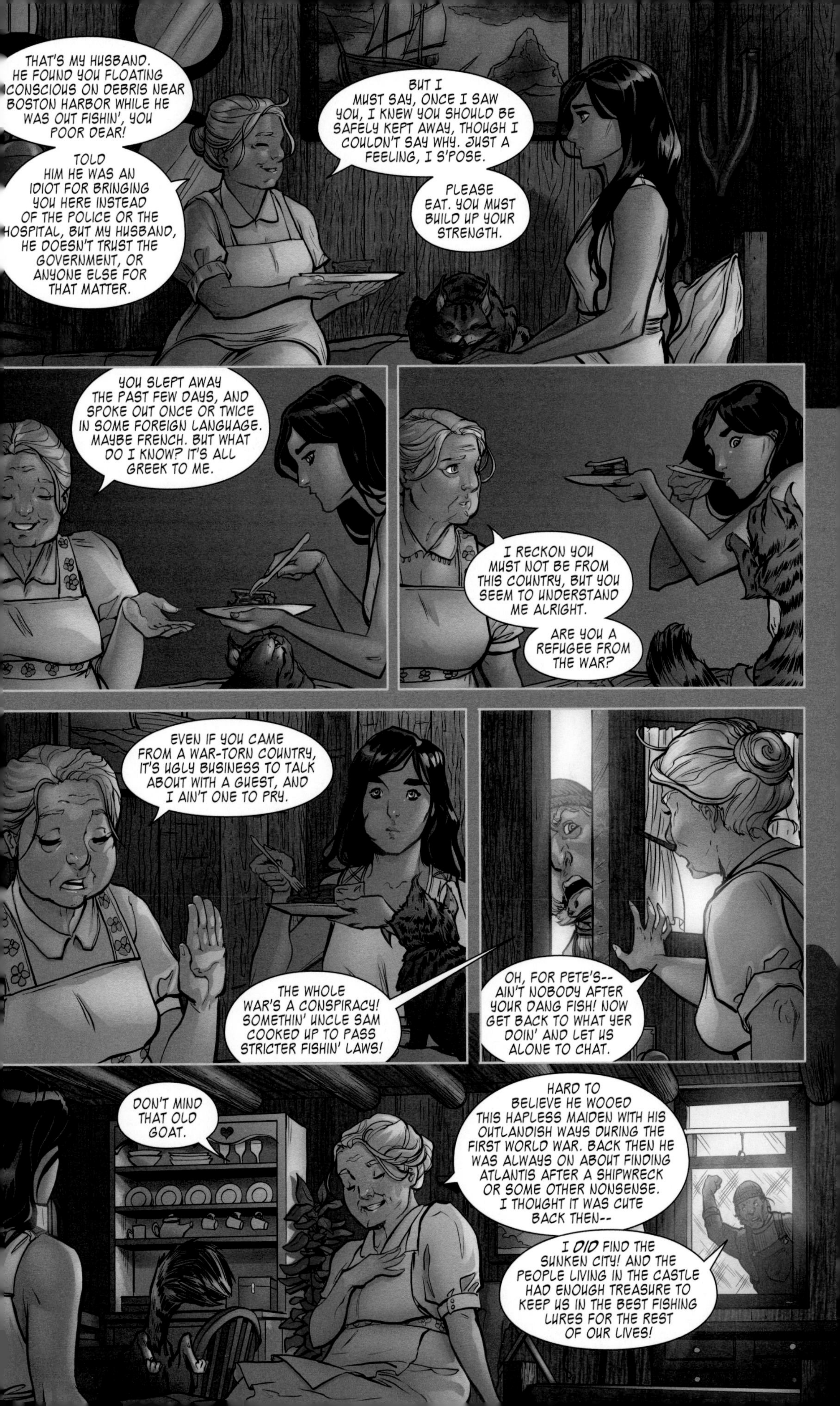

THAT'S MY HUSBAND. HE FOUND YOU FLOATING CONSCIOUS ON DEBRIS NEAR BOSTON HARBOR WHILE HE WAS OUT FISHIN', YOU POOR DEAR!
TOLD HIM HE WAS AN IDIOT FOR BRINGING YOU HERE INSTEAD OF THE POLICE OR THE HOSPITAL, BUT MY HUSBAND, HE DOESN'T TRUST THE GOVERNMENT, OR ANYONE ELSE FOR THAT MATTER.
BUT I MUST SAY, ONCE I SAW YOU, I KNEW YOU SHOULD BE SAFELY KEPT AWAY, THOUGH I COULDN'T SAY WHY. JUST A FEELING, I S'POSE.
PLEASE EAT. YOU MUST BUILD UP YOUR STRENGTH.
YOU SLEPT AWAY THE PAST FEW DAYS, AND SPOKE OUT ONCE OR TWICE IN SOME FOREIGN LANGUAGE. MAYBE FRENCH. BUT WHAT DO I KNOW? IT'S ALL GREEK TO ME.
I RECKON YOU MUST NOT BE FROM THIS COUNTRY, BUT YOU SEEM TO UNDERSTAND ME ALRIGHT.
ARE YOU A REFUGEE FROM THE WAR?
EVEN IF YOU CAME FROM A WAR-TORN COUNTRY, IT'S UGLY BUSINESS TO TALK ABOUT WITH A GUEST, AND I AIN'T ONE TO PRY.
THE WHOLE WAR'S A CONSPIRACY! SOMETHIN' UNCLE SAM COOKED UP TO PASS STRICTER FISHIN' LAWS!
OH, FOR PETE'S-- AIN'T NOBODY AFTER YOUR DANG FISH! NOW GET BACK TO WHAT YER DOIN' AND LET US ALONE TO CHAT.
DON'T MIND THAT OLD GOAT.
HARD TO BELIEVE HE WOOED THIS HAPLESS MAIDEN WITH HIS OUTLANDISH WAYS DURING THE FIRST WORLD WAR. BACK THEN HE WAS ALWAYS ON ABOUT FINDING ATLANTIS AFTER A SHIPWRECK OR SOME OTHER NONSENSE. I THOUGHT IT WAS CUTE BACK THEN--
I *DID* FIND THE SUNKEN CITY! AND THE PEOPLE LIVING IN THE CASTLE HAD ENOUGH TREASURE TO KEEP US IN THE BEST FISHING LURES FOR THE REST OF OUR LIVES!

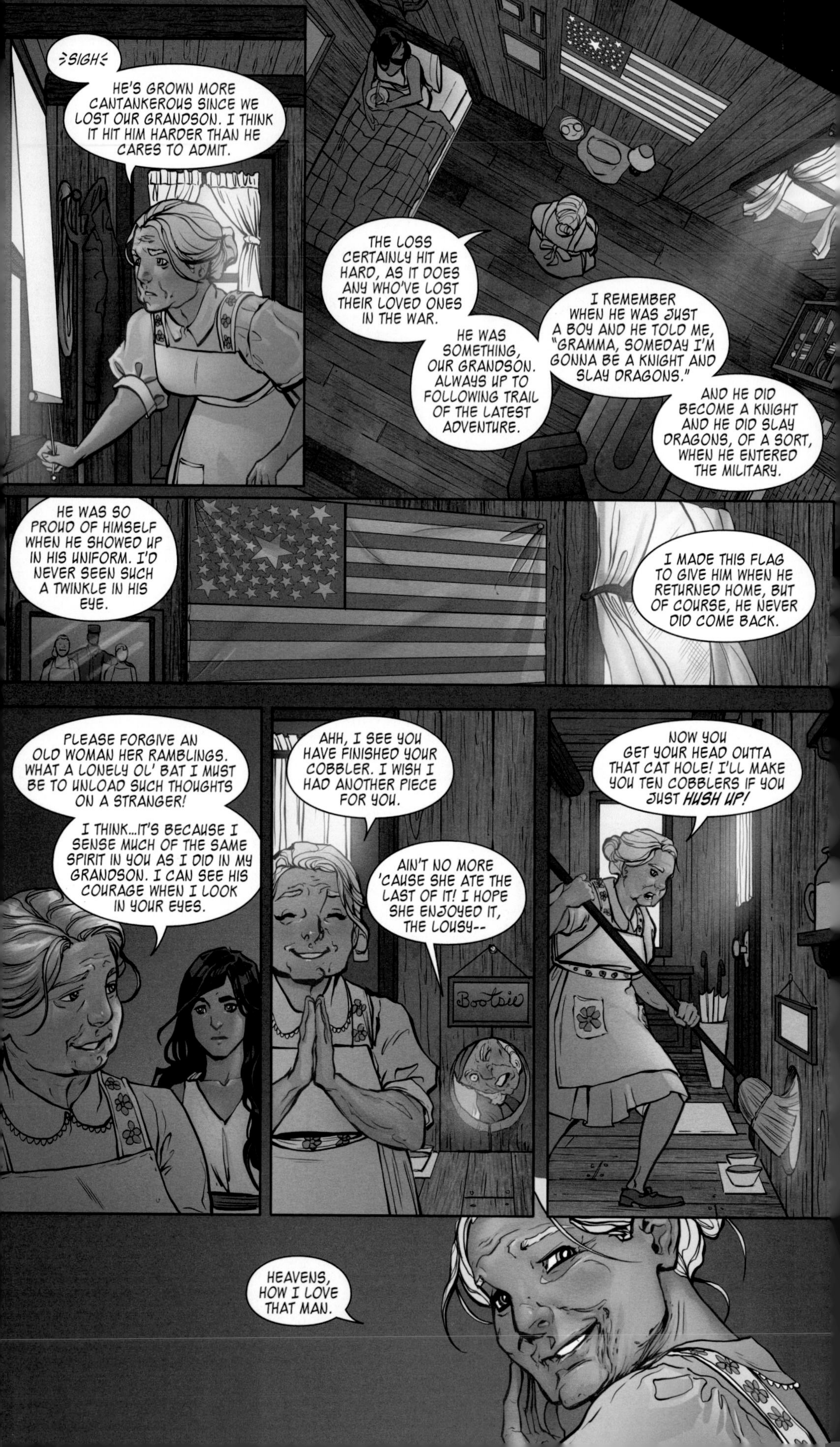

SIGH
HE'S GROWN MORE CANTANKEROUS SINCE WE LOST OUR GRANDSON. I THINK IT HIT HIM HARDER THAN HE CARES TO ADMIT.
THE LOSS CERTAINLY HIT ME HARD, AS IT DOES ANY WHO'VE LOST THEIR LOVED ONES IN THE WAR.
HE WAS SOMETHING, OUR GRANDSON. ALWAYS UP TO FOLLOWING TRAIL OF THE LATEST ADVENTURE.
I REMEMBER WHEN HE WAS JUST A BOY AND HE TOLD ME, "GRAMMA, SOMEDAY I'M GONNA BE A KNIGHT AND SLAY DRAGONS."
AND HE DID BECOME A KNIGHT AND HE DID SLAY DRAGONS, OF A SORT, WHEN HE ENTERED THE MILITARY.
HE WAS SO PROUD OF HIMSELF WHEN HE SHOWED UP IN HIS UNIFORM. I'D NEVER SEEN SUCH A TWINKLE IN HIS EYE.
I MADE THIS FLAG TO GIVE HIM WHEN HE RETURNED HOME, BUT OF COURSE, HE NEVER DID COME BACK.
PLEASE FORGIVE AN OLD WOMAN HER RAMBLINGS. WHAT A LONELY OL' BAT I MUST BE TO UNLOAD SUCH THOUGHTS ON A STRANGER!
I THINK...IT'S BECAUSE I SENSE MUCH OF THE SAME SPIRIT IN YOU AS I DID IN MY GRANDSON. I CAN SEE HIS COURAGE WHEN I LOOK IN YOUR EYES.
AHH, I SEE YOU HAVE FINISHED YOUR COBBLER. I WISH I HAD ANOTHER PIECE FOR YOU.
AIN'T NO MORE 'CAUSE SHE ATE THE LAST OF IT! I HOPE SHE ENJOYED IT, THE LOUSY--
Bootsie
NOW YOU GET YOUR HEAD OUTTA THAT CAT HOLE! I'LL MAKE YOU TEN COBBLERS IF YOU JUST HUSH UP!
HEAVENS, HOW I LOVE THAT MAN.

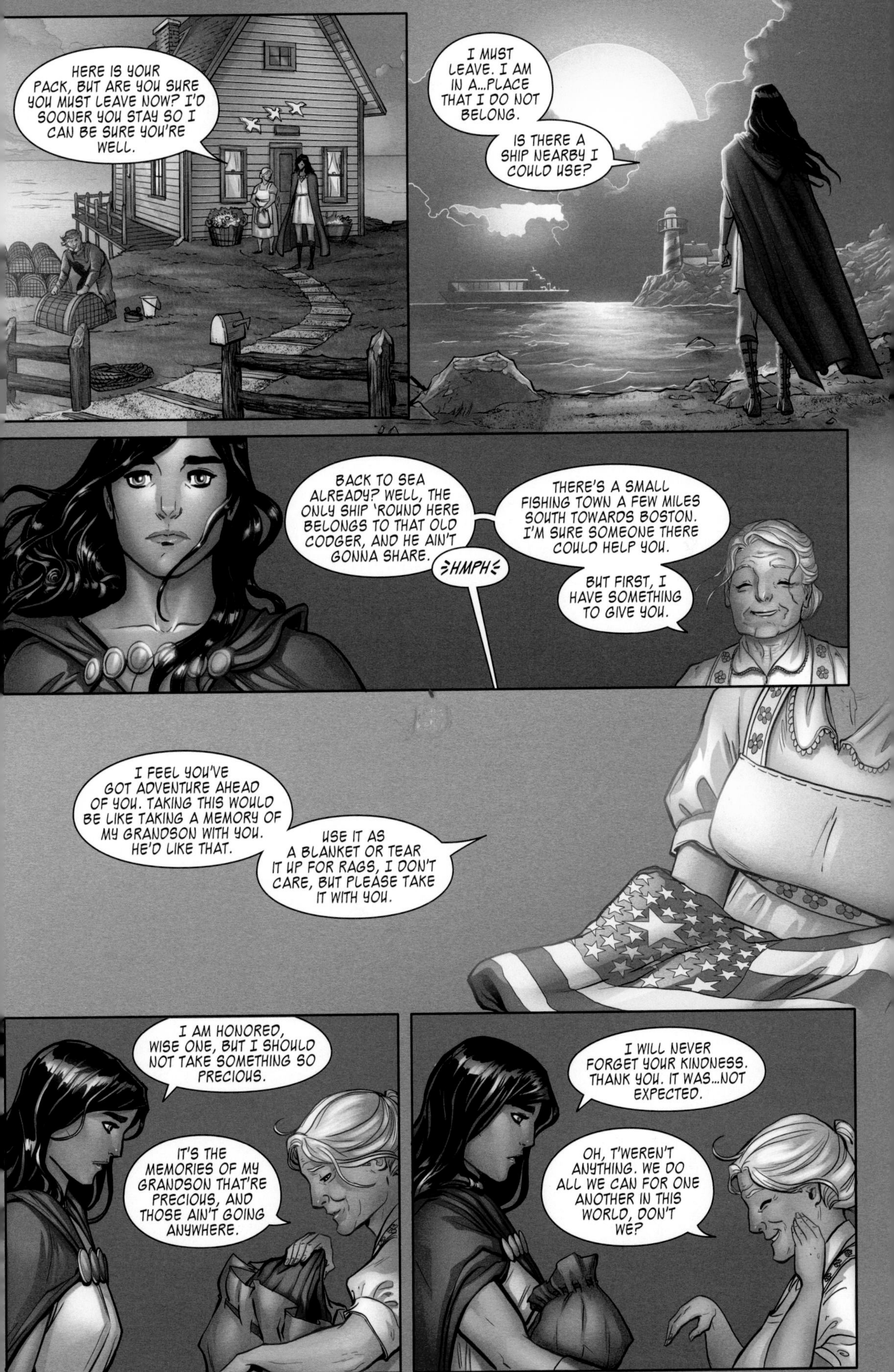
HERE IS YOUR PACK, BUT ARE YOU SURE YOU MUST LEAVE NOW? I'D SOONER YOU STAY SO I CAN BE SURE YOU'RE WELL.
I MUST LEAVE. I AM IN A...PLACE THAT I DO NOT BELONG.
IS THERE A SHIP NEARBY I COULD USE?
BACK TO SEA ALREADY? WELL, THE ONLY SHIP 'ROUND HERE BELONGS TO THAT OLD CODGER, AND HE AIN'T GONNA SHARE.
HMPH
THERE'S A SMALL FISHING TOWN A FEW MILES SOUTH TOWARDS BOSTON. I'M SURE SOMEONE THERE COULD HELP YOU.
BUT FIRST, I HAVE SOMETHING TO GIVE YOU.
I FEEL YOU'VE GOT ADVENTURE AHEAD OF YOU. TAKING THIS WOULD BE LIKE TAKING A MEMORY OF MY GRANDSON WITH YOU. HE'D LIKE THAT.
USE IT AS A BLANKET OR TEAR IT UP FOR RAGS, I DON'T CARE, BUT PLEASE TAKE IT WITH YOU.
I AM HONORED, WISE ONE, BUT I SHOULD NOT TAKE SOMETHING SO PRECIOUS.
IT'S THE MEMORIES OF MY GRANDSON THAT'RE PRECIOUS, AND THOSE AIN'T GOING ANYWHERE.
I WILL NEVER FORGET YOUR KINDNESS. THANK YOU. IT WAS...NOT EXPECTED.
OH, T'WEREN'T ANYTHING. WE DO ALL WE CAN FOR ONE ANOTHER IN THIS WORLD, DON'T WE?

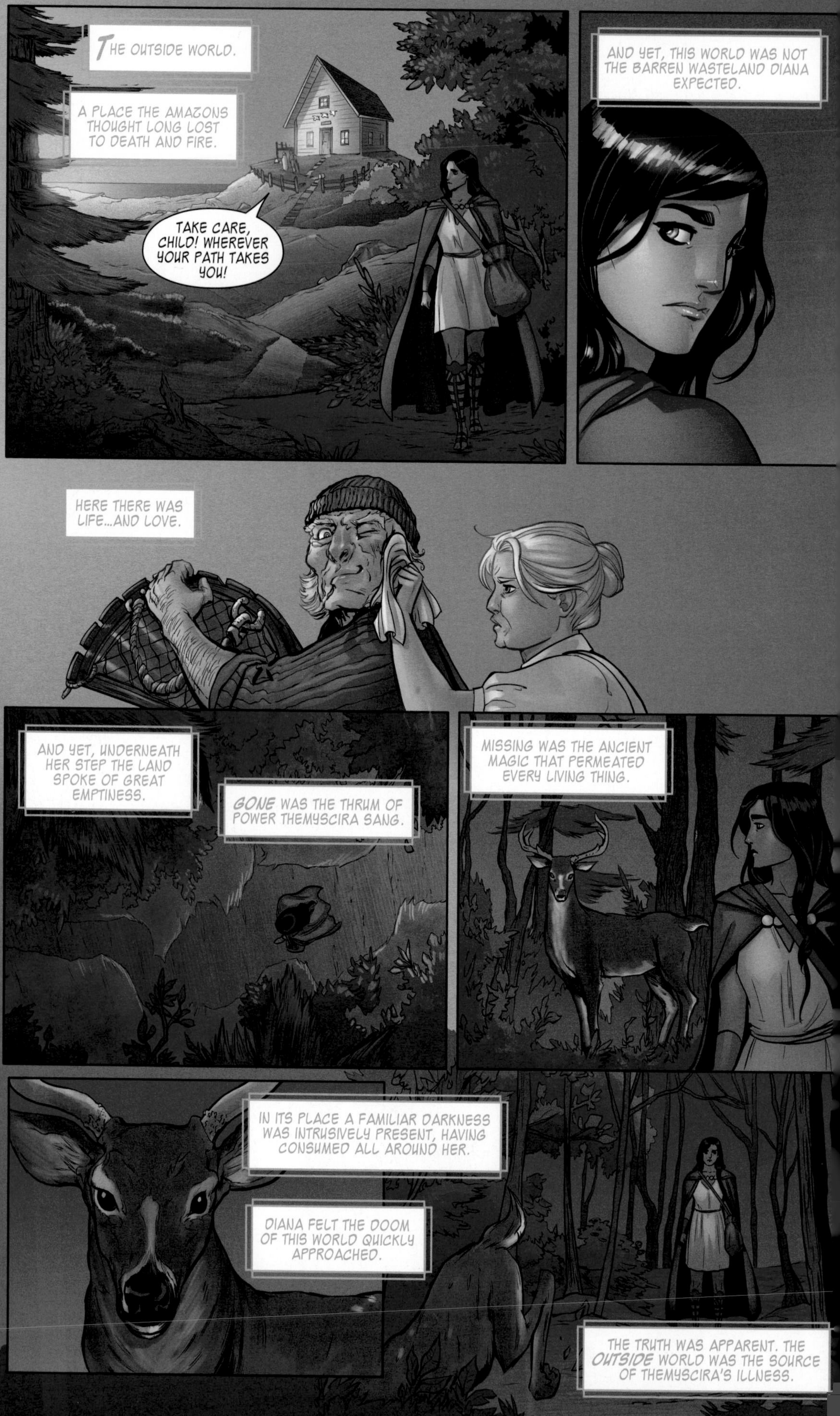
THE OUTSIDE WORLD.
A PLACE THE AMAZONS THOUGHT LONG LOST TO DEATH AND FIRE.
TAKE CARE, CHILD! WHEREVER YOUR PATH TAKES YOU!
AND YET, THIS WORLD WAS NOT THE BARREN WASTELAND DIANA EXPECTED.
HERE THERE WAS LIFE...AND LOVE.
AND YET, UNDERNEATH HER STEP THE LAND SPOKE OF GREAT EMPTINESS.
GONE WAS THE THRUM OF POWER THEMYSCIRA SANG.
MISSING WAS THE ANCIENT MAGIC THAT PERMEATED EVERY LIVING THING.
IN ITS PLACE A FAMILIAR DARKNESS WAS INTRUSIVELY PRESENT, HAVING CONSUMED ALL AROUND HER.
DIANA FELT THE DOOM OF THIS WORLD QUICKLY APPROACHED.
THE TRUTH WAS APPARENT. THE OUTSIDE WORLD WAS THE SOURCE OF THEMYSCIRA'S ILLNESS.

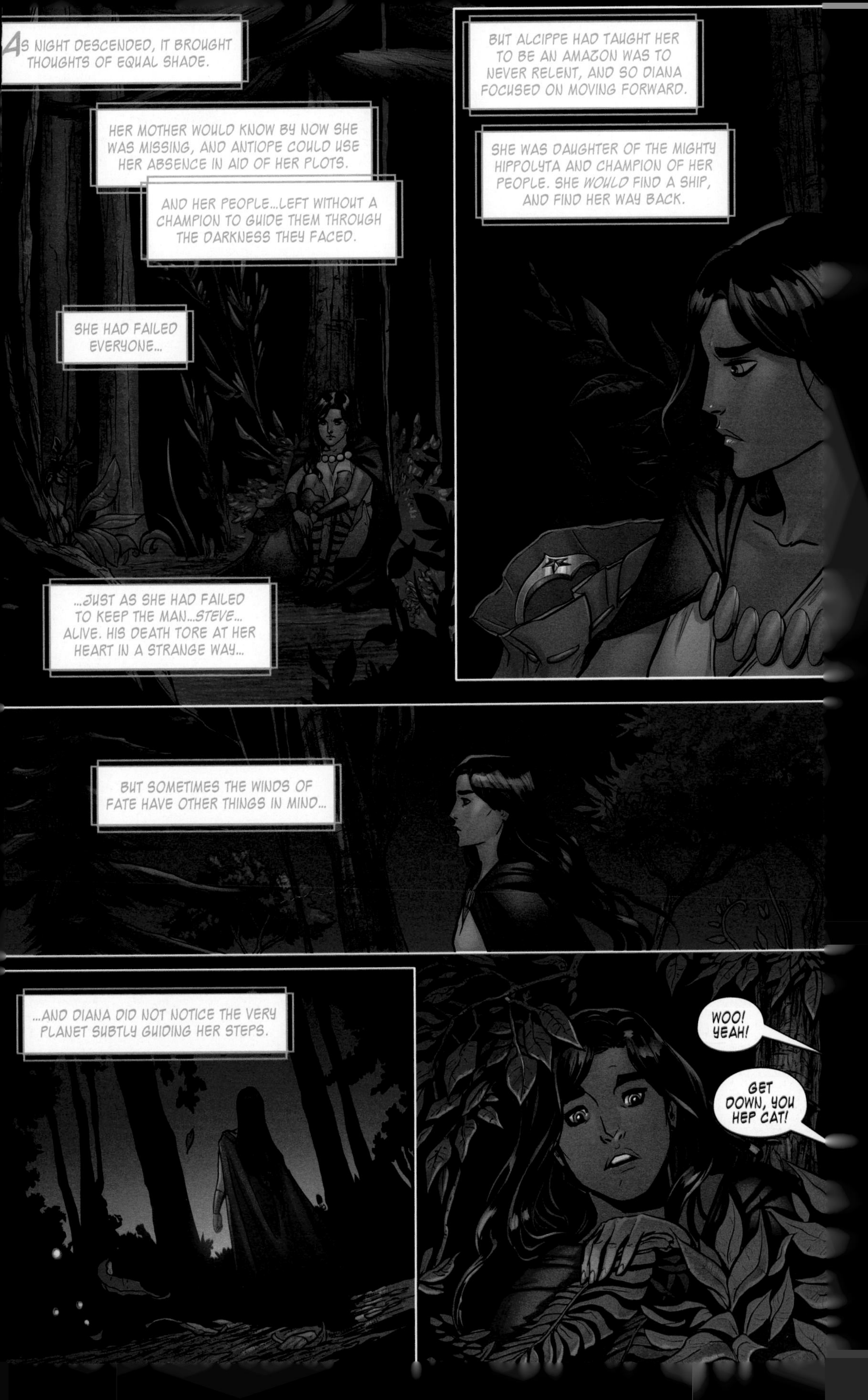
AS NIGHT DESCENDED, IT BROUGHT THOUGHTS OF EQUAL SHADE.
HER MOTHER WOULD KNOW BY NOW SHE WAS MISSING, AND ANTIOPE COULD USE HER ABSENCE IN AID OF HER PLOTS.
AND HER PEOPLE...LEFT WITHOUT A CHAMPION TO GUIDE THEM THROUGH THE DARKNESS THEY FACED.
SHE HAD FAILED EVERYONE...
...JUST AS SHE HAD FAILED TO KEEP THE MAN...*STEVE*... ALIVE. HIS DEATH TORE AT HER HEART IN A STRANGE WAY...
BUT ALCIPPE HAD TAUGHT HER TO BE AN AMAZON WAS TO NEVER RELENT, AND SO DIANA FOCUSED ON MOVING FORWARD.
SHE WAS DAUGHTER OF THE MIGHTY HIPPOLYTA AND CHAMPION OF HER PEOPLE. SHE *WOULD* FIND A SHIP, AND FIND HER WAY BACK.
BUT SOMETIMES THE WINDS OF FATE HAVE OTHER THINGS IN MIND...
...AND DIANA DID NOT NOTICE THE VERY PLANET SUBTLY GUIDING HER STEPS.
WOO! YEAH!
GET DOWN, YOU HEP CAT!

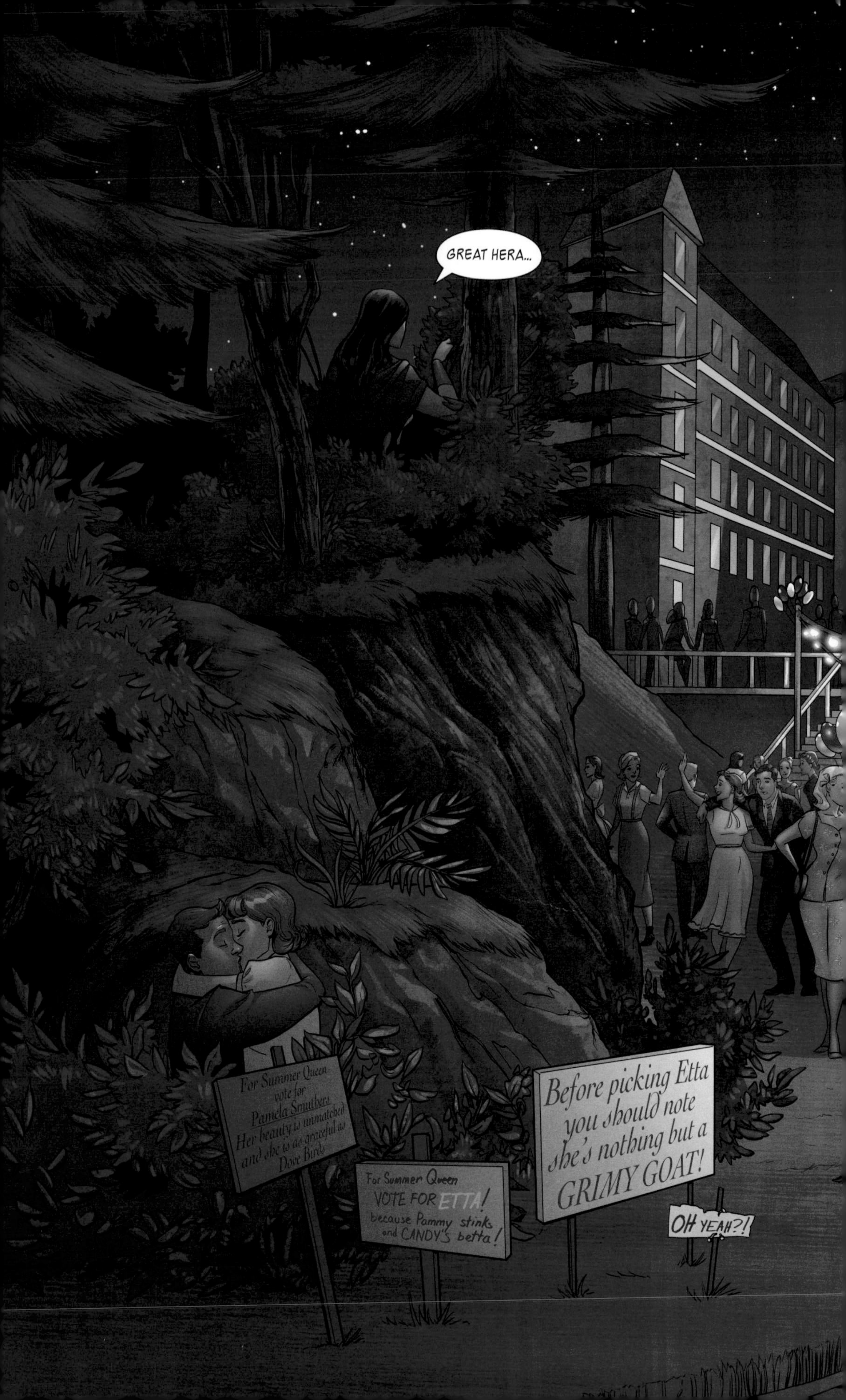
GREAT HERA...
For Summer Queen vote for Pamela Smuthers Her beauty is unmatched and she is as graceful as Dove Birds
For Summer Queen VOTE FOR ETTA! because Pammy stinks and CANDY'S betta!
Before picking Etta you should note she's nothing but a GRIMY GOAT!
OH YEAH?!

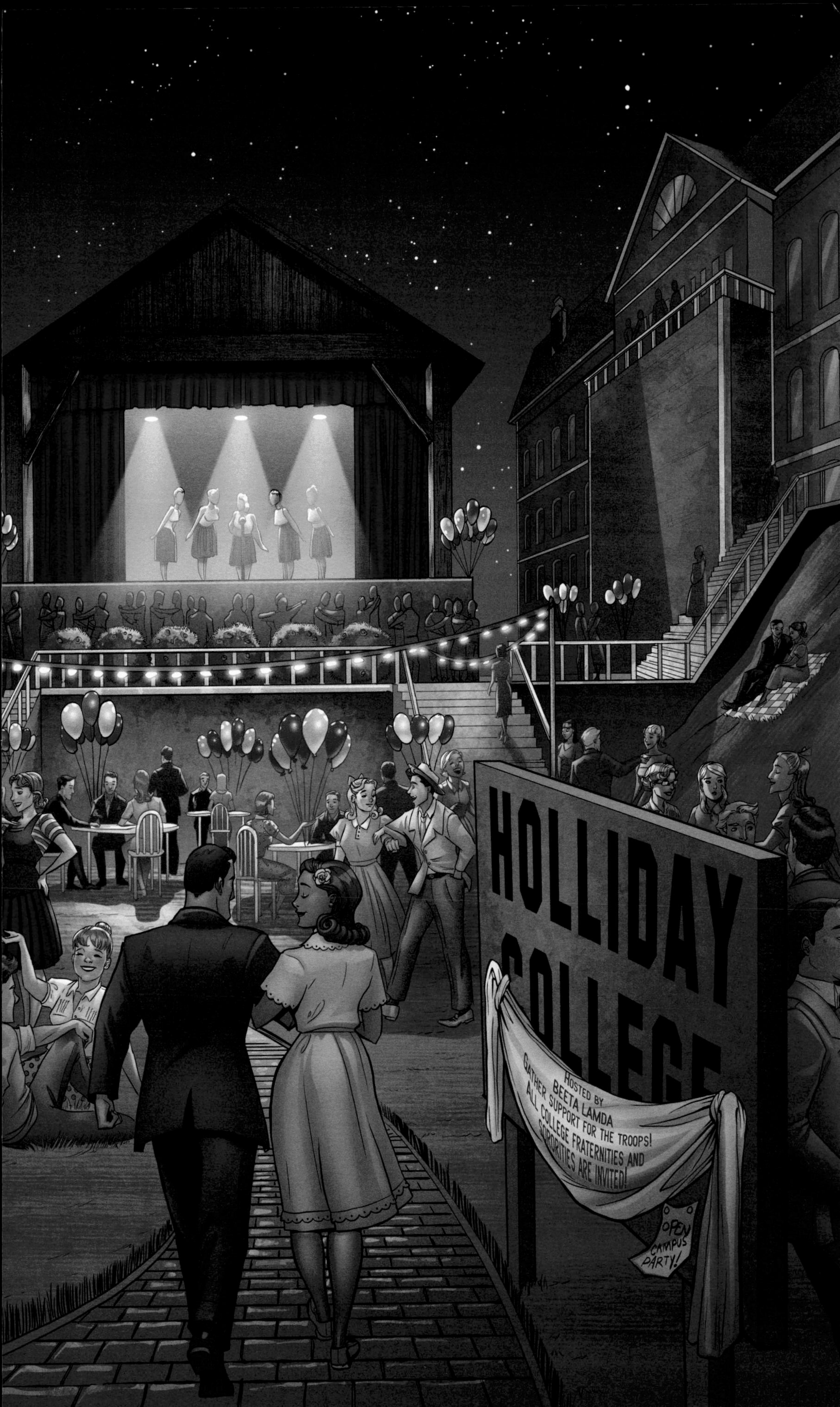
HOLLIDAY COLLEGE
HOSTED BY BEETA LAMDA
GATHER SUPPORT FOR THE TROOPS!
ALL COLLEGE FRATERNITIES AND SORORITIES ARE INVITED!
OPEN CAMPUS PARTY!

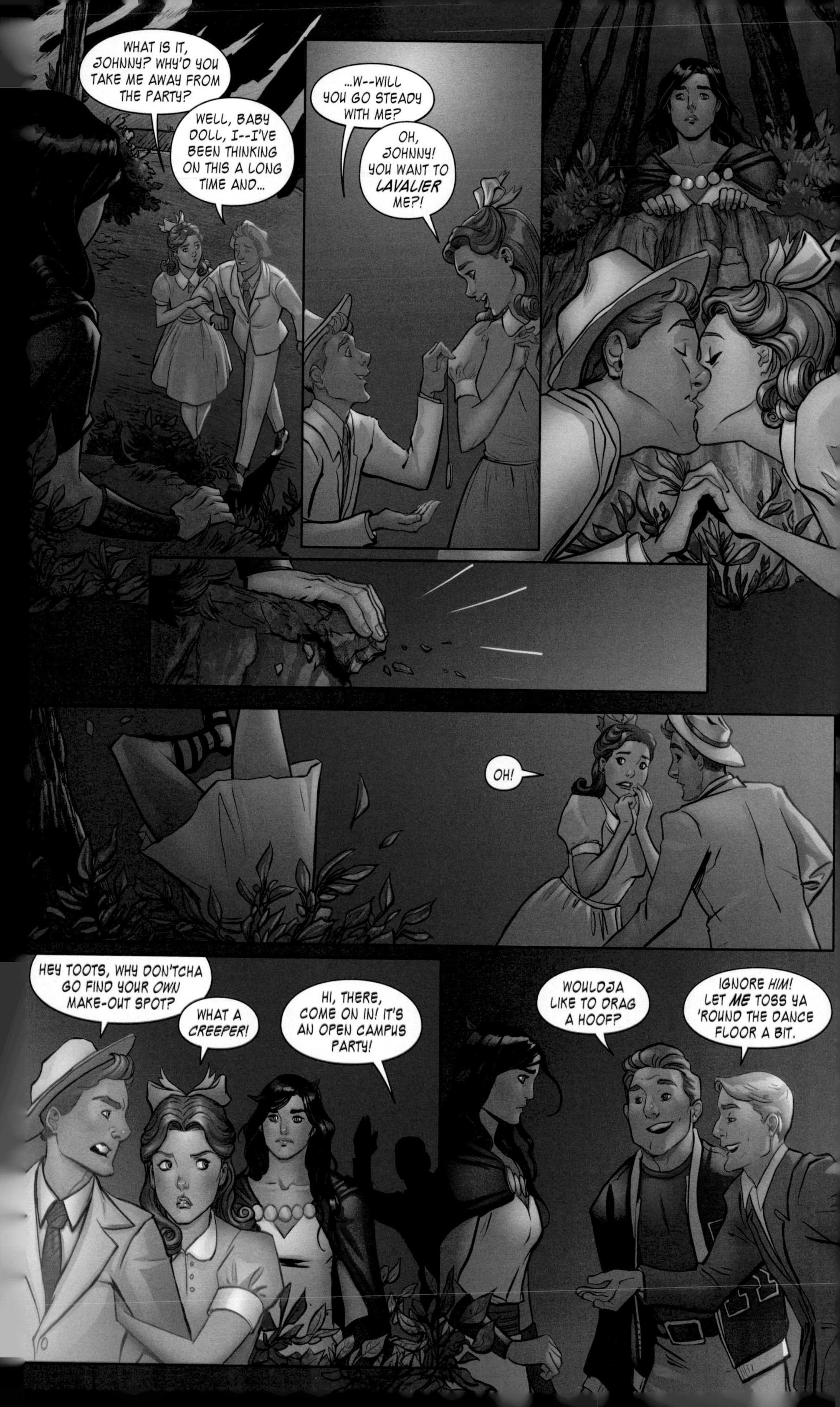
WHAT IS IT, JOHNNY? WHY'D YOU TAKE ME AWAY FROM THE PARTY?
WELL, BABY DOLL, I--I'VE BEEN THINKING ON THIS A LONG TIME AND...
...W--WILL YOU GO STEADY WITH ME?
OH, JOHNNY! YOU WANT TO LAVALIER ME?!
OH!
HEY TOOTS, WHY DON'TCHA GO FIND YOUR OWN MAKE-OUT SPOT?
WHAT A CREEPER!
HI, THERE, COME ON IN! IT'S AN OPEN CAMPUS PARTY!
WOULDJA LIKE TO DRAG A HOOF?
IGNORE HIM! LET ME TOSS YA 'ROUND THE DANCE FLOOR A BIT.

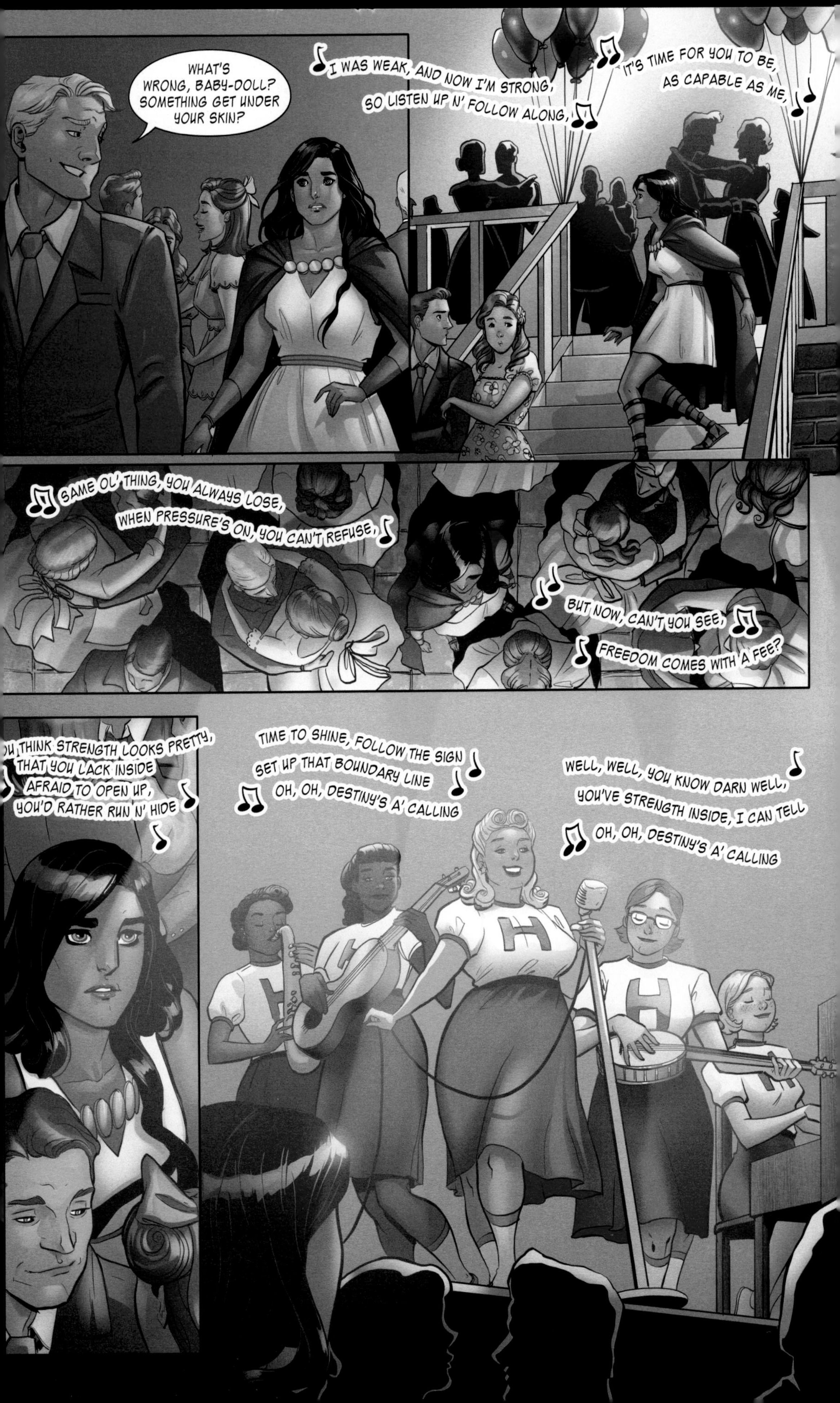
WHAT'S WRONG, BABY-DOLL? SOMETHING GET UNDER YOUR SKIN?
I WAS WEAK, AND NOW I'M STRONG, SO LISTEN UP N' FOLLOW ALONG,
IT'S TIME FOR YOU TO BE, AS CAPABLE AS ME,
SAME OL' THING, YOU ALWAYS LOSE, WHEN PRESSURE'S ON, YOU CAN'T REFUSE,
BUT NOW, CAN'T YOU SEE,
FREEDOM COMES WITH A FEE?
THINK STRENGTH LOOKS PRETTY, THAT YOU LACK INSIDE AFRAID TO OPEN UP, YOU'D RATHER RUN N' HIDE
TIME TO SHINE, FOLLOW THE SIGN SET UP THAT BOUNDARY LINE
OH, OH, DESTINY'S A' CALLING
WELL, WELL, YOU KNOW DARN WELL, YOU'VE STRENGTH INSIDE, I CAN TELL
OH, OH, DESTINY'S A' CALLING

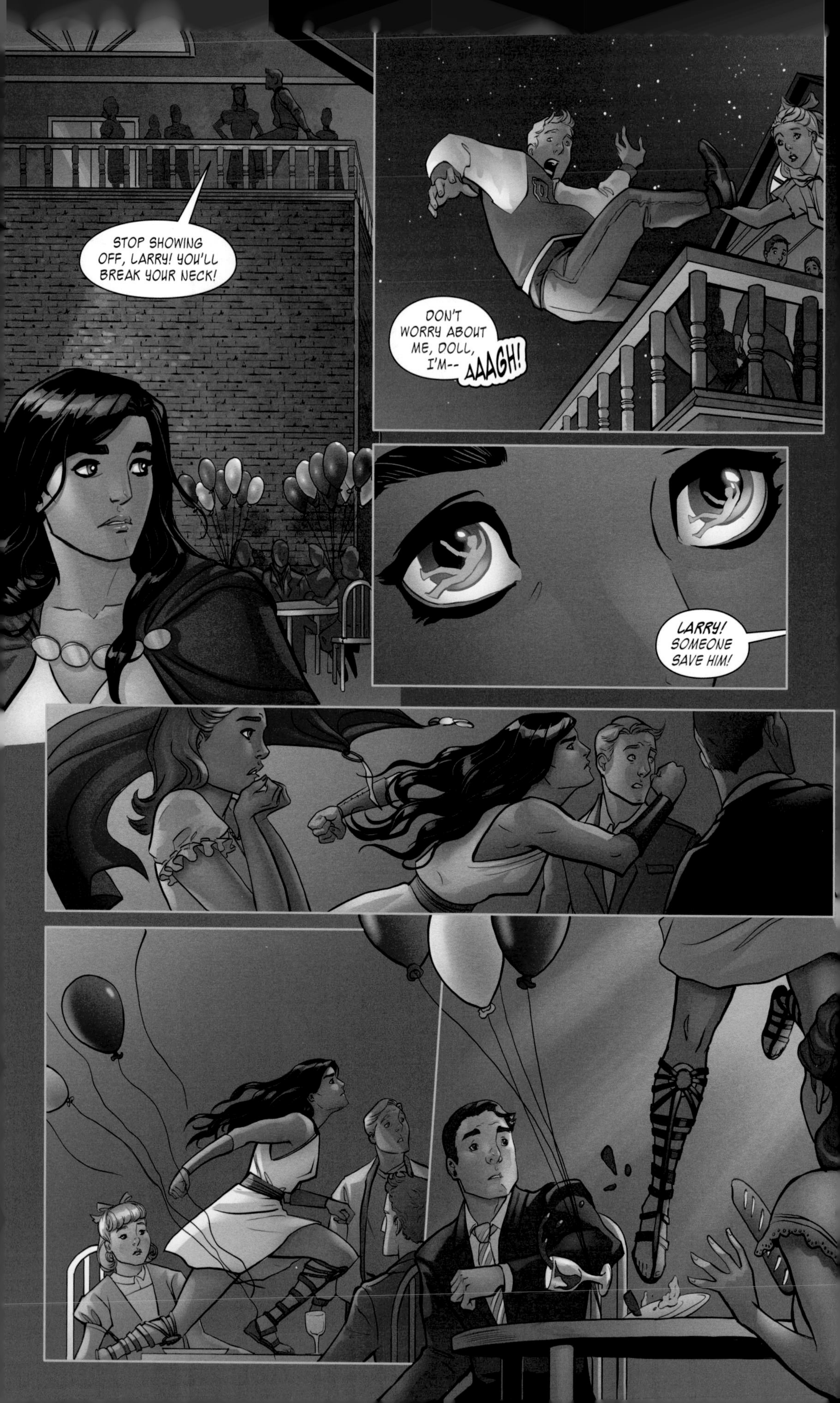
STOP SHOWING OFF, LARRY! YOU'LL BREAK YOUR NECK!
DON'T WORRY ABOUT ME, DOLL, I'M-- AAAGH!
LARRY! SOMEONE SAVE HIM!

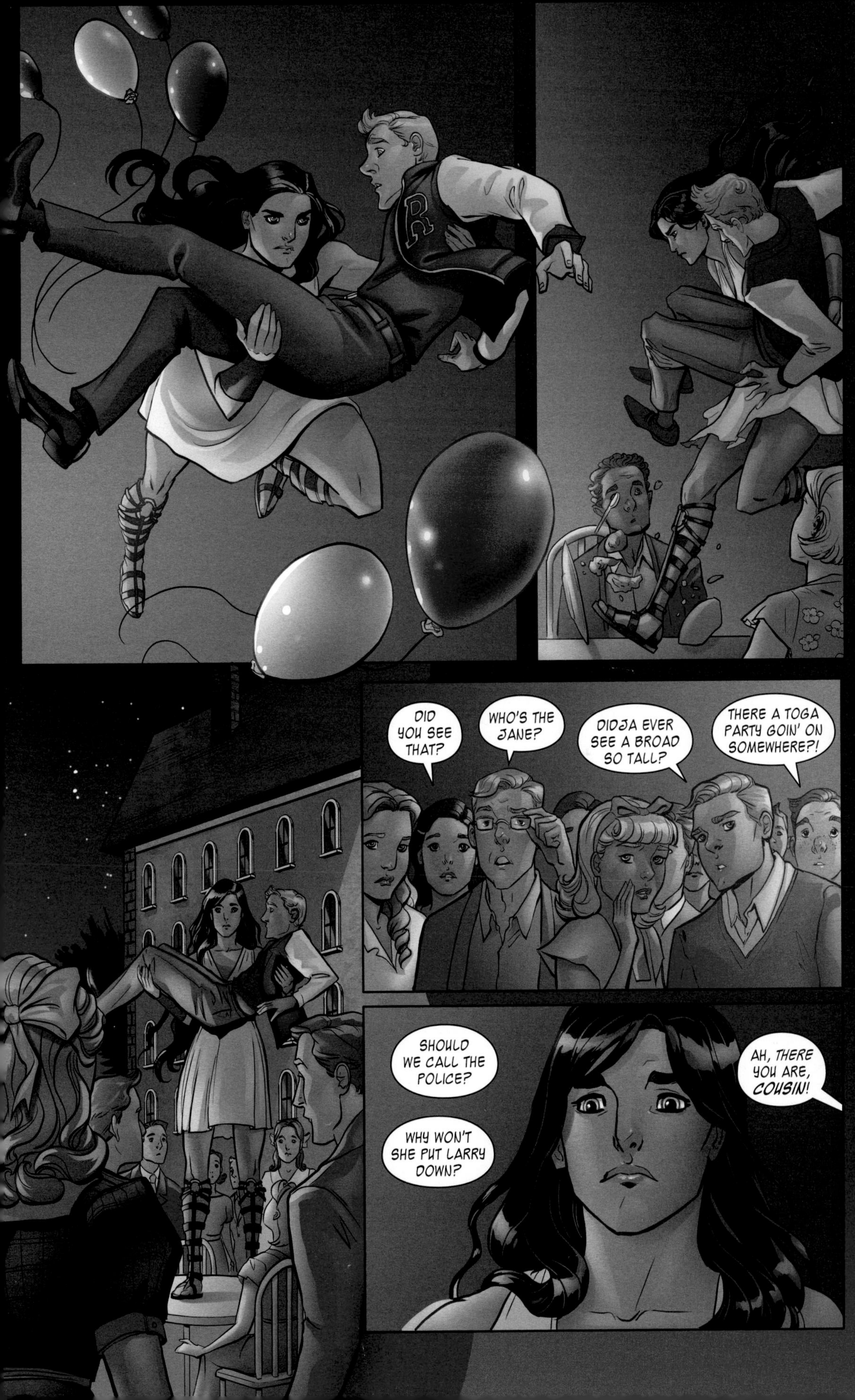
DID YOU SEE THAT?
WHO'S THE JANE?
DIDJA EVER SEE A BROAD SO TALL?
THERE A TOGA PARTY GOIN' ON SOMEWHERE?!
SHOULD WE CALL THE POLICE?
WHY WON'T SHE PUT LARRY DOWN?
AH, THERE YOU ARE, *COUSIN!*

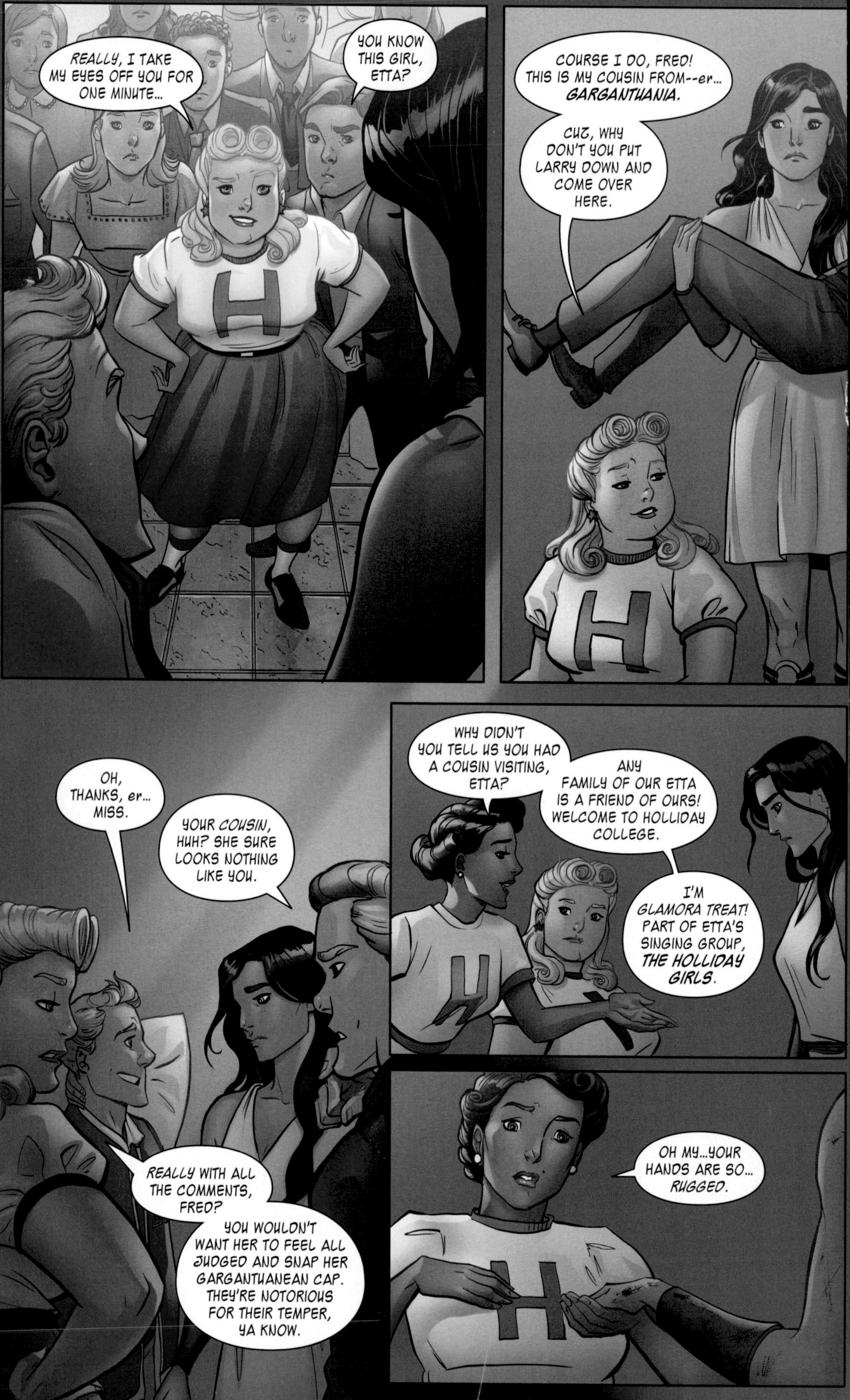
REALLY, I TAKE MY EYES OFF YOU FOR ONE MINUTE...
YOU KNOW THIS GIRL, ETTA?
COURSE I DO, FRED! THIS IS MY COUSIN FROM--er... GARGANTUANIA.
CUZ, WHY DON'T YOU PUT LARRY DOWN AND COME OVER HERE.
OH, THANKS, er... MISS.
YOUR COUSIN, HUH? SHE SURE LOOKS NOTHING LIKE YOU.
REALLY WITH ALL THE COMMENTS, FRED?
YOU WOULDN'T WANT HER TO FEEL ALL JUDGED AND SNAP HER GARGANTUANEAN CAP. THEY'RE NOTORIOUS FOR THEIR TEMPER, YA KNOW.
WHY DIDN'T YOU TELL US YOU HAD A COUSIN VISITING, ETTA?
ANY FAMILY OF OUR ETTA IS A FRIEND OF OURS! WELCOME TO HOLLIDAY COLLEGE.
I'M GLAMORA TREAT! PART OF ETTA'S SINGING GROUP, THE HOLLIDAY GIRLS.
OH MY...YOUR HANDS ARE SO... RUGGED.

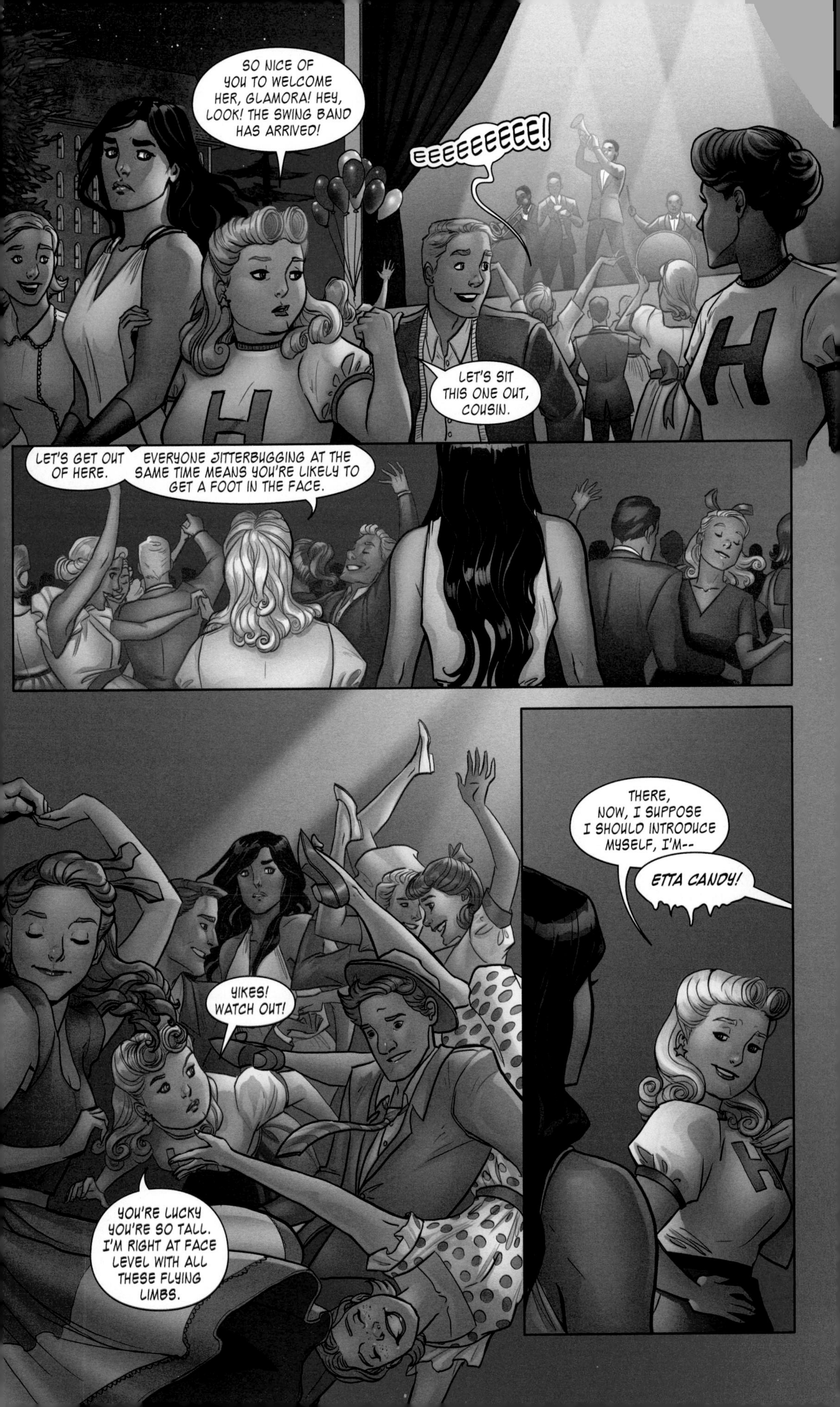

SO NICE OF YOU TO WELCOME HER, GLAMORA! HEY, LOOK! THE SWING BAND HAS ARRIVED!
EEEEEEEEEE!
LET'S SIT THIS ONE OUT, COUSIN.
LET'S GET OUT OF HERE.
EVERYONE JITTERBUGGING AT THE SAME TIME MEANS YOU'RE LIKELY TO GET A FOOT IN THE FACE.
YIKES! WATCH OUT!
YOU'RE LUCKY YOU'RE SO TALL. I'M RIGHT AT FACE LEVEL WITH ALL THESE FLYING LIMBS.
THERE, NOW, I SUPPOSE I SHOULD INTRODUCE MYSELF, I'M--
ETTA CANDY!

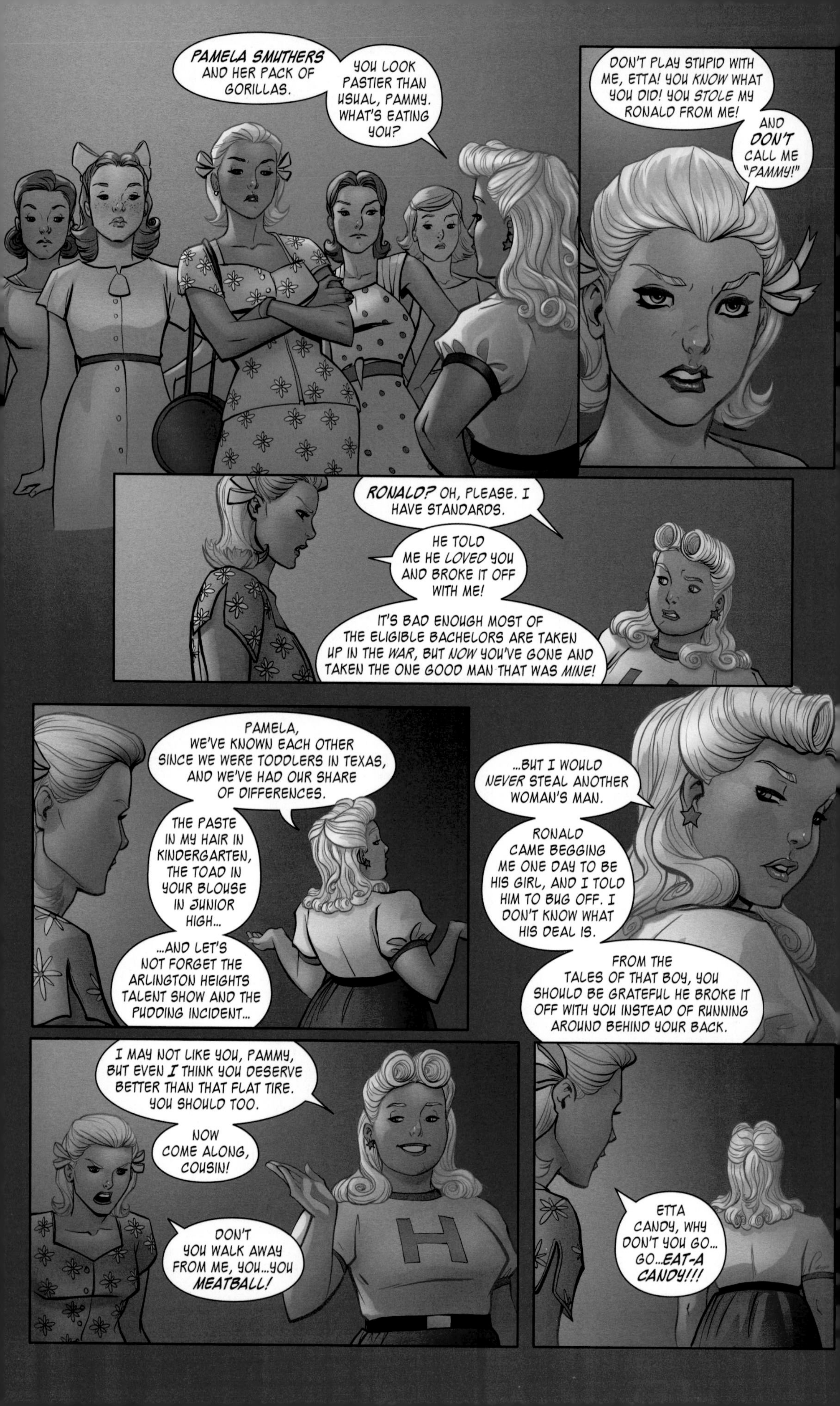
PAMELA SMUTHERS AND HER PACK OF GORILLAS.
YOU LOOK PASTIER THAN USUAL, PAMMY. WHAT'S EATING YOU?
DON'T PLAY STUPID WITH ME, ETTA! YOU KNOW WHAT YOU DID! YOU STOLE MY RONALD FROM ME!
AND DON'T CALL ME "PAMMY!"
RONALD? OH, PLEASE. I HAVE STANDARDS.
HE TOLD ME HE LOVED YOU AND BROKE IT OFF WITH ME!
IT'S BAD ENOUGH MOST OF THE ELIGIBLE BACHELORS ARE TAKEN UP IN THE WAR, BUT NOW YOU'VE GONE AND TAKEN THE ONE GOOD MAN THAT WAS MINE!
PAMELA, WE'VE KNOWN EACH OTHER SINCE WE WERE TODDLERS IN TEXAS, AND WE'VE HAD OUR SHARE OF DIFFERENCES.
THE PASTE IN MY HAIR IN KINDERGARTEN, THE TOAD IN YOUR BLOUSE IN JUNIOR HIGH...
...AND LET'S NOT FORGET THE ARLINGTON HEIGHTS TALENT SHOW AND THE PUDDING INCIDENT...
...BUT I WOULD NEVER STEAL ANOTHER WOMAN'S MAN.
RONALD CAME BEGGING ME ONE DAY TO BE HIS GIRL, AND I TOLD HIM TO BUG OFF. I DON'T KNOW WHAT HIS DEAL IS.
FROM THE TALES OF THAT BOY, YOU SHOULD BE GRATEFUL HE BROKE IT OFF WITH YOU INSTEAD OF RUNNING AROUND BEHIND YOUR BACK.
I MAY NOT LIKE YOU, PAMMY, BUT EVEN I THINK YOU DESERVE BETTER THAN THAT FLAT TIRE. YOU SHOULD TOO.
NOW COME ALONG, COUSIN!
DON'T YOU WALK AWAY FROM ME, YOU...YOU MEATBALL!
ETTA CANDY, WHY DON'T YOU GO... GO...EAT-A CANDY!!!

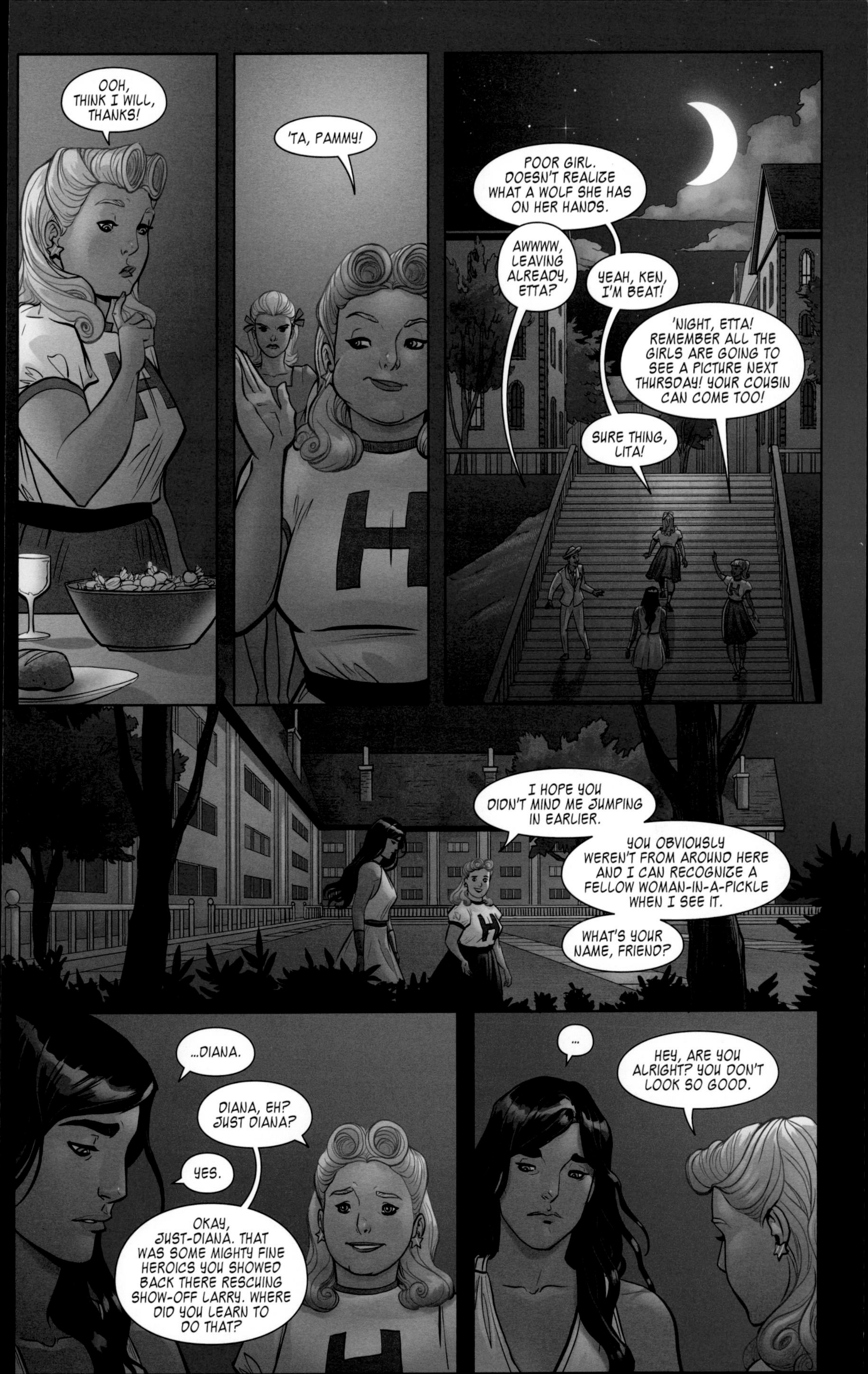
OOH, THINK I WILL, THANKS!
'TA, PAMMY!
POOR GIRL. DOESN'T REALIZE WHAT A WOLF SHE HAS ON HER HANDS.
AWWWW, LEAVING ALREADY, ETTA?
YEAH, KEN, I'M BEAT!
'NIGHT, ETTA! REMEMBER ALL THE GIRLS ARE GOING TO SEE A PICTURE NEXT THURSDAY! YOUR COUSIN CAN COME TOO!
SURE THING, LITA!
I HOPE YOU DIDN'T MIND ME JUMPING IN EARLIER.
YOU OBVIOUSLY WEREN'T FROM AROUND HERE AND I CAN RECOGNIZE A FELLOW WOMAN-IN-A-PICKLE WHEN I SEE IT.
WHAT'S YOUR NAME, FRIEND?
...DIANA.
DIANA, EH? JUST DIANA?
YES.
OKAY, JUST-DIANA. THAT WAS SOME MIGHTY FINE HEROICS YOU SHOWED BACK THERE RESCUING SHOW-OFF LARRY. WHERE DID YOU LEARN TO DO THAT?
...
HEY, ARE YOU ALRIGHT? YOU DON'T LOOK SO GOOD.

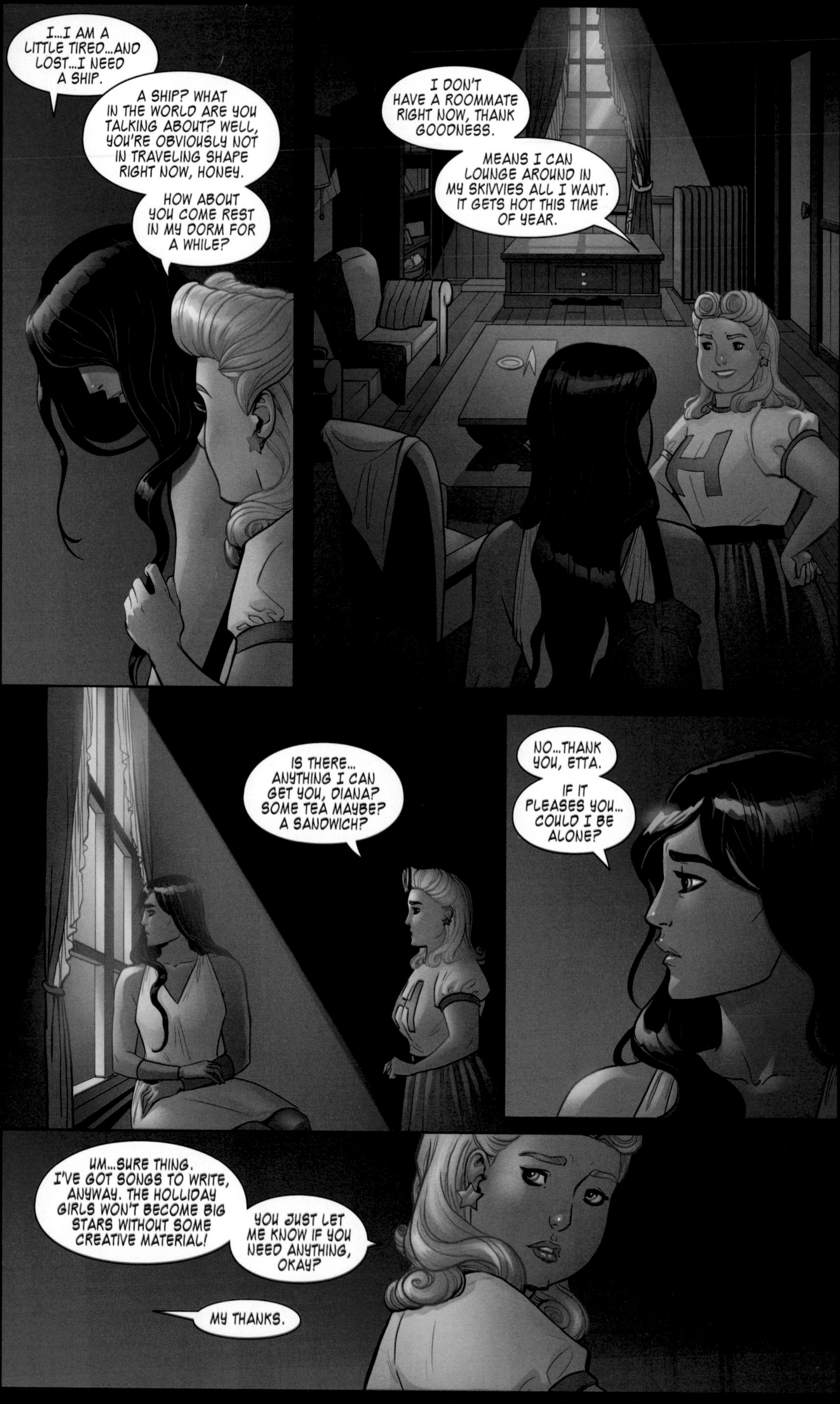

I...I AM A LITTLE TIRED...AND LOST...I NEED A SHIP.
A SHIP? WHAT IN THE WORLD ARE YOU TALKING ABOUT? WELL, YOU'RE OBVIOUSLY NOT IN TRAVELING SHAPE RIGHT NOW, HONEY.
HOW ABOUT YOU COME REST IN MY DORM FOR A WHILE?
I DON'T HAVE A ROOMMATE RIGHT NOW, THANK GOODNESS.
MEANS I CAN LOUNGE AROUND IN MY SKIVVIES ALL I WANT. IT GETS HOT THIS TIME OF YEAR.
IS THERE... ANYTHING I CAN GET YOU, DIANA? SOME TEA MAYBE? A SANDWICH?
NO...THANK YOU, ETTA.
IF IT PLEASES YOU... COULD I BE ALONE?
UM...SURE THING. I'VE GOT SONGS TO WRITE, ANYWAY. THE HOLLIDAY GIRLS WON'T BECOME BIG STARS WITHOUT SOME CREATIVE MATERIAL!
YOU JUST LET ME KNOW IF YOU NEED ANYTHING, OKAY?
MY THANKS.

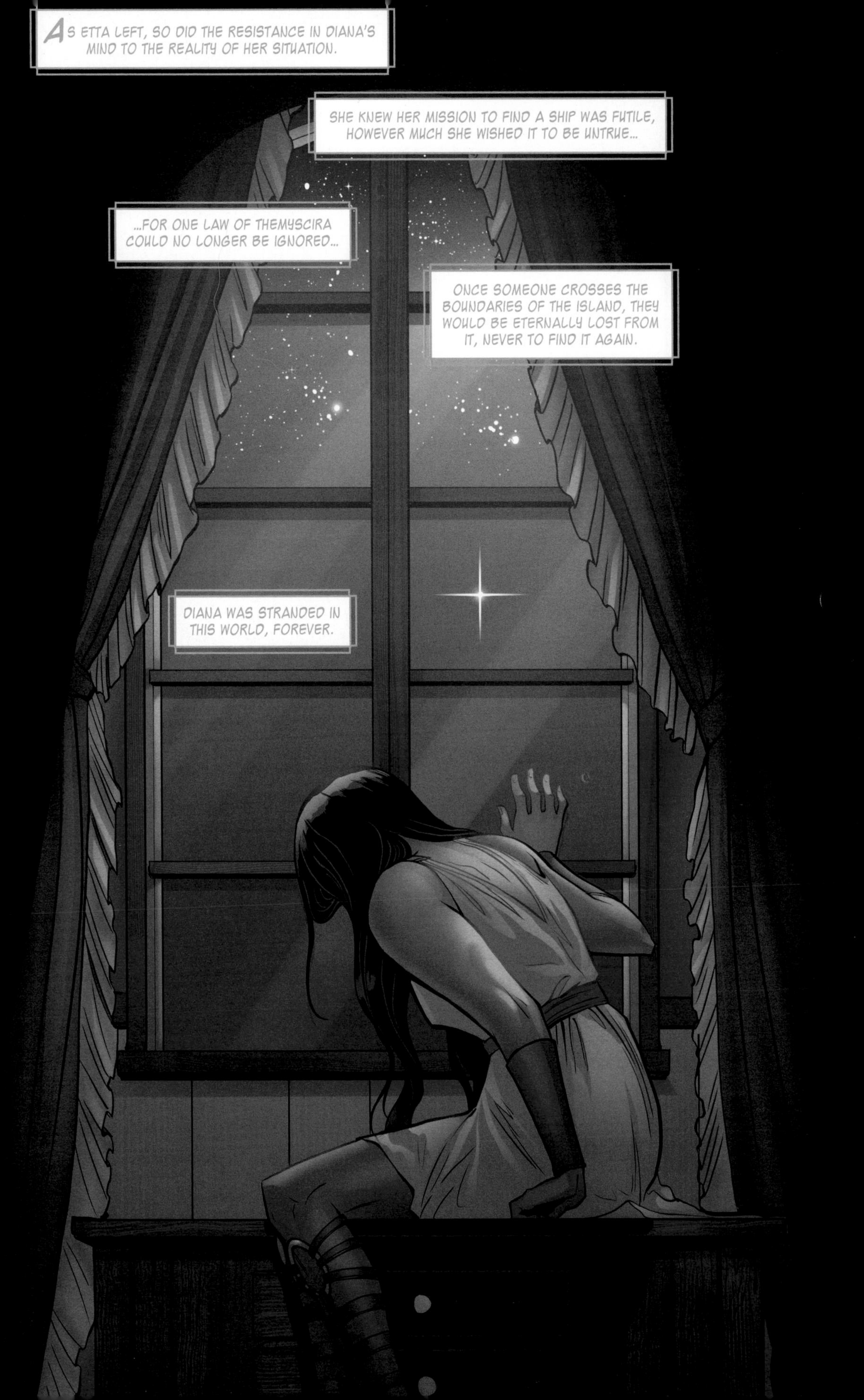

AS ETTA LEFT, SO DID THE RESISTANCE IN DIANA'S MIND TO THE REALITY OF HER SITUATION.
SHE KNEW HER MISSION TO FIND A SHIP WAS FUTILE, HOWEVER MUCH SHE WISHED IT TO BE UNTRUE...
...FOR ONE LAW OF THEMYSCIRA COULD NO LONGER BE IGNORED...
ONCE SOMEONE CROSSES THE BOUNDARIES OF THE ISLAND, THEY WOULD BE ETERNALLY LOST FROM IT, NEVER TO FIND IT AGAIN.
DIANA WAS STRANDED IN THIS WORLD, FOREVER.

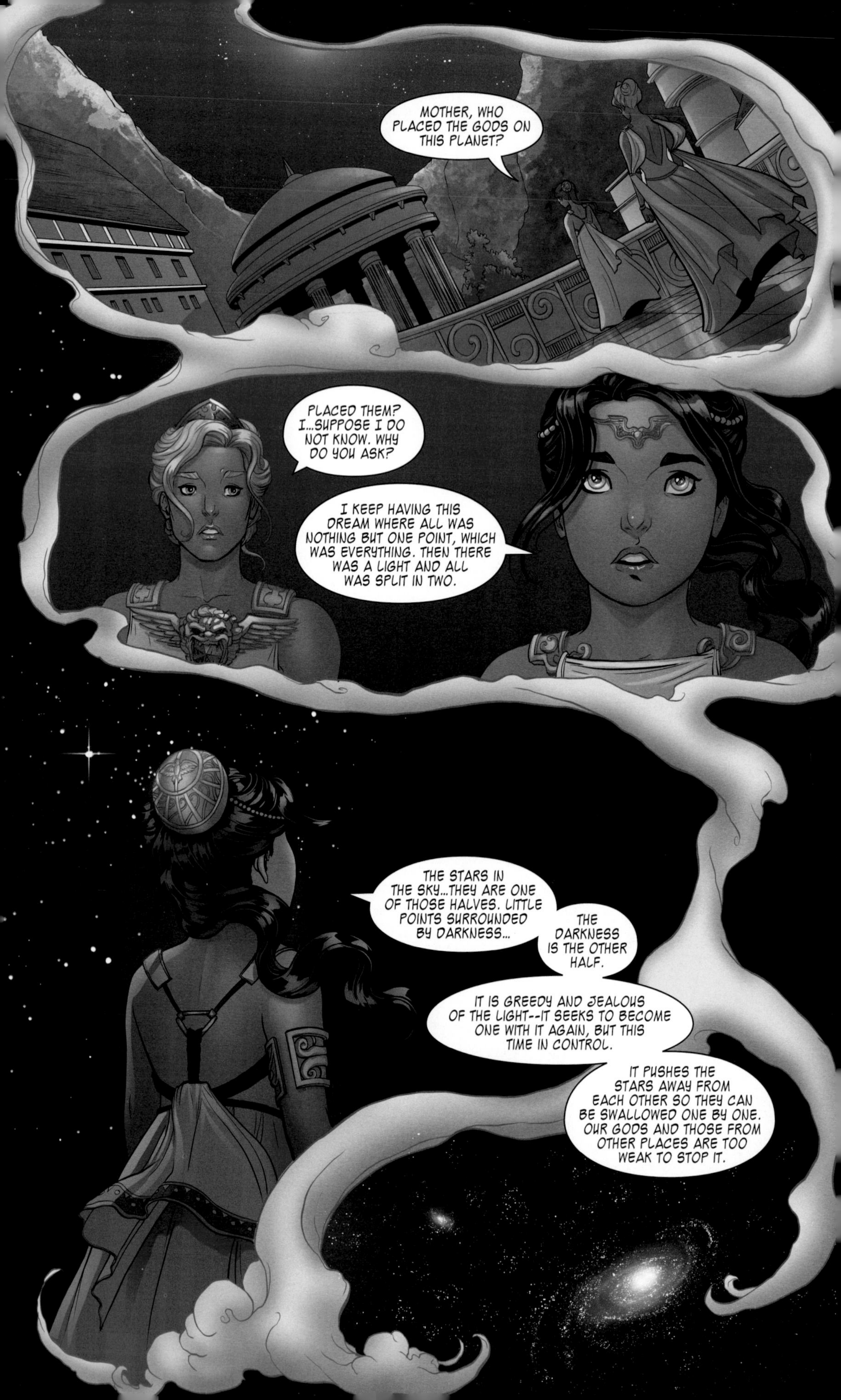
MOTHER, WHO PLACED THE GODS ON THIS PLANET?
PLACED THEM? I...SUPPOSE I DO NOT KNOW. WHY DO YOU ASK?
I KEEP HAVING THIS DREAM WHERE ALL WAS NOTHING BUT ONE POINT, WHICH WAS EVERYTHING. THEN THERE WAS A LIGHT AND ALL WAS SPLIT IN TWO.
THE STARS IN THE SKY...THEY ARE ONE OF THOSE HALVES. LITTLE POINTS SURROUNDED BY DARKNESS...
THE DARKNESS IS THE OTHER HALF.
IT IS GREEDY AND JEALOUS OF THE LIGHT--IT SEEKS TO BECOME ONE WITH IT AGAIN, BUT THIS TIME IN CONTROL.
IT PUSHES THE STARS AWAY FROM EACH OTHER SO THEY CAN BE SWALLOWED ONE BY ONE. OUR GODS AND THOSE FROM OTHER PLACES ARE TOO WEAK TO STOP IT.

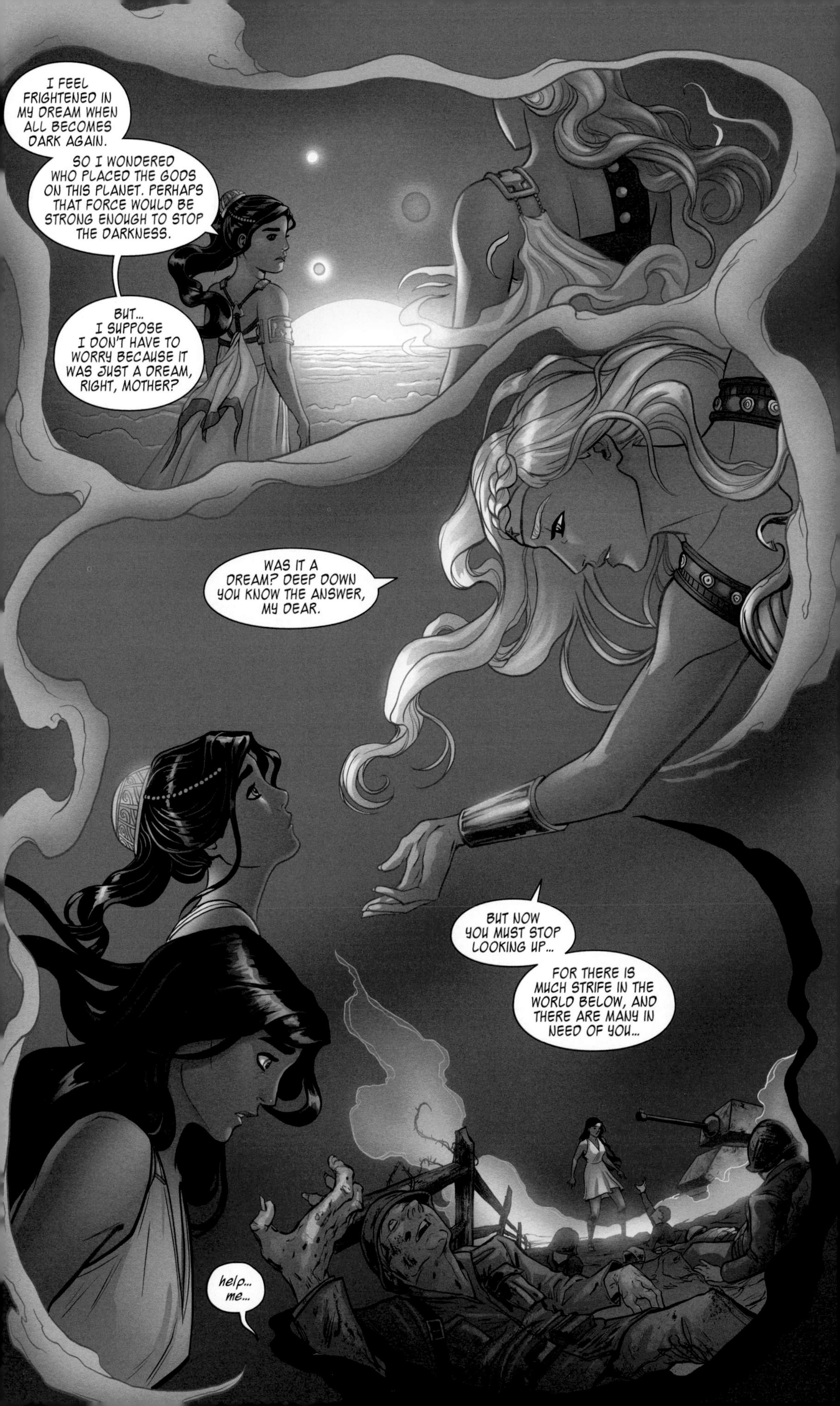

I FEEL FRIGHTENED IN MY DREAM WHEN ALL BECOMES DARK AGAIN.
SO I WONDERED WHO PLACED THE GODS ON THIS PLANET. PERHAPS THAT FORCE WOULD BE STRONG ENOUGH TO STOP THE DARKNESS.
BUT... I SUPPOSE I DON'T HAVE TO WORRY BECAUSE IT WAS JUST A DREAM, RIGHT, MOTHER?
WAS IT A DREAM? DEEP DOWN YOU KNOW THE ANSWER, MY DEAR.
BUT NOW YOU MUST STOP LOOKING UP...
FOR THERE IS MUCH STRIFE IN THE WORLD BELOW, AND THERE ARE MANY IN NEED OF YOU...
help... me...

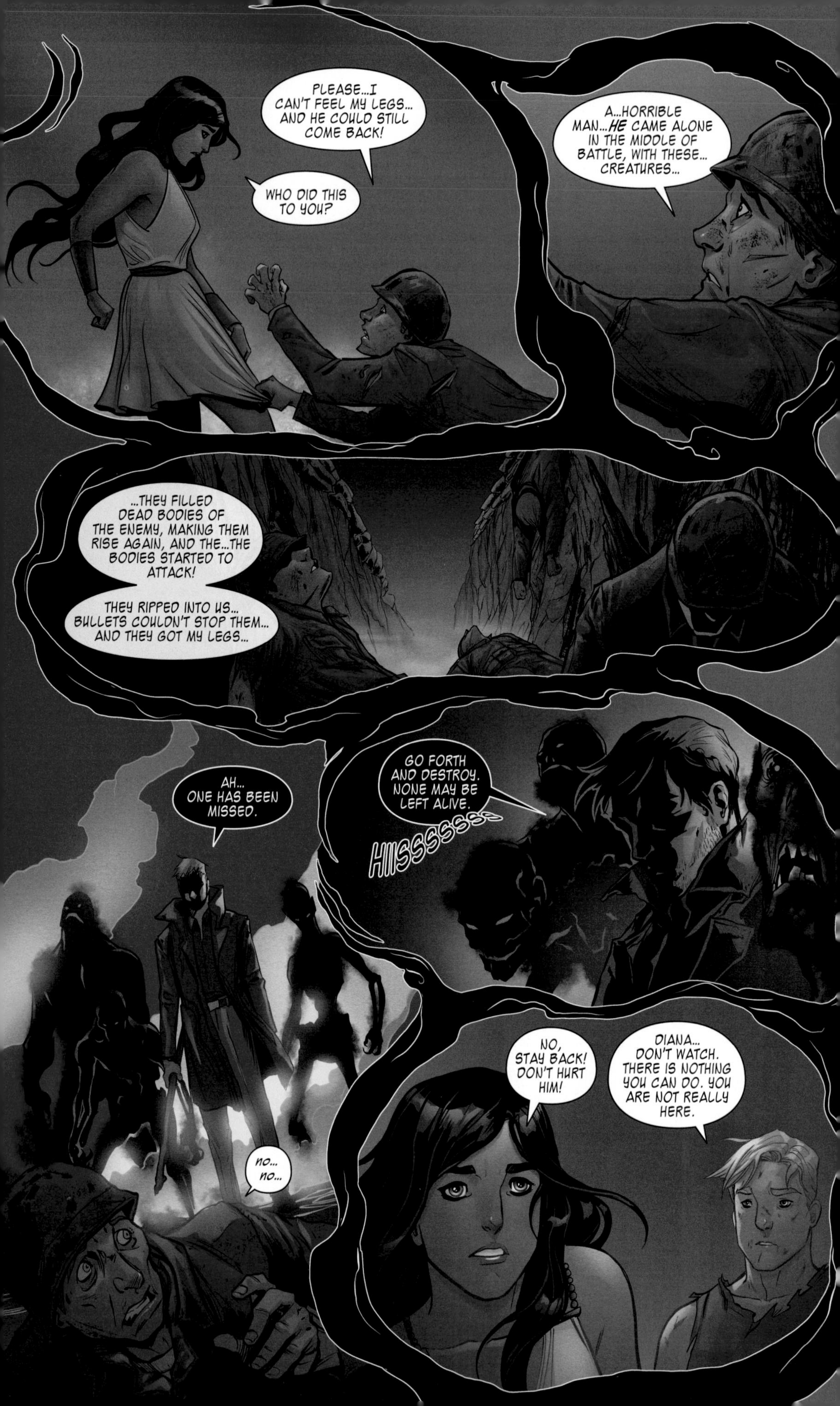
PLEASE...I CAN'T FEEL MY LEGS... AND HE COULD STILL COME BACK!
WHO DID THIS TO YOU?
A...HORRIBLE MAN...HE CAME ALONE IN THE MIDDLE OF BATTLE, WITH THESE... CREATURES...
...THEY FILLED DEAD BODIES OF THE ENEMY, MAKING THEM RISE AGAIN, AND THE...THE BODIES STARTED TO ATTACK!
THEY RIPPED INTO US... BULLETS COULDN'T STOP THEM... AND THEY GOT MY LEGS...
AH... ONE HAS BEEN MISSED.
no... no...
GO FORTH AND DESTROY. NONE MAY BE LEFT ALIVE.
HIISSSSSSS
NO, STAY BACK! DON'T HURT HIM!
DIANA... DON'T WATCH. THERE IS NOTHING YOU CAN DO. YOU ARE NOT REALLY HERE.

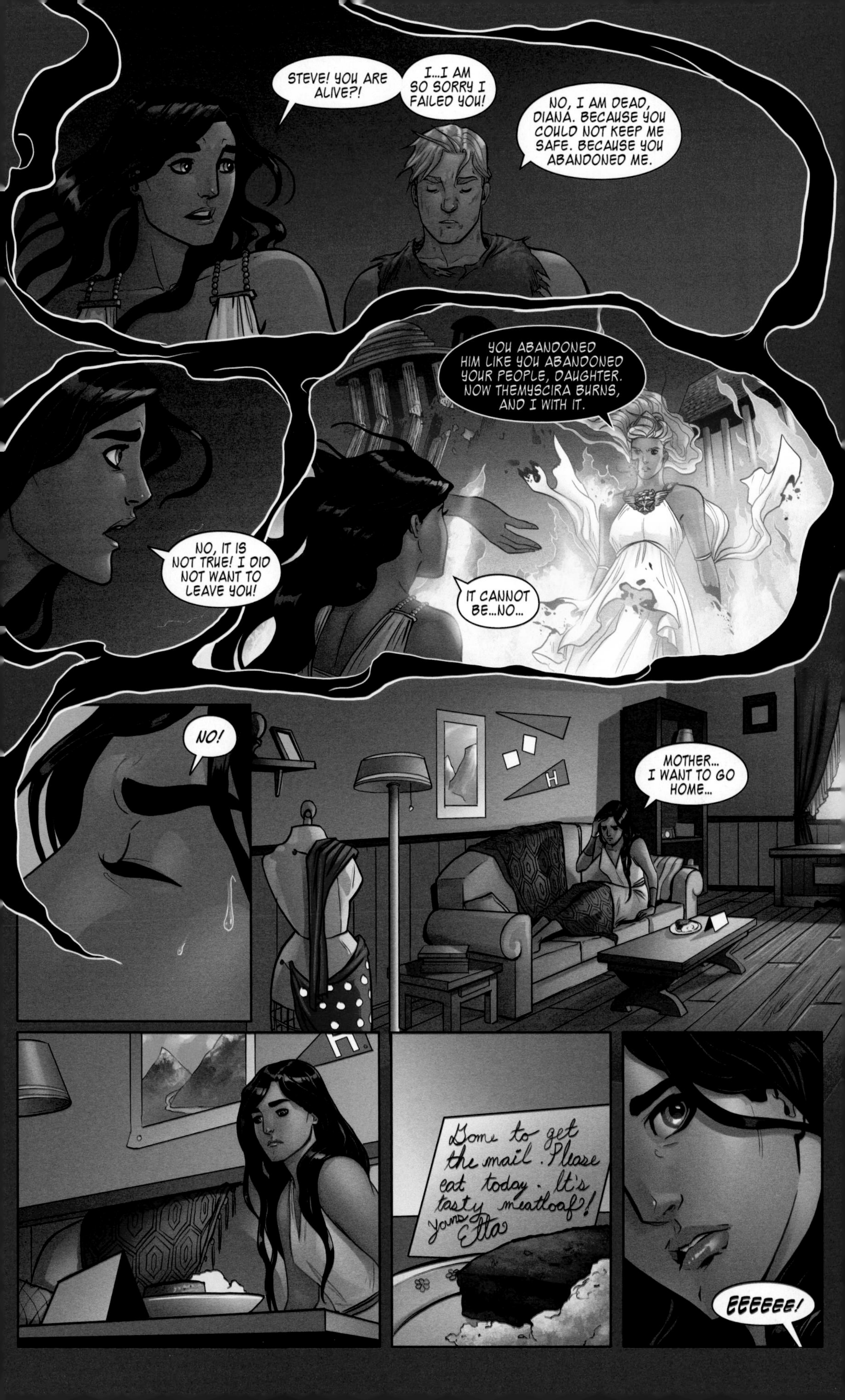
STEVE! YOU ARE ALIVE?!
I...I AM SO SORRY I FAILED YOU!
NO, I AM DEAD, DIANA. BECAUSE YOU COULD NOT KEEP ME SAFE. BECAUSE YOU ABANDONED ME.
YOU ABANDONED HIM LIKE YOU ABANDONED YOUR PEOPLE, DAUGHTER. NOW THEMYSCIRA BURNS, AND I WITH IT.
NO, IT IS NOT TRUE! I DID NOT WANT TO LEAVE YOU!
IT CANNOT BE...NO...
NO!
MOTHER... I WANT TO GO HOME...
Gone to get the mail. Please eat today. It's tasty meatloaf! Yours, Etta
EEEEEE!

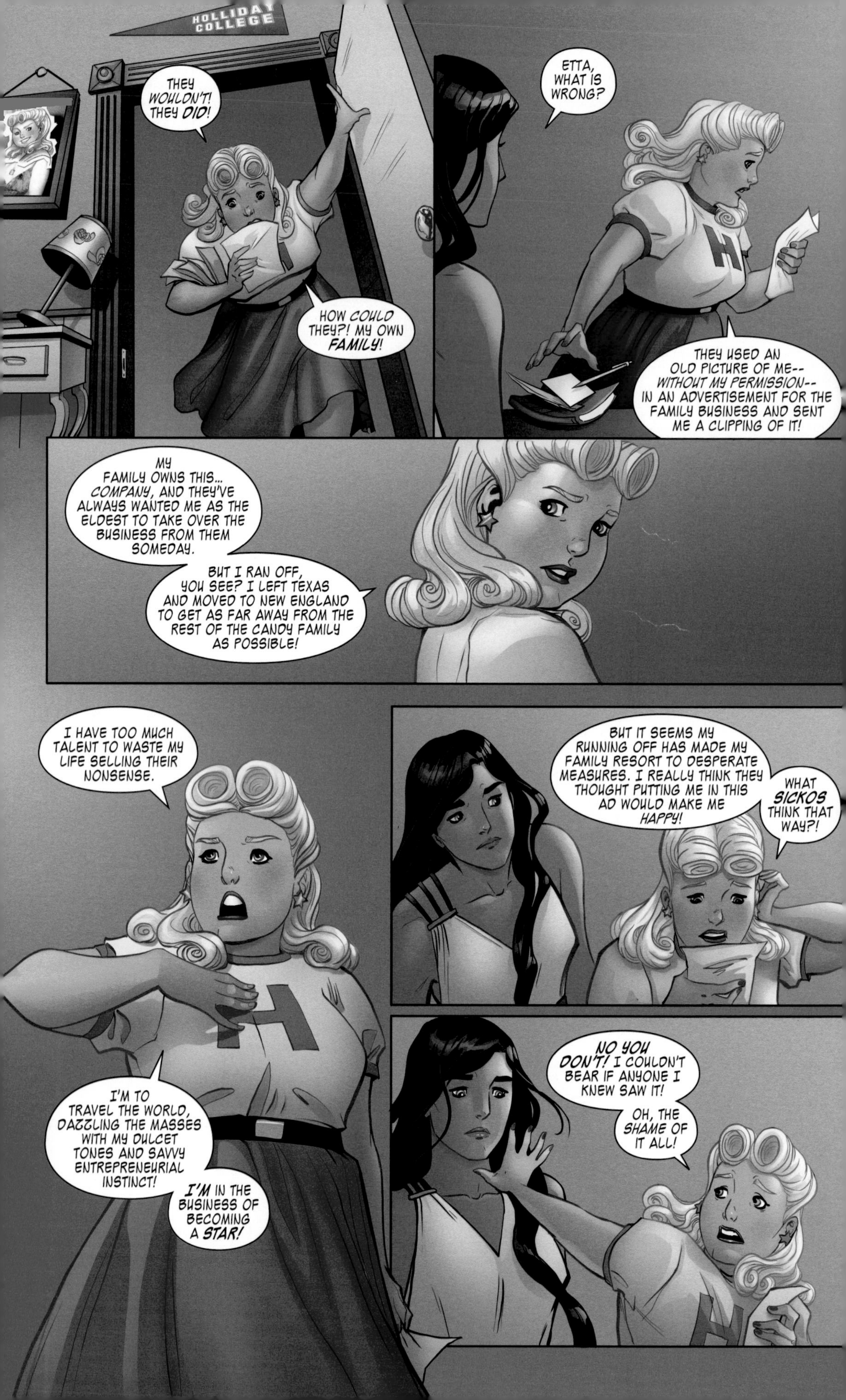
HOLLIDAY COLLEGE
THEY WOULDN'T! THEY DID!
HOW COULD THEY?! MY OWN FAMILY!
ETTA, WHAT IS WRONG?
THEY USED AN OLD PICTURE OF ME-- WITHOUT MY PERMISSION-- IN AN ADVERTISEMENT FOR THE FAMILY BUSINESS AND SENT ME A CLIPPING OF IT!
MY FAMILY OWNS THIS... COMPANY, AND THEY'VE ALWAYS WANTED ME AS THE ELDEST TO TAKE OVER THE BUSINESS FROM THEM SOMEDAY.
BUT I RAN OFF, YOU SEE? I LEFT TEXAS AND MOVED TO NEW ENGLAND TO GET AS FAR AWAY FROM THE REST OF THE CANDY FAMILY AS POSSIBLE!
I HAVE TOO MUCH TALENT TO WASTE MY LIFE SELLING THEIR NONSENSE.
I'M TO TRAVEL THE WORLD, DAZZLING THE MASSES WITH MY DULCET TONES AND SAVVY ENTREPRENEURIAL INSTINCT!
I'M IN THE BUSINESS OF BECOMING A STAR!
BUT IT SEEMS MY RUNNING OFF HAS MADE MY FAMILY RESORT TO DESPERATE MEASURES. I REALLY THINK THEY THOUGHT PUTTING ME IN THIS AD WOULD MAKE ME HAPPY!
WHAT SICKOS THINK THAT WAY?!
NO YOU DON'T! I COULDN'T BEAR IF ANYONE I KNEW SAW IT!
OH, THE SHAME OF IT ALL!

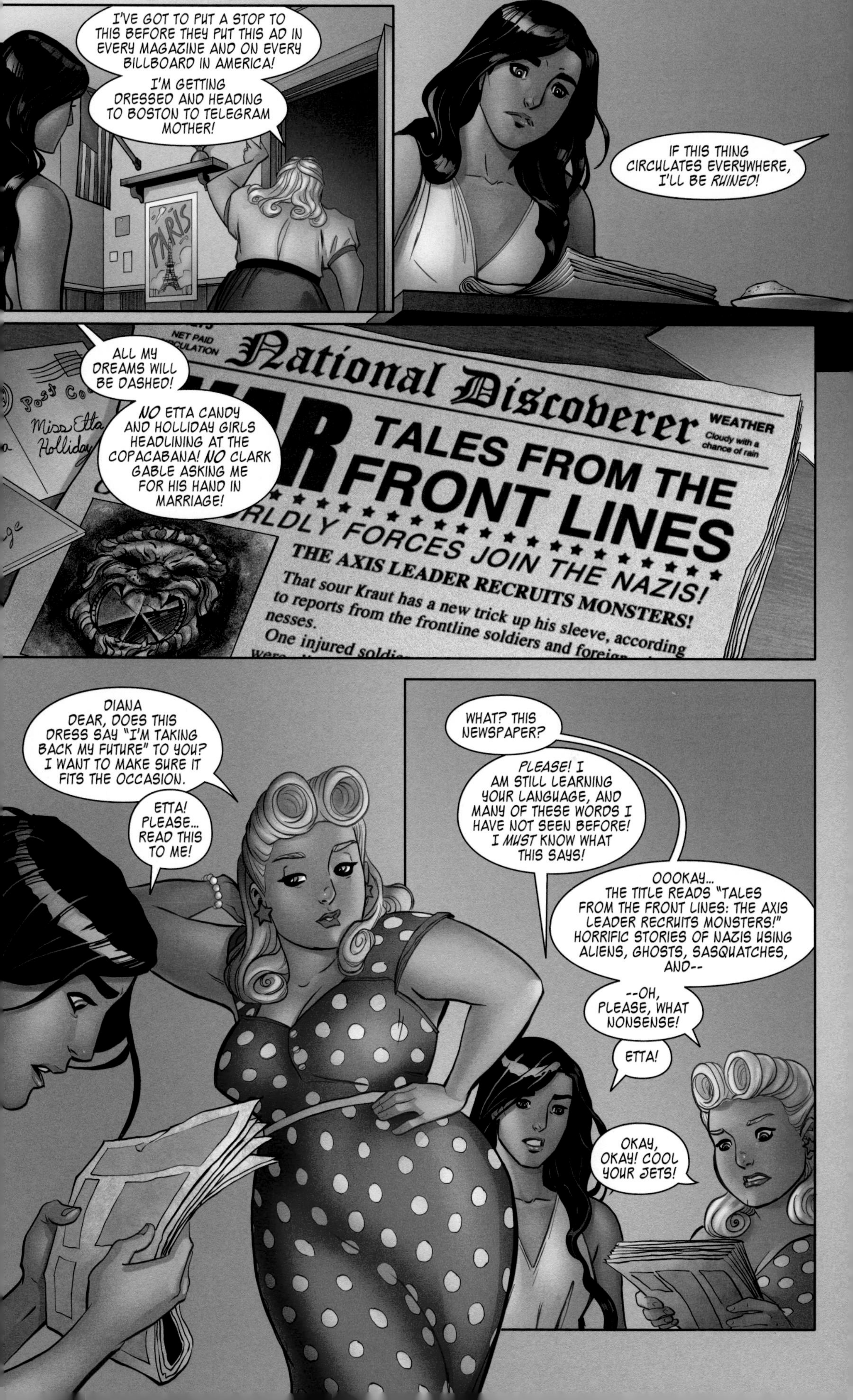
I'VE GOT TO PUT A STOP TO THIS BEFORE THEY PUT THIS AD IN EVERY MAGAZINE AND ON EVERY BILLBOARD IN AMERICA!
I'M GETTING DRESSED AND HEADING TO BOSTON TO TELEGRAM MOTHER!
IF THIS THING CIRCULATES EVERYWHERE, I'LL BE RUINED!
ALL MY DREAMS WILL BE DASHED!
NO ETTA CANDY AND HOLLIDAY GIRLS HEADLINING AT THE COPACABANA! NO CLARK GABLE ASKING ME FOR HIS HAND IN MARRIAGE!
Post Card
Miss Etta Holliday
NET PAID CIRCULATION
National Discoverer
WEATHER
Cloudy with a chance of rain
TALES FROM THE FRONT LINES
ORLDLY FORCES JOIN THE NAZIS!
THE AXIS LEADER RECRUITS MONSTERS!
That sour Kraut has a new trick up his sleeve, according to reports from the frontline soldiers and foreign
nesses.
One injured soldi
DIANA DEAR, DOES THIS DRESS SAY "I'M TAKING BACK MY FUTURE" TO YOU? I WANT TO MAKE SURE IT FITS THE OCCASION.
ETTA! PLEASE... READ THIS TO ME!
WHAT? THIS NEWSPAPER?
PLEASE! I AM STILL LEARNING YOUR LANGUAGE, AND MANY OF THESE WORDS I HAVE NOT SEEN BEFORE! I MUST KNOW WHAT THIS SAYS!
OOOKAY... THE TITLE READS "TALES FROM THE FRONT LINES: THE AXIS LEADER RECRUITS MONSTERS!" HORRIFIC STORIES OF NAZIS USING ALIENS, GHOSTS, SASQUATCHES, AND--
--OH, PLEASE, WHAT NONSENSE!
ETTA!
OKAY, OKAY! COOL YOUR JETS!

"TALES FROM THE FRONT LINES: THE AXIS LEADER RECRUITS MONSTERS! THAT SOUR KRAUT HAS A NEW TRICK UP HIS SLEEVE, ACCORDING TO REPORTS FROM FRONTLINE SOLDIERS AND FOREIGN WITNESSES.

"ONE INJURED SOLDIER SOUTH OF KIEV SPOKE FRANKLY, 'THERE WERE ALIENS COMING DOWN OUT OF THE CLOUDS WITH NAZI INSIGNIA ON THEIR FLYING SAUCERS. BEFORE I KNEW IT WE WERE BLOWN AWAY BY THEIR RAY GUNS!'"

OH, BROTHER!

"ANOTHER REPORT COMES FROM AN AMERICAN COMBAT PHOTOGRAPHER WHO TELLS OF NAZI SASQUATCH ATTACKS AT THE SEVASTAPOL PORT ON THE BLACK SEA ON ALLIED FORCES, WHO MYSTERIOUSLY DISAPPEARED MID-BATTLE. AS WE KNOW, THAT BATTLE WAS WON BY THE ALLIES, BUT WOULD IT HAVE BEEN IF THE BIGFOOT BRIGADE HAD REMAINED?

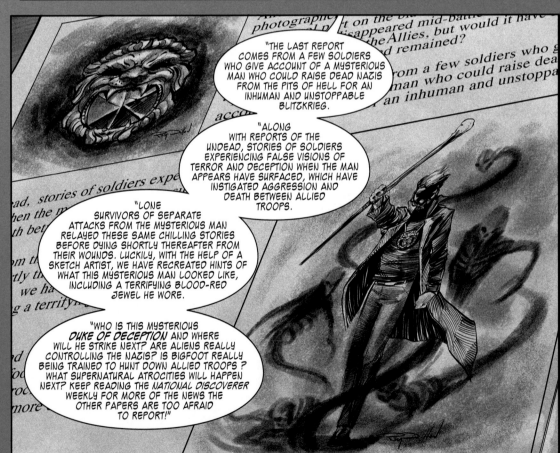

"THE LAST REPORT COMES FROM A FEW SOLDIERS WHO GIVE ACCOUNT OF A MYSTERIOUS MAN WHO COULD RAISE DEAD NAZIS FROM THE PITS OF HELL FOR AN INHUMAN AND UNSTOPPABLE BLITZKRIEG.

"ALONG WITH REPORTS OF THE UNDEAD, STORIES OF SOLDIERS EXPERIENCING FALSE VISIONS OF TERROR AND DECEPTION WHEN THE MAN APPEARS HAVE SURFACED, WHICH HAVE INSTIGATED AGGRESSION AND DEATH BETWEEN ALLIED TROOPS.

"LONE SURVIVORS OF SEPARATE ATTACKS FROM THE MYSTERIOUS MAN RELAYED THESE SAME CHILLING STORIES BEFORE DYING SHORTLY THEREAFTER FROM THEIR WOUNDS. LUCKILY, WITH THE HELP OF A SKETCH ARTIST, WE HAVE RECREATED HINTS OF WHAT THIS MYSTERIOUS MAN LOOKED LIKE, INCLUDING A TERRIFYING BLOOD-RED JEWEL HE WORE.

"WHO IS THIS MYSTERIOUS *DUKE OF DECEPTION* AND WHERE WILL HE STRIKE NEXT? ARE ALIENS REALLY CONTROLLING THE NAZIS? IS BIGFOOT REALLY BEING TRAINED TO HUNT DOWN ALLIED TROOPS? WHAT SUPERNATURAL ATROCITIES WILL HAPPEN NEXT? KEEP READING THE *NATIONAL DISCOVERER* WEEKLY FOR MORE OF THE NEWS THE OTHER PAPERS ARE TOO AFRAID TO REPORT!"

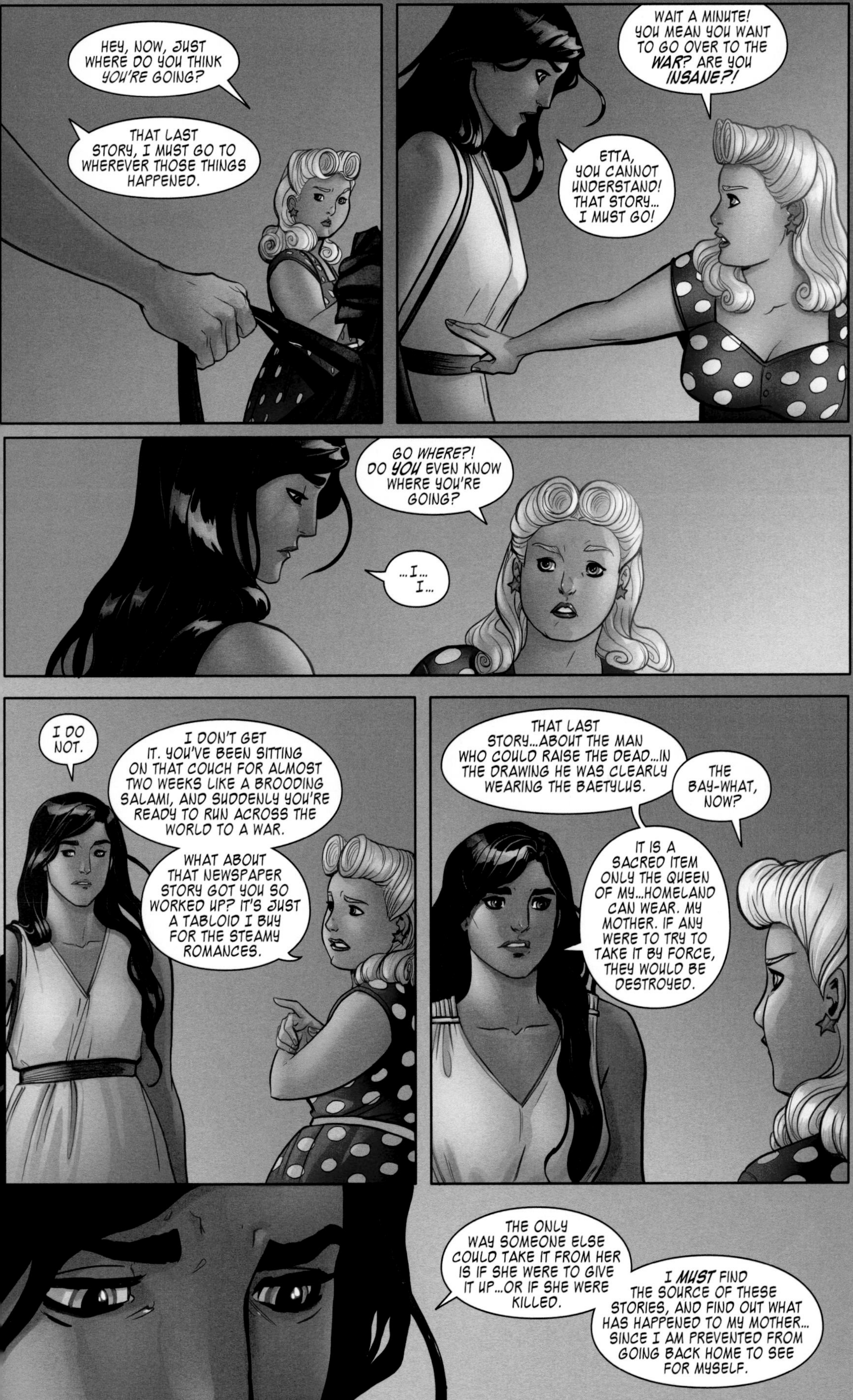
HEY, NOW, JUST WHERE DO YOU THINK YOU'RE GOING?
THAT LAST STORY, I MUST GO TO WHEREVER THOSE THINGS HAPPENED.
WAIT A MINUTE! YOU MEAN YOU WANT TO GO OVER TO THE WAR? ARE YOU INSANE?!
ETTA, YOU CANNOT UNDERSTAND! THAT STORY... I MUST GO!
GO WHERE?! DO YOU EVEN KNOW WHERE YOU'RE GOING?
...I... I...
I DO NOT.
I DON'T GET IT. YOU'VE BEEN SITTING ON THAT COUCH FOR ALMOST TWO WEEKS LIKE A BROODING SALAMI, AND SUDDENLY YOU'RE READY TO RUN ACROSS THE WORLD TO A WAR.
WHAT ABOUT THAT NEWSPAPER STORY GOT YOU SO WORKED UP? IT'S JUST A TABLOID I BUY FOR THE STEAMY ROMANCES.
THAT LAST STORY...ABOUT THE MAN WHO COULD RAISE THE DEAD...IN THE DRAWING HE WAS CLEARLY WEARING THE BAETYLUS.
THE BAY-WHAT, NOW?
IT IS A SACRED ITEM ONLY THE QUEEN OF MY...HOMELAND CAN WEAR. MY MOTHER. IF ANY WERE TO TRY TO TAKE IT BY FORCE, THEY WOULD BE DESTROYED.
THE ONLY WAY SOMEONE ELSE COULD TAKE IT FROM HER IS IF SHE WERE TO GIVE IT UP...OR IF SHE WERE KILLED.
I MUST FIND THE SOURCE OF THESE STORIES, AND FIND OUT WHAT HAS HAPPENED TO MY MOTHER... SINCE I AM PREVENTED FROM GOING BACK HOME TO SEE FOR MYSELF.

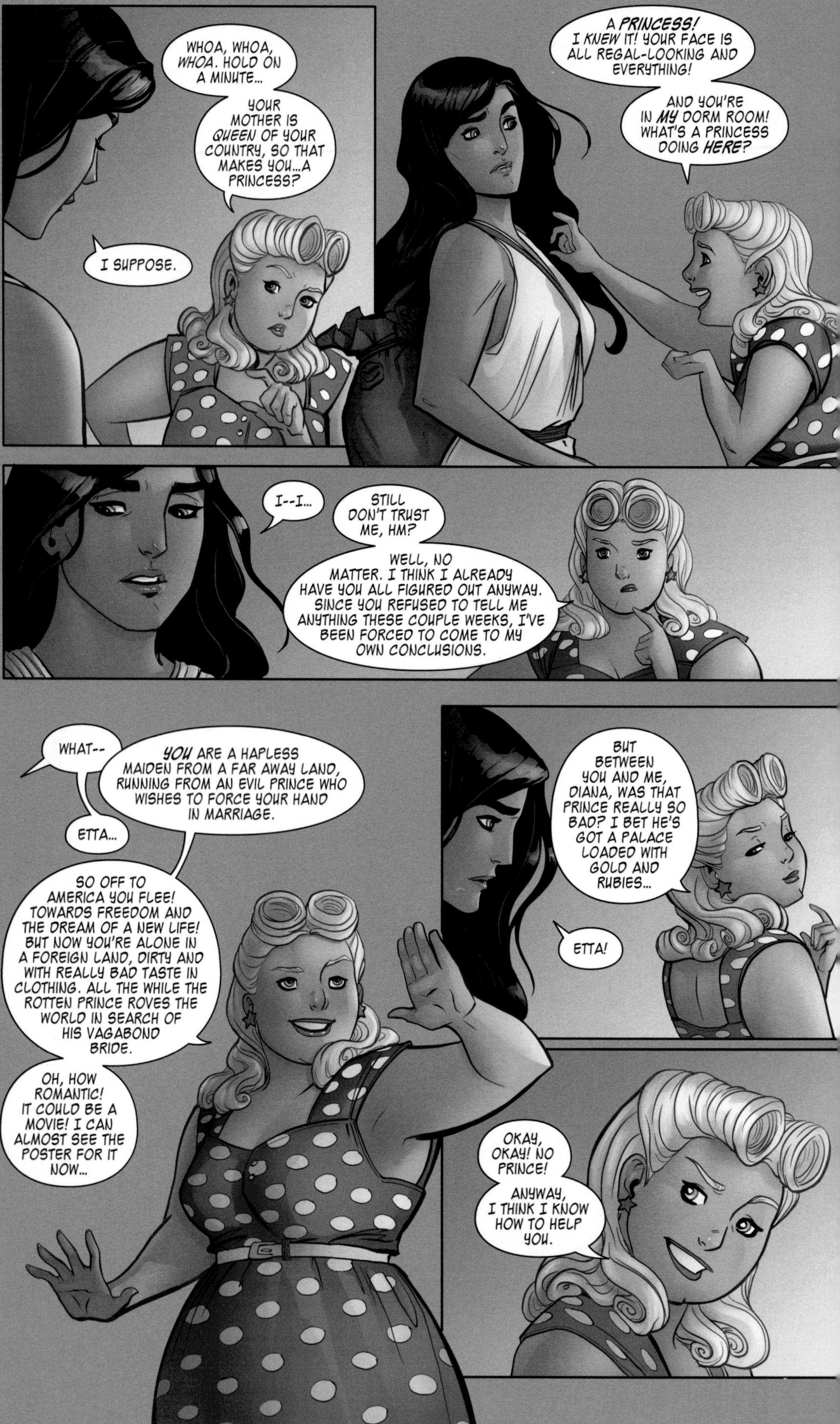
WHOA, WHOA, WHOA. HOLD ON A MINUTE...
YOUR MOTHER IS QUEEN OF YOUR COUNTRY, SO THAT MAKES YOU...A PRINCESS?
I SUPPOSE.
A PRINCESS! I KNEW IT! YOUR FACE IS ALL REGAL-LOOKING AND EVERYTHING!
AND YOU'RE IN MY DORM ROOM! WHAT'S A PRINCESS DOING HERE?
I--I...
STILL DON'T TRUST ME, HM?
WELL, NO MATTER. I THINK I ALREADY HAVE YOU ALL FIGURED OUT ANYWAY. SINCE YOU REFUSED TO TELL ME ANYTHING THESE COUPLE WEEKS, I'VE BEEN FORCED TO COME TO MY OWN CONCLUSIONS.
WHAT--
YOU ARE A HAPLESS MAIDEN FROM A FAR AWAY LAND, RUNNING FROM AN EVIL PRINCE WHO WISHES TO FORCE YOUR HAND IN MARRIAGE.
ETTA...
SO OFF TO AMERICA YOU FLEE! TOWARDS FREEDOM AND THE DREAM OF A NEW LIFE! BUT NOW YOU'RE ALONE IN A FOREIGN LAND, DIRTY AND WITH REALLY BAD TASTE IN CLOTHING. ALL THE WHILE THE ROTTEN PRINCE ROVES THE WORLD IN SEARCH OF HIS VAGABOND BRIDE.
OH, HOW ROMANTIC! IT COULD BE A MOVIE! I CAN ALMOST SEE THE POSTER FOR IT NOW...
BUT BETWEEN YOU AND ME, DIANA, WAS THAT PRINCE REALLY SO BAD? I BET HE'S GOT A PALACE LOADED WITH GOLD AND RUBIES...
ETTA!
OKAY, OKAY! NO PRINCE!
ANYWAY, I THINK I KNOW HOW TO HELP YOU.

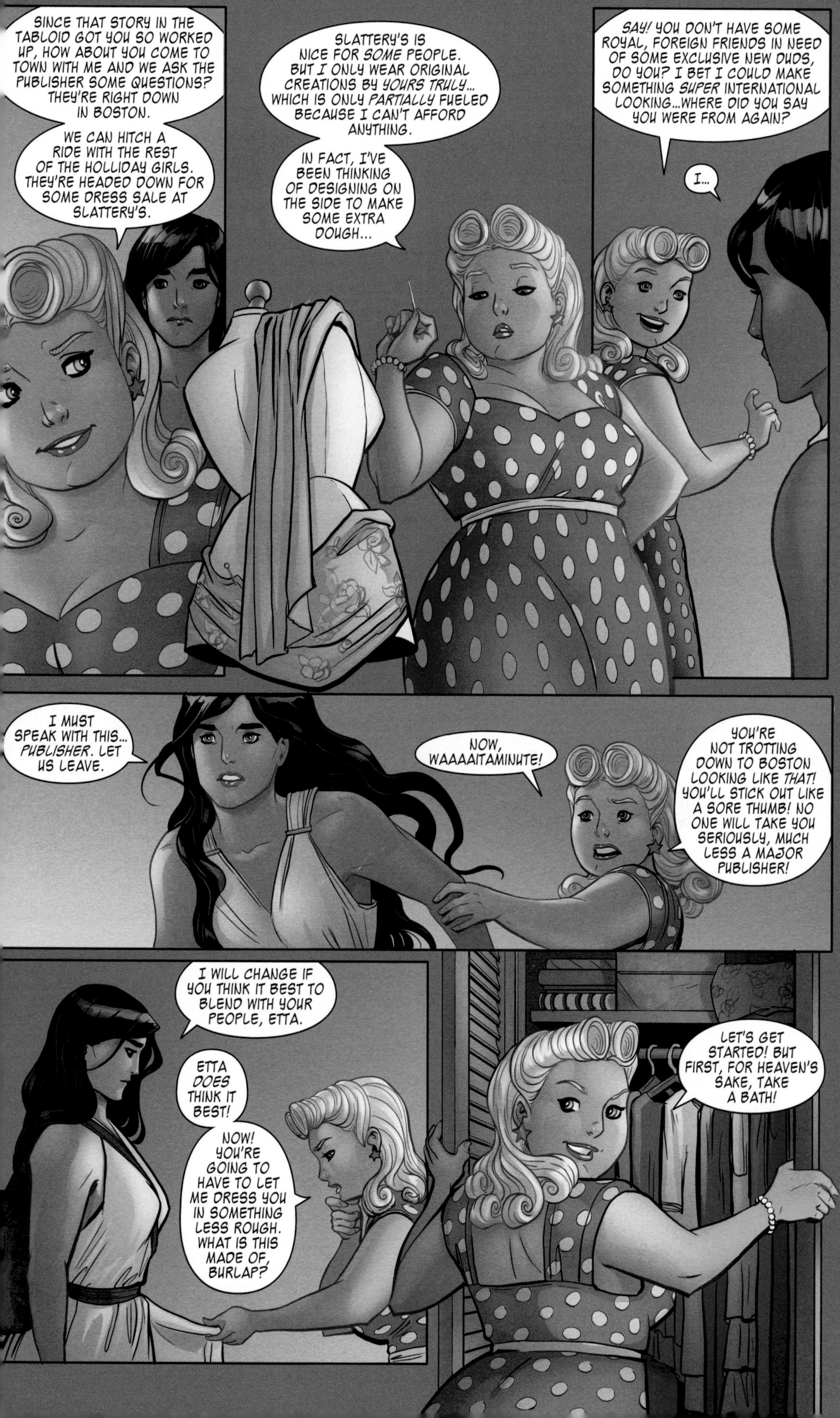
SINCE THAT STORY IN THE TABLOID GOT YOU SO WORKED UP, HOW ABOUT YOU COME TO TOWN WITH ME AND WE ASK THE PUBLISHER SOME QUESTIONS? THEY'RE RIGHT DOWN IN BOSTON.
WE CAN HITCH A RIDE WITH THE REST OF THE HOLLIDAY GIRLS. THEY'RE HEADED DOWN FOR SOME DRESS SALE AT SLATTERY'S.
SLATTERY'S IS NICE FOR *SOME* PEOPLE. BUT *I* ONLY WEAR ORIGINAL CREATIONS BY *YOURS TRULY*... WHICH IS ONLY *PARTIALLY* FUELED BECAUSE I CAN'T AFFORD ANYTHING.
IN FACT, I'VE BEEN THINKING OF DESIGNING ON THE SIDE TO MAKE SOME EXTRA DOUGH...
SAY! YOU DON'T HAVE SOME ROYAL, FOREIGN FRIENDS IN NEED OF SOME EXCLUSIVE NEW DUDS, DO YOU? I BET I COULD MAKE SOMETHING *SUPER* INTERNATIONAL LOOKING...WHERE DID YOU SAY YOU WERE FROM AGAIN?
I...
I MUST SPEAK WITH THIS... *PUBLISHER*. LET US LEAVE.
NOW, WAAAAITAMINUTE!
YOU'RE NOT TROTTING DOWN TO BOSTON LOOKING LIKE *THAT!* YOU'LL STICK OUT LIKE A SORE THUMB! NO ONE WILL TAKE YOU SERIOUSLY, MUCH LESS A MAJOR PUBLISHER!
I WILL CHANGE IF YOU THINK IT BEST TO BLEND WITH YOUR PEOPLE, ETTA.
ETTA *DOES* THINK IT BEST!
NOW! YOU'RE GOING TO HAVE TO LET ME DRESS YOU IN SOMETHING LESS ROUGH. WHAT IS THIS MADE OF, BURLAP?
LET'S GET STARTED! BUT FIRST, FOR HEAVEN'S SAKE, TAKE A BATH!

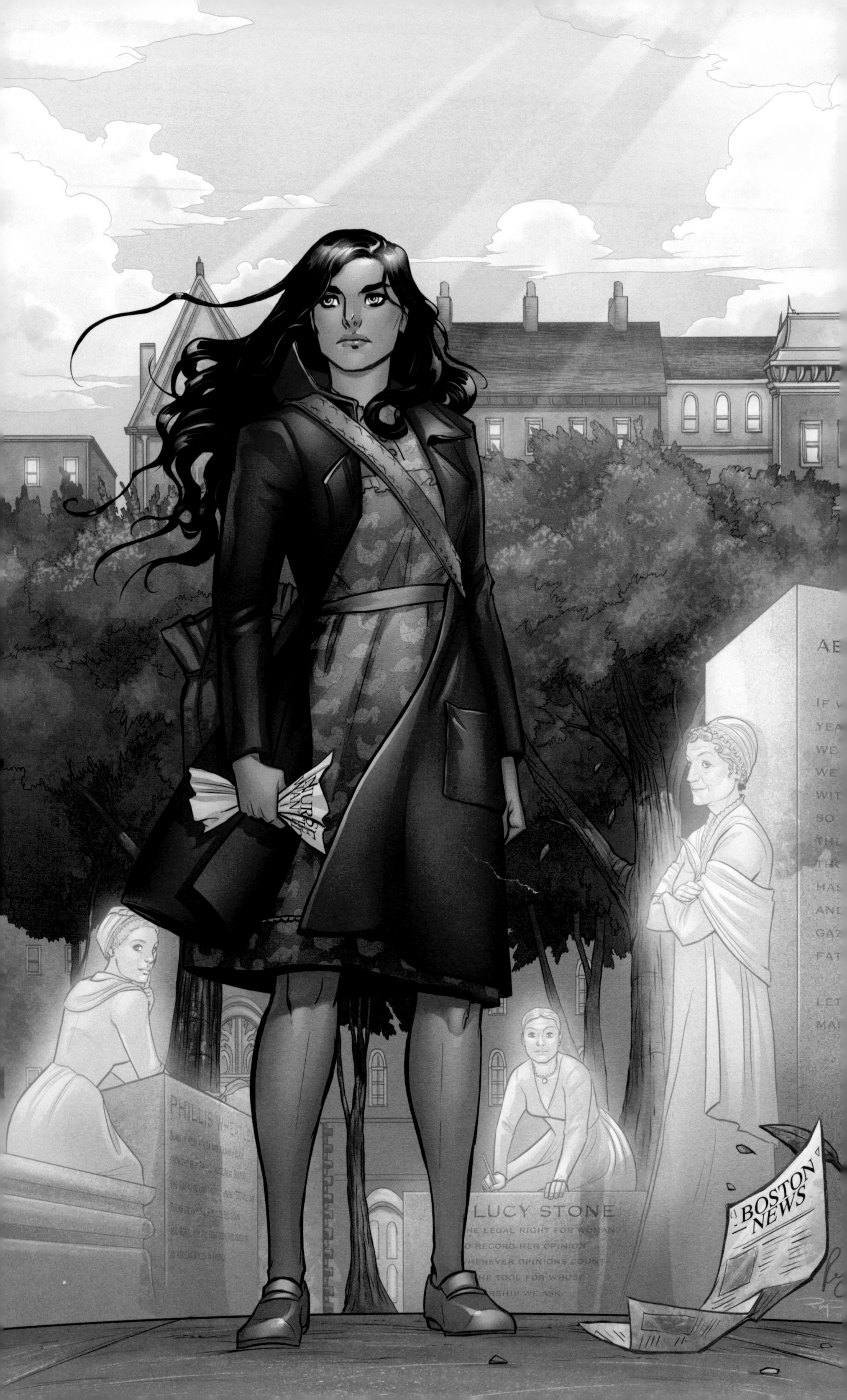
LUCY STONE
BOSTON NEWS

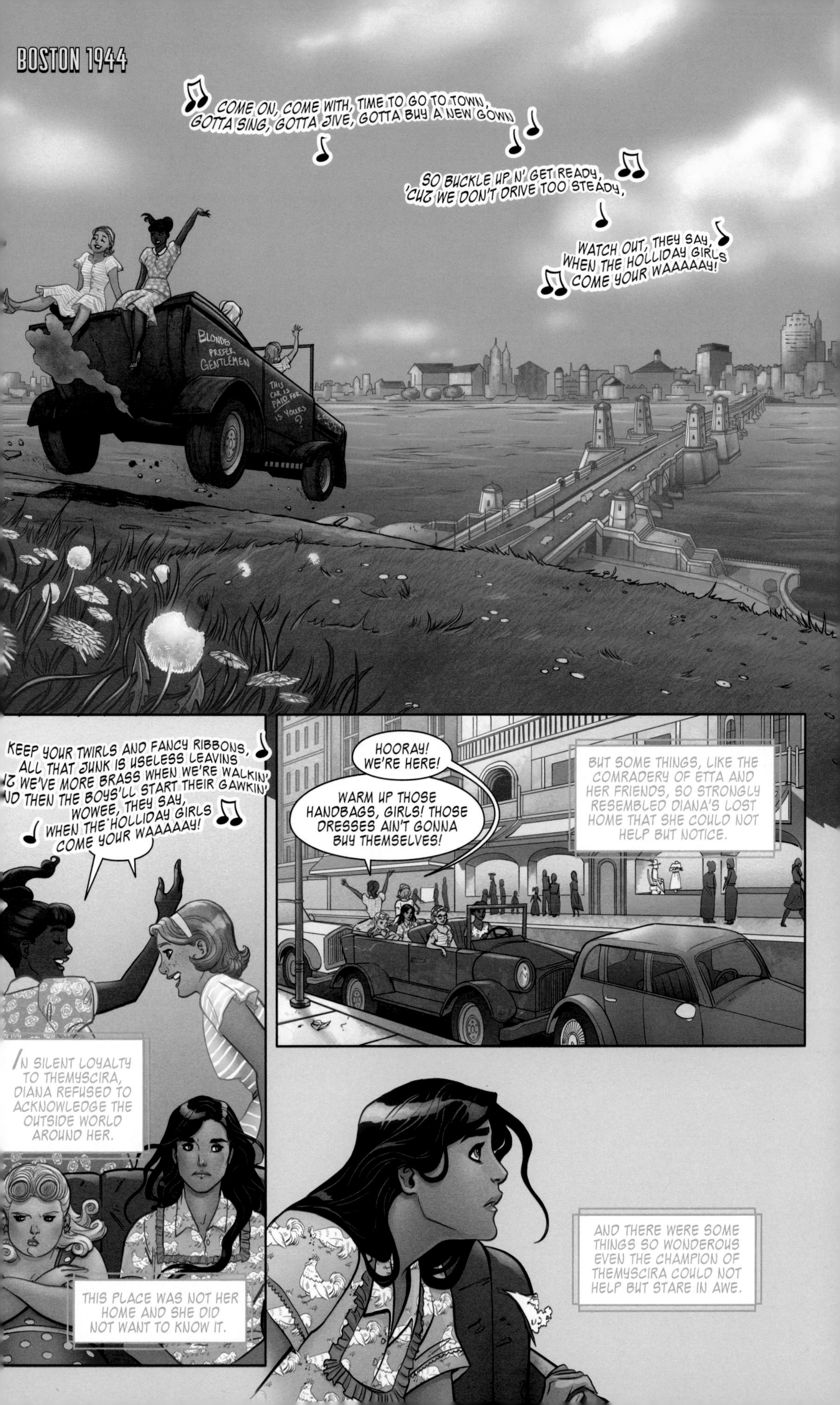
BOSTON 1944
COME ON, COME WITH, TIME TO GO TO TOWN, GOTTA SING, GOTTA JIVE, GOTTA BUY A NEW GOWN
SO BUCKLE UP N' GET READY, 'CUZ WE DON'T DRIVE TOO STEADY,
WATCH OUT, THEY SAY, WHEN THE HOLLIDAY GIRLS COME YOUR WAAAAAY!
BLONDES PREFER GENTLEMEN
THIS CAR IS PAID FOR IS YOURS?
KEEP YOUR TWIRLS AND FANCY RIBBONS, ALL THAT JUNK IS USELESS LEAVINS
'Z WE'VE MORE BRASS WHEN WE'RE WALKIN'
ND THEN THE BOYS'LL START THEIR GAWKIN'
WOWEE, THEY SAY, WHEN THE HOLLIDAY GIRLS COME YOUR WAAAAAY!
HOORAY! WE'RE HERE!
WARM UP THOSE HANDBAGS, GIRLS! THOSE DRESSES AIN'T GONNA BUY THEMSELVES!
BUT SOME THINGS, LIKE THE COMRADERY OF ETTA AND HER FRIENDS, SO STRONGLY RESEMBLED DIANA'S LOST HOME THAT SHE COULD NOT HELP BUT NOTICE.
IN SILENT LOYALTY TO THEMYSCIRA, DIANA REFUSED TO ACKNOWLEDGE THE OUTSIDE WORLD AROUND HER.
THIS PLACE WAS NOT HER HOME AND SHE DID NOT WANT TO KNOW IT.
AND THERE WERE SOME THINGS SO WONDEROUS EVEN THE CHAMPION OF THEMYSCIRA COULD NOT HELP BUT STARE IN AWE.

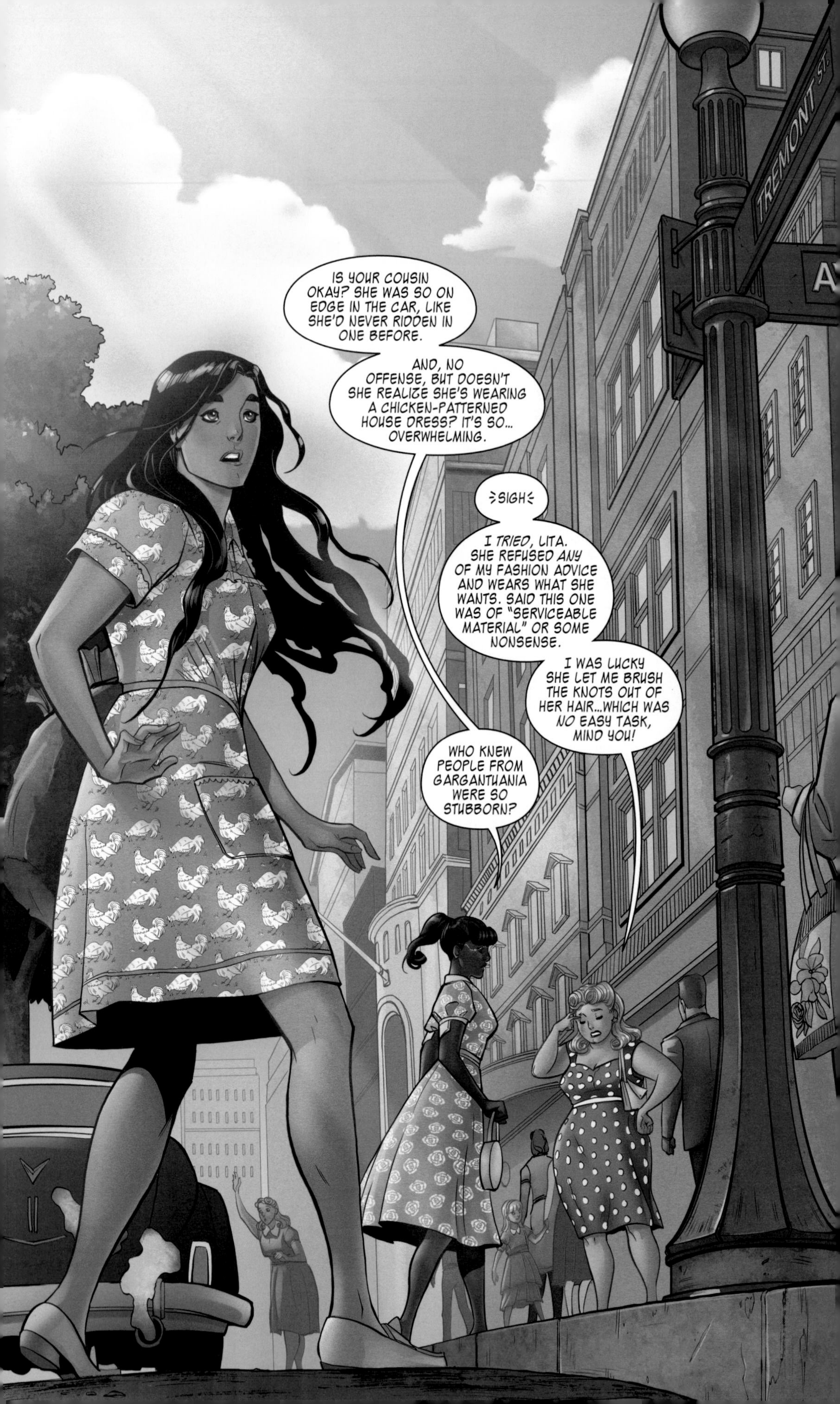
TREMONT ST.
IS YOUR COUSIN OKAY? SHE WAS SO ON EDGE IN THE CAR, LIKE SHE'D NEVER RIDDEN IN ONE BEFORE.
AND, NO OFFENSE, BUT DOESN'T SHE REALIZE SHE'S WEARING A CHICKEN-PATTERNED HOUSE DRESS? IT'S SO... OVERWHELMING.
SIGH
I *TRIED*, LITA. SHE REFUSED *ANY* OF MY FASHION ADVICE AND WEARS WHAT SHE WANTS. SAID THIS ONE WAS OF "SERVICEABLE MATERIAL" OR SOME NONSENSE.
I WAS LUCKY SHE LET ME BRUSH THE KNOTS OUT OF HER HAIR...WHICH WAS *NO* EASY TASK, MIND YOU!
WHO KNEW PEOPLE FROM GARGANTUANIA WERE SO STUBBORN?

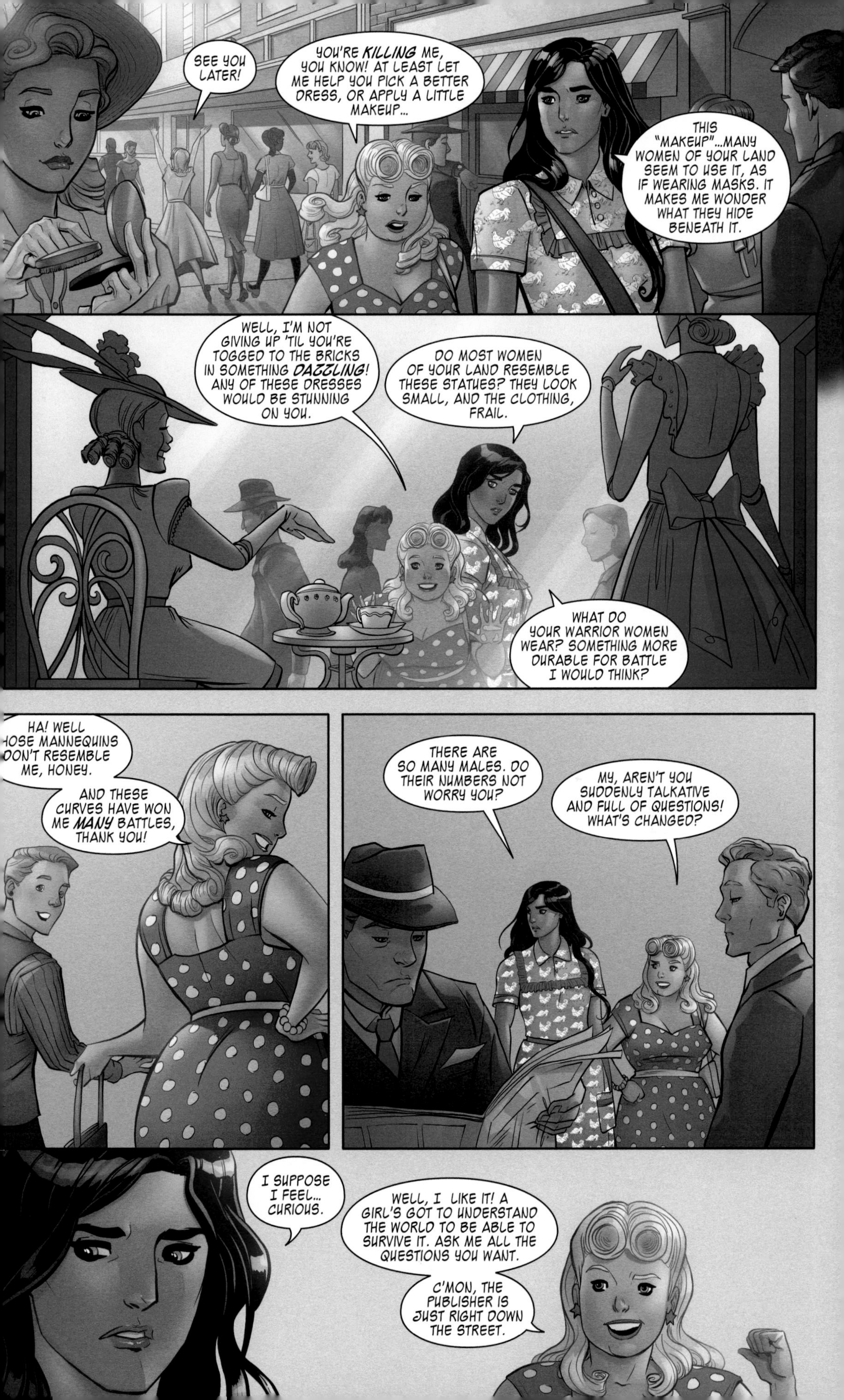
SEE YOU LATER!
YOU'RE KILLING ME, YOU KNOW! AT LEAST LET ME HELP YOU PICK A BETTER DRESS, OR APPLY A LITTLE MAKEUP...
THIS "MAKEUP"...MANY WOMEN OF YOUR LAND SEEM TO USE IT, AS IF WEARING MASKS. IT MAKES ME WONDER WHAT THEY HIDE BENEATH IT.
WELL, I'M NOT GIVING UP 'TIL YOU'RE TOGGED TO THE BRICKS IN SOMETHING DAZZLING! ANY OF THESE DRESSES WOULD BE STUNNING ON YOU.
DO MOST WOMEN OF YOUR LAND RESEMBLE THESE STATUES? THEY LOOK SMALL, AND THE CLOTHING, FRAIL.
WHAT DO YOUR WARRIOR WOMEN WEAR? SOMETHING MORE DURABLE FOR BATTLE I WOULD THINK?
HA! WELL HOSE MANNEQUINS DON'T RESEMBLE ME, HONEY.
AND THESE CURVES HAVE WON ME MANY BATTLES, THANK YOU!
THERE ARE SO MANY MALES. DO THEIR NUMBERS NOT WORRY YOU?
MY, AREN'T YOU SUDDENLY TALKATIVE AND FULL OF QUESTIONS! WHAT'S CHANGED?
I SUPPOSE I FEEL... CURIOUS.
WELL, I LIKE IT! A GIRL'S GOT TO UNDERSTAND THE WORLD TO BE ABLE TO SURVIVE IT. ASK ME ALL THE QUESTIONS YOU WANT.
C'MON, THE PUBLISHER IS JUST RIGHT DOWN THE STREET.

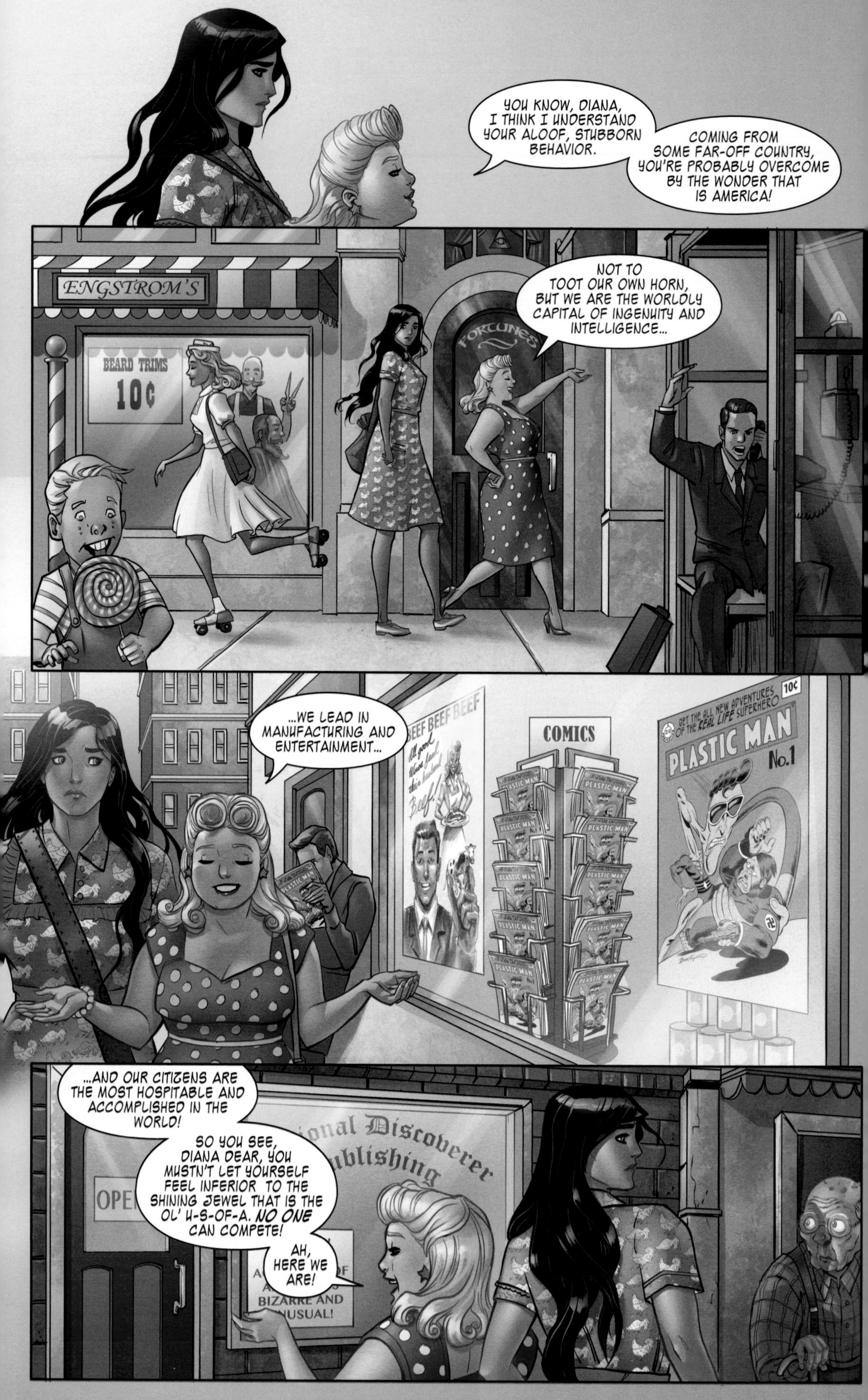
YOU KNOW, DIANA, I THINK I UNDERSTAND YOUR ALOOF, STUBBORN BEHAVIOR.
COMING FROM SOME FAR-OFF COUNTRY, YOU'RE PROBABLY OVERCOME BY THE WONDER THAT IS AMERICA!
ENGSTROM'S
BEARD TRIMS
10¢
FORTUNES
NOT TO TOOT OUR OWN HORN, BUT WE ARE THE WORLDLY CAPITAL OF INGENUITY AND INTELLIGENCE...
...WE LEAD IN MANUFACTURING AND ENTERTAINMENT...
BEEF BEEF BEEF
COMICS
10¢
GET THE ALL NEW ADVENTURES OF THE REAL LIFE SUPERHERO
PLASTIC MAN
No.1
...AND OUR CITIZENS ARE THE MOST HOSPITABLE AND ACCOMPLISHED IN THE WORLD!
SO YOU SEE, DIANA DEAR, YOU MUSTN'T LET YOURSELF FEEL INFERIOR TO THE SHINING JEWEL THAT IS THE OL' U-S-OF-A. *NO ONE* CAN COMPETE!
AH, HERE WE ARE!
BIZARRE AND

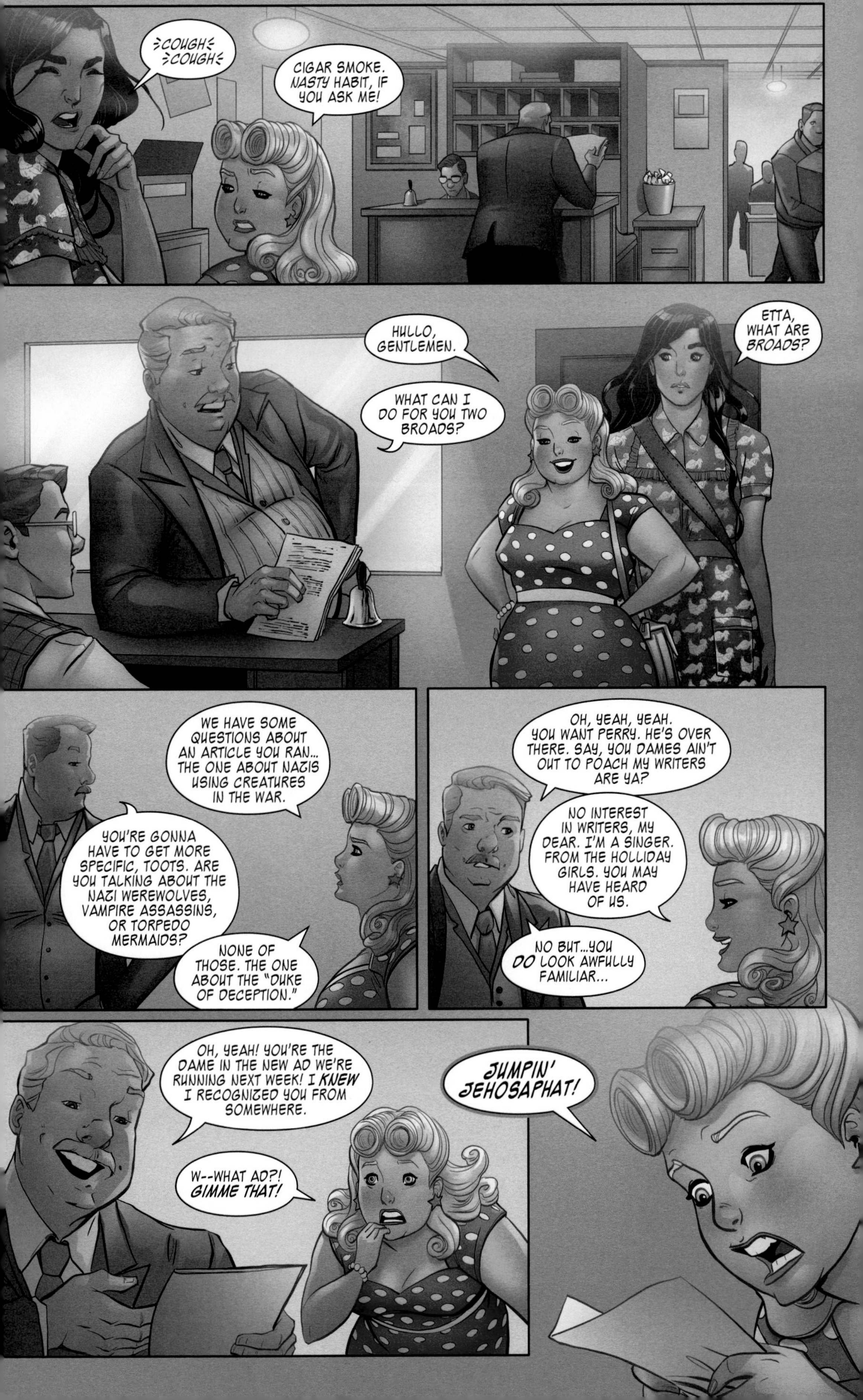

>COUGH< >COUGH<
CIGAR SMOKE. NASTY HABIT, IF YOU ASK ME!
HULLO, GENTLEMEN.
WHAT CAN I DO FOR YOU TWO BROADS?
ETTA, WHAT ARE BROADS?
WE HAVE SOME QUESTIONS ABOUT AN ARTICLE YOU RAN... THE ONE ABOUT NAZIS USING CREATURES IN THE WAR.
YOU'RE GONNA HAVE TO GET MORE SPECIFIC, TOOTS. ARE YOU TALKING ABOUT THE NAZI WEREWOLVES, VAMPIRE ASSASSINS, OR TORPEDO MERMAIDS?
NONE OF THOSE. THE ONE ABOUT THE "DUKE OF DECEPTION."
OH, YEAH, YEAH. YOU WANT PERRY. HE'S OVER THERE. SAY, YOU DAMES AIN'T OUT TO POACH MY WRITERS ARE YA?
NO INTEREST IN WRITERS, MY DEAR. I'M A SINGER. FROM THE HOLLIDAY GIRLS. YOU MAY HAVE HEARD OF US.
NO BUT...YOU DO LOOK AWFULLY FAMILIAR...
OH, YEAH! YOU'RE THE DAME IN THE NEW AD WE'RE RUNNING NEXT WEEK! I KNEW I RECOGNIZED YOU FROM SOMEWHERE.
W--WHAT AD?! GIMME THAT!
JUMPIN' JEHOSAPHAT!

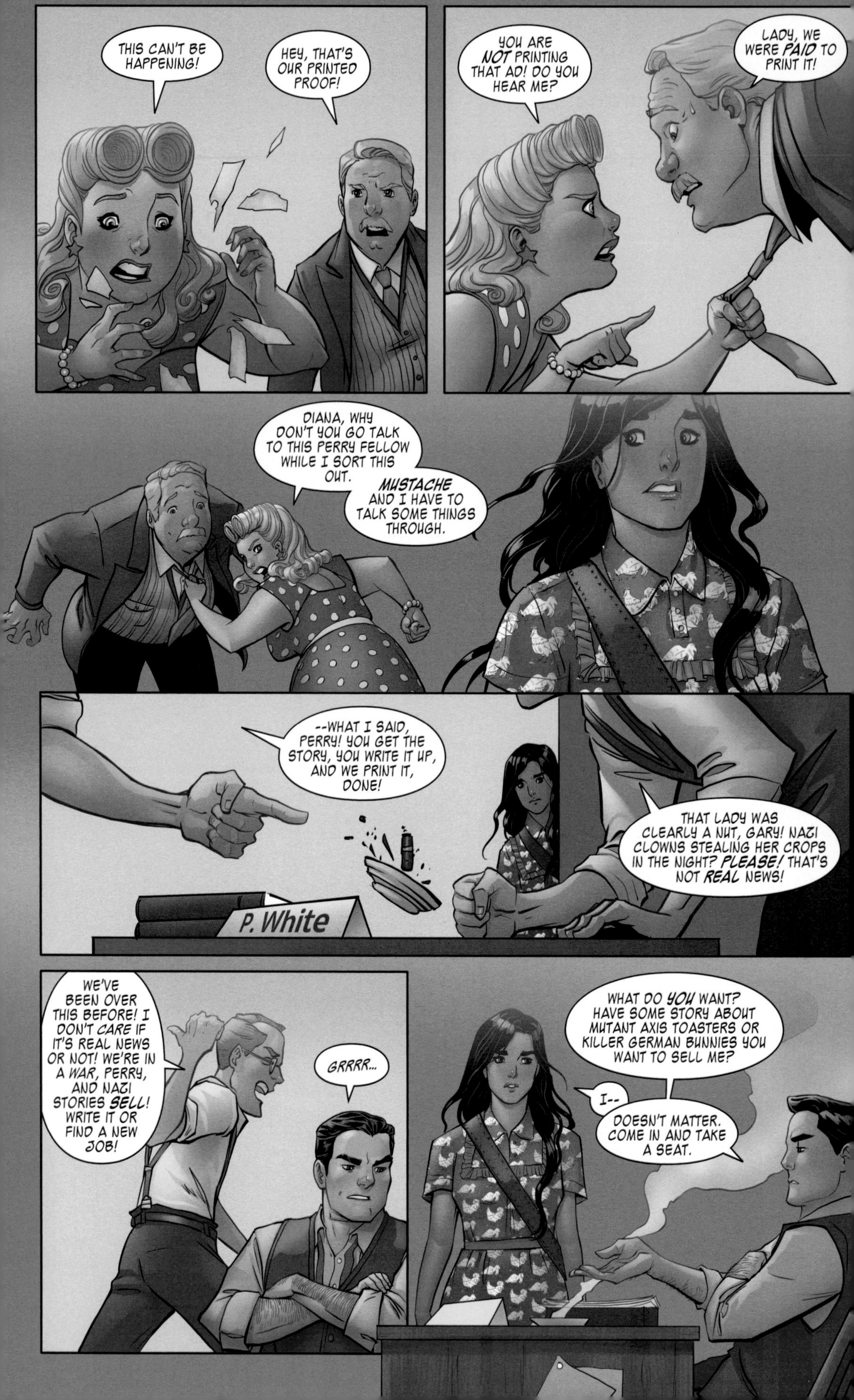

THIS CAN'T BE HAPPENING!
HEY, THAT'S OUR PRINTED PROOF!
YOU ARE NOT PRINTING THAT AD! DO YOU HEAR ME?
LADY, WE WERE PAID TO PRINT IT!
DIANA, WHY DON'T YOU GO TALK TO THIS PERRY FELLOW WHILE I SORT THIS OUT.
MUSTACHE AND I HAVE TO TALK SOME THINGS THROUGH.
--WHAT I SAID, PERRY! YOU GET THE STORY, YOU WRITE IT UP, AND WE PRINT IT, DONE!
THAT LADY WAS CLEARLY A NUT, GARY! NAZI CLOWNS STEALING HER CROPS IN THE NIGHT? PLEASE! THAT'S NOT REAL NEWS!
P. White
WE'VE BEEN OVER THIS BEFORE! I DON'T CARE IF IT'S REAL NEWS OR NOT! WE'RE IN A WAR, PERRY, AND NAZI STORIES SELL! WRITE IT OR FIND A NEW JOB!
GRRRR...
WHAT DO YOU WANT? HAVE SOME STORY ABOUT MUTANT AXIS TOASTERS OR KILLER GERMAN BUNNIES YOU WANT TO SELL ME?
I--
DOESN'T MATTER. COME IN AND TAKE A SEAT.

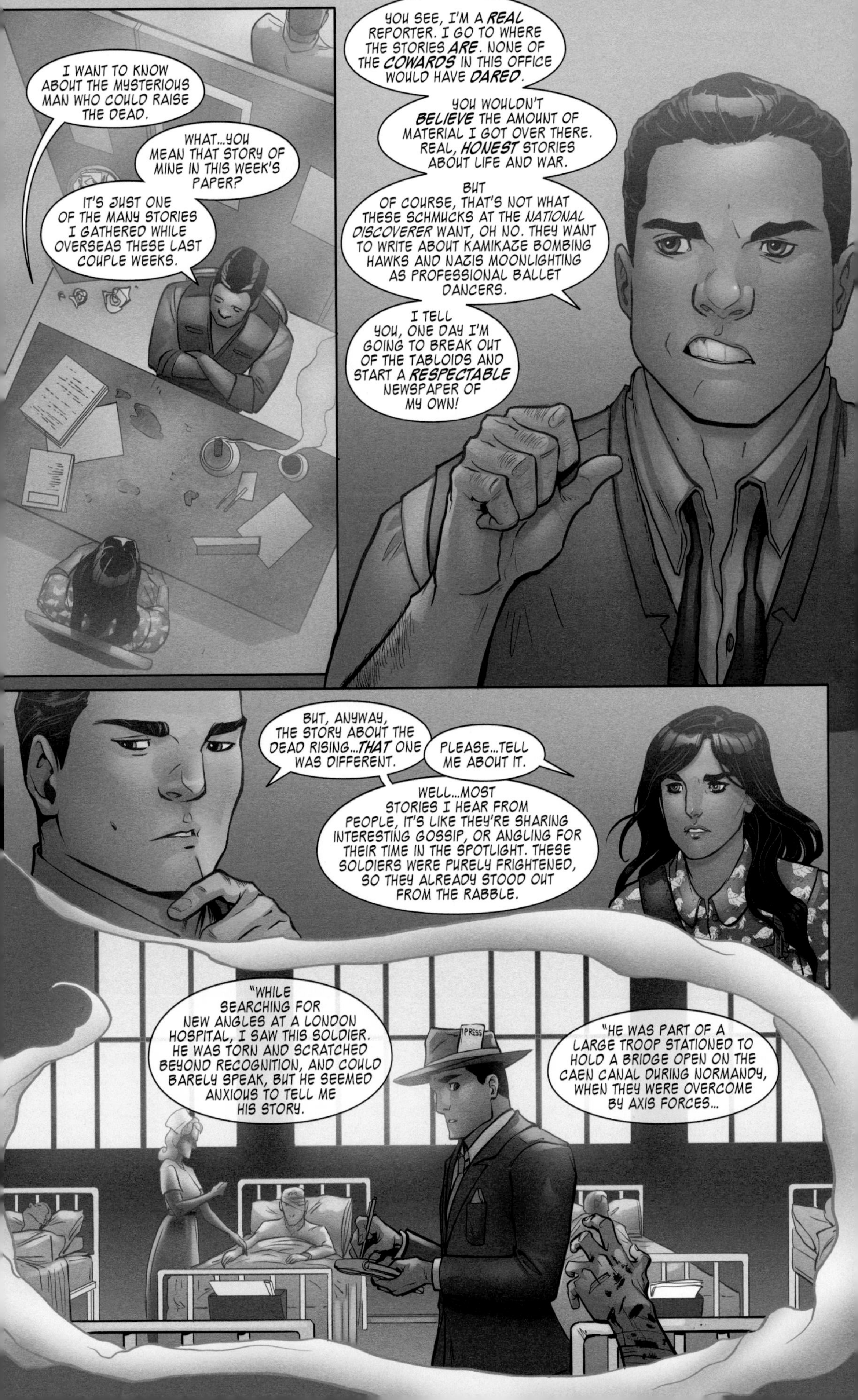

I WANT TO KNOW ABOUT THE MYSTERIOUS MAN WHO COULD RAISE THE DEAD.
WHAT...YOU MEAN THAT STORY OF MINE IN THIS WEEK'S PAPER?
IT'S JUST ONE OF THE MANY STORIES I GATHERED WHILE OVERSEAS THESE LAST COUPLE WEEKS.
YOU SEE, I'M A REAL REPORTER. I GO TO WHERE THE STORIES ARE. NONE OF THE COWARDS IN THIS OFFICE WOULD HAVE DARED.
YOU WOULDN'T BELIEVE THE AMOUNT OF MATERIAL I GOT OVER THERE. REAL, HONEST STORIES ABOUT LIFE AND WAR.
BUT OF COURSE, THAT'S NOT WHAT THESE SCHMUCKS AT THE NATIONAL DISCOVERER WANT, OH NO. THEY WANT TO WRITE ABOUT KAMIKAZE BOMBING HAWKS AND NAZIS MOONLIGHTING AS PROFESSIONAL BALLET DANCERS.
I TELL YOU, ONE DAY I'M GOING TO BREAK OUT OF THE TABLOIDS AND START A RESPECTABLE NEWSPAPER OF MY OWN!
BUT, ANYWAY, THE STORY ABOUT THE DEAD RISING...THAT ONE WAS DIFFERENT.
PLEASE...TELL ME ABOUT IT.
WELL...MOST STORIES I HEAR FROM PEOPLE, IT'S LIKE THEY'RE SHARING INTERESTING GOSSIP, OR ANGLING FOR THEIR TIME IN THE SPOTLIGHT. THESE SOLDIERS WERE PURELY FRIGHTENED, SO THEY ALREADY STOOD OUT FROM THE RABBLE.
"WHILE SEARCHING FOR NEW ANGLES AT A LONDON HOSPITAL, I SAW THIS SOLDIER. HE WAS TORN AND SCRATCHED BEYOND RECOGNITION, AND COULD BARELY SPEAK, BUT HE SEEMED ANXIOUS TO TELL ME HIS STORY.
PRESS
"HE WAS PART OF A LARGE TROOP STATIONED TO HOLD A BRIDGE OPEN ON THE CAEN CANAL DURING NORMANDY, WHEN THEY WERE OVERCOME BY AXIS FORCES...

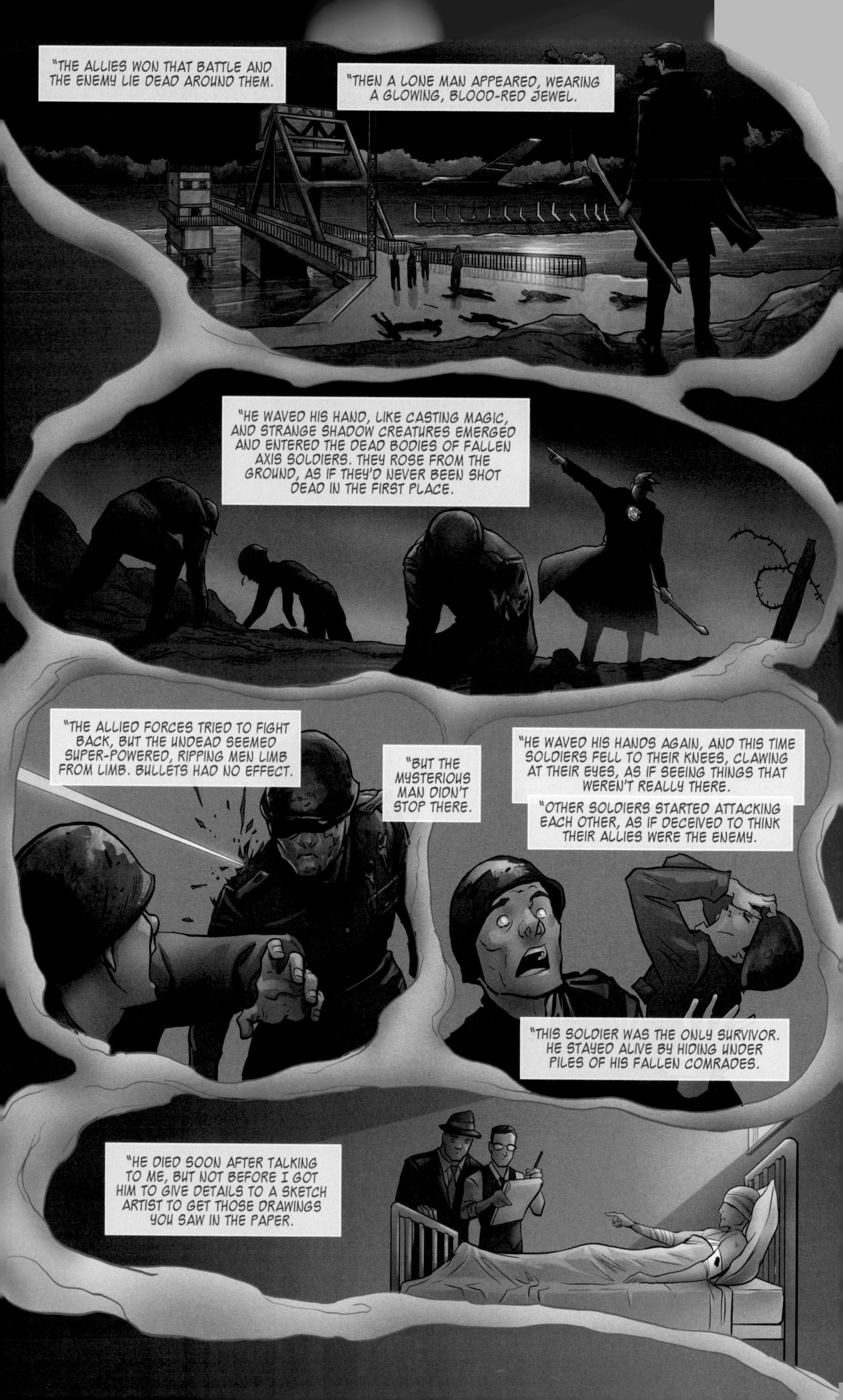
"THE ALLIES WON THAT BATTLE AND THE ENEMY LIE DEAD AROUND THEM.
"THEN A LONE MAN APPEARED, WEARING A GLOWING, BLOOD-RED JEWEL.
"HE WAVED HIS HAND, LIKE CASTING MAGIC, AND STRANGE SHADOW CREATURES EMERGED AND ENTERED THE DEAD BODIES OF FALLEN AXIS SOLDIERS. THEY ROSE FROM THE GROUND, AS IF THEY'D NEVER BEEN SHOT DEAD IN THE FIRST PLACE.
"THE ALLIED FORCES TRIED TO FIGHT BACK, BUT THE UNDEAD SEEMED SUPER-POWERED, RIPPING MEN LIMB FROM LIMB. BULLETS HAD NO EFFECT.
"BUT THE MYSTERIOUS MAN DIDN'T STOP THERE.
"HE WAVED HIS HANDS AGAIN, AND THIS TIME SOLDIERS FELL TO THEIR KNEES, CLAWING AT THEIR EYES, AS IF SEEING THINGS THAT WEREN'T REALLY THERE.
"OTHER SOLDIERS STARTED ATTACKING EACH OTHER, AS IF DECEIVED TO THINK THEIR ALLIES WERE THE ENEMY.
"THIS SOLDIER WAS THE ONLY SURVIVOR. HE STAYED ALIVE BY HIDING UNDER PILES OF HIS FALLEN COMRADES.
"HE DIED SOON AFTER TALKING TO ME, BUT NOT BEFORE I GOT HIM TO GIVE DETAILS TO A SKETCH ARTIST TO GET THOSE DRAWINGS YOU SAW IN THE PAPER.

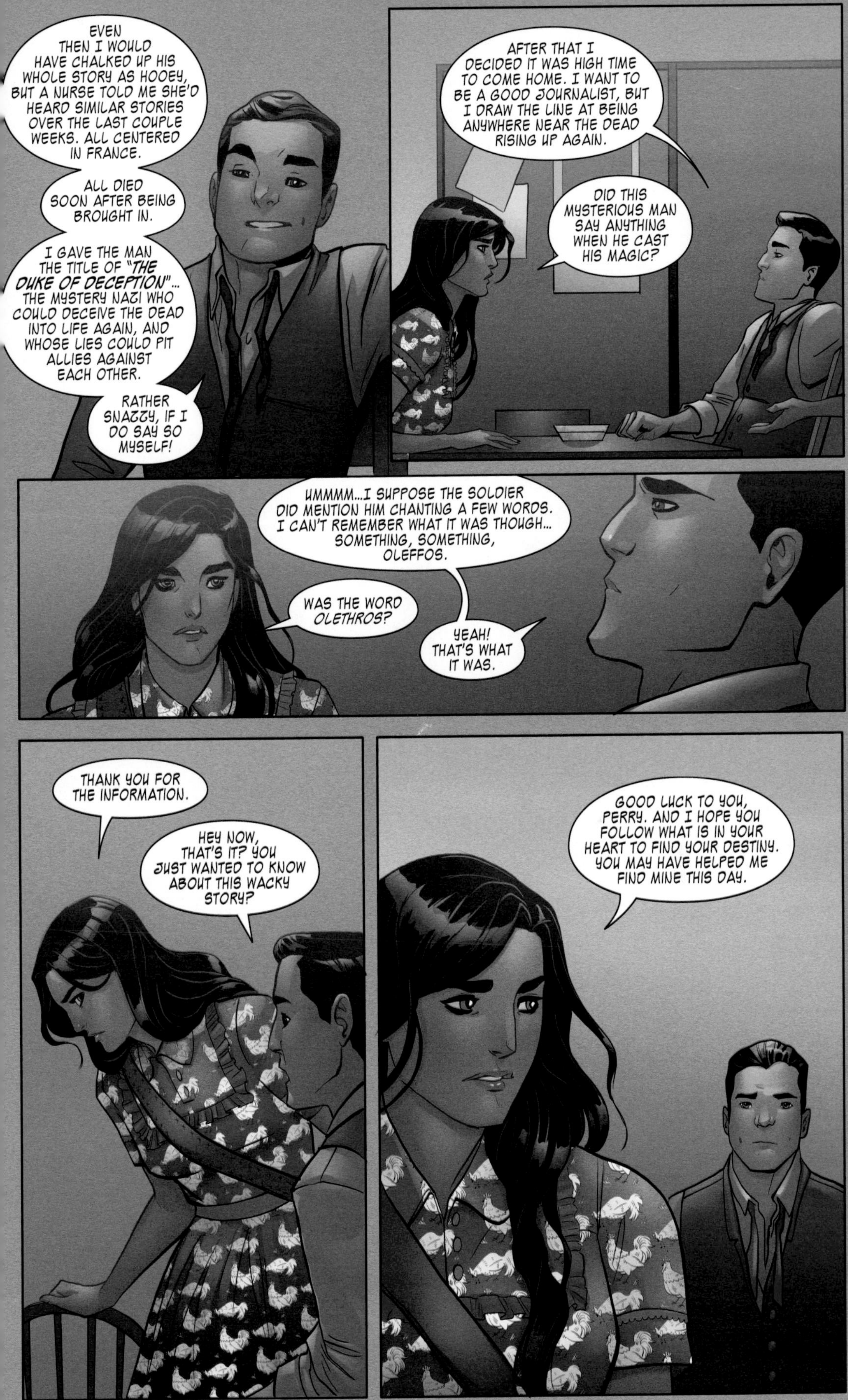
EVEN THEN I WOULD HAVE CHALKED UP HIS WHOLE STORY AS HOOEY, BUT A NURSE TOLD ME SHE'D HEARD SIMILAR STORIES OVER THE LAST COUPLE WEEKS. ALL CENTERED IN FRANCE.
ALL DIED SOON AFTER BEING BROUGHT IN.
I GAVE THE MAN THE TITLE OF "THE DUKE OF DECEPTION"... THE MYSTERY NAZI WHO COULD DECEIVE THE DEAD INTO LIFE AGAIN, AND WHOSE LIES COULD PIT ALLIES AGAINST EACH OTHER.
RATHER SNAZZY, IF I DO SAY SO MYSELF!
AFTER THAT I DECIDED IT WAS HIGH TIME TO COME HOME. I WANT TO BE A GOOD JOURNALIST, BUT I DRAW THE LINE AT BEING ANYWHERE NEAR THE DEAD RISING UP AGAIN.
DID THIS MYSTERIOUS MAN SAY ANYTHING WHEN HE CAST HIS MAGIC?
UMMMM...I SUPPOSE THE SOLDIER DID MENTION HIM CHANTING A FEW WORDS. I CAN'T REMEMBER WHAT IT WAS THOUGH... SOMETHING, SOMETHING, OLEFFOS.
WAS THE WORD OLETHROS?
YEAH! THAT'S WHAT IT WAS.
THANK YOU FOR THE INFORMATION.
HEY NOW, THAT'S IT? YOU JUST WANTED TO KNOW ABOUT THIS WACKY STORY?
GOOD LUCK TO YOU, PERRY. AND I HOPE YOU FOLLOW WHAT IS IN YOUR HEART TO FIND YOUR DESTINY. YOU MAY HAVE HELPED ME FIND MINE THIS DAY.

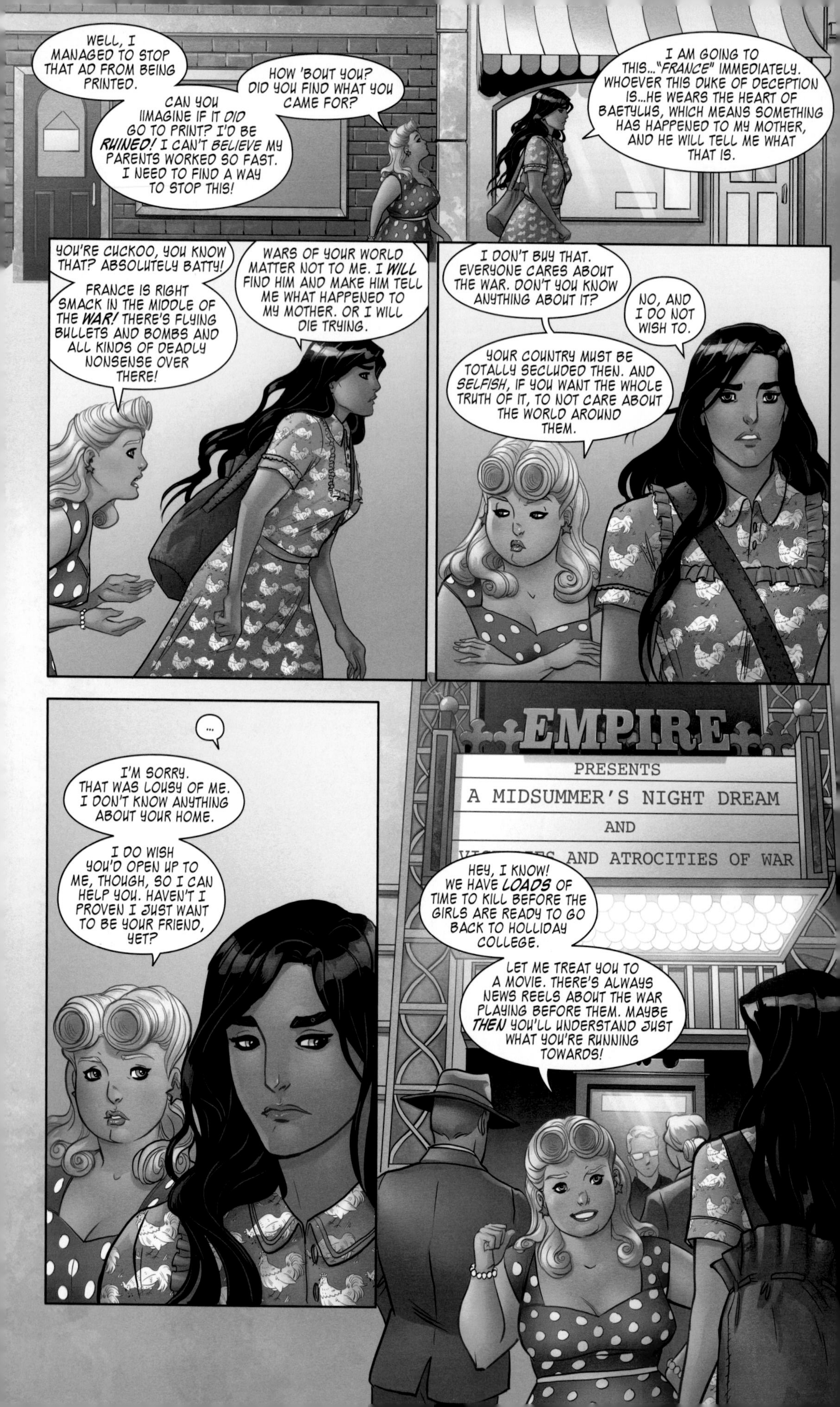

WELL, I MANAGED TO STOP THAT AD FROM BEING PRINTED.
CAN YOU IMAGINE IF IT DID GO TO PRINT? I'D BE RUINED! I CAN'T BELIEVE MY PARENTS WORKED SO FAST. I NEED TO FIND A WAY TO STOP THIS!
HOW 'BOUT YOU? DID YOU FIND WHAT YOU CAME FOR?
I AM GOING TO THIS..."FRANCE" IMMEDIATELY. WHOEVER THIS DUKE OF DECEPTION IS...HE WEARS THE HEART OF BAETYLUS, WHICH MEANS SOMETHING HAS HAPPENED TO MY MOTHER, AND HE WILL TELL ME WHAT THAT IS.
YOU'RE CUCKOO, YOU KNOW THAT? ABSOLUTELY BATTY!
FRANCE IS RIGHT SMACK IN THE MIDDLE OF THE WAR! THERE'S FLYING BULLETS AND BOMBS AND ALL KINDS OF DEADLY NONSENSE OVER THERE!
WARS OF YOUR WORLD MATTER NOT TO ME. I WILL FIND HIM AND MAKE HIM TELL ME WHAT HAPPENED TO MY MOTHER. OR I WILL DIE TRYING.
I DON'T BUY THAT. EVERYONE CARES ABOUT THE WAR. DON'T YOU KNOW ANYTHING ABOUT IT?
NO, AND I DO NOT WISH TO.
YOUR COUNTRY MUST BE TOTALLY SECLUDED THEN. AND SELFISH, IF YOU WANT THE WHOLE TRUTH OF IT, TO NOT CARE ABOUT THE WORLD AROUND THEM.
...
I'M SORRY. THAT WAS LOUSY OF ME. I DON'T KNOW ANYTHING ABOUT YOUR HOME.
I DO WISH YOU'D OPEN UP TO ME, THOUGH, SO I CAN HELP YOU. HAVEN'T I PROVEN I JUST WANT TO BE YOUR FRIEND, YET?
EMPIRE
PRESENTS
A MIDSUMMER'S NIGHT DREAM
AND
AND ATROCITIES OF WAR
HEY, I KNOW! WE HAVE LOADS OF TIME TO KILL BEFORE THE GIRLS ARE READY TO GO BACK TO HOLLIDAY COLLEGE.
LET ME TREAT YOU TO A MOVIE. THERE'S ALWAYS NEWS REELS ABOUT THE WAR PLAYING BEFORE THEM. MAYBE THEN YOU'LL UNDERSTAND JUST WHAT YOU'RE RUNNING TOWARDS!

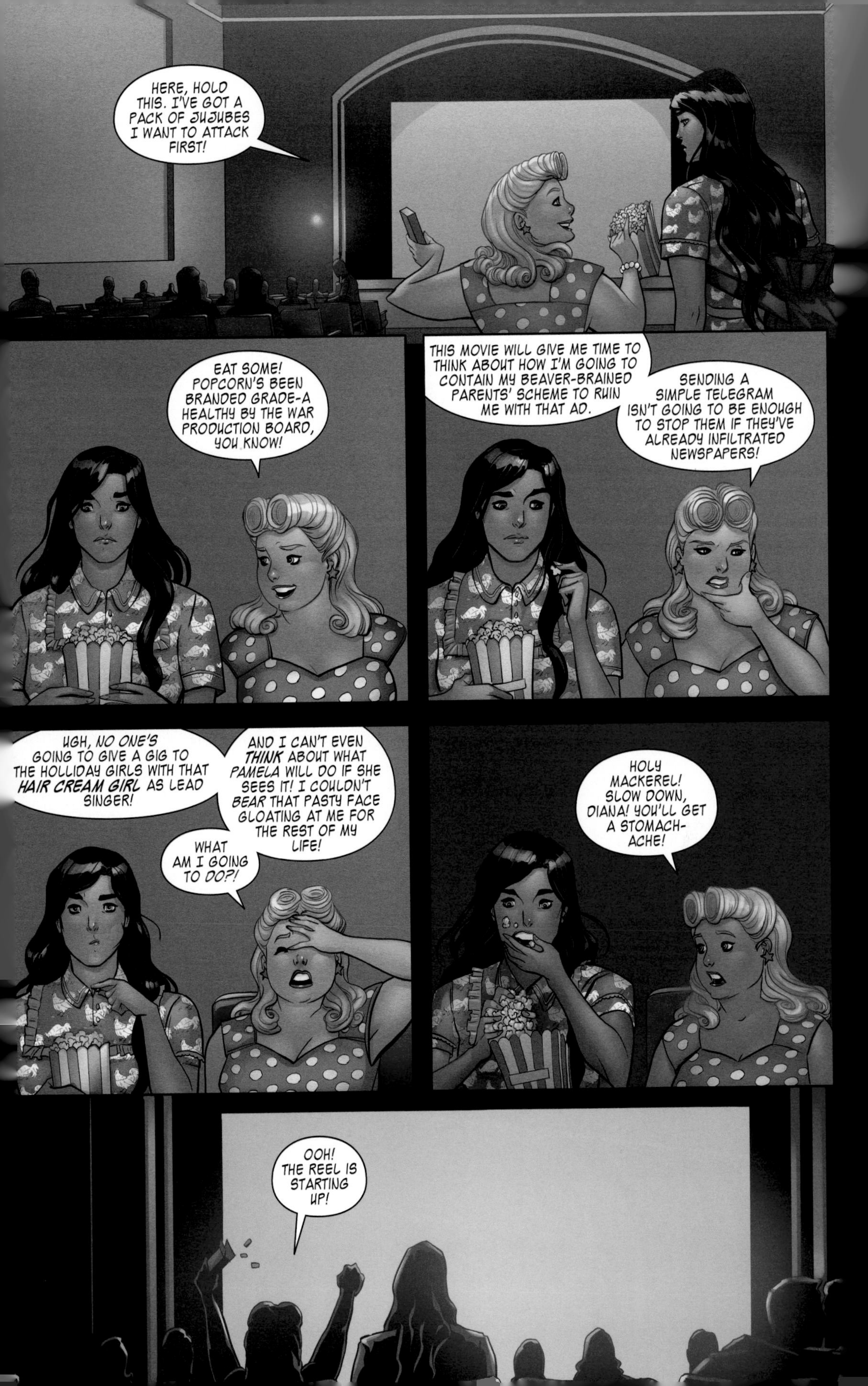
HERE, HOLD THIS. I'VE GOT A PACK OF JUJUBES I WANT TO ATTACK FIRST!
EAT SOME! POPCORN'S BEEN BRANDED GRADE-A HEALTHY BY THE WAR PRODUCTION BOARD, YOU KNOW!
THIS MOVIE WILL GIVE ME TIME TO THINK ABOUT HOW I'M GOING TO CONTAIN MY BEAVER-BRAINED PARENTS' SCHEME TO RUIN ME WITH THAT AD.
SENDING A SIMPLE TELEGRAM ISN'T GOING TO BE ENOUGH TO STOP THEM IF THEY'VE ALREADY INFILTRATED NEWSPAPERS!
UGH, NO ONE'S GOING TO GIVE A GIG TO THE HOLLIDAY GIRLS WITH THAT HAIR CREAM GIRL AS LEAD SINGER!
AND I CAN'T EVEN THINK ABOUT WHAT PAMELA WILL DO IF SHE SEES IT! I COULDN'T BEAR THAT PASTY FACE GLOATING AT ME FOR THE REST OF MY LIFE!
WHAT AM I GOING TO DO?!
HOLY MACKEREL! SLOW DOWN, DIANA! YOU'LL GET A STOMACH-ACHE!
OOH! THE REEL IS STARTING UP!

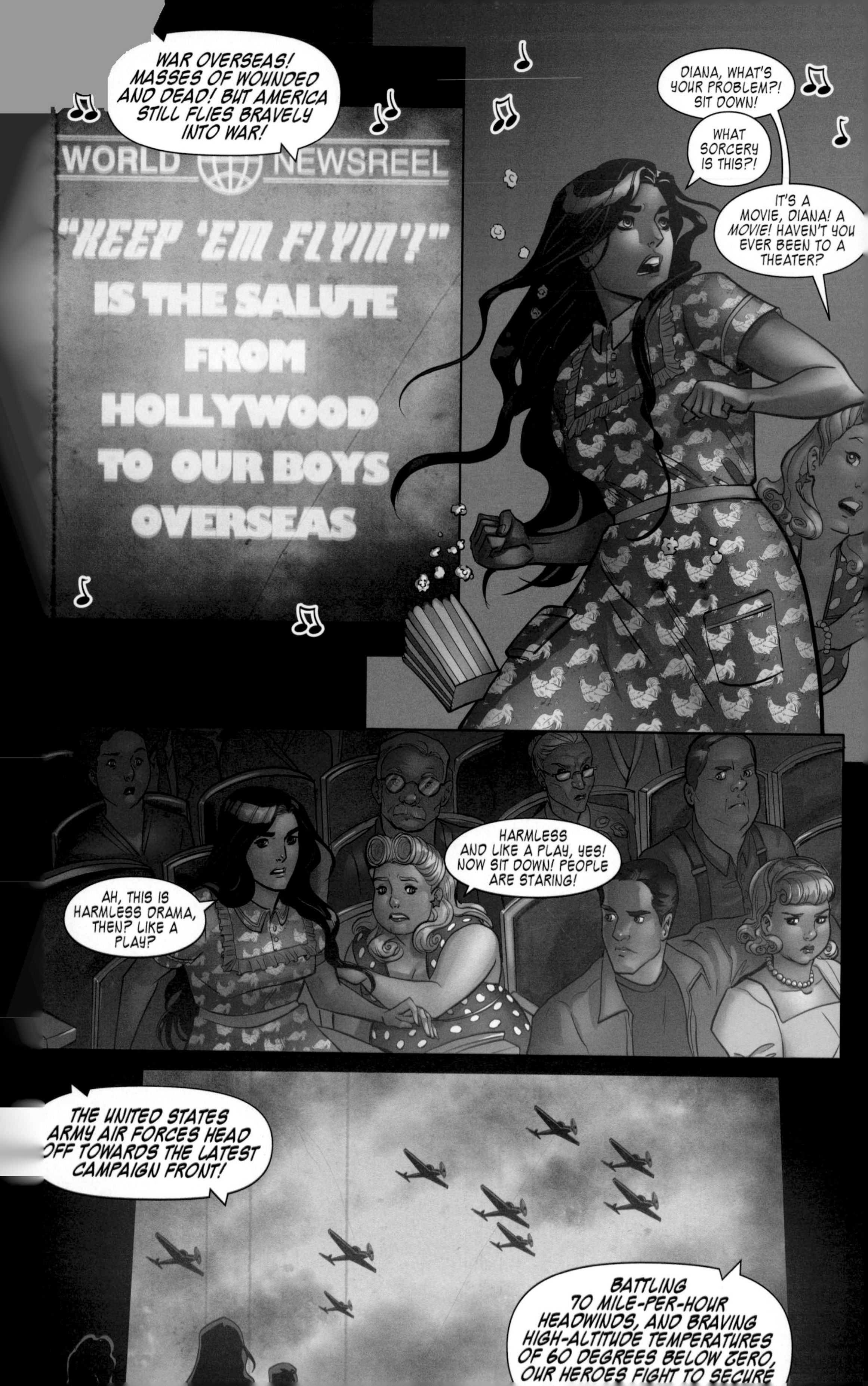
WAR OVERSEAS! MASSES OF WOUNDED AND DEAD! BUT AMERICA STILL FLIES BRAVELY INTO WAR!
WORLD NEWSREEL
"KEEP 'EM FLYIN'!" IS THE SALUTE FROM HOLLYWOOD TO OUR BOYS OVERSEAS
DIANA, WHAT'S YOUR PROBLEM?! SIT DOWN!
WHAT SORCERY IS THIS?!
IT'S A MOVIE, DIANA! A MOVIE! HAVEN'T YOU EVER BEEN TO A THEATER?
AH, THIS IS HARMLESS DRAMA, THEN? LIKE A PLAY?
HARMLESS AND LIKE A PLAY, YES! NOW SIT DOWN! PEOPLE ARE STARING!
THE UNITED STATES ARMY AIR FORCES HEAD OFF TOWARDS THE LATEST CAMPAIGN FRONT!
BATTLING 70 MILE-PER-HOUR HEADWINDS, AND BRAVING HIGH-ALTITUDE TEMPERATURES OF 60 DEGREES BELOW ZERO, OUR HEROES FIGHT TO SECURE

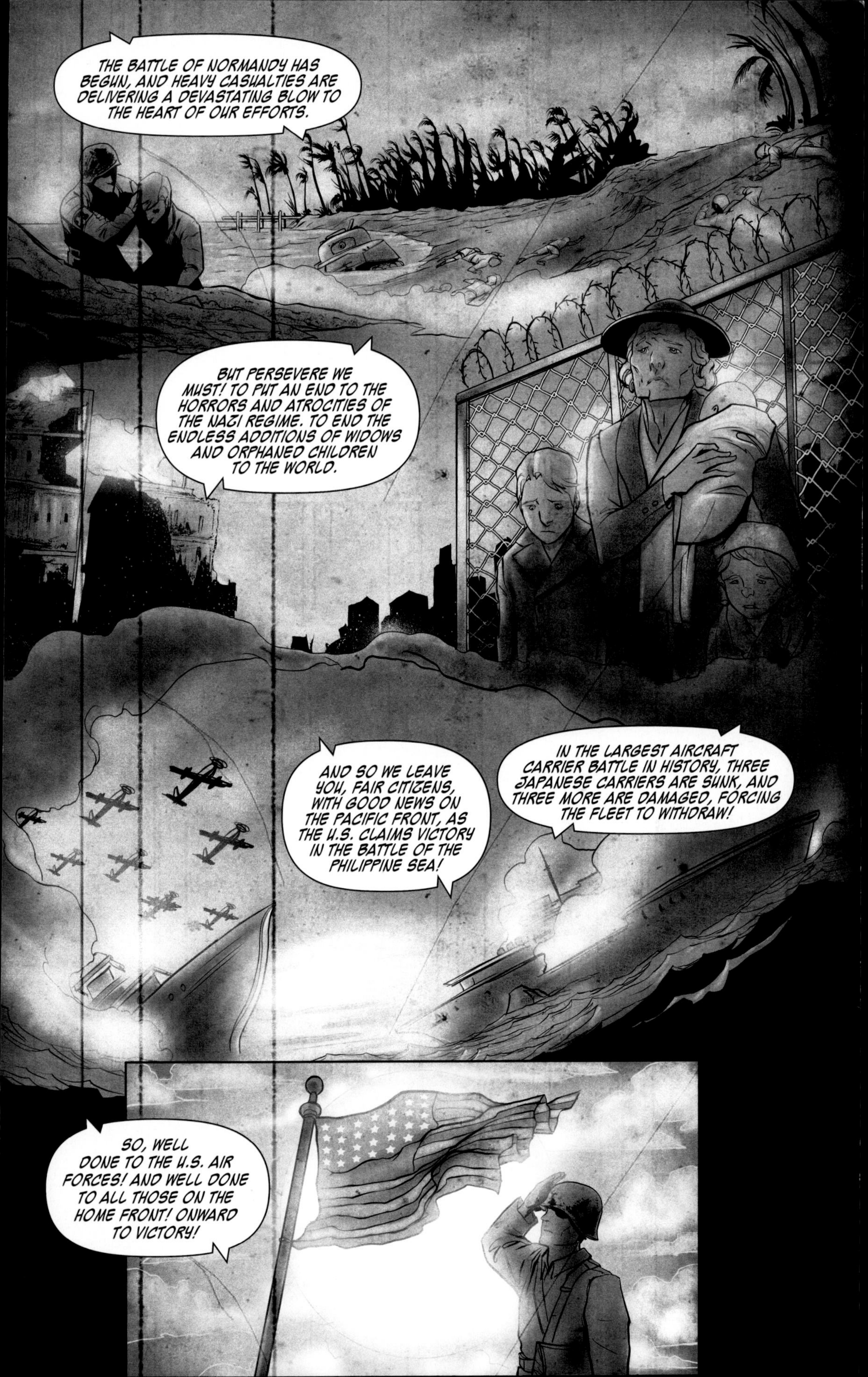
THE BATTLE OF NORMANDY HAS BEGUN, AND HEAVY CASUALTIES ARE DELIVERING A DEVASTATING BLOW TO THE HEART OF OUR EFFORTS.
BUT PERSEVERE WE MUST! TO PUT AN END TO THE HORRORS AND ATROCITIES OF THE NAZI REGIME. TO END THE ENDLESS ADDITIONS OF WIDOWS AND ORPHANED CHILDREN TO THE WORLD.
AND SO WE LEAVE YOU, FAIR CITIZENS, WITH GOOD NEWS ON THE PACIFIC FRONT, AS THE U.S. CLAIMS VICTORY IN THE BATTLE OF THE PHILIPPINE SEA!
IN THE LARGEST AIRCRAFT CARRIER BATTLE IN HISTORY, THREE JAPANESE CARRIERS ARE SUNK, AND THREE MORE ARE DAMAGED, FORCING THE FLEET TO WITHDRAW!
SO, WELL DONE TO THE U.S. AIR FORCES! AND WELL DONE TO ALL THOSE ON THE HOME FRONT! ONWARD TO VICTORY!

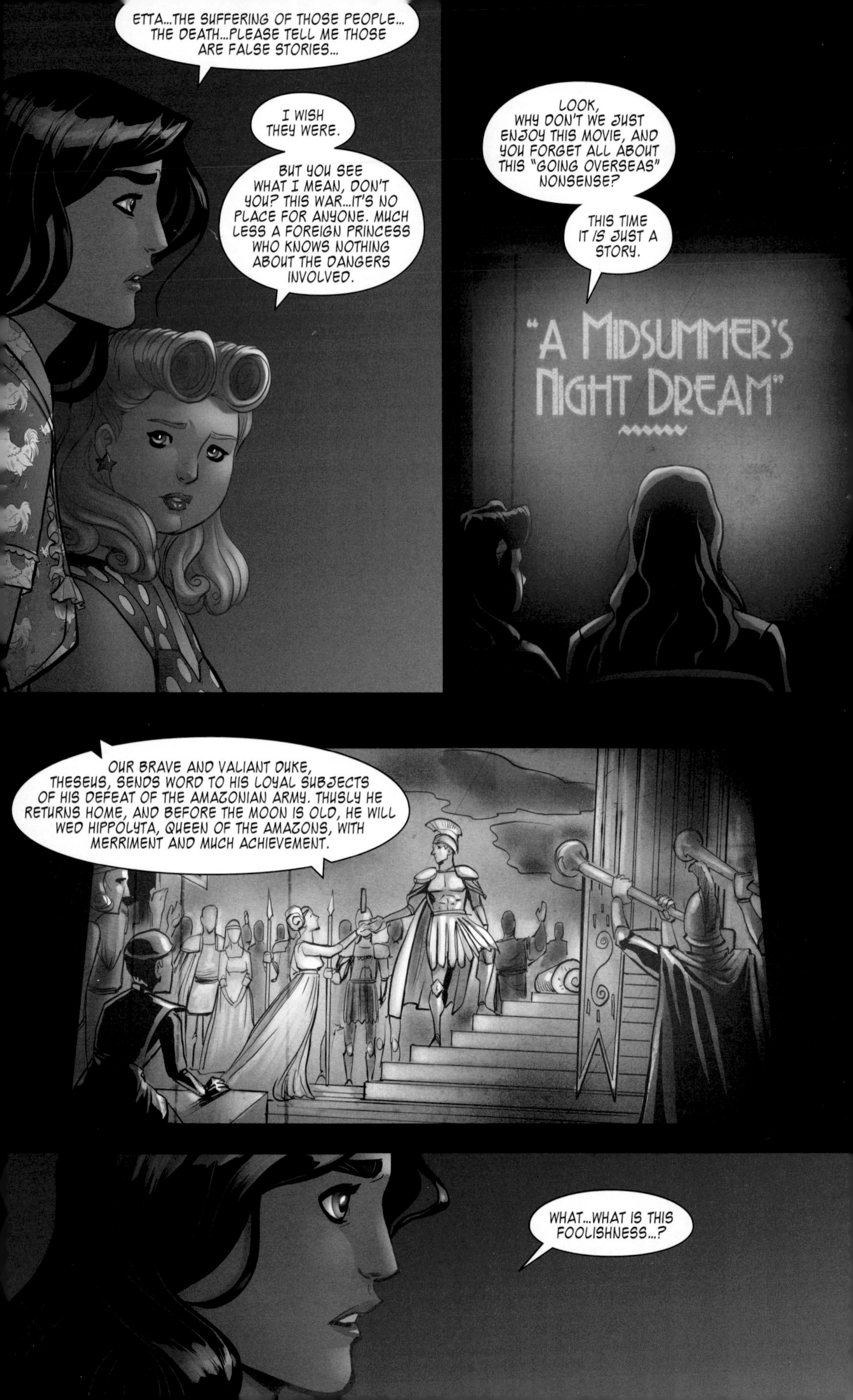
ETTA...THE SUFFERING OF THOSE PEOPLE... THE DEATH...PLEASE TELL ME THOSE ARE FALSE STORIES...
I WISH THEY WERE.
BUT YOU SEE WHAT I MEAN, DON'T YOU? THIS WAR...IT'S NO PLACE FOR ANYONE. MUCH LESS A FOREIGN PRINCESS WHO KNOWS NOTHING ABOUT THE DANGERS INVOLVED.
LOOK, WHY DON'T WE JUST ENJOY THIS MOVIE, AND YOU FORGET ALL ABOUT THIS "GOING OVERSEAS" NONSENSE?
THIS TIME IT IS JUST A STORY.
"A MIDSUMMER'S NIGHT DREAM"
OUR BRAVE AND VALIANT DUKE, THESEUS, SENDS WORD TO HIS LOYAL SUBJECTS OF HIS DEFEAT OF THE AMAZONIAN ARMY. THUSLY HE RETURNS HOME, AND BEFORE THE MOON IS OLD, HE WILL WED HIPPOLYTA, QUEEN OF THE AMAZONS, WITH MERRIMENT AND MUCH ACHIEVEMENT.
WHAT...WHAT IS THIS FOOLISHNESS...?

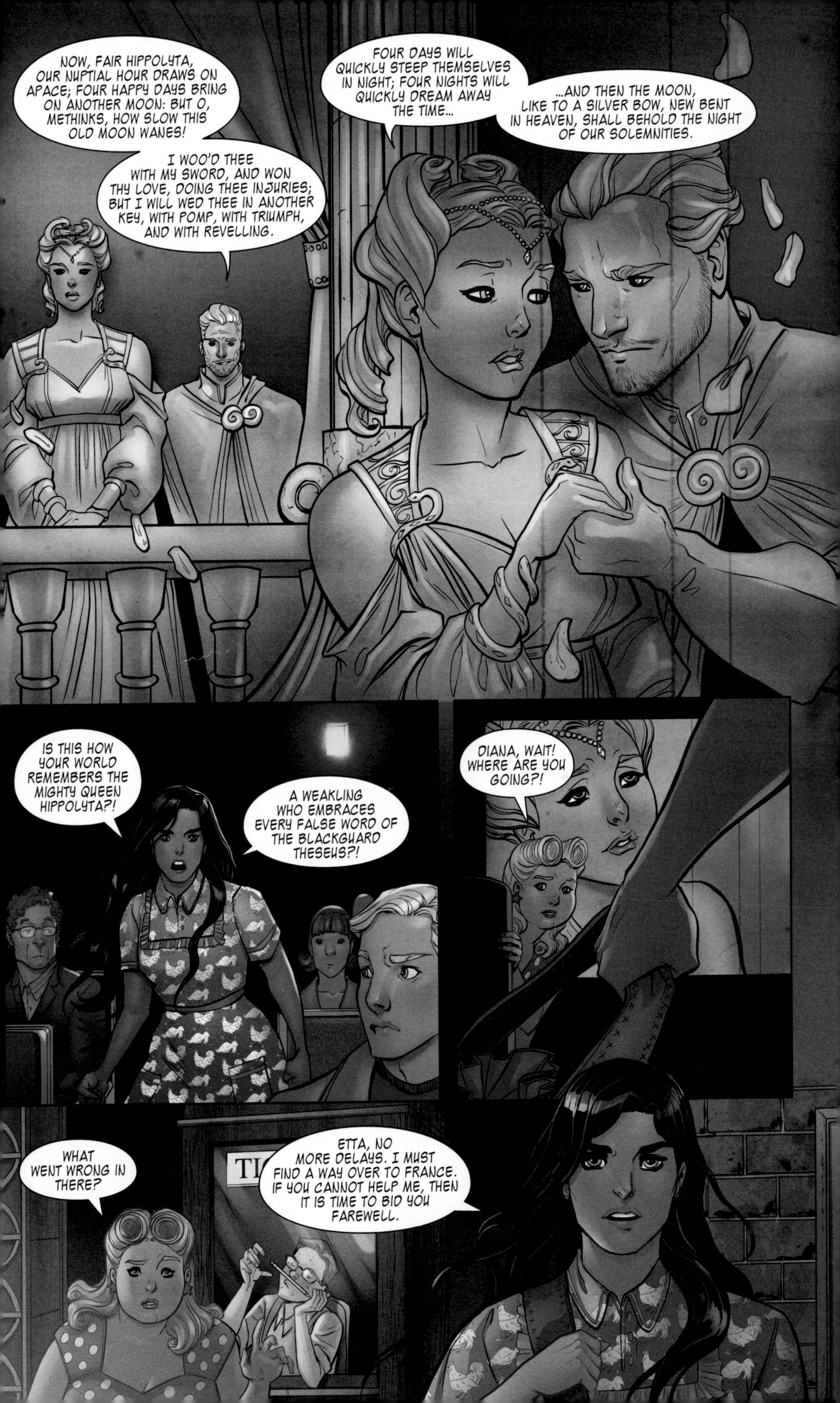

NOW, FAIR HIPPOLYTA, OUR NUPTIAL HOUR DRAWS ON APACE; FOUR HAPPY DAYS BRING ON ANOTHER MOON: BUT O, METHINKS, HOW SLOW THIS OLD MOON WANES!
I WOO'D THEE WITH MY SWORD, AND WON THY LOVE, DOING THEE INJURIES; BUT I WILL WED THEE IN ANOTHER KEY, WITH POMP, WITH TRIUMPH, AND WITH REVELLING.
FOUR DAYS WILL QUICKLY STEEP THEMSELVES IN NIGHT; FOUR NIGHTS WILL QUICKLY DREAM AWAY THE TIME...
...AND THEN THE MOON, LIKE TO A SILVER BOW, NEW BENT IN HEAVEN, SHALL BEHOLD THE NIGHT OF OUR SOLEMNITIES.
IS THIS HOW YOUR WORLD REMEMBERS THE MIGHTY QUEEN HIPPOLYTA?!
A WEAKLING WHO EMBRACES EVERY FALSE WORD OF THE BLACKGUARD THESEUS?!
DIANA, WAIT! WHERE ARE YOU GOING?!
WHAT WENT WRONG IN THERE?
ETTA, NO MORE DELAYS. I MUST FIND A WAY OVER TO FRANCE. IF YOU CANNOT HELP ME, THEN IT IS TIME TO BID YOU FAREWELL.

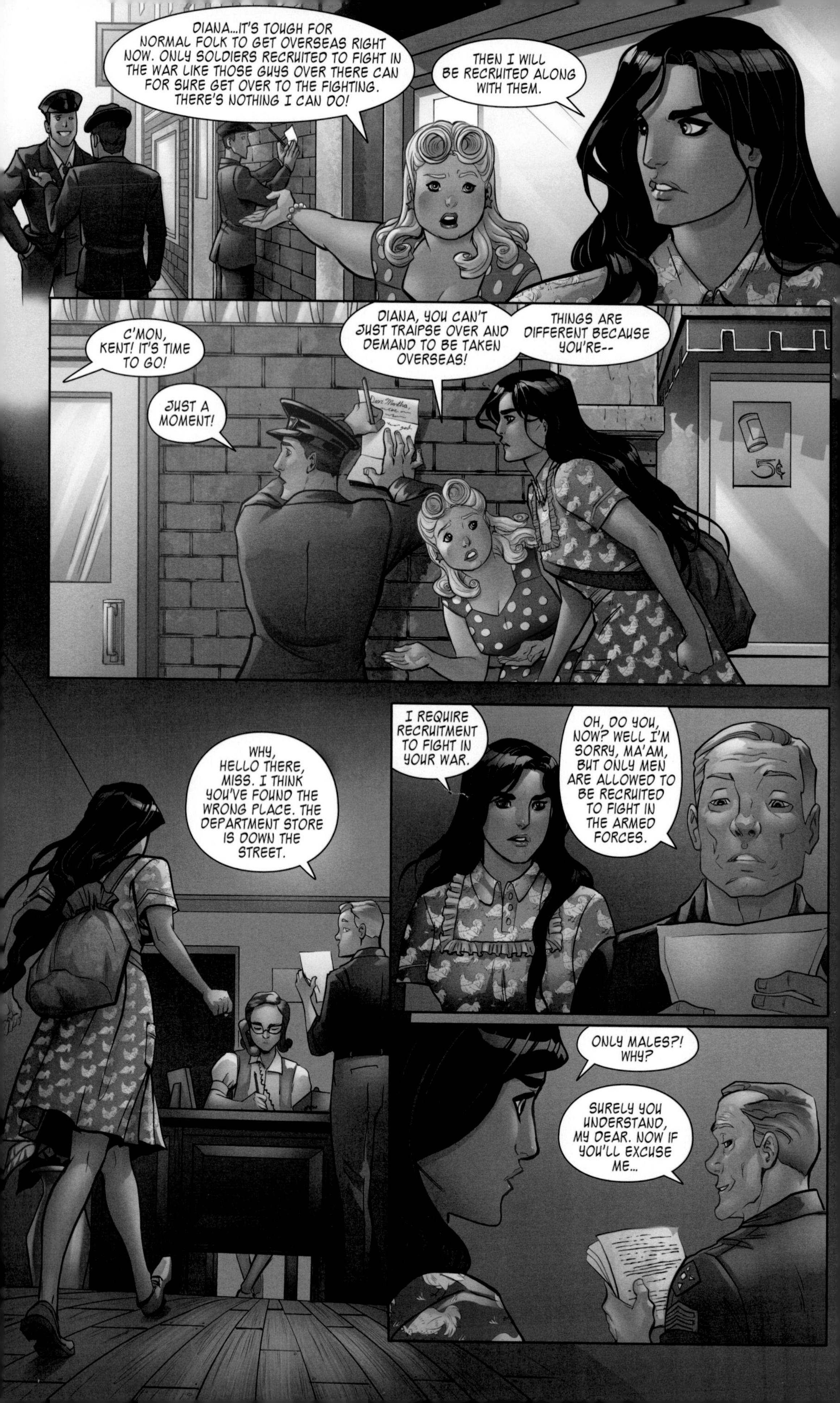
DIANA...IT'S TOUGH FOR NORMAL FOLK TO GET OVERSEAS RIGHT NOW. ONLY SOLDIERS RECRUITED TO FIGHT IN THE WAR LIKE THOSE GUYS OVER THERE CAN FOR SURE GET OVER TO THE FIGHTING. THERE'S NOTHING I CAN DO!
THEN I WILL BE RECRUITED ALONG WITH THEM.
C'MON, KENT! IT'S TIME TO GO!
JUST A MOMENT!
DIANA, YOU CAN'T JUST TRAIPSE OVER AND DEMAND TO BE TAKEN OVERSEAS!
THINGS ARE DIFFERENT BECAUSE YOU'RE--
5¢
WHY, HELLO THERE, MISS. I THINK YOU'VE FOUND THE WRONG PLACE. THE DEPARTMENT STORE IS DOWN THE STREET.
I REQUIRE RECRUITMENT TO FIGHT IN YOUR WAR.
OH, DO YOU, NOW? WELL I'M SORRY, MA'AM, BUT ONLY MEN ARE ALLOWED TO BE RECRUITED TO FIGHT IN THE ARMED FORCES.
ONLY MALES?! WHY?
SURELY YOU UNDERSTAND, MY DEAR. NOW IF YOU'LL EXCUSE ME...

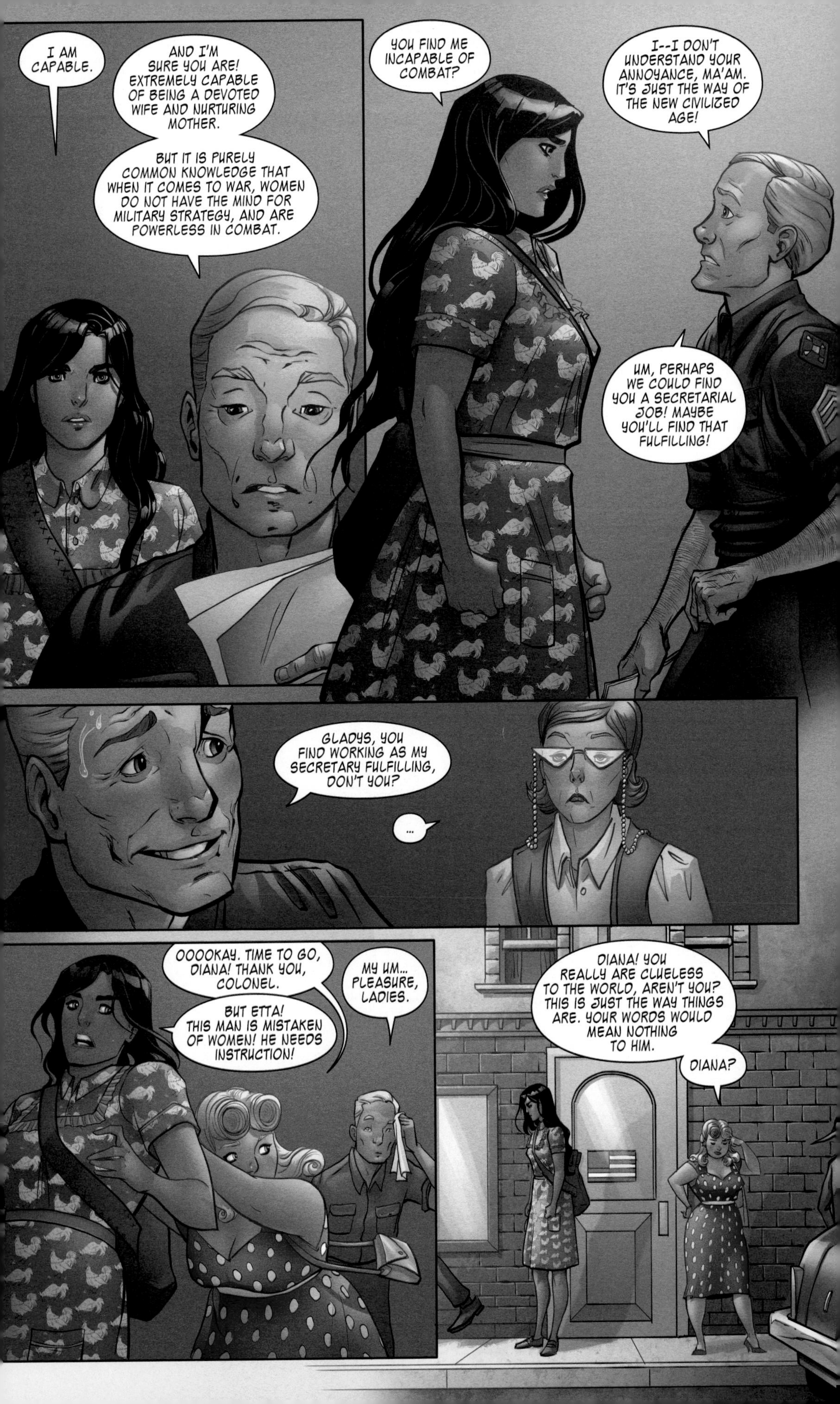
I AM CAPABLE.
AND I'M SURE YOU ARE! EXTREMELY CAPABLE OF BEING A DEVOTED WIFE AND NURTURING MOTHER.
BUT IT IS PURELY COMMON KNOWLEDGE THAT WHEN IT COMES TO WAR, WOMEN DO NOT HAVE THE MIND FOR MILITARY STRATEGY, AND ARE POWERLESS IN COMBAT.
YOU FIND ME INCAPABLE OF COMBAT?
I--I DON'T UNDERSTAND YOUR ANNOYANCE, MA'AM. IT'S JUST THE WAY OF THE NEW CIVILIZED AGE!
UM, PERHAPS WE COULD FIND YOU A SECRETARIAL JOB! MAYBE YOU'LL FIND THAT FULFILLING!
GLADYS, YOU FIND WORKING AS MY SECRETARY FULFILLING, DON'T YOU?
...
OOOOKAY. TIME TO GO, DIANA! THANK YOU, COLONEL.
BUT ETTA! THIS MAN IS MISTAKEN OF WOMEN! HE NEEDS INSTRUCTION!
MY UM... PLEASURE, LADIES.
DIANA! YOU REALLY ARE CLUELESS TO THE WORLD, AREN'T YOU? THIS IS JUST THE WAY THINGS ARE. YOUR WORDS WOULD MEAN NOTHING TO HIM.
DIANA?

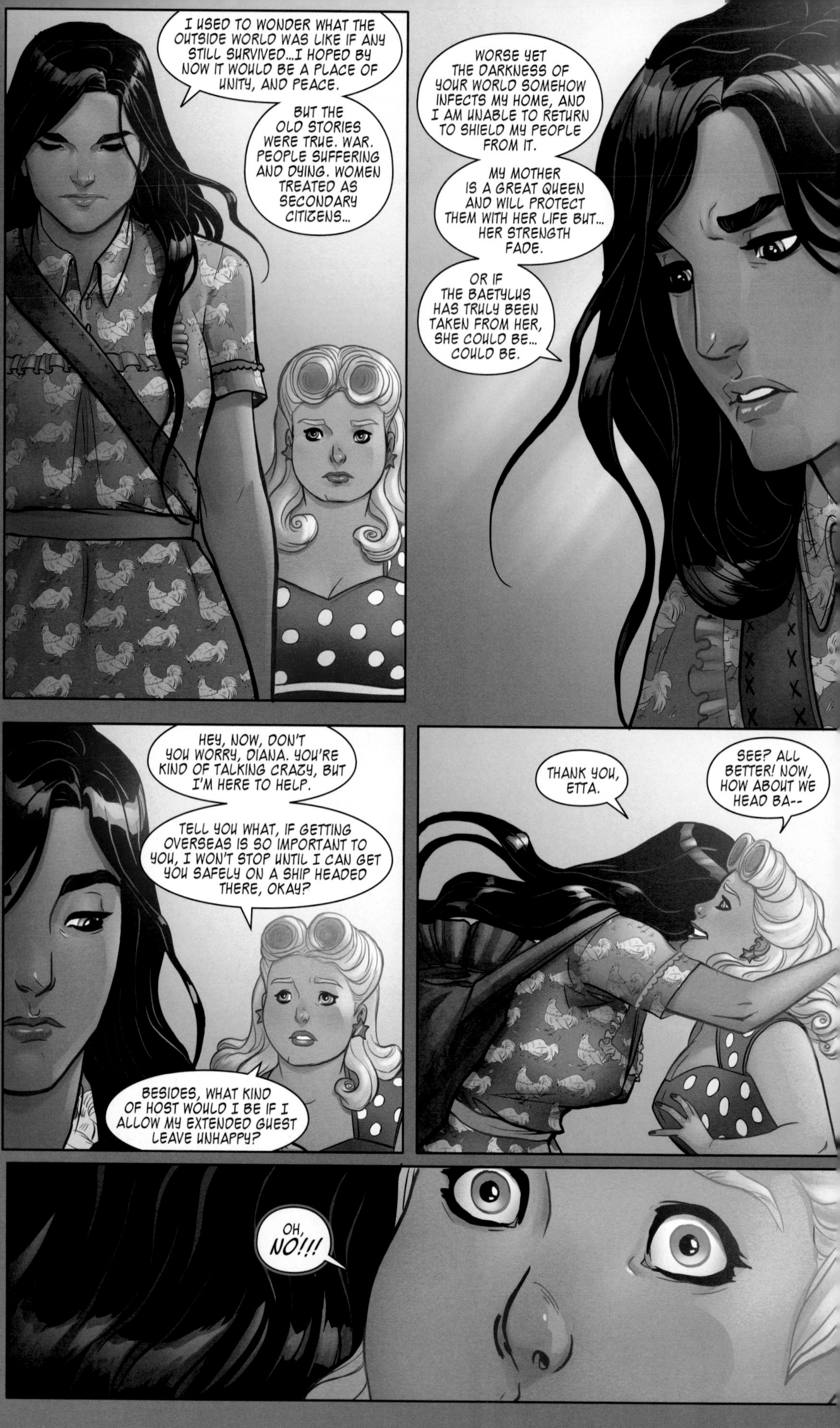
I USED TO WONDER WHAT THE OUTSIDE WORLD WAS LIKE IF ANY STILL SURVIVED...I HOPED BY NOW IT WOULD BE A PLACE OF UNITY, AND PEACE.
BUT THE OLD STORIES WERE TRUE. WAR. PEOPLE SUFFERING AND DYING. WOMEN TREATED AS SECONDARY CITIZENS...
WORSE YET THE DARKNESS OF YOUR WORLD SOMEHOW INFECTS MY HOME, AND I AM UNABLE TO RETURN TO SHIELD MY PEOPLE FROM IT.
MY MOTHER IS A GREAT QUEEN AND WILL PROTECT THEM WITH HER LIFE BUT... HER STRENGTH FADE.
OR IF THE BAETYLUS HAS TRULY BEEN TAKEN FROM HER, SHE COULD BE... COULD BE.
HEY, NOW, DON'T YOU WORRY, DIANA. YOU'RE KIND OF TALKING CRAZY, BUT I'M HERE TO HELP.
TELL YOU WHAT, IF GETTING OVERSEAS IS SO IMPORTANT TO YOU, I WON'T STOP UNTIL I CAN GET YOU SAFELY ON A SHIP HEADED THERE, OKAY?
BESIDES, WHAT KIND OF HOST WOULD I BE IF I ALLOW MY EXTENDED GUEST LEAVE UNHAPPY?
THANK YOU, ETTA.
SEE? ALL BETTER! NOW, HOW ABOUT WE HEAD BA--
OH, NO!!!

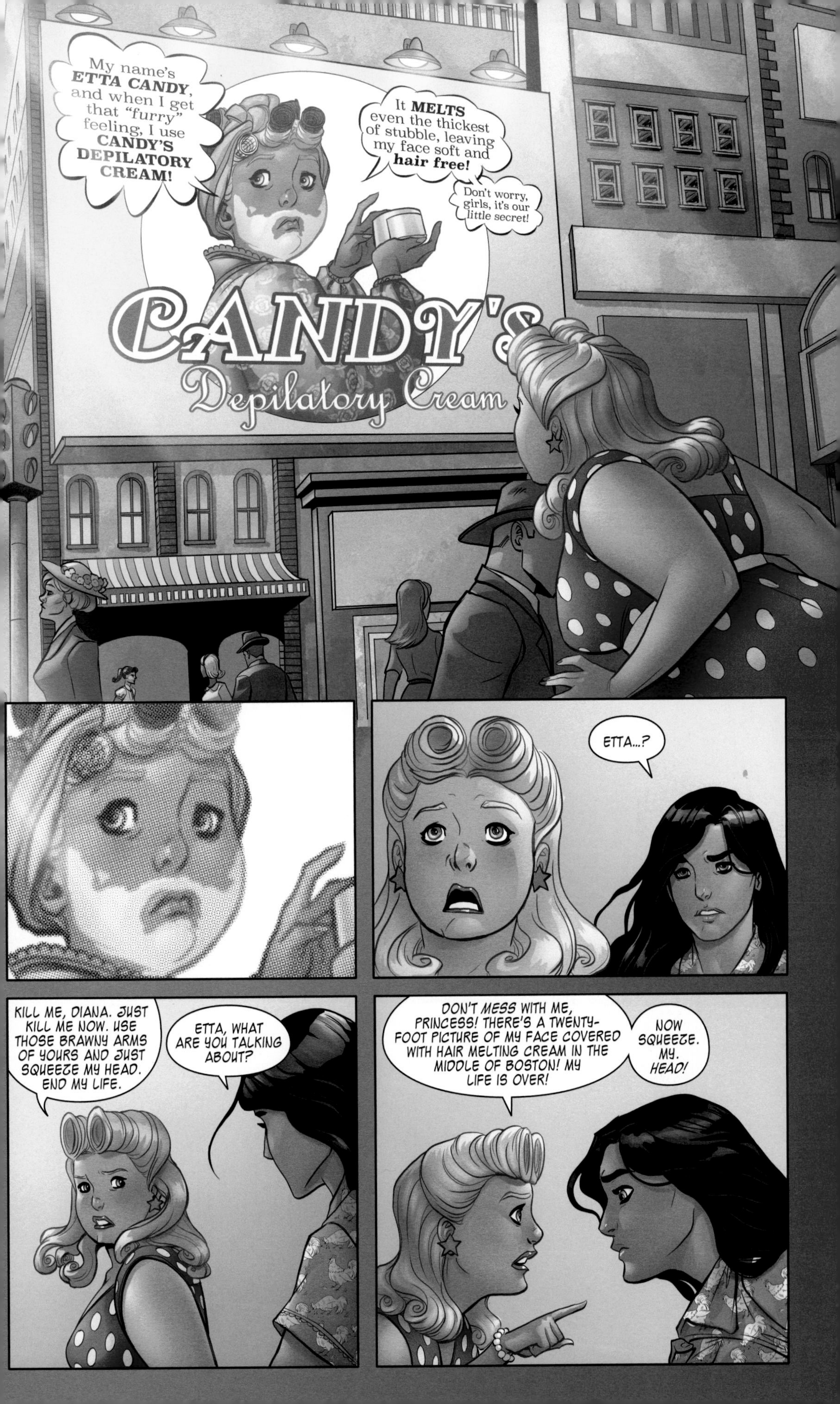
My name's ETTA CANDY, and when I get that "furry" feeling, I use CANDY'S DEPILATORY CREAM!
It MELTS even the thickest of stubble, leaving my face soft and hair free!
Don't worry, girls, it's our little secret!
CANDY'S
Depilatory Cream
ETTA...?
KILL ME, DIANA. JUST KILL ME NOW. USE THOSE BRAWNY ARMS OF YOURS AND JUST SQUEEZE MY HEAD. END MY LIFE.
ETTA, WHAT ARE YOU TALKING ABOUT?
DON'T MESS WITH ME, PRINCESS! THERE'S A TWENTY-FOOT PICTURE OF MY FACE COVERED WITH HAIR MELTING CREAM IN THE MIDDLE OF BOSTON! MY LIFE IS OVER!
NOW SQUEEZE. MY. HEAD!

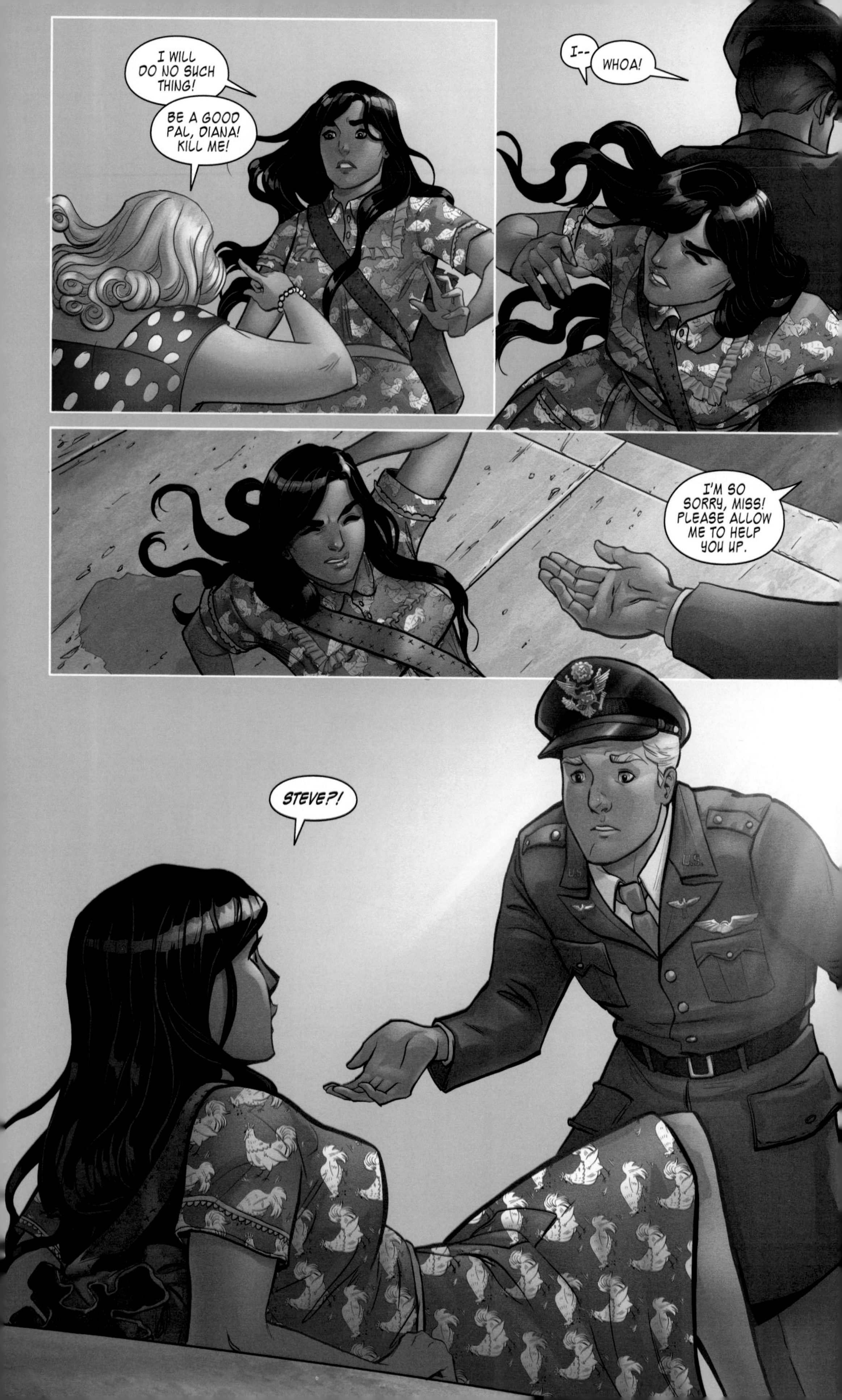
I WILL DO NO SUCH THING!
BE A GOOD PAL, DIANA! KILL ME!
I--
WHOA!
I'M SO SORRY, MISS! PLEASE ALLOW ME TO HELP YOU UP.
STEVE?!

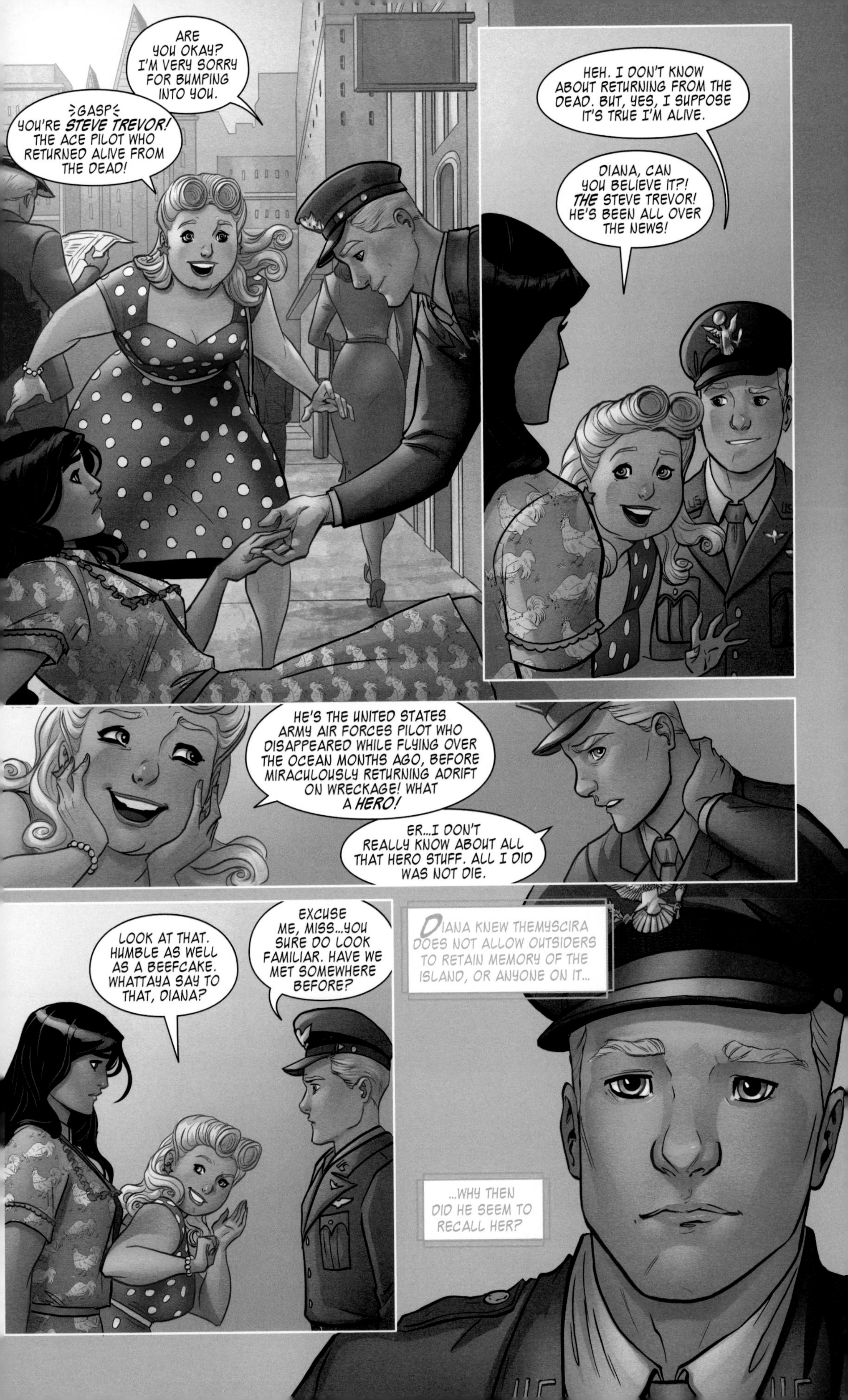
ARE YOU OKAY? I'M VERY SORRY FOR BUMPING INTO YOU.
GASP YOU'RE STEVE TREVOR! THE ACE PILOT WHO RETURNED ALIVE FROM THE DEAD!
HEH. I DON'T KNOW ABOUT RETURNING FROM THE DEAD. BUT, YES, I SUPPOSE IT'S TRUE I'M ALIVE.
DIANA, CAN YOU BELIEVE IT?! THE STEVE TREVOR! HE'S BEEN ALL OVER THE NEWS!
HE'S THE UNITED STATES ARMY AIR FORCES PILOT WHO DISAPPEARED WHILE FLYING OVER THE OCEAN MONTHS AGO, BEFORE MIRACULOUSLY RETURNING ADRIFT ON WRECKAGE! WHAT A HERO!
ER...I DON'T REALLY KNOW ABOUT ALL THAT HERO STUFF. ALL I DID WAS NOT DIE.
LOOK AT THAT. HUMBLE AS WELL AS A BEEFCAKE. WHATTAYA SAY TO THAT, DIANA?
EXCUSE ME, MISS...YOU SURE DO LOOK FAMILIAR. HAVE WE MET SOMEWHERE BEFORE?
DIANA KNEW THEMYSCIRA DOES NOT ALLOW OUTSIDERS TO RETAIN MEMORY OF THE ISLAND, OR ANYONE ON IT...
...WHY THEN DID HE SEEM TO RECALL HER?

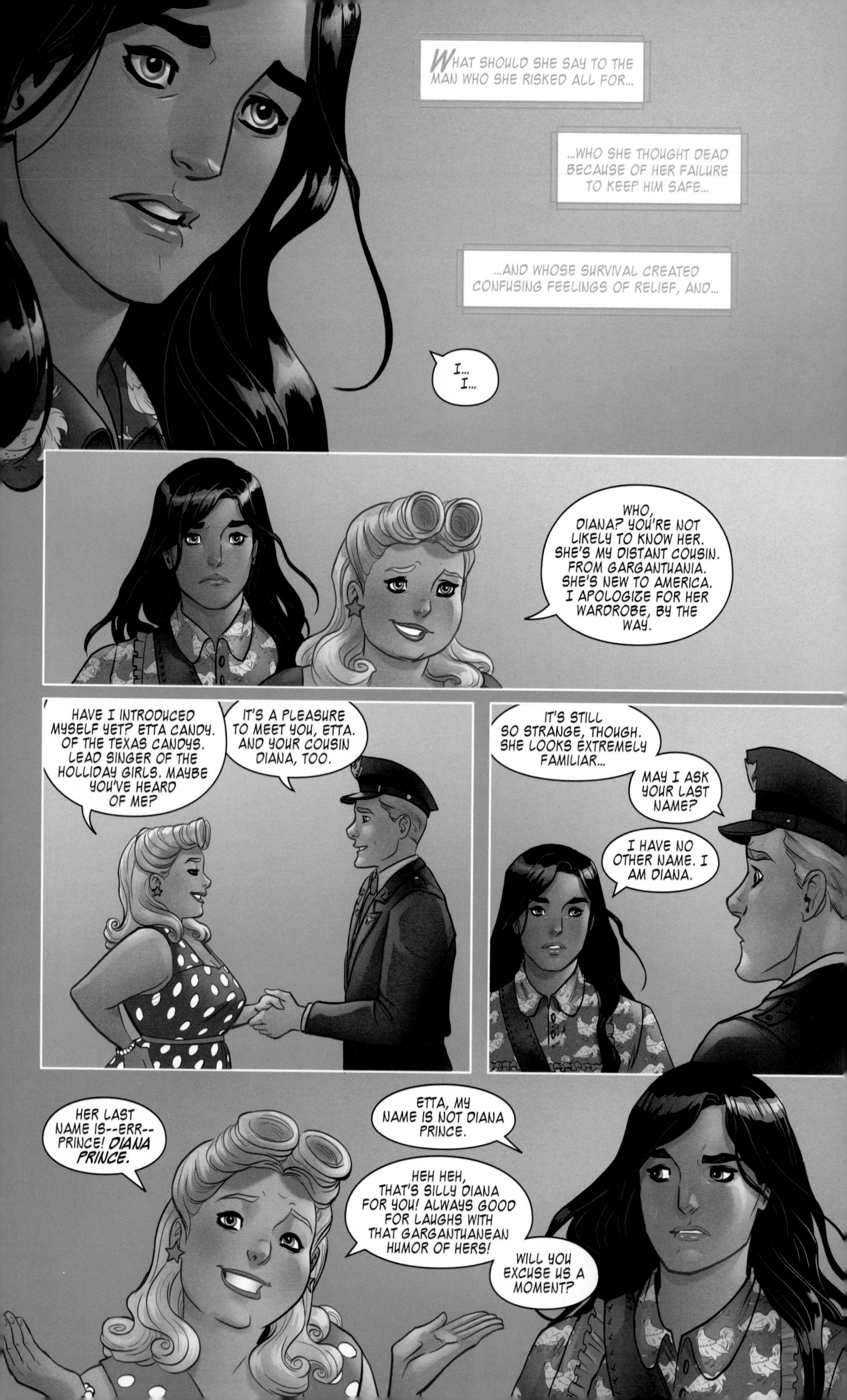
WHAT SHOULD SHE SAY TO THE MAN WHO SHE RISKED ALL FOR...
...WHO SHE THOUGHT DEAD BECAUSE OF HER FAILURE TO KEEP HIM SAFE...
...AND WHOSE SURVIVAL CREATED CONFUSING FEELINGS OF RELIEF, AND...
I... I...
WHO, DIANA? YOU'RE NOT LIKELY TO KNOW HER. SHE'S MY DISTANT COUSIN. FROM GARGANTHANIA. SHE'S NEW TO AMERICA. I APOLOGIZE FOR HER WARDROBE, BY THE WAY.
HAVE I INTRODUCED MYSELF YET? ETTA CANDY. OF THE TEXAS CANDYS. LEAD SINGER OF THE HOLLIDAY GIRLS. MAYBE YOU'VE HEARD OF ME?
IT'S A PLEASURE TO MEET YOU, ETTA. AND YOUR COUSIN DIANA, TOO.
IT'S STILL SO STRANGE, THOUGH. SHE LOOKS EXTREMELY FAMILIAR...
MAY I ASK YOUR LAST NAME?
I HAVE NO OTHER NAME. I AM DIANA.
HER LAST NAME IS--ERR-- PRINCE! *DIANA PRINCE.*
ETTA, MY NAME IS NOT DIANA PRINCE.
HEH HEH, THAT'S SILLY DIANA FOR YOU! ALWAYS GOOD FOR LAUGHS WITH THAT GARGANTHANEAN HUMOR OF HERS!
WILL YOU EXCUSE US A MOMENT?

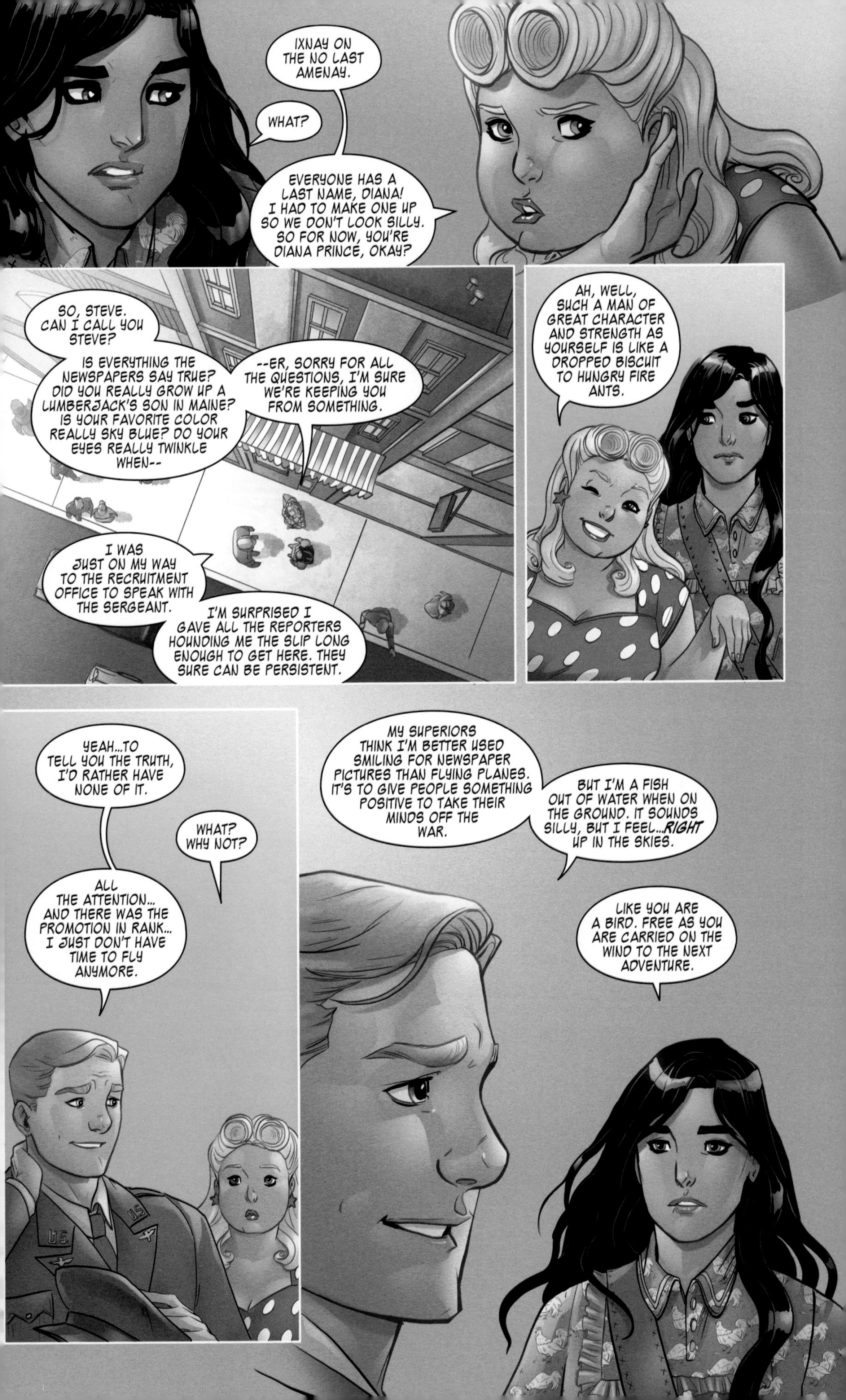
IXNAY ON THE NO LAST AMENAY.
WHAT?
EVERYONE HAS A LAST NAME, DIANA! I HAD TO MAKE ONE UP SO WE DON'T LOOK SILLY. SO FOR NOW, YOU'RE DIANA PRINCE, OKAY?
SO, STEVE. CAN I CALL YOU STEVE?
IS EVERYTHING THE NEWSPAPERS SAY TRUE? DID YOU REALLY GROW UP A LUMBERJACK'S SON IN MAINE? IS YOUR FAVORITE COLOR REALLY SKY BLUE? DO YOUR EYES REALLY TWINKLE WHEN--
--ER, SORRY FOR ALL THE QUESTIONS, I'M SURE WE'RE KEEPING YOU FROM SOMETHING.
I WAS JUST ON MY WAY TO THE RECRUITMENT OFFICE TO SPEAK WITH THE SERGEANT.
I'M SURPRISED I GAVE ALL THE REPORTERS HOUNDING ME THE SLIP LONG ENOUGH TO GET HERE. THEY SURE CAN BE PERSISTENT.
AH, WELL, SUCH A MAN OF GREAT CHARACTER AND STRENGTH AS YOURSELF IS LIKE A DROPPED BISCUIT TO HUNGRY FIRE ANTS.
YEAH...TO TELL YOU THE TRUTH, I'D RATHER HAVE NONE OF IT.
WHAT? WHY NOT?
ALL THE ATTENTION... AND THERE WAS THE PROMOTION IN RANK... I JUST DON'T HAVE TIME TO FLY ANYMORE.
MY SUPERIORS THINK I'M BETTER USED SMILING FOR NEWSPAPER PICTURES THAN FLYING PLANES. IT'S TO GIVE PEOPLE SOMETHING POSITIVE TO TAKE THEIR MINDS OFF THE WAR.
BUT I'M A FISH OUT OF WATER WHEN ON THE GROUND. IT SOUNDS SILLY, BUT I FEEL...*RIGHT* UP IN THE SKIES.
LIKE YOU ARE A BIRD. FREE AS YOU ARE CARRIED ON THE WIND TO THE NEXT ADVENTURE.
U.S.
U.S.

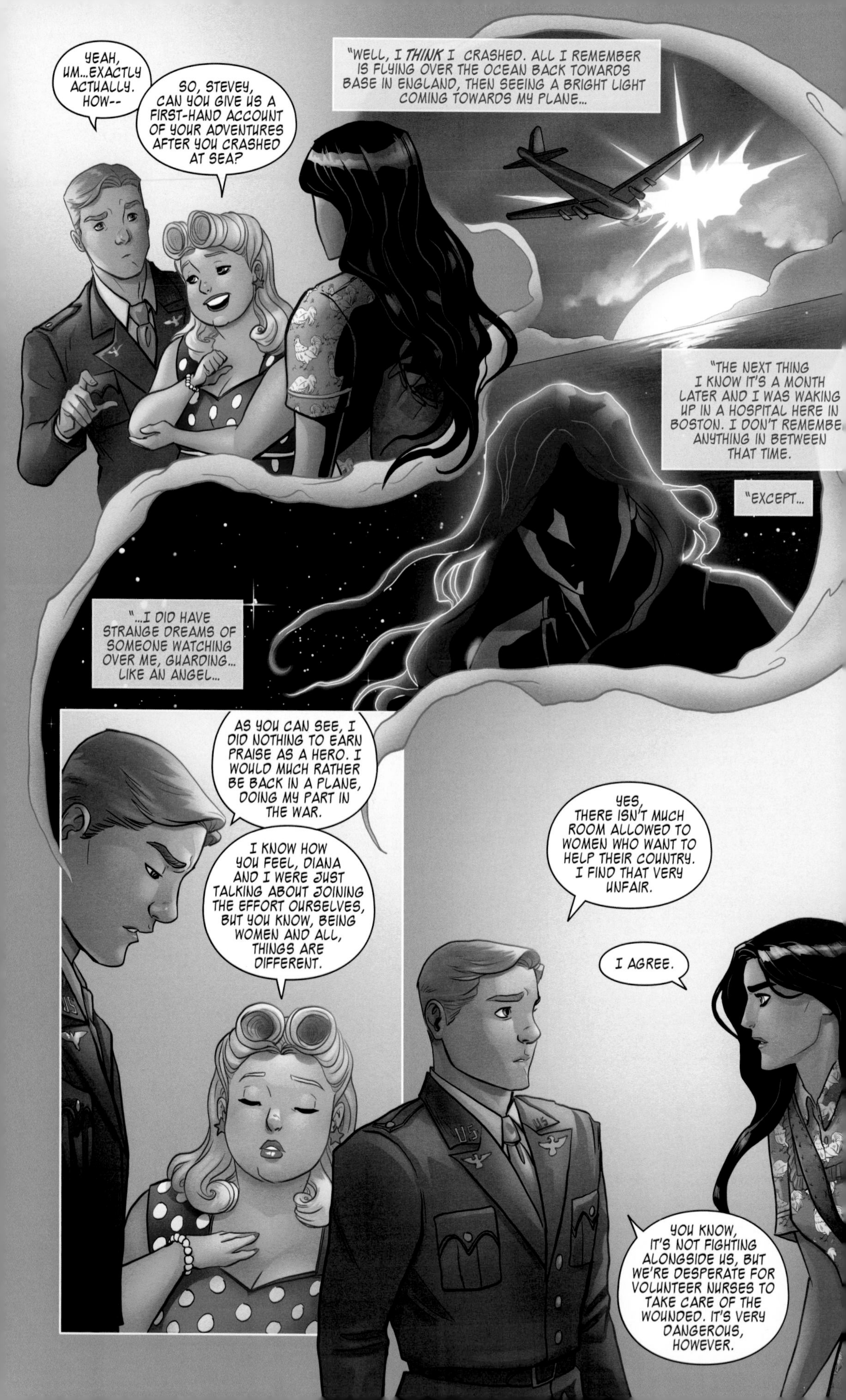
YEAH, UM...EXACTLY ACTUALLY. HOW--
SO, STEVEY, CAN YOU GIVE US A FIRST-HAND ACCOUNT OF YOUR ADVENTURES AFTER YOU CRASHED AT SEA?
"WELL, I THINK I CRASHED. ALL I REMEMBER IS FLYING OVER THE OCEAN BACK TOWARDS BASE IN ENGLAND, THEN SEEING A BRIGHT LIGHT COMING TOWARDS MY PLANE...
"THE NEXT THING I KNOW IT'S A MONTH LATER AND I WAS WAKING UP IN A HOSPITAL HERE IN BOSTON. I DON'T REMEMBE ANYTHING IN BETWEEN THAT TIME.
"EXCEPT...
"...I DID HAVE STRANGE DREAMS OF SOMEONE WATCHING OVER ME, GUARDING... LIKE AN ANGEL...
AS YOU CAN SEE, I DID NOTHING TO EARN PRAISE AS A HERO. I WOULD MUCH RATHER BE BACK IN A PLANE, DOING MY PART IN THE WAR.
I KNOW HOW YOU FEEL, DIANA AND I WERE JUST TALKING ABOUT JOINING THE EFFORT OURSELVES, BUT YOU KNOW, BEING WOMEN AND ALL, THINGS ARE DIFFERENT.
YES, THERE ISN'T MUCH ROOM ALLOWED TO WOMEN WHO WANT TO HELP THEIR COUNTRY. I FIND THAT VERY UNFAIR.
I AGREE.
YOU KNOW, IT'S NOT FIGHTING ALONGSIDE US, BUT WE'RE DESPERATE FOR VOLUNTEER NURSES TO TAKE CARE OF THE WOUNDED. IT'S VERY DANGEROUS, HOWEVER.

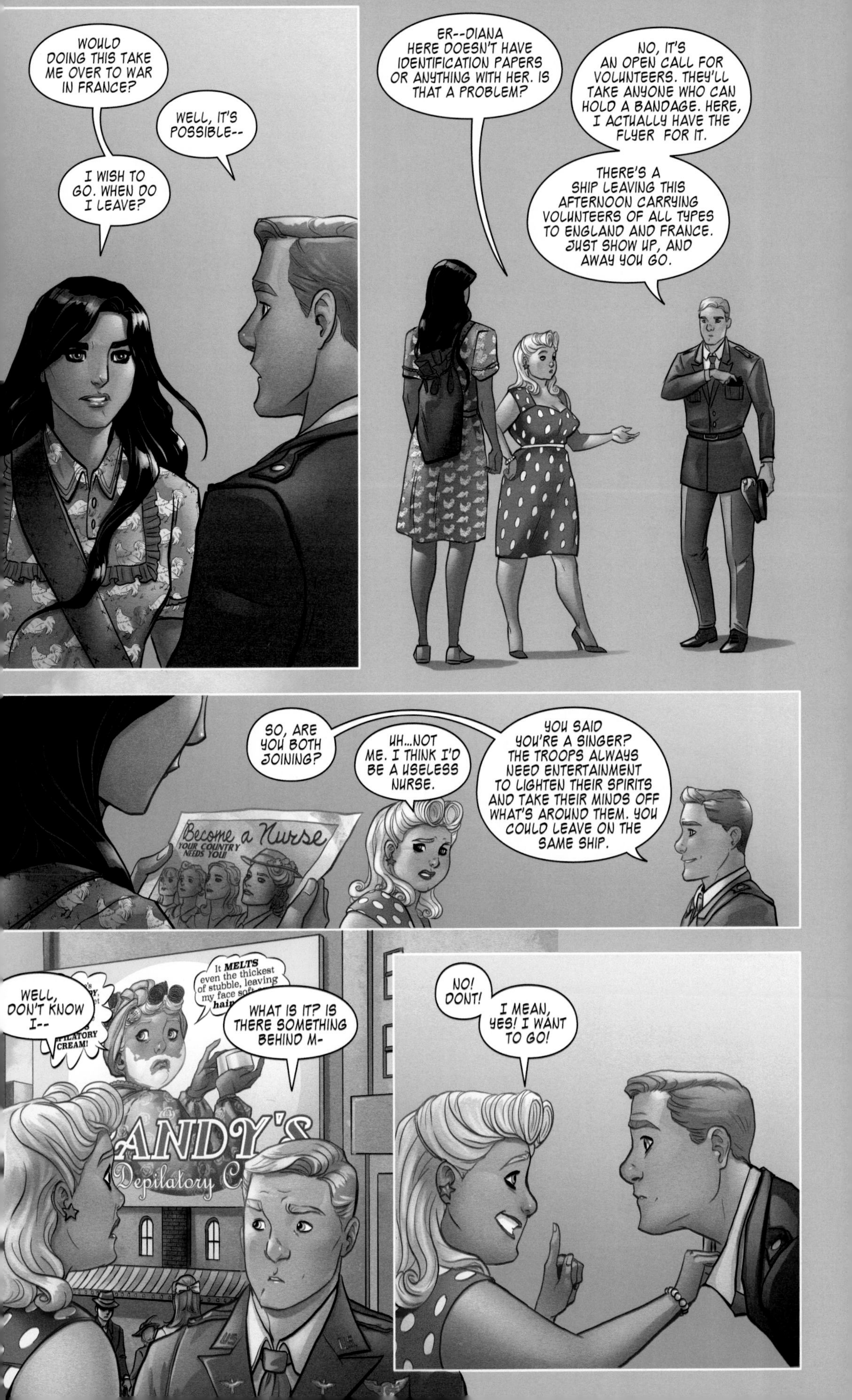
WOULD DOING THIS TAKE ME OVER TO WAR IN FRANCE?
WELL, IT'S POSSIBLE--
I WISH TO GO. WHEN DO I LEAVE?
ER--DIANA HERE DOESN'T HAVE IDENTIFICATION PAPERS OR ANYTHING WITH HER. IS THAT A PROBLEM?
NO, IT'S AN OPEN CALL FOR VOLUNTEERS. THEY'LL TAKE ANYONE WHO CAN HOLD A BANDAGE. HERE, I ACTUALLY HAVE THE FLYER FOR IT.
THERE'S A SHIP LEAVING THIS AFTERNOON CARRYING VOLUNTEERS OF ALL TYPES TO ENGLAND AND FRANCE. JUST SHOW UP, AND AWAY YOU GO.
Become a Nurse
YOUR COUNTRY NEEDS YOU!
SO, ARE YOU BOTH JOINING?
UH...NOT ME. I THINK I'D BE A USELESS NURSE.
YOU SAID YOU'RE A SINGER? THE TROOPS ALWAYS NEED ENTERTAINMENT TO LIGHTEN THEIR SPIRITS AND TAKE THEIR MINDS OFF WHAT'S AROUND THEM. YOU COULD LEAVE ON THE SAME SHIP.
WELL, DON'T KNOW I--
It MELTS even the thickest of stubble, leaving my face
CREAM!
WHAT IS IT? IS THERE SOMETHING BEHIND M-
Depilatory
NO! DONT!
I MEAN, YES! I WANT TO GO!

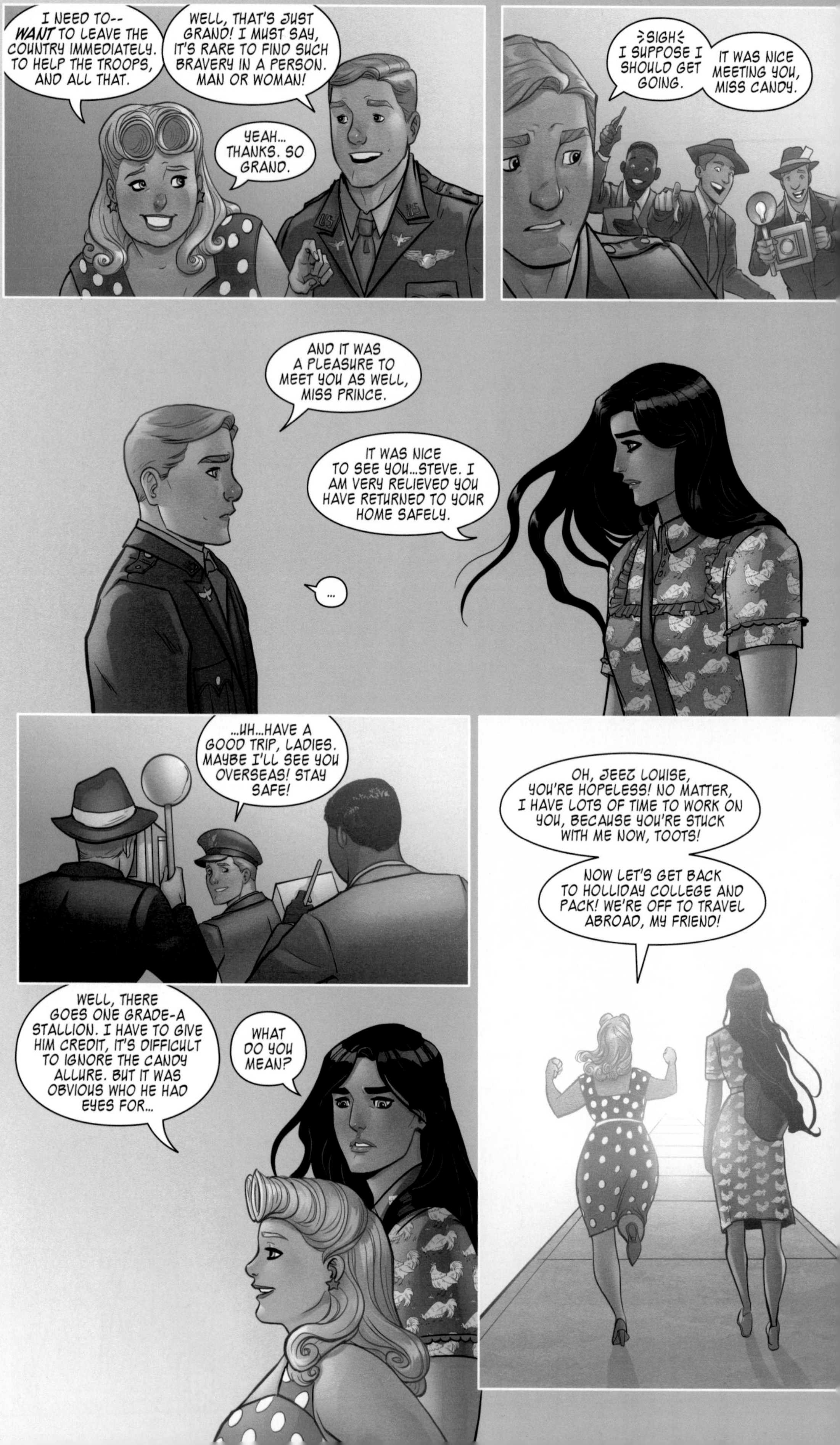
I NEED TO-- *WANT* TO LEAVE THE COUNTRY IMMEDIATELY. TO HELP THE TROOPS, AND ALL THAT.
WELL, THAT'S JUST GRAND! I MUST SAY, IT'S RARE TO FIND SUCH BRAVERY IN A PERSON. MAN OR WOMAN!
YEAH... THANKS. SO GRAND.
>SIGH< I SUPPOSE I SHOULD GET GOING.
IT WAS NICE MEETING YOU, MISS CANDY.
AND IT WAS A PLEASURE TO MEET YOU AS WELL, MISS PRINCE.
IT WAS NICE TO SEE YOU...STEVE. I AM VERY RELIEVED YOU HAVE RETURNED TO YOUR HOME SAFELY.
...
...UH...HAVE A GOOD TRIP, LADIES. MAYBE I'LL SEE YOU OVERSEAS! STAY SAFE!
WELL, THERE GOES ONE GRADE-A STALLION. I HAVE TO GIVE HIM CREDIT, IT'S DIFFICULT TO IGNORE THE CANDY ALLURE. BUT IT WAS OBVIOUS WHO HE HAD EYES FOR...
WHAT DO YOU MEAN?
OH, JEEZ LOUISE, YOU'RE HOPELESS! NO MATTER, I HAVE LOTS OF TIME TO WORK ON YOU, BECAUSE YOU'RE STUCK WITH ME NOW, TOOTS!
NOW LET'S GET BACK TO HOLLIDAY COLLEGE AND PACK! WE'RE OFF TO TRAVEL ABROAD, MY FRIEND!

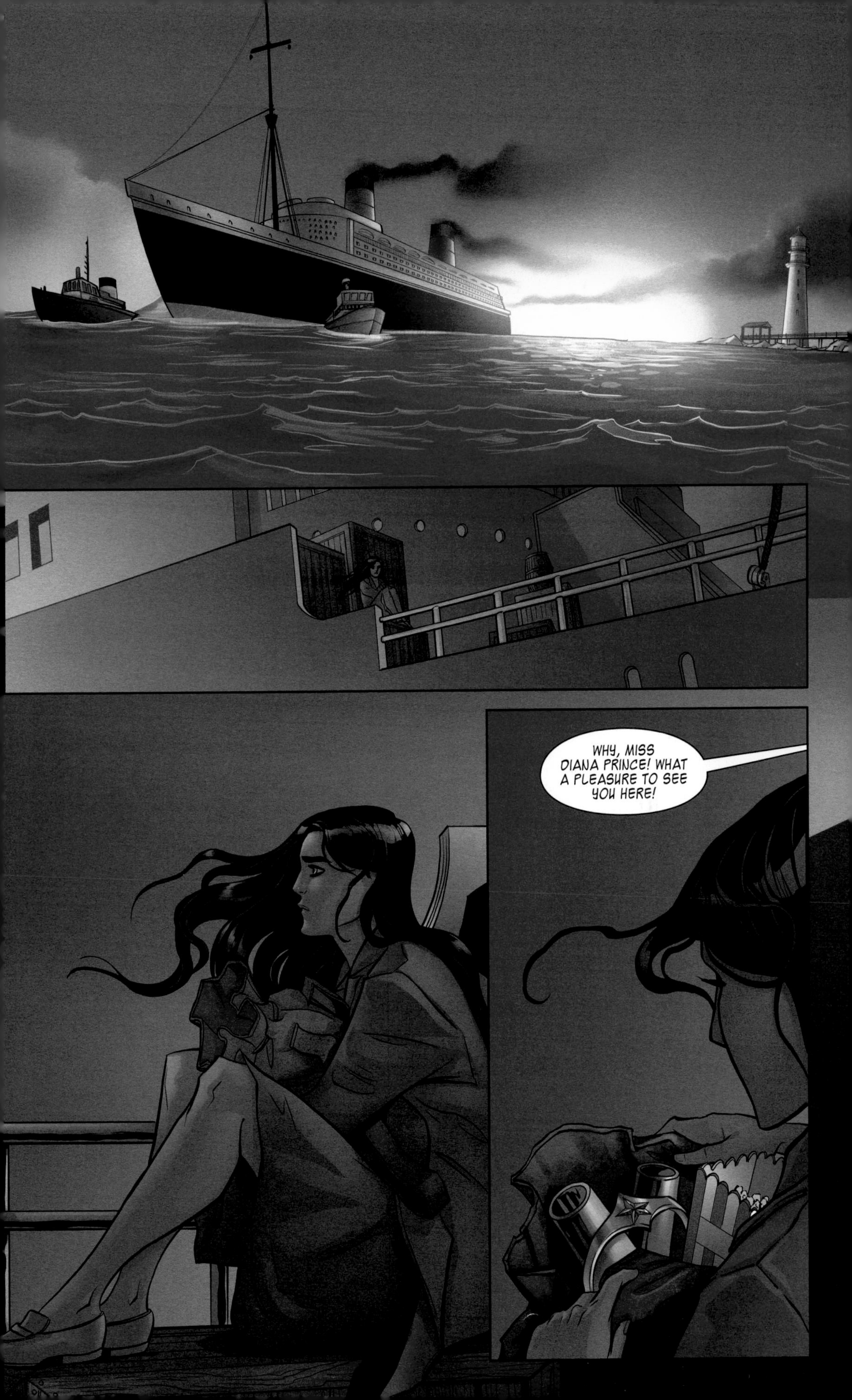
WHY, MISS DIANA PRINCE! WHAT A PLEASURE TO SEE YOU HERE!

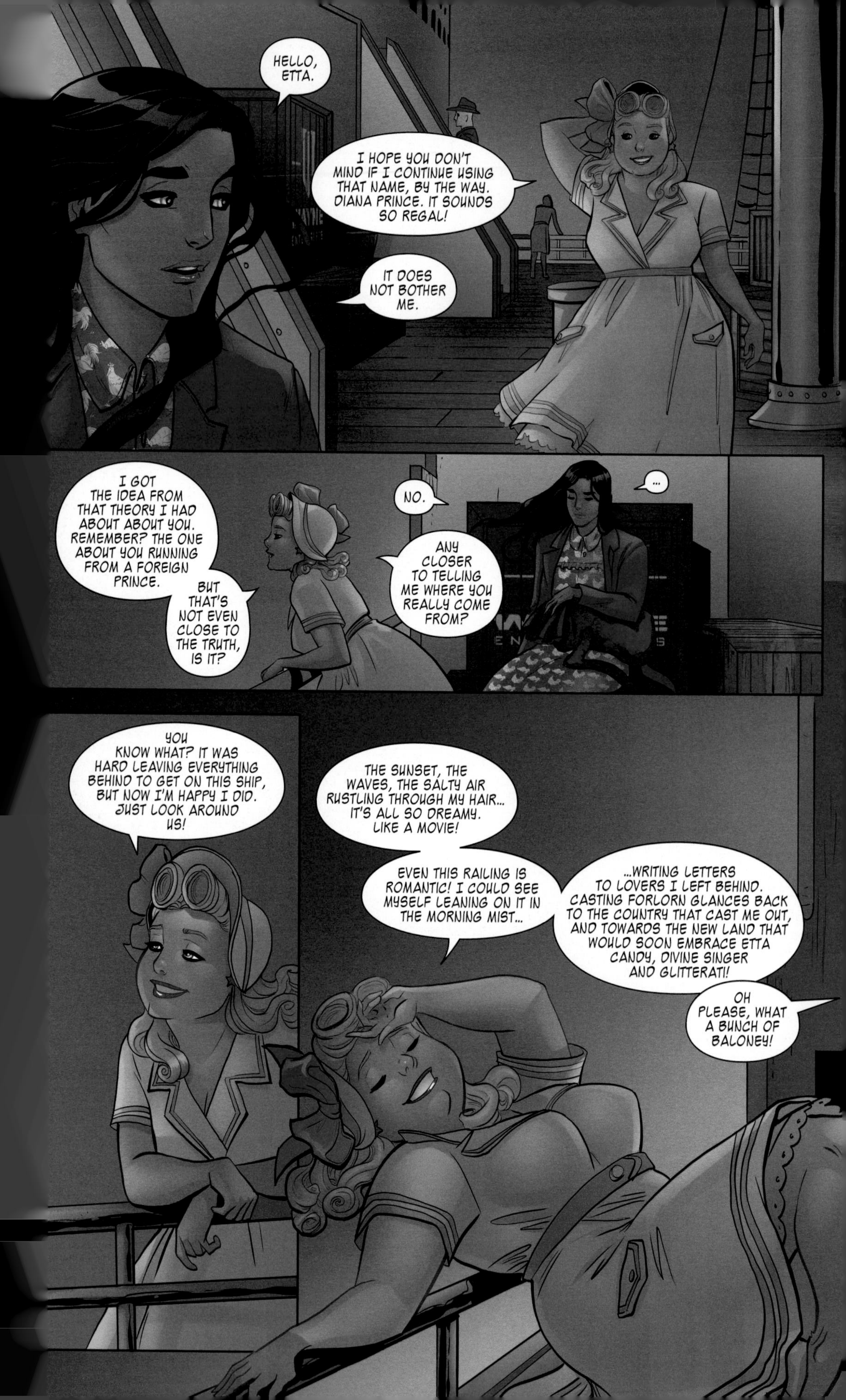
HELLO, ETTA.
I HOPE YOU DON'T MIND IF I CONTINUE USING THAT NAME, BY THE WAY. DIANA PRINCE. IT SOUNDS SO REGAL!
IT DOES NOT BOTHER ME.
I GOT THE IDEA FROM THAT THEORY I HAD ABOUT ABOUT YOU. REMEMBER? THE ONE ABOUT YOU RUNNING FROM A FOREIGN PRINCE.
BUT THAT'S NOT EVEN CLOSE TO THE TRUTH, IS IT?
NO.
ANY CLOSER TO TELLING ME WHERE YOU REALLY COME FROM?
...
YOU KNOW WHAT? IT WAS HARD LEAVING EVERYTHING BEHIND TO GET ON THIS SHIP, BUT NOW I'M HAPPY I DID. JUST LOOK AROUND US!
THE SUNSET, THE WAVES, THE SALTY AIR RUSTLING THROUGH MY HAIR... IT'S ALL SO DREAMY. LIKE A MOVIE!
EVEN THIS RAILING IS ROMANTIC! I COULD SEE MYSELF LEANING ON IT IN THE MORNING MIST...
...WRITING LETTERS TO LOVERS I LEFT BEHIND. CASTING FORLORN GLANCES BACK TO THE COUNTRY THAT CAST ME OUT, AND TOWARDS THE NEW LAND THAT WOULD SOON EMBRACE ETTA CANDY, DIVINE SINGER AND GLITTERATI!
OH PLEASE, WHAT A BUNCH OF BALONEY!

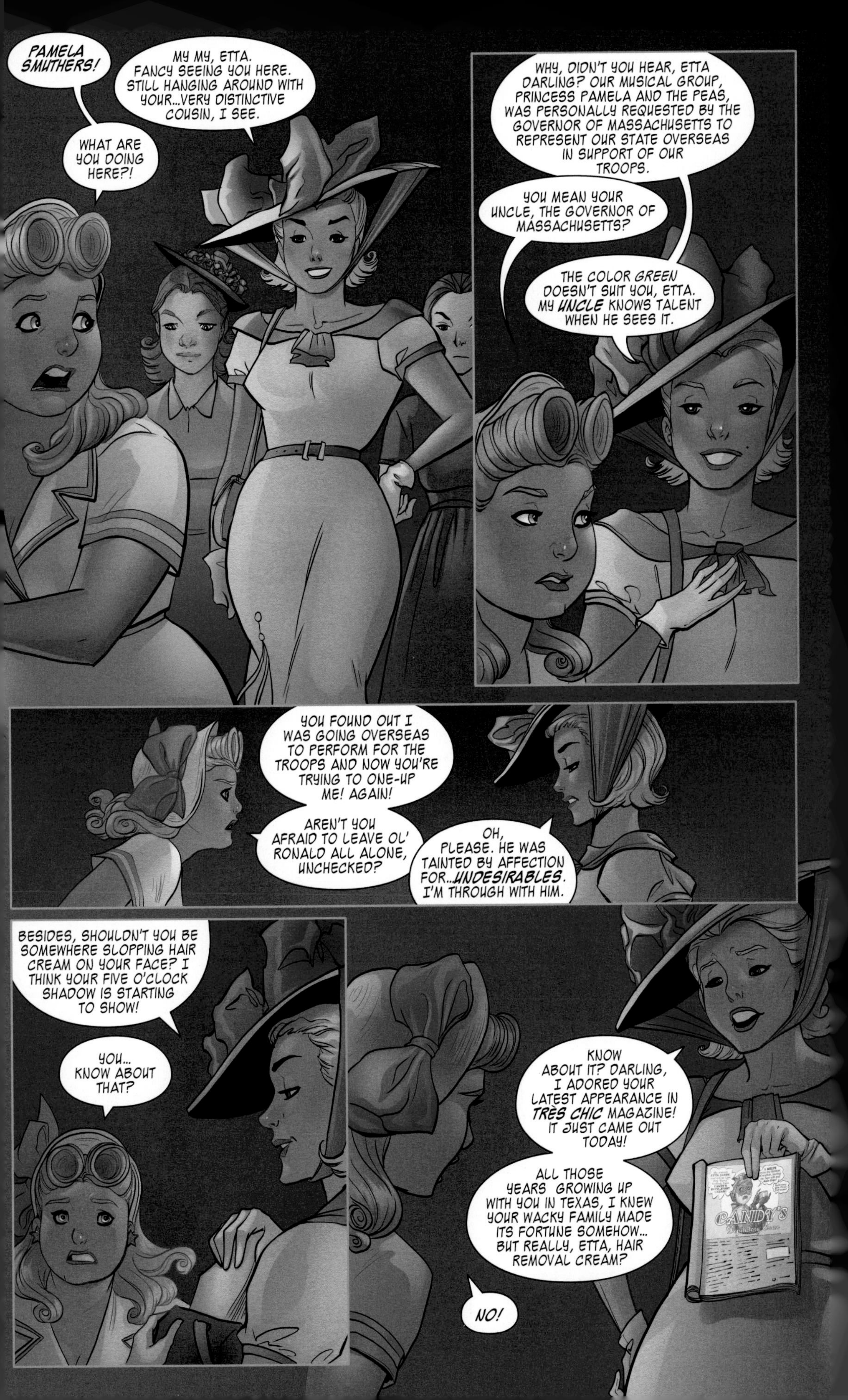
PAMELA SMUTHERS!
WHAT ARE YOU DOING HERE?!
MY MY, ETTA. FANCY SEEING YOU HERE. STILL HANGING AROUND WITH YOUR...VERY DISTINCTIVE COUSIN, I SEE.
WHY, DIDN'T YOU HEAR, ETTA DARLING? OUR MUSICAL GROUP, PRINCESS PAMELA AND THE PEAS, WAS PERSONALLY REQUESTED BY THE GOVERNOR OF MASSACHUSETTS TO REPRESENT OUR STATE OVERSEAS IN SUPPORT OF OUR TROOPS.
YOU MEAN YOUR UNCLE, THE GOVERNOR OF MASSACHUSETTS?
THE COLOR GREEN DOESN'T SUIT YOU, ETTA. MY UNCLE KNOWS TALENT WHEN HE SEES IT.
YOU FOUND OUT I WAS GOING OVERSEAS TO PERFORM FOR THE TROOPS AND NOW YOU'RE TRYING TO ONE-UP ME! AGAIN!
AREN'T YOU AFRAID TO LEAVE OL' RONALD ALL ALONE, UNCHECKED?
OH, PLEASE. HE WAS TAINTED BY AFFECTION FOR...UNDESIRABLES. I'M THROUGH WITH HIM.
BESIDES, SHOULDN'T YOU BE SOMEWHERE SLOPPING HAIR CREAM ON YOUR FACE? I THINK YOUR FIVE O'CLOCK SHADOW IS STARTING TO SHOW!
YOU... KNOW ABOUT THAT?
KNOW ABOUT IT? DARLING, I ADORED YOUR LATEST APPEARANCE IN TRÈS CHIC MAGAZINE! IT JUST CAME OUT TODAY!
ALL THOSE YEARS GROWING UP WITH YOU IN TEXAS, I KNEW YOUR WACKY FAMILY MADE ITS FORTUNE SOMEHOW... BUT REALLY, ETTA, HAIR REMOVAL CREAM?
CANDY'S
NO!

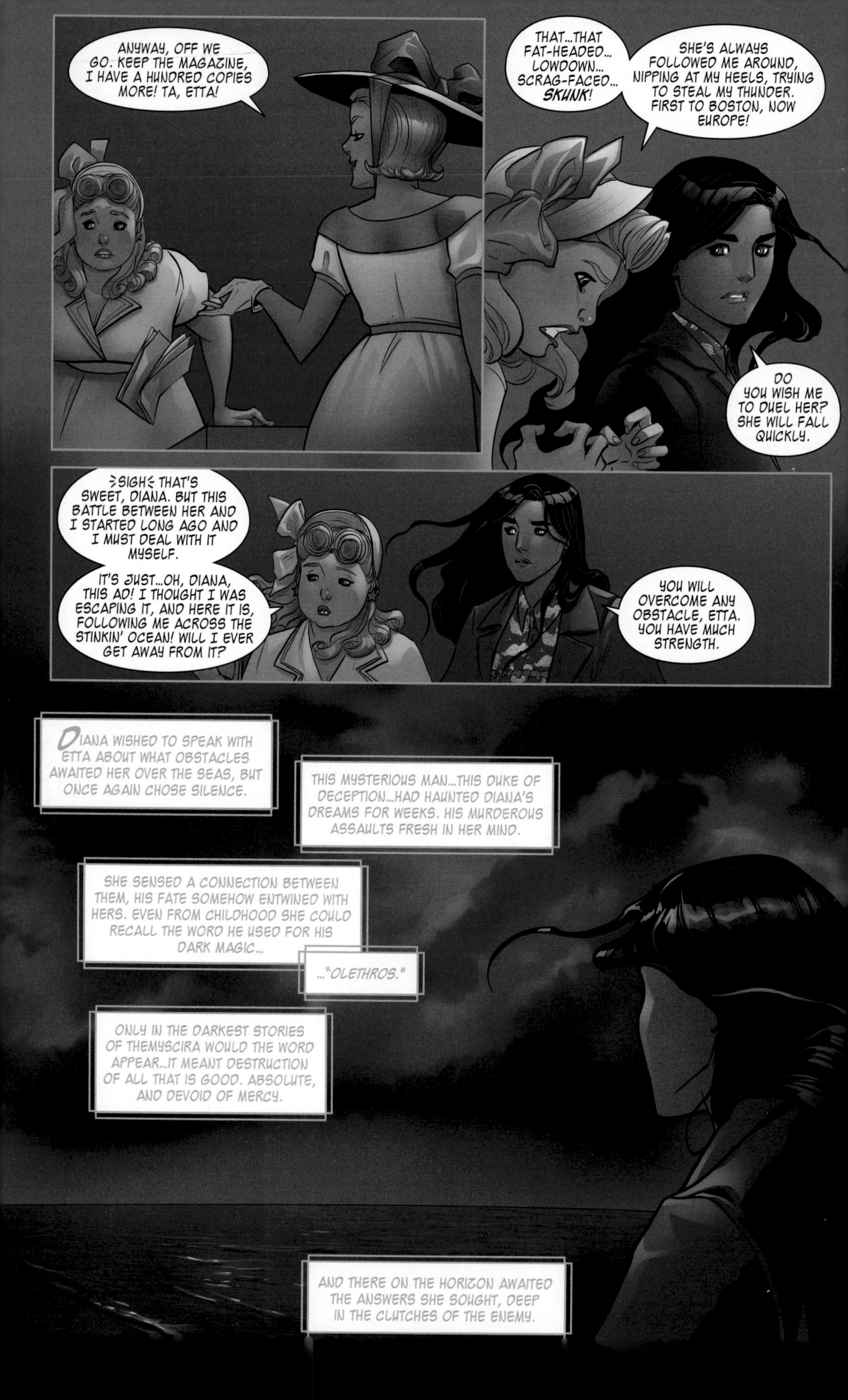

ANYWAY, OFF WE GO. KEEP THE MAGAZINE, I HAVE A HUNDRED COPIES MORE! TA, ETTA!
THAT...THAT FAT-HEADED... LOWDOWN... SCRAG-FACED... SKUNK!
SHE'S ALWAYS FOLLOWED ME AROUND, NIPPING AT MY HEELS, TRYING TO STEAL MY THUNDER. FIRST TO BOSTON, NOW EUROPE!
DO YOU WISH ME TO DUEL HER? SHE WILL FALL QUICKLY.
>SIGH< THAT'S SWEET, DIANA. BUT THIS BATTLE BETWEEN HER AND I STARTED LONG AGO AND I MUST DEAL WITH IT MYSELF.
IT'S JUST...OH, DIANA, THIS AD! I THOUGHT I WAS ESCAPING IT, AND HERE IT IS, FOLLOWING ME ACROSS THE STINKIN' OCEAN! WILL I EVER GET AWAY FROM IT?
YOU WILL OVERCOME ANY OBSTACLE, ETTA. YOU HAVE MUCH STRENGTH.
DIANA WISHED TO SPEAK WITH ETTA ABOUT WHAT OBSTACLES AWAITED HER OVER THE SEAS, BUT ONCE AGAIN CHOSE SILENCE.
THIS MYSTERIOUS MAN...THIS DUKE OF DECEPTION...HAD HAUNTED DIANA'S DREAMS FOR WEEKS. HIS MURDEROUS ASSAULTS FRESH IN HER MIND.
SHE SENSED A CONNECTION BETWEEN THEM, HIS FATE SOMEHOW ENTWINED WITH HERS. EVEN FROM CHILDHOOD SHE COULD RECALL THE WORD HE USED FOR HIS DARK MAGIC...
..."OLETHROS."
ONLY IN THE DARKEST STORIES OF THEMYSCIRA WOULD THE WORD APPEAR...IT MEANT DESTRUCTION OF ALL THAT IS GOOD. ABSOLUTE, AND DEVOID OF MERCY.
AND THERE ON THE HORIZON AWAITED THE ANSWERS SHE SOUGHT, DEEP IN THE CLUTCHES OF THE ENEMY.

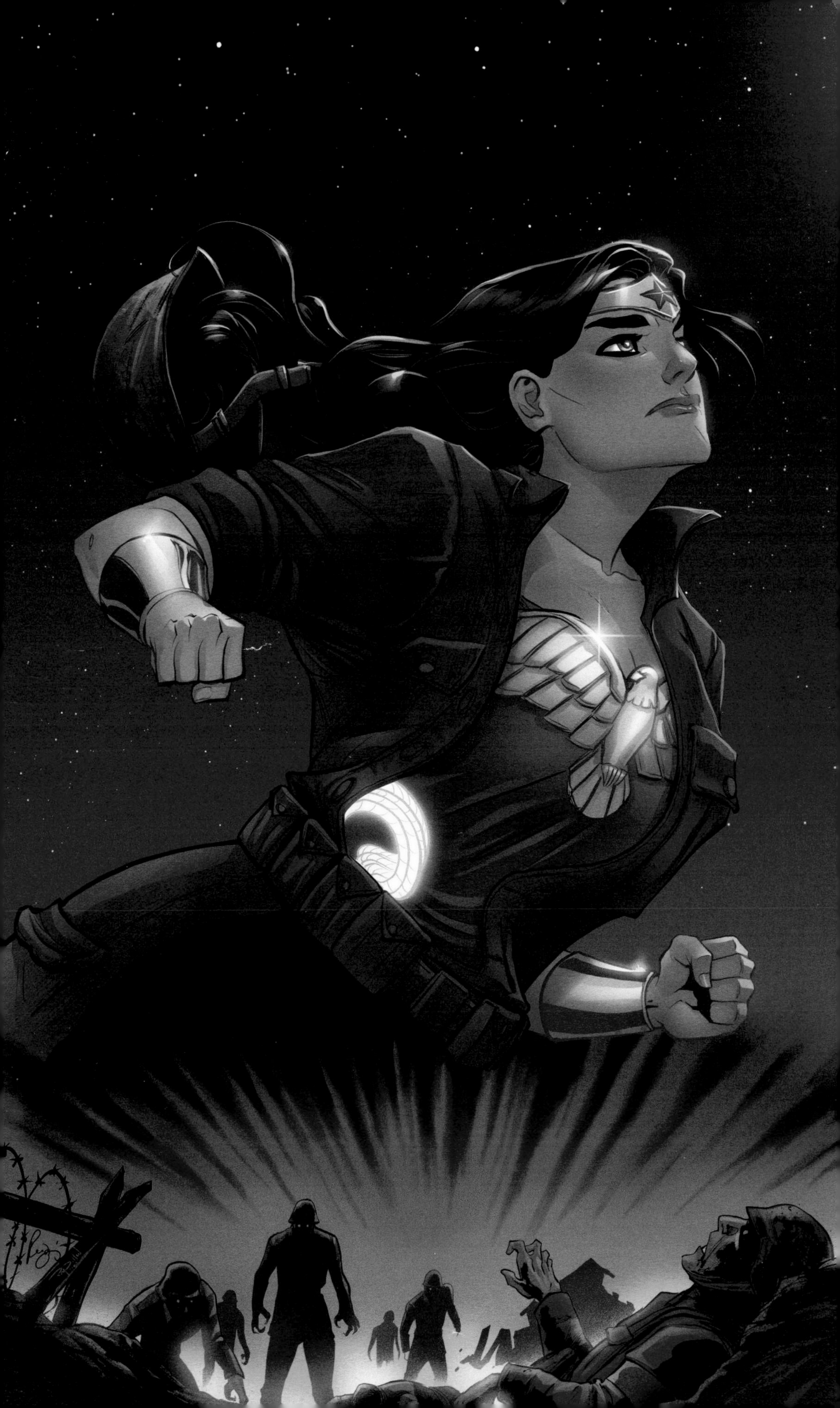

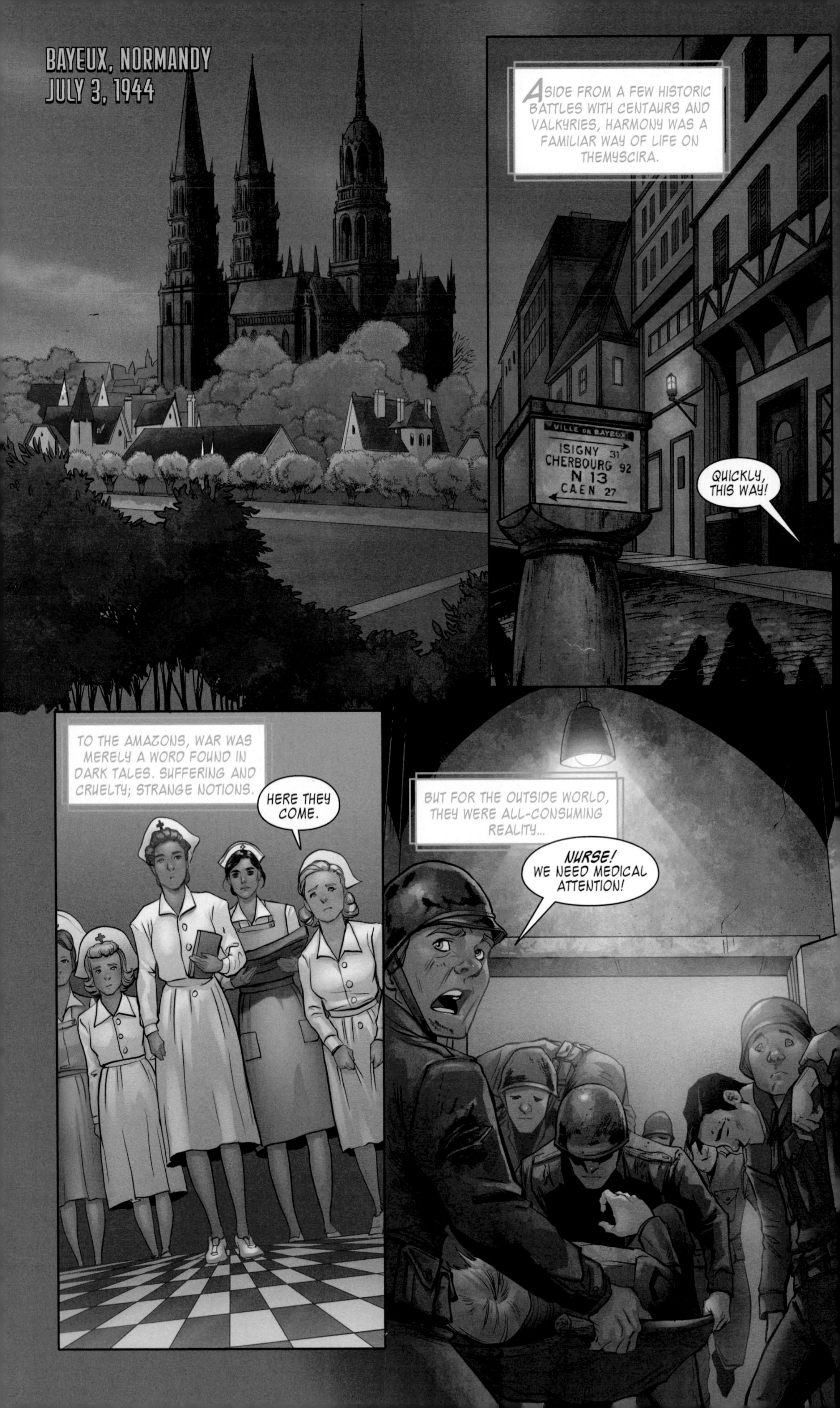
BAYEUX, NORMANDY
JULY 3, 1944
ASIDE FROM A FEW HISTORIC BATTLES WITH CENTAURS AND VALKYRIES, HARMONY WAS A FAMILIAR WAY OF LIFE ON THEMYSCIRA.
VILLE DE BAYEUX
ISIGNY 31
CHERBOURG 92
N 13
CAEN 27
QUICKLY, THIS WAY!
TO THE AMAZONS, WAR WAS MERELY A WORD FOUND IN DARK TALES. SUFFERING AND CRUELTY; STRANGE NOTIONS.
HERE THEY COME.
BUT FOR THE OUTSIDE WORLD, THEY WERE ALL-CONSUMING REALITY...
NURSE! WE NEED MEDICAL ATTENTION!

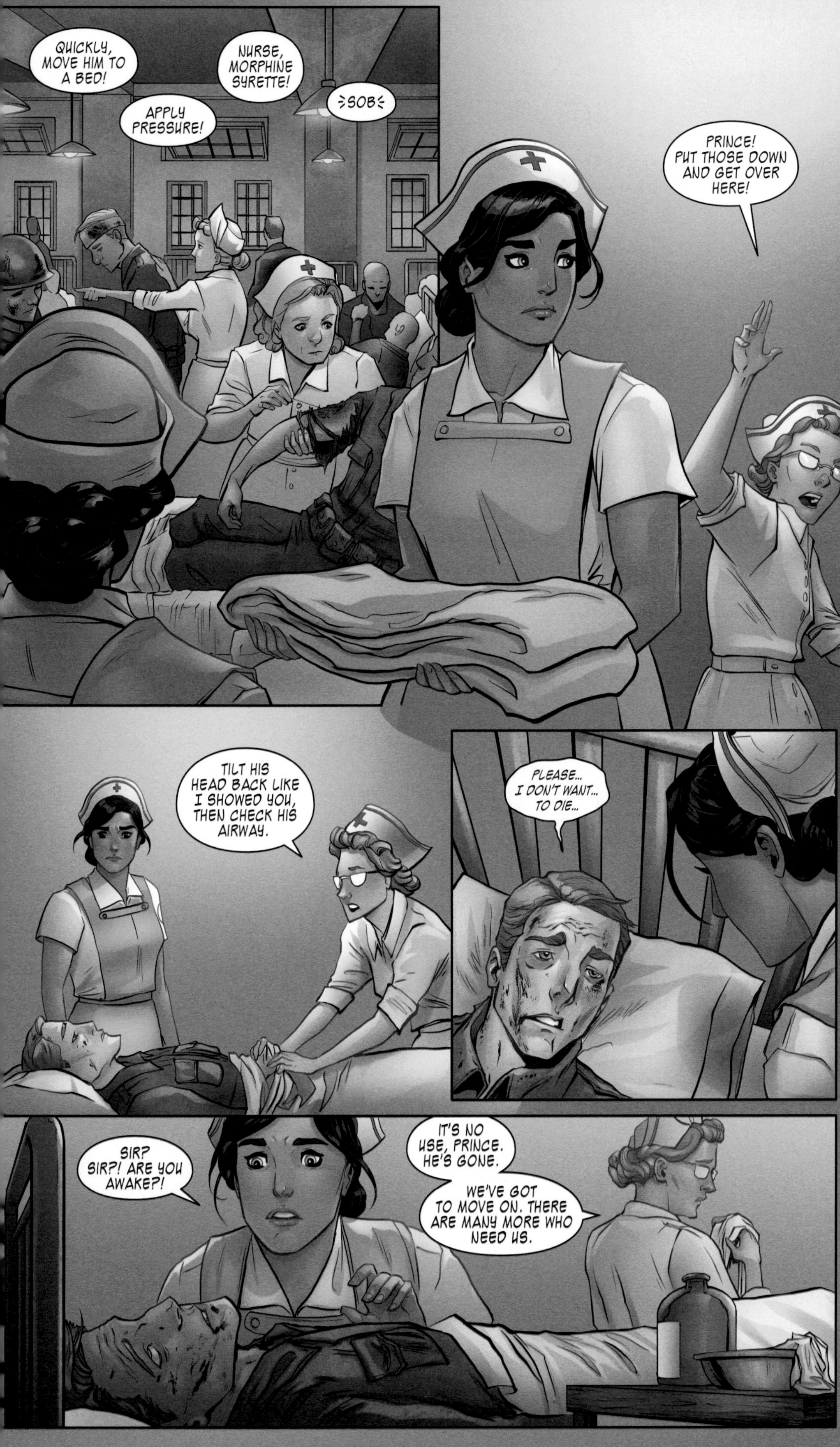
QUICKLY, MOVE HIM TO A BED!
NURSE, MORPHINE SYRETTE!
APPLY PRESSURE!
SOB
PRINCE! PUT THOSE DOWN AND GET OVER HERE!
TILT HIS HEAD BACK LIKE I SHOWED YOU, THEN CHECK HIS AIRWAY.
PLEASE... I DON'T WANT... TO DIE...
SIR? SIR?! ARE YOU AWAKE?!
IT'S NO USE, PRINCE. HE'S GONE.
WE'VE GOT TO MOVE ON. THERE ARE MANY MORE WHO NEED US.

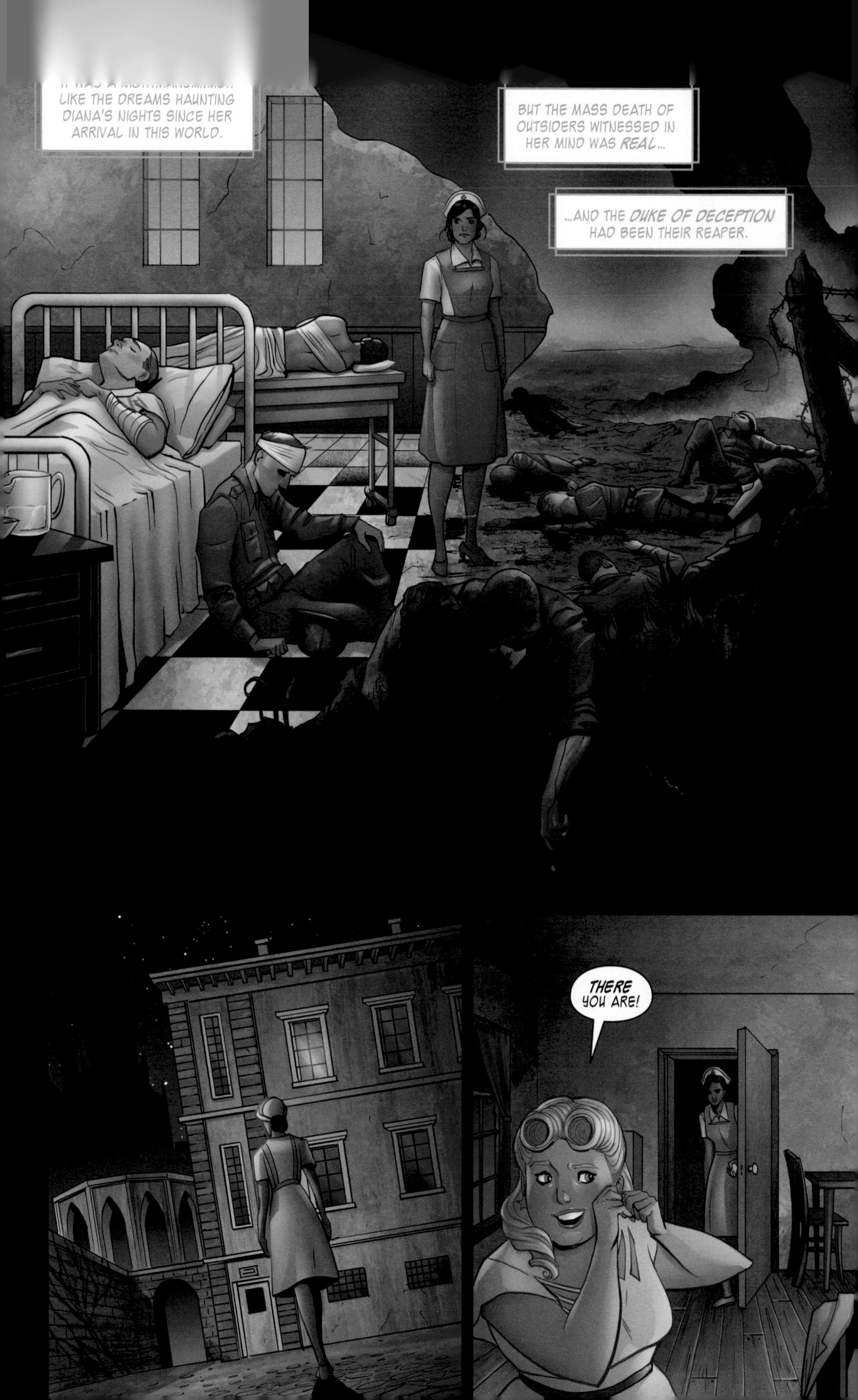
LIKE THE DREAMS HAUNTING DIANA'S NIGHTS SINCE HER ARRIVAL IN THIS WORLD.
BUT THE MASS DEATH OF OUTSIDERS WITNESSED IN HER MIND WAS REAL...
...AND THE DUKE OF DECEPTION HAD BEEN THEIR REAPER.
THERE YOU ARE!

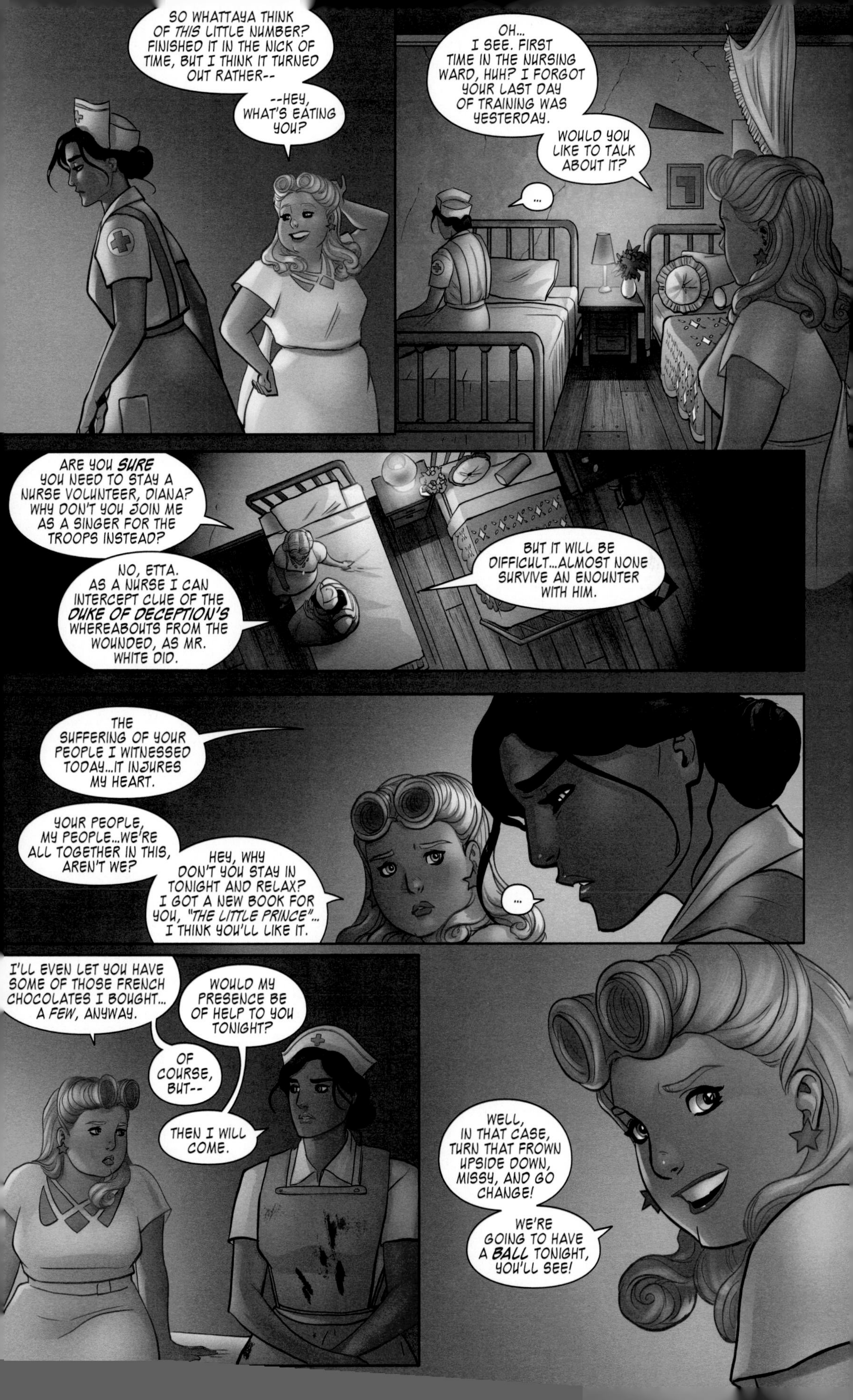
SO WHATTAYA THINK OF *THIS* LITTLE NUMBER? FINISHED IT IN THE NICK OF TIME, BUT I THINK IT TURNED OUT RATHER--
--HEY, WHAT'S EATING YOU?
OH... I SEE. FIRST TIME IN THE NURSING WARD, HUH? I FORGOT YOUR LAST DAY OF TRAINING WAS YESTERDAY.
WOULD YOU LIKE TO TALK ABOUT IT?
...
ARE YOU ***SURE*** YOU NEED TO STAY A NURSE VOLUNTEER, DIANA? WHY DON'T YOU JOIN ME AS A SINGER FOR THE TROOPS INSTEAD?
NO, ETTA. AS A NURSE I CAN INTERCEPT CLUE OF THE ***DUKE OF DECEPTION'S*** WHEREABOUTS FROM THE WOUNDED, AS MR. WHITE DID.
BUT IT WILL BE DIFFICULT...ALMOST NONE SURVIVE AN ENOUNTER WITH HIM.
THE SUFFERING OF YOUR PEOPLE I WITNESSED TODAY...IT INJURES MY HEART.
YOUR PEOPLE, MY PEOPLE...WE'RE ALL TOGETHER IN THIS, AREN'T WE?
HEY, WHY DON'T YOU STAY IN TONIGHT AND RELAX? I GOT A NEW BOOK FOR YOU, *"THE LITTLE PRINCE"*... I THINK YOU'LL LIKE IT.
...
I'LL EVEN LET YOU HAVE SOME OF THOSE FRENCH CHOCOLATES I BOUGHT... A *FEW*, ANYWAY.
WOULD MY PRESENCE BE OF HELP TO YOU TONIGHT?
OF COURSE, BUT--
THEN I WILL COME.
WELL, IN THAT CASE, TURN THAT FROWN UPSIDE DOWN, MISSY, AND GO CHANGE!
WE'RE GOING TO HAVE A ***BALL*** TONIGHT, YOU'LL SEE!

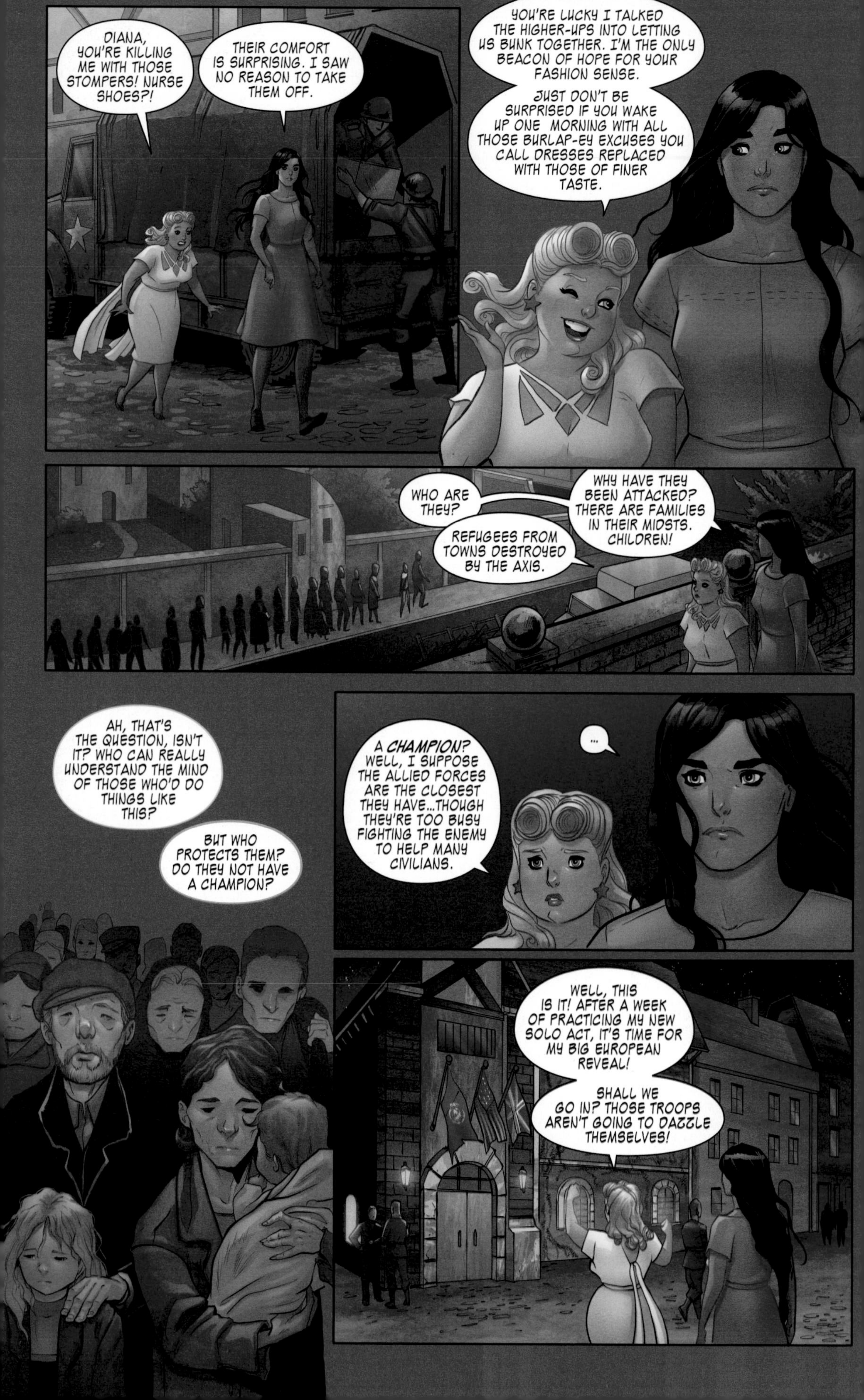
DIANA, YOU'RE KILLING ME WITH THOSE STOMPERS! NURSE SHOES?!
THEIR COMFORT IS SURPRISING. I SAW NO REASON TO TAKE THEM OFF.
YOU'RE LUCKY I TALKED THE HIGHER-UPS INTO LETTING US BUNK TOGETHER. I'M THE ONLY BEACON OF HOPE FOR YOUR FASHION SENSE.
JUST DON'T BE SURPRISED IF YOU WAKE UP ONE MORNING WITH ALL THOSE BURLAP-EY EXCUSES YOU CALL DRESSES REPLACED WITH THOSE OF FINER TASTE.
WHO ARE THEY?
REFUGEES FROM TOWNS DESTROYED BY THE AXIS.
WHY HAVE THEY BEEN ATTACKED? THERE ARE FAMILIES IN THEIR MIDSTS. CHILDREN!
AH, THAT'S THE QUESTION, ISN'T IT? WHO CAN REALLY UNDERSTAND THE MIND OF THOSE WHO'D DO THINGS LIKE THIS?
BUT WHO PROTECTS THEM? DO THEY NOT HAVE A CHAMPION?
A CHAMPION? WELL, I SUPPOSE THE ALLIED FORCES ARE THE CLOSEST THEY HAVE...THOUGH THEY'RE TOO BUSY FIGHTING THE ENEMY TO HELP MANY CIVILIANS.
...
WELL, THIS IS IT! AFTER A WEEK OF PRACTICING MY NEW SOLO ACT, IT'S TIME FOR MY BIG EUROPEAN REVEAL!
SHALL WE GO IN? THOSE TROOPS AREN'T GOING TO DAZZLE THEMSELVES!

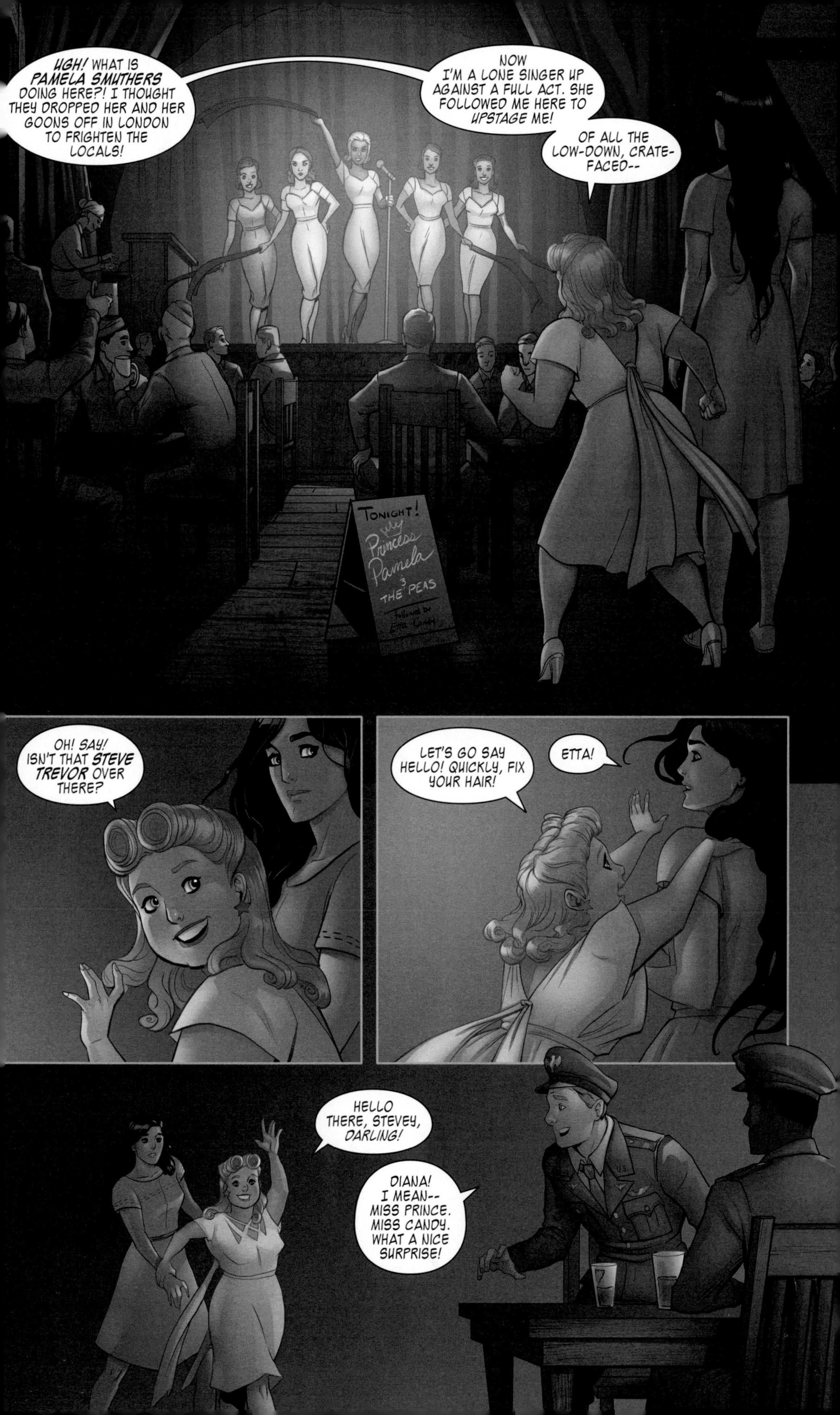
UGH! WHAT IS PAMELA SMUTHERS DOING HERE?! I THOUGHT THEY DROPPED HER AND HER GOONS OFF IN LONDON TO FRIGHTEN THE LOCALS!
NOW I'M A LONE SINGER UP AGAINST A FULL ACT. SHE FOLLOWED ME HERE TO UPSTAGE ME!
OF ALL THE LOW-DOWN, CRATE-FACED--
TONIGHT! Princess Pamela & THE PEAS
Followed by Etta Candy
OH! SAY! ISN'T THAT STEVE TREVOR OVER THERE?
LET'S GO SAY HELLO! QUICKLY, FIX YOUR HAIR!
ETTA!
HELLO THERE, STEVEY, DARLING!
DIANA! I MEAN-- MISS PRINCE. MISS CANDY. WHAT A NICE SURPRISE!

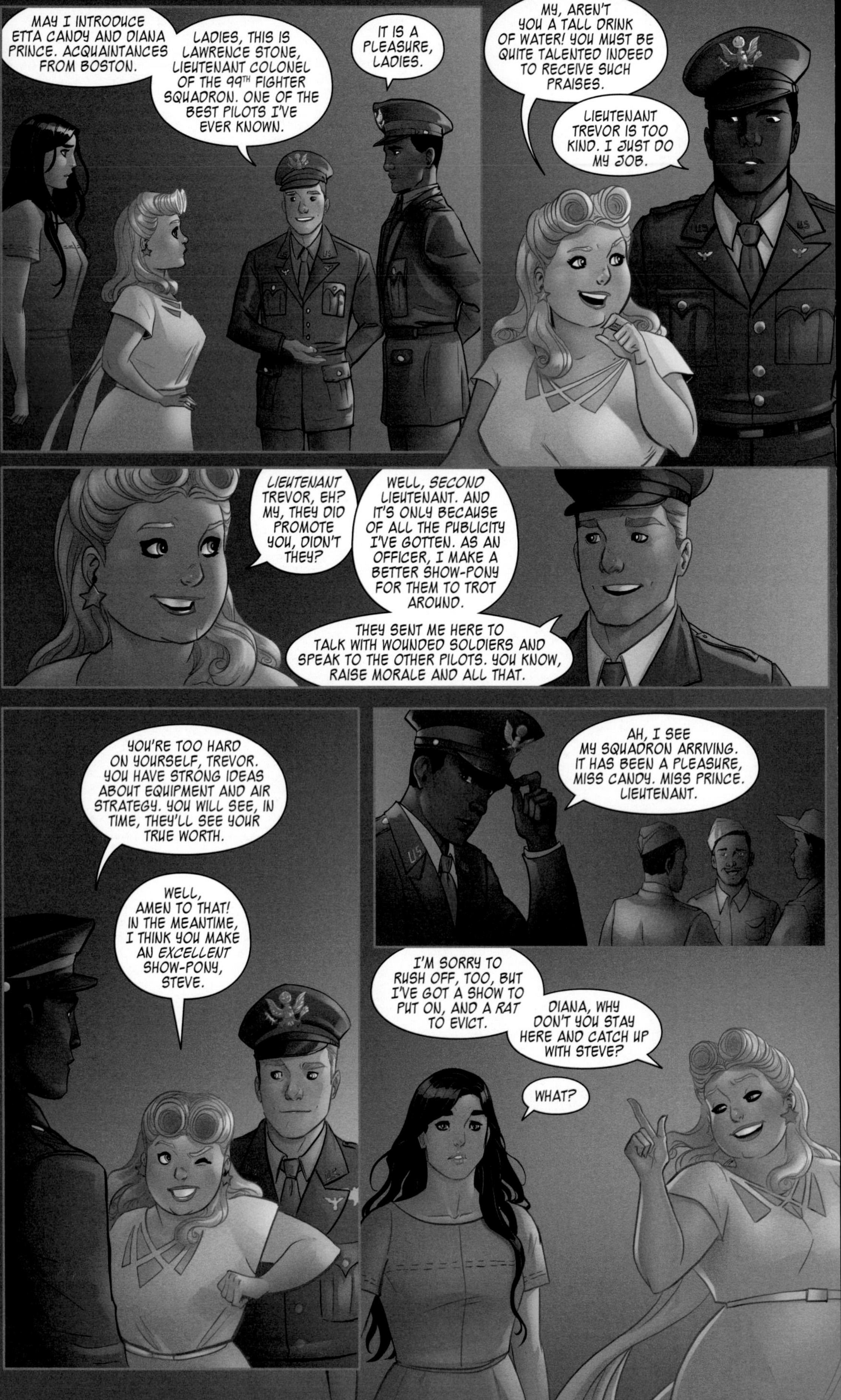

MAY I INTRODUCE ETTA CANDY AND DIANA PRINCE. ACQUAINTANCES FROM BOSTON.
LADIES, THIS IS LAWRENCE STONE, LIEUTENANT COLONEL OF THE 99TH FIGHTER SQUADRON. ONE OF THE BEST PILOTS I'VE EVER KNOWN.
IT IS A PLEASURE, LADIES.
MY, AREN'T YOU A TALL DRINK OF WATER! YOU MUST BE QUITE TALENTED INDEED TO RECEIVE SUCH PRAISES.
LIEUTENANT TREVOR IS TOO KIND. I JUST DO MY JOB.
LIEUTENANT TREVOR, EH? MY, THEY DID PROMOTE YOU, DIDN'T THEY?
WELL, SECOND LIEUTENANT. AND IT'S ONLY BECAUSE OF ALL THE PUBLICITY I'VE GOTTEN. AS AN OFFICER, I MAKE A BETTER SHOW-PONY FOR THEM TO TROT AROUND.
THEY SENT ME HERE TO TALK WITH WOUNDED SOLDIERS AND SPEAK TO THE OTHER PILOTS. YOU KNOW, RAISE MORALE AND ALL THAT.
YOU'RE TOO HARD ON YOURSELF, TREVOR. YOU HAVE STRONG IDEAS ABOUT EQUIPMENT AND AIR STRATEGY. YOU WILL SEE, IN TIME, THEY'LL SEE YOUR TRUE WORTH.
WELL, AMEN TO THAT! IN THE MEANTIME, I THINK YOU MAKE AN EXCELLENT SHOW-PONY, STEVE.
AH, I SEE MY SQUADRON ARRIVING. IT HAS BEEN A PLEASURE, MISS CANDY. MISS PRINCE. LIEUTENANT.
I'M SORRY TO RUSH OFF, TOO, BUT I'VE GOT A SHOW TO PUT ON, AND A RAT TO EVICT.
DIANA, WHY DON'T YOU STAY HERE AND CATCH UP WITH STEVE?
WHAT?

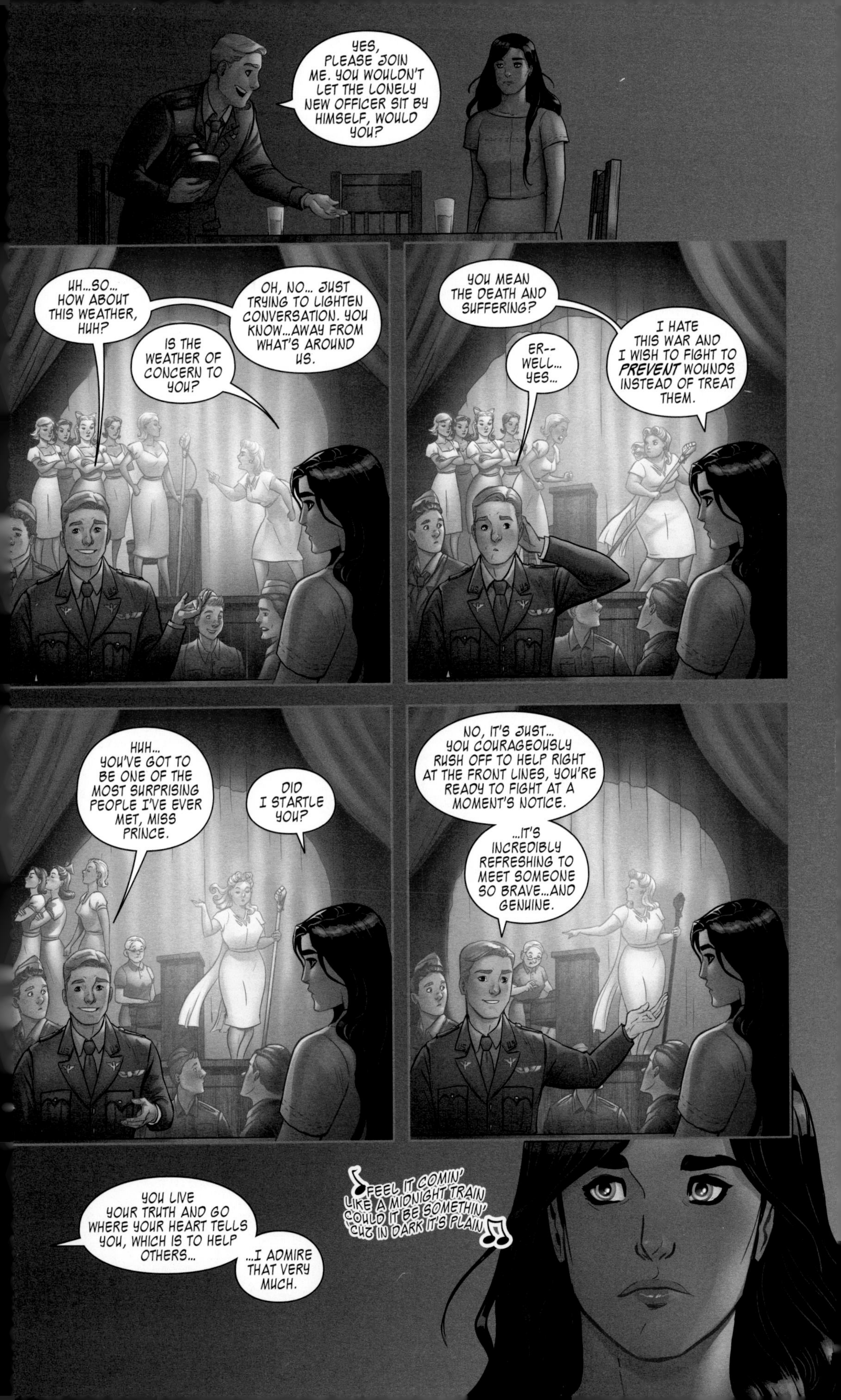
YES, PLEASE JOIN ME. YOU WOULDN'T LET THE LONELY NEW OFFICER SIT BY HIMSELF, WOULD YOU?
UH...SO... HOW ABOUT THIS WEATHER, HUH?
IS THE WEATHER OF CONCERN TO YOU?
OH, NO... JUST TRYING TO LIGHTEN CONVERSATION. YOU KNOW...AWAY FROM WHAT'S AROUND US.
YOU MEAN THE DEATH AND SUFFERING?
ER-- WELL... YES...
I HATE THIS WAR AND I WISH TO FIGHT TO *PREVENT* WOUNDS INSTEAD OF TREAT THEM.
HUH... YOU'VE GOT TO BE ONE OF THE MOST SURPRISING PEOPLE I'VE EVER MET, MISS PRINCE.
DID I STARTLE YOU?
NO, IT'S JUST... YOU COURAGEOUSLY RUSH OFF TO HELP RIGHT AT THE FRONT LINES, YOU'RE READY TO FIGHT AT A MOMENT'S NOTICE.
...IT'S INCREDIBLY REFRESHING TO MEET SOMEONE SO BRAVE...AND GENUINE.
YOU LIVE YOUR TRUTH AND GO WHERE YOUR HEART TELLS YOU, WHICH IS TO HELP OTHERS...
...I ADMIRE THAT VERY MUCH.
FEEL IT COMIN' LIKE A MIDNIGHT TRAIN COULD IT BE SOMETHIN' 'CUZ IN DARK IT'S PLAIN

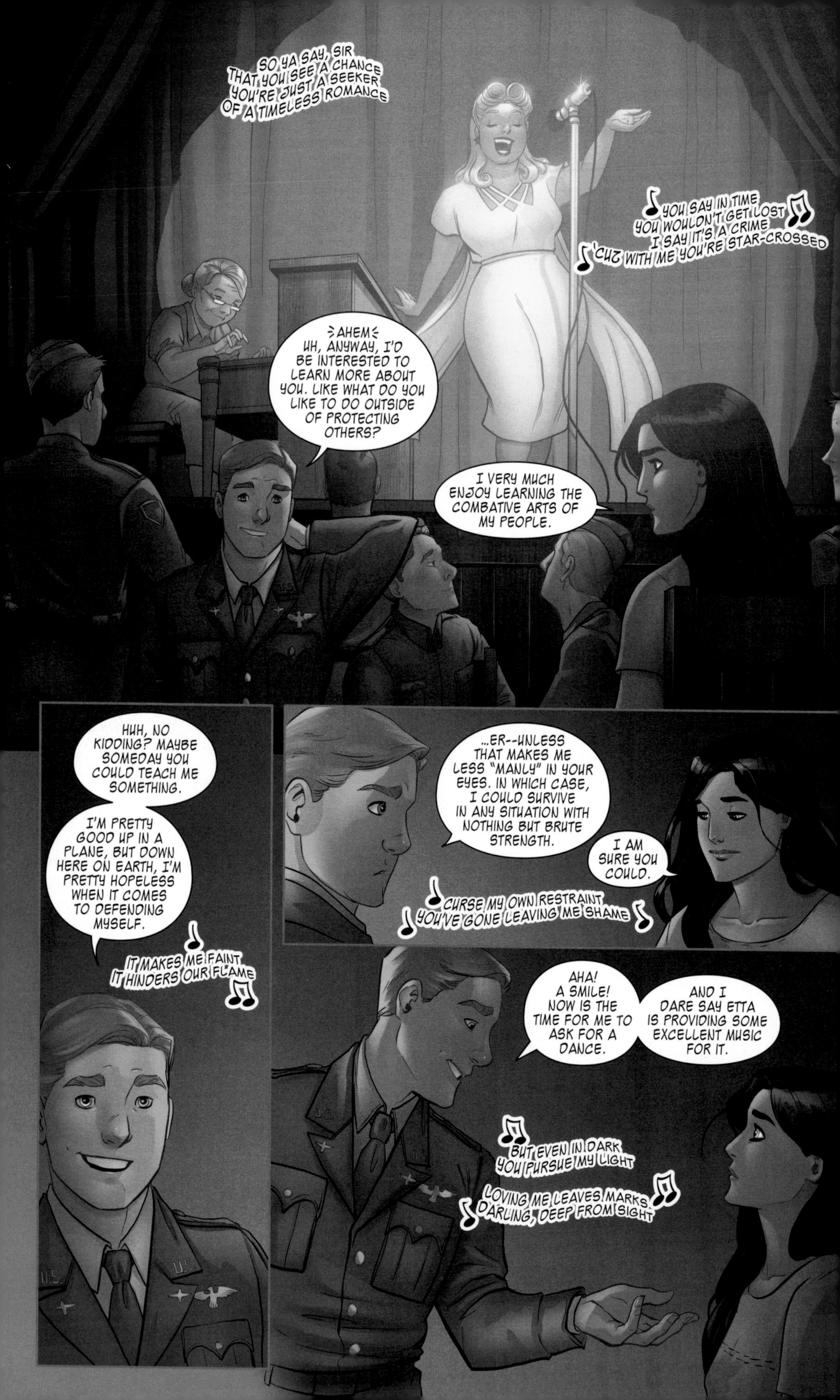

SO YA SAY, SIR THAT YOU SEE A CHANCE YOU'RE JUST A SEEKER OF A TIMELESS ROMANCE
YOU SAY IN TIME YOU WOULDN'T GET LOST I SAY IT'S A CRIME 'CUZ WITH ME YOU'RE STAR-CROSSED
AHEM UH, ANYWAY, I'D BE INTERESTED TO LEARN MORE ABOUT YOU. LIKE WHAT DO YOU LIKE TO DO OUTSIDE OF PROTECTING OTHERS?
I VERY MUCH ENJOY LEARNING THE COMBATIVE ARTS OF MY PEOPLE.
HUH, NO KIDDING? MAYBE SOMEDAY YOU COULD TEACH ME SOMETHING.
I'M PRETTY GOOD UP IN A PLANE, BUT DOWN HERE ON EARTH, I'M PRETTY HOPELESS WHEN IT COMES TO DEFENDING MYSELF.
IT MAKES ME FAINT IT HINDERS OUR FLAME
...ER--UNLESS THAT MAKES ME LESS "MANLY" IN YOUR EYES. IN WHICH CASE, I COULD SURVIVE IN ANY SITUATION WITH NOTHING BUT BRUTE STRENGTH.
I AM SURE YOU COULD.
CURSE MY OWN RESTRAINT YOU'VE GONE LEAVING ME SHAME
AHA! A SMILE! NOW IS THE TIME FOR ME TO ASK FOR A DANCE.
AND I DARE SAY ETTA IS PROVIDING SOME EXCELLENT MUSIC FOR IT.
BUT EVEN IN DARK YOU PURSUE MY LIGHT
LOVING ME LEAVES MARKS DARLING, DEEP FROM SIGHT

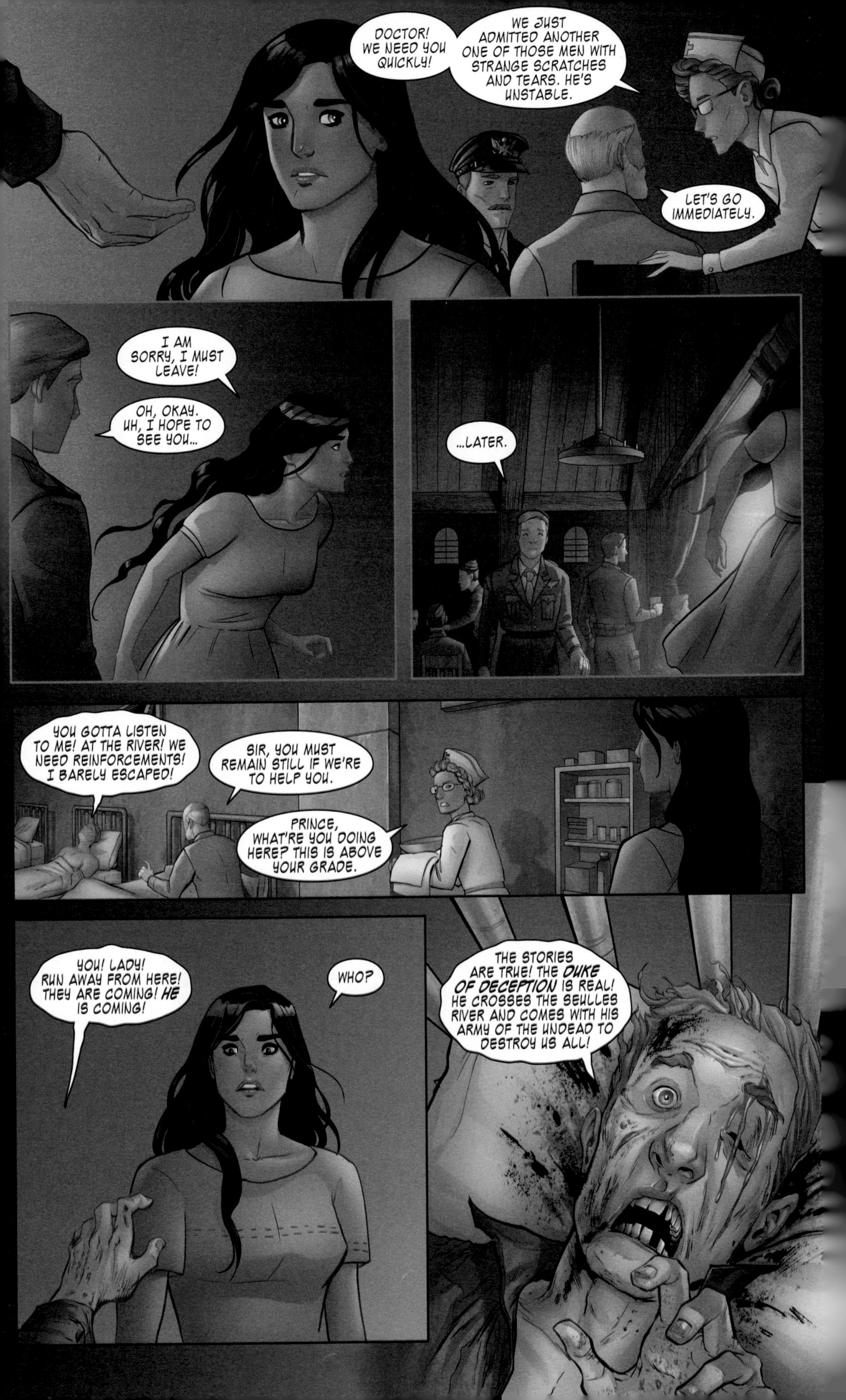
DOCTOR! WE NEED YOU QUICKLY!
WE JUST ADMITTED ANOTHER ONE OF THOSE MEN WITH STRANGE SCRATCHES AND TEARS. HE'S UNSTABLE.
LET'S GO IMMEDIATELY.
I AM SORRY, I MUST LEAVE!
OH, OKAY. UH, I HOPE TO SEE YOU...
...LATER.
YOU GOTTA LISTEN TO ME! AT THE RIVER! WE NEED REINFORCEMENTS! I BARELY ESCAPED!
SIR, YOU MUST REMAIN STILL IF WE'RE TO HELP YOU.
PRINCE, WHAT'RE YOU DOING HERE? THIS IS ABOVE YOUR GRADE.
YOU! LADY! RUN AWAY FROM HERE! THEY ARE COMING! *HE* IS COMING!
WHO?
THE STORIES ARE TRUE! THE *DUKE OF DECEPTION* IS REAL! HE CROSSES THE SEULLES RIVER AND COMES WITH HIS ARMY OF THE UNDEAD TO DESTROY US ALL!

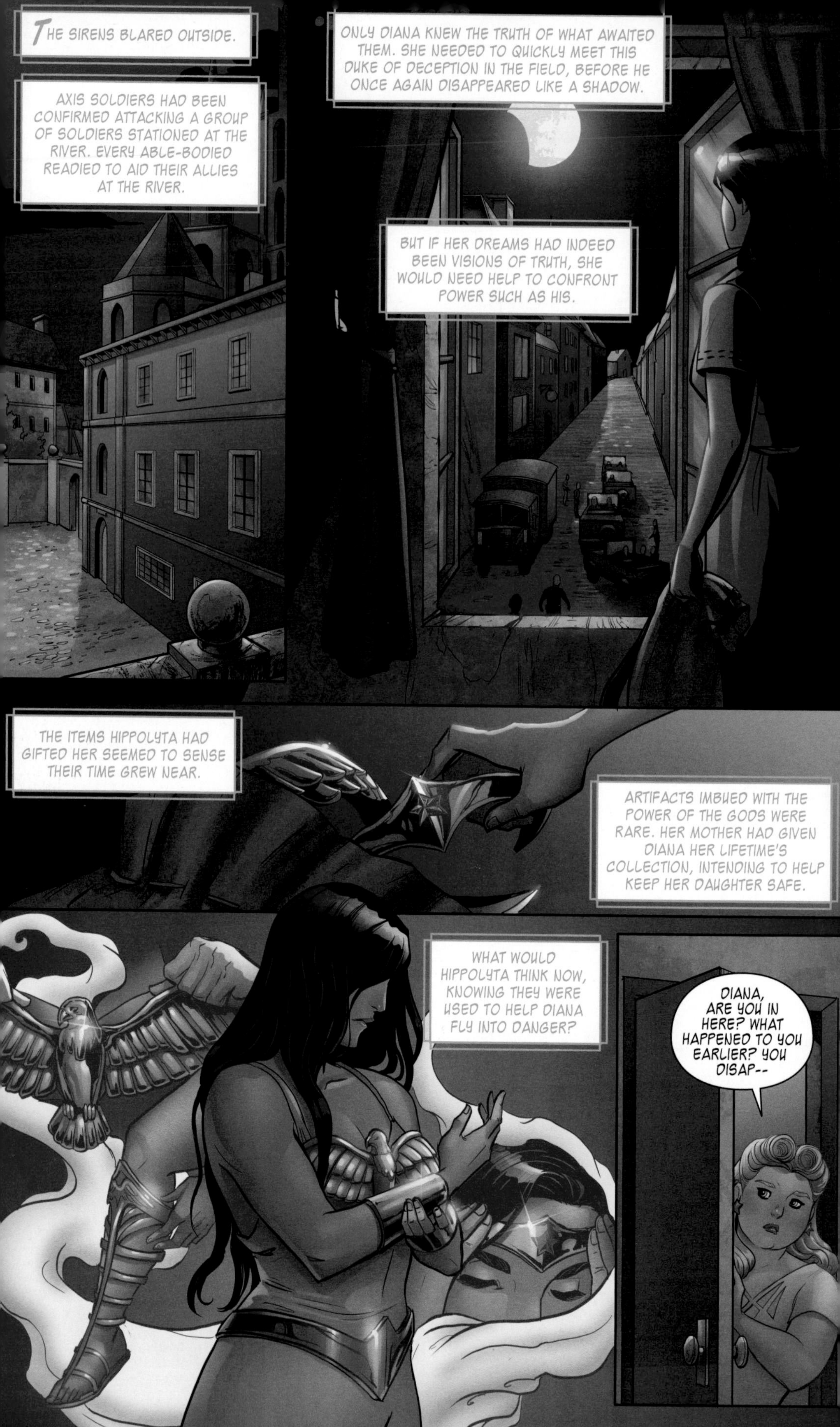
THE SIRENS BLARED OUTSIDE.
AXIS SOLDIERS HAD BEEN CONFIRMED ATTACKING A GROUP OF SOLDIERS STATIONED AT THE RIVER. EVERY ABLE-BODIED READIED TO AID THEIR ALLIES AT THE RIVER.
ONLY DIANA KNEW THE TRUTH OF WHAT AWAITED THEM. SHE NEEDED TO QUICKLY MEET THIS DUKE OF DECEPTION IN THE FIELD, BEFORE HE ONCE AGAIN DISAPPEARED LIKE A SHADOW.
BUT IF HER DREAMS HAD INDEED BEEN VISIONS OF TRUTH, SHE WOULD NEED HELP TO CONFRONT POWER SUCH AS HIS.
THE ITEMS HIPPOLYTA HAD GIFTED HER SEEMED TO SENSE THEIR TIME GREW NEAR.
ARTIFACTS IMBUED WITH THE POWER OF THE GODS WERE RARE. HER MOTHER HAD GIVEN DIANA HER LIFETIME'S COLLECTION, INTENDING TO HELP KEEP HER DAUGHTER SAFE.
WHAT WOULD HIPPOLYTA THINK NOW, KNOWING THEY WERE USED TO HELP DIANA FLY INTO DANGER?
DIANA, ARE YOU IN HERE? WHAT HAPPENED TO YOU EARLIER? YOU DISAP--

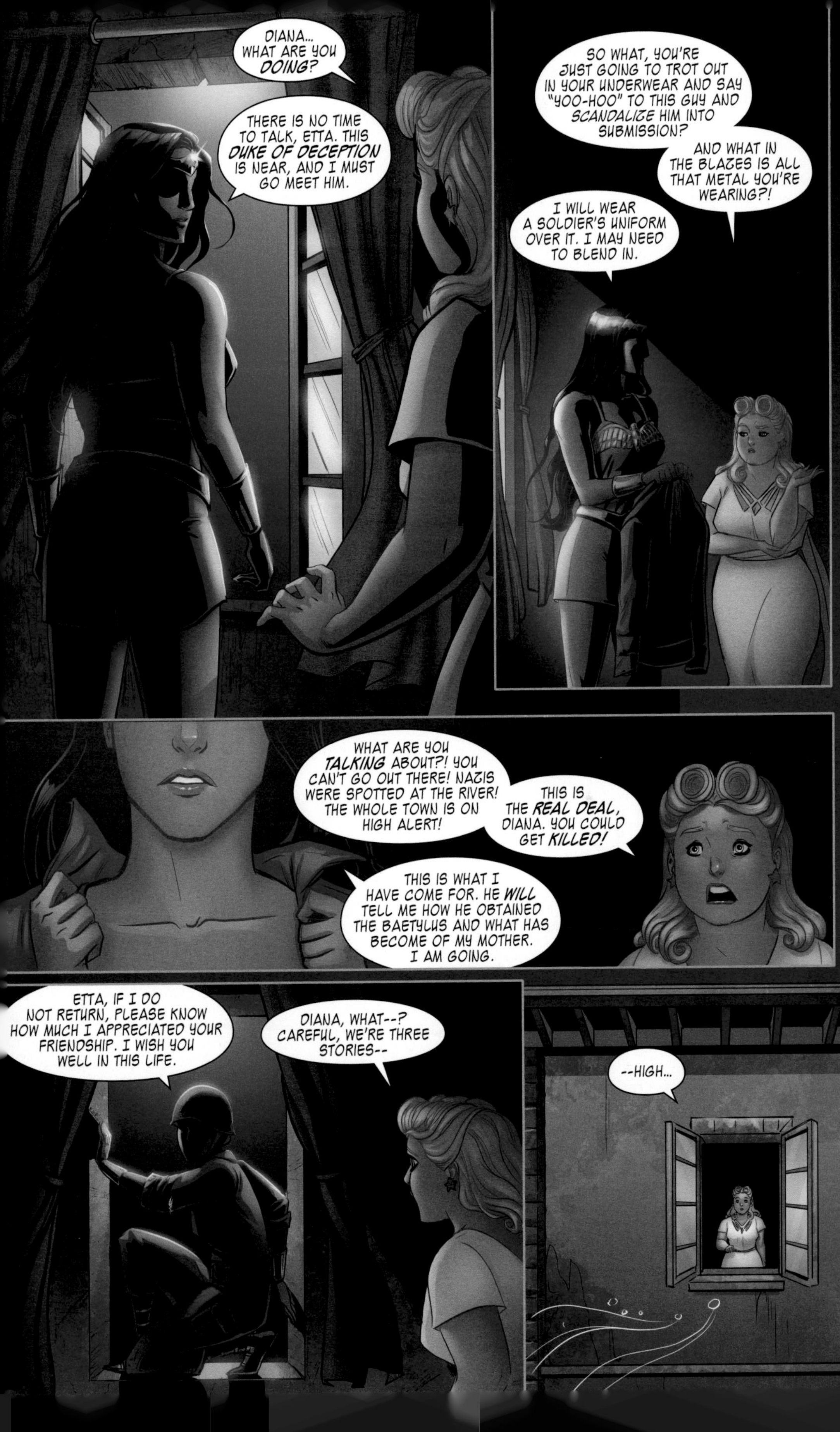
DIANA... WHAT ARE YOU DOING?
THERE IS NO TIME TO TALK, ETTA. THIS DUKE OF DECEPTION IS NEAR, AND I MUST GO MEET HIM.
SO WHAT, YOU'RE JUST GOING TO TROT OUT IN YOUR UNDERWEAR AND SAY "YOO-HOO" TO THIS GUY AND SCANDALIZE HIM INTO SUBMISSION?
AND WHAT IN THE BLAZES IS ALL THAT METAL YOU'RE WEARING?!
I WILL WEAR A SOLDIER'S UNIFORM OVER IT. I MAY NEED TO BLEND IN.
WHAT ARE YOU TALKING ABOUT?! YOU CAN'T GO OUT THERE! NAZIS WERE SPOTTED AT THE RIVER! THE WHOLE TOWN IS ON HIGH ALERT!
THIS IS THE REAL DEAL, DIANA. YOU COULD GET KILLED!
THIS IS WHAT I HAVE COME FOR. HE WILL TELL ME HOW HE OBTAINED THE BAETYLUS AND WHAT HAS BECOME OF MY MOTHER. I AM GOING.
ETTA, IF I DO NOT RETURN, PLEASE KNOW HOW MUCH I APPRECIATED YOUR FRIENDSHIP. I WISH YOU WELL IN THIS LIFE.
DIANA, WHAT--? CAREFUL, WE'RE THREE STORIES--
--HIGH...

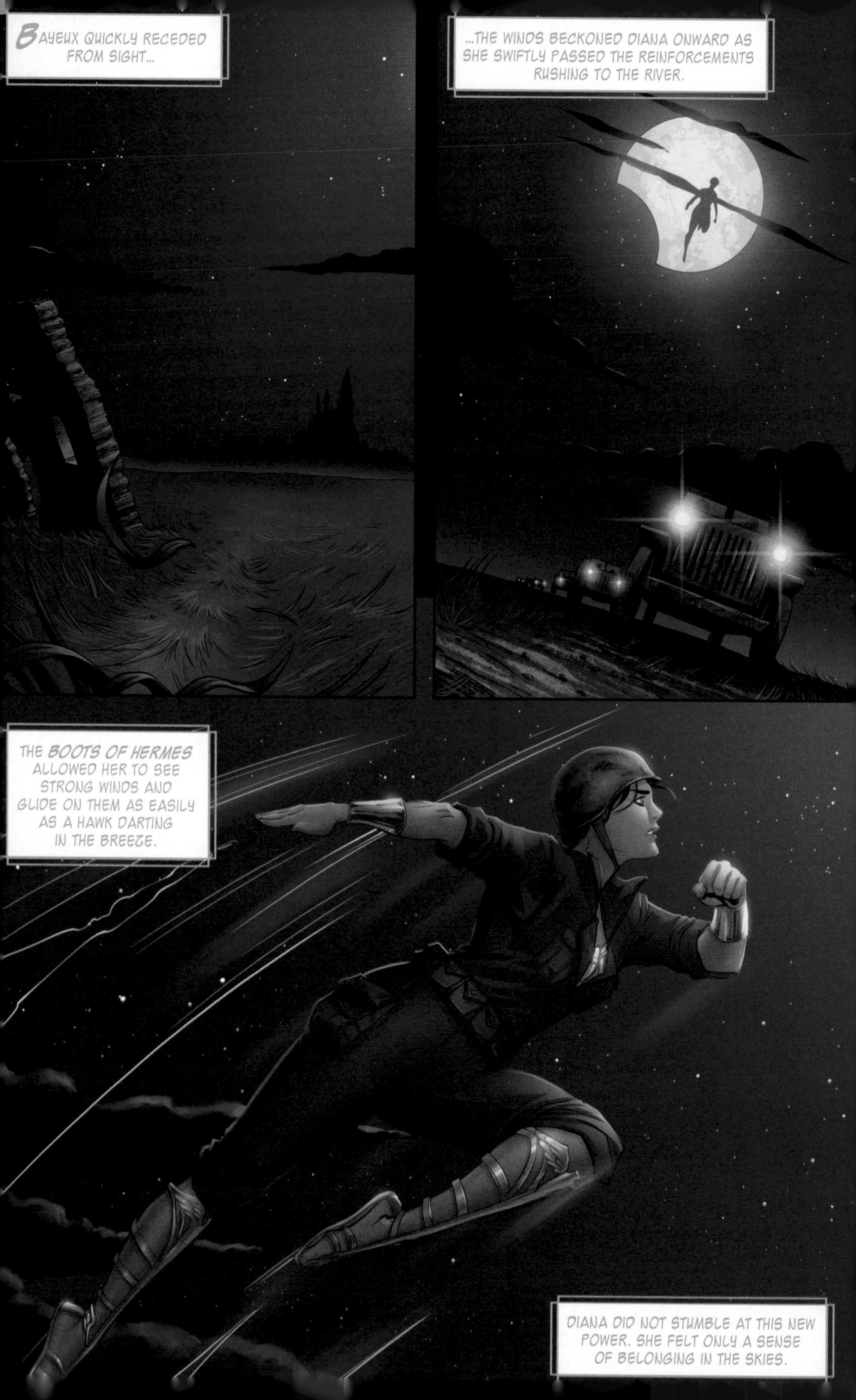
BAYEUX QUICKLY RECEDED FROM SIGHT...
...THE WINDS BECKONED DIANA ONWARD AS SHE SWIFTLY PASSED THE REINFORCEMENTS RUSHING TO THE RIVER.
THE BOOTS OF HERMES ALLOWED HER TO SEE STRONG WINDS AND GLIDE ON THEM AS EASILY AS A HAWK DARTING IN THE BREEZE.
DIANA DID NOT STUMBLE AT THIS NEW POWER. SHE FELT ONLY A SENSE OF BELONGING IN THE SKIES.

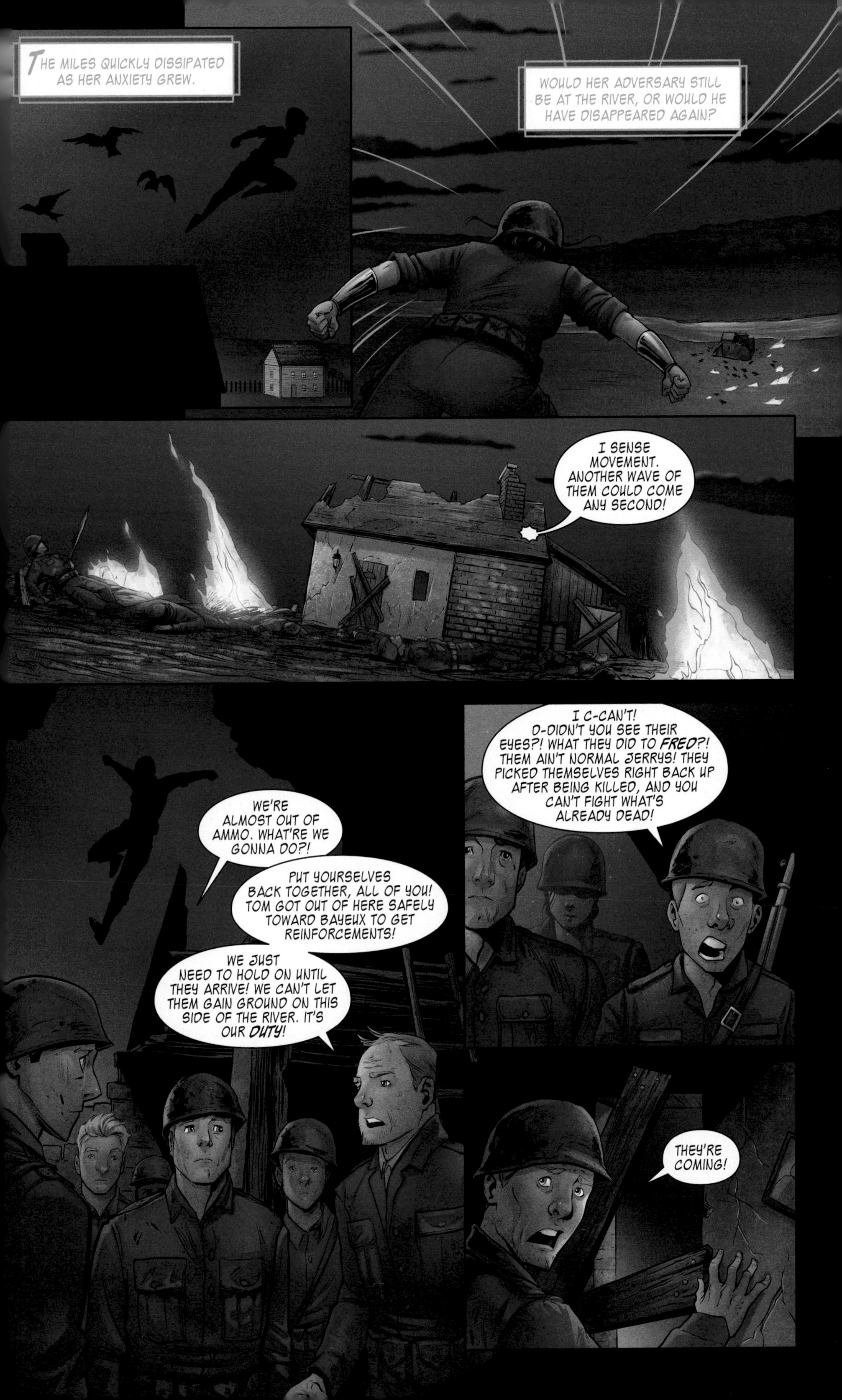
THE MILES QUICKLY DISSIPATED AS HER ANXIETY GREW.
WOULD HER ADVERSARY STILL BE AT THE RIVER, OR WOULD HE HAVE DISAPPEARED AGAIN?
I SENSE MOVEMENT. ANOTHER WAVE OF THEM COULD COME ANY SECOND!
WE'RE ALMOST OUT OF AMMO. WHAT'RE WE GONNA DO?!
PUT YOURSELVES BACK TOGETHER, ALL OF YOU! TOM GOT OUT OF HERE SAFELY TOWARD BAYEUX TO GET REINFORCEMENTS!
WE JUST NEED TO HOLD ON UNTIL THEY ARRIVE! WE CAN'T LET THEM GAIN GROUND ON THIS SIDE OF THE RIVER. IT'S OUR *DUTY*!
I C-CAN'T! D-DIDN'T YOU SEE THEIR EYES?! WHAT THEY DID TO *FRED*?! THEM AIN'T NORMAL JERRYS! THEY PICKED THEMSELVES RIGHT BACK UP AFTER BEING KILLED, AND YOU CAN'T FIGHT WHAT'S ALREADY DEAD!
THEY'RE COMING!

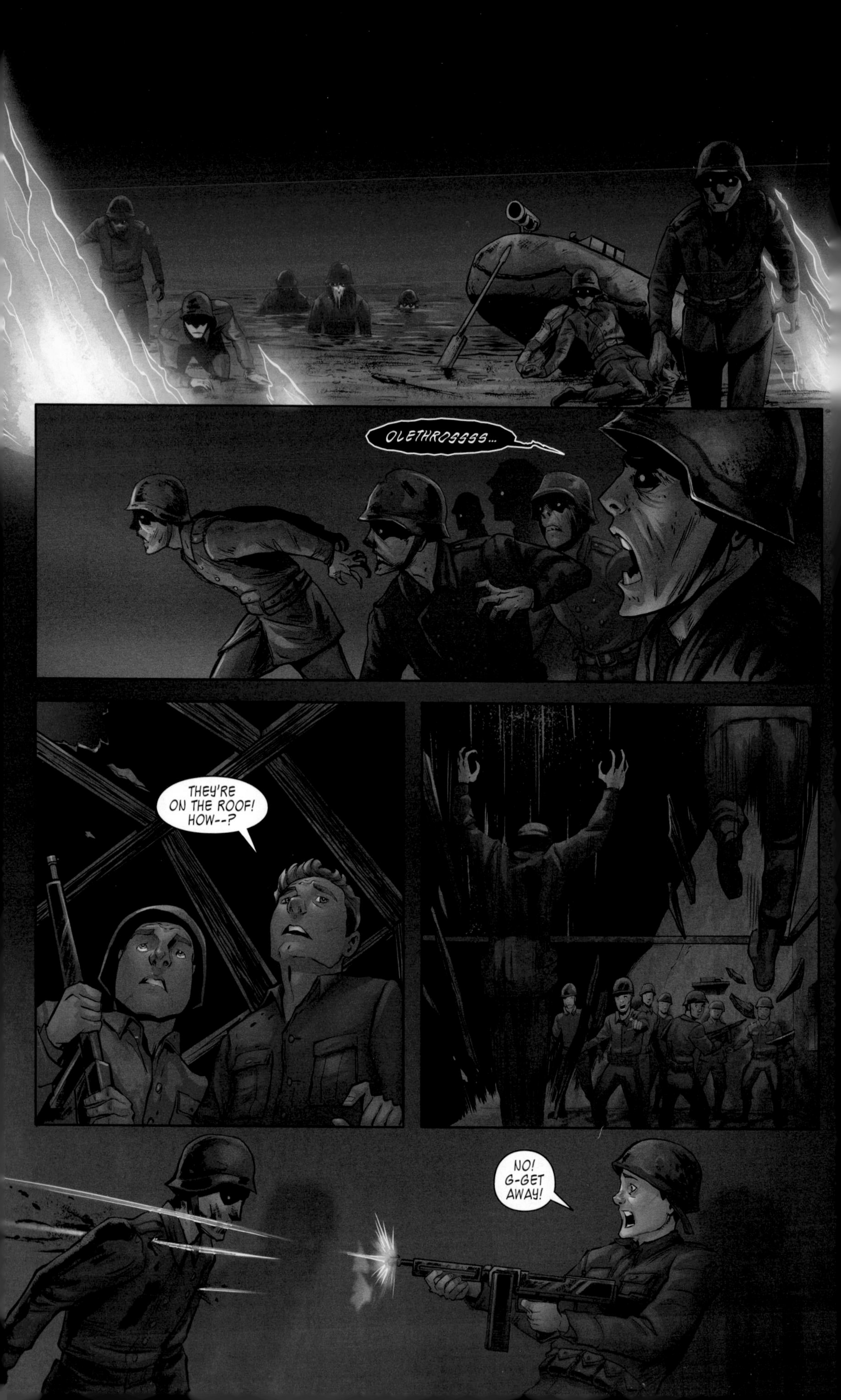
OLETHROSSSS...
THEY'RE ON THE ROOF! HOW--?
NO! G-GET AWAY!

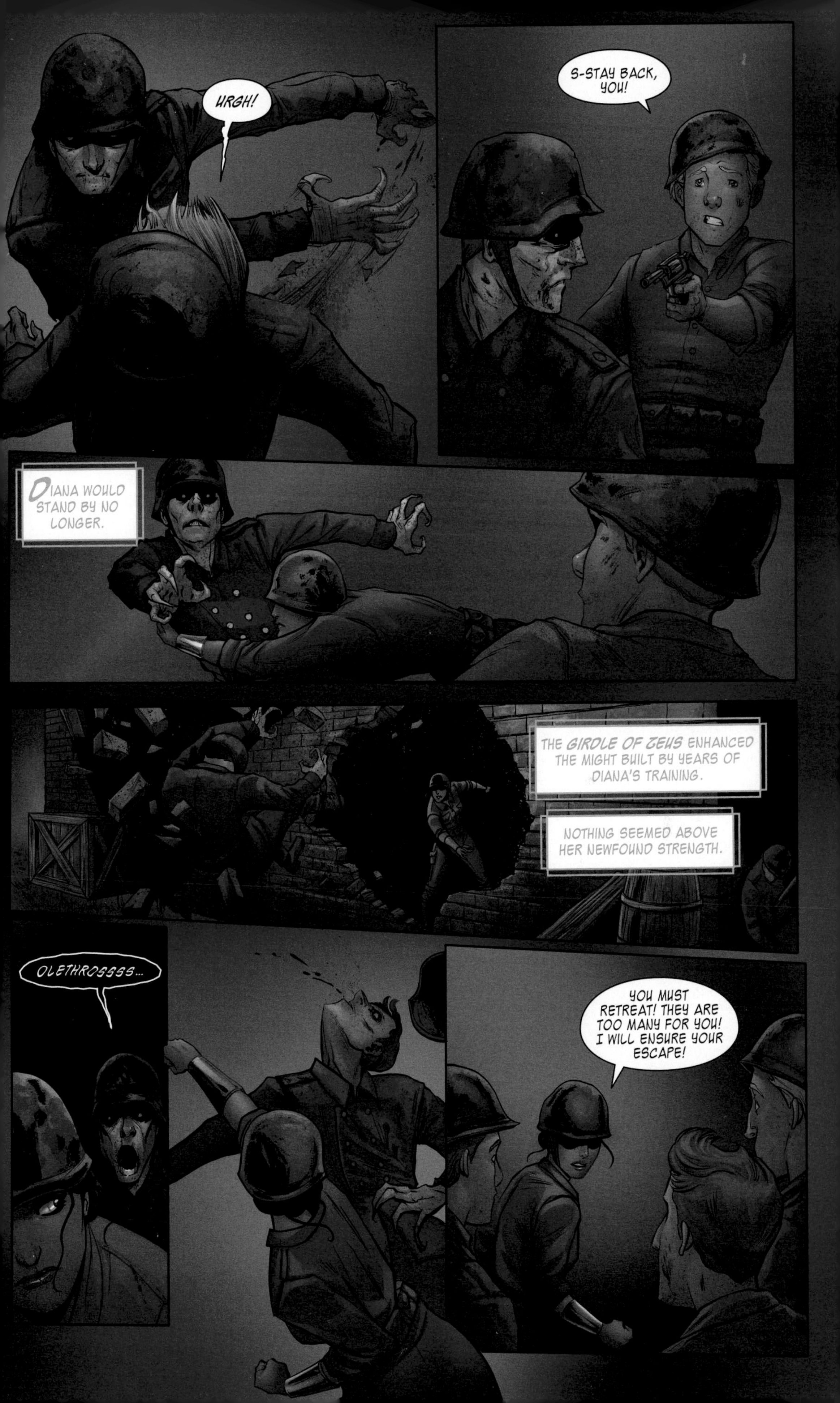
URGH!
S-STAY BACK, YOU!
DIANA WOULD STAND BY NO LONGER.
THE GIRDLE OF ZEUS ENHANCED THE MIGHT BUILT BY YEARS OF DIANA'S TRAINING.
NOTHING SEEMED ABOVE HER NEWFOUND STRENGTH.
OLETHROSSSS...
YOU MUST RETREAT! THEY ARE TOO MANY FOR YOU! I WILL ENSURE YOUR ESCAPE!

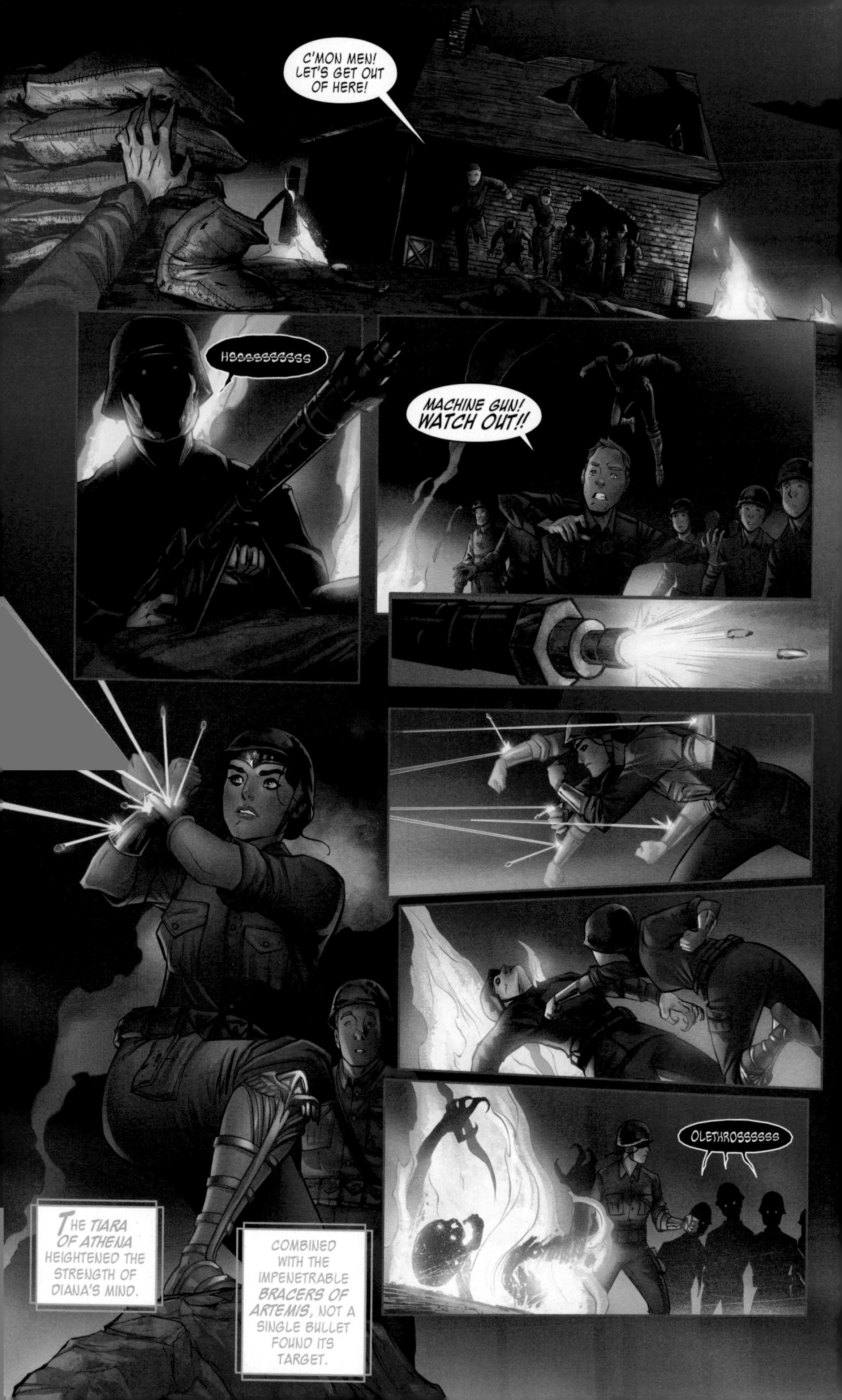
C'MON MEN! LET'S GET OUT OF HERE!
HSSSSSSSSSS
MACHINE GUN! WATCH OUT!!
THE TIARA OF ATHENA HEIGHTENED THE STRENGTH OF DIANA'S MIND.
COMBINED WITH THE IMPENETRABLE BRACERS OF ARTEMIS, NOT A SINGLE BULLET FOUND ITS TARGET.
OLETHROSSSSSS

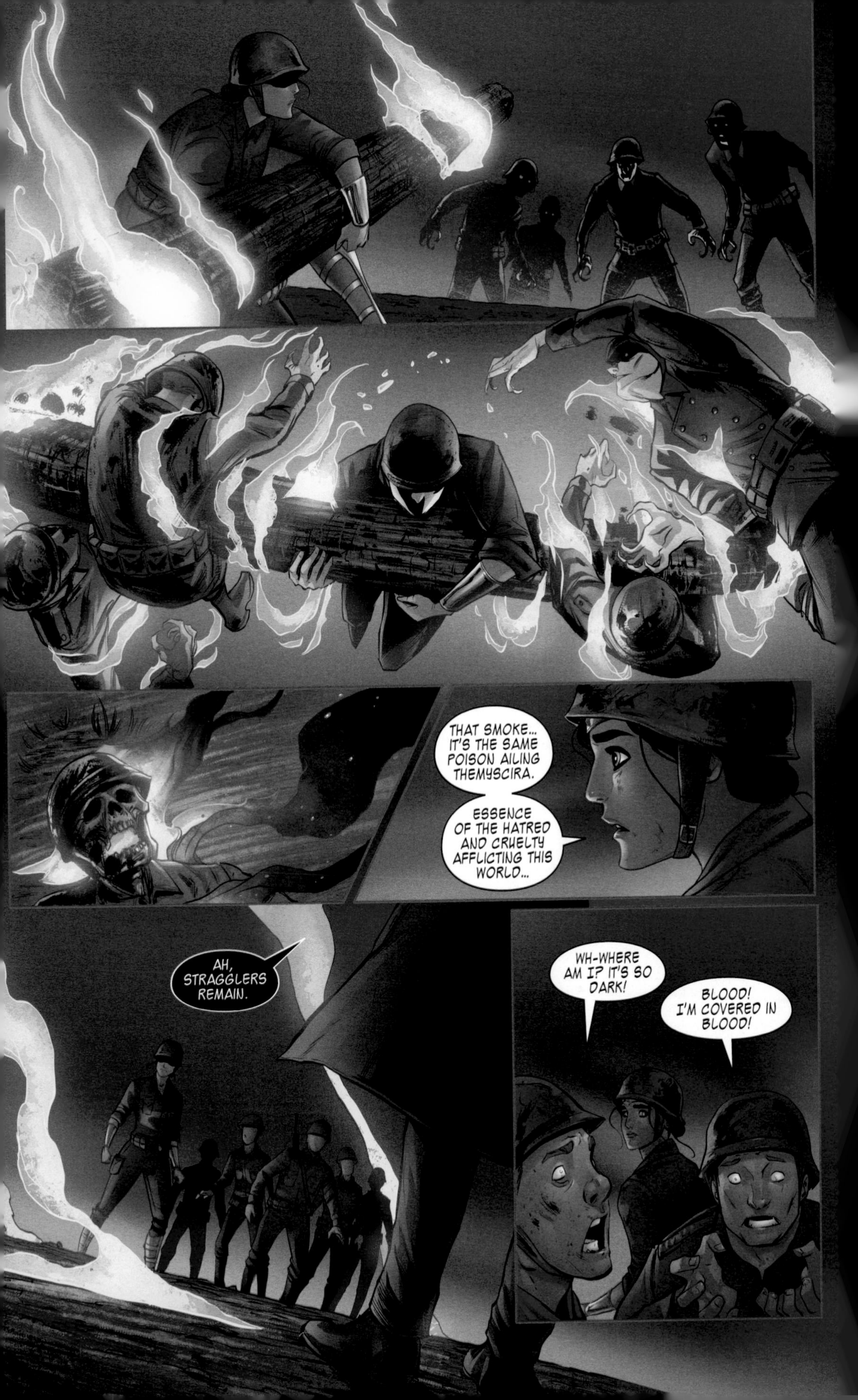
THAT SMOKE... IT'S THE SAME POISON AILING THEMYSCIRA.
ESSENCE OF THE HATRED AND CRUELTY AFFLICTING THIS WORLD...
AH, STRAGGLERS REMAIN.
WH-WHERE AM I? IT'S SO DARK!
BLOOD! I'M COVERED IN BLOOD!

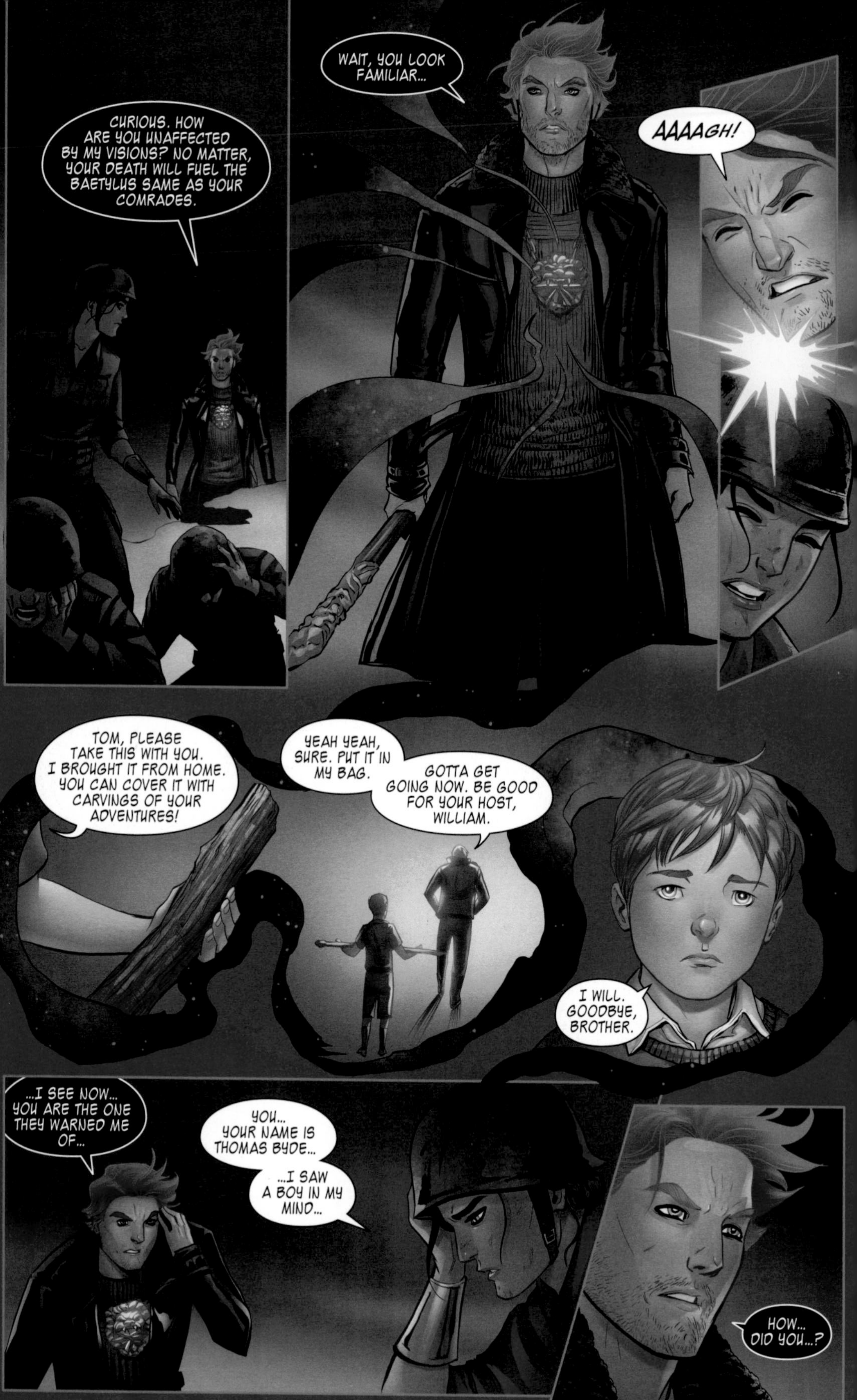
CURIOUS. HOW ARE YOU UNAFFECTED BY MY VISIONS? NO MATTER, YOUR DEATH WILL FUEL THE BAETYLUS SAME AS YOUR COMRADES.
WAIT, YOU LOOK FAMILIAR...
AAAAGH!
TOM, PLEASE TAKE THIS WITH YOU. I BROUGHT IT FROM HOME. YOU CAN COVER IT WITH CARVINGS OF YOUR ADVENTURES!
YEAH YEAH, SURE. PUT IT IN MY BAG.
GOTTA GET GOING NOW. BE GOOD FOR YOUR HOST, WILLIAM.
I WILL. GOODBYE, BROTHER.
...I SEE NOW... YOU ARE THE ONE THEY WARNED ME OF...
YOU... YOUR NAME IS THOMAS BYDE...
...I SAW A BOY IN MY MIND...
HOW... DID YOU...?

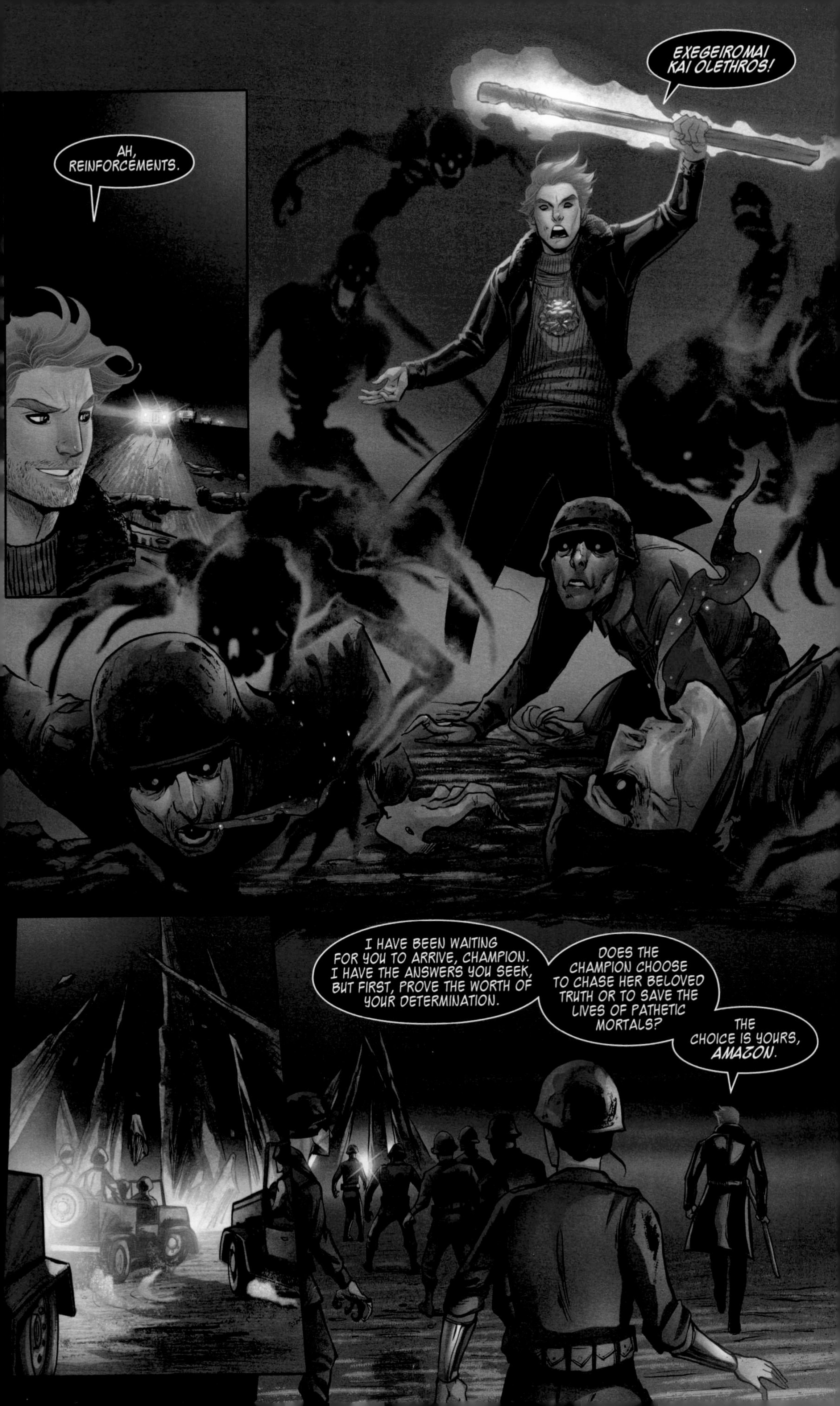
AH, REINFORCEMENTS.
EXEGEIROMAI KAI OLETHROS!
I HAVE BEEN WAITING FOR YOU TO ARRIVE, CHAMPION. I HAVE THE ANSWERS YOU SEEK, BUT FIRST, PROVE THE WORTH OF YOUR DETERMINATION.
DOES THE CHAMPION CHOOSE TO CHASE HER BELOVED TRUTH OR TO SAVE THE LIVES OF PATHETIC MORTALS?
THE CHOICE IS YOURS, AMAZON.

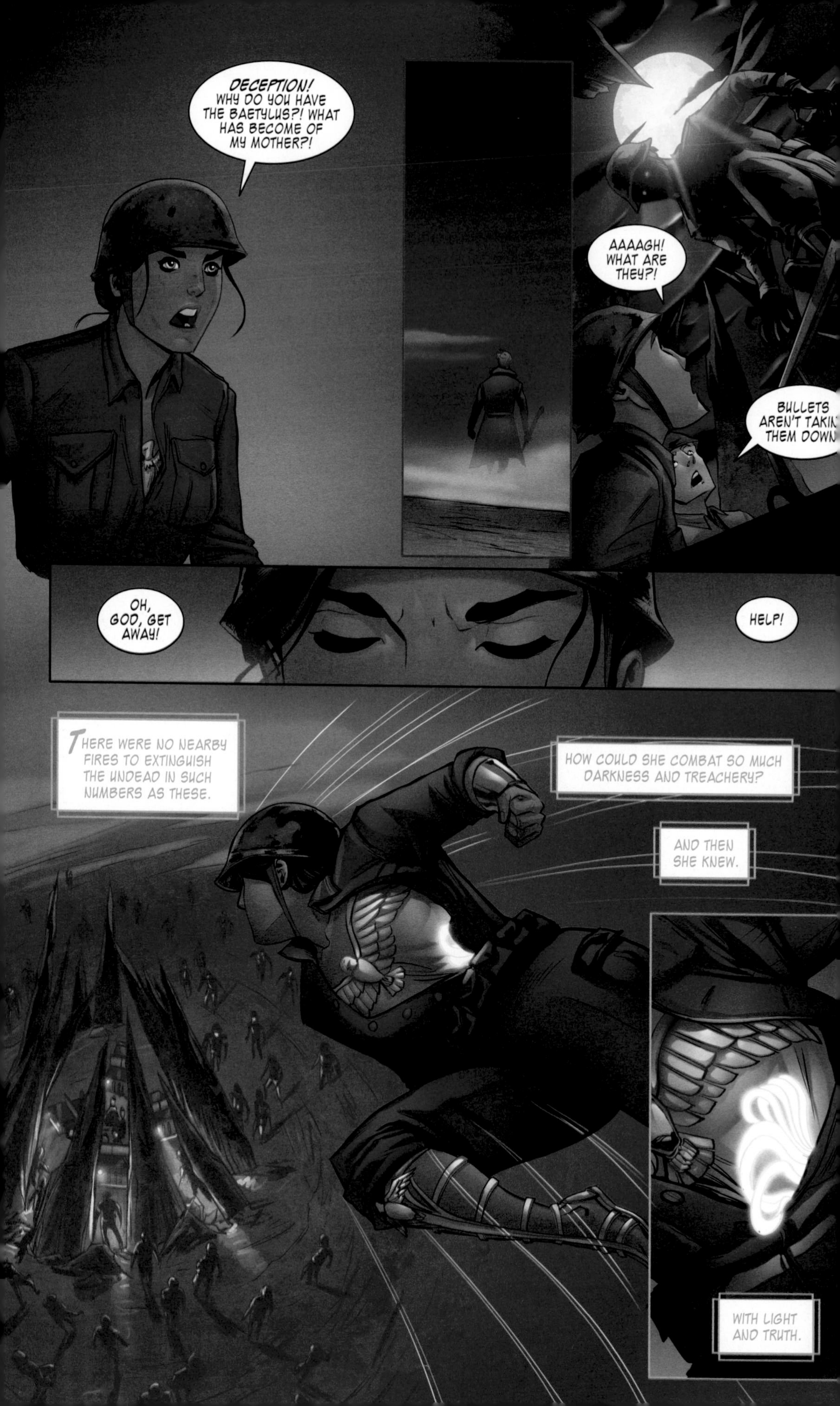
DECEPTION! WHY DO YOU HAVE THE BAETYLUS?! WHAT HAS BECOME OF MY MOTHER?!
AAAAGH! WHAT ARE THEY?!
BULLETS AREN'T TAKIN THEM DOWN
OH, GOD, GET AWAY!
HELP!
THERE WERE NO NEARBY FIRES TO EXTINGUISH THE UNDEAD IN SUCH NUMBERS AS THESE.
HOW COULD SHE COMBAT SO MUCH DARKNESS AND TREACHERY?
AND THEN SHE KNEW.
WITH LIGHT AND TRUTH.

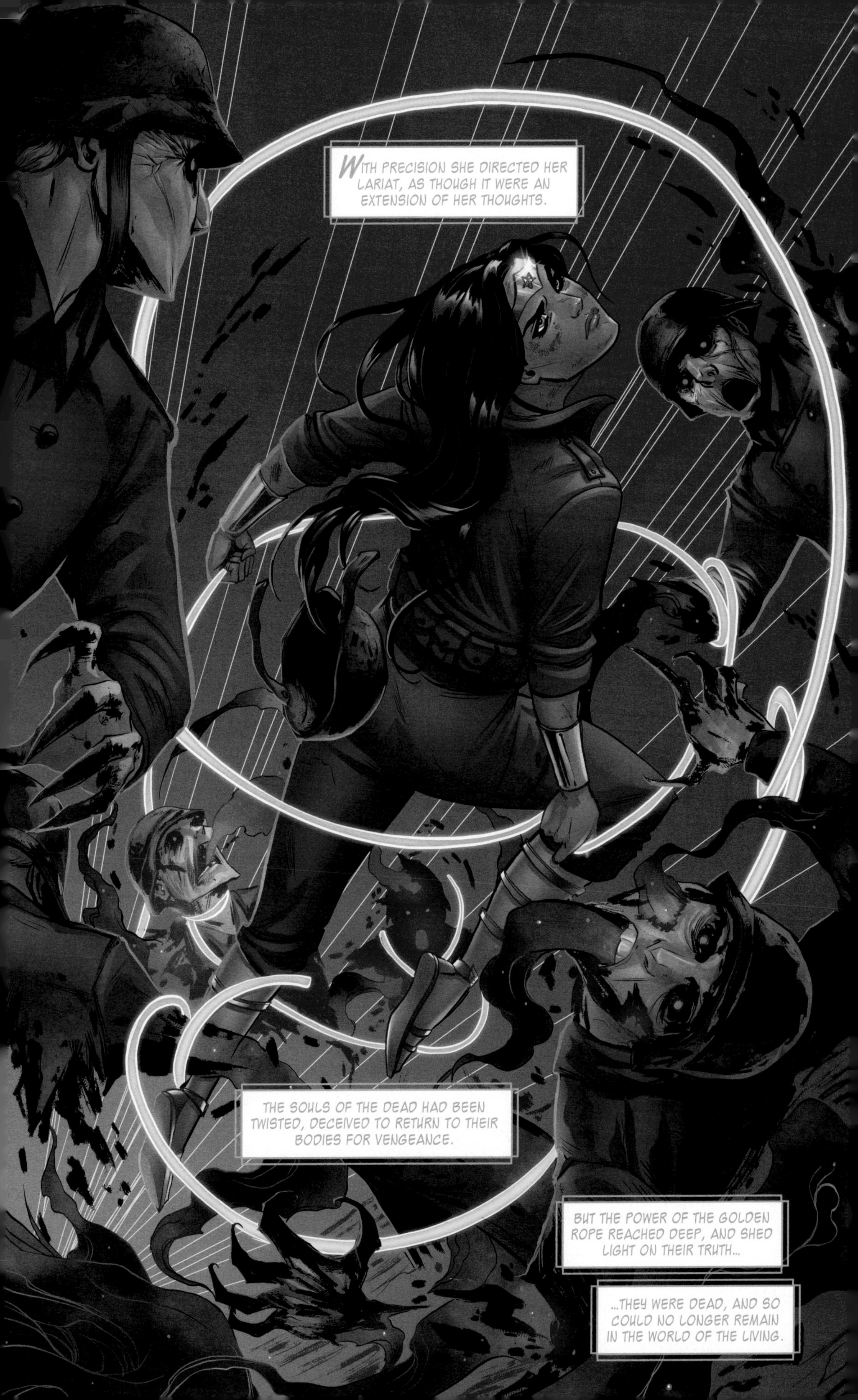
WITH PRECISION SHE DIRECTED HER LARIAT, AS THOUGH IT WERE AN EXTENSION OF HER THOUGHTS.
THE SOULS OF THE DEAD HAD BEEN TWISTED, DECEIVED TO RETURN TO THEIR BODIES FOR VENGEANCE.
BUT THE POWER OF THE GOLDEN ROPE REACHED DEEP, AND SHED LIGHT ON THEIR TRUTH...
...THEY WERE DEAD, AND SO COULD NO LONGER REMAIN IN THE WORLD OF THE LIVING.

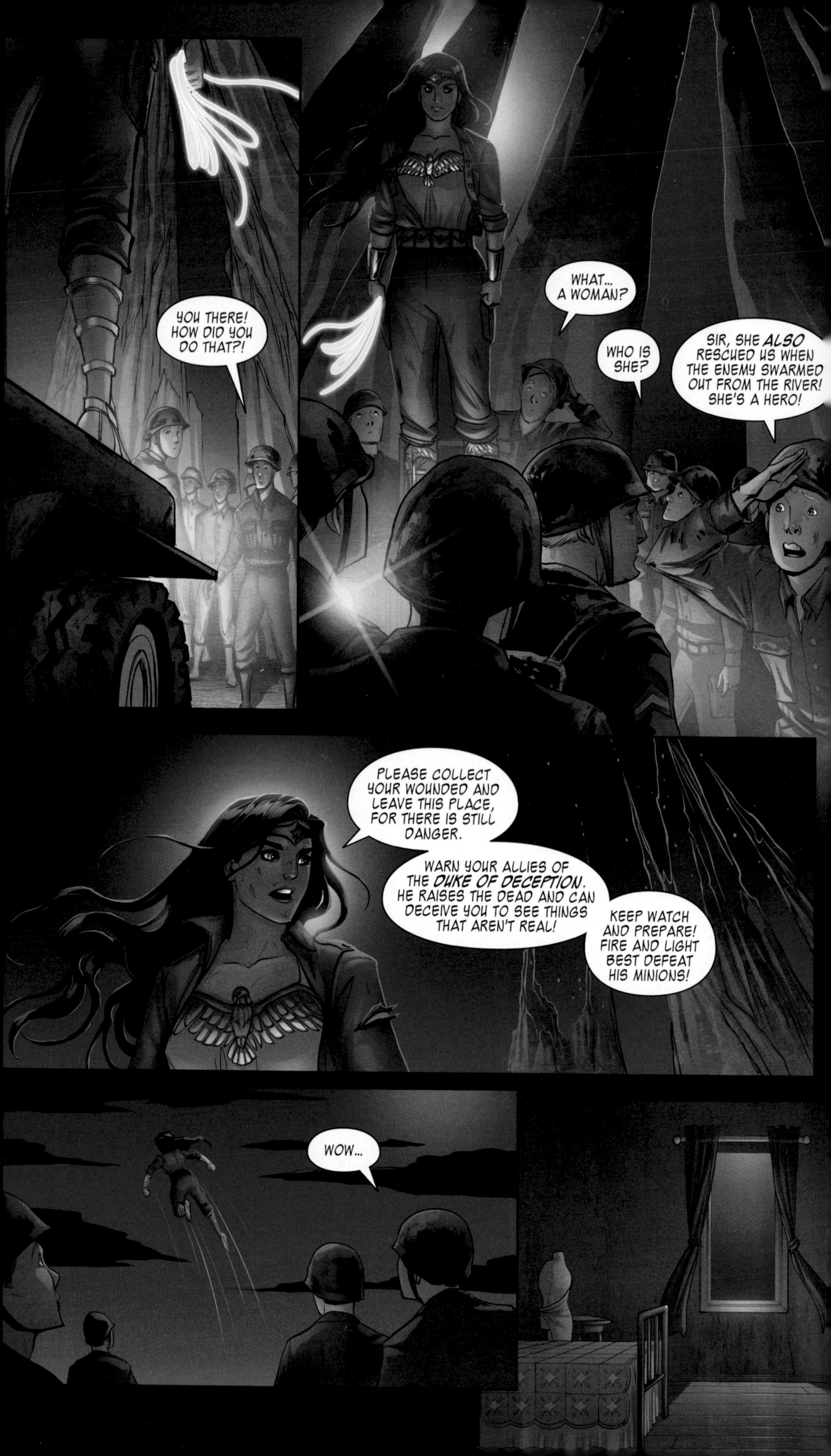
YOU THERE! HOW DID YOU DO THAT?!
WHAT... A WOMAN?
WHO IS SHE?
SIR, SHE ALSO RESCUED US WHEN THE ENEMY SWARMED OUT FROM THE RIVER! SHE'S A HERO!
PLEASE COLLECT YOUR WOUNDED AND LEAVE THIS PLACE, FOR THERE IS STILL DANGER.
WARN YOUR ALLIES OF THE DUKE OF DECEPTION. HE RAISES THE DEAD AND CAN DECEIVE YOU TO SEE THINGS THAT AREN'T REAL!
KEEP WATCH AND PREPARE! FIRE AND LIGHT BEST DEFEAT HIS MINIONS!
WOW...

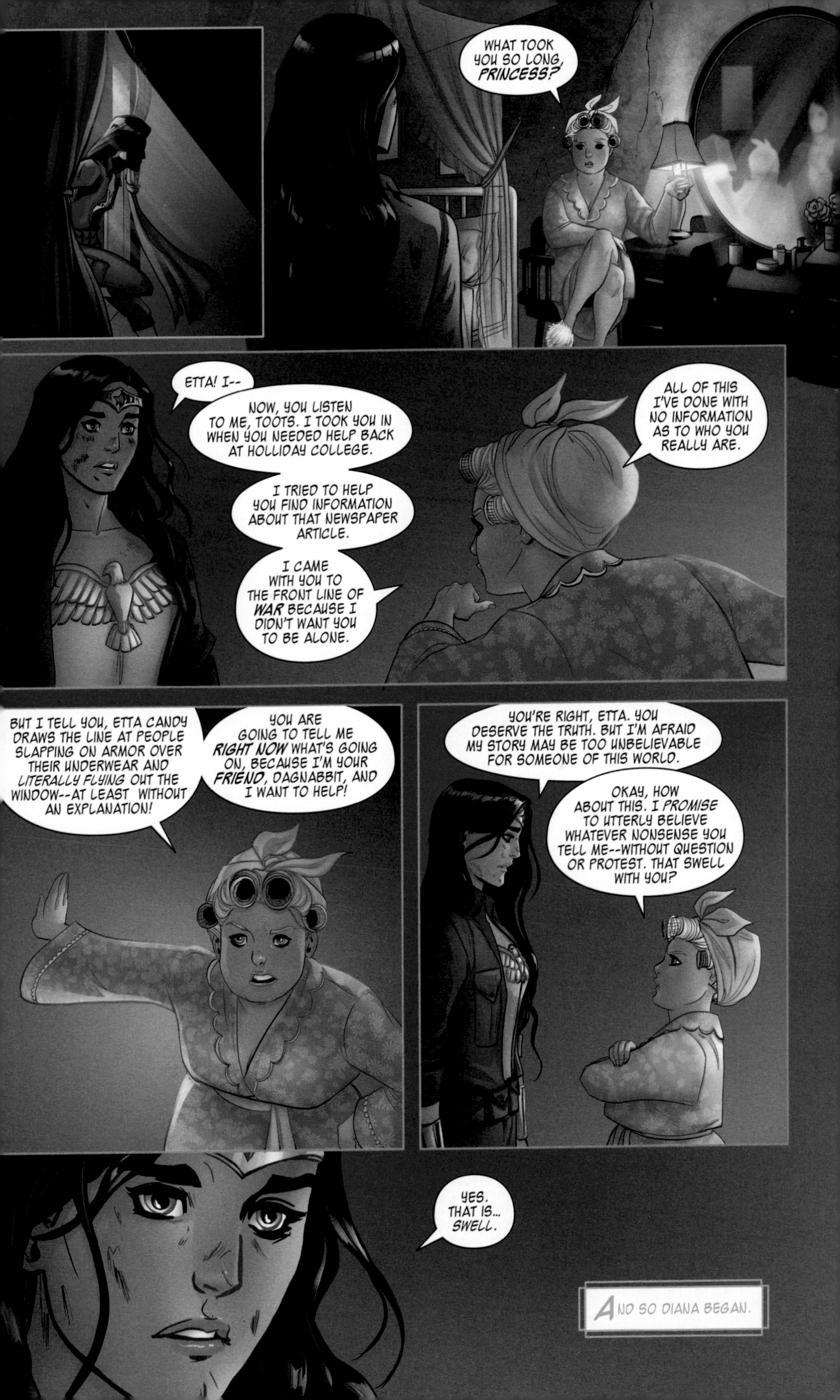

WHAT TOOK YOU SO LONG, *PRINCESS?*
ETTA! I--
NOW, YOU LISTEN TO ME, TOOTS. I TOOK YOU IN WHEN YOU NEEDED HELP BACK AT HOLLIDAY COLLEGE.
I TRIED TO HELP YOU FIND INFORMATION ABOUT THAT NEWSPAPER ARTICLE.
I CAME WITH YOU TO THE FRONT LINE OF *WAR* BECAUSE I DIDN'T WANT YOU TO BE ALONE.
ALL OF THIS I'VE DONE WITH NO INFORMATION AS TO WHO YOU REALLY ARE.
BUT I TELL YOU, ETTA CANDY DRAWS THE LINE AT PEOPLE SLAPPING ON ARMOR OVER THEIR UNDERWEAR AND *LITERALLY FLYING* OUT THE WINDOW--AT LEAST WITHOUT AN EXPLANATION!
YOU ARE GOING TO TELL ME *RIGHT NOW* WHAT'S GOING ON, BECAUSE I'M YOUR *FRIEND*, DAGNABBIT, AND I WANT TO HELP!
YOU'RE RIGHT, ETTA. YOU DESERVE THE TRUTH. BUT I'M AFRAID MY STORY MAY BE TOO UNBELIEVABLE FOR SOMEONE OF THIS WORLD.
OKAY, HOW ABOUT THIS. I *PROMISE* TO UTTERLY BELIEVE WHATEVER NONSENSE YOU TELL ME--WITHOUT QUESTION OR PROTEST. THAT SWELL WITH YOU?
YES. THAT IS... *SWELL.*
AND SO DIANA BEGAN.

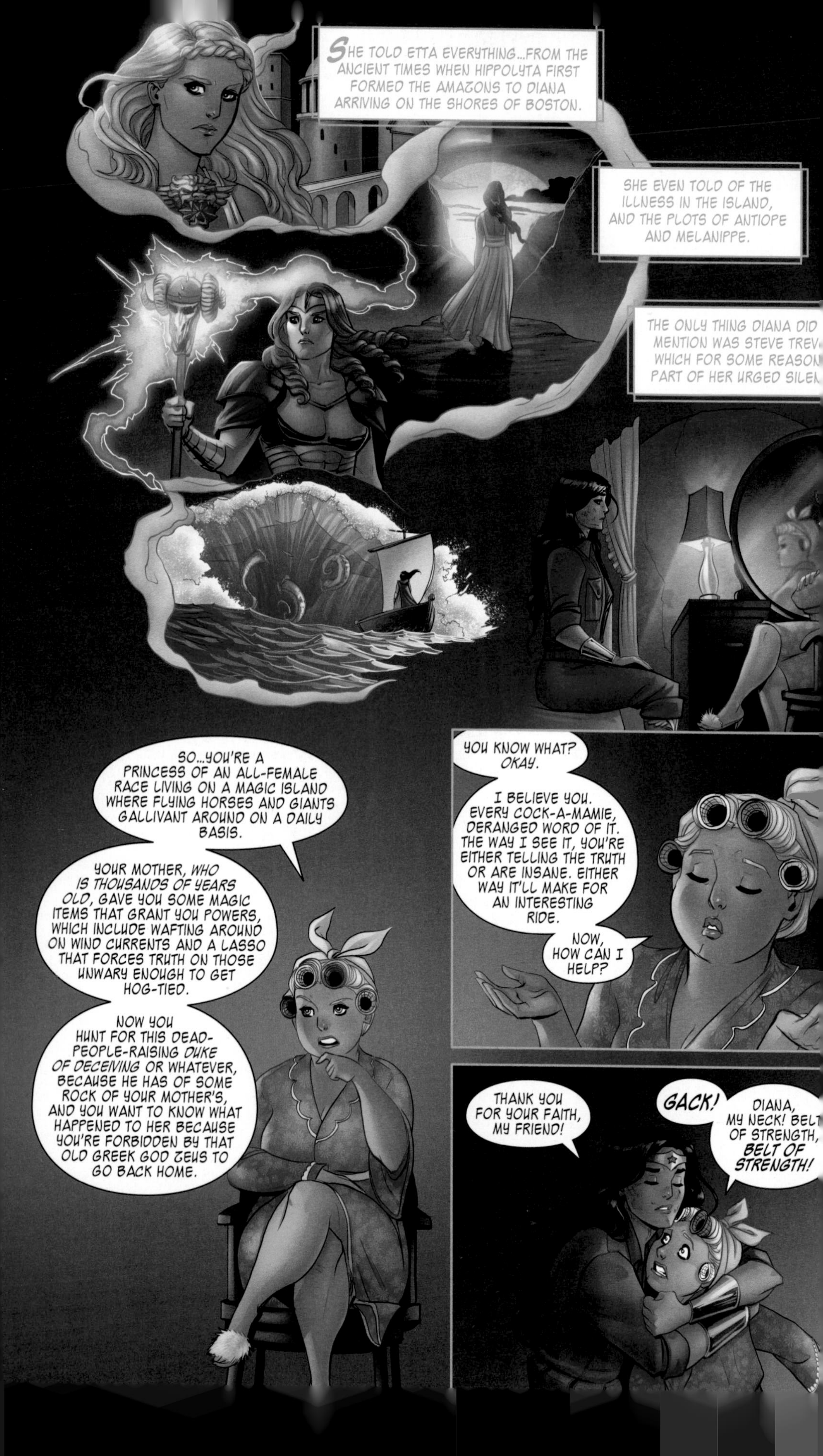
SHE TOLD ETTA EVERYTHING...FROM THE ANCIENT TIMES WHEN HIPPOLYTA FIRST FORMED THE AMAZONS TO DIANA ARRIVING ON THE SHORES OF BOSTON.
SHE EVEN TOLD OF THE ILLNESS IN THE ISLAND, AND THE PLOTS OF ANTIOPE AND MELANIPPE.
THE ONLY THING DIANA DID MENTION WAS STEVE TREV WHICH FOR SOME REASON PART OF HER URGED SILEN
SO...YOU'RE A PRINCESS OF AN ALL-FEMALE RACE LIVING ON A MAGIC ISLAND WHERE FLYING HORSES AND GIANTS GALLIVANT AROUND ON A DAILY BASIS.
YOUR MOTHER, WHO IS THOUSANDS OF YEARS OLD, GAVE YOU SOME MAGIC ITEMS THAT GRANT YOU POWERS, WHICH INCLUDE WAFTING AROUND ON WIND CURRENTS AND A LASSO THAT FORCES TRUTH ON THOSE UNWARY ENOUGH TO GET HOG-TIED.
NOW YOU HUNT FOR THIS DEAD-PEOPLE-RAISING DUKE OF DECEIVING OR WHATEVER, BECAUSE HE HAS OF SOME ROCK OF YOUR MOTHER'S, AND YOU WANT TO KNOW WHAT HAPPENED TO HER BECAUSE YOU'RE FORBIDDEN BY THAT OLD GREEK GOD ZEUS TO GO BACK HOME.
YOU KNOW WHAT? OKAY.
I BELIEVE YOU. EVERY COCK-A-MAMIE, DERANGED WORD OF IT. THE WAY I SEE IT, YOU'RE EITHER TELLING THE TRUTH OR ARE INSANE. EITHER WAY IT'LL MAKE FOR AN INTERESTING RIDE.
NOW, HOW CAN I HELP?
THANK YOU FOR YOUR FAITH, MY FRIEND!
GACK!
DIANA, MY NECK! BELT OF STRENGTH, BELT OF STRENGTH!

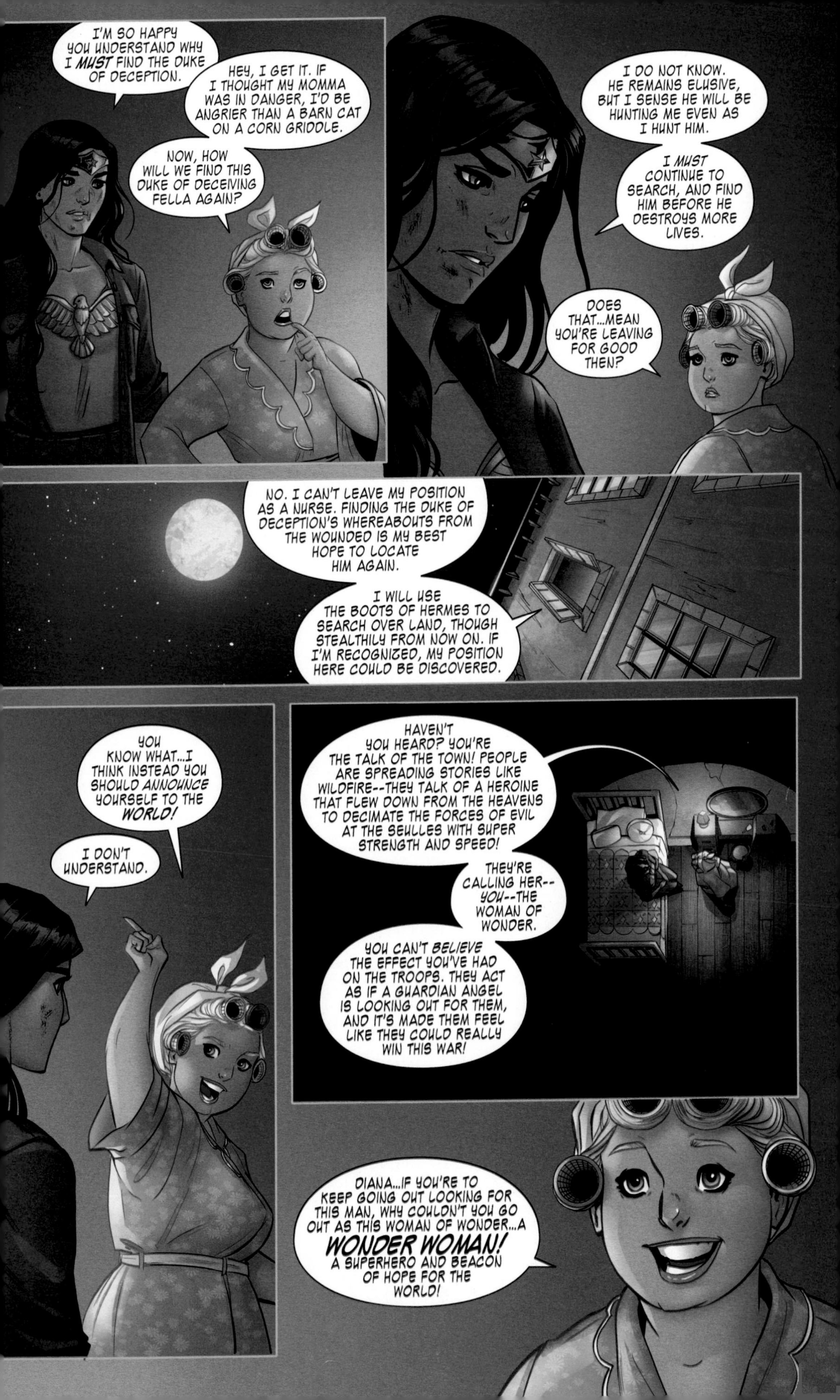

I'M SO HAPPY YOU UNDERSTAND WHY I *MUST* FIND THE DUKE OF DECEPTION.
HEY, I GET IT. IF I THOUGHT MY MOMMA WAS IN DANGER, I'D BE ANGRIER THAN A BARN CAT ON A CORN GRIDDLE.
NOW, HOW WILL WE FIND THIS DUKE OF DECEIVING FELLA AGAIN?
I DO NOT KNOW. HE REMAINS ELUSIVE, BUT I SENSE HE WILL BE HUNTING ME EVEN AS I HUNT HIM.
I *MUST* CONTINUE TO SEARCH, AND FIND HIM BEFORE HE DESTROYS MORE LIVES.
DOES THAT...MEAN YOU'RE LEAVING FOR GOOD THEN?
NO. I CAN'T LEAVE MY POSITION AS A NURSE. FINDING THE DUKE OF DECEPTION'S WHEREABOUTS FROM THE WOUNDED IS MY BEST HOPE TO LOCATE HIM AGAIN.
I WILL USE THE BOOTS OF HERMES TO SEARCH OVER LAND, THOUGH STEALTHILY FROM NOW ON. IF I'M RECOGNIZED, MY POSITION HERE COULD BE DISCOVERED.
YOU KNOW WHAT...I THINK INSTEAD YOU SHOULD *ANNOUNCE* YOURSELF TO THE *WORLD!*
I DON'T UNDERSTAND.
HAVEN'T YOU HEARD? YOU'RE THE TALK OF THE TOWN! PEOPLE ARE SPREADING STORIES LIKE WILDFIRE--THEY TALK OF A HEROINE THAT FLEW DOWN FROM THE HEAVENS TO DECIMATE THE FORCES OF EVIL AT THE SEULLES WITH SUPER STRENGTH AND SPEED!
THEY'RE CALLING HER-- *YOU*--THE WOMAN OF WONDER.
YOU CAN'T *BELIEVE* THE EFFECT YOU'VE HAD ON THE TROOPS. THEY ACT AS IF A GUARDIAN ANGEL IS LOOKING OUT FOR THEM, AND IT'S MADE THEM FEEL LIKE THEY COULD REALLY WIN THIS WAR!
DIANA...IF YOU'RE TO KEEP GOING OUT LOOKING FOR THIS MAN, WHY COULDN'T YOU GO OUT AS THIS WOMAN OF WONDER...A
WONDER WOMAN!
A SUPERHERO AND BEACON OF HOPE FOR THE WORLD!

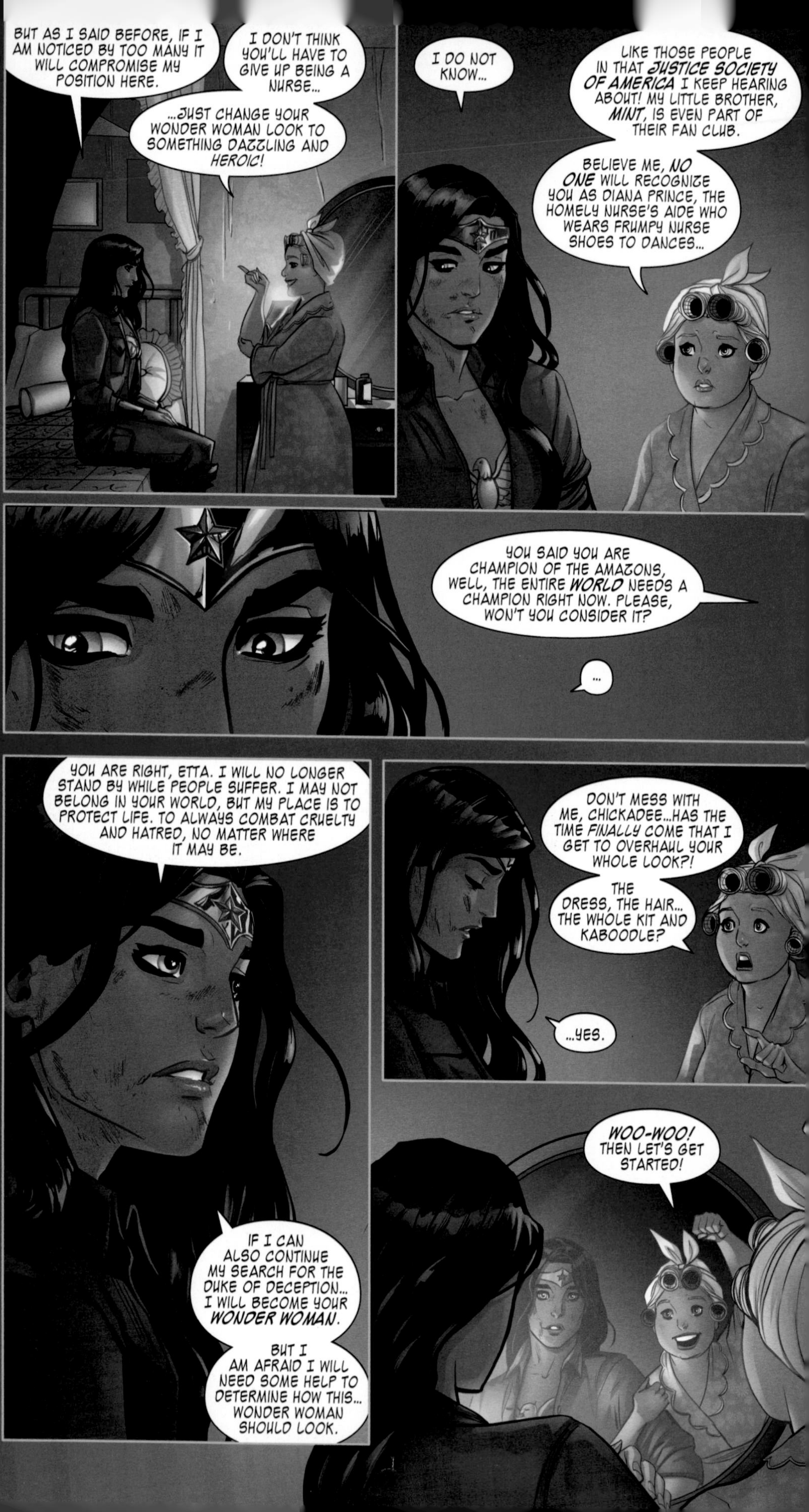
BUT AS I SAID BEFORE, IF I AM NOTICED BY TOO MANY IT WILL COMPROMISE MY POSITION HERE.
I DON'T THINK YOU'LL HAVE TO GIVE UP BEING A NURSE...
...JUST CHANGE YOUR WONDER WOMAN LOOK TO SOMETHING DAZZLING AND HEROIC!
I DO NOT KNOW...
LIKE THOSE PEOPLE IN THAT JUSTICE SOCIETY OF AMERICA I KEEP HEARING ABOUT! MY LITTLE BROTHER, MINT, IS EVEN PART OF THEIR FAN CLUB.
BELIEVE ME, NO ONE WILL RECOGNIZE YOU AS DIANA PRINCE, THE HOMELY NURSE'S AIDE WHO WEARS FRUMPY NURSE SHOES TO DANCES...
YOU SAID YOU ARE CHAMPION OF THE AMAZONS, WELL, THE ENTIRE WORLD NEEDS A CHAMPION RIGHT NOW. PLEASE, WON'T YOU CONSIDER IT?
...
YOU ARE RIGHT, ETTA. I WILL NO LONGER STAND BY WHILE PEOPLE SUFFER. I MAY NOT BELONG IN YOUR WORLD, BUT MY PLACE IS TO PROTECT LIFE. TO ALWAYS COMBAT CRUELTY AND HATRED, NO MATTER WHERE IT MAY BE.
IF I CAN ALSO CONTINUE MY SEARCH FOR THE DUKE OF DECEPTION... I WILL BECOME YOUR WONDER WOMAN.
BUT I AM AFRAID I WILL NEED SOME HELP TO DETERMINE HOW THIS... WONDER WOMAN SHOULD LOOK.
DON'T MESS WITH ME, CHICKADEE...HAS THE TIME FINALLY COME THAT I GET TO OVERHAUL YOUR WHOLE LOOK?!
THE DRESS, THE HAIR... THE WHOLE KIT AND KABOODLE?
...YES.
WOO-WOO! THEN LET'S GET STARTED!

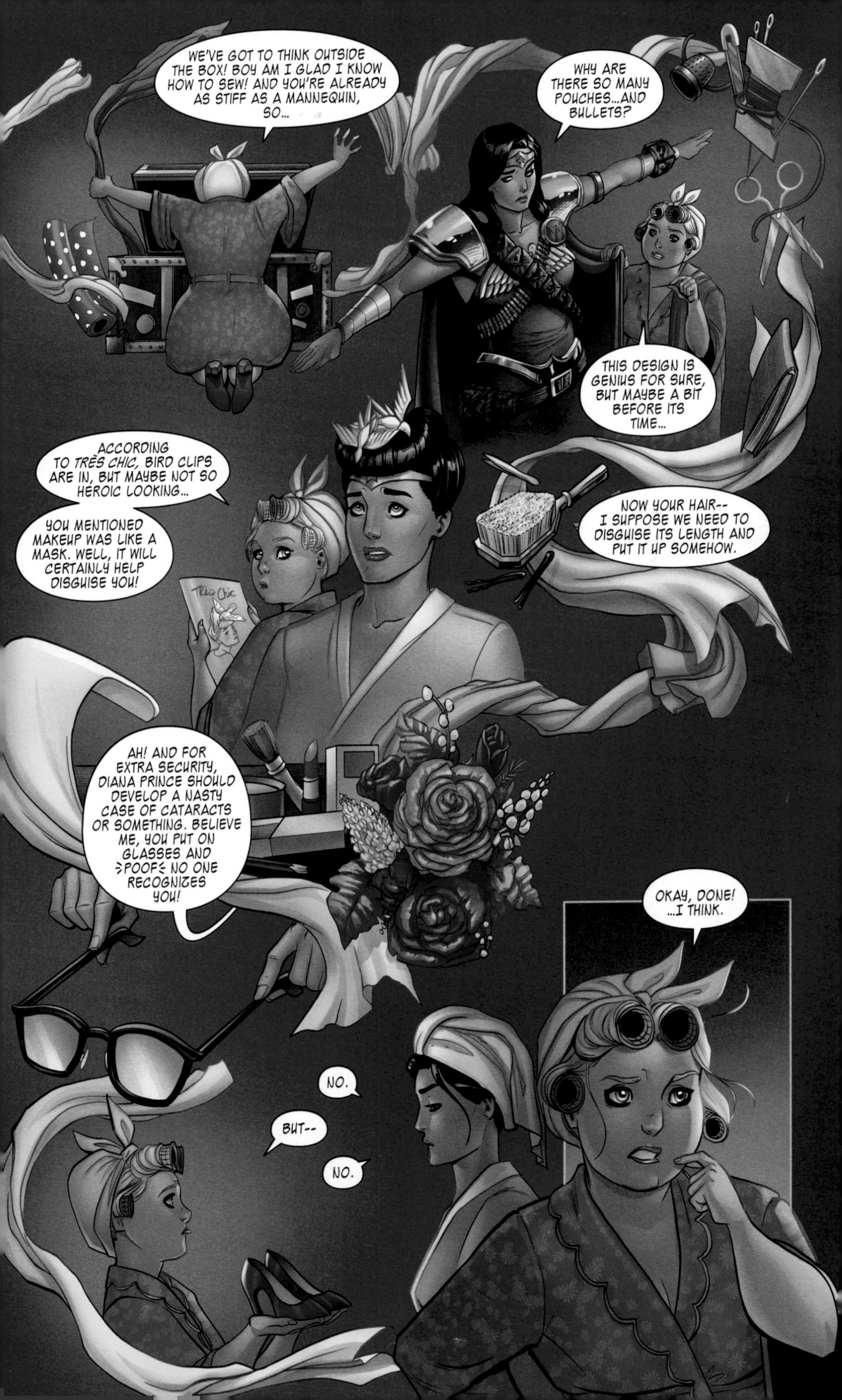
WE'VE GOT TO THINK OUTSIDE THE BOX! BOY AM I GLAD I KNOW HOW TO SEW! AND YOU'RE ALREADY AS STIFF AS A MANNEQUIN, SO...
WHY ARE THERE SO MANY POUCHES...AND BULLETS?
THIS DESIGN IS GENIUS FOR SURE, BUT MAYBE A BIT BEFORE ITS TIME...
ACCORDING TO *TRÈS CHIC*, BIRD CLIPS ARE IN, BUT MAYBE NOT SO HEROIC LOOKING...
YOU MENTIONED MAKEUP WAS LIKE A MASK. WELL, IT WILL CERTAINLY HELP DISGUISE YOU!
NOW YOUR HAIR-- I SUPPOSE WE NEED TO DISGUISE ITS LENGTH AND PUT IT UP SOMEHOW.
TRÈS CHIC
AH! AND FOR EXTRA SECURITY, DIANA PRINCE SHOULD DEVELOP A NASTY CASE OF CATARACTS OR SOMETHING. BELIEVE ME, YOU PUT ON GLASSES AND *POOF* NO ONE RECOGNIZES YOU!
OKAY, DONE! ...I THINK.
NO.
BUT--
NO.

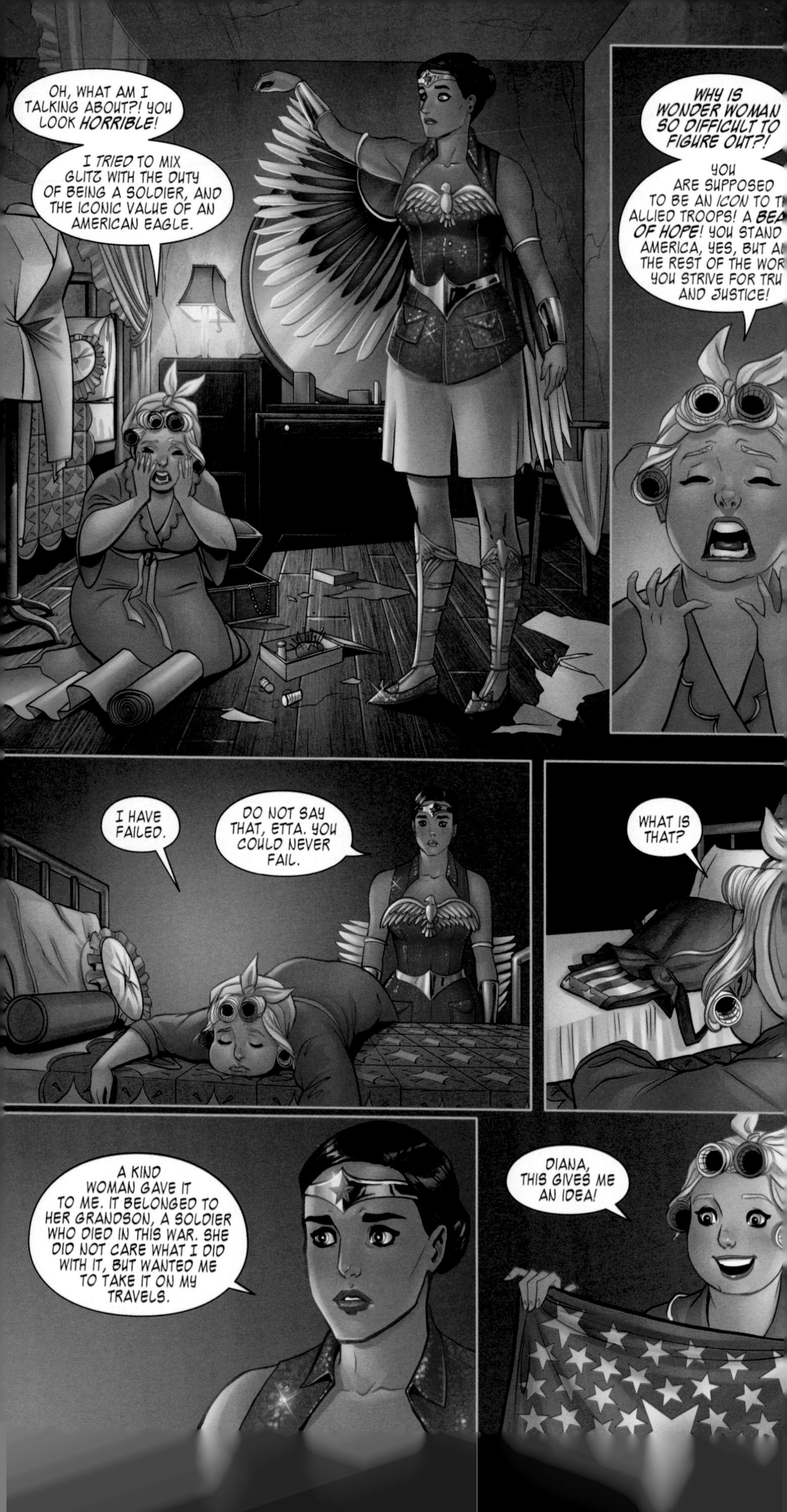

OH, WHAT AM I TALKING ABOUT?! YOU LOOK *HORRIBLE!*
I *TRIED* TO MIX GLITZ WITH THE DUTY OF BEING A SOLDIER, AND THE ICONIC VALUE OF AN AMERICAN EAGLE.
WHY IS WONDER WOMAN SO DIFFICULT TO FIGURE OUT?!
YOU ARE SUPPOSED TO BE AN *ICON* TO T
ALLIED TROOPS! A *BEA*
OF HOPE! YOU STAND
AMERICA, YES, BUT A
THE REST OF THE WOR
YOU STRIVE FOR TRU
AND JUSTICE!
I HAVE FAILED.
DO NOT SAY THAT, ETTA. YOU COULD NEVER FAIL.
WHAT IS THAT?
A KIND WOMAN GAVE IT TO ME. IT BELONGED TO HER GRANDSON, A SOLDIER WHO DIED IN THIS WAR. SHE DID NOT CARE WHAT I DID WITH IT, BUT WANTED ME TO TAKE IT ON MY TRAVELS.
DIANA, THIS GIVES ME AN IDEA!

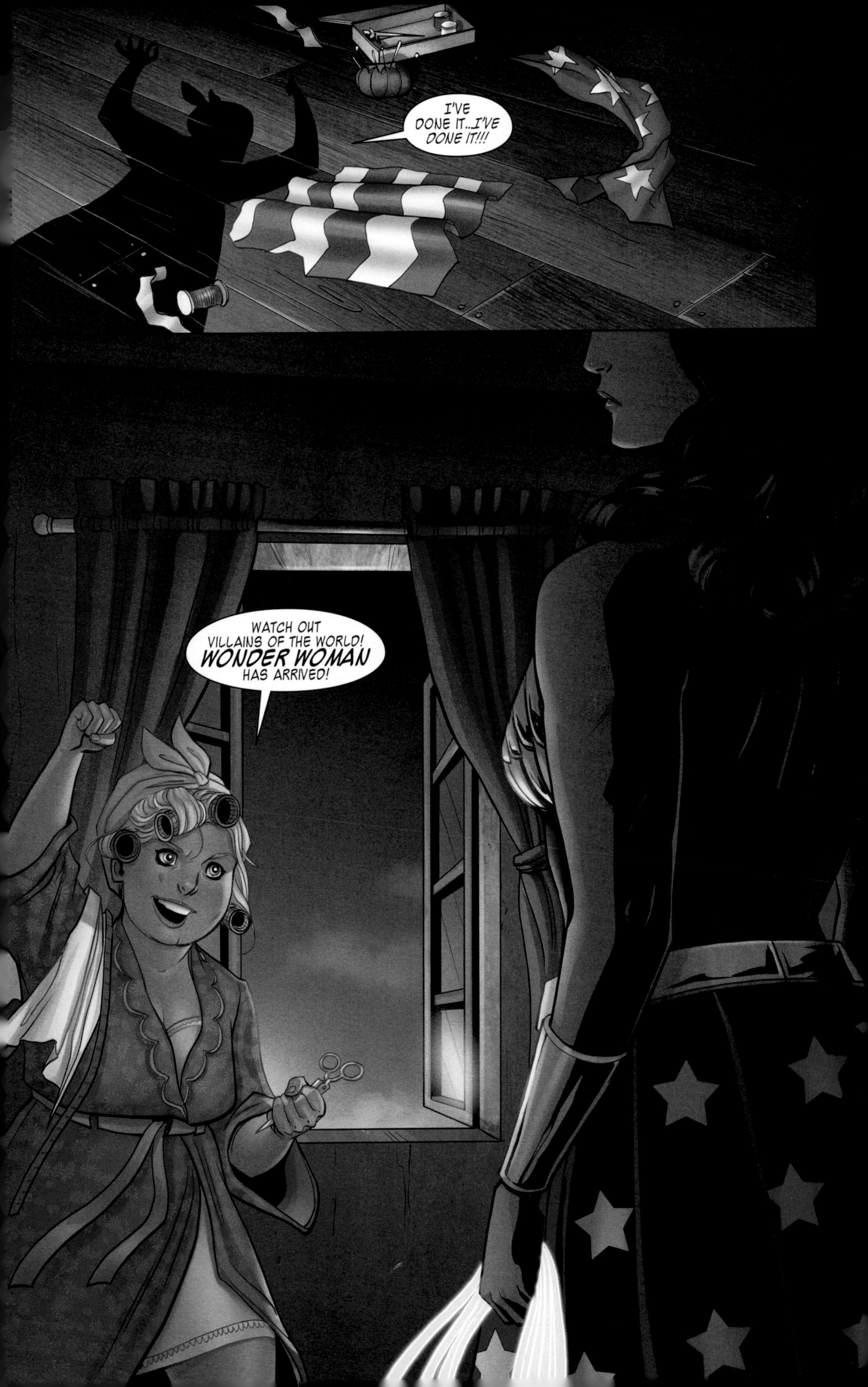
I'VE DONE IT...I'VE DONE IT!!!
WATCH OUT VILLAINS OF THE WORLD! WONDER WOMAN HAS ARRIVED!

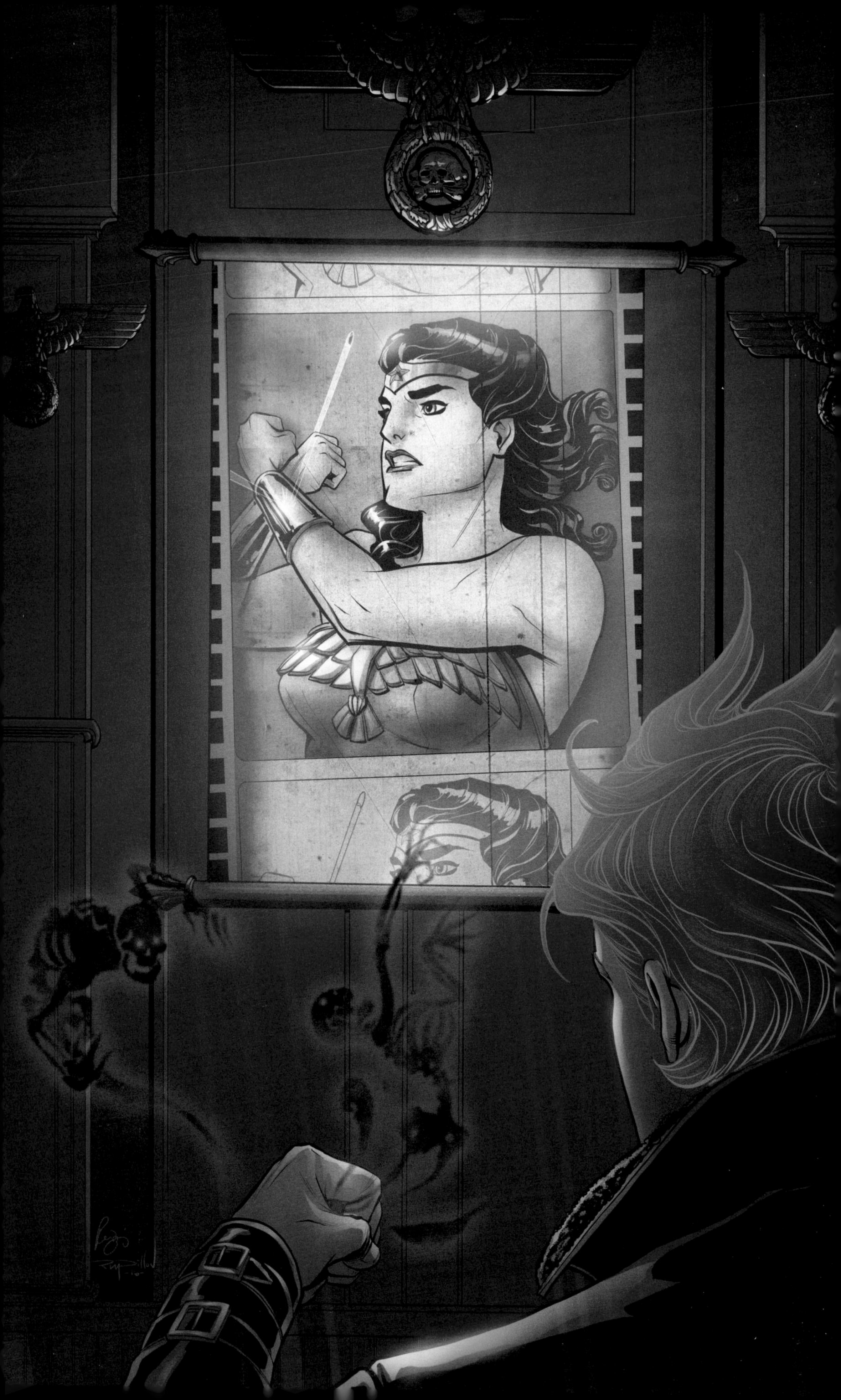

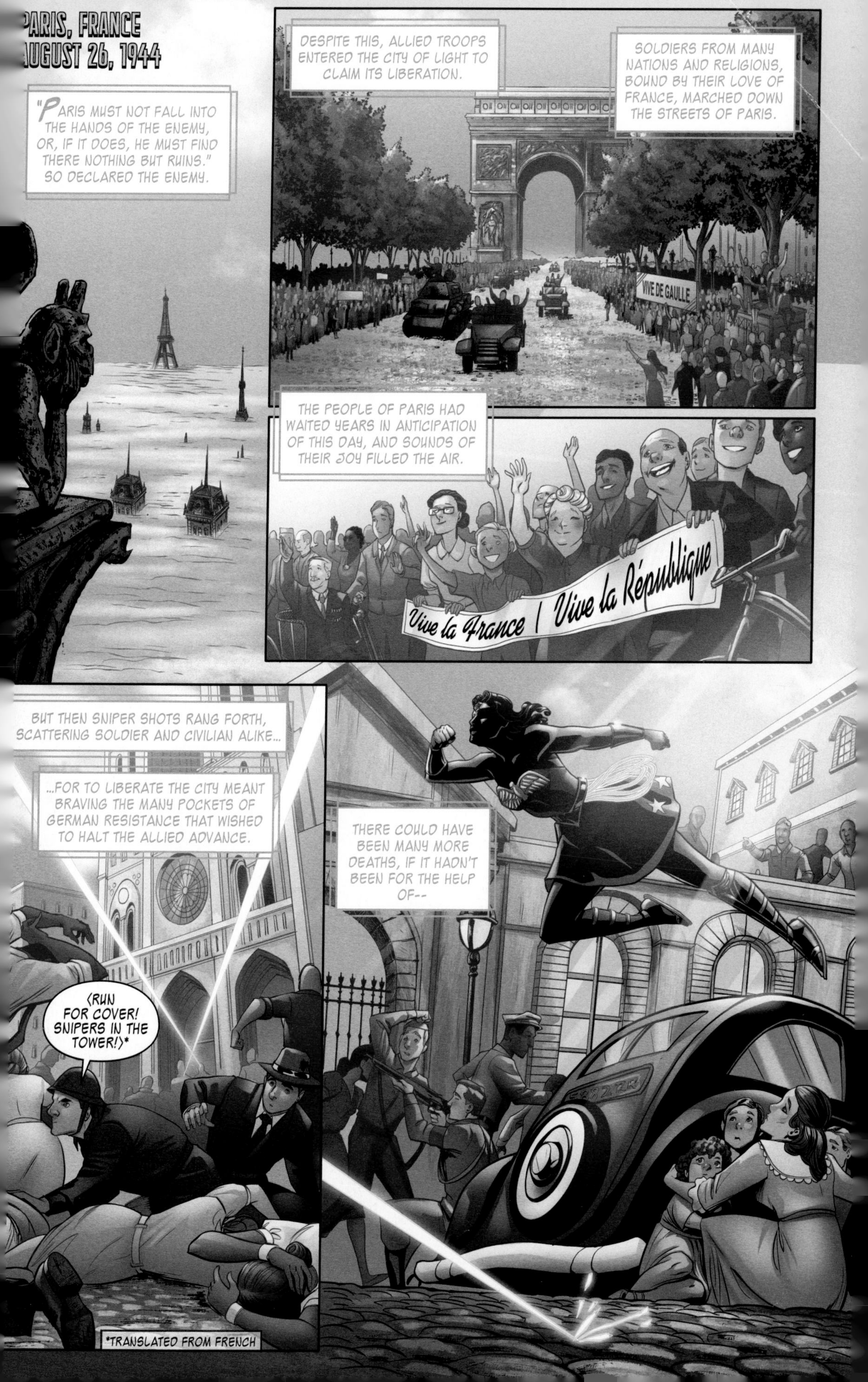
PARIS, FRANCE
AUGUST 26, 1944
"PARIS MUST NOT FALL INTO THE HANDS OF THE ENEMY, OR, IF IT DOES, HE MUST FIND THERE NOTHING BUT RUINS." SO DECLARED THE ENEMY.
DESPITE THIS, ALLIED TROOPS ENTERED THE CITY OF LIGHT TO CLAIM ITS LIBERATION.
SOLDIERS FROM MANY NATIONS AND RELIGIONS, BOUND BY THEIR LOVE OF FRANCE, MARCHED DOWN THE STREETS OF PARIS.
VIVE DE GAULLE
THE PEOPLE OF PARIS HAD WAITED YEARS IN ANTICIPATION OF THIS DAY, AND SOUNDS OF THEIR JOY FILLED THE AIR.
Vive la France ! Vive la République
BUT THEN SNIPER SHOTS RANG FORTH, SCATTERING SOLDIER AND CIVILIAN ALIKE...
...FOR TO LIBERATE THE CITY MEANT BRAVING THE MANY POCKETS OF GERMAN RESISTANCE THAT WISHED TO HALT THE ALLIED ADVANCE.
<RUN FOR COVER! SNIPERS IN THE TOWER!>*
*TRANSLATED FROM FRENCH
THERE COULD HAVE BEEN MANY MORE DEATHS, IF IT HADN'T BEEN FOR THE HELP OF--

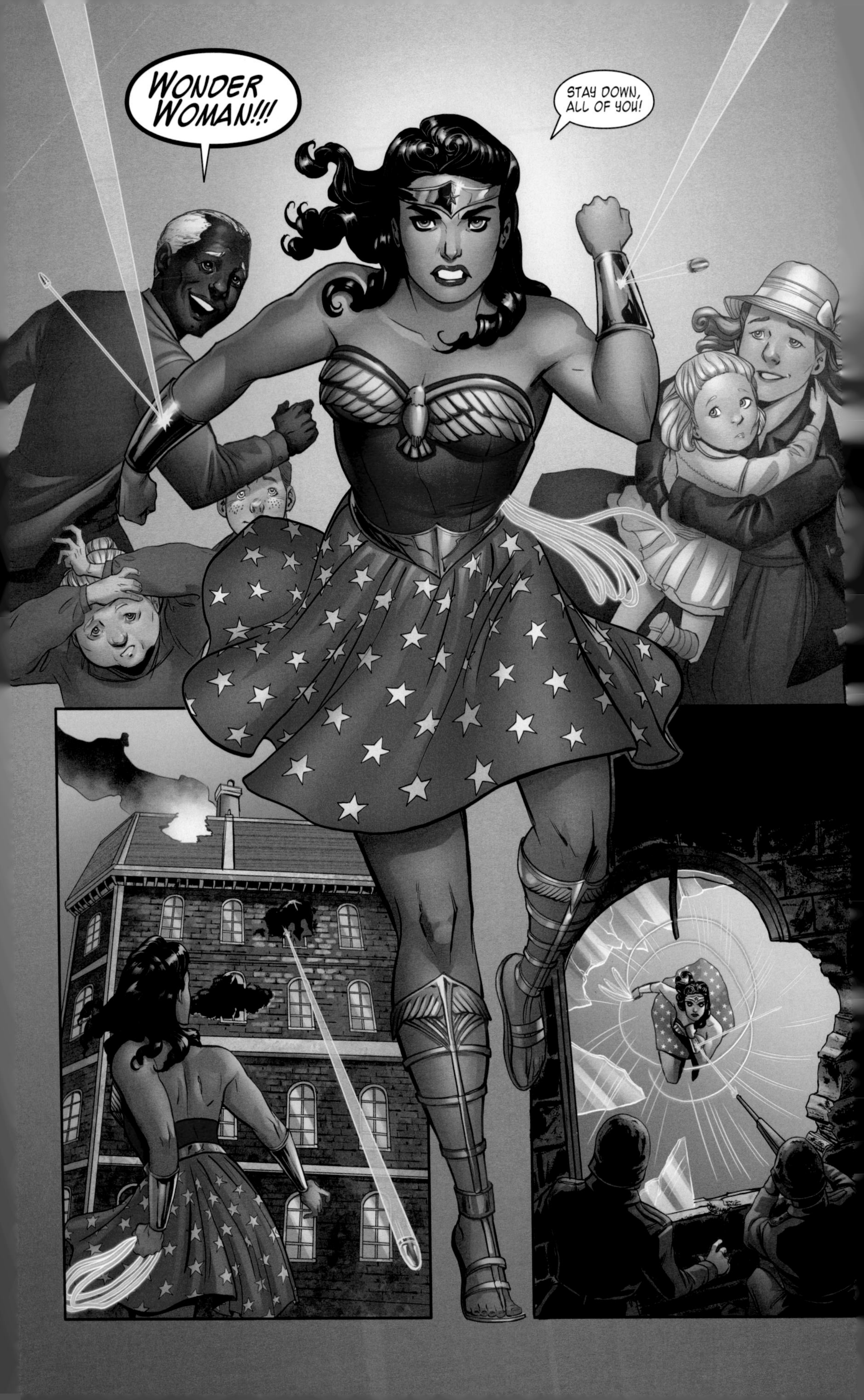
WONDER WOMAN!!!
STAY DOWN, ALL OF YOU!

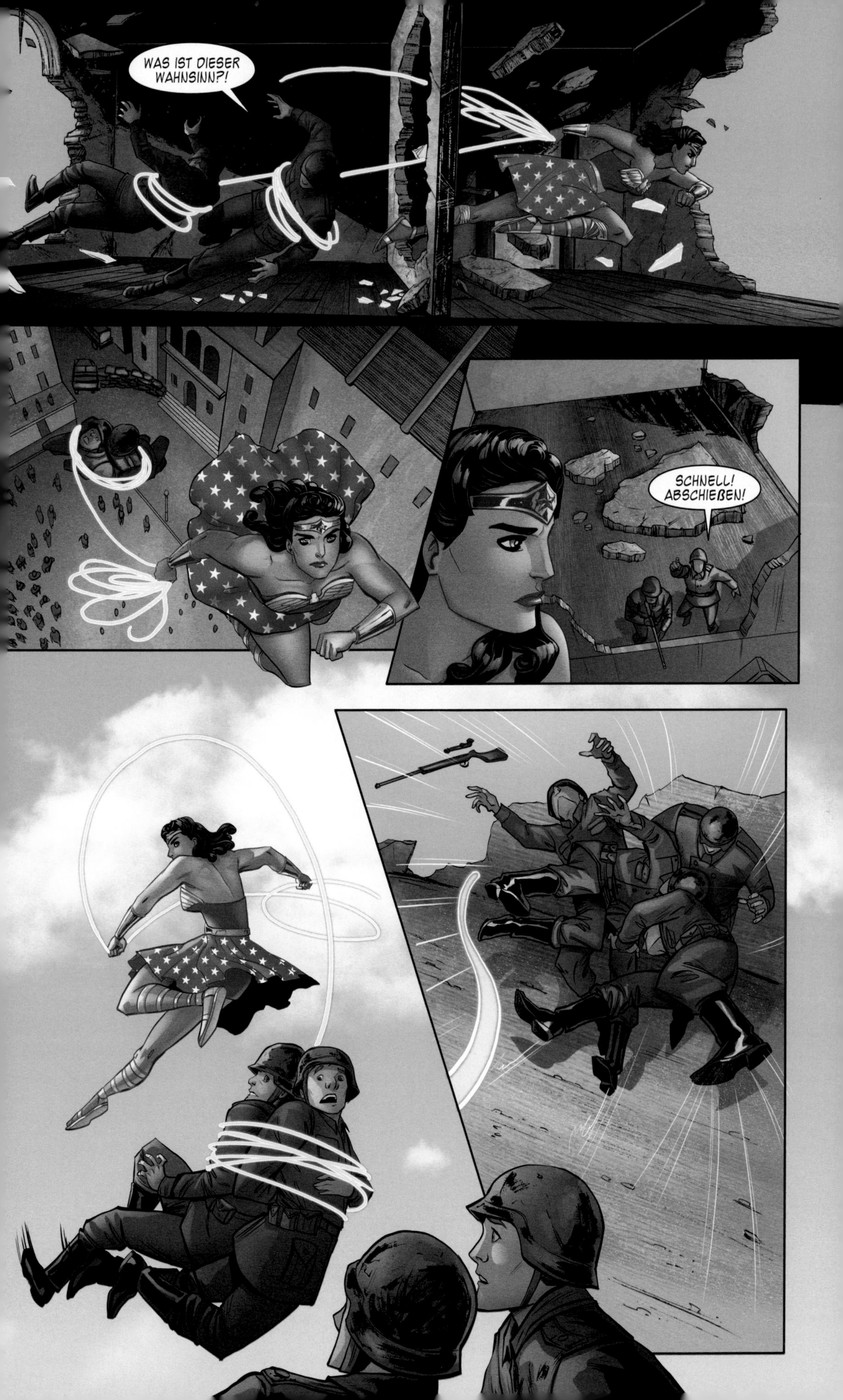
WAS IST DIESER WAHNSINN?!
SCHNELL! ABSCHIEẞEN!

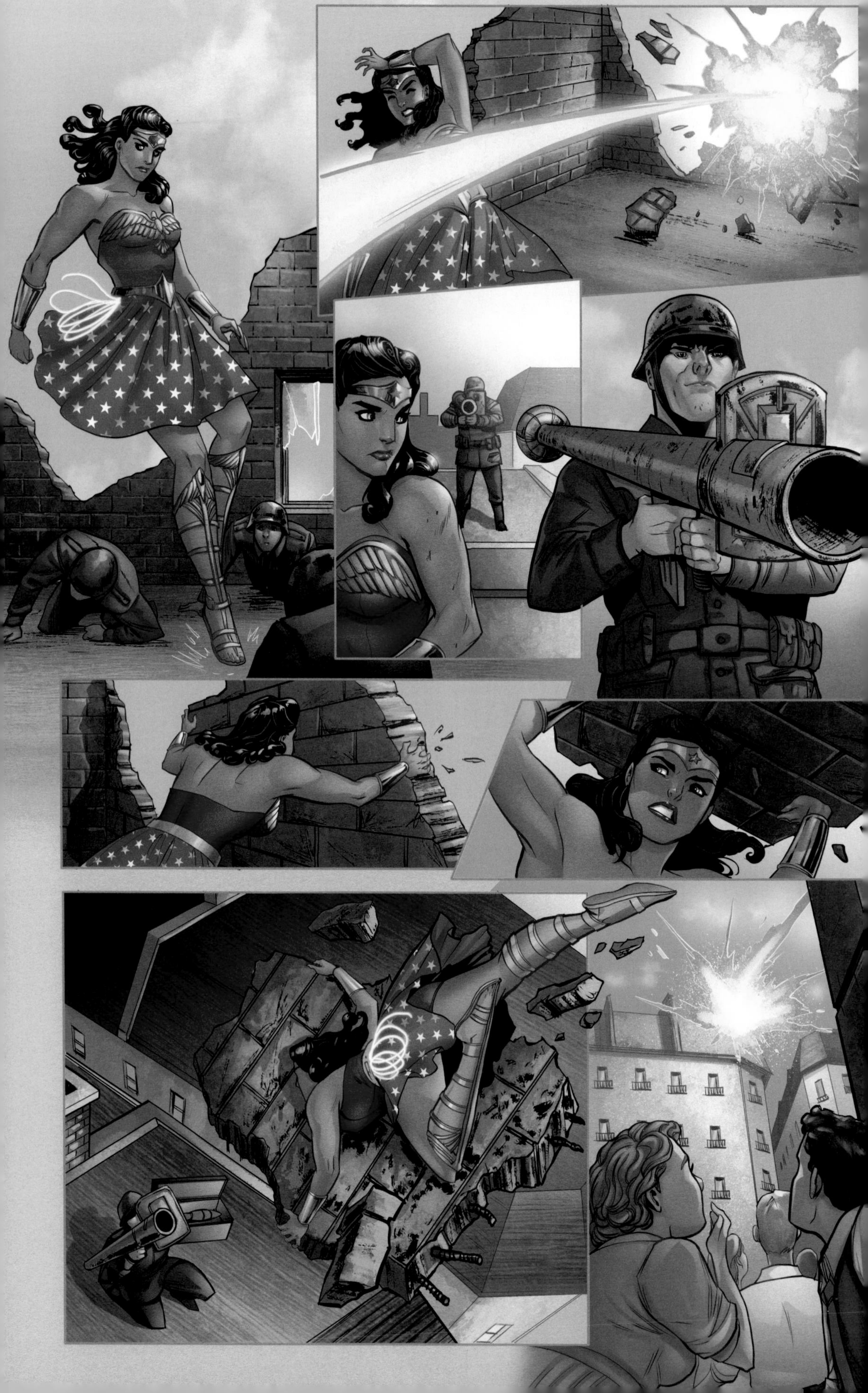

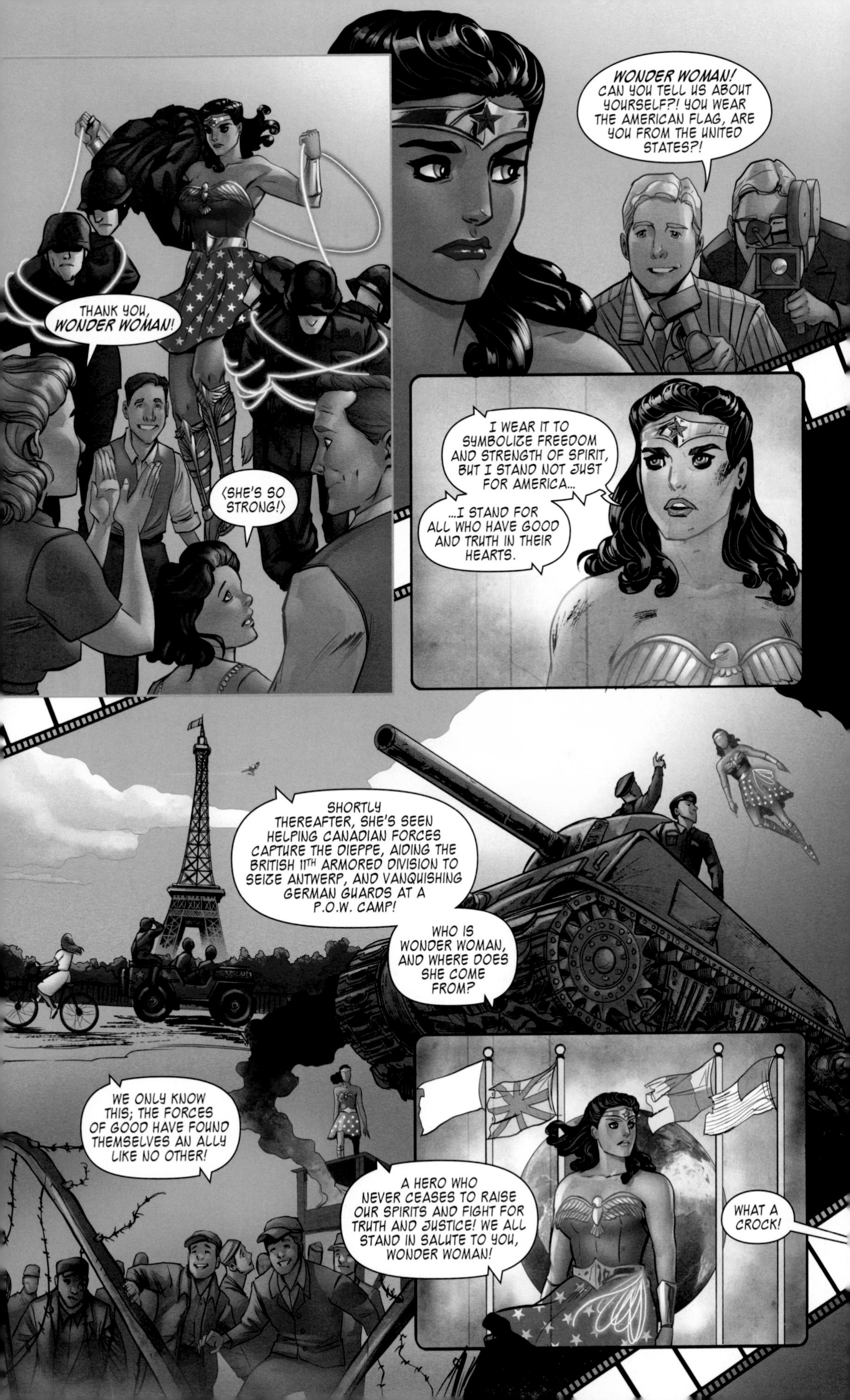
WONDER WOMAN! CAN YOU TELL US ABOUT YOURSELF?! YOU WEAR THE AMERICAN FLAG, ARE YOU FROM THE UNITED STATES?!
THANK YOU, WONDER WOMAN!
I WEAR IT TO SYMBOLIZE FREEDOM AND STRENGTH OF SPIRIT, BUT I STAND NOT JUST FOR AMERICA...
...I STAND FOR ALL WHO HAVE GOOD AND TRUTH IN THEIR HEARTS.
<SHE'S SO STRONG!>
SHORTLY THEREAFTER, SHE'S SEEN HELPING CANADIAN FORCES CAPTURE THE DIEPPE, AIDING THE BRITISH 11TH ARMORED DIVISION TO SEIZE ANTWERP, AND VANQUISHING GERMAN GUARDS AT A P.O.W. CAMP!
WHO IS WONDER WOMAN, AND WHERE DOES SHE COME FROM?
WE ONLY KNOW THIS; THE FORCES OF GOOD HAVE FOUND THEMSELVES AN ALLY LIKE NO OTHER!
A HERO WHO NEVER CEASES TO RAISE OUR SPIRITS AND FIGHT FOR TRUTH AND JUSTICE! WE ALL STAND IN SALUTE TO YOU, WONDER WOMAN!
WHAT A CROCK!

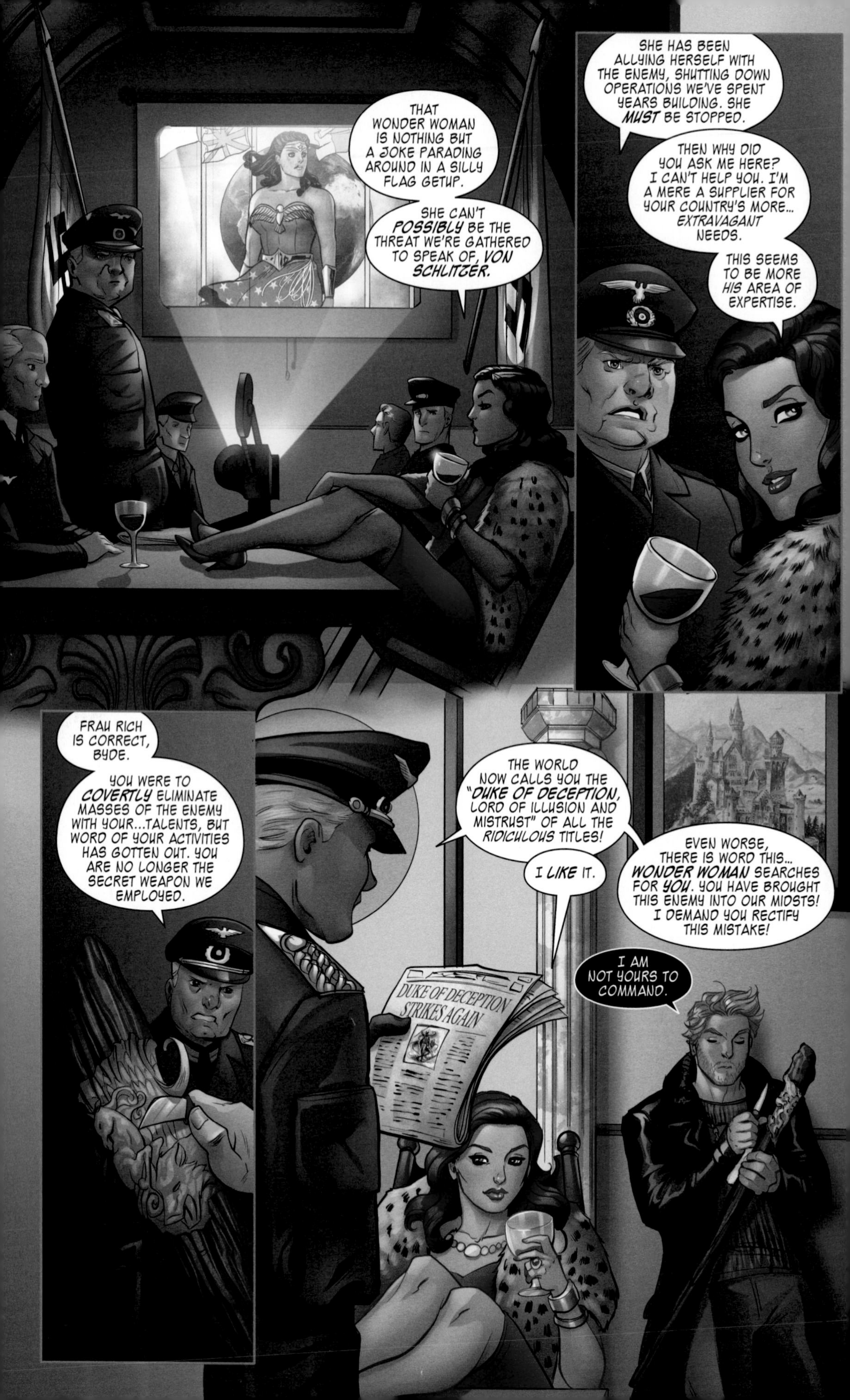
THAT WONDER WOMAN IS NOTHING BUT A JOKE PARADING AROUND IN A SILLY FLAG GETUP.
SHE CAN'T POSSIBLY BE THE THREAT WE'RE GATHERED TO SPEAK OF, VON SCHLITZER.
SHE HAS BEEN ALLYING HERSELF WITH THE ENEMY, SHUTTING DOWN OPERATIONS WE'VE SPENT YEARS BUILDING. SHE MUST BE STOPPED.
THEN WHY DID YOU ASK ME HERE? I CAN'T HELP YOU. I'M A MERE A SUPPLIER FOR YOUR COUNTRY'S MORE... EXTRAVAGANT NEEDS.
THIS SEEMS TO BE MORE HIS AREA OF EXPERTISE.
FRAU RICH IS CORRECT, BYDE.
YOU WERE TO COVERTLY ELIMINATE MASSES OF THE ENEMY WITH YOUR...TALENTS, BUT WORD OF YOUR ACTIVITIES HAS GOTTEN OUT. YOU ARE NO LONGER THE SECRET WEAPON WE EMPLOYED.
THE WORLD NOW CALLS YOU THE "DUKE OF DECEPTION, LORD OF ILLUSION AND MISTRUST" OF ALL THE RIDICULOUS TITLES!
I LIKE IT.
EVEN WORSE, THERE IS WORD THIS... WONDER WOMAN SEARCHES FOR YOU. YOU HAVE BROUGHT THIS ENEMY INTO OUR MIDSTS! I DEMAND YOU RECTIFY THIS MISTAKE!
DUKE OF DECEPTION STRIKES AGAIN
I AM NOT YOURS TO COMMAND.

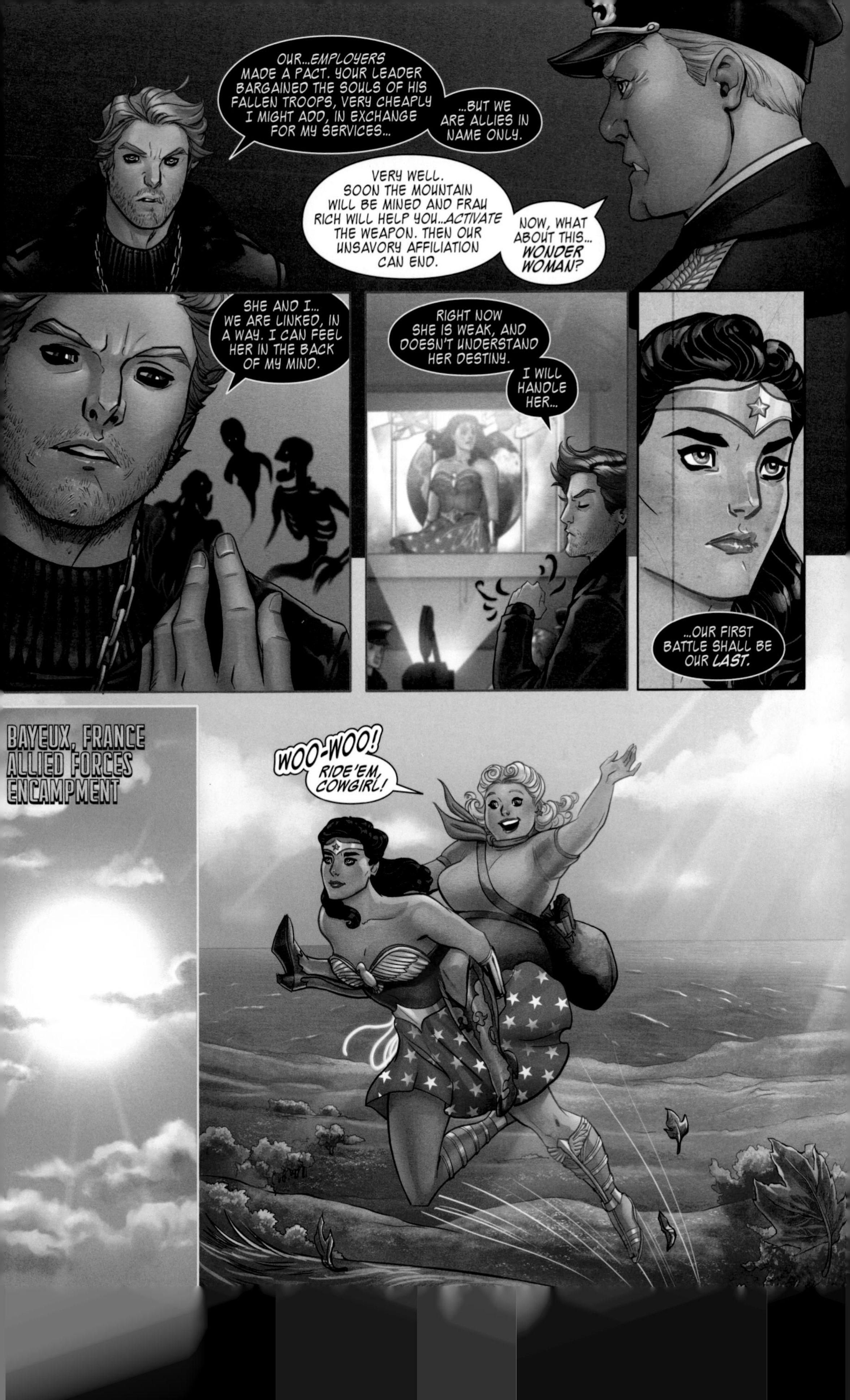

OUR...EMPLOYERS MADE A PACT. YOUR LEADER BARGAINED THE SOULS OF HIS FALLEN TROOPS, VERY CHEAPLY I MIGHT ADD, IN EXCHANGE FOR MY SERVICES...
...BUT WE ARE ALLIES IN NAME ONLY.
VERY WELL. SOON THE MOUNTAIN WILL BE MINED AND FRAU RICH WILL HELP YOU...ACTIVATE THE WEAPON. THEN OUR UNSAVORY AFFILIATION CAN END.
NOW, WHAT ABOUT THIS... WONDER WOMAN?
SHE AND I... WE ARE LINKED, IN A WAY. I CAN FEEL HER IN THE BACK OF MY MIND.
RIGHT NOW SHE IS WEAK, AND DOESN'T UNDERSTAND HER DESTINY.
I WILL HANDLE HER...
...OUR FIRST BATTLE SHALL BE OUR LAST.
BAYEUX, FRANCE ALLIED FORCES ENCAMPMENT
WOO-WOO! RIDE'EM, COWGIRL!

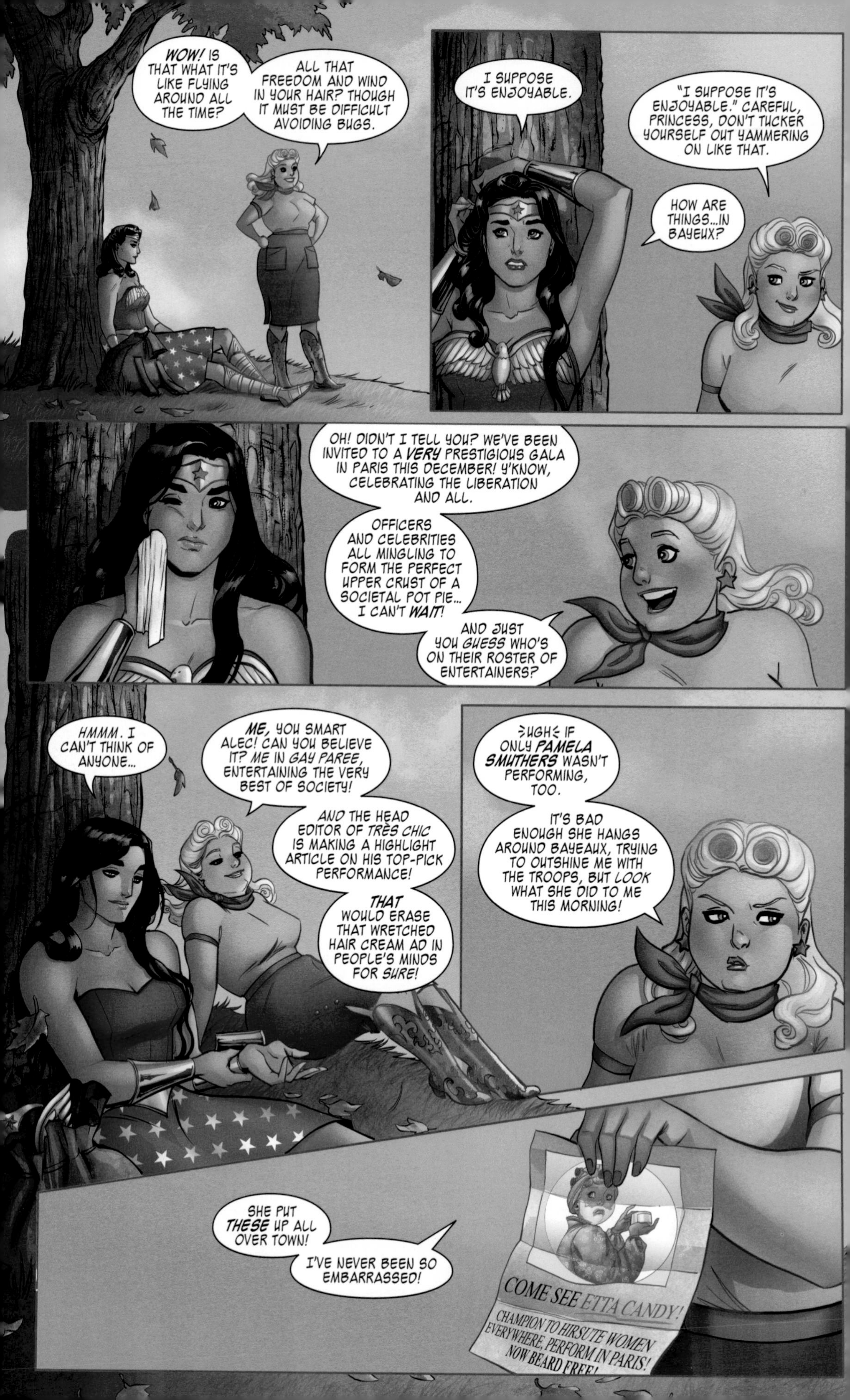

WOW! IS THAT WHAT IT'S LIKE FLYING AROUND ALL THE TIME?
ALL THAT FREEDOM AND WIND IN YOUR HAIR? THOUGH IT MUST BE DIFFICULT AVOIDING BUGS.
I SUPPOSE IT'S ENJOYABLE.
"I SUPPOSE IT'S ENJOYABLE." CAREFUL, PRINCESS, DON'T TUCKER YOURSELF OUT YAMMERING ON LIKE THAT.
HOW ARE THINGS...IN BAYEUX?
OH! DIDN'T I TELL YOU? WE'VE BEEN INVITED TO A VERY PRESTIGIOUS GALA IN PARIS THIS DECEMBER! Y'KNOW, CELEBRATING THE LIBERATION AND ALL.
OFFICERS AND CELEBRITIES ALL MINGLING TO FORM THE PERFECT UPPER CRUST OF A SOCIETAL POT PIE... I CAN'T WAIT!
AND JUST YOU GUESS WHO'S ON THEIR ROSTER OF ENTERTAINERS?
HMMM. I CAN'T THINK OF ANYONE...
ME, YOU SMART ALEC! CAN YOU BELIEVE IT? ME IN GAY PAREE, ENTERTAINING THE VERY BEST OF SOCIETY!
AND THE HEAD EDITOR OF TRÈS CHIC IS MAKING A HIGHLIGHT ARTICLE ON HIS TOP-PICK PERFORMANCE!
THAT WOULD ERASE THAT WRETCHED HAIR CREAM AD IN PEOPLE'S MINDS FOR SURE!
>UGH< IF ONLY PAMELA SMUTHERS WASN'T PERFORMING, TOO.
IT'S BAD ENOUGH SHE HANGS AROUND BAYEAUX, TRYING TO OUTSHINE ME WITH THE TROOPS, BUT LOOK WHAT SHE DID TO ME THIS MORNING!
SHE PUT THESE UP ALL OVER TOWN!
I'VE NEVER BEEN SO EMBARRASSED!
COME SEE ETTA CANDY!
CHAMPION TO HIRSUTE WOMEN EVERYWHERE, PERFORM IN PARIS! NOW BEARD FREE!

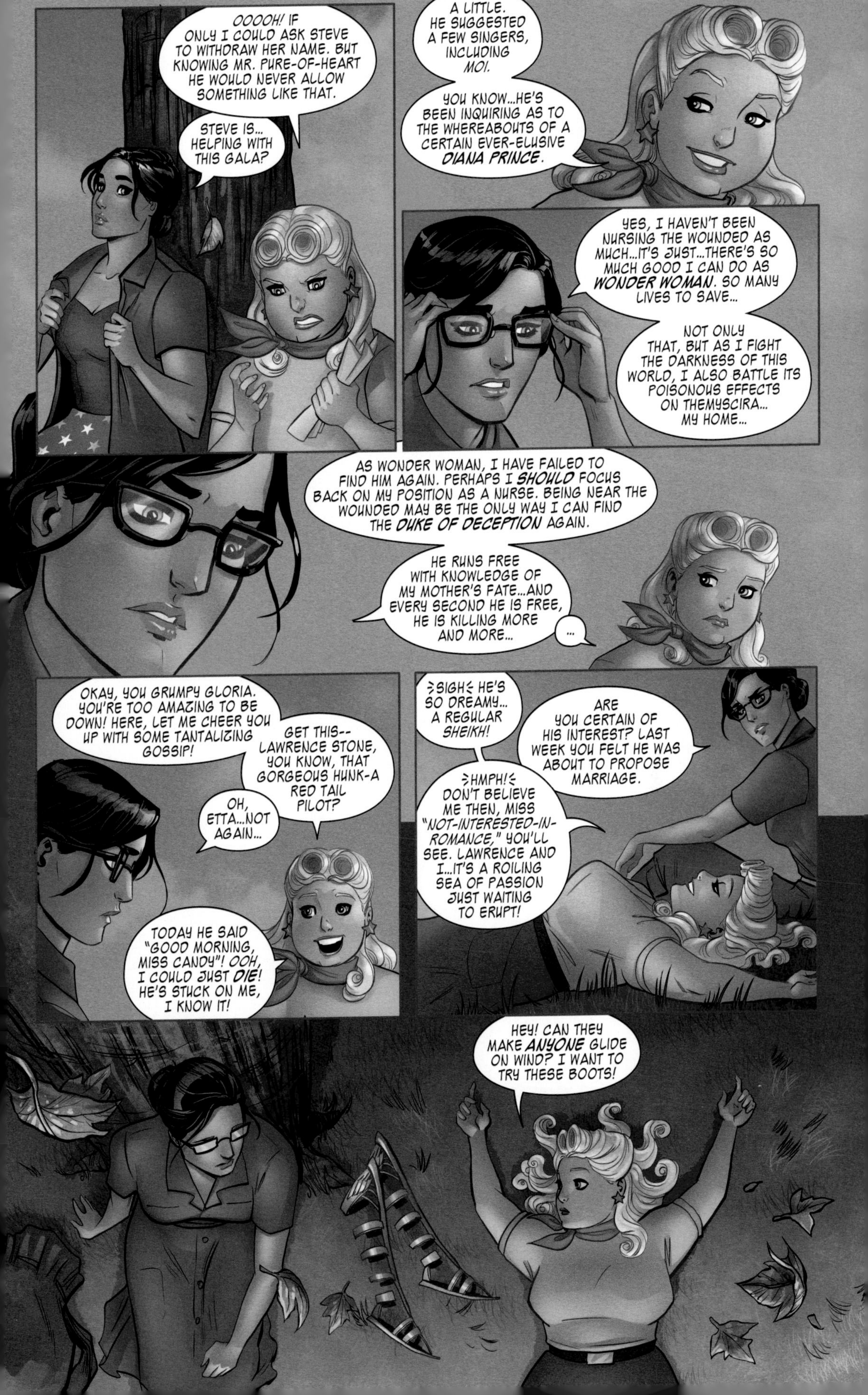
OOOOH! IF ONLY I COULD ASK STEVE TO WITHDRAW HER NAME. BUT KNOWING MR. PURE-OF-HEART HE WOULD NEVER ALLOW SOMETHING LIKE THAT.
STEVE IS... HELPING WITH THIS GALA?
A LITTLE. HE SUGGESTED A FEW SINGERS, INCLUDING MOI.
YOU KNOW...HE'S BEEN INQUIRING AS TO THE WHEREABOUTS OF A CERTAIN EVER-ELUSIVE DIANA PRINCE.
YES, I HAVEN'T BEEN NURSING THE WOUNDED AS MUCH...IT'S JUST...THERE'S SO MUCH GOOD I CAN DO AS WONDER WOMAN. SO MANY LIVES TO SAVE...
NOT ONLY THAT, BUT AS I FIGHT THE DARKNESS OF THIS WORLD, I ALSO BATTLE ITS POISONOUS EFFECTS ON THEMYSCIRA... MY HOME...
AS WONDER WOMAN, I HAVE FAILED TO FIND HIM AGAIN. PERHAPS I SHOULD FOCUS BACK ON MY POSITION AS A NURSE. BEING NEAR THE WOUNDED MAY BE THE ONLY WAY I CAN FIND THE DUKE OF DECEPTION AGAIN.
HE RUNS FREE WITH KNOWLEDGE OF MY MOTHER'S FATE...AND EVERY SECOND HE IS FREE, HE IS KILLING MORE AND MORE...
...
OKAY, YOU GRUMPY GLORIA. YOU'RE TOO AMAZING TO BE DOWN! HERE, LET ME CHEER YOU UP WITH SOME TANTALIZING GOSSIP!
GET THIS--LAWRENCE STONE, YOU KNOW, THAT GORGEOUS HUNK-A RED TAIL PILOT?
OH, ETTA...NOT AGAIN...
TODAY HE SAID "GOOD MORNING, MISS CANDY"! OOH, I COULD JUST DIE! HE'S STUCK ON ME, I KNOW IT!
>SIGH< HE'S SO DREAMY... A REGULAR SHEIKH!
ARE YOU CERTAIN OF HIS INTEREST? LAST WEEK YOU FELT HE WAS ABOUT TO PROPOSE MARRIAGE.
>HMPH!< DON'T BELIEVE ME THEN, MISS "NOT-INTERESTED-IN-ROMANCE," YOU'LL SEE. LAWRENCE AND I...IT'S A ROILING SEA OF PASSION JUST WAITING TO ERUPT!
HEY! CAN THEY MAKE ANYONE GLIDE ON WIND? I WANT TO TRY THESE BOOTS!

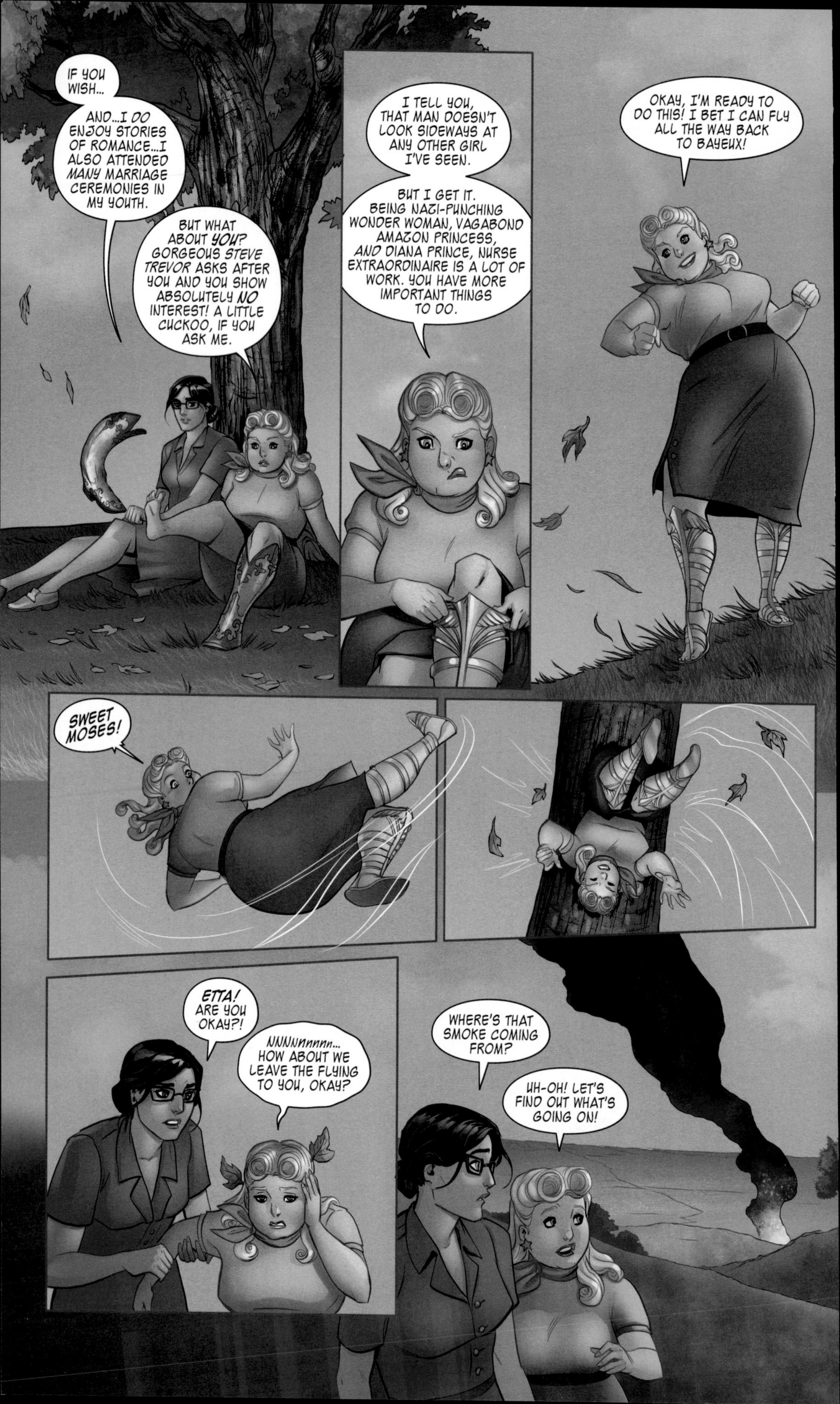
IF YOU WISH...
AND...I DO ENJOY STORIES OF ROMANCE...I ALSO ATTENDED MANY MARRIAGE CEREMONIES IN MY YOUTH.
BUT WHAT ABOUT YOU? GORGEOUS STEVE TREVOR ASKS AFTER YOU AND YOU SHOW ABSOLUTELY NO INTEREST! A LITTLE CUCKOO, IF YOU ASK ME.
I TELL YOU, THAT MAN DOESN'T LOOK SIDEWAYS AT ANY OTHER GIRL I'VE SEEN.
BUT I GET IT. BEING NAZI-PUNCHING WONDER WOMAN, VAGABOND AMAZON PRINCESS, AND DIANA PRINCE, NURSE EXTRAORDINAIRE IS A LOT OF WORK. YOU HAVE MORE IMPORTANT THINGS TO DO.
OKAY, I'M READY TO DO THIS! I BET I CAN FLY ALL THE WAY BACK TO BAYEUX!
SWEET MOSES!
ETTA! ARE YOU OKAY?!
NNNNnnnnn... HOW ABOUT WE LEAVE THE FLYING TO YOU, OKAY?
WHERE'S THAT SMOKE COMING FROM?
UH-OH! LET'S FIND OUT WHAT'S GOING ON!

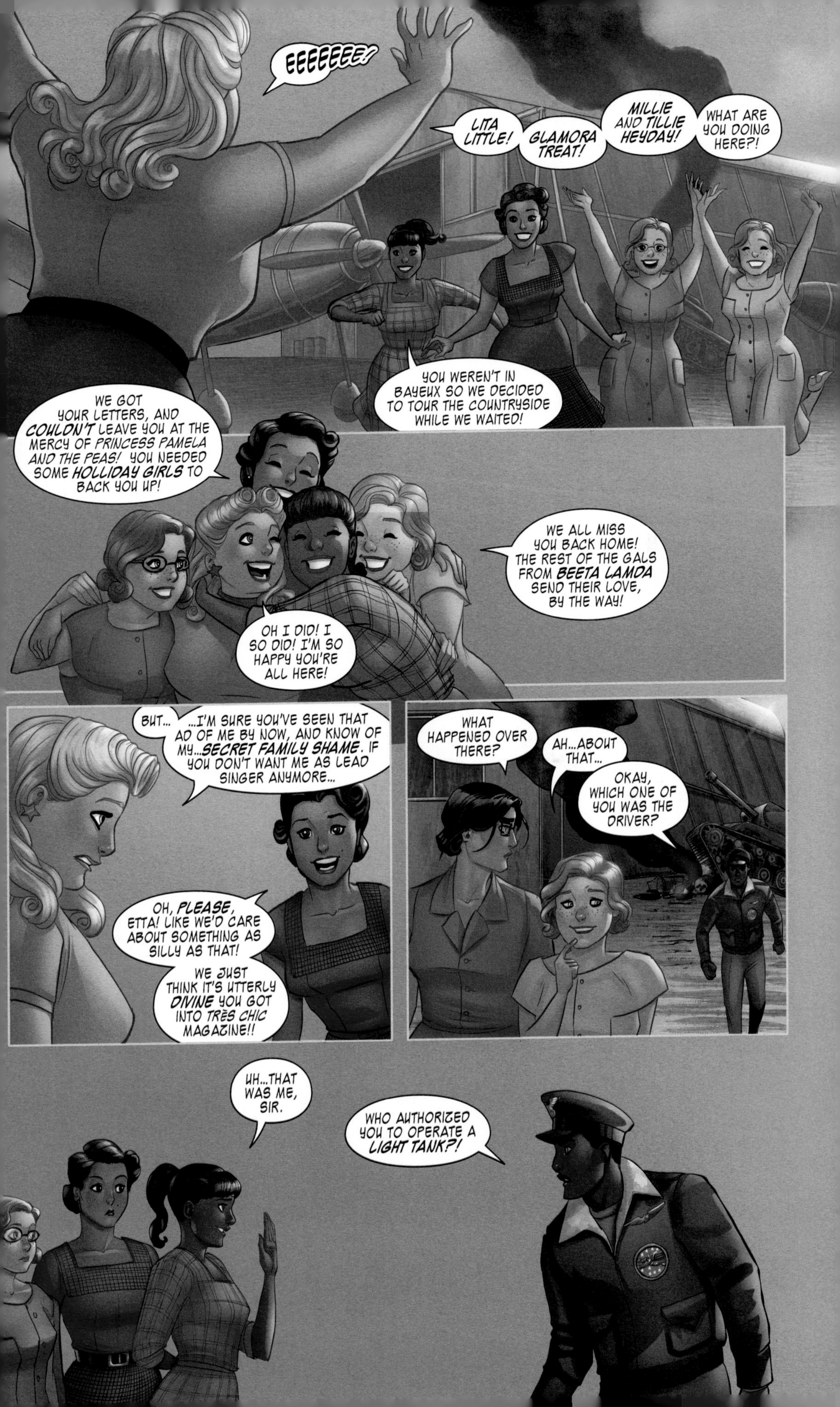
EEEEEEE!
LITA LITTLE!
GLAMORA TREAT!
MILLIE AND TILLIE HEYDAY!
WHAT ARE YOU DOING HERE?!
YOU WEREN'T IN BAYEUX SO WE DECIDED TO TOUR THE COUNTRYSIDE WHILE WE WAITED!
WE GOT YOUR LETTERS, AND COULDN'T LEAVE YOU AT THE MERCY OF PRINCESS PAMELA AND THE PEAS! YOU NEEDED SOME HOLLIDAY GIRLS TO BACK YOU UP!
WE ALL MISS YOU BACK HOME! THE REST OF THE GALS FROM BEETA LAMDA SEND THEIR LOVE, BY THE WAY!
OH I DID! I SO DID! I'M SO HAPPY YOU'RE ALL HERE!
BUT...
...I'M SURE YOU'VE SEEN THAT AD OF ME BY NOW, AND KNOW OF MY...SECRET FAMILY SHAME. IF YOU DON'T WANT ME AS LEAD SINGER ANYMORE...
OH, PLEASE, ETTA! LIKE WE'D CARE ABOUT SOMETHING AS SILLY AS THAT!
WE JUST THINK IT'S UTTERLY DIVINE YOU GOT INTO TRÈS CHIC MAGAZINE!!
WHAT HAPPENED OVER THERE?
AH...ABOUT THAT...
OKAY, WHICH ONE OF YOU WAS THE DRIVER?
UH...THAT WAS ME, SIR.
WHO AUTHORIZED YOU TO OPERATE A LIGHT TANK?!

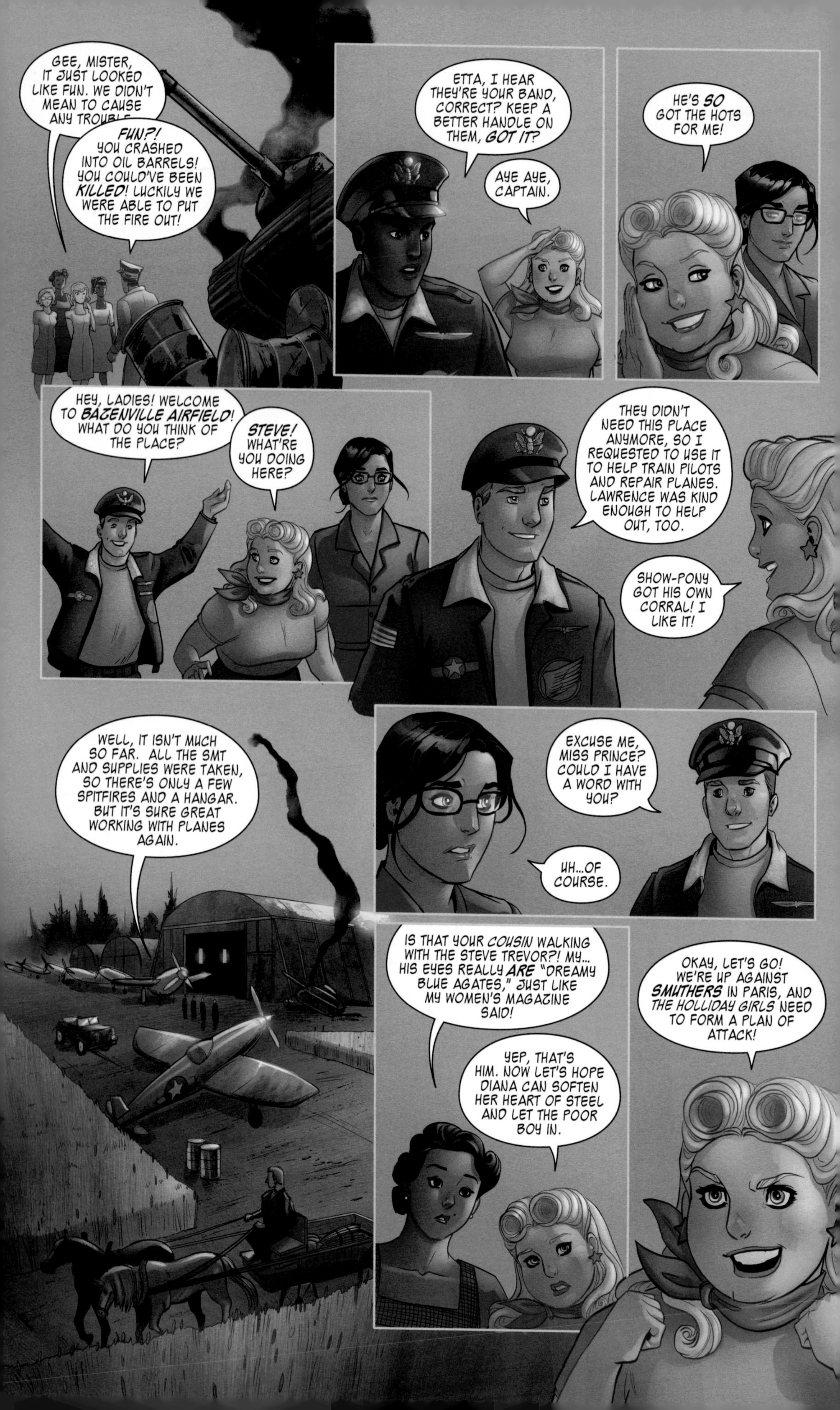
GEE, MISTER, IT JUST LOOKED LIKE FUN. WE DIDN'T MEAN TO CAUSE ANY TROUBLE...
FUN?! YOU CRASHED INTO OIL BARRELS! YOU COULD'VE BEEN KILLED! LUCKILY WE WERE ABLE TO PUT THE FIRE OUT!
ETTA, I HEAR THEY'RE YOUR BAND, CORRECT? KEEP A BETTER HANDLE ON THEM, GOT IT?
AYE AYE, CAPTAIN.
HE'S SO GOT THE HOTS FOR ME!
HEY, LADIES! WELCOME TO BAZENVILLE AIRFIELD! WHAT DO YOU THINK OF THE PLACE?
STEVE! WHAT'RE YOU DOING HERE?
THEY DIDN'T NEED THIS PLACE ANYMORE, SO I REQUESTED TO USE IT TO HELP TRAIN PILOTS AND REPAIR PLANES. LAWRENCE WAS KIND ENOUGH TO HELP OUT, TOO.
SHOW-PONY GOT HIS OWN CORRAL! I LIKE IT!
WELL, IT ISN'T MUCH SO FAR. ALL THE SMT AND SUPPLIES WERE TAKEN, SO THERE'S ONLY A FEW SPITFIRES AND A HANGAR. BUT IT'S SURE GREAT WORKING WITH PLANES AGAIN.
EXCUSE ME, MISS PRINCE? COULD I HAVE A WORD WITH YOU?
UH...OF COURSE.
IS THAT YOUR COUSIN WALKING WITH THE STEVE TREVOR?! MY... HIS EYES REALLY ARE "DREAMY BLUE AGATES," JUST LIKE MY WOMEN'S MAGAZINE SAID!
YEP, THAT'S HIM. NOW LET'S HOPE DIANA CAN SOFTEN HER HEART OF STEEL AND LET THE POOR BOY IN.
OKAY, LET'S GO! WE'RE UP AGAINST SMUTHERS IN PARIS, AND THE HOLLIDAY GIRLS NEED TO FORM A PLAN OF ATTACK!

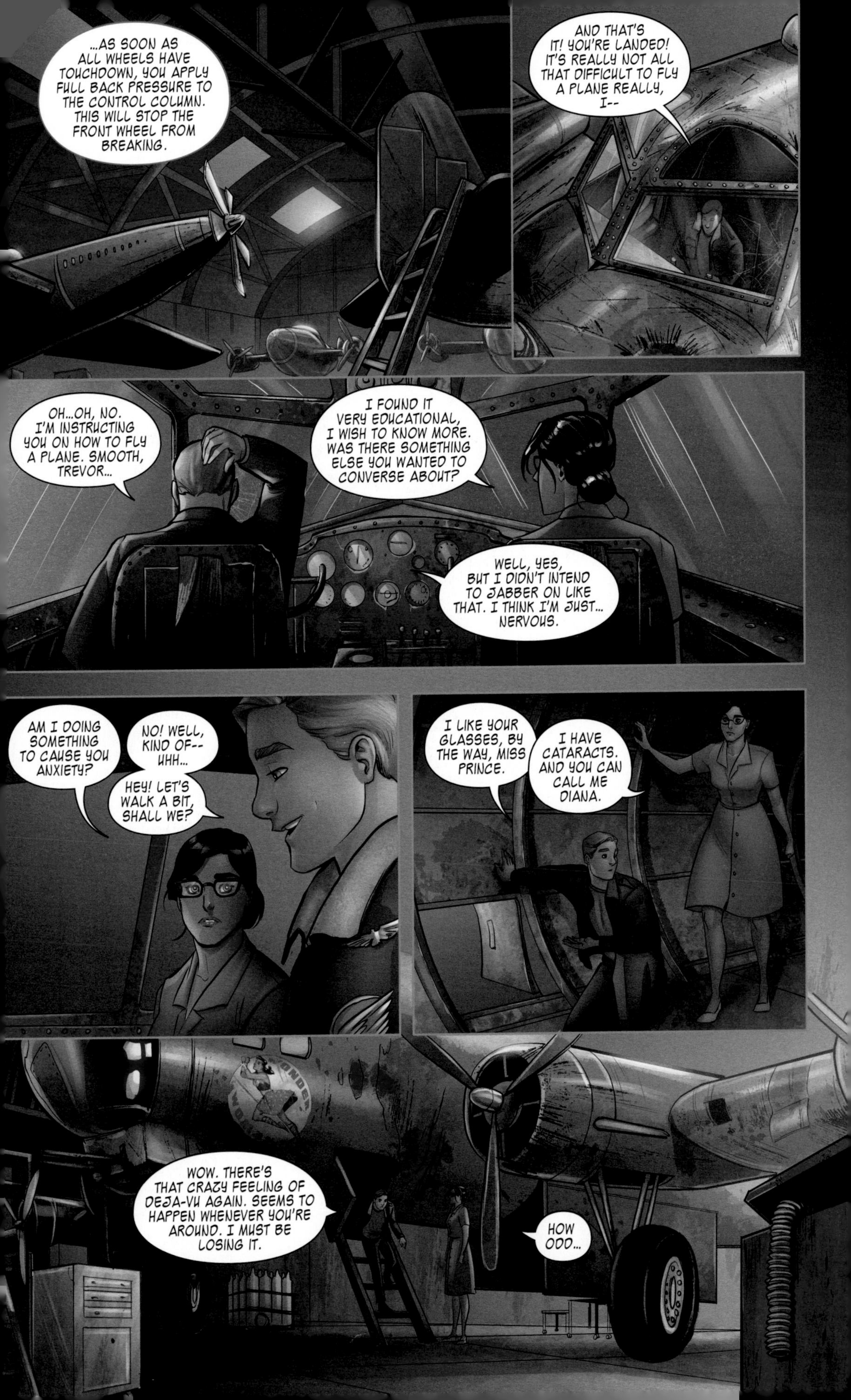
...AS SOON AS ALL WHEELS HAVE TOUCHDOWN, YOU APPLY FULL BACK PRESSURE TO THE CONTROL COLUMN. THIS WILL STOP THE FRONT WHEEL FROM BREAKING.
AND THAT'S IT! YOU'RE LANDED! IT'S REALLY NOT ALL THAT DIFFICULT TO FLY A PLANE REALLY, I--
OH...OH, NO. I'M INSTRUCTING YOU ON HOW TO FLY A PLANE. SMOOTH, TREVOR...
I FOUND IT VERY EDUCATIONAL, I WISH TO KNOW MORE. WAS THERE SOMETHING ELSE YOU WANTED TO CONVERSE ABOUT?
WELL, YES, BUT I DIDN'T INTEND TO JABBER ON LIKE THAT. I THINK I'M JUST... NERVOUS.
AM I DOING SOMETHING TO CAUSE YOU ANXIETY?
NO! WELL, KIND OF-- UHH...
HEY! LET'S WALK A BIT, SHALL WE?
I LIKE YOUR GLASSES, BY THE WAY, MISS PRINCE.
I HAVE CATARACTS. AND YOU CAN CALL ME DIANA.
WOW. THERE'S THAT CRAZY FEELING OF DEJA-VU AGAIN. SEEMS TO HAPPEN WHENEVER YOU'RE AROUND. I MUST BE LOSING IT.
HOW ODD...

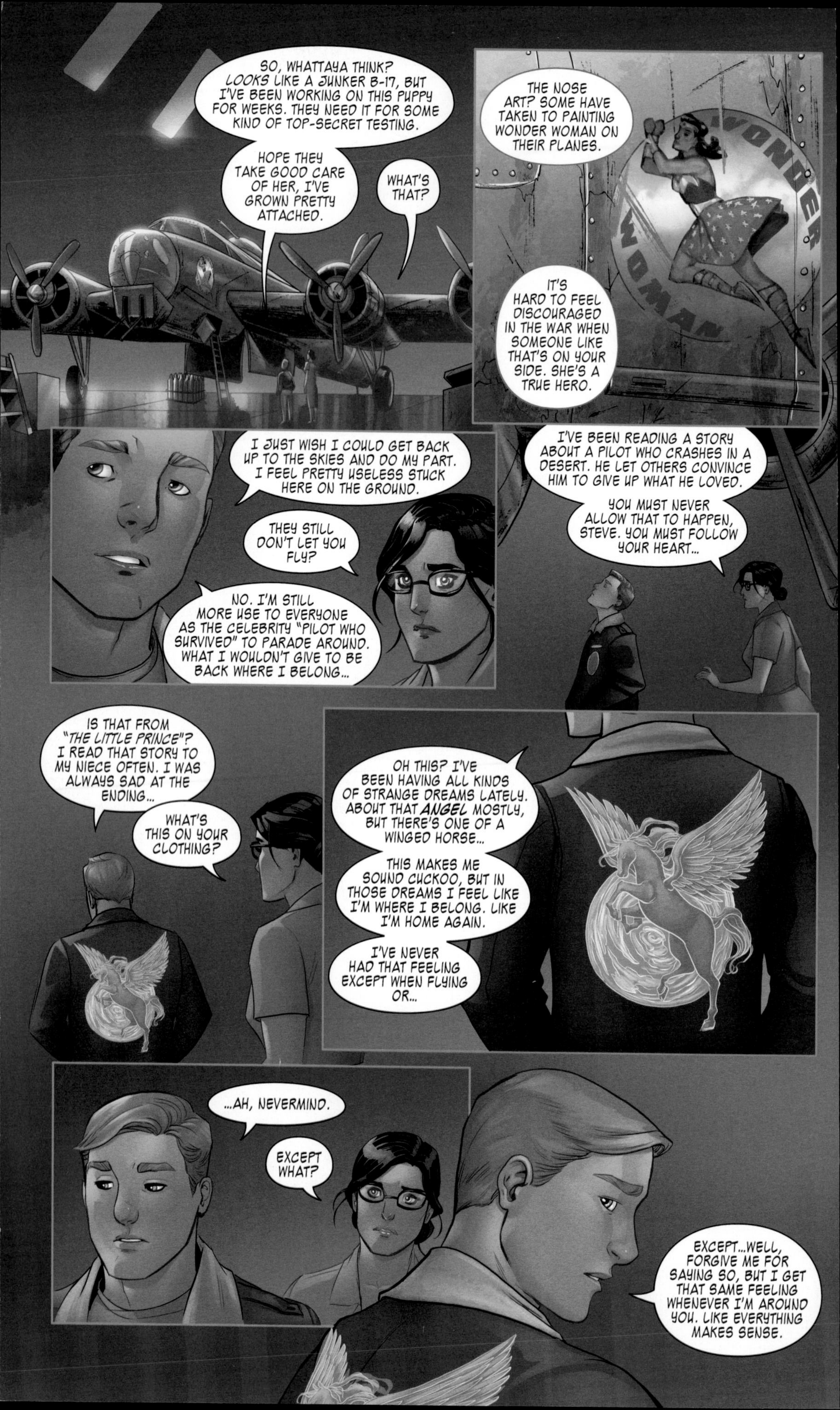

SO, WHATTAYA THINK? LOOKS LIKE A JUNKER B-17, BUT I'VE BEEN WORKING ON THIS PUPPY FOR WEEKS. THEY NEED IT FOR SOME KIND OF TOP-SECRET TESTING.
HOPE THEY TAKE GOOD CARE OF HER, I'VE GROWN PRETTY ATTACHED.
WHAT'S THAT?
THE NOSE ART? SOME HAVE TAKEN TO PAINTING WONDER WOMAN ON THEIR PLANES.
WONDER WOMAN
IT'S HARD TO FEEL DISCOURAGED IN THE WAR WHEN SOMEONE LIKE THAT'S ON YOUR SIDE. SHE'S A TRUE HERO.
I JUST WISH I COULD GET BACK UP TO THE SKIES AND DO MY PART. I FEEL PRETTY USELESS STUCK HERE ON THE GROUND.
THEY STILL DON'T LET YOU FLY?
NO. I'M STILL MORE USE TO EVERYONE AS THE CELEBRITY "PILOT WHO SURVIVED" TO PARADE AROUND. WHAT I WOULDN'T GIVE TO BE BACK WHERE I BELONG...
I'VE BEEN READING A STORY ABOUT A PILOT WHO CRASHES IN A DESERT. HE LET OTHERS CONVINCE HIM TO GIVE UP WHAT HE LOVED.
YOU MUST NEVER ALLOW THAT TO HAPPEN, STEVE. YOU MUST FOLLOW YOUR HEART...
IS THAT FROM "THE LITTLE PRINCE"? I READ THAT STORY TO MY NIECE OFTEN. I WAS ALWAYS SAD AT THE ENDING...
WHAT'S THIS ON YOUR CLOTHING?
OH THIS? I'VE BEEN HAVING ALL KINDS OF STRANGE DREAMS LATELY. ABOUT THAT ANGEL MOSTLY, BUT THERE'S ONE OF A WINGED HORSE...
THIS MAKES ME SOUND CUCKOO, BUT IN THOSE DREAMS I FEEL LIKE I'M WHERE I BELONG. LIKE I'M HOME AGAIN.
I'VE NEVER HAD THAT FEELING EXCEPT WHEN FLYING OR...
...AH, NEVERMIND.
EXCEPT WHAT?
EXCEPT...WELL, FORGIVE ME FOR SAYING SO, BUT I GET THAT SAME FEELING WHENEVER I'M AROUND YOU. LIKE EVERYTHING MAKES SENSE.

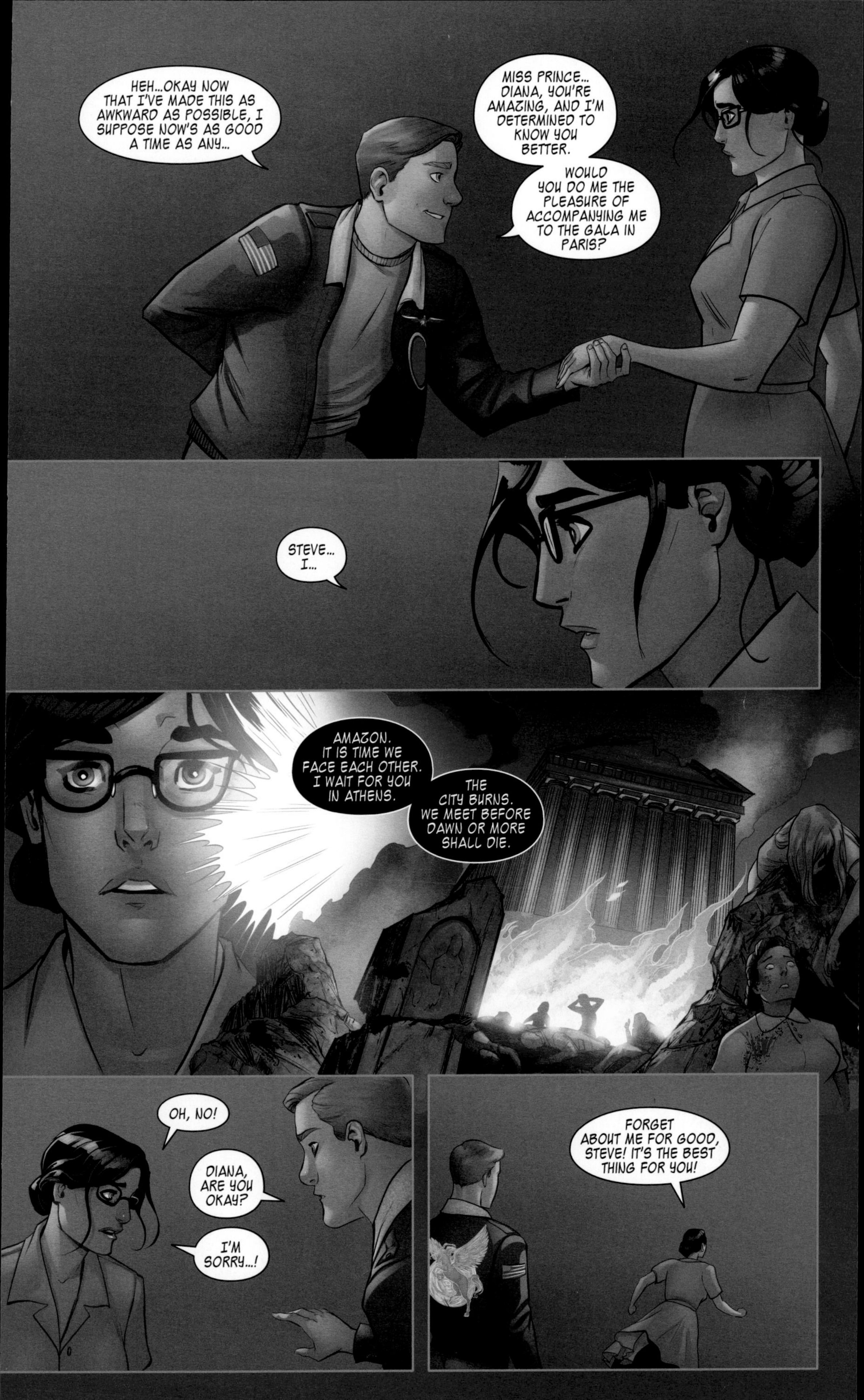
HEH...OKAY NOW THAT I'VE MADE THIS AS AWKWARD AS POSSIBLE, I SUPPOSE NOW'S AS GOOD A TIME AS ANY...
MISS PRINCE... DIANA, YOU'RE AMAZING, AND I'M DETERMINED TO KNOW YOU BETTER.
WOULD YOU DO ME THE PLEASURE OF ACCOMPANYING ME TO THE GALA IN PARIS?
STEVE... I...
AMAZON. IT IS TIME WE FACE EACH OTHER. I WAIT FOR YOU IN ATHENS.
THE CITY BURNS. WE MEET BEFORE DAWN OR MORE SHALL DIE.
OH, NO!
DIANA, ARE YOU OKAY?
I'M SORRY...!
FORGET ABOUT ME FOR GOOD, STEVE! IT'S THE BEST THING FOR YOU!

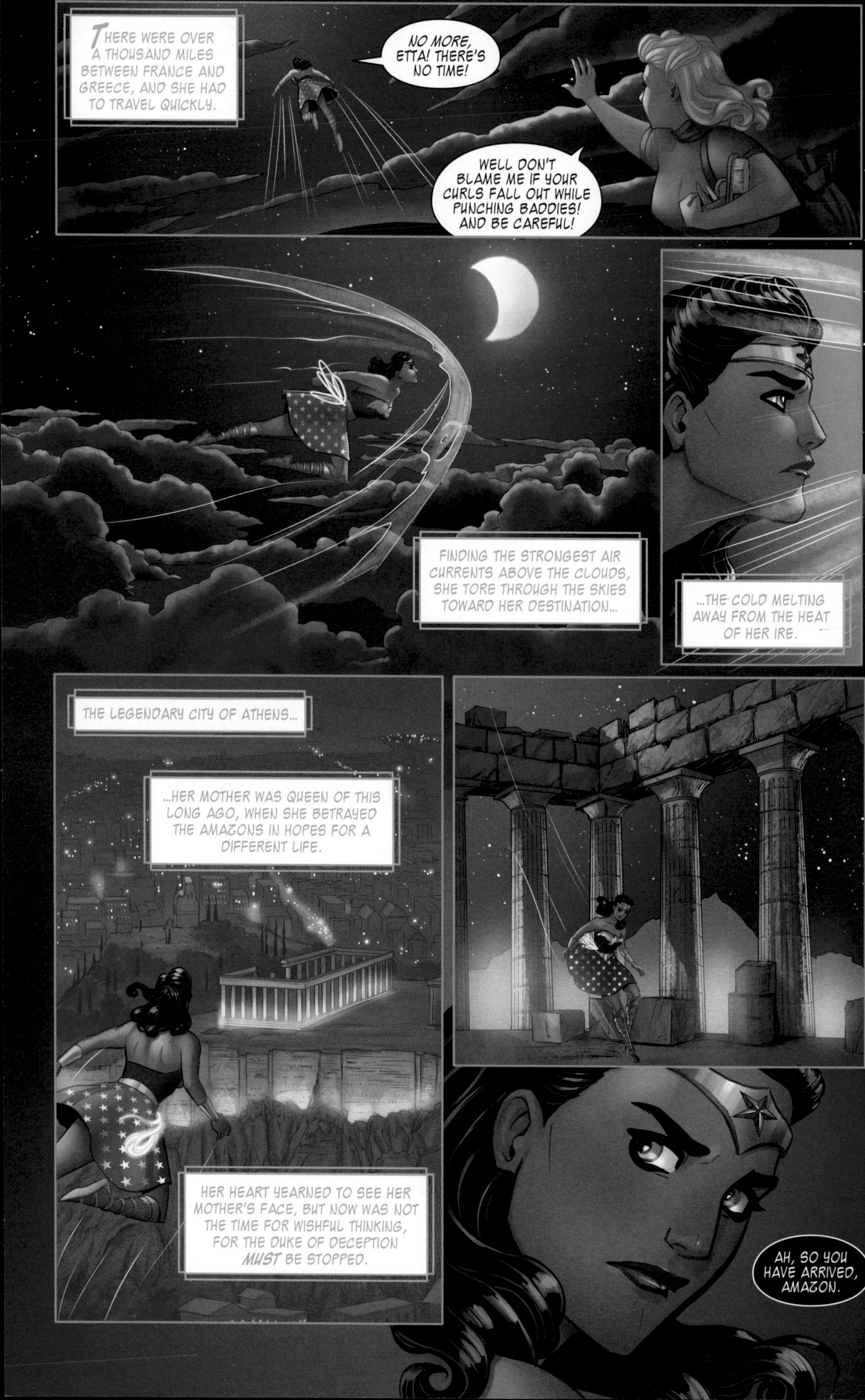
THERE WERE OVER A THOUSAND MILES BETWEEN FRANCE AND GREECE, AND SHE HAD TO TRAVEL QUICKLY.
NO MORE, ETTA! THERE'S NO TIME!
WELL DON'T BLAME ME IF YOUR CURLS FALL OUT WHILE PUNCHING BADDIES! AND BE CAREFUL!
FINDING THE STRONGEST AIR CURRENTS ABOVE THE CLOUDS, SHE TORE THROUGH THE SKIES TOWARD HER DESTINATION...
...THE COLD MELTING AWAY FROM THE HEAT OF HER IRE.
THE LEGENDARY CITY OF ATHENS...
...HER MOTHER WAS QUEEN OF THIS LONG AGO, WHEN SHE BETRAYED THE AMAZONS IN HOPES FOR A DIFFERENT LIFE.
HER HEART YEARNED TO SEE HER MOTHER'S FACE, BUT NOW WAS NOT THE TIME FOR WISHFUL THINKING, FOR THE DUKE OF DECEPTION *MUST* BE STOPPED.
AH, SO YOU HAVE ARRIVED, AMAZON.

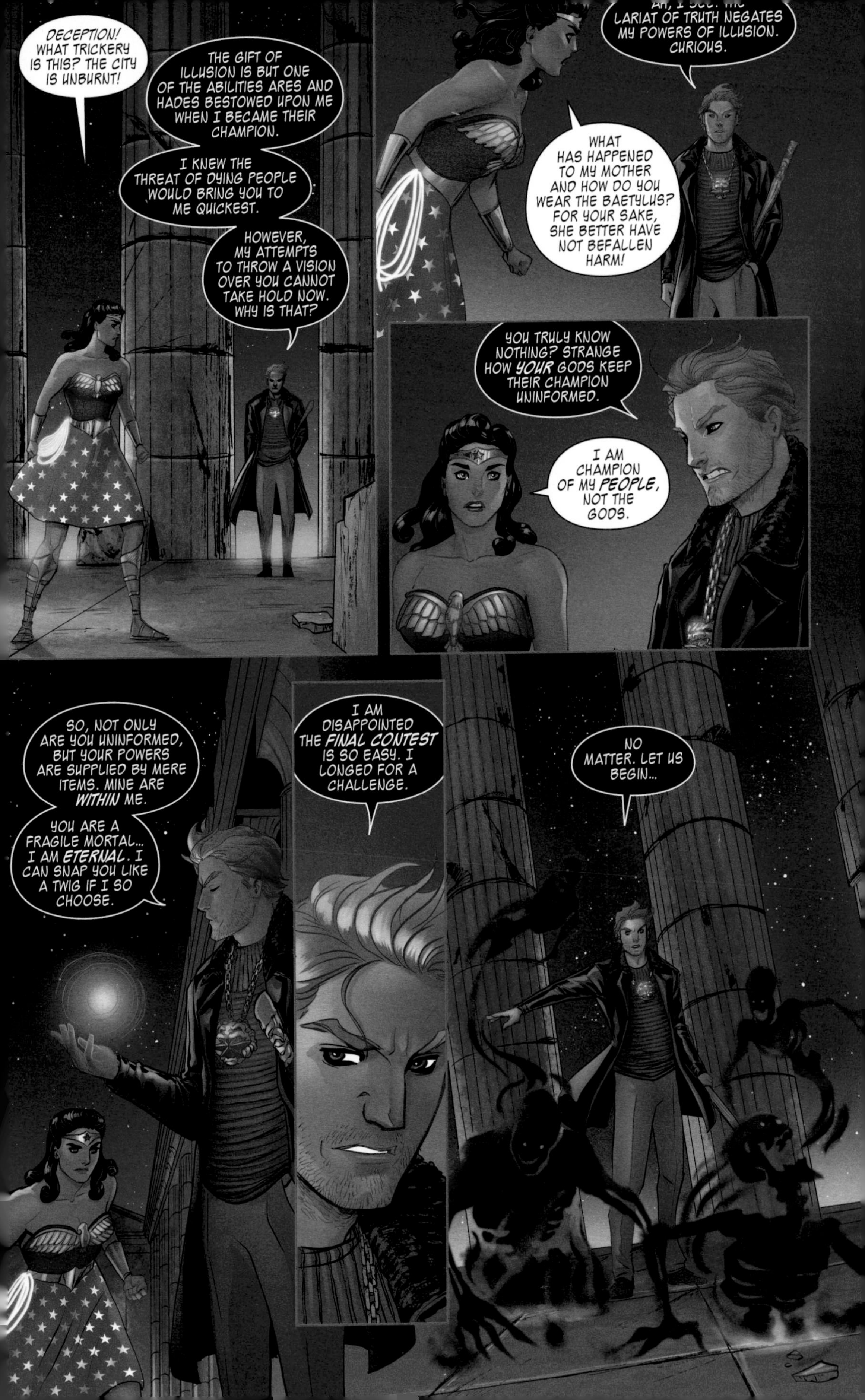
DECEPTION! WHAT TRICKERY IS THIS? THE CITY IS UNBURNT!
THE GIFT OF ILLUSION IS BUT ONE OF THE ABILITIES ARES AND HADES BESTOWED UPON ME WHEN I BECAME THEIR CHAMPION.
I KNEW THE THREAT OF DYING PEOPLE WOULD BRING YOU TO ME QUICKEST.
HOWEVER, MY ATTEMPTS TO THROW A VISION OVER YOU CANNOT TAKE HOLD NOW. WHY IS THAT?
LARIAT OF TRUTH NEGATES MY POWERS OF ILLUSION. CURIOUS.
WHAT HAS HAPPENED TO MY MOTHER AND HOW DO YOU WEAR THE BAETYLUS? FOR YOUR SAKE, SHE BETTER HAVE NOT BEFALLEN HARM!
YOU TRULY KNOW NOTHING? STRANGE HOW YOUR GODS KEEP THEIR CHAMPION UNINFORMED.
I AM CHAMPION OF MY PEOPLE, NOT THE GODS.
SO, NOT ONLY ARE YOU UNINFORMED, BUT YOUR POWERS ARE SUPPLIED BY MERE ITEMS. MINE ARE WITHIN ME.
YOU ARE A FRAGILE MORTAL... I AM ETERNAL. I CAN SNAP YOU LIKE A TWIG IF I SO CHOOSE.
I AM DISAPPOINTED THE FINAL CONTEST IS SO EASY. I LONGED FOR A CHALLENGE.
NO MATTER. LET US BEGIN...

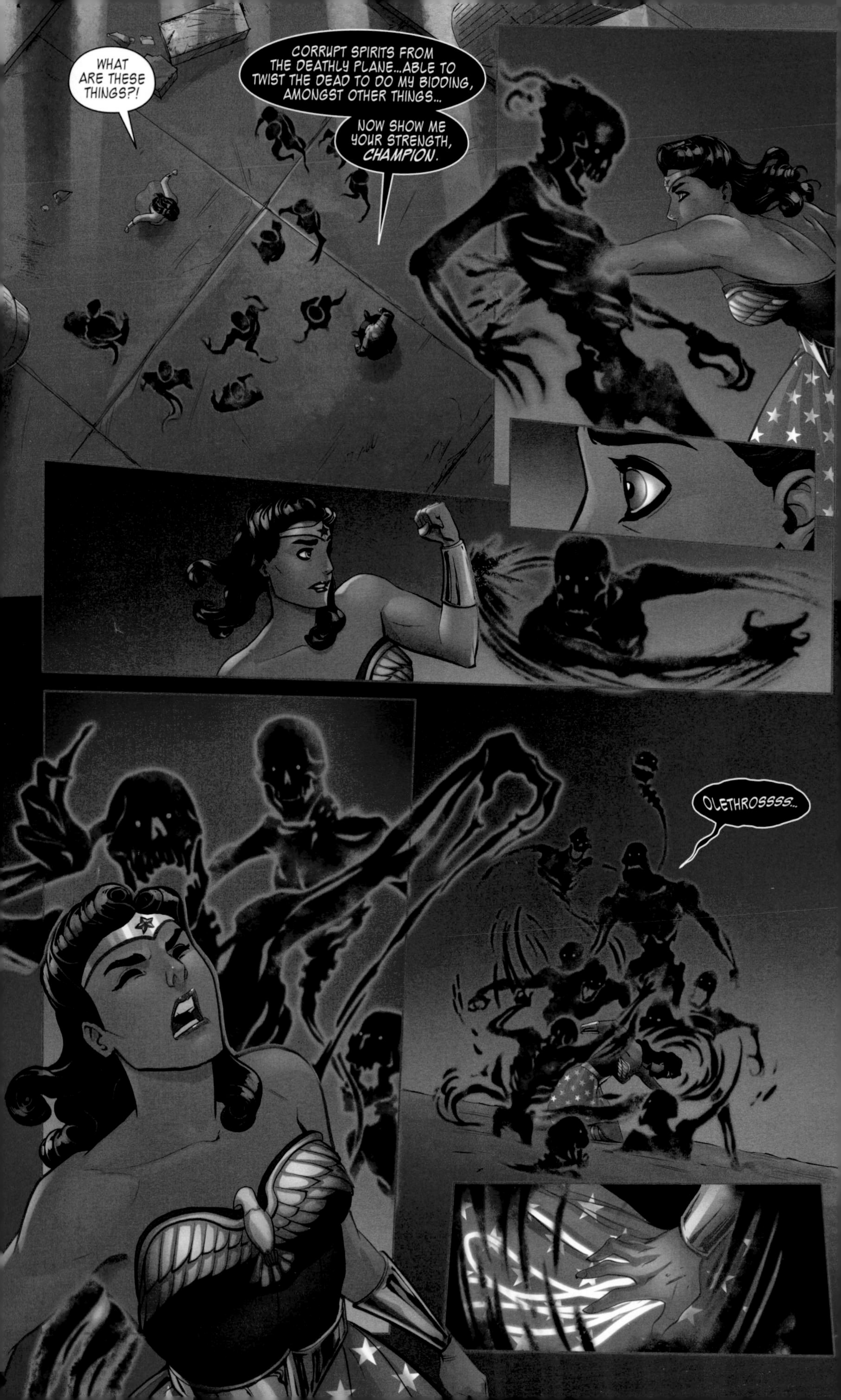
WHAT ARE THESE THINGS?!
CORRUPT SPIRITS FROM THE DEATHLY PLANE...ABLE TO TWIST THE DEAD TO DO MY BIDDING, AMONGST OTHER THINGS...
NOW SHOW ME YOUR STRENGTH, *CHAMPION*.
OLETHROSSSS...

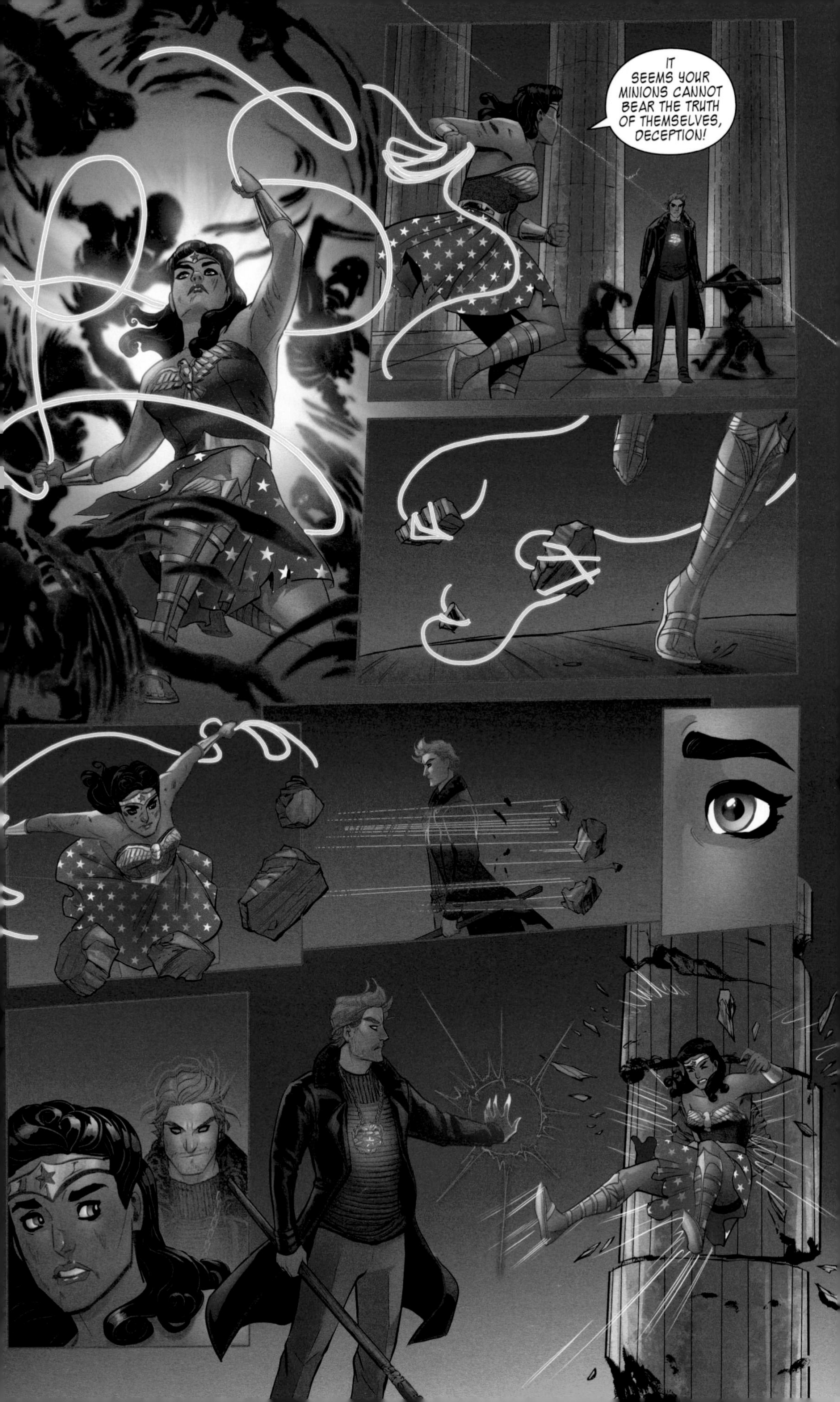
IT SEEMS YOUR MINIONS CANNOT BEAR THE TRUTH OF THEMSELVES, DECEPTION!

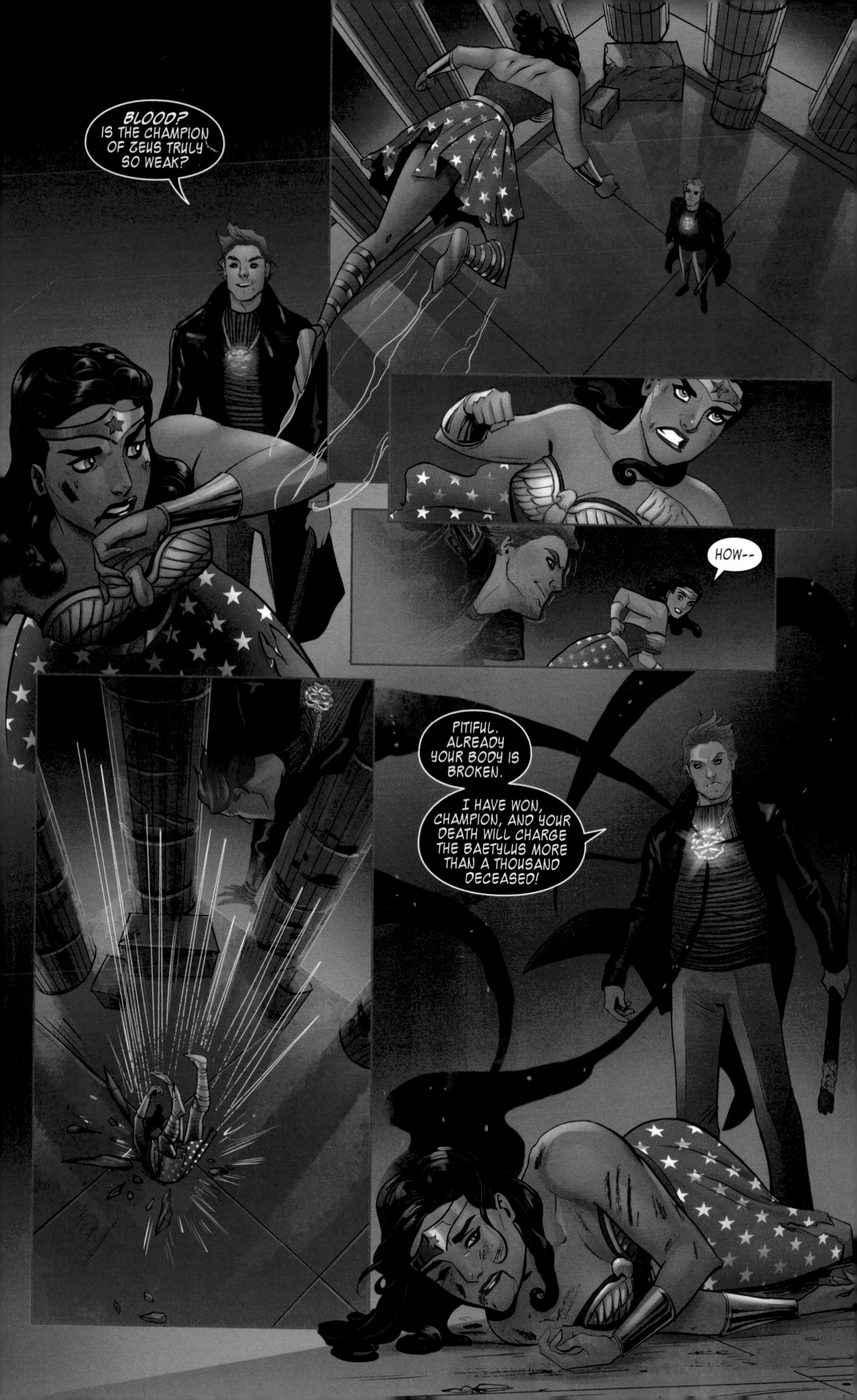
BLOOD? IS THE CHAMPION OF ZEUS TRULY SO WEAK?
HOW--
PITIFUL. ALREADY YOUR BODY IS BROKEN.
I HAVE WON, CHAMPION, AND YOUR DEATH WILL CHARGE THE BAETYLUS MORE THAN A THOUSAND DECEASED!

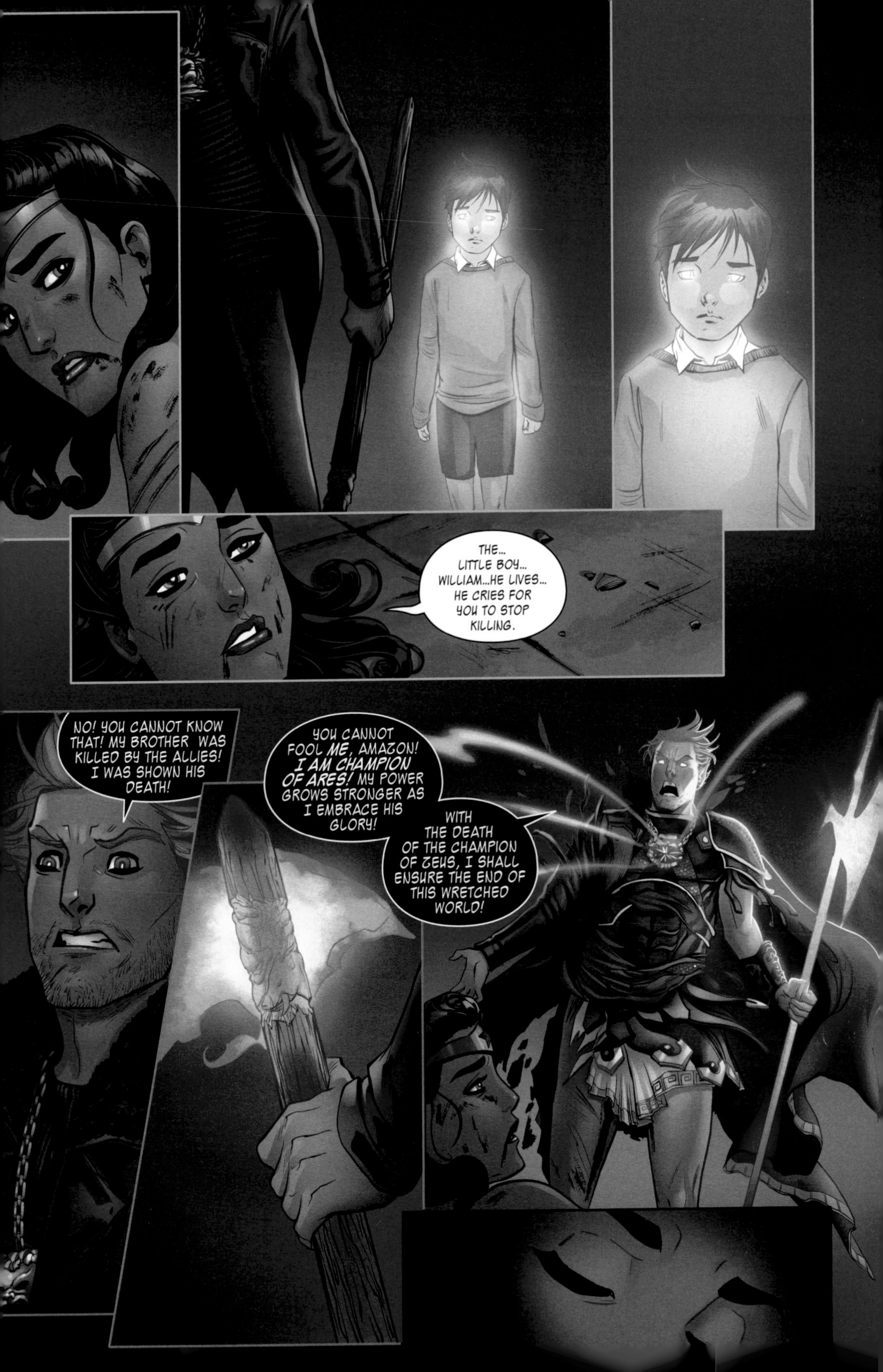
THE... LITTLE BOY... WILLIAM...HE LIVES... HE CRIES FOR YOU TO STOP KILLING.
NO! YOU CANNOT KNOW THAT! MY BROTHER WAS KILLED BY THE ALLIES! I WAS SHOWN HIS DEATH!
YOU CANNOT FOOL ME, AMAZON! I AM CHAMPION OF ARES! MY POWER GROWS STRONGER AS I EMBRACE HIS GLORY!
WITH THE DEATH OF THE CHAMPION OF ZEUS, I SHALL ENSURE THE END OF THIS WRETCHED WORLD!

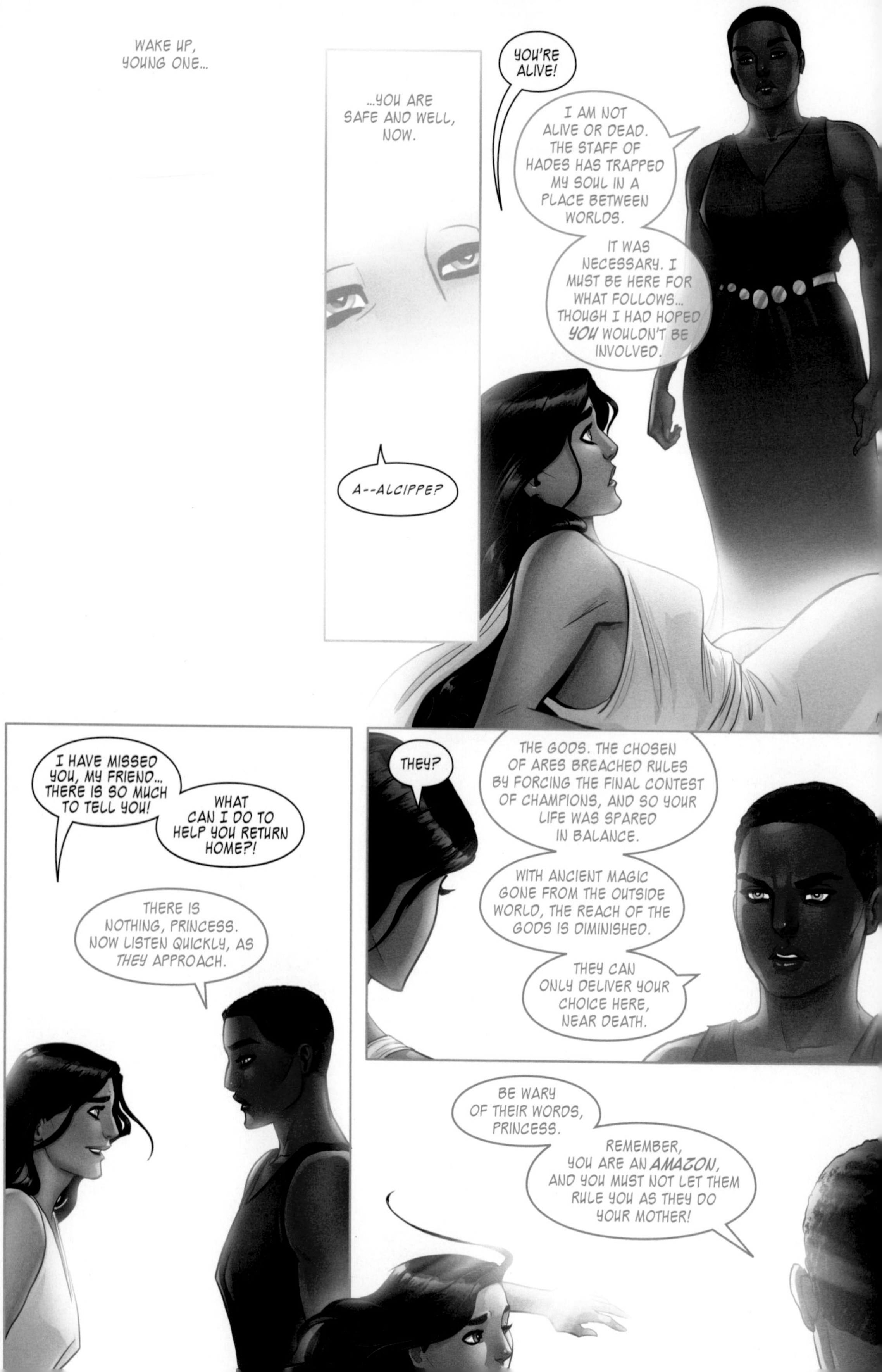
WAKE UP, YOUNG ONE...
...YOU ARE SAFE AND WELL, NOW.
A--ALCIPPE?
YOU'RE ALIVE!
I AM NOT ALIVE OR DEAD. THE STAFF OF HADES HAS TRAPPED MY SOUL IN A PLACE BETWEEN WORLDS.
IT WAS NECESSARY. I MUST BE HERE FOR WHAT FOLLOWS... THOUGH I HAD HOPED *YOU* WOULDN'T BE INVOLVED.
I HAVE MISSED YOU, MY FRIEND... THERE IS SO MUCH TO TELL YOU!
WHAT CAN I DO TO HELP YOU RETURN HOME?!
THERE IS NOTHING, PRINCESS. NOW LISTEN QUICKLY, AS *THEY* APPROACH.
THEY?
THE GODS. THE CHOSEN OF ARES BREACHED RULES BY FORCING THE FINAL CONTEST OF CHAMPIONS, AND SO YOUR LIFE WAS SPARED IN BALANCE.
WITH ANCIENT MAGIC GONE FROM THE OUTSIDE WORLD, THE REACH OF THE GODS IS DIMINISHED.
THEY CAN ONLY DELIVER YOUR CHOICE HERE, NEAR DEATH.
BE WARY OF THEIR WORDS, PRINCESS.
REMEMBER, YOU ARE AN *AMAZON*, AND YOU MUST NOT LET THEM RULE YOU AS THEY DO YOUR MOTHER!

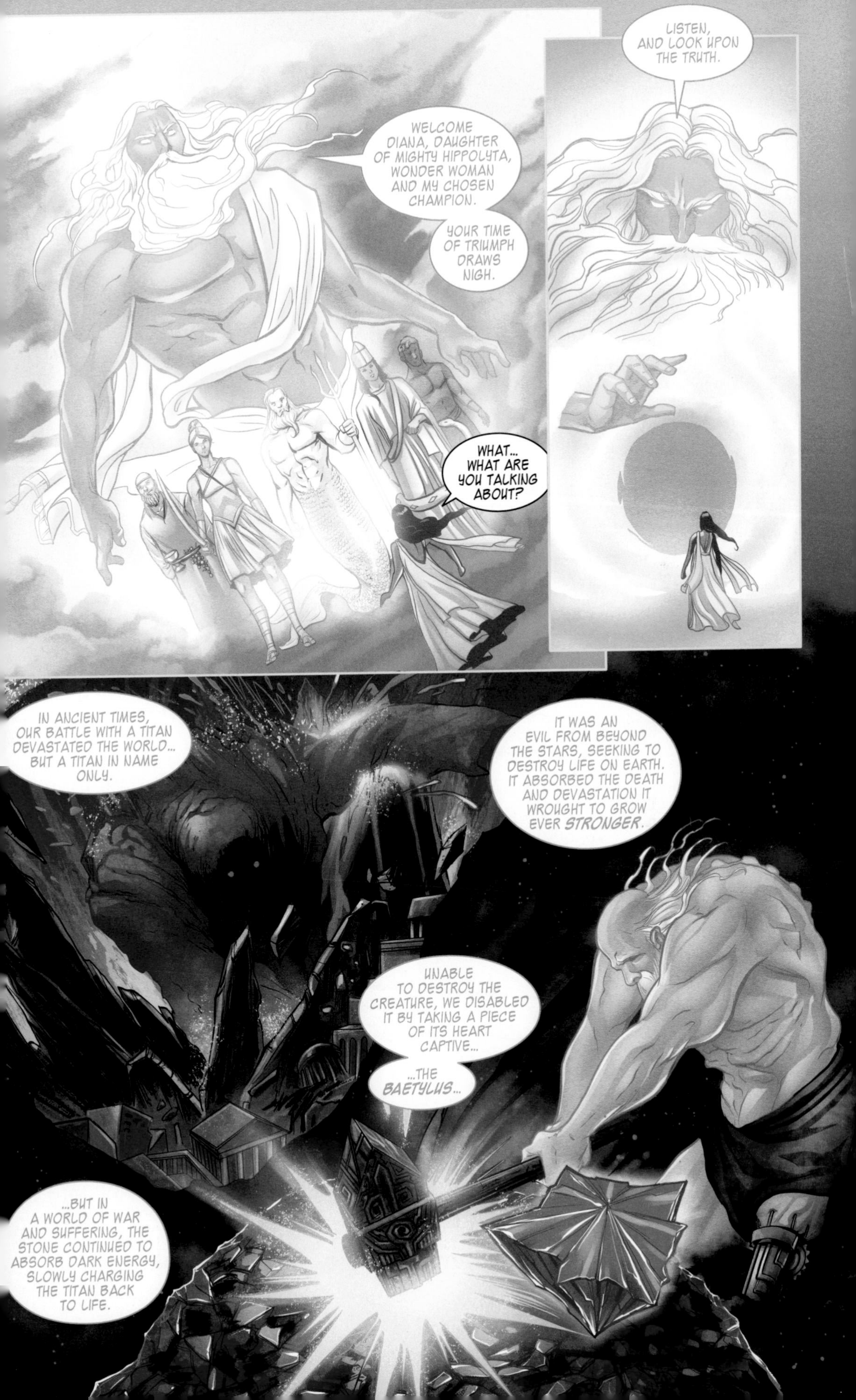
WELCOME DIANA, DAUGHTER OF MIGHTY HIPPOLYTA, WONDER WOMAN AND MY CHOSEN CHAMPION.
YOUR TIME OF TRIUMPH DRAWS NIGH.
WHAT... WHAT ARE YOU TALKING ABOUT?
LISTEN, AND LOOK UPON THE TRUTH.
IN ANCIENT TIMES, OUR BATTLE WITH A TITAN DEVASTATED THE WORLD... BUT A TITAN IN NAME ONLY.
IT WAS AN EVIL FROM BEYOND THE STARS, SEEKING TO DESTROY LIFE ON EARTH. IT ABSORBED THE DEATH AND DEVASTATION IT WROUGHT TO GROW EVER STRONGER.
UNABLE TO DESTROY THE CREATURE, WE DISABLED IT BY TAKING A PIECE OF ITS HEART CAPTIVE...
...THE BAETYLUS...
...BUT IN A WORLD OF WAR AND SUFFERING, THE STONE CONTINUED TO ABSORB DARK ENERGY, SLOWLY CHARGING THE TITAN BACK TO LIFE.

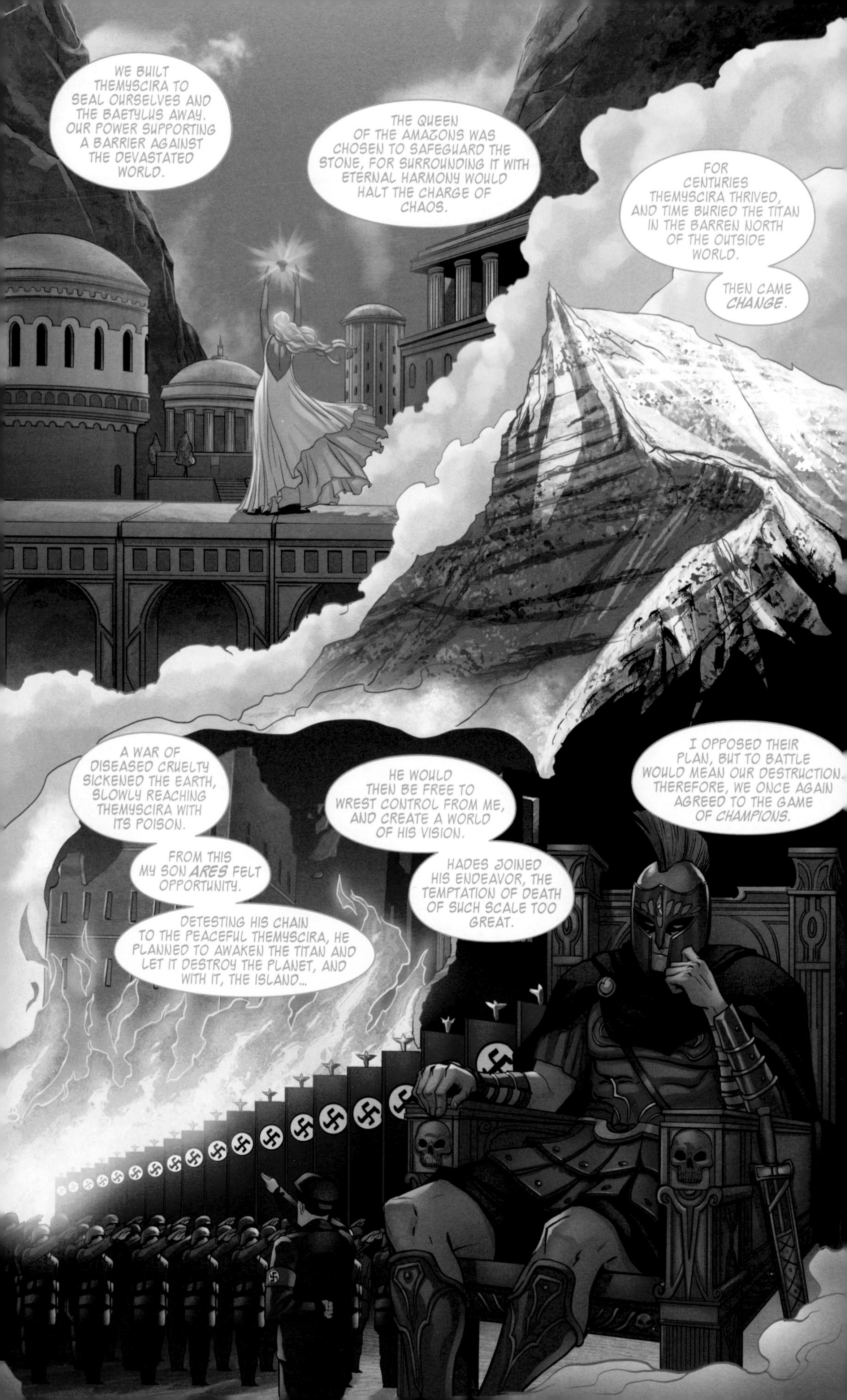
WE BUILT THEMYSCIRA TO SEAL OURSELVES AND THE BAETYLUS AWAY. OUR POWER SUPPORTING A BARRIER AGAINST THE DEVASTATED WORLD.
THE QUEEN OF THE AMAZONS WAS CHOSEN TO SAFEGUARD THE STONE, FOR SURROUNDING IT WITH ETERNAL HARMONY WOULD HALT THE CHARGE OF CHAOS.
FOR CENTURIES THEMYSCIRA THRIVED, AND TIME BURIED THE TITAN IN THE BARREN NORTH OF THE OUTSIDE WORLD.
THEN CAME *CHANGE*.
A WAR OF DISEASED CRUELTY SICKENED THE EARTH, SLOWLY REACHING THEMYSCIRA WITH ITS POISON.
FROM THIS MY SON *ARES* FELT OPPORTUNITY.
DETESTING HIS CHAIN TO THE PEACEFUL THEMYSCIRA, HE PLANNED TO AWAKEN THE TITAN AND LET IT DESTROY THE PLANET, AND WITH IT, THE ISLAND...
HE WOULD THEN BE FREE TO WREST CONTROL FROM ME, AND CREATE A WORLD OF HIS VISION.
HADES JOINED HIS ENDEAVOR, THE TEMPTATION OF DEATH OF SUCH SCALE TOO GREAT.
I OPPOSED THEIR PLAN, BUT TO BATTLE WOULD MEAN OUR DESTRUCTION. THEREFORE, WE ONCE AGAIN AGREED TO THE GAME OF *CHAMPIONS*.

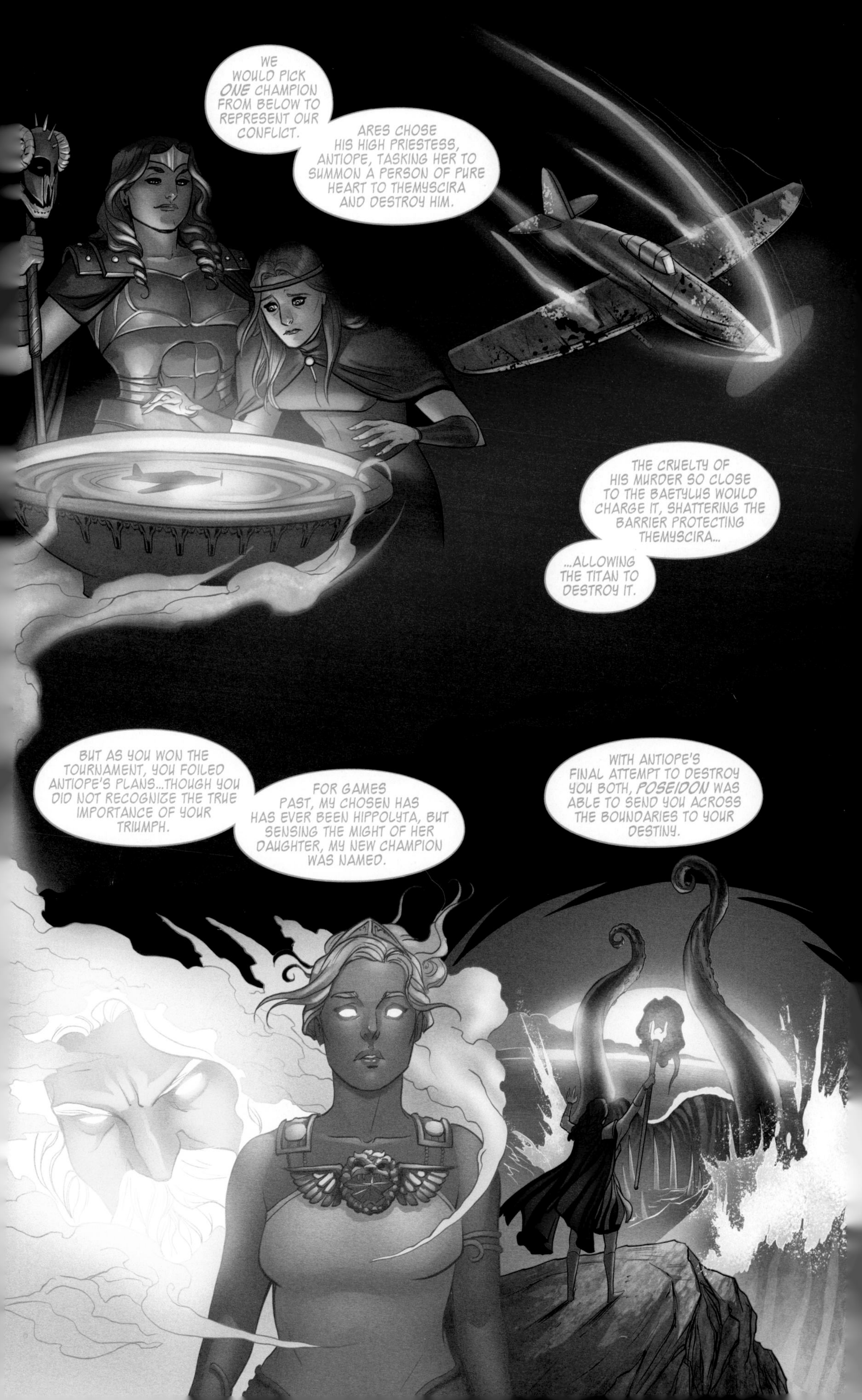
WE WOULD PICK ONE CHAMPION FROM BELOW TO REPRESENT OUR CONFLICT.
ARES CHOSE HIS HIGH PRIESTESS, ANTIOPE, TASKING HER TO SUMMON A PERSON OF PURE HEART TO THEMYSCIRA AND DESTROY HIM.
THE CRUELTY OF HIS MURDER SO CLOSE TO THE BAETYLUS WOULD CHARGE IT, SHATTERING THE BARRIER PROTECTING THEMYSCIRA...
...ALLOWING THE TITAN TO DESTROY IT.
BUT AS YOU WON THE TOURNAMENT, YOU FOILED ANTIOPE'S PLANS...THOUGH YOU DID NOT RECOGNIZE THE TRUE IMPORTANCE OF YOUR TRIUMPH.
FOR GAMES PAST, MY CHOSEN HAS HAS EVER BEEN HIPPOLYTA, BUT SENSING THE MIGHT OF HER DAUGHTER, MY NEW CHAMPION WAS NAMED.
WITH ANTIOPE'S FINAL ATTEMPT TO DESTROY YOU BOTH, POSEIDON WAS ABLE TO SEND YOU ACROSS THE BOUNDARIES TO YOUR DESTINY.

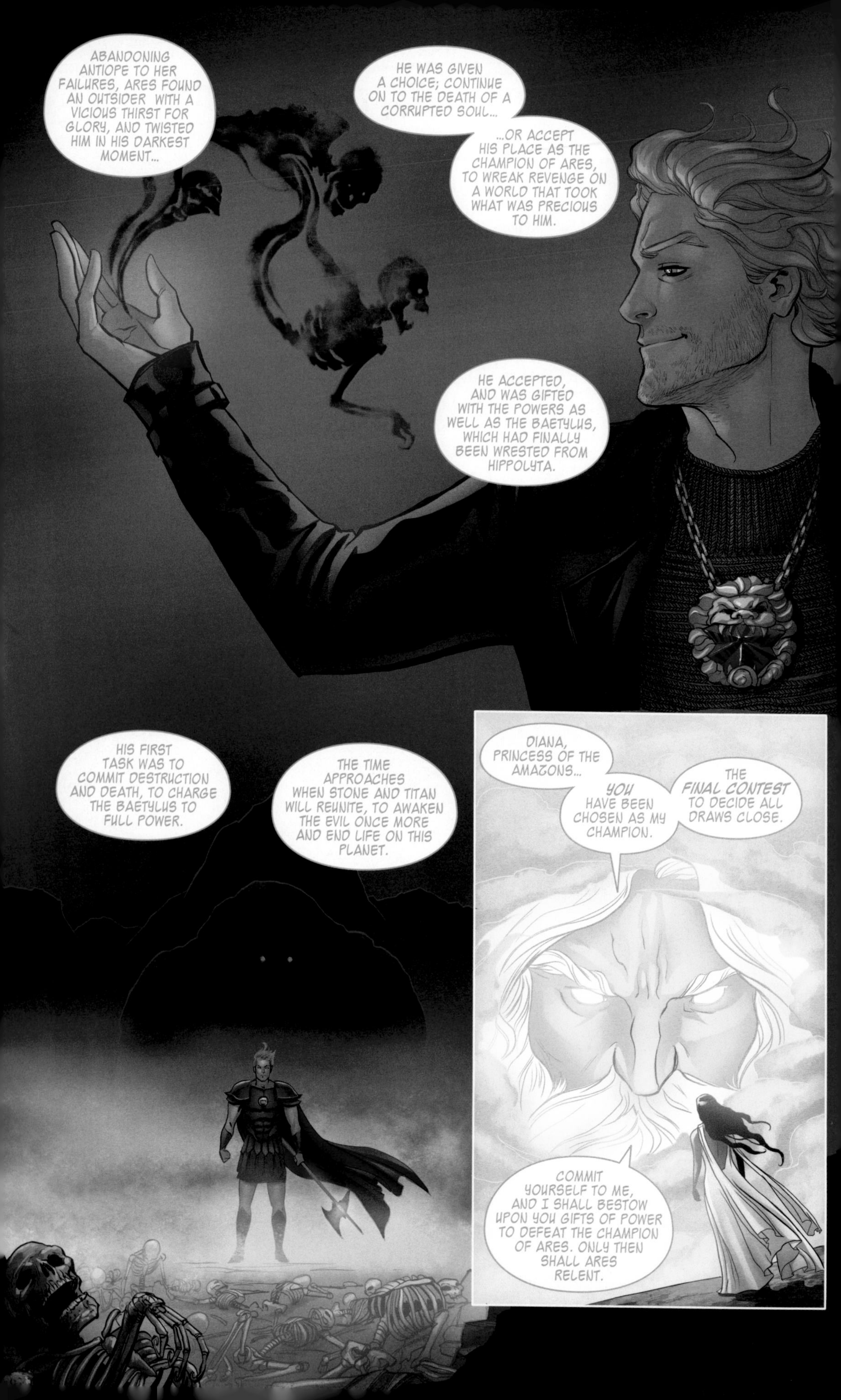
ABANDONING ANTIOPE TO HER FAILURES, ARES FOUND AN OUTSIDER WITH A VICIOUS THIRST FOR GLORY, AND TWISTED HIM IN HIS DARKEST MOMENT...
HE WAS GIVEN A CHOICE; CONTINUE ON TO THE DEATH OF A CORRUPTED SOUL...
...OR ACCEPT HIS PLACE AS THE CHAMPION OF ARES, TO WREAK REVENGE ON A WORLD THAT TOOK WHAT WAS PRECIOUS TO HIM.
HE ACCEPTED, AND WAS GIFTED WITH THE POWERS AS WELL AS THE BAETYLUS, WHICH HAD FINALLY BEEN WRESTED FROM HIPPOLYTA.
HIS FIRST TASK WAS TO COMMIT DESTRUCTION AND DEATH, TO CHARGE THE BAETYLUS TO FULL POWER.
THE TIME APPROACHES WHEN STONE AND TITAN WILL REUNITE, TO AWAKEN THE EVIL ONCE MORE AND END LIFE ON THIS PLANET.
DIANA, PRINCESS OF THE AMAZONS...
YOU HAVE BEEN CHOSEN AS MY CHAMPION.
THE FINAL CONTEST TO DECIDE ALL DRAWS CLOSE.
COMMIT YOURSELF TO ME, AND I SHALL BESTOW UPON YOU GIFTS OF POWER TO DEFEAT THE CHAMPION OF ARES. ONLY THEN SHALL ARES RELENT.

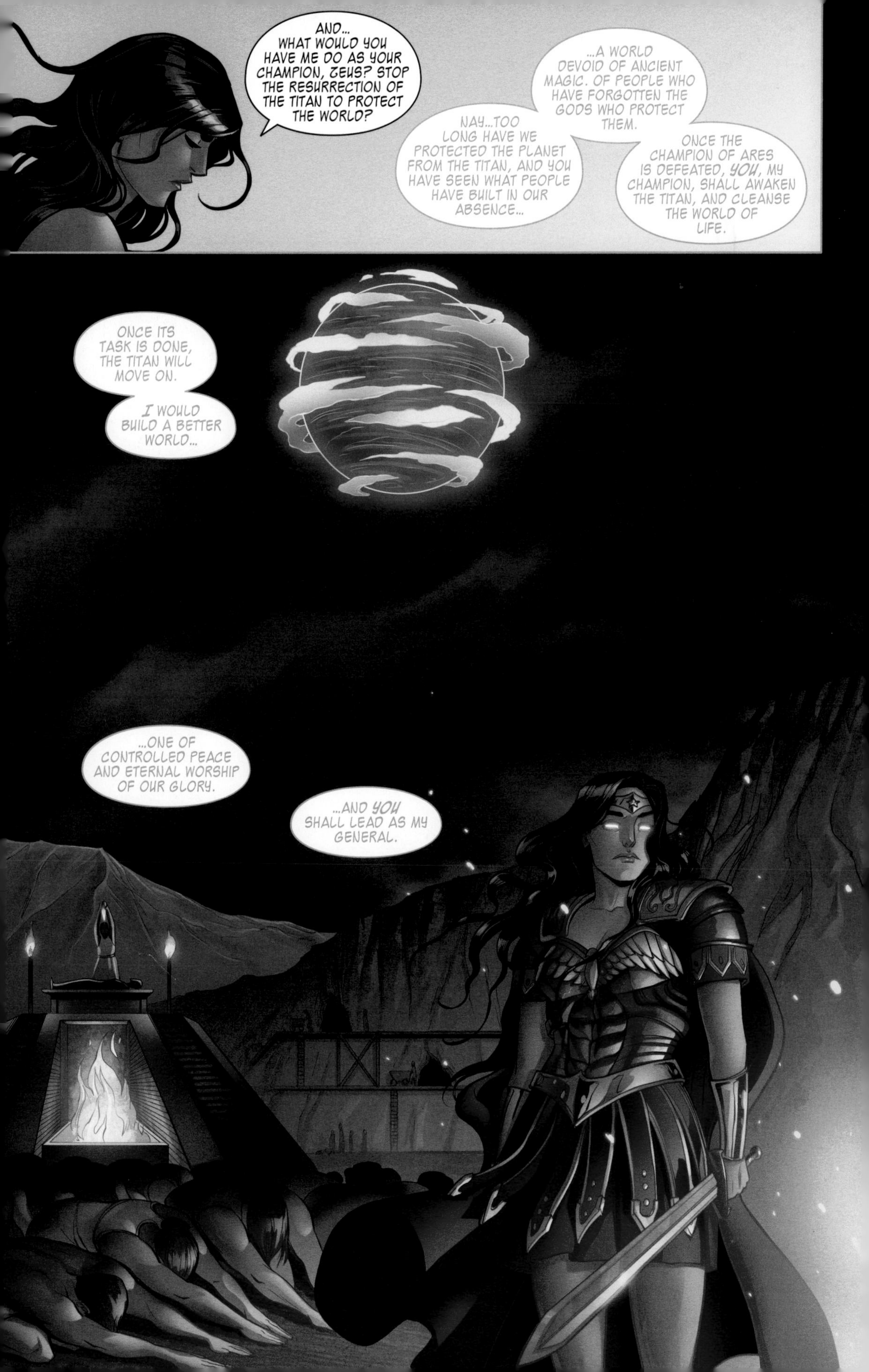
AND... WHAT WOULD YOU HAVE ME DO AS YOUR CHAMPION, ZEUS? STOP THE RESURRECTION OF THE TITAN TO PROTECT THE WORLD?
NAY...TOO LONG HAVE WE PROTECTED THE PLANET FROM THE TITAN, AND YOU HAVE SEEN WHAT PEOPLE HAVE BUILT IN OUR ABSENCE...
...A WORLD DEVOID OF ANCIENT MAGIC. OF PEOPLE WHO HAVE FORGOTTEN THE GODS WHO PROTECT THEM.
ONCE THE CHAMPION OF ARES IS DEFEATED, YOU, MY CHAMPION, SHALL AWAKEN THE TITAN, AND CLEANSE THE WORLD OF LIFE.
ONCE ITS TASK IS DONE, THE TITAN WILL MOVE ON.
I WOULD BUILD A BETTER WORLD...
...ONE OF CONTROLLED PEACE AND ETERNAL WORSHIP OF OUR GLORY.
...AND YOU SHALL LEAD AS MY GENERAL.

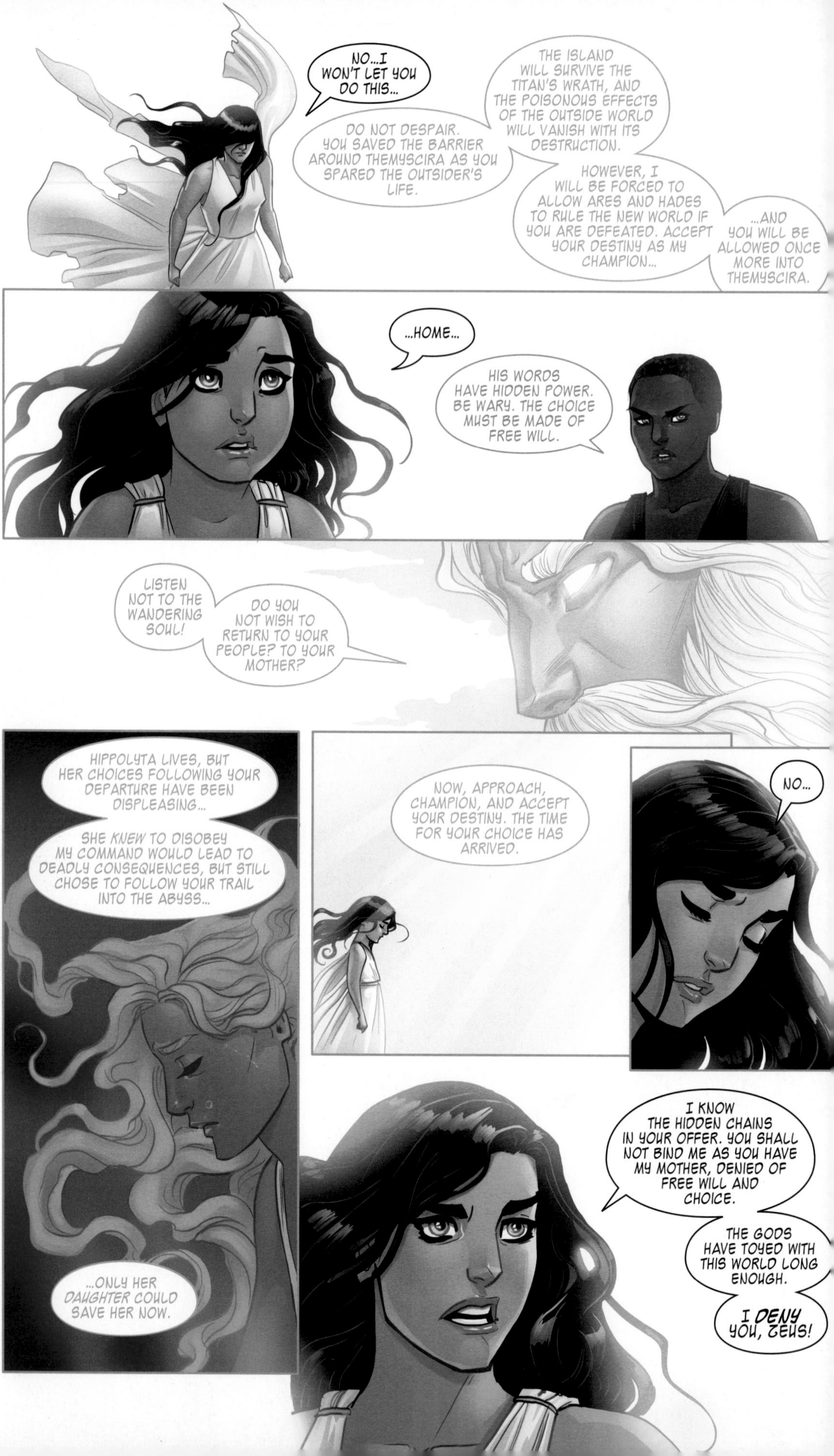
NO...I WON'T LET YOU DO THIS...
DO NOT DESPAIR. YOU SAVED THE BARRIER AROUND THEMYSCIRA AS YOU SPARED THE OUTSIDER'S LIFE.
THE ISLAND WILL SURVIVE THE TITAN'S WRATH, AND THE POISONOUS EFFECTS OF THE OUTSIDE WORLD WILL VANISH WITH ITS DESTRUCTION.
HOWEVER, I WILL BE FORCED TO ALLOW ARES AND HADES TO RULE THE NEW WORLD IF YOU ARE DEFEATED. ACCEPT YOUR DESTINY AS MY CHAMPION...
...AND YOU WILL BE ALLOWED ONCE MORE INTO THEMYSCIRA.
...HOME...
HIS WORDS HAVE HIDDEN POWER. BE WARY. THE CHOICE MUST BE MADE OF FREE WILL.
LISTEN NOT TO THE WANDERING SOUL!
DO YOU NOT WISH TO RETURN TO YOUR PEOPLE? TO YOUR MOTHER?
HIPPOLYTA LIVES, BUT HER CHOICES FOLLOWING YOUR DEPARTURE HAVE BEEN DISPLEASING...
SHE KNEW TO DISOBEY MY COMMAND WOULD LEAD TO DEADLY CONSEQUENCES, BUT STILL CHOSE TO FOLLOW YOUR TRAIL INTO THE ABYSS...
...ONLY HER DAUGHTER COULD SAVE HER NOW.
NOW, APPROACH, CHAMPION, AND ACCEPT YOUR DESTINY. THE TIME FOR YOUR CHOICE HAS ARRIVED.
NO...
I KNOW THE HIDDEN CHAINS IN YOUR OFFER. YOU SHALL NOT BIND ME AS YOU HAVE MY MOTHER, DENIED OF FREE WILL AND CHOICE.
THE GODS HAVE TOYED WITH THIS WORLD LONG ENOUGH.
I DENY YOU, ZEUS!

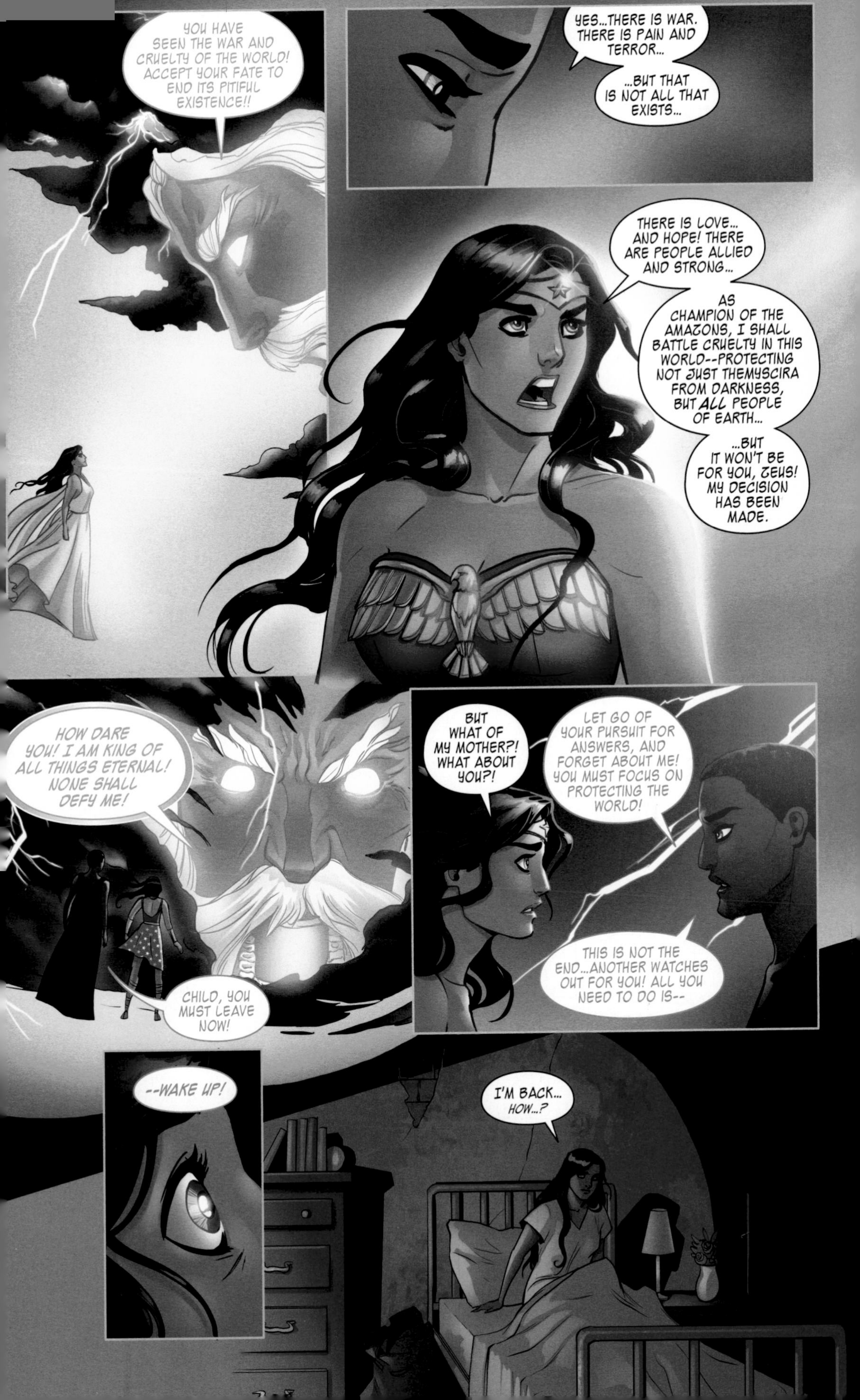

YOU HAVE SEEN THE WAR AND CRUELTY OF THE WORLD! ACCEPT YOUR FATE TO END ITS PITIFUL EXISTENCE!!
YES...THERE IS WAR. THERE IS PAIN AND TERROR...
...BUT THAT IS NOT ALL THAT EXISTS...
THERE IS LOVE... AND HOPE! THERE ARE PEOPLE ALLIED AND STRONG...
AS CHAMPION OF THE AMAZONS, I SHALL BATTLE CRUELTY IN THIS WORLD--PROTECTING NOT JUST THEMYSCIRA FROM DARKNESS, BUT ALL PEOPLE OF EARTH...
...BUT IT WON'T BE FOR YOU, ZEUS! MY DECISION HAS BEEN MADE.
HOW DARE YOU! I AM KING OF ALL THINGS ETERNAL! NONE SHALL DEFY ME!
CHILD, YOU MUST LEAVE NOW!
BUT WHAT OF MY MOTHER?! WHAT ABOUT YOU?!
LET GO OF YOUR PURSUIT FOR ANSWERS, AND FORGET ABOUT ME! YOU MUST FOCUS ON PROTECTING THE WORLD!
THIS IS NOT THE END...ANOTHER WATCHES OUT FOR YOU! ALL YOU NEED TO DO IS--
--WAKE UP!
I'M BACK... HOW...?

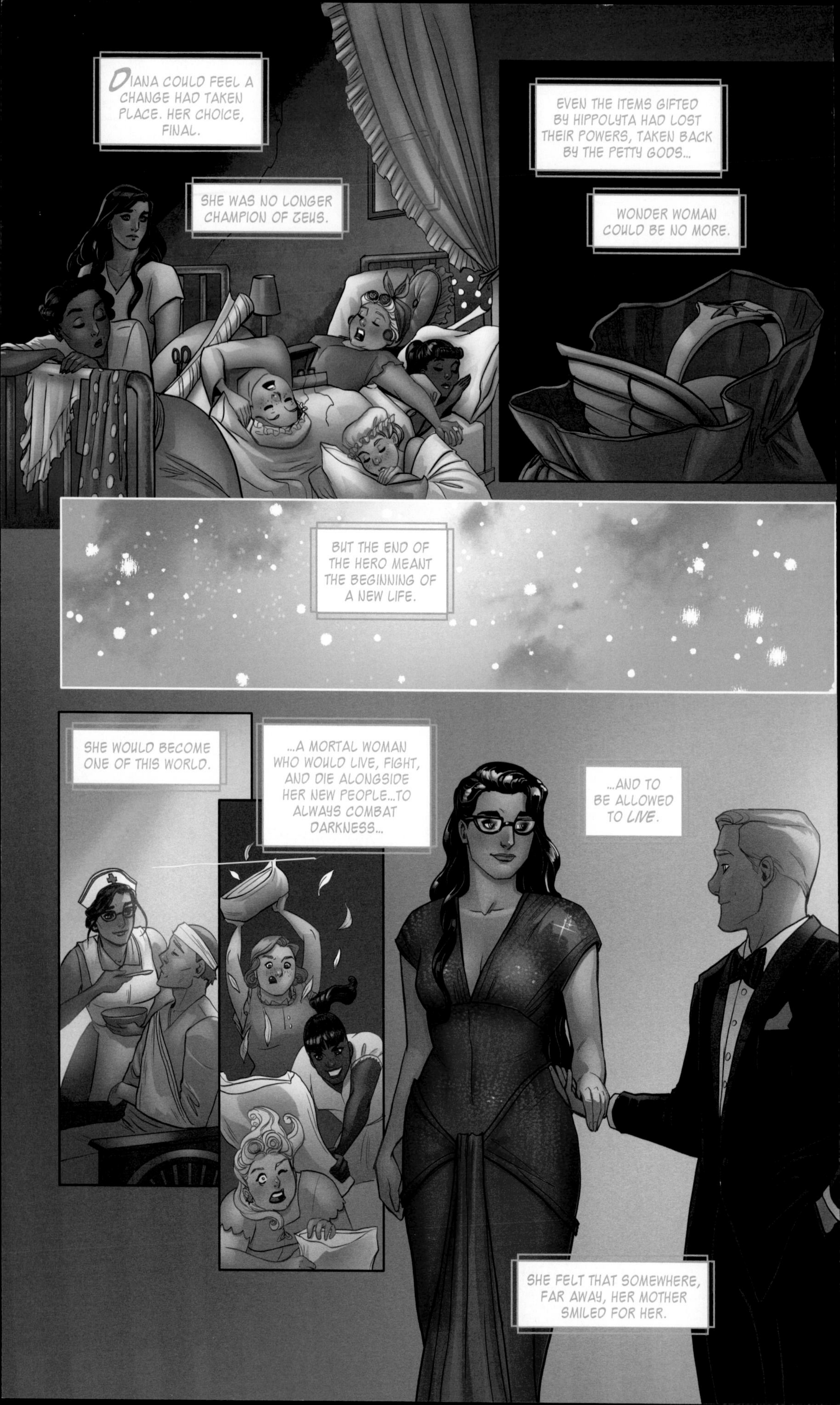
DIANA COULD FEEL A CHANGE HAD TAKEN PLACE. HER CHOICE, FINAL.
SHE WAS NO LONGER CHAMPION OF ZEUS.
EVEN THE ITEMS GIFTED BY HIPPOLYTA HAD LOST THEIR POWERS, TAKEN BACK BY THE PETTY GODS...
WONDER WOMAN COULD BE NO MORE.
BUT THE END OF THE HERO MEANT THE BEGINNING OF A NEW LIFE.
SHE WOULD BECOME ONE OF THIS WORLD.
...A MORTAL WOMAN WHO WOULD LIVE, FIGHT, AND DIE ALONGSIDE HER NEW PEOPLE...TO ALWAYS COMBAT DARKNESS...
...AND TO BE ALLOWED TO *LIVE*.
SHE FELT THAT SOMEWHERE, FAR AWAY, HER MOTHER SMILED FOR HER.

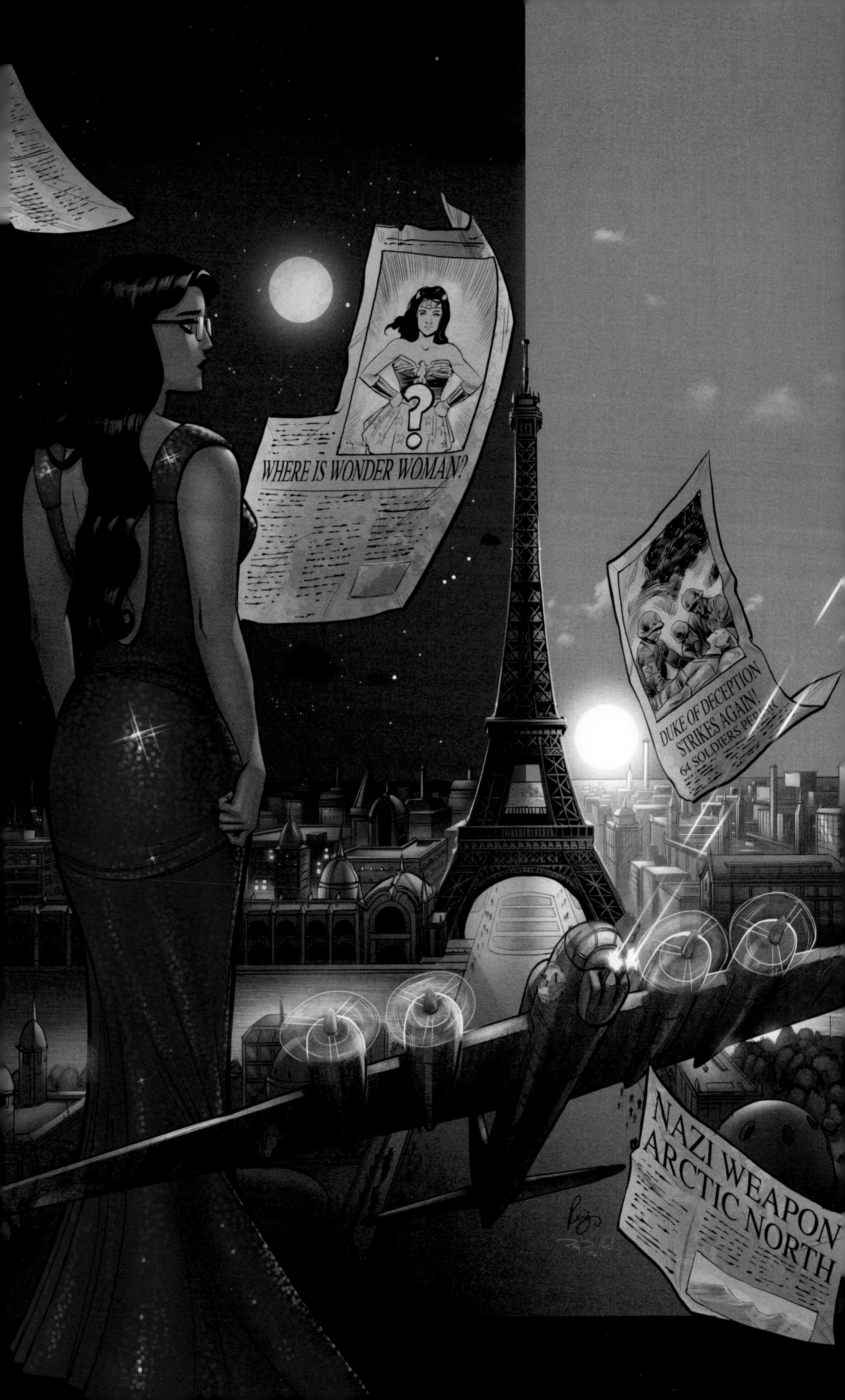
WHERE IS WONDER WOMAN?
DUKE OF DECEPTION
STRIKES AGAIN!
64 SOLDIERS
NAZI WEAPON
ARCTIC NORTH

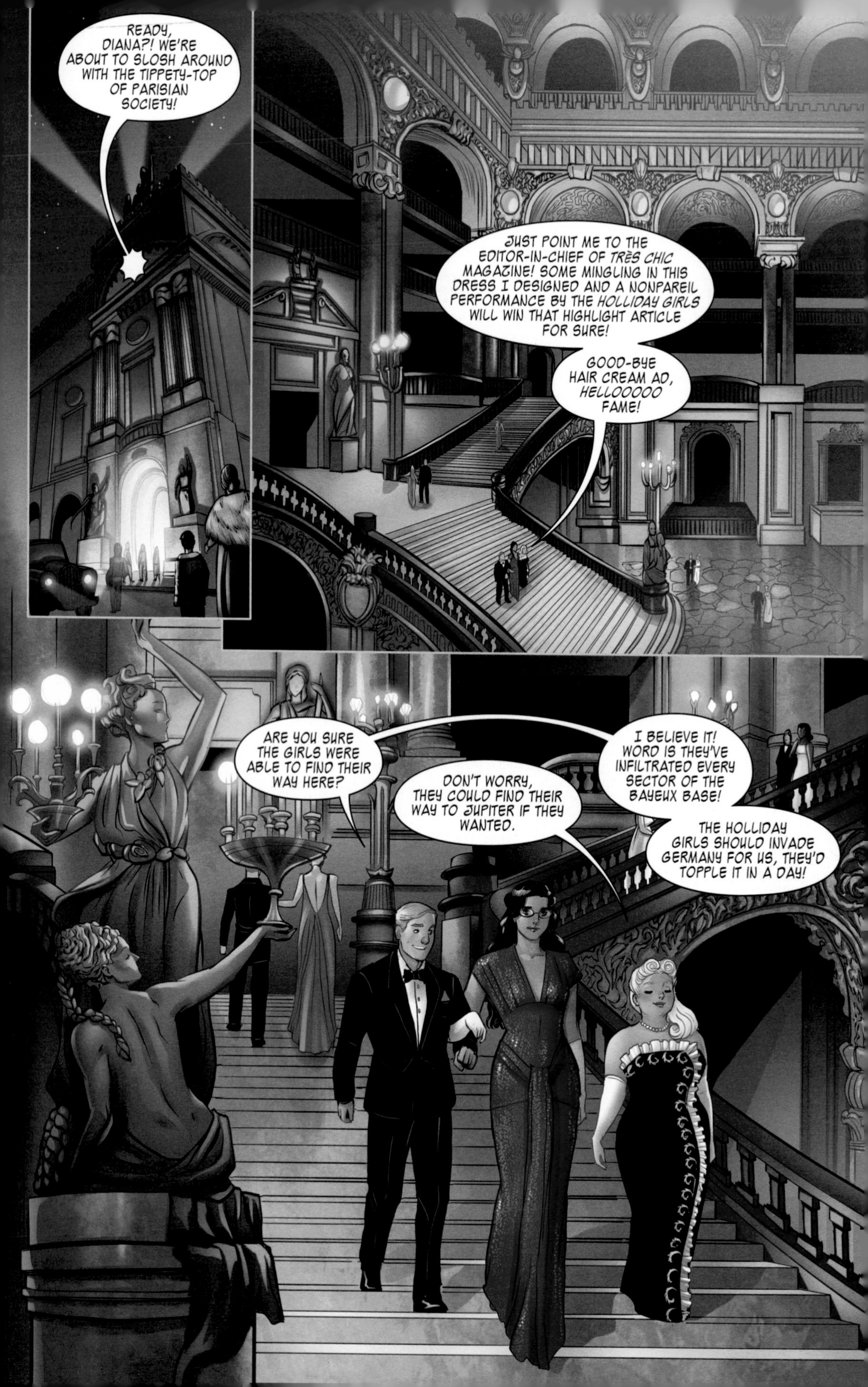
READY, DIANA?! WE'RE ABOUT TO SLOSH AROUND WITH THE TIPPETY-TOP OF PARISIAN SOCIETY!
JUST POINT ME TO THE EDITOR-IN-CHIEF OF *TRÈS CHIC* MAGAZINE! SOME MINGLING IN THIS DRESS I DESIGNED AND A NONPAREIL PERFORMANCE BY THE *HOLLIDAY GIRLS* WILL WIN THAT HIGHLIGHT ARTICLE FOR SURE!
GOOD-BYE HAIR CREAM AD, *HELLOOOOO* FAME!
ARE YOU SURE THE GIRLS WERE ABLE TO FIND THEIR WAY HERE?
DON'T WORRY, THEY COULD FIND THEIR WAY TO JUPITER IF THEY WANTED.
I BELIEVE IT! WORD IS THEY'VE INFILTRATED EVERY SECTOR OF THE BAYEUX BASE!
THE HOLLIDAY GIRLS SHOULD INVADE GERMANY FOR US, THEY'D TOPPLE IT IN A DAY!

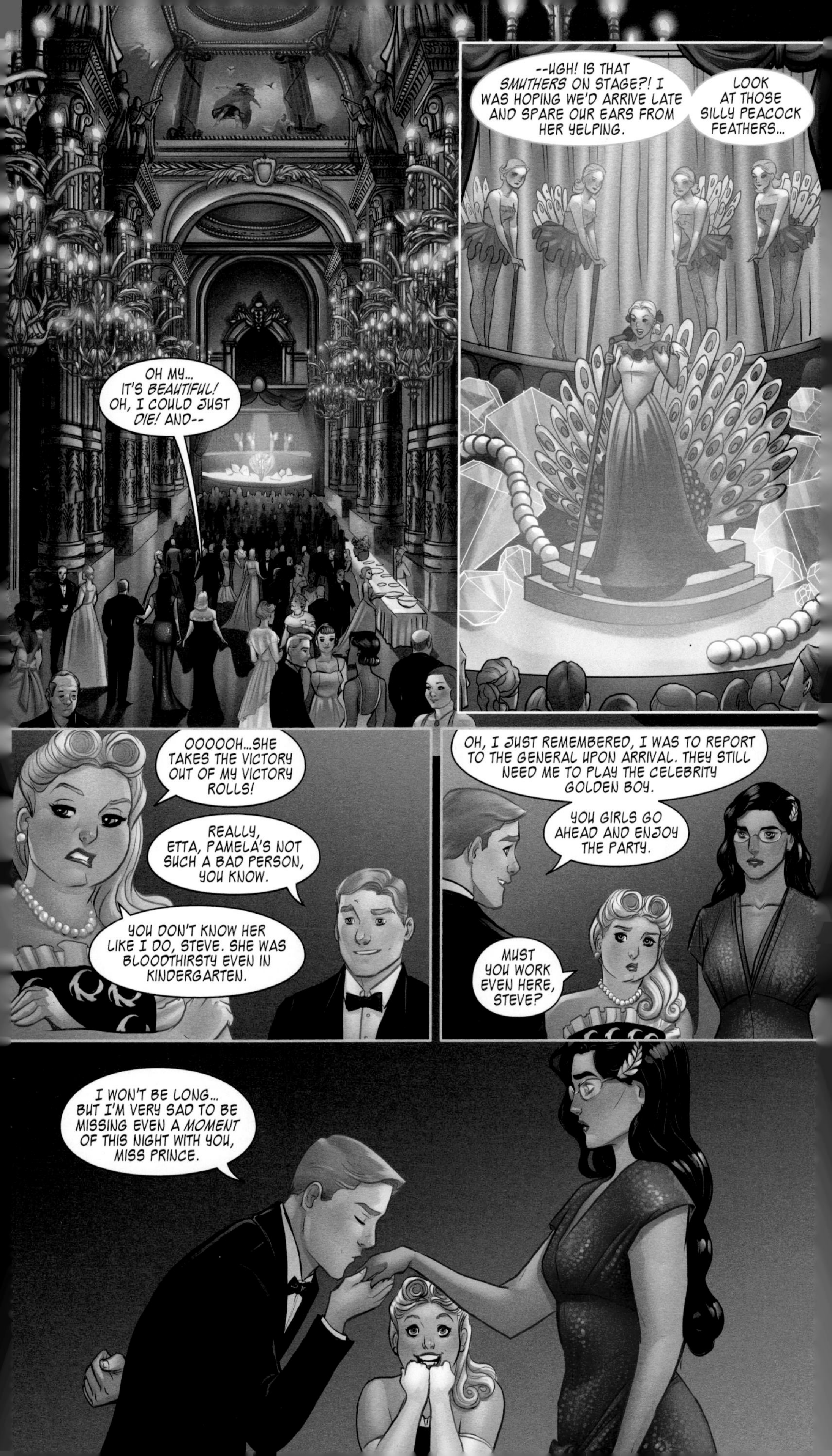
OH MY... IT'S BEAUTIFUL! OH, I COULD JUST DIE! AND--
--UGH! IS THAT SMUTHERS ON STAGE?! I WAS HOPING WE'D ARRIVE LATE AND SPARE OUR EARS FROM HER YELPING.
LOOK AT THOSE SILLY PEACOCK FEATHERS...
OOOOOH...SHE TAKES THE VICTORY OUT OF MY VICTORY ROLLS!
REALLY, ETTA, PAMELA'S NOT SUCH A BAD PERSON, YOU KNOW.
YOU DON'T KNOW HER LIKE I DO, STEVE. SHE WAS BLOODTHIRSTY EVEN IN KINDERGARTEN.
OH, I JUST REMEMBERED, I WAS TO REPORT TO THE GENERAL UPON ARRIVAL. THEY STILL NEED ME TO PLAY THE CELEBRITY GOLDEN BOY.
YOU GIRLS GO AHEAD AND ENJOY THE PARTY.
MUST YOU WORK EVEN HERE, STEVE?
I WON'T BE LONG... BUT I'M VERY SAD TO BE MISSING EVEN A MOMENT OF THIS NIGHT WITH YOU, MISS PRINCE.

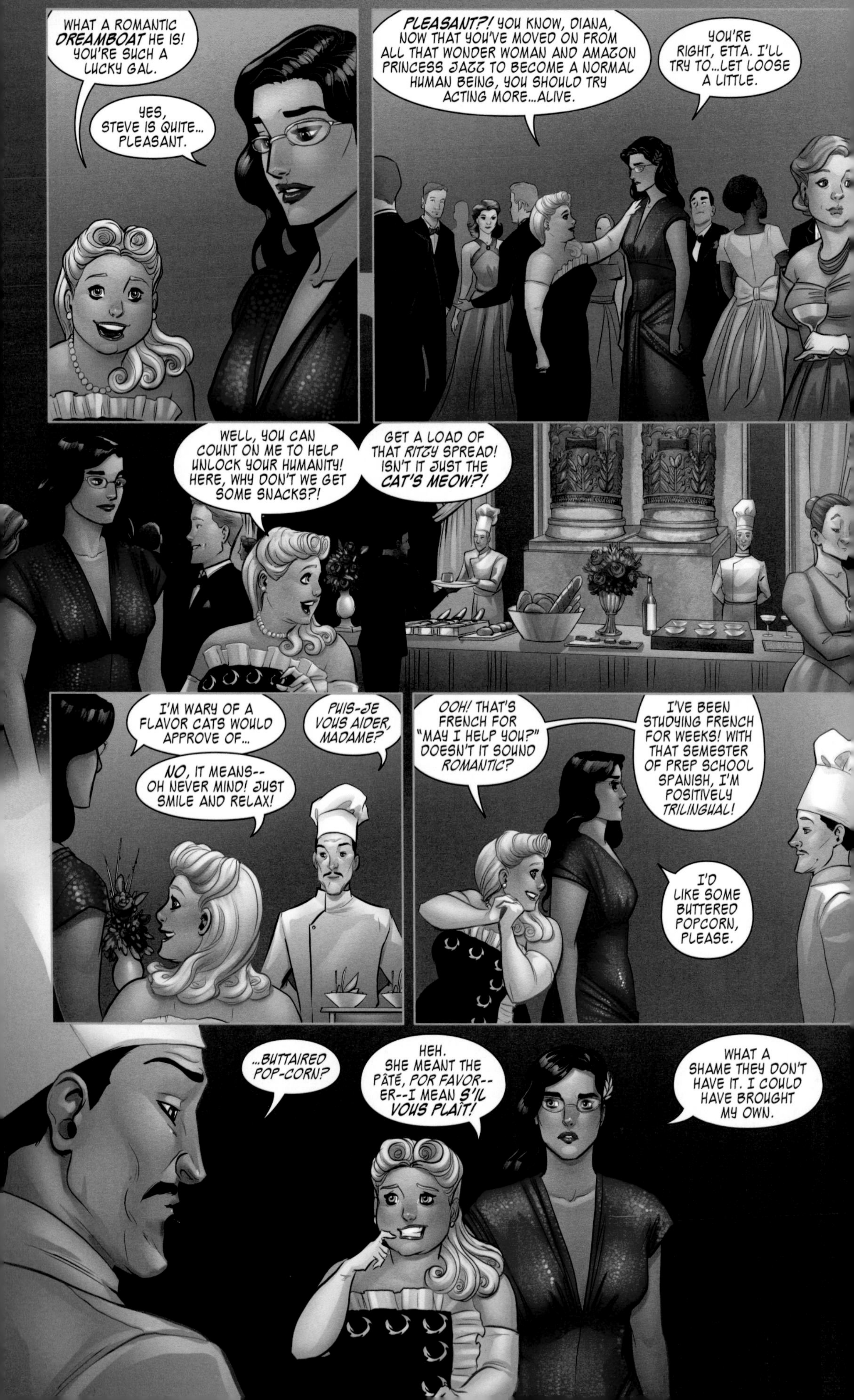
WHAT A ROMANTIC DREAMBOAT HE IS! YOU'RE SUCH A LUCKY GAL.
YES, STEVE IS QUITE... PLEASANT.
PLEASANT?! YOU KNOW, DIANA, NOW THAT YOU'VE MOVED ON FROM ALL THAT WONDER WOMAN AND AMAZON PRINCESS JAZZ TO BECOME A NORMAL HUMAN BEING, YOU SHOULD TRY ACTING MORE...ALIVE.
YOU'RE RIGHT, ETTA. I'LL TRY TO...LET LOOSE A LITTLE.
WELL, YOU CAN COUNT ON ME TO HELP UNLOCK YOUR HUMANITY! HERE, WHY DON'T WE GET SOME SNACKS?!
GET A LOAD OF THAT RITZY SPREAD! ISN'T IT JUST THE CAT'S MEOW?!
I'M WARY OF A FLAVOR CATS WOULD APPROVE OF...
NO, IT MEANS-- OH NEVER MIND! JUST SMILE AND RELAX!
PUIS-JE VOUS AIDER, MADAME?
OOH! THAT'S FRENCH FOR "MAY I HELP YOU?" DOESN'T IT SOUND ROMANTIC?
I'VE BEEN STUDYING FRENCH FOR WEEKS! WITH THAT SEMESTER OF PREP SCHOOL SPANISH, I'M POSITIVELY TRILINGUAL!
I'D LIKE SOME BUTTERED POPCORN, PLEASE.
...BUTTAIRED POP-CORN?
HEH. SHE MEANT THE PÂTÉ, POR FAVOR-- ER--I MEAN S'IL VOUS PLAÎT!
WHAT A SHAME THEY DON'T HAVE IT. I COULD HAVE BROUGHT MY OWN.

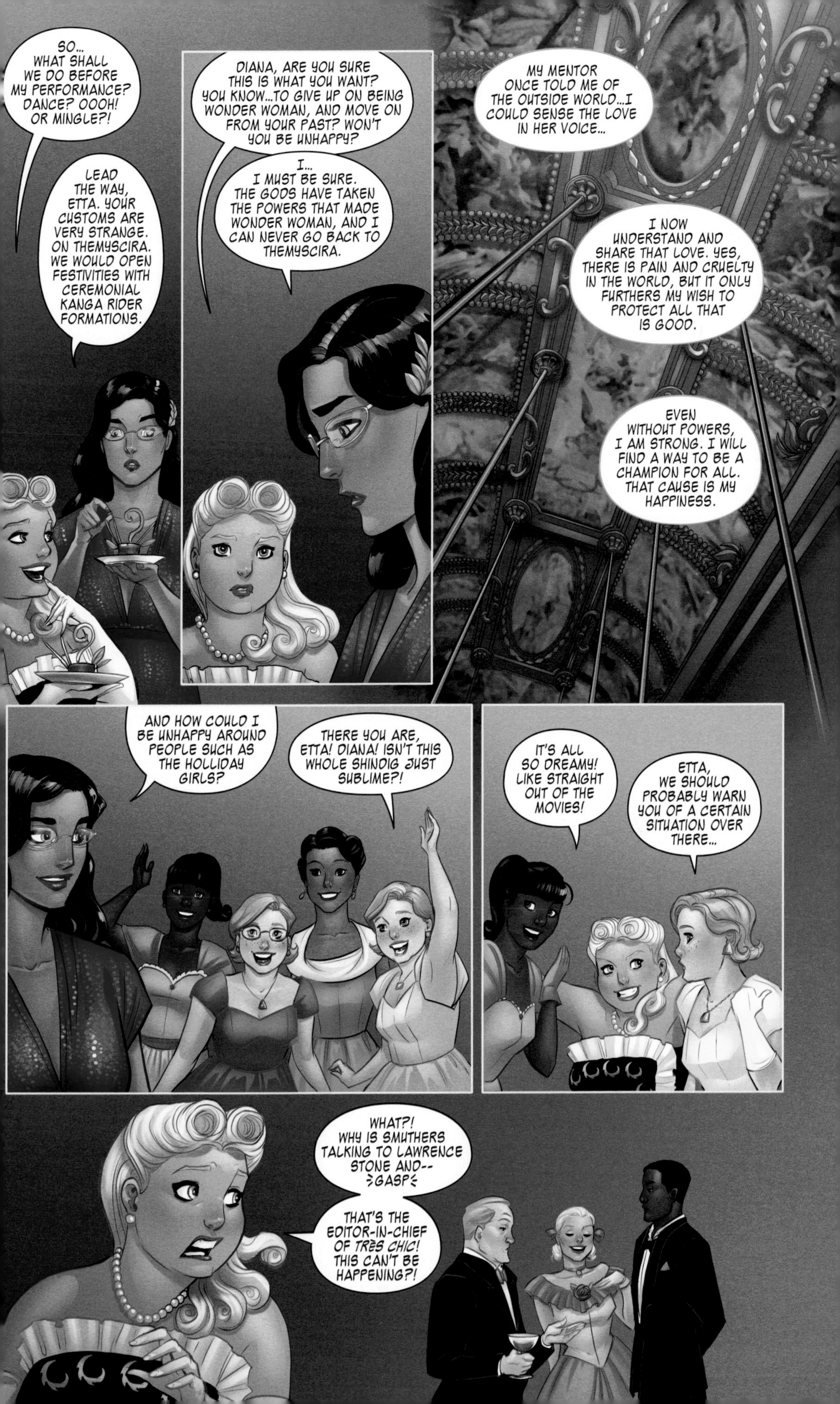
SO... WHAT SHALL WE DO BEFORE MY PERFORMANCE? DANCE? OOOH! OR MINGLE?!
LEAD THE WAY, ETTA. YOUR CUSTOMS ARE VERY STRANGE. ON THEMYSCIRA. WE WOULD OPEN FESTIVITIES WITH CEREMONIAL KANGA RIDER FORMATIONS.
DIANA, ARE YOU SURE THIS IS WHAT YOU WANT? YOU KNOW...TO GIVE UP ON BEING WONDER WOMAN, AND MOVE ON FROM YOUR PAST? WON'T YOU BE UNHAPPY?
I... I MUST BE SURE. THE GODS HAVE TAKEN THE POWERS THAT MADE WONDER WOMAN, AND I CAN NEVER GO BACK TO THEMYSCIRA.
MY MENTOR ONCE TOLD ME OF THE OUTSIDE WORLD...I COULD SENSE THE LOVE IN HER VOICE...
I NOW UNDERSTAND AND SHARE THAT LOVE. YES, THERE IS PAIN AND CRUELTY IN THE WORLD, BUT IT ONLY FURTHERS MY WISH TO PROTECT ALL THAT IS GOOD.
EVEN WITHOUT POWERS, I AM STRONG. I WILL FIND A WAY TO BE A CHAMPION FOR ALL. THAT CAUSE IS MY HAPPINESS.
AND HOW COULD I BE UNHAPPY AROUND PEOPLE SUCH AS THE HOLLIDAY GIRLS?
THERE YOU ARE, ETTA! DIANA! ISN'T THIS WHOLE SHINDIG JUST SUBLIME?!
IT'S ALL SO DREAMY! LIKE STRAIGHT OUT OF THE MOVIES!
ETTA, WE SHOULD PROBABLY WARN YOU OF A CERTAIN SITUATION OVER THERE...
WHAT?! WHY IS SMUTHERS TALKING TO LAWRENCE STONE AND-- ⋛GASP⋚
THAT'S THE EDITOR-IN-CHIEF OF *TRÈS CHIC*! THIS CAN'T BE HAPPENING?!

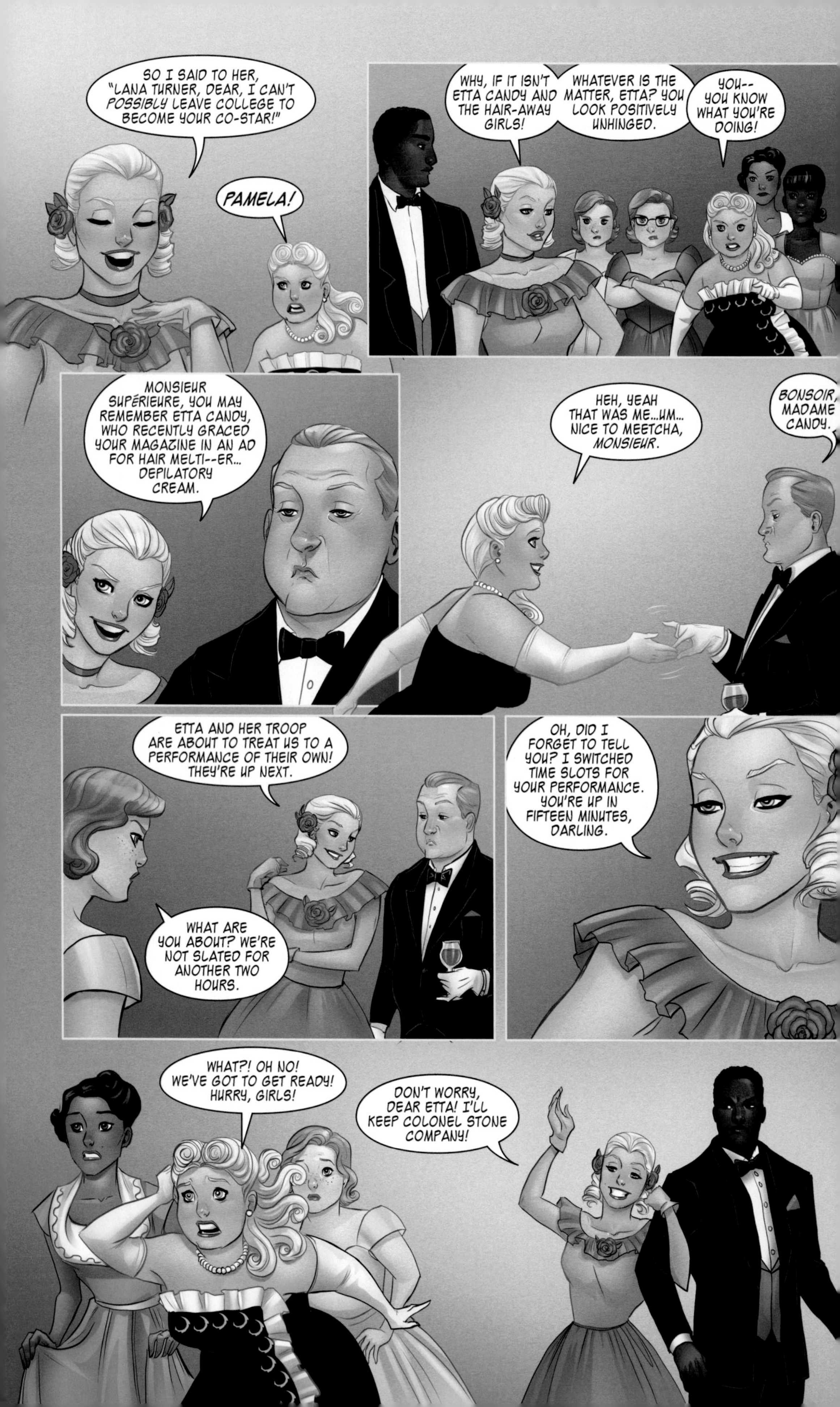

SO I SAID TO HER, "LANA TURNER, DEAR, I CAN'T POSSIBLY LEAVE COLLEGE TO BECOME YOUR CO-STAR!"
PAMELA!
WHY, IF IT ISN'T ETTA CANDY AND THE HAIR-AWAY GIRLS!
WHATEVER IS THE MATTER, ETTA? YOU LOOK POSITIVELY UNHINGED.
YOU-- YOU KNOW WHAT YOU'RE DOING!
MONSIEUR SUPÉRIEURE, YOU MAY REMEMBER ETTA CANDY, WHO RECENTLY GRACED YOUR MAGAZINE IN AN AD FOR HAIR MELTI--ER... DEPILATORY CREAM.
HEH, YEAH THAT WAS ME...UM... NICE TO MEETCHA, MONSIEUR.
BONSOIR, MADAME CANDY.
ETTA AND HER TROOP ARE ABOUT TO TREAT US TO A PERFORMANCE OF THEIR OWN! THEY'RE UP NEXT.
WHAT ARE YOU ABOUT? WE'RE NOT SLATED FOR ANOTHER TWO HOURS.
OH, DID I FORGET TO TELL YOU? I SWITCHED TIME SLOTS FOR YOUR PERFORMANCE. YOU'RE UP IN FIFTEEN MINUTES, DARLING.
WHAT?! OH NO! WE'VE GOT TO GET READY! HURRY, GIRLS!
DON'T WORRY, DEAR ETTA! I'LL KEEP COLONEL STONE COMPANY!

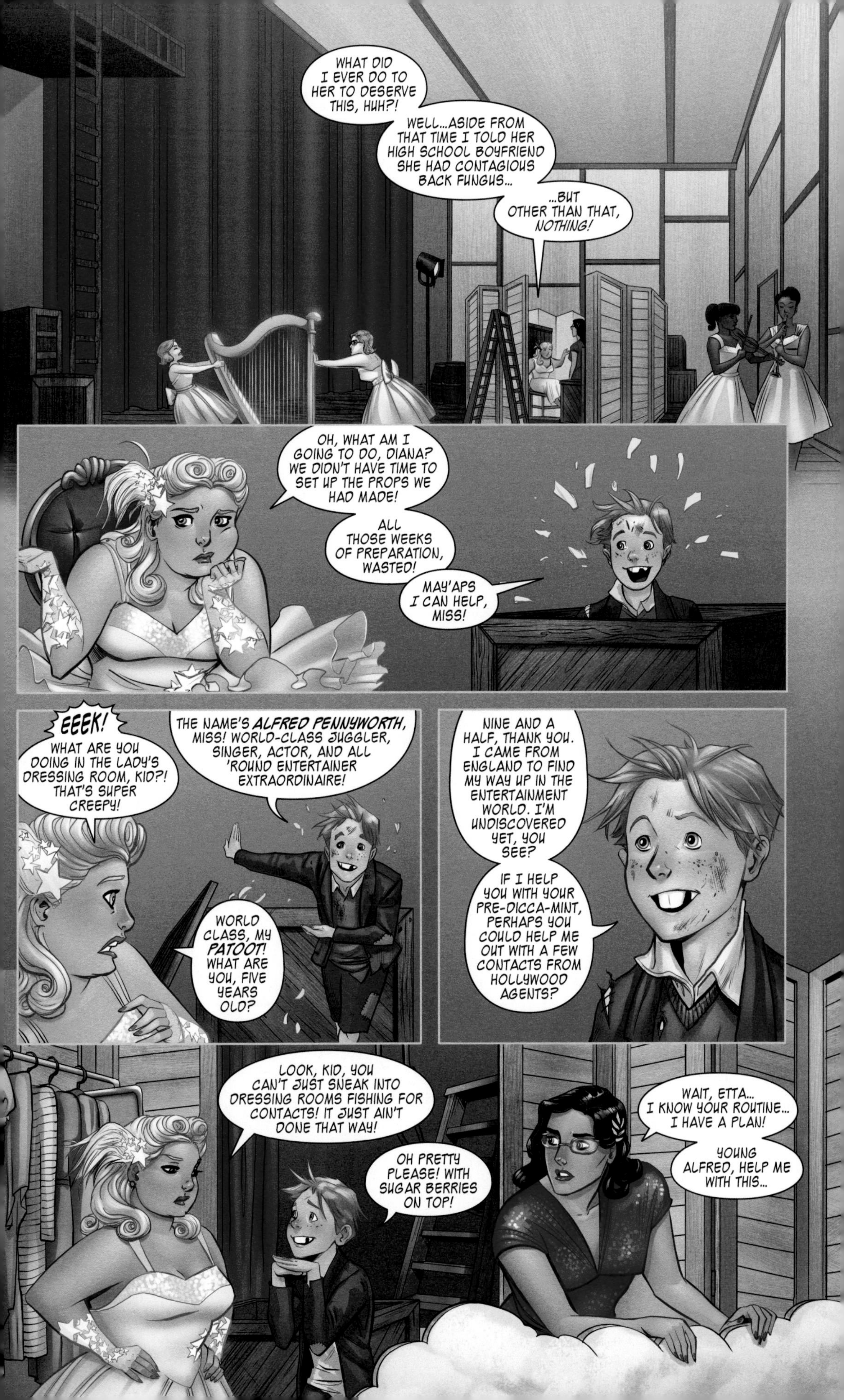
WHAT DID I EVER DO TO HER TO DESERVE THIS, HUH?!
WELL...ASIDE FROM THAT TIME I TOLD HER HIGH SCHOOL BOYFRIEND SHE HAD CONTAGIOUS BACK FUNGUS...
...BUT OTHER THAN THAT, *NOTHING!*
OH, WHAT AM I GOING TO DO, DIANA? WE DIDN'T HAVE TIME TO SET UP THE PROPS WE HAD MADE!
ALL THOSE WEEKS OF PREPARATION, WASTED!
MAY'APS I CAN HELP, MISS!
EEEK!
WHAT ARE YOU DOING IN THE LADY'S DRESSING ROOM, KID?! THAT'S SUPER CREEPY!
THE NAME'S *ALFRED PENNYWORTH*, MISS! WORLD-CLASS JUGGLER, SINGER, ACTOR, AND ALL 'ROUND ENTERTAINER EXTRAORDINAIRE!
WORLD CLASS, MY *PATOOT*! WHAT ARE YOU, FIVE YEARS OLD?
NINE AND A HALF, THANK YOU. I CAME FROM ENGLAND TO FIND MY WAY UP IN THE ENTERTAINMENT WORLD. I'M UNDISCOVERED YET, YOU SEE?
IF I HELP YOU WITH YOUR PRE-DICCA-MINT, PERHAPS YOU COULD HELP ME OUT WITH A FEW CONTACTS FROM HOLLYWOOD AGENTS?
LOOK, KID, YOU CAN'T JUST SNEAK INTO DRESSING ROOMS FISHING FOR CONTACTS! IT JUST AIN'T DONE THAT WAY!
OH PRETTY PLEASE! WITH SUGAR BERRIES ON TOP!
WAIT, ETTA... I KNOW YOUR ROUTINE... I HAVE A PLAN!
YOUNG ALFRED, HELP ME WITH THIS...

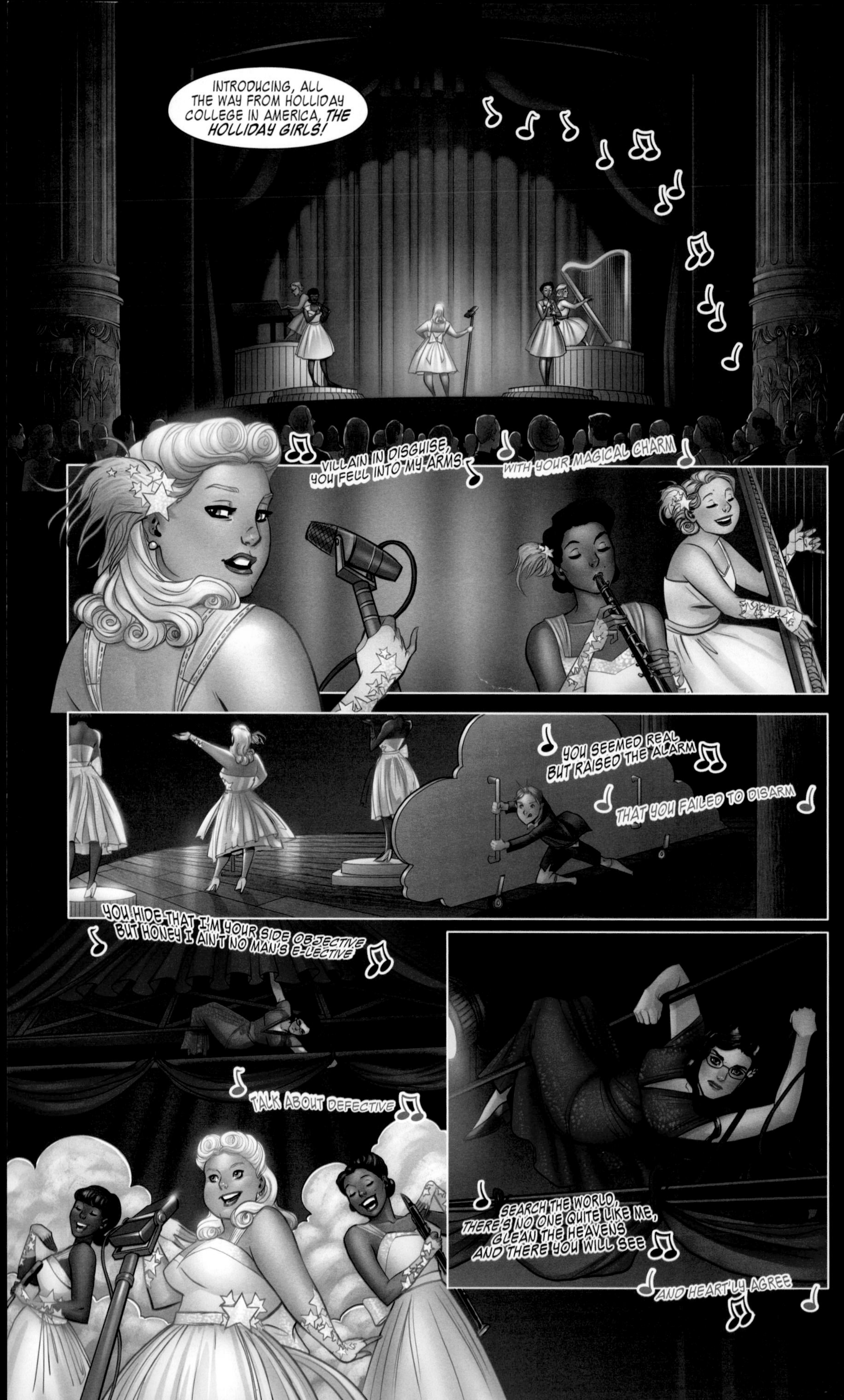

INTRODUCING, ALL THE WAY FROM HOLLIDAY COLLEGE IN AMERICA, THE HOLLIDAY GIRLS!
VILLAIN IN DISGUISE, YOU FELL INTO MY ARMS
WITH YOUR MAGICAL CHARM
YOU SEEMED REAL BUT RAISED THE ALARM
THAT YOU FAILED TO DISARM
YOU HIDE THAT I'M YOUR SIDE OBJECTIVE
BUT HONEY I AIN'T NO MAN'S E-LECTIVE
TALK ABOUT DEFECTIVE
SEARCH THE WORLD, THERE'S NO ONE QUITE LIKE ME, CLEAN THE HEAVENS AND THERE YOU WILL SEE
AND HEART'LY AGREE

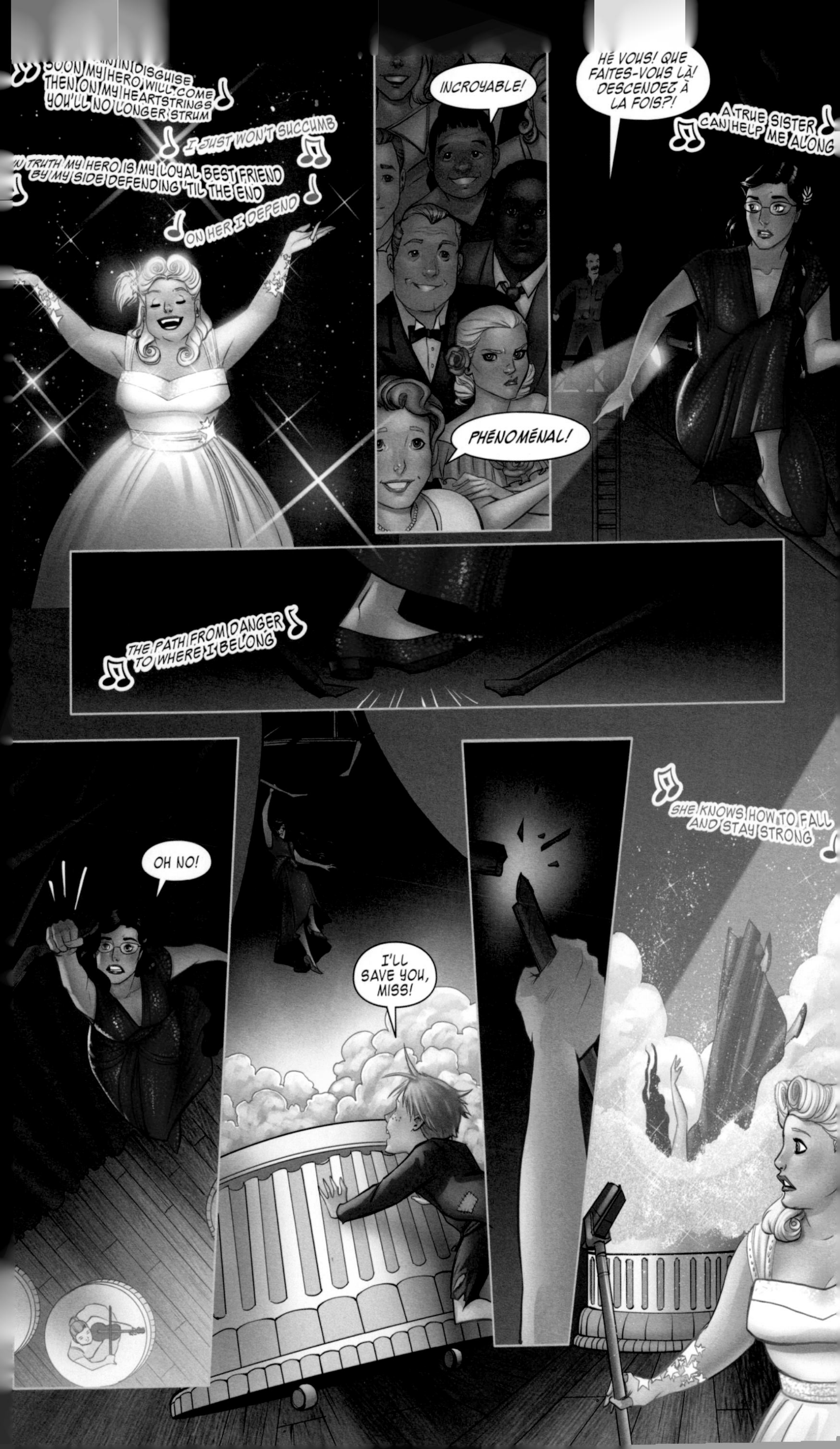

SOON IN DISGUISE
THEN ON MY HERO WILL COME
ON MY HEARTSTRINGS
YOU'LL NO LONGER STRUM
I JUST WON'T SUCCUMB
TRUTH MY HERO IS MY LOYAL BEST FRIEND
BY MY SIDE DEFENDING 'TIL THE END
ON HER I DEPEND
INCROYABLE!
PHÉNOMÉNAL!
HÉ VOUS! QUE FAITES-VOUS LÀ! DESCENDEZ À LA FOIS?!
A TRUE SISTER CAN HELP ME ALONG
THE PATH FROM DANGER TO WHERE I BELONG
OH NO!
I'LL SAVE YOU, MISS!
SHE KNOWS HOW TO FALL AND STAY STRONG

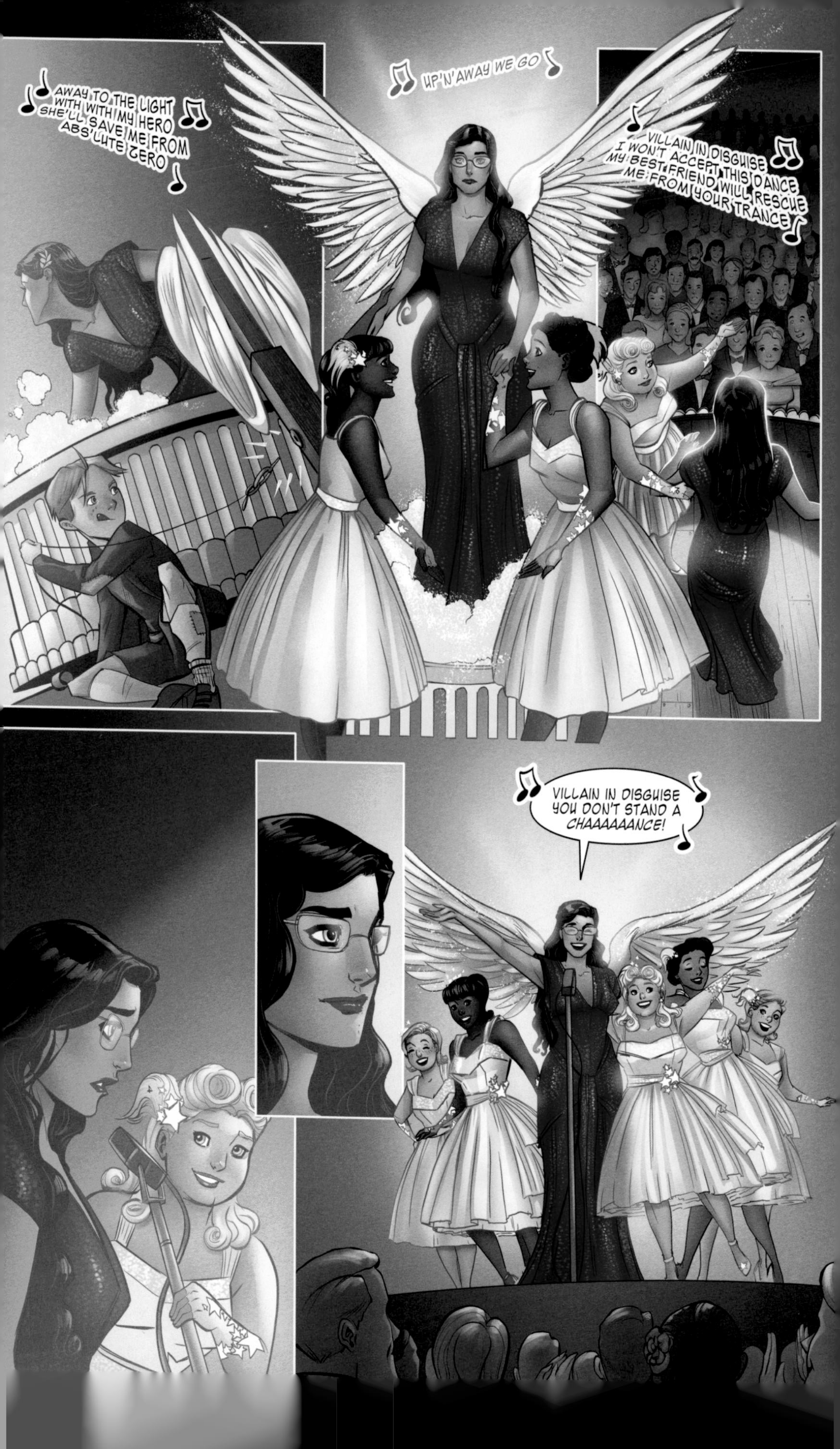
AWAY TO THE LIGHT WITH WITH MY HERO SHE'LL SAVE ME FROM ABS'LUTE ZERO
UP'N'AWAY WE GO
VILLAIN IN DISGUISE I WON'T ACCEPT THIS DANCE MY BEST FRIEND WILL RESCUE ME FROM YOUR TRANCE
VILLAIN IN DISGUISE YOU DON'T STAND A CHAAAAAAANCE!

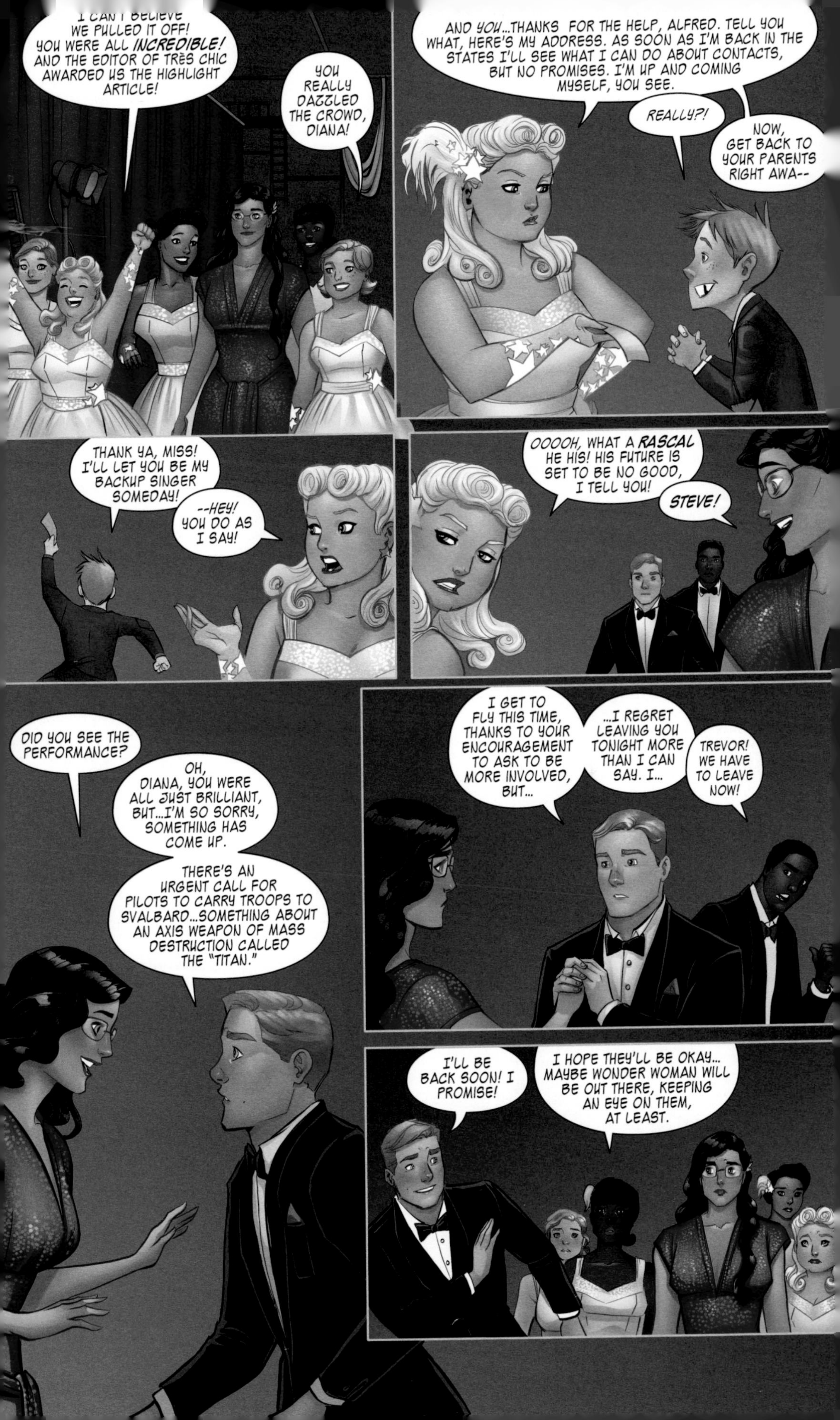

I CAN'T BELIEVE WE PULLED IT OFF! YOU WERE ALL INCREDIBLE! AND THE EDITOR OF TRÈS CHIC AWARDED US THE HIGHLIGHT ARTICLE!
YOU REALLY DAZZLED THE CROWD, DIANA!
AND YOU...THANKS FOR THE HELP, ALFRED. TELL YOU WHAT, HERE'S MY ADDRESS. AS SOON AS I'M BACK IN THE STATES I'LL SEE WHAT I CAN DO ABOUT CONTACTS, BUT NO PROMISES. I'M UP AND COMING MYSELF, YOU SEE.
REALLY?!
NOW, GET BACK TO YOUR PARENTS RIGHT AWA--
THANK YA, MISS! I'LL LET YOU BE MY BACKUP SINGER SOMEDAY!
--HEY! YOU DO AS I SAY!
OOOOH, WHAT A RASCAL HE HIS! HIS FUTURE IS SET TO BE NO GOOD, I TELL YOU!
STEVE!
DID YOU SEE THE PERFORMANCE?
OH, DIANA, YOU WERE ALL JUST BRILLIANT, BUT...I'M SO SORRY, SOMETHING HAS COME UP.
THERE'S AN URGENT CALL FOR PILOTS TO CARRY TROOPS TO SVALBARD...SOMETHING ABOUT AN AXIS WEAPON OF MASS DESTRUCTION CALLED THE "TITAN."
I GET TO FLY THIS TIME, THANKS TO YOUR ENCOURAGEMENT TO ASK TO BE MORE INVOLVED, BUT...
...I REGRET LEAVING YOU TONIGHT MORE THAN I CAN SAY. I...
TREVOR! WE HAVE TO LEAVE NOW!
I'LL BE BACK SOON! I PROMISE!
I HOPE THEY'LL BE OKAY... MAYBE WONDER WOMAN WILL BE OUT THERE, KEEPING AN EYE ON THEM, AT LEAST.

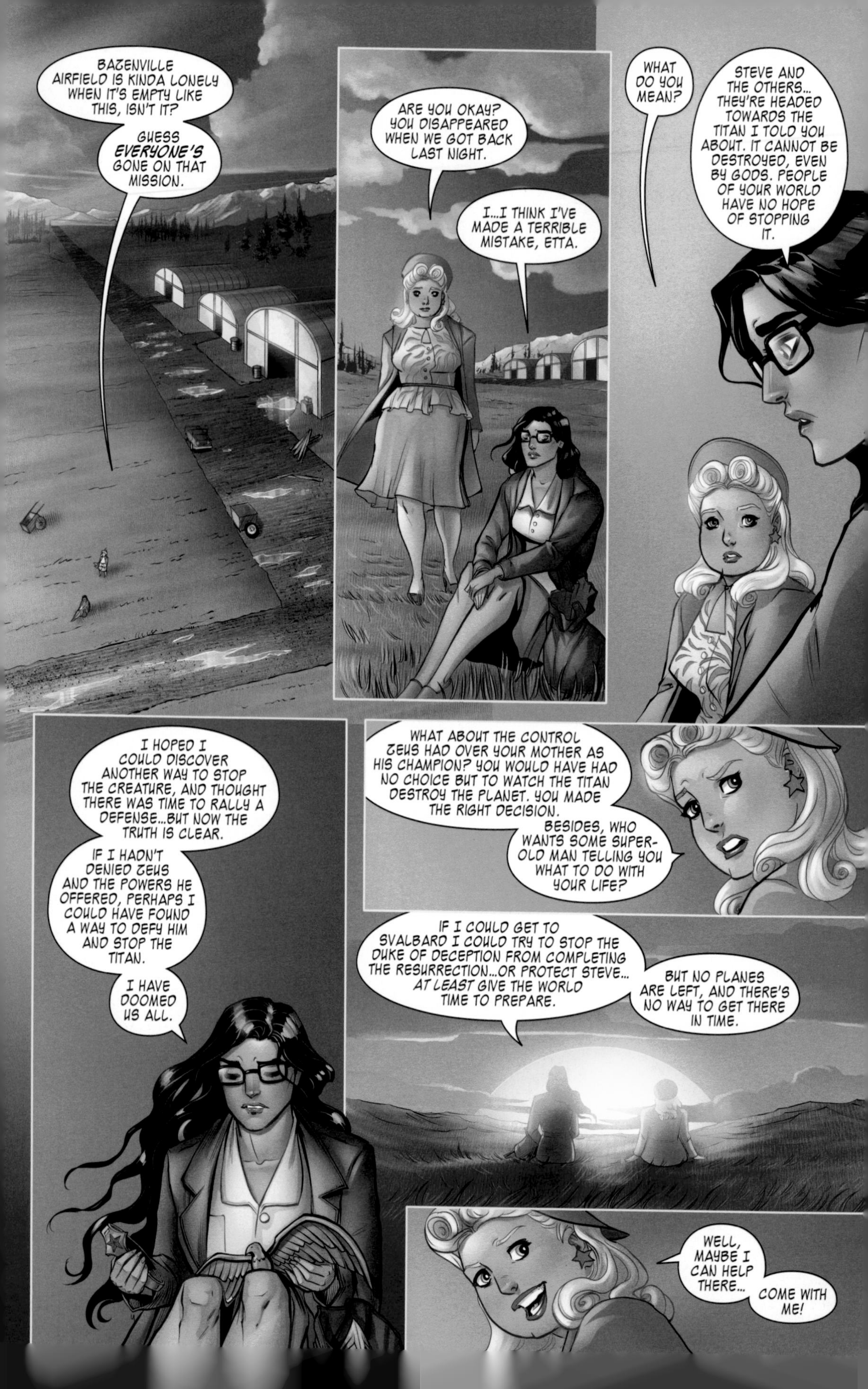

BAZENVILLE AIRFIELD IS KINDA LONELY WHEN IT'S EMPTY LIKE THIS, ISN'T IT?
GUESS *EVERYONE'S* GONE ON THAT MISSION.
ARE YOU OKAY? YOU DISAPPEARED WHEN WE GOT BACK LAST NIGHT.
I...I THINK I'VE MADE A TERRIBLE MISTAKE, ETTA.
WHAT DO YOU MEAN?
STEVE AND THE OTHERS... THEY'RE HEADED TOWARDS THE TITAN I TOLD YOU ABOUT. IT CANNOT BE DESTROYED, EVEN BY GODS. PEOPLE OF YOUR WORLD HAVE NO HOPE OF STOPPING IT.
I HOPED I COULD DISCOVER ANOTHER WAY TO STOP THE CREATURE, AND THOUGHT THERE WAS TIME TO RALLY A DEFENSE...BUT NOW THE TRUTH IS CLEAR.
IF I HADN'T DENIED ZEUS AND THE POWERS HE OFFERED, PERHAPS I COULD HAVE FOUND A WAY TO DEFY HIM AND STOP THE TITAN.
I HAVE DOOMED US ALL.
WHAT ABOUT THE CONTROL ZEUS HAD OVER YOUR MOTHER AS HIS CHAMPION? YOU WOULD HAVE HAD NO CHOICE BUT TO WATCH THE TITAN DESTROY THE PLANET. YOU MADE THE RIGHT DECISION.
BESIDES, WHO WANTS SOME SUPER-OLD MAN TELLING YOU WHAT TO DO WITH YOUR LIFE?
IF I COULD GET TO SVALBARD I COULD TRY TO STOP THE DUKE OF DECEPTION FROM COMPLETING THE RESURRECTION...OR PROTECT STEVE... *AT LEAST* GIVE THE WORLD TIME TO PREPARE.
BUT NO PLANES ARE LEFT, AND THERE'S NO WAY TO GET THERE IN TIME.
WELL, MAYBE I CAN HELP THERE...
COME WITH ME!

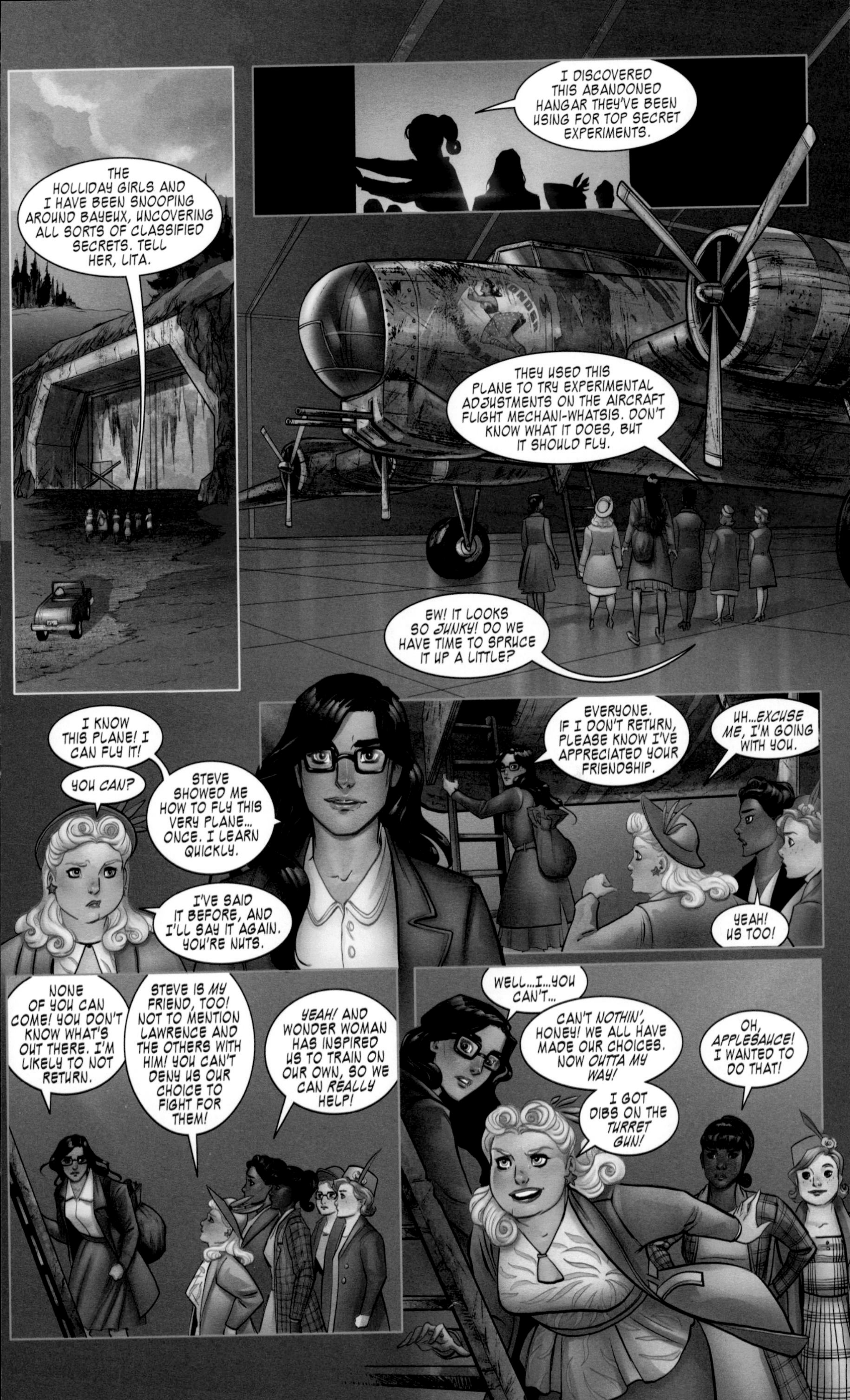

THE HOLLIDAY GIRLS AND I HAVE BEEN SNOOPING AROUND BAYEUX, UNCOVERING ALL SORTS OF CLASSIFIED SECRETS. TELL HER, LITA.
I DISCOVERED THIS ABANDONED HANGAR THEY'VE BEEN USING FOR TOP SECRET EXPERIMENTS.
THEY USED THIS PLANE TO TRY EXPERIMENTAL ADJUSTMENTS ON THE AIRCRAFT FLIGHT MECHANI-WHATSIS. DON'T KNOW WHAT IT DOES, BUT IT SHOULD FLY.
EW! IT LOOKS SO JUNKY! DO WE HAVE TIME TO SPRUCE IT UP A LITTLE?
I KNOW THIS PLANE! I CAN FLY IT!
YOU CAN?
STEVE SHOWED ME HOW TO FLY THIS VERY PLANE... ONCE. I LEARN QUICKLY.
I'VE SAID IT BEFORE, AND I'LL SAY IT AGAIN. YOU'RE NUTS.
EVERYONE. IF I DON'T RETURN, PLEASE KNOW I'VE APPRECIATED YOUR FRIENDSHIP.
UH...EXCUSE ME, I'M GOING WITH YOU.
YEAH! US TOO!
NONE OF YOU CAN COME! YOU DON'T KNOW WHAT'S OUT THERE. I'M LIKELY TO NOT RETURN.
STEVE IS MY FRIEND, TOO! NOT TO MENTION LAWRENCE AND THE OTHERS WITH HIM! YOU CAN'T DENY US OUR CHOICE TO FIGHT FOR THEM!
YEAH! AND WONDER WOMAN HAS INSPIRED US TO TRAIN ON OUR OWN, SO WE CAN REALLY HELP!
WELL...I...YOU CAN'T...
CAN'T NOTHIN', HONEY! WE ALL HAVE MADE OUR CHOICES. NOW OUTTA MY WAY!
I GOT DIBS ON THE TURRET GUN!
OH, APPLESAUCE! I WANTED TO DO THAT!

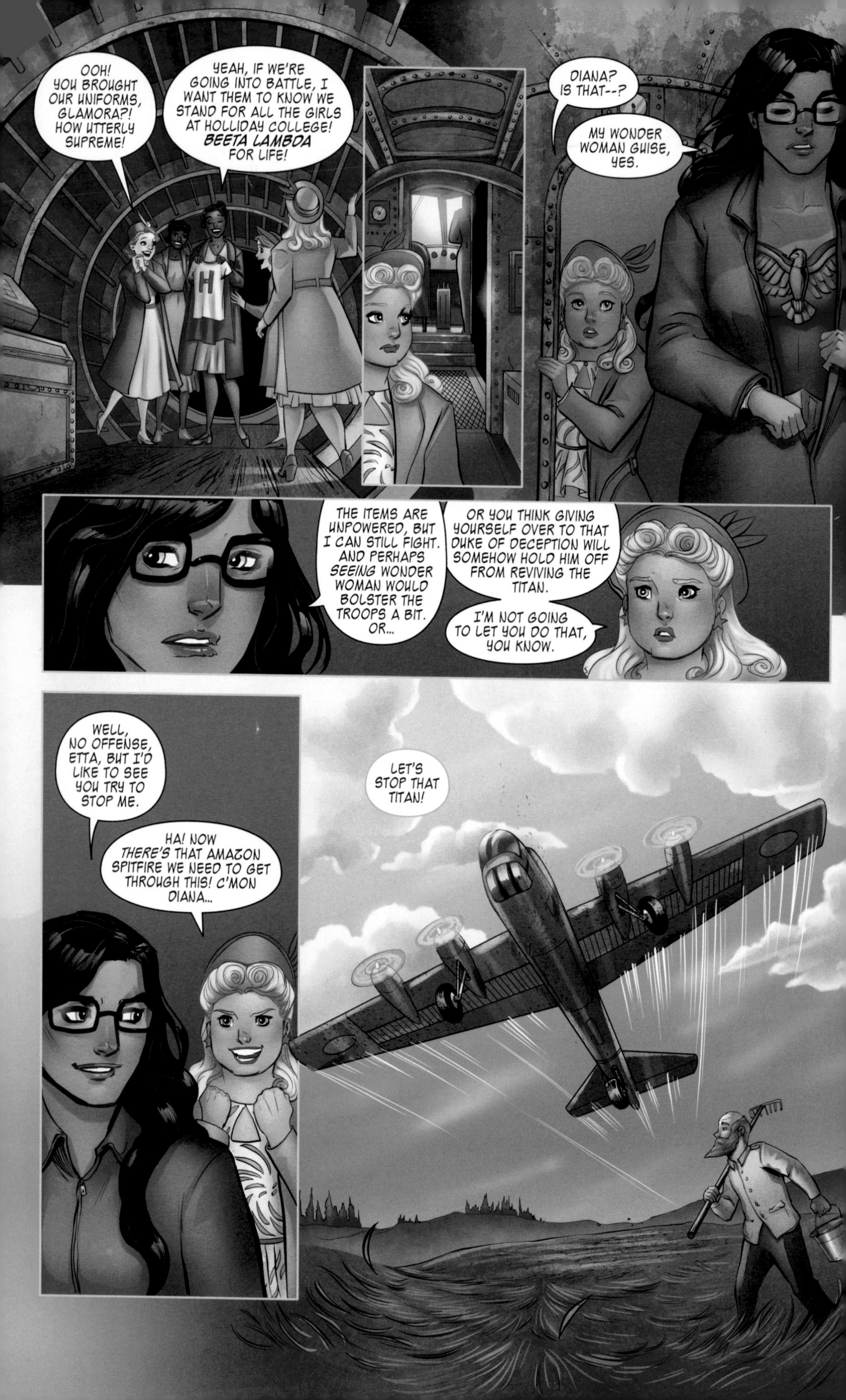
OOH! YOU BROUGHT OUR UNIFORMS, GLAMORA?! HOW UTTERLY SUPREME!
YEAH, IF WE'RE GOING INTO BATTLE, I WANT THEM TO KNOW WE STAND FOR ALL THE GIRLS AT HOLLIDAY COLLEGE! BEETA LAMBDA FOR LIFE!
H
DIANA? IS THAT--?
MY WONDER WOMAN GUISE, YES.
THE ITEMS ARE UNPOWERED, BUT I CAN STILL FIGHT. AND PERHAPS SEEING WONDER WOMAN WOULD BOLSTER THE TROOPS A BIT. OR...
OR YOU THINK GIVING YOURSELF OVER TO THAT DUKE OF DECEPTION WILL SOMEHOW HOLD HIM OFF FROM REVIVING THE TITAN.
I'M NOT GOING TO LET YOU DO THAT, YOU KNOW.
WELL, NO OFFENSE, ETTA, BUT I'D LIKE TO SEE YOU TRY TO STOP ME.
HA! NOW THERE'S THAT AMAZON SPITFIRE WE NEED TO GET THROUGH THIS! C'MON DIANA...
LET'S STOP THAT TITAN!

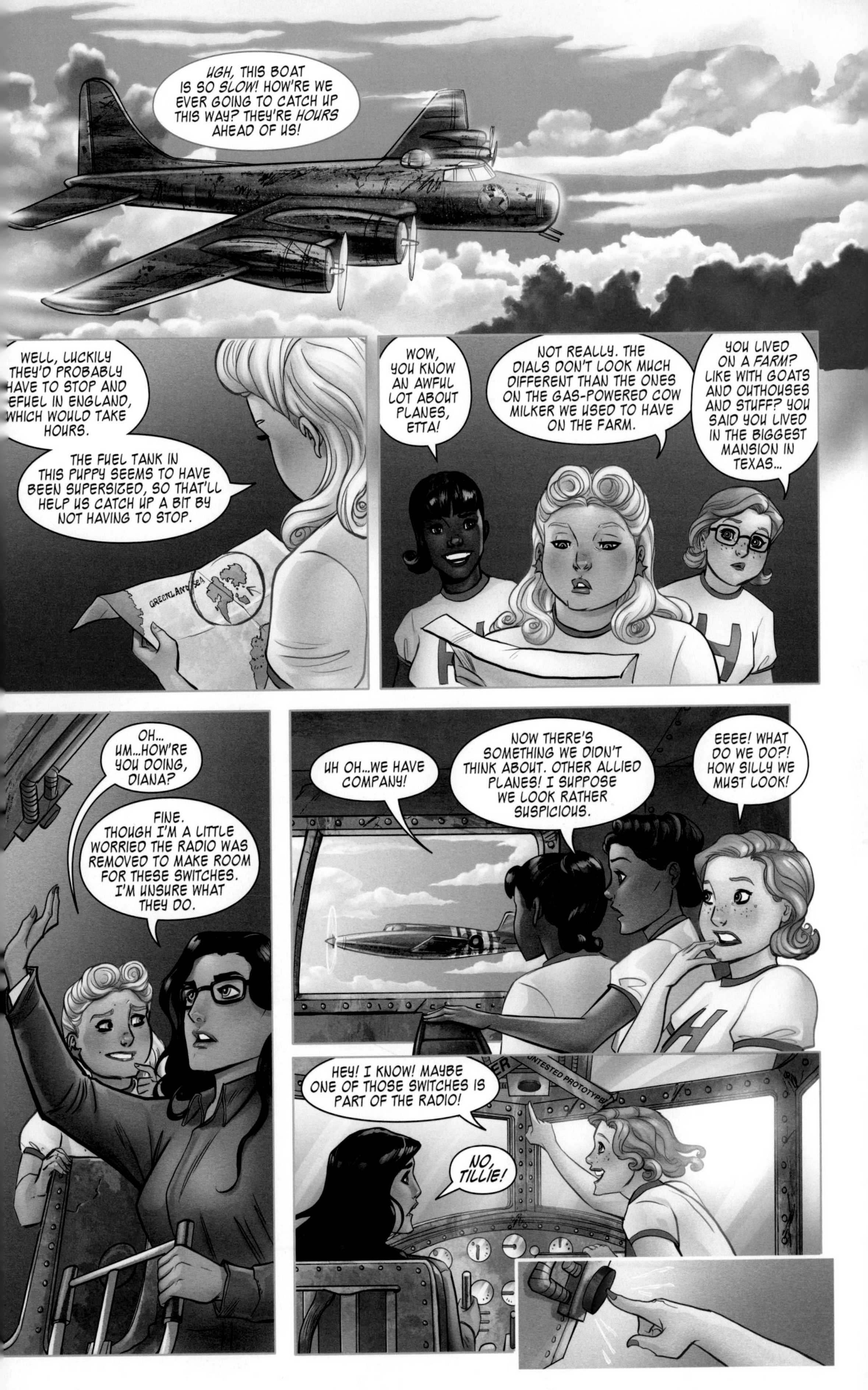
UGH, THIS BOAT IS SO SLOW! HOW'RE WE EVER GOING TO CATCH UP THIS WAY? THEY'RE HOURS AHEAD OF US!
WELL, LUCKILY THEY'D PROBABLY HAVE TO STOP AND REFUEL IN ENGLAND, WHICH WOULD TAKE HOURS.
THE FUEL TANK IN THIS PUPPY SEEMS TO HAVE BEEN SUPERSIZED, SO THAT'LL HELP US CATCH UP A BIT BY NOT HAVING TO STOP.
WOW, YOU KNOW AN AWFUL LOT ABOUT PLANES, ETTA!
NOT REALLY. THE DIALS DON'T LOOK MUCH DIFFERENT THAN THE ONES ON THE GAS-POWERED COW MILKER WE USED TO HAVE ON THE FARM.
YOU LIVED ON A FARM? LIKE WITH GOATS AND OUTHOUSES AND STUFF? YOU SAID YOU LIVED IN THE BIGGEST MANSION IN TEXAS...
OH... UM...HOW'RE YOU DOING, DIANA?
FINE. THOUGH I'M A LITTLE WORRIED THE RADIO WAS REMOVED TO MAKE ROOM FOR THESE SWITCHES. I'M UNSURE WHAT THEY DO.
UH OH...WE HAVE COMPANY!
NOW THERE'S SOMETHING WE DIDN'T THINK ABOUT. OTHER ALLIED PLANES! I SUPPOSE WE LOOK RATHER SUSPICIOUS.
EEEE! WHAT DO WE DO?! HOW SILLY WE MUST LOOK!
HEY! I KNOW! MAYBE ONE OF THOSE SWITCHES IS PART OF THE RADIO!
UNTESTED PROTOTYPE
NO, TILLIE!

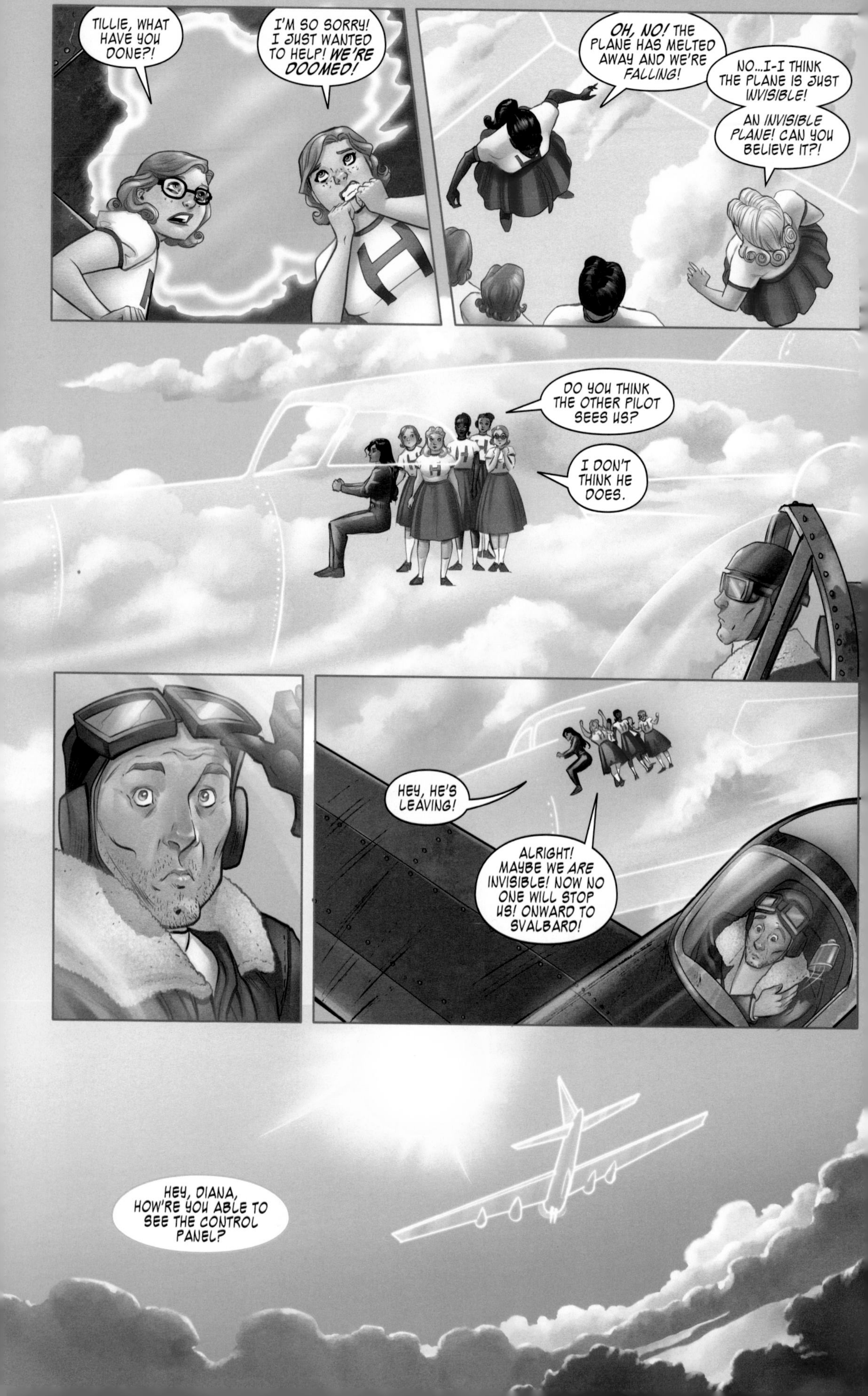
TILLIE, WHAT HAVE YOU DONE?!
I'M SO SORRY! I JUST WANTED TO HELP! WE'RE DOOMED!
OH, NO! THE PLANE HAS MELTED AWAY AND WE'RE FALLING!
NO...I-I THINK THE PLANE IS JUST INVISIBLE!
AN INVISIBLE PLANE! CAN YOU BELIEVE IT?!
DO YOU THINK THE OTHER PILOT SEES US?
I DON'T THINK HE DOES.
HEY, HE'S LEAVING!
ALRIGHT! MAYBE WE ARE INVISIBLE! NOW NO ONE WILL STOP US! ONWARD TO SVALBARD!
HEY, DIANA, HOW'RE YOU ABLE TO SEE THE CONTROL PANEL?

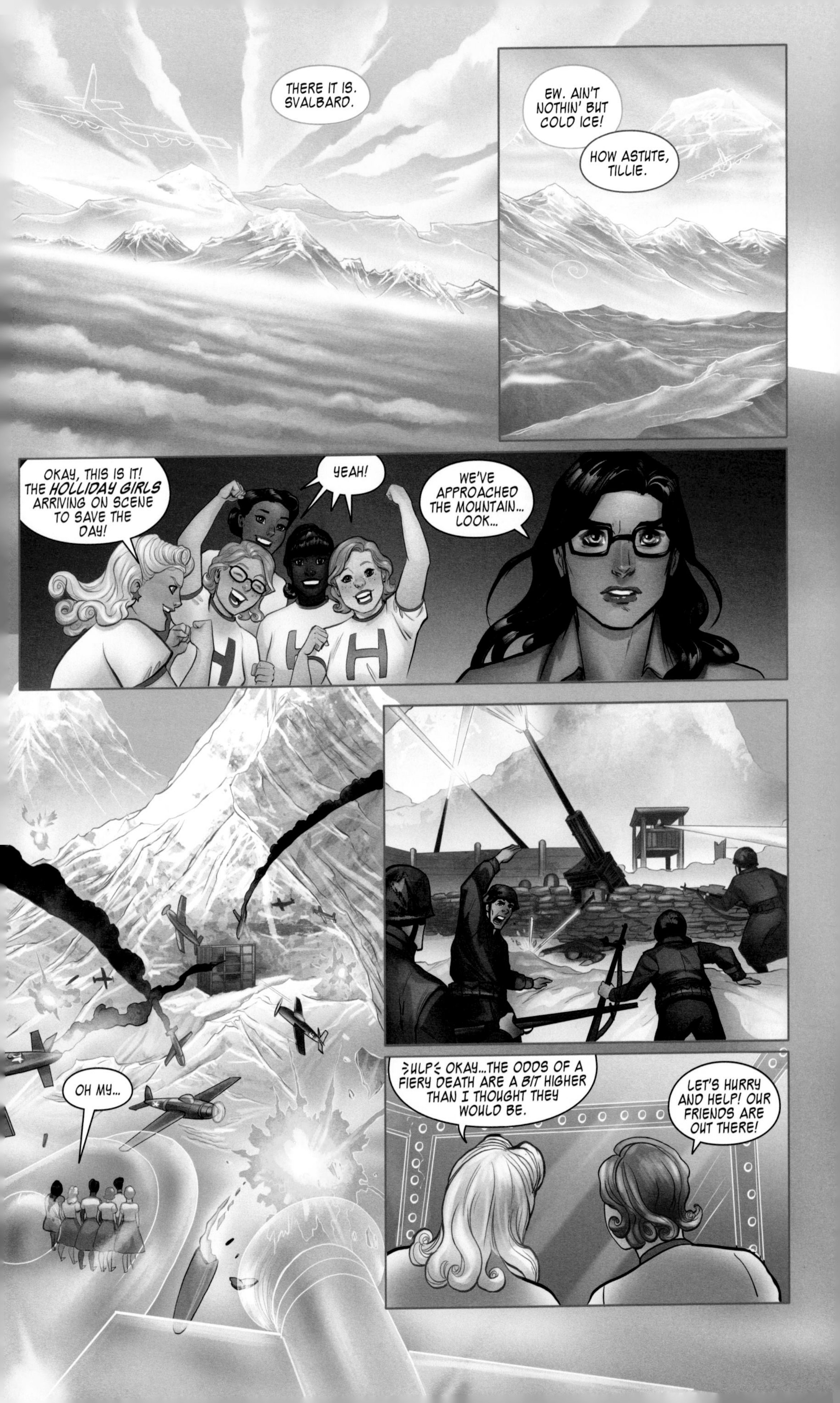
THERE IT IS. SVALBARD.
EW. AIN'T NOTHIN' BUT COLD ICE!
HOW ASTUTE, TILLIE.
OKAY, THIS IS IT! THE HOLLIDAY GIRLS ARRIVING ON SCENE TO SAVE THE DAY!
YEAH!
WE'VE APPROACHED THE MOUNTAIN... LOOK...
OH MY...
GULP OKAY...THE ODDS OF A FIERY DEATH ARE A BIT HIGHER THAN I THOUGHT THEY WOULD BE.
LET'S HURRY AND HELP! OUR FRIENDS ARE OUT THERE!

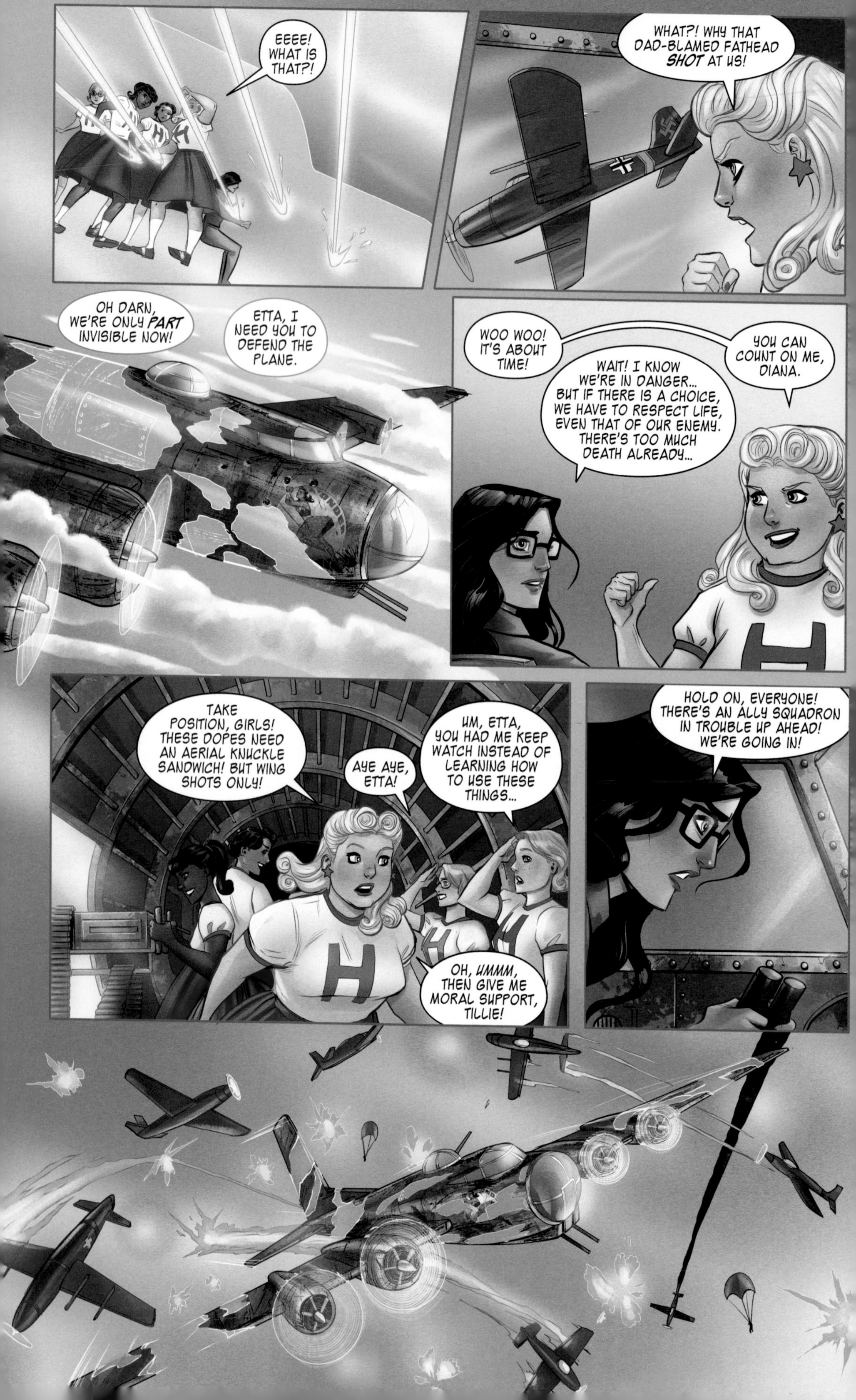
EEEE! WHAT IS THAT?!
WHAT?! WHY THAT DAD-BLAMED FATHEAD SHOT AT US!
OH DARN, WE'RE ONLY PART INVISIBLE NOW!
ETTA, I NEED YOU TO DEFEND THE PLANE.
WOO WOO! IT'S ABOUT TIME!
YOU CAN COUNT ON ME, DIANA.
WAIT! I KNOW WE'RE IN DANGER... BUT IF THERE IS A CHOICE, WE HAVE TO RESPECT LIFE, EVEN THAT OF OUR ENEMY. THERE'S TOO MUCH DEATH ALREADY...
TAKE POSITION, GIRLS! THESE DOPES NEED AN AERIAL KNUCKLE SANDWICH! BUT WING SHOTS ONLY!
AYE AYE, ETTA!
UM, ETTA, YOU HAD ME KEEP WATCH INSTEAD OF LEARNING HOW TO USE THESE THINGS...
OH, UMMM, THEN GIVE ME MORAL SUPPORT, TILLIE!
HOLD ON, EVERYONE! THERE'S AN ALLY SQUADRON IN TROUBLE UP AHEAD! WE'RE GOING IN!

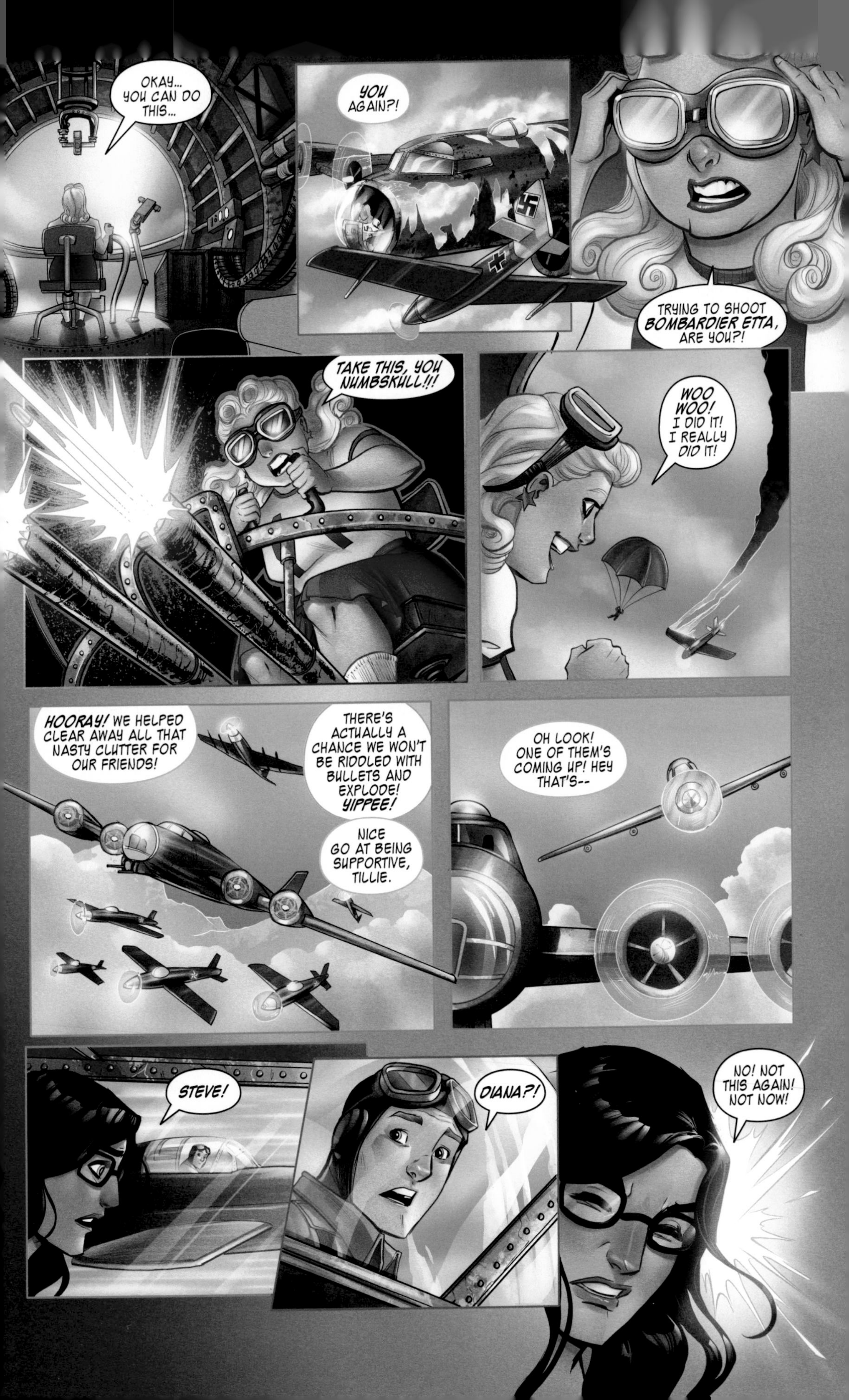
OKAY... YOU CAN DO THIS...
YOU AGAIN?!
TRYING TO SHOOT BOMBARDIER ETTA, ARE YOU?!
TAKE THIS, YOU NUMBSKULL!!!
WOO WOO! I DID IT! I REALLY DID IT!
HOORAY! WE HELPED CLEAR AWAY ALL THAT NASTY CLUTTER FOR OUR FRIENDS!
THERE'S ACTUALLY A CHANCE WE WON'T BE RIDDLED WITH BULLETS AND EXPLODE! YIPPEE!
NICE GO AT BEING SUPPORTIVE, TILLIE.
OH LOOK! ONE OF THEM'S COMING UP! HEY THAT'S--
STEVE!
DIANA?!
NO! NOT THIS AGAIN! NOT NOW!

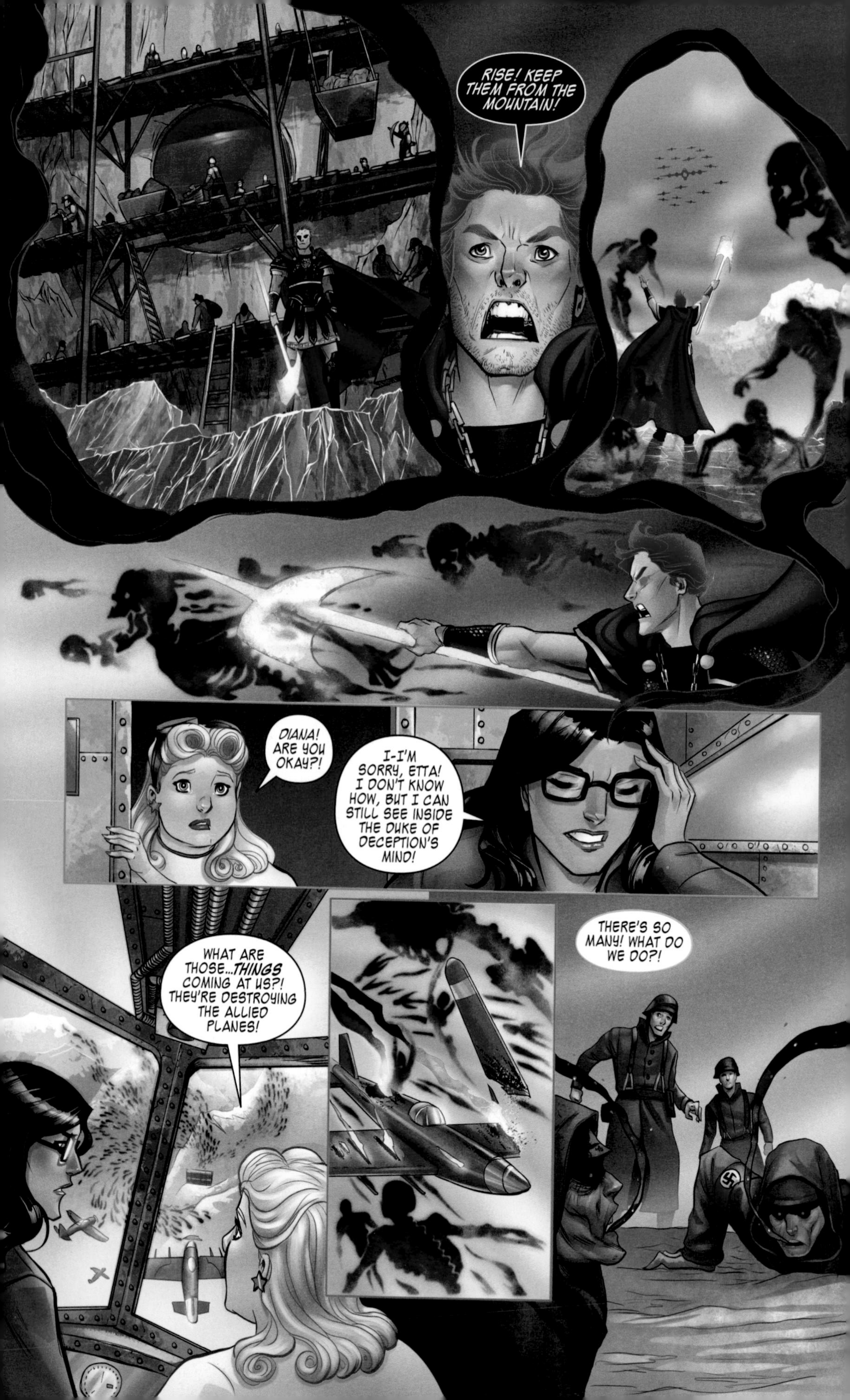
RISE! KEEP THEM FROM THE MOUNTAIN!
DIANA! ARE YOU OKAY?!
I-I'M SORRY, ETTA! I DON'T KNOW HOW, BUT I CAN STILL SEE INSIDE THE DUKE OF DECEPTION'S MIND!
WHAT ARE THOSE...THINGS COMING AT US?! THEY'RE DESTROYING THE ALLIED PLANES!
THERE'S SO MANY! WHAT DO WE DO?!

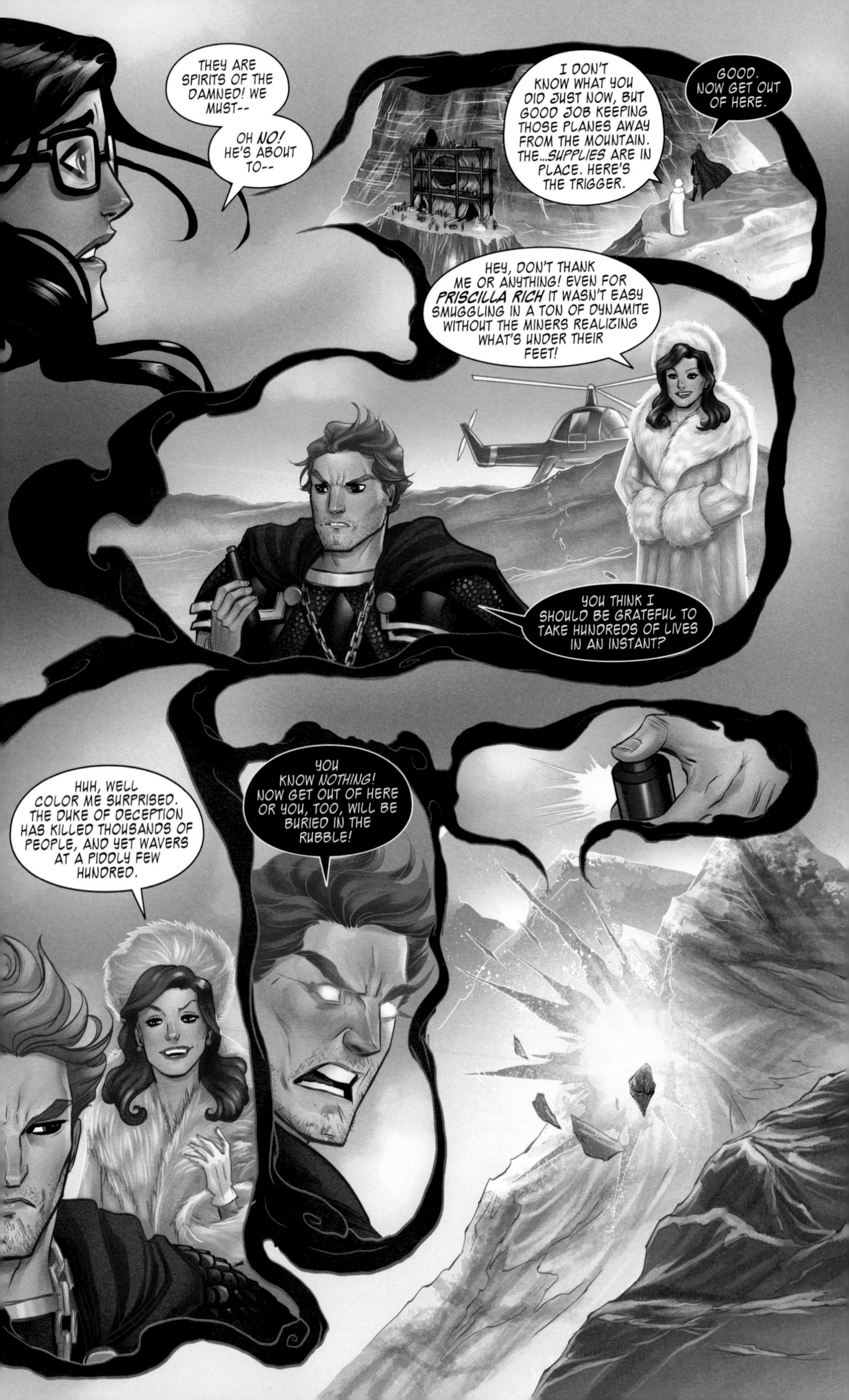
THEY ARE SPIRITS OF THE DAMNED! WE MUST--
OH NO! HE'S ABOUT TO--
I DON'T KNOW WHAT YOU DID JUST NOW, BUT GOOD JOB KEEPING THOSE PLANES AWAY FROM THE MOUNTAIN. THE...SUPPLIES ARE IN PLACE. HERE'S THE TRIGGER.
GOOD. NOW GET OUT OF HERE.
HEY, DON'T THANK ME OR ANYTHING! EVEN FOR PRISCILLA RICH IT WASN'T EASY SMUGGLING IN A TON OF DYNAMITE WITHOUT THE MINERS REALIZING WHAT'S UNDER THEIR FEET!
YOU THINK I SHOULD BE GRATEFUL TO TAKE HUNDREDS OF LIVES IN AN INSTANT?
HUH, WELL COLOR ME SURPRISED. THE DUKE OF DECEPTION HAS KILLED THOUSANDS OF PEOPLE, AND YET WAVERS AT A PIDDLY FEW HUNDRED.
YOU KNOW NOTHING! NOW GET OUT OF HERE OR YOU, TOO, WILL BE BURIED IN THE RUBBLE!

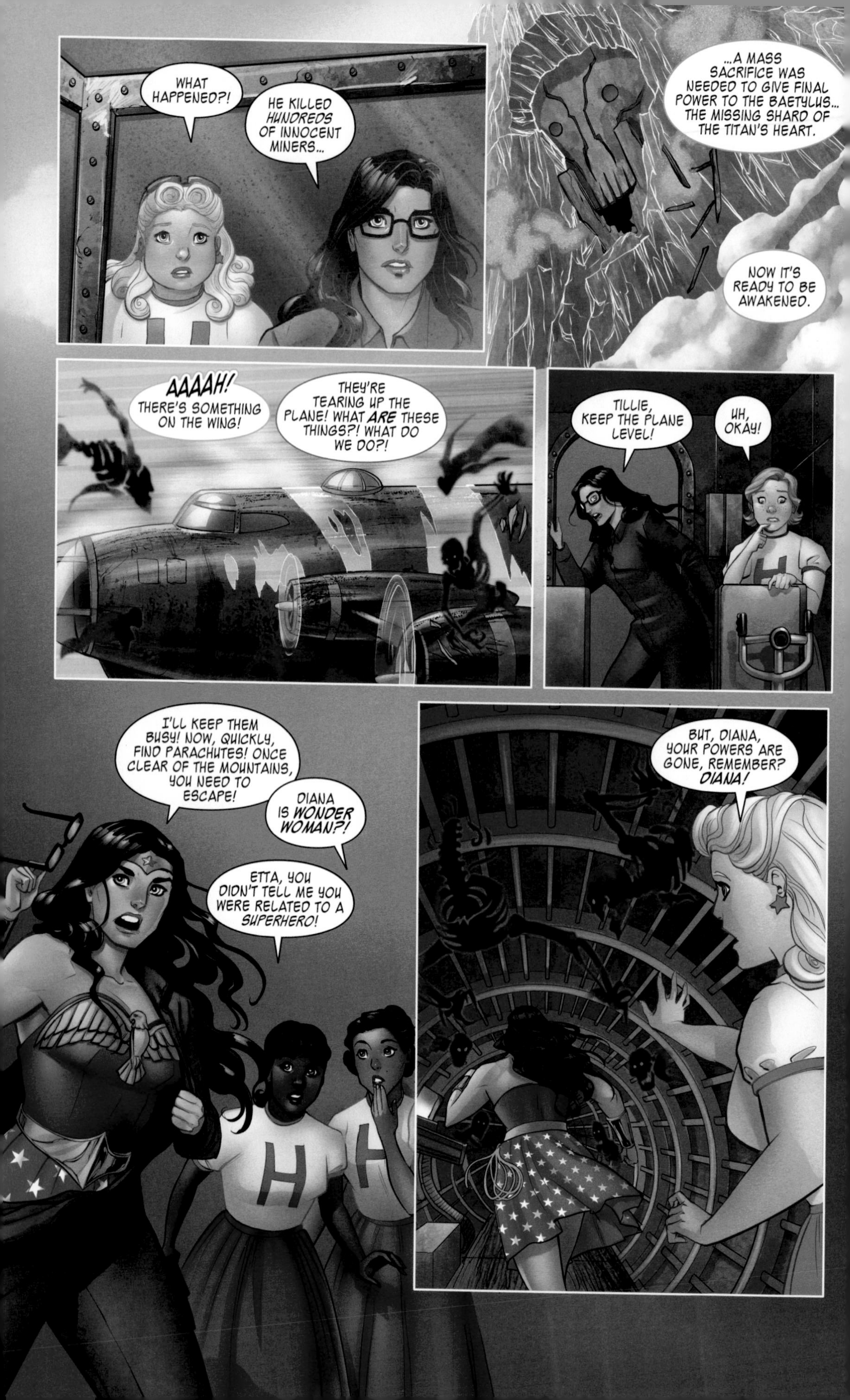

WHAT HAPPENED?!
HE KILLED HUNDREDS OF INNOCENT MINERS...
...A MASS SACRIFICE WAS NEEDED TO GIVE FINAL POWER TO THE BAETYLUS... THE MISSING SHARD OF THE TITAN'S HEART.
NOW IT'S READY TO BE AWAKENED.
AAAAH! THERE'S SOMETHING ON THE WING!
THEY'RE TEARING UP THE PLANE! WHAT ARE THESE THINGS?! WHAT DO WE DO?!
TILLIE, KEEP THE PLANE LEVEL!
UH, OKAY!
I'LL KEEP THEM BUSY! NOW, QUICKLY, FIND PARACHUTES! ONCE CLEAR OF THE MOUNTAINS, YOU NEED TO ESCAPE!
DIANA IS WONDER WOMAN?!
ETTA, YOU DIDN'T TELL ME YOU WERE RELATED TO A SUPERHERO!
BUT, DIANA, YOUR POWERS ARE GONE, REMEMBER? DIANA!

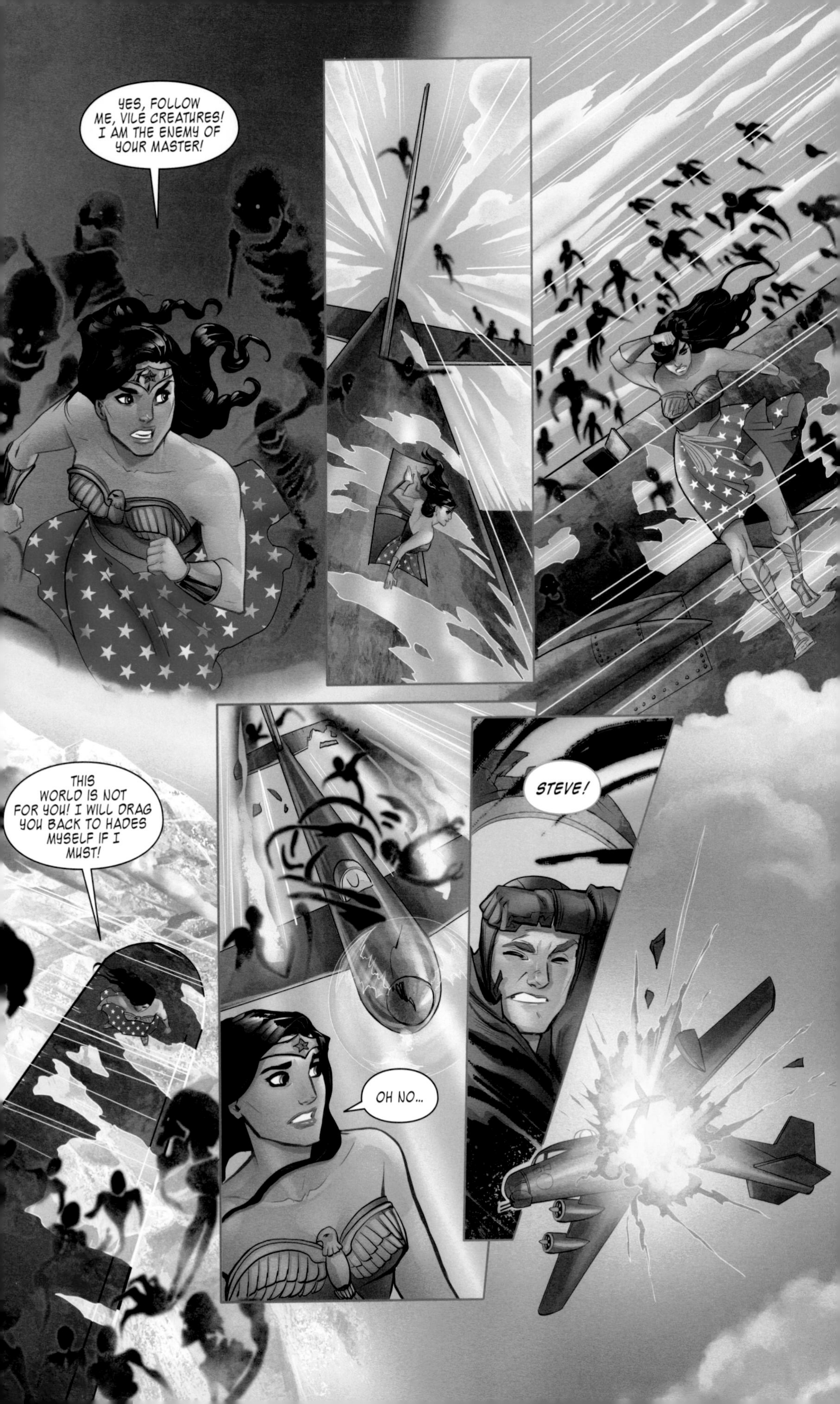
YES, FOLLOW ME, VILE CREATURES! I AM THE ENEMY OF YOUR MASTER!
THIS WORLD IS NOT FOR YOU! I WILL DRAG YOU BACK TO HADES MYSELF IF I MUST!
OH NO...
STEVE!

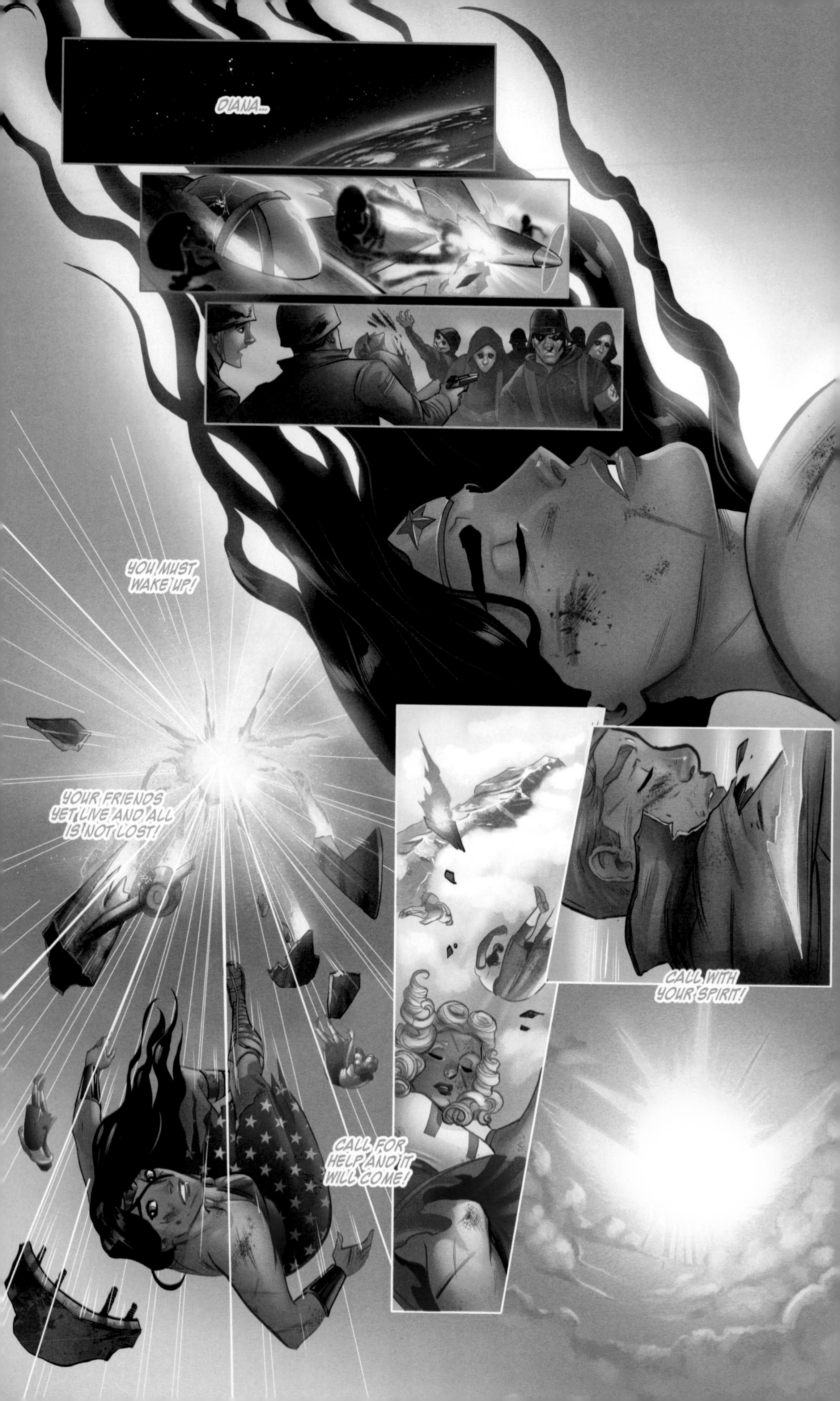
DIANA...
YOU MUST WAKE UP!
YOUR FRIENDS YET LIVE AND ALL IS NOT LOST!
CALL WITH YOUR SPIRIT!
CALL FOR HELP AND IT WILL COME!

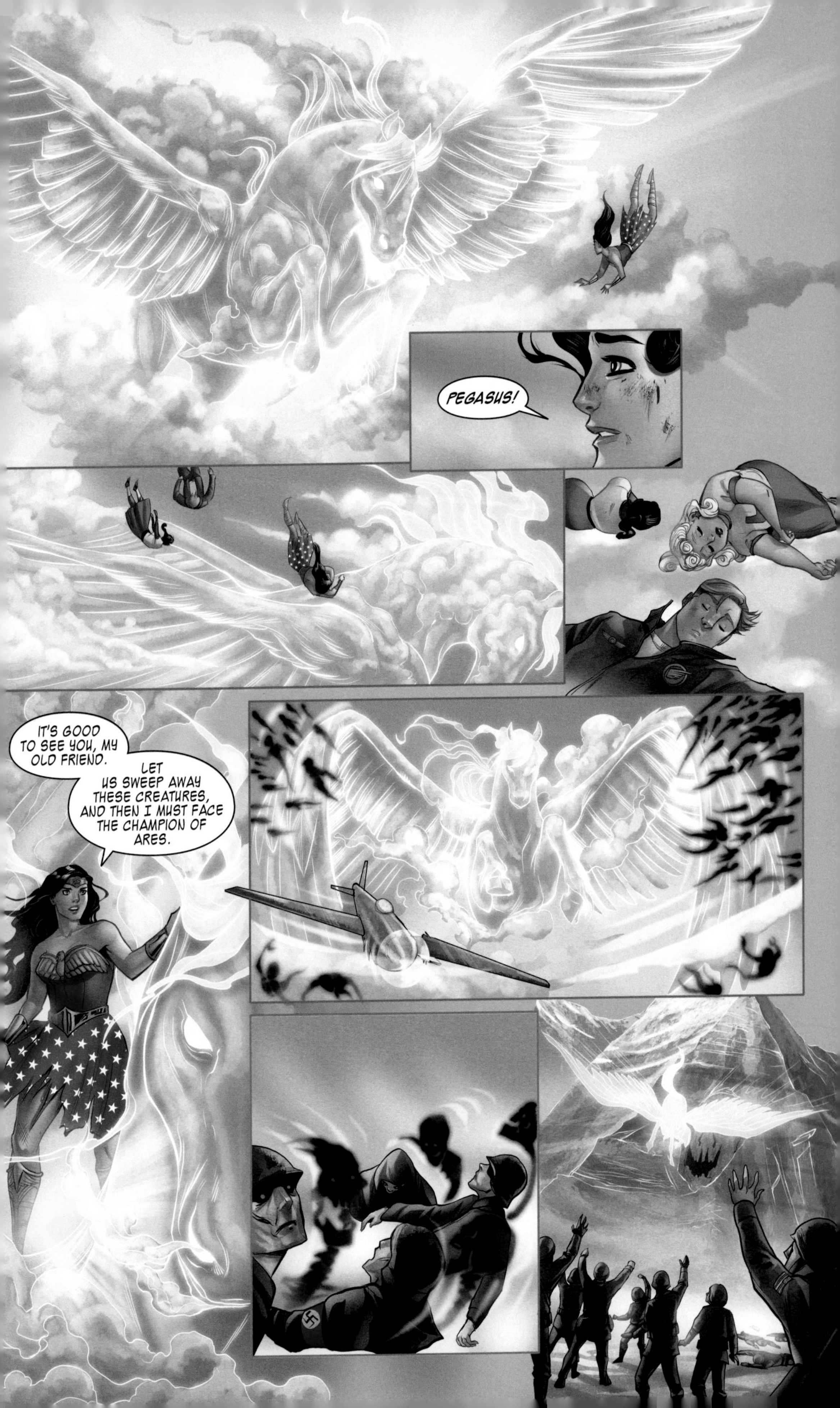
PEGASUS!
IT'S GOOD TO SEE YOU, MY OLD FRIEND.
LET US SWEEP AWAY THESE CREATURES, AND THEN I MUST FACE THE CHAMPION OF ARES.

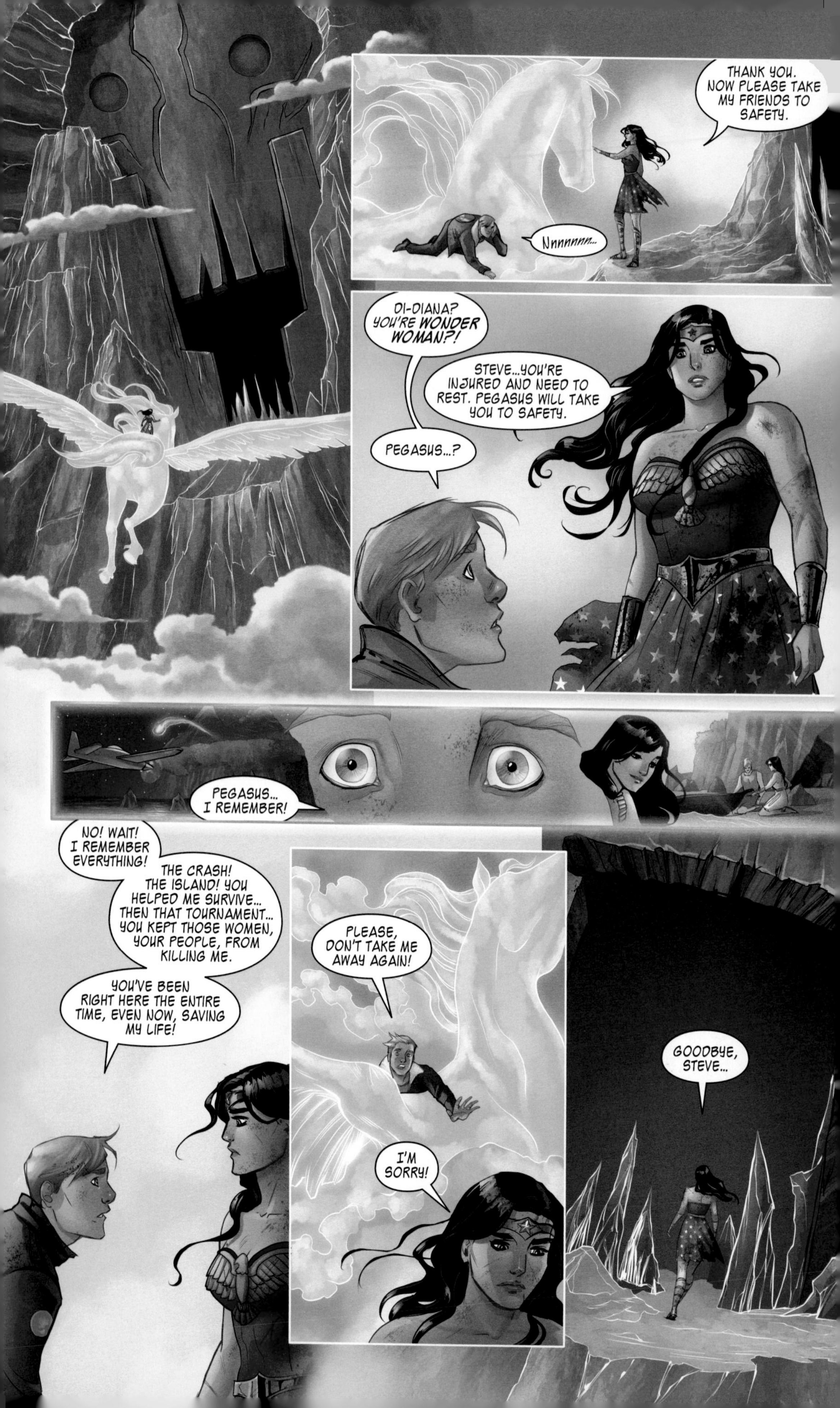
THANK YOU. NOW PLEASE TAKE MY FRIENDS TO SAFETY.
Nnnnnnn...
DI-DIANA? YOU'RE WONDER WOMAN?!
STEVE...YOU'RE INJURED AND NEED TO REST. PEGASUS WILL TAKE YOU TO SAFETY.
PEGASUS...?
PEGASUS... I REMEMBER!
NO! WAIT! I REMEMBER EVERYTHING!
THE CRASH! THE ISLAND! YOU HELPED ME SURVIVE... THEN THAT TOURNAMENT... YOU KEPT THOSE WOMEN, YOUR PEOPLE, FROM KILLING ME.
YOU'VE BEEN RIGHT HERE THE ENTIRE TIME, EVEN NOW, SAVING MY LIFE!
PLEASE, DON'T TAKE ME AWAY AGAIN!
I'M SORRY!
GOODBYE, STEVE...

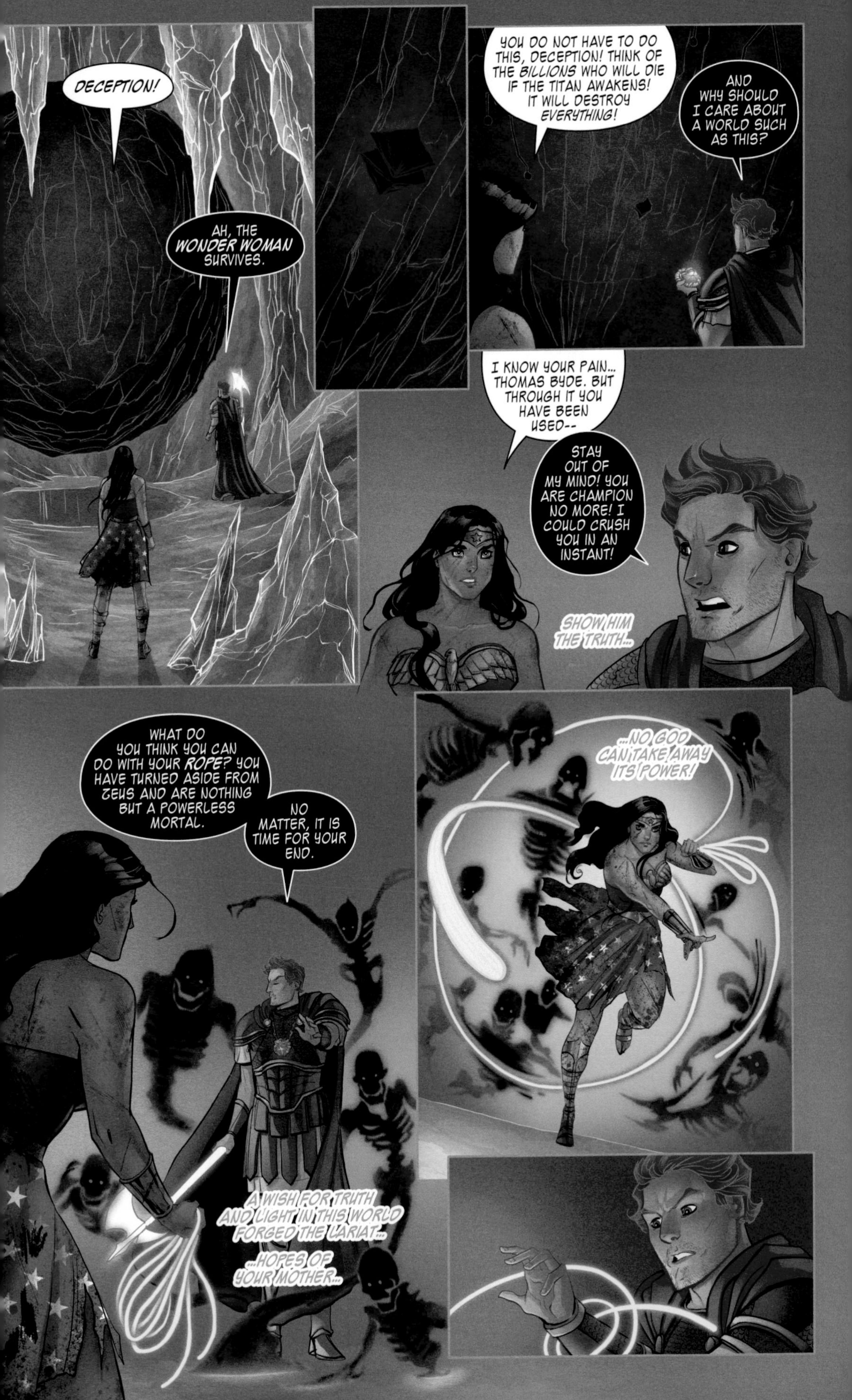
DECEPTION!
AH, THE WONDER WOMAN SURVIVES.
YOU DO NOT HAVE TO DO THIS, DECEPTION! THINK OF THE BILLIONS WHO WILL DIE IF THE TITAN AWAKENS! IT WILL DESTROY EVERYTHING!
AND WHY SHOULD I CARE ABOUT A WORLD SUCH AS THIS?
I KNOW YOUR PAIN... THOMAS BYDE. BUT THROUGH IT YOU HAVE BEEN USED--
STAY OUT OF MY MIND! YOU ARE CHAMPION NO MORE! I COULD CRUSH YOU IN AN INSTANT!
SHOW HIM THE TRUTH...
WHAT DO YOU THINK YOU CAN DO WITH YOUR ROPE? YOU HAVE TURNED ASIDE FROM ZEUS AND ARE NOTHING BUT A POWERLESS MORTAL.
NO MATTER, IT IS TIME FOR YOUR END.
A WISH FOR TRUTH AND LIGHT IN THIS WORLD FORGED THE LARIAT...
...HOPES OF YOUR MOTHER...
...NO GOD CAN TAKE AWAY ITS POWER!

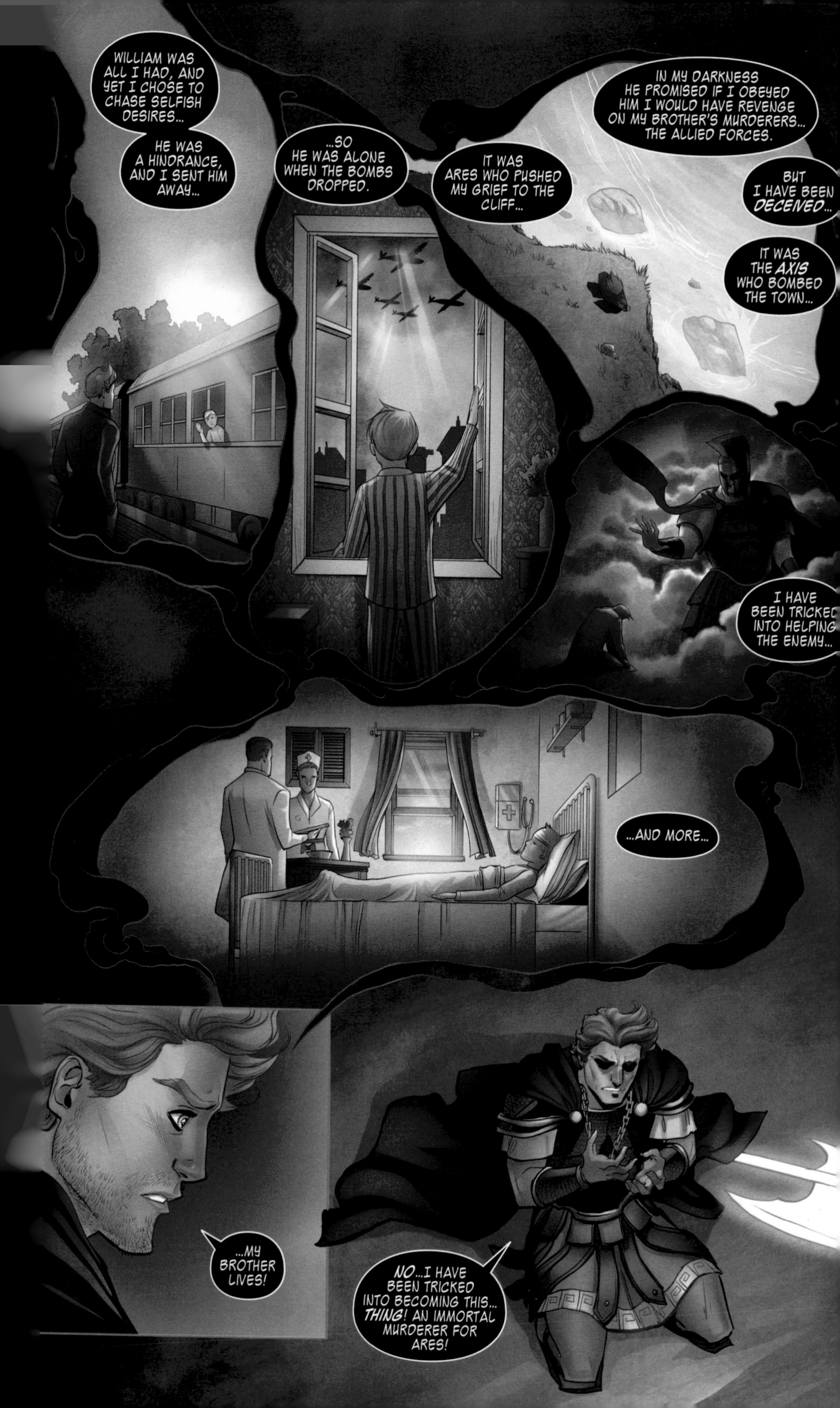
WILLIAM WAS ALL I HAD, AND YET I CHOSE TO CHASE SELFISH DESIRES...
HE WAS A HINDRANCE, AND I SENT HIM AWAY...
...SO HE WAS ALONE WHEN THE BOMBS DROPPED.
IT WAS ARES WHO PUSHED MY GRIEF TO THE CLIFF...
IN MY DARKNESS HE PROMISED IF I OBEYED HIM I WOULD HAVE REVENGE ON MY BROTHER'S MURDERERS... THE ALLIED FORCES.
BUT I HAVE BEEN DECEIVED...
IT WAS THE AXIS WHO BOMBED THE TOWN...
I HAVE BEEN TRICKED INTO HELPING THE ENEMY...
...AND MORE...
...MY BROTHER LIVES!
NO...I HAVE BEEN TRICKED INTO BECOMING THIS... THING! AN IMMORTAL MURDERER FOR ARES!

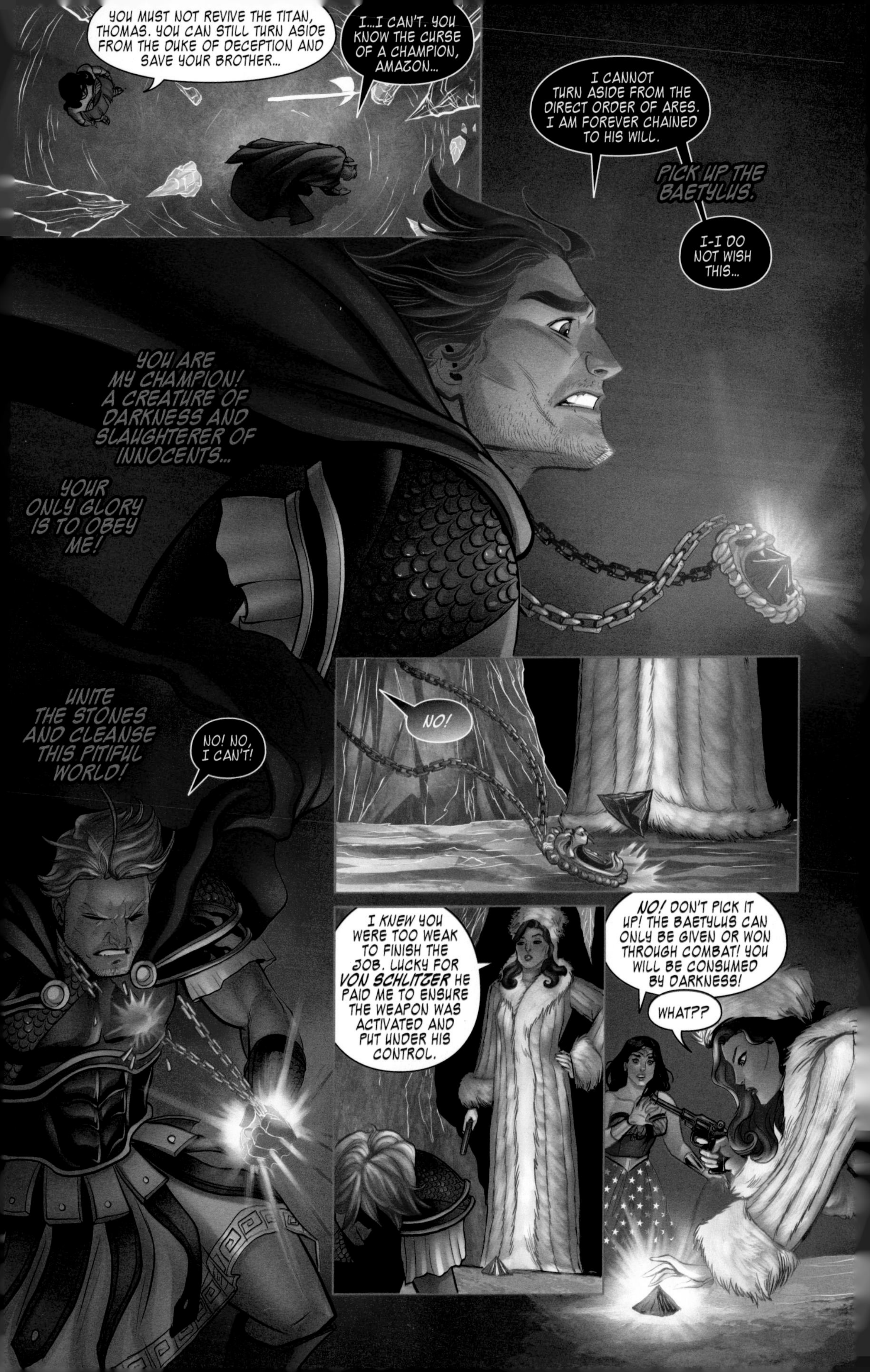
YOU MUST NOT REVIVE THE TITAN, THOMAS. YOU CAN STILL TURN ASIDE FROM THE DUKE OF DECEPTION AND SAVE YOUR BROTHER...
I...I CAN'T. YOU KNOW THE CURSE OF A CHAMPION, AMAZON...
I CANNOT TURN ASIDE FROM THE DIRECT ORDER OF ARES. I AM FOREVER CHAINED TO HIS WILL.
PICK UP THE BAETYLUS.
I-I DO NOT WISH THIS...
YOU ARE MY CHAMPION! A CREATURE OF DARKNESS AND SLAUGHTERER OF INNOCENTS...
YOUR ONLY GLORY IS TO OBEY ME!
UNITE THE STONES AND CLEANSE THIS PITIFUL WORLD!
NO! NO, I CAN'T!
NO!
I KNEW YOU WERE TOO WEAK TO FINISH THE JOB. LUCKY FOR VON SCHLITZER HE PAID ME TO ENSURE THE WEAPON WAS ACTIVATED AND PUT UNDER HIS CONTROL.
NO! DON'T PICK IT UP! THE BAETYLUS CAN ONLY BE GIVEN OR WON THROUGH COMBAT! YOU WILL BE CONSUMED BY DARKNESS!
WHAT??

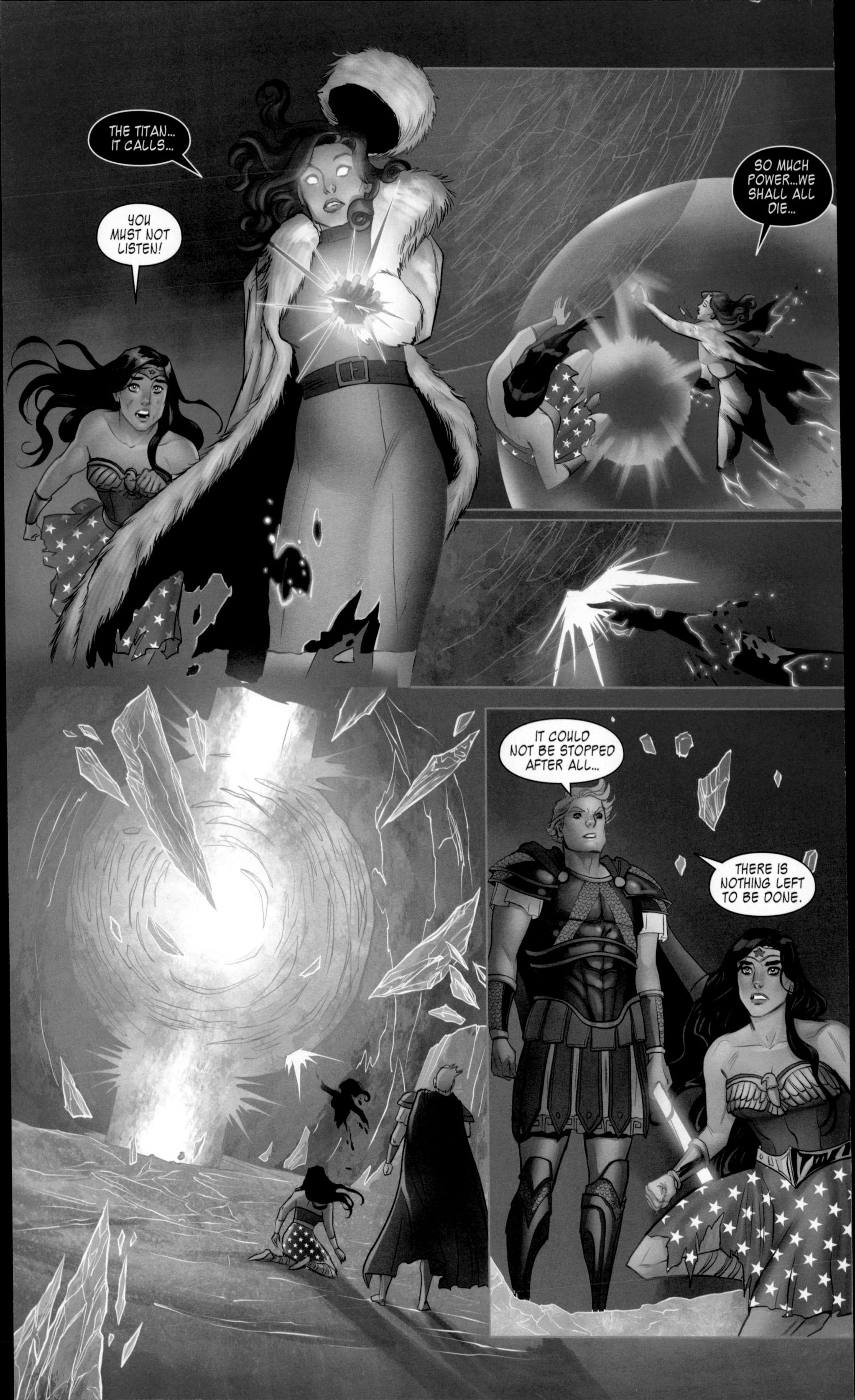
THE TITAN... IT CALLS...
YOU MUST NOT LISTEN!
SO MUCH POWER...WE SHALL ALL DIE...
IT COULD NOT BE STOPPED AFTER ALL...
THERE IS NOTHING LEFT TO BE DONE.

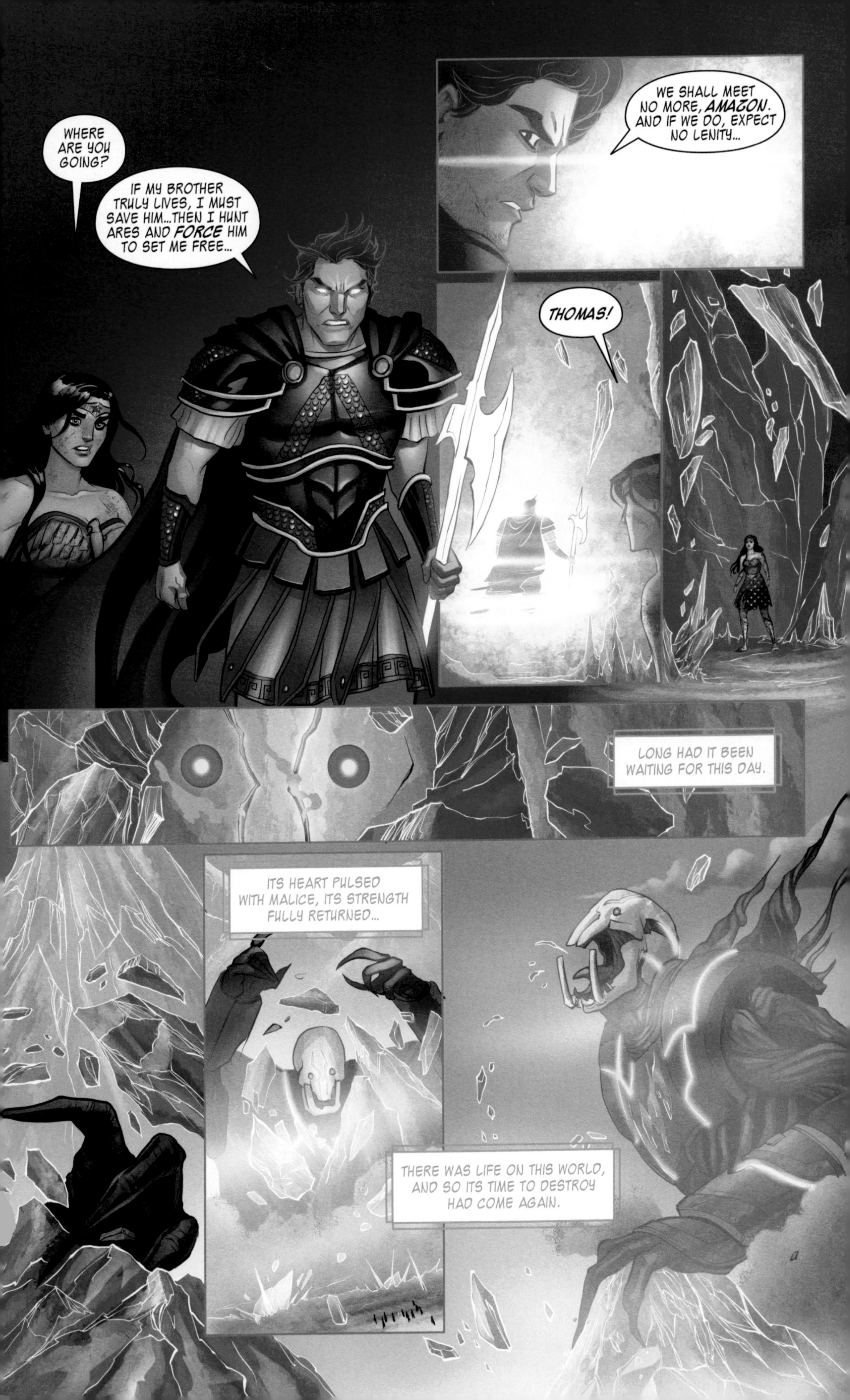

WHERE ARE YOU GOING?
IF MY BROTHER TRULY LIVES, I MUST SAVE HIM...THEN I HUNT ARES AND FORCE HIM TO SET ME FREE...
WE SHALL MEET NO MORE, AMAZON. AND IF WE DO, EXPECT NO LENITY...
THOMAS!
LONG HAD IT BEEN WAITING FOR THIS DAY.
ITS HEART PULSED WITH MALICE, ITS STRENGTH FULLY RETURNED...
THERE WAS LIFE ON THIS WORLD, AND SO ITS TIME TO DESTROY HAD COME AGAIN.

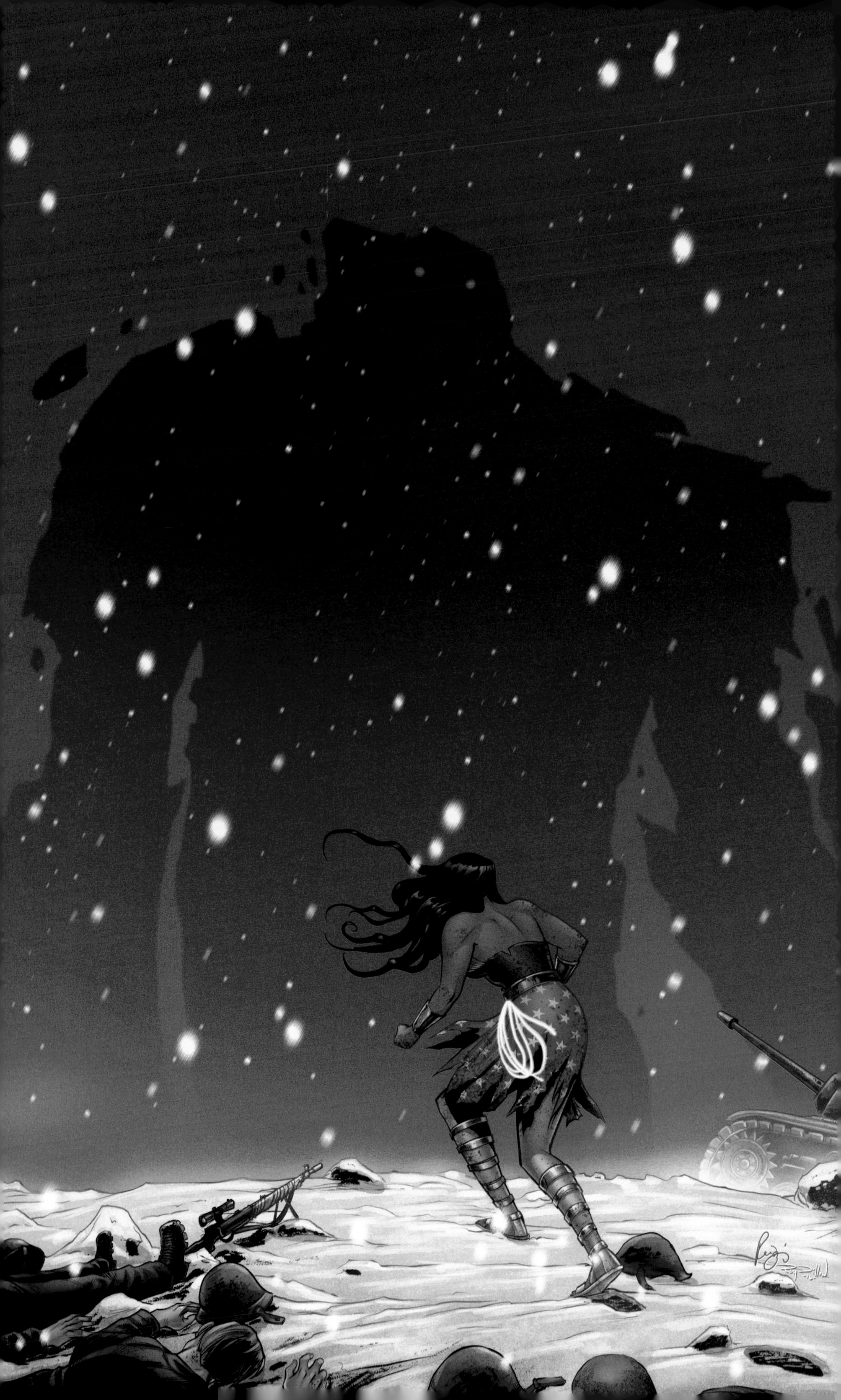

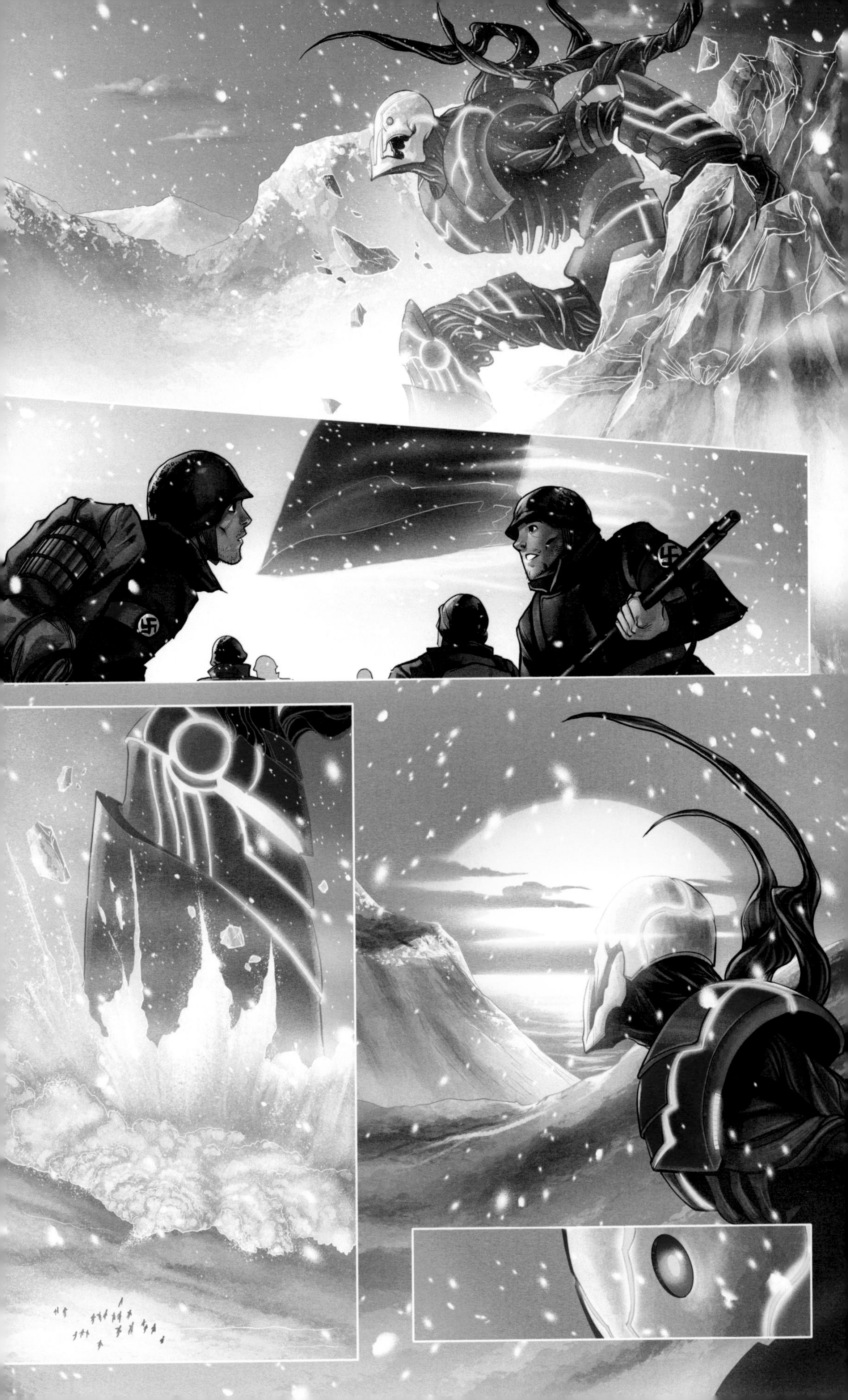

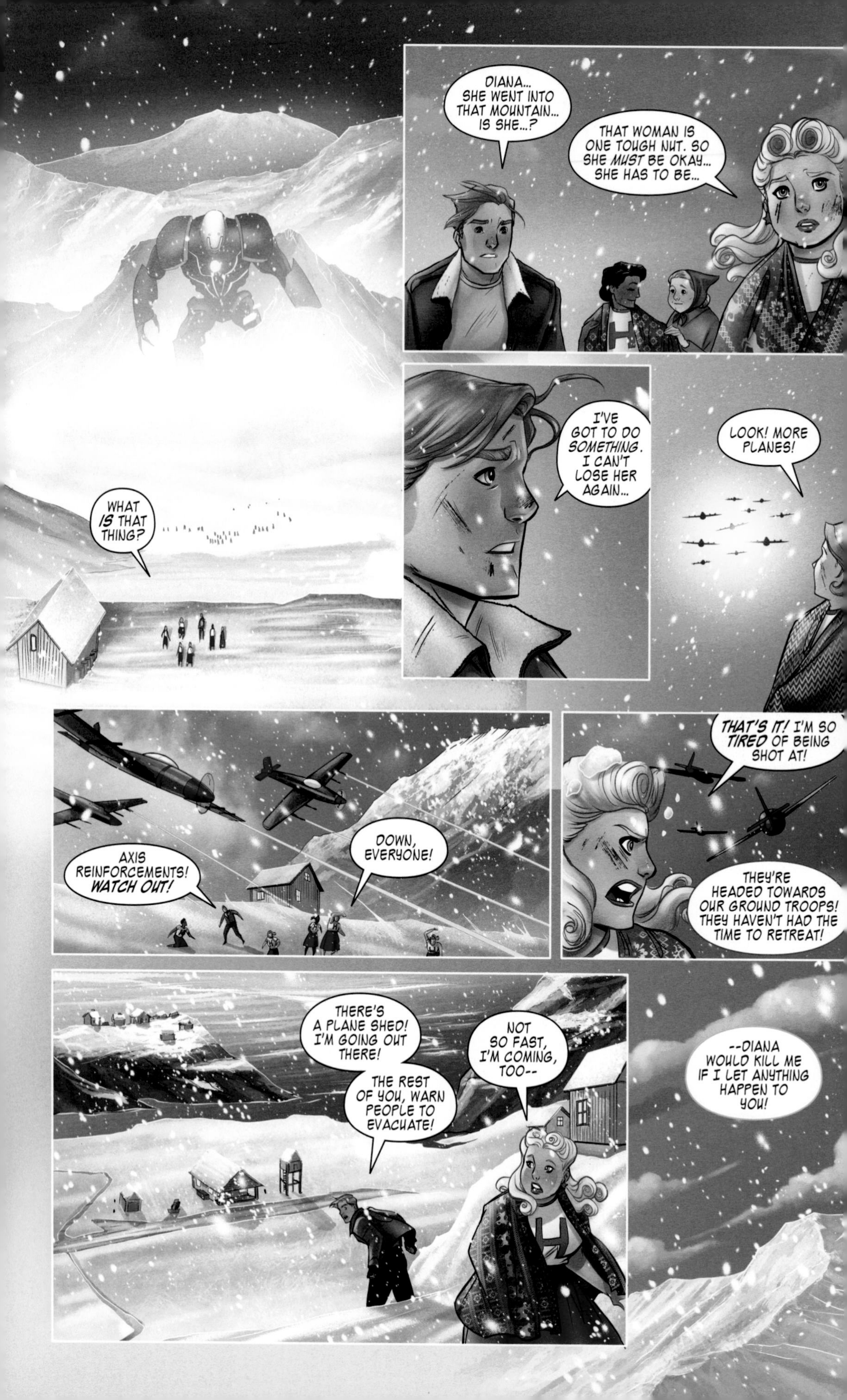
DIANA... SHE WENT INTO THAT MOUNTAIN... IS SHE...?
THAT WOMAN IS ONE TOUGH NUT. SO SHE MUST BE OKAY... SHE HAS TO BE...
WHAT IS THAT THING?
I'VE GOT TO DO SOMETHING. I CAN'T LOSE HER AGAIN...
LOOK! MORE PLANES!
AXIS REINFORCEMENTS! WATCH OUT!
DOWN, EVERYONE!
THAT'S IT! I'M SO TIRED OF BEING SHOT AT!
THEY'RE HEADED TOWARDS OUR GROUND TROOPS! THEY HAVEN'T HAD THE TIME TO RETREAT!
THERE'S A PLANE SHED! I'M GOING OUT THERE!
THE REST OF YOU, WARN PEOPLE TO EVACUATE!
NOT SO FAST, I'M COMING, TOO--
--DIANA WOULD KILL ME IF I LET ANYTHING HAPPEN TO YOU!

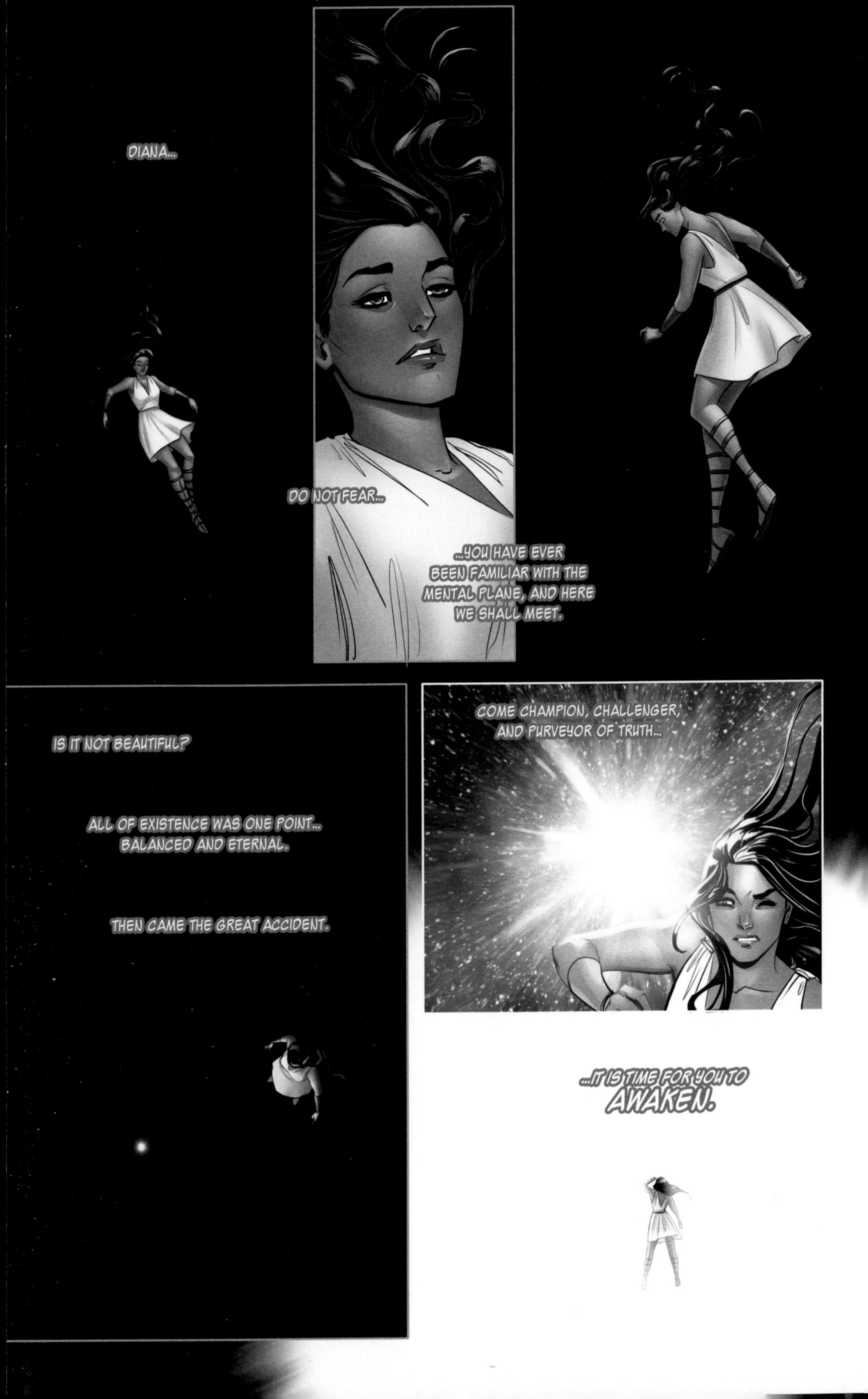
DIANA...
DO NOT FEAR...
...YOU HAVE EVER BEEN FAMILIAR WITH THE MENTAL PLANE, AND HERE WE SHALL MEET.
IS IT NOT BEAUTIFUL?
ALL OF EXISTENCE WAS ONE POINT... BALANCED AND ETERNAL.
THEN CAME THE GREAT ACCIDENT.
COME CHAMPION, CHALLENGER, AND PURVEYOR OF TRUTH...
...IT IS TIME FOR YOU TO AWAKEN.

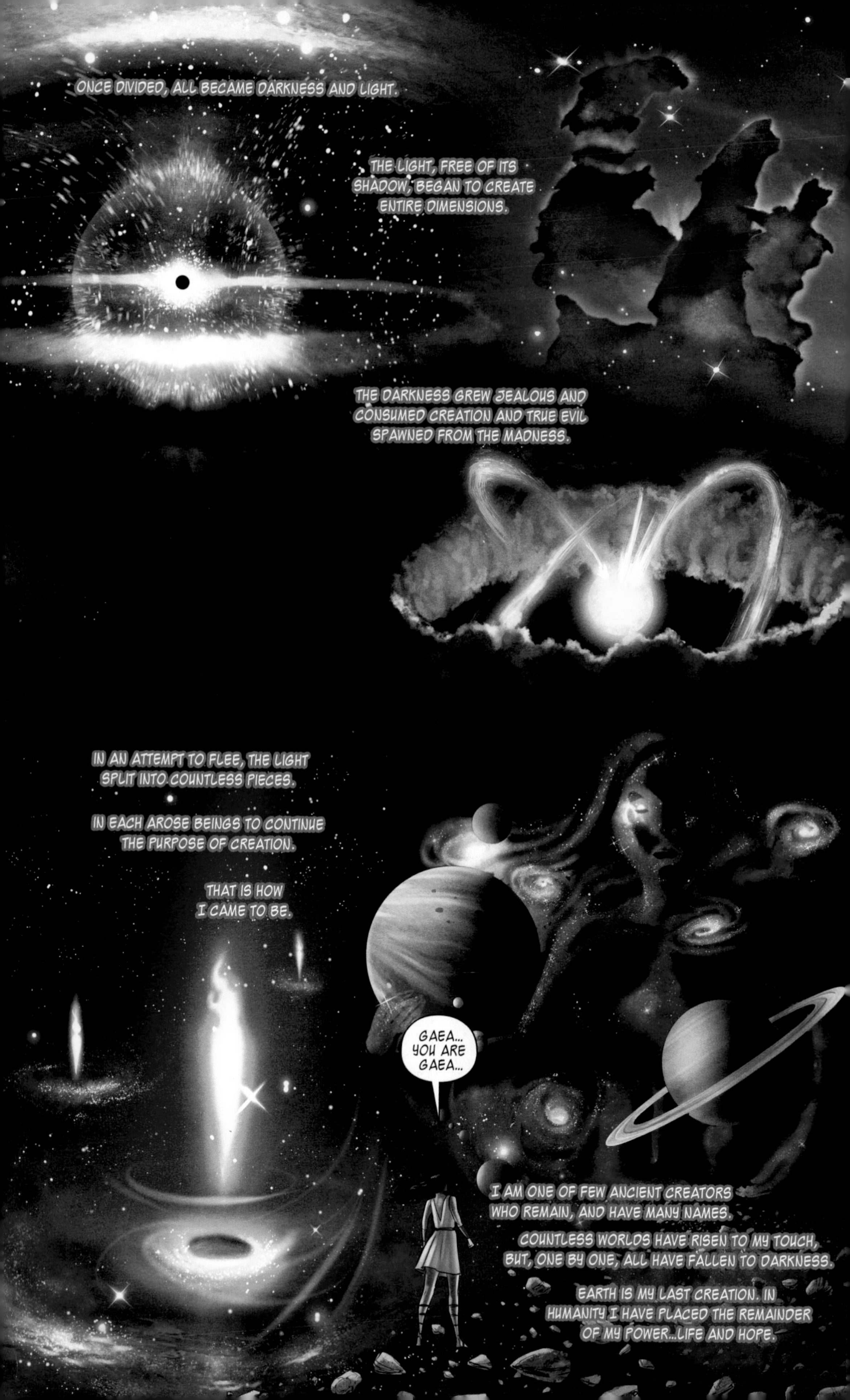

ONCE DIVIDED, ALL BECAME DARKNESS AND LIGHT.
THE LIGHT, FREE OF ITS SHADOW, BEGAN TO CREATE ENTIRE DIMENSIONS.
THE DARKNESS GREW JEALOUS AND CONSUMED CREATION AND TRUE EVIL SPAWNED FROM THE MADNESS.
IN AN ATTEMPT TO FLEE, THE LIGHT SPLIT INTO COUNTLESS PIECES.
IN EACH AROSE BEINGS TO CONTINUE THE PURPOSE OF CREATION.
THAT IS HOW I CAME TO BE.
GAEA... YOU ARE GAEA...
I AM ONE OF FEW ANCIENT CREATORS WHO REMAIN, AND HAVE MANY NAMES.
COUNTLESS WORLDS HAVE RISEN TO MY TOUCH, BUT, ONE BY ONE, ALL HAVE FALLEN TO DARKNESS.
EARTH IS MY LAST CREATION. IN HUMANITY I HAVE PLACED THE REMAINDER OF MY POWER...LIFE AND HOPE.

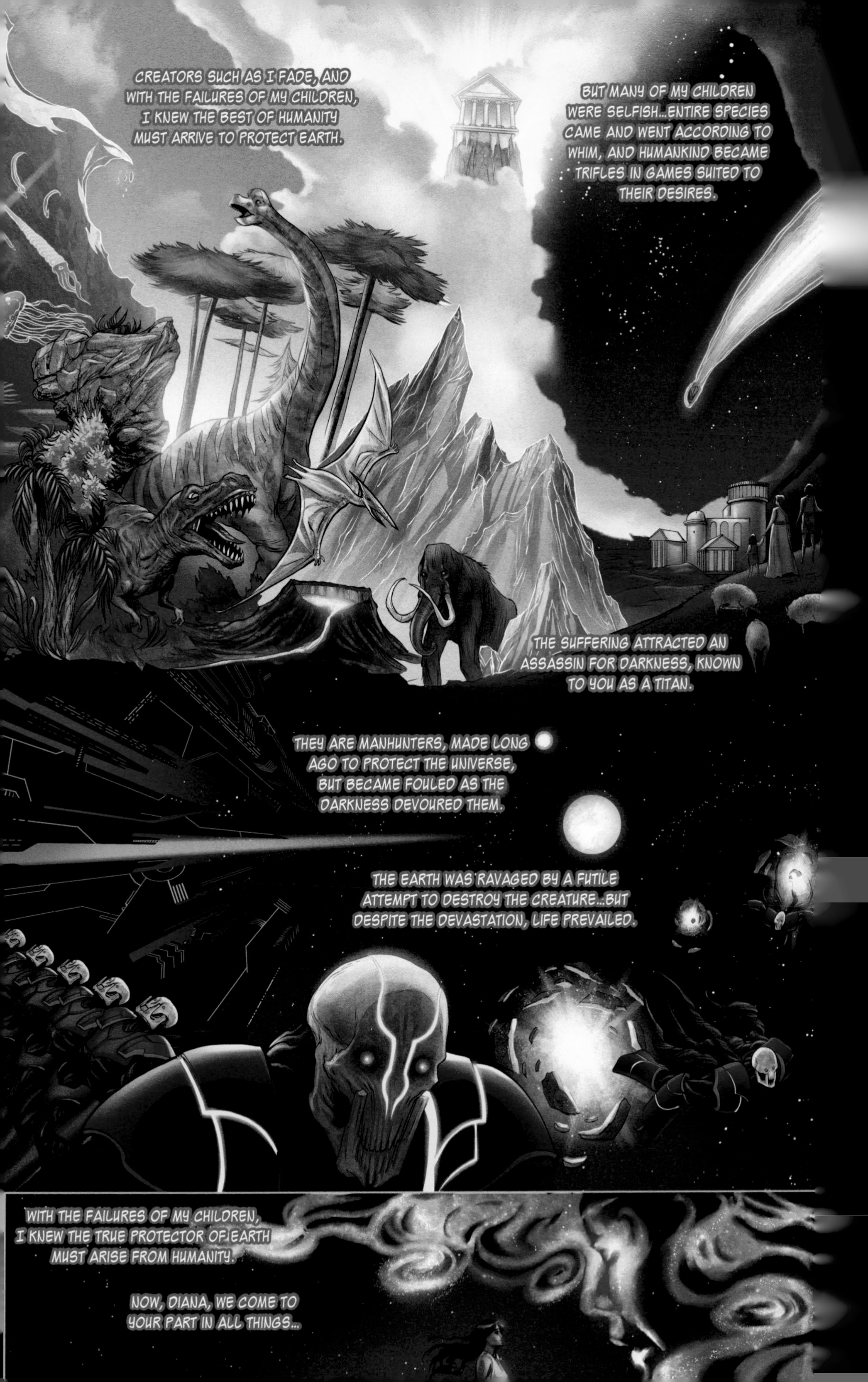
CREATORS SUCH AS I FADE, AND WITH THE FAILURES OF MY CHILDREN, I KNEW THE BEST OF HUMANITY MUST ARRIVE TO PROTECT EARTH.
BUT MANY OF MY CHILDREN WERE SELFISH...ENTIRE SPECIES CAME AND WENT ACCORDING TO WHIM, AND HUMANKIND BECAME TRIFLES IN GAMES SUITED TO THEIR DESIRES.
THE SUFFERING ATTRACTED AN ASSASSIN FOR DARKNESS, KNOWN TO YOU AS A TITAN.
THEY ARE MANHUNTERS, MADE LONG AGO TO PROTECT THE UNIVERSE, BUT BECAME FOULED AS THE DARKNESS DEVOURED THEM.
THE EARTH WAS RAVAGED BY A FUTILE ATTEMPT TO DESTROY THE CREATURE...BUT DESPITE THE DEVASTATION, LIFE PREVAILED.
WITH THE FAILURES OF MY CHILDREN, I KNEW THE TRUE PROTECTOR OF EARTH MUST ARISE FROM HUMANITY.
NOW, DIANA, WE COME TO YOUR PART IN ALL THINGS...

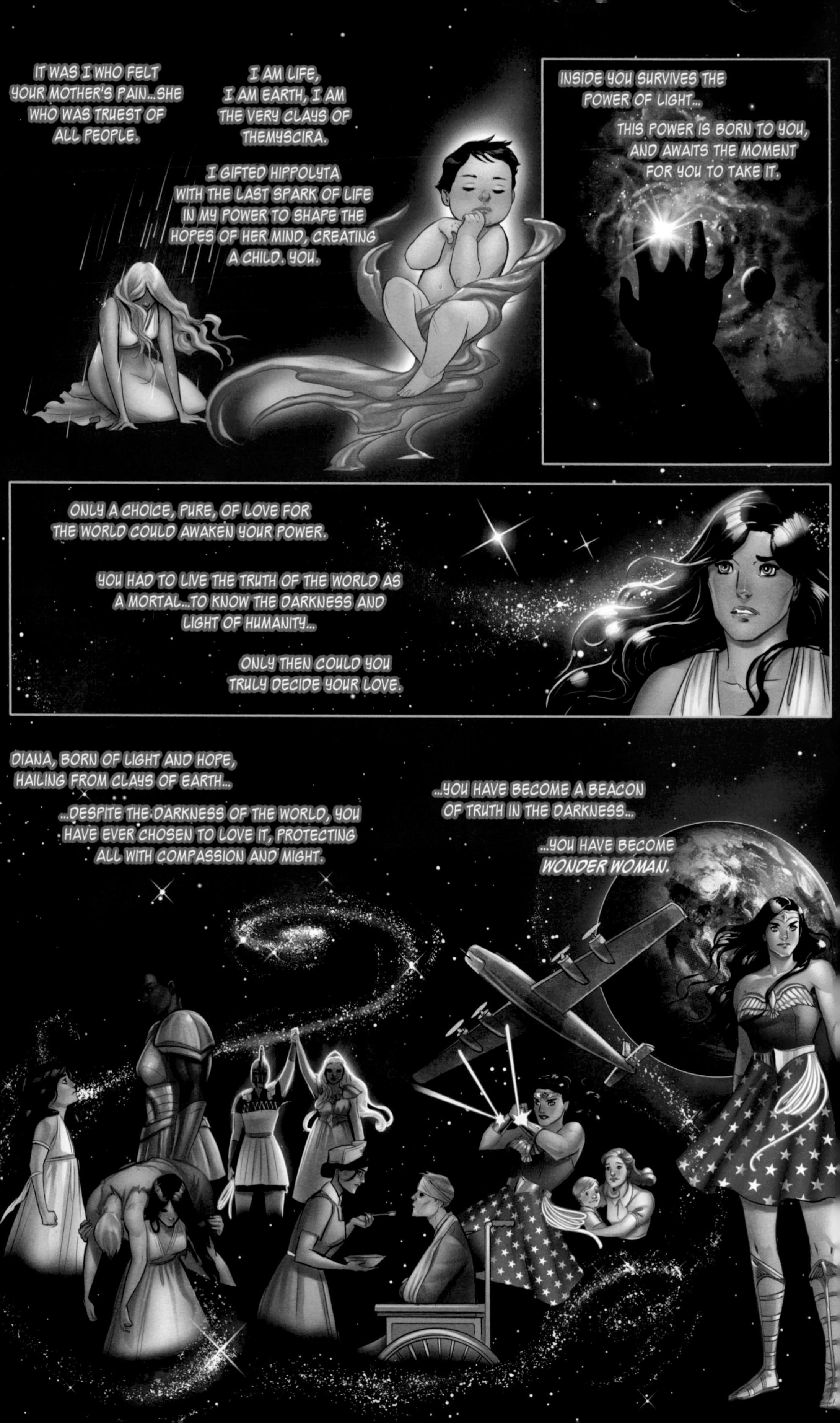
IT WAS I WHO FELT YOUR MOTHER'S PAIN...SHE WHO WAS TRUEST OF ALL PEOPLE.
I AM LIFE, I AM EARTH, I AM THE VERY CLAYS OF THEMYSCIRA.
I GIFTED HIPPOLYTA WITH THE LAST SPARK OF LIFE IN MY POWER TO SHAPE THE HOPES OF HER MIND, CREATING A CHILD. YOU.
INSIDE YOU SURVIVES THE POWER OF LIGHT...
THIS POWER IS BORN TO YOU, AND AWAITS THE MOMENT FOR YOU TO TAKE IT.
ONLY A CHOICE, PURE, OF LOVE FOR THE WORLD COULD AWAKEN YOUR POWER.
YOU HAD TO LIVE THE TRUTH OF THE WORLD AS A MORTAL...TO KNOW THE DARKNESS AND LIGHT OF HUMANITY...
ONLY THEN COULD YOU TRULY DECIDE YOUR LOVE.
DIANA, BORN OF LIGHT AND HOPE, HAILING FROM CLAYS OF EARTH...
...DESPITE THE DARKNESS OF THE WORLD, YOU HAVE EVER CHOSEN TO LOVE IT, PROTECTING ALL WITH COMPASSION AND MIGHT.
...YOU HAVE BECOME A BEACON OF TRUTH IN THE DARKNESS...
...YOU HAVE BECOME WONDER WOMAN.

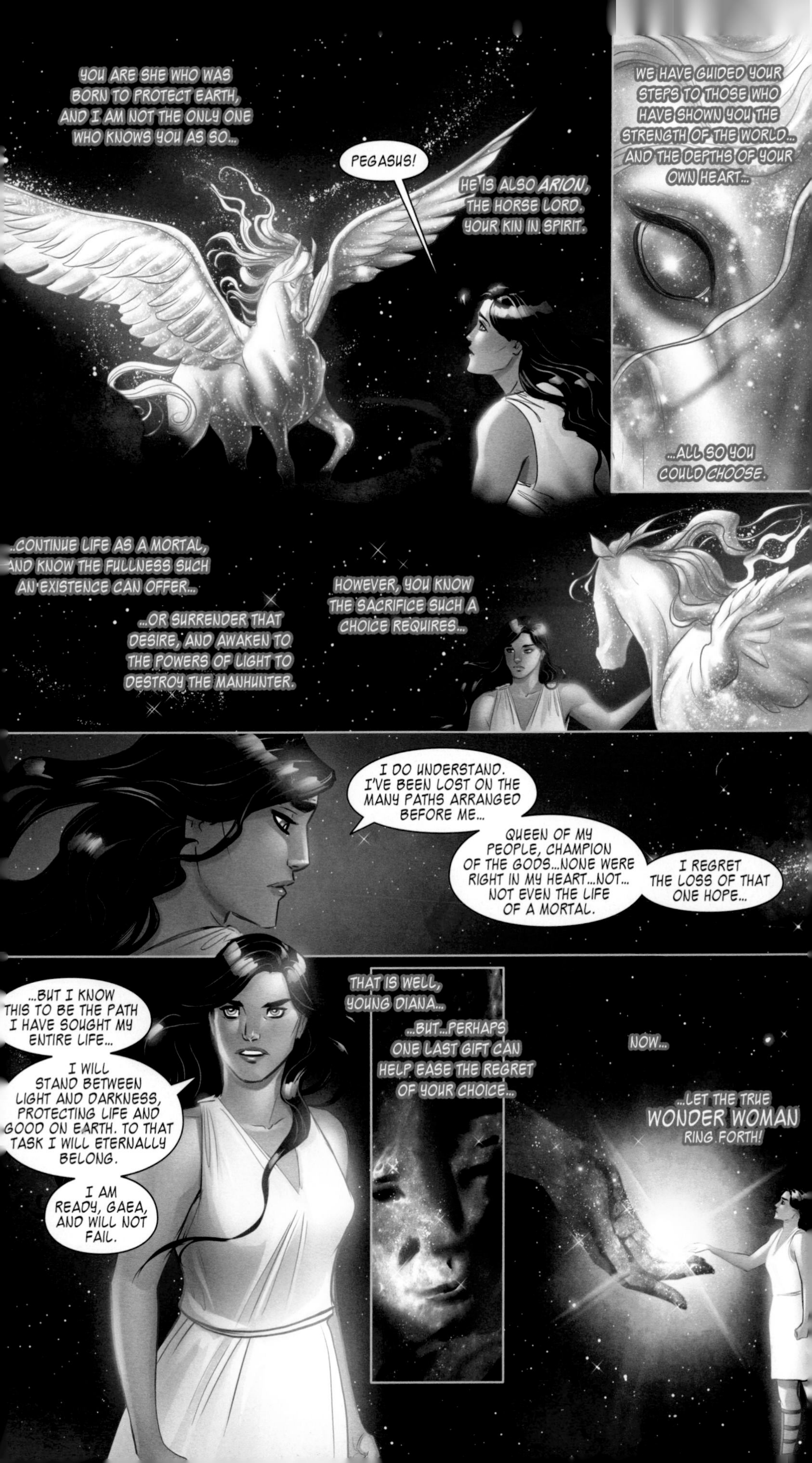
YOU ARE SHE WHO WAS BORN TO PROTECT EARTH, AND I AM NOT THE ONLY ONE WHO KNOWS YOU AS SO...
PEGASUS!
HE IS ALSO ARION, THE HORSE LORD. YOUR KIN IN SPIRIT.
WE HAVE GUIDED YOUR STEPS TO THOSE WHO HAVE SHOWN YOU THE STRENGTH OF THE WORLD... AND THE DEPTHS OF YOUR OWN HEART...
...ALL SO YOU COULD CHOOSE.
..CONTINUE LIFE AS A MORTAL, AND KNOW THE FULLNESS SUCH AN EXISTENCE CAN OFFER...
...OR SURRENDER THAT DESIRE, AND AWAKEN TO THE POWERS OF LIGHT TO DESTROY THE MANHUNTER.
HOWEVER, YOU KNOW THE SACRIFICE SUCH A CHOICE REQUIRES...
I DO UNDERSTAND. I'VE BEEN LOST ON THE MANY PATHS ARRANGED BEFORE ME...
QUEEN OF MY PEOPLE, CHAMPION OF THE GODS...NONE WERE RIGHT IN MY HEART...NOT... NOT EVEN THE LIFE OF A MORTAL.
I REGRET THE LOSS OF THAT ONE HOPE...
...BUT I KNOW THIS TO BE THE PATH I HAVE SOUGHT MY ENTIRE LIFE...
I WILL STAND BETWEEN LIGHT AND DARKNESS, PROTECTING LIFE AND GOOD ON EARTH. TO THAT TASK I WILL ETERNALLY BELONG.
I AM READY, GAEA, AND WILL NOT FAIL.
THAT IS WELL, YOUNG DIANA...
...BUT...PERHAPS ONE LAST GIFT CAN HELP EASE THE REGRET OF YOUR CHOICE...
NOW...
...LET THE TRUE WONDER WOMAN RING FORTH!

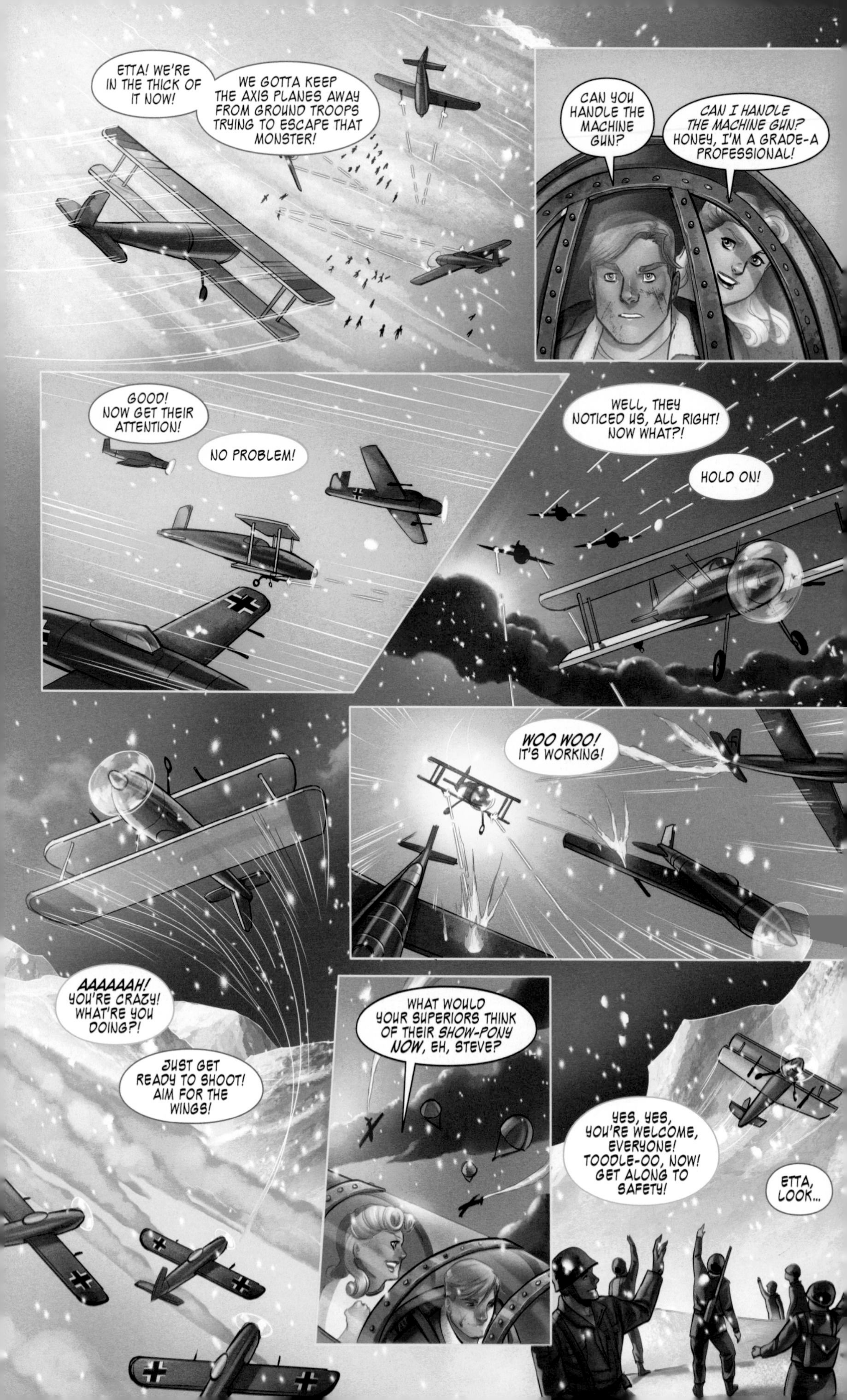
ETTA! WE'RE IN THE THICK OF IT NOW!
WE GOTTA KEEP THE AXIS PLANES AWAY FROM GROUND TROOPS TRYING TO ESCAPE THAT MONSTER!
CAN YOU HANDLE THE MACHINE GUN?
CAN I HANDLE THE MACHINE GUN? HONEY, I'M A GRADE-A PROFESSIONAL!
GOOD! NOW GET THEIR ATTENTION!
NO PROBLEM!
WELL, THEY NOTICED US, ALL RIGHT! NOW WHAT?!
HOLD ON!
WOO WOO! IT'S WORKING!
AAAAAAH! YOU'RE CRAZY! WHAT'RE YOU DOING?!
JUST GET READY TO SHOOT! AIM FOR THE WINGS!
WHAT WOULD YOUR SUPERIORS THINK OF THEIR SHOW-PONY NOW, EH, STEVE?
YES, YES, YOU'RE WELCOME, EVERYONE! TOODLE-OO, NOW! GET ALONG TO SAFETY!
ETTA, LOOK...

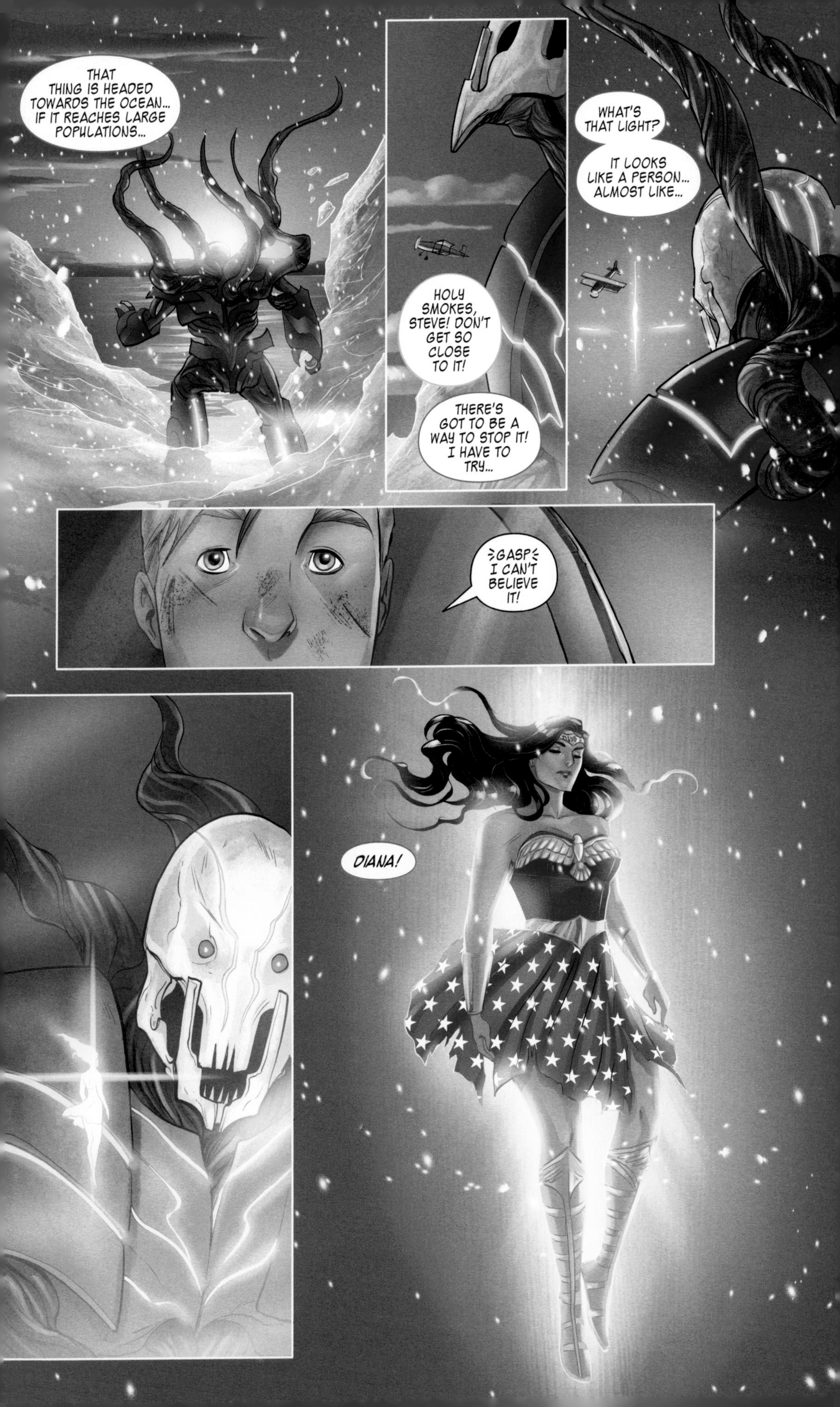
THAT THING IS HEADED TOWARDS THE OCEAN... IF IT REACHES LARGE POPULATIONS...
HOLY SMOKES, STEVE! DON'T GET SO CLOSE TO IT!
THERE'S GOT TO BE A WAY TO STOP IT! I HAVE TO TRY...
WHAT'S THAT LIGHT?
IT LOOKS LIKE A PERSON... ALMOST LIKE...
GASP I CAN'T BELIEVE IT!
DIANA!

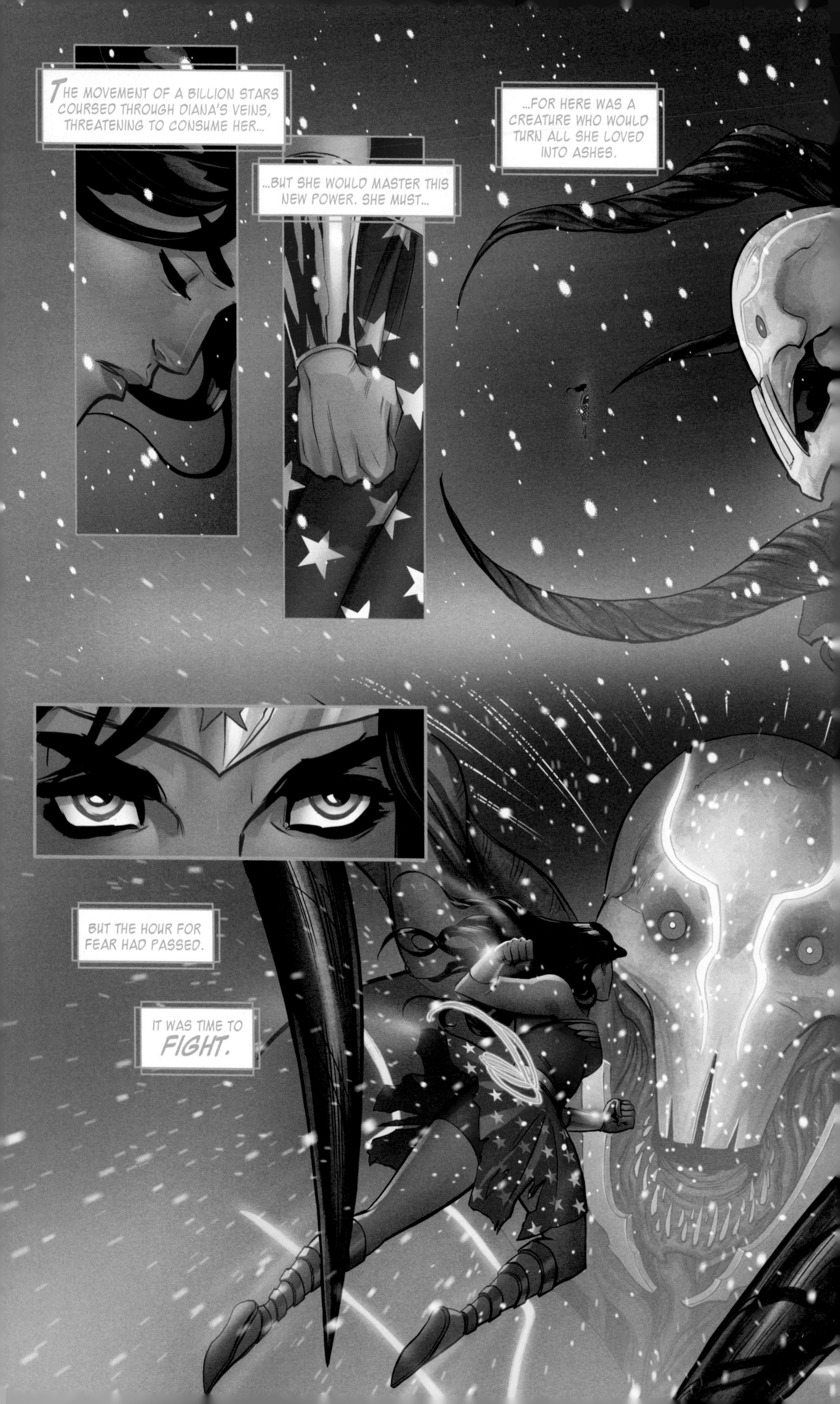
THE MOVEMENT OF A BILLION STARS COURSED THROUGH DIANA'S VEINS, THREATENING TO CONSUME HER...
...BUT SHE WOULD MASTER THIS NEW POWER. SHE MUST...
...FOR HERE WAS A CREATURE WHO WOULD TURN ALL SHE LOVED INTO ASHES.
BUT THE HOUR FOR FEAR HAD PASSED.
IT WAS TIME TO FIGHT.

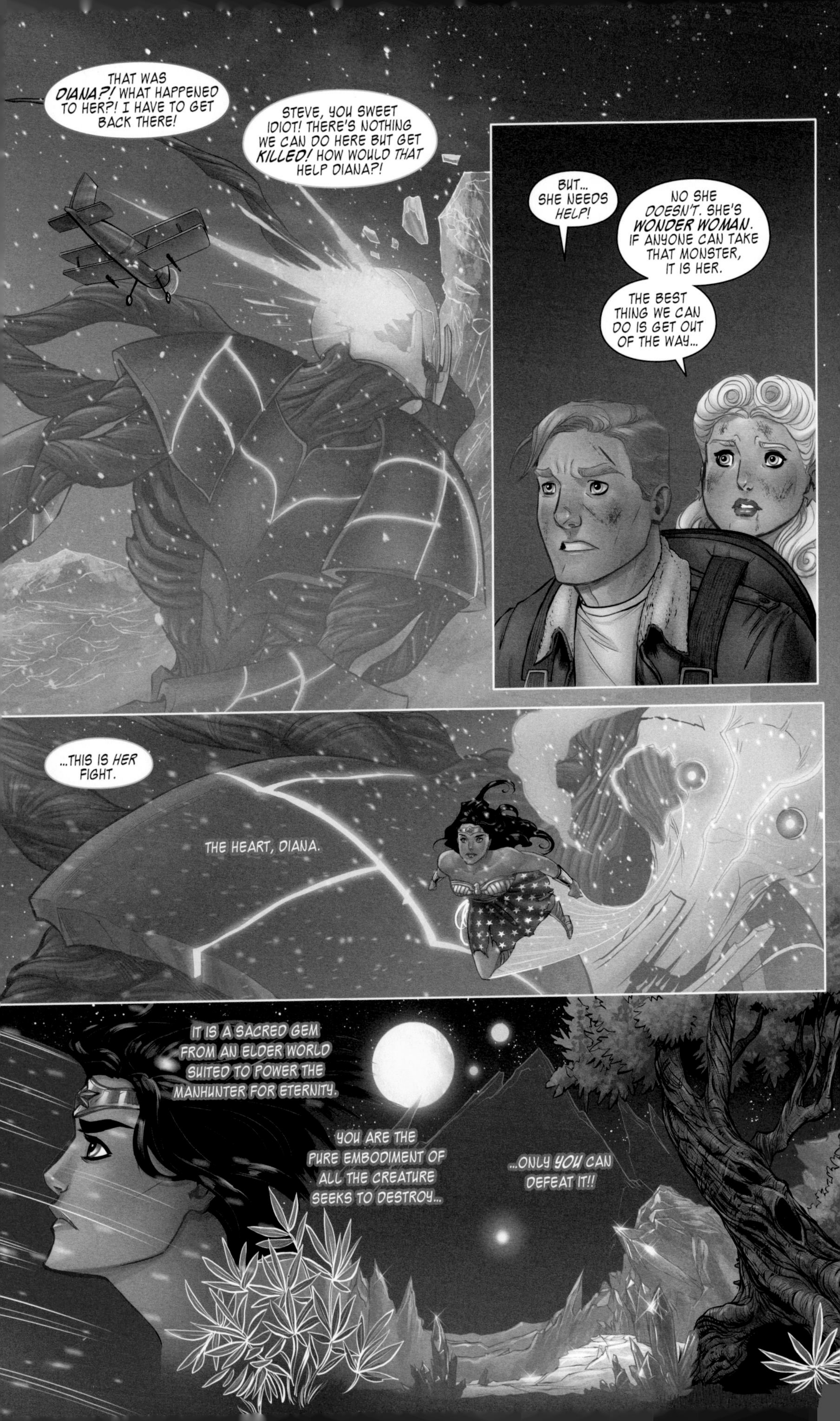

THAT WAS DIANA?! WHAT HAPPENED TO HER?! I HAVE TO GET BACK THERE!
STEVE, YOU SWEET IDIOT! THERE'S NOTHING WE CAN DO HERE BUT GET KILLED! HOW WOULD THAT HELP DIANA?!
BUT... SHE NEEDS HELP!
NO SHE DOESN'T. SHE'S WONDER WOMAN. IF ANYONE CAN TAKE THAT MONSTER, IT IS HER.
THE BEST THING WE CAN DO IS GET OUT OF THE WAY...
...THIS IS HER FIGHT.
THE HEART, DIANA.
IT IS A SACRED GEM FROM AN ELDER WORLD SUITED TO POWER THE MANHUNTER FOR ETERNITY.
YOU ARE THE PURE EMBODIMENT OF ALL THE CREATURE SEEKS TO DESTROY...
...ONLY YOU CAN DEFEAT IT!!

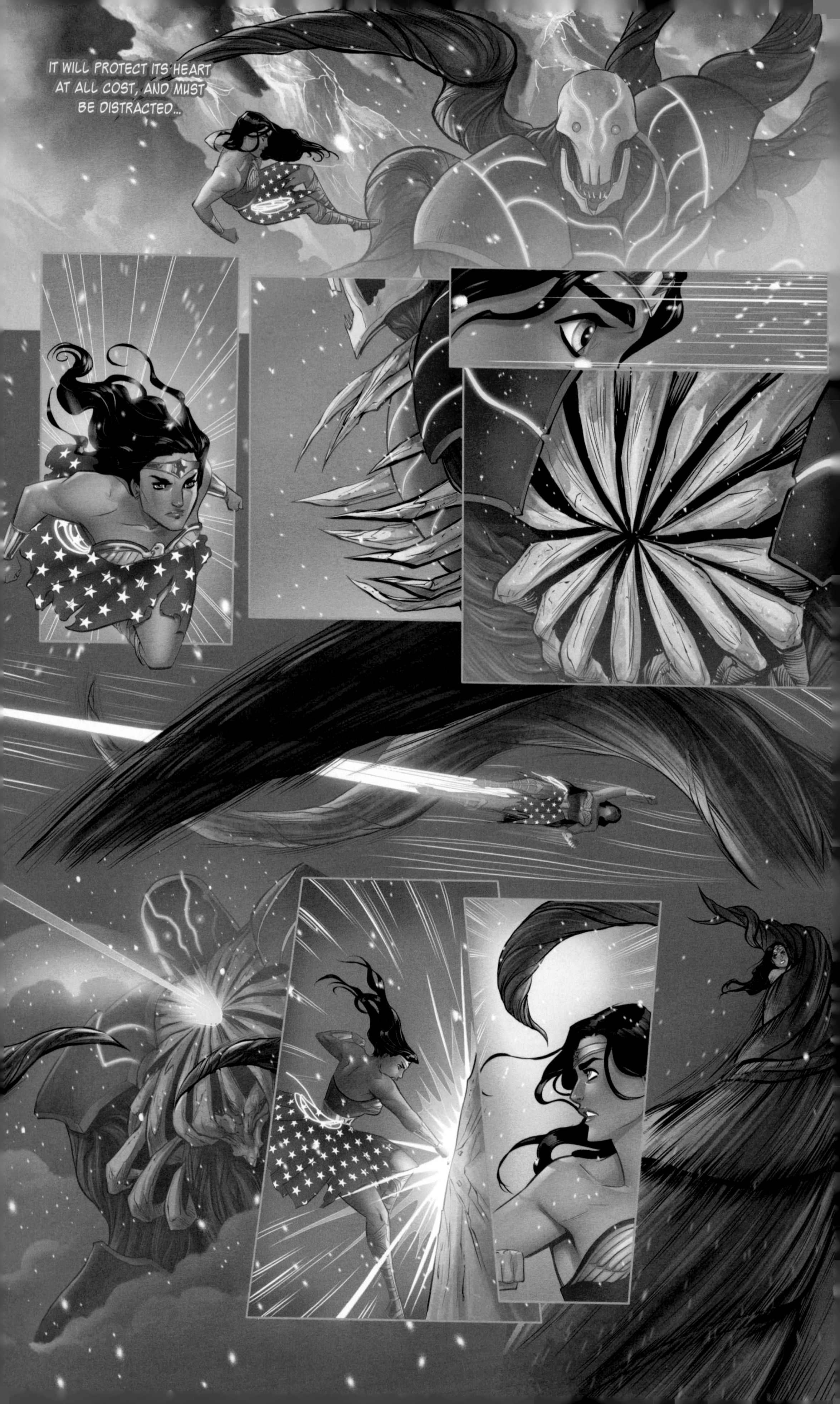
IT WILL PROTECT ITS HEART AT ALL COST, AND MUST BE DISTRACTED...

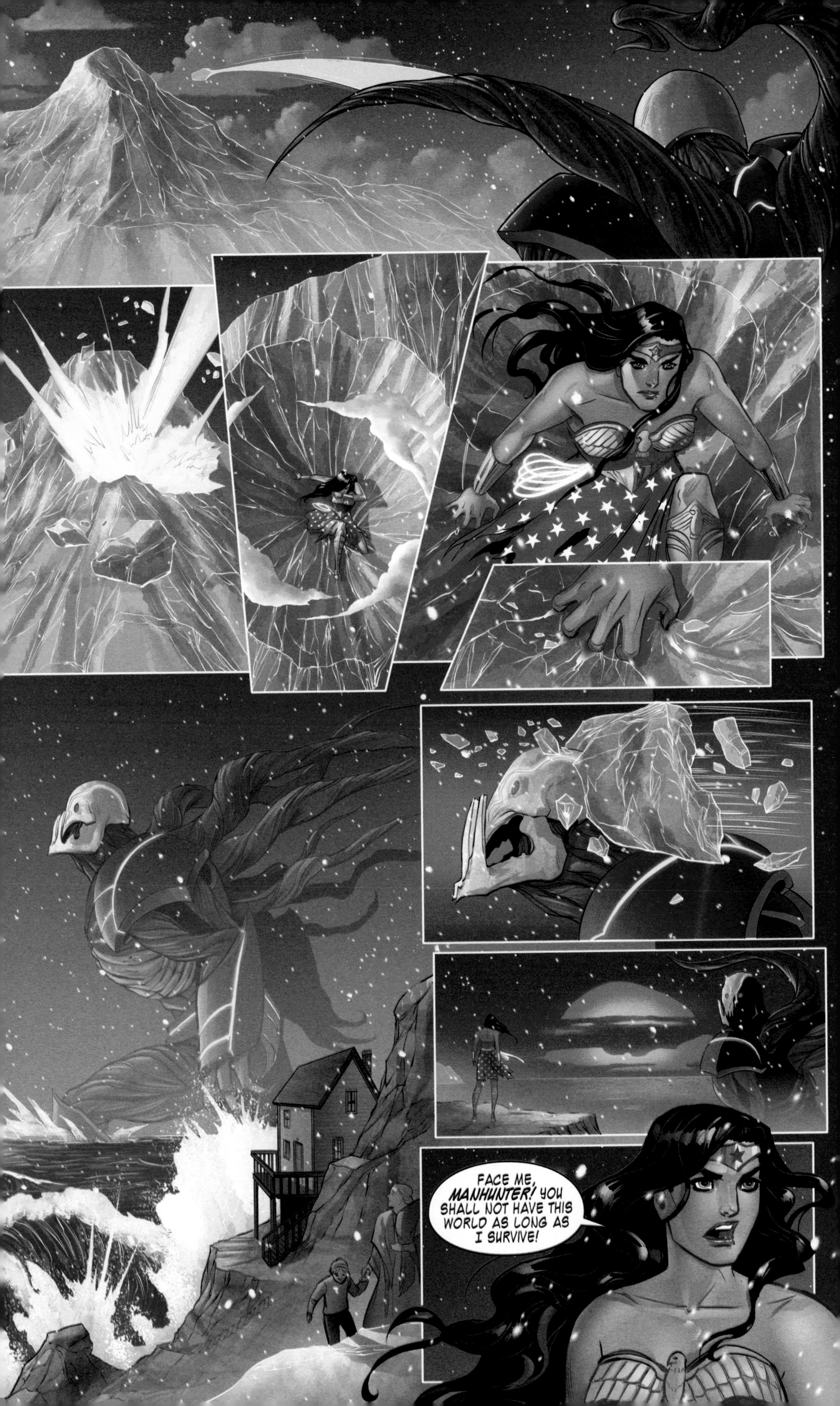
FACE ME, MANHUNTER! YOU SHALL NOT HAVE THIS WORLD AS LONG AS I SURVIVE!

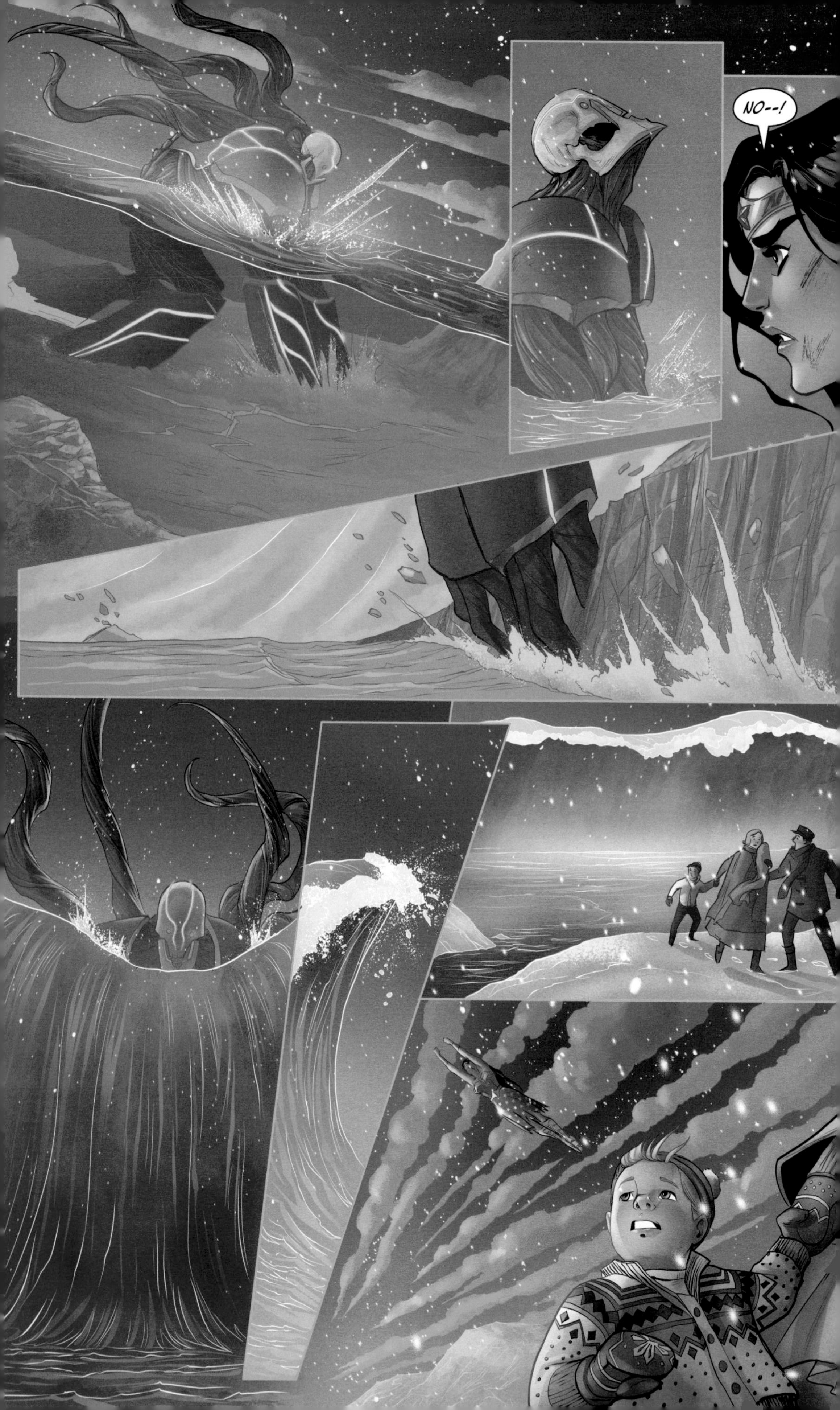
NO--!

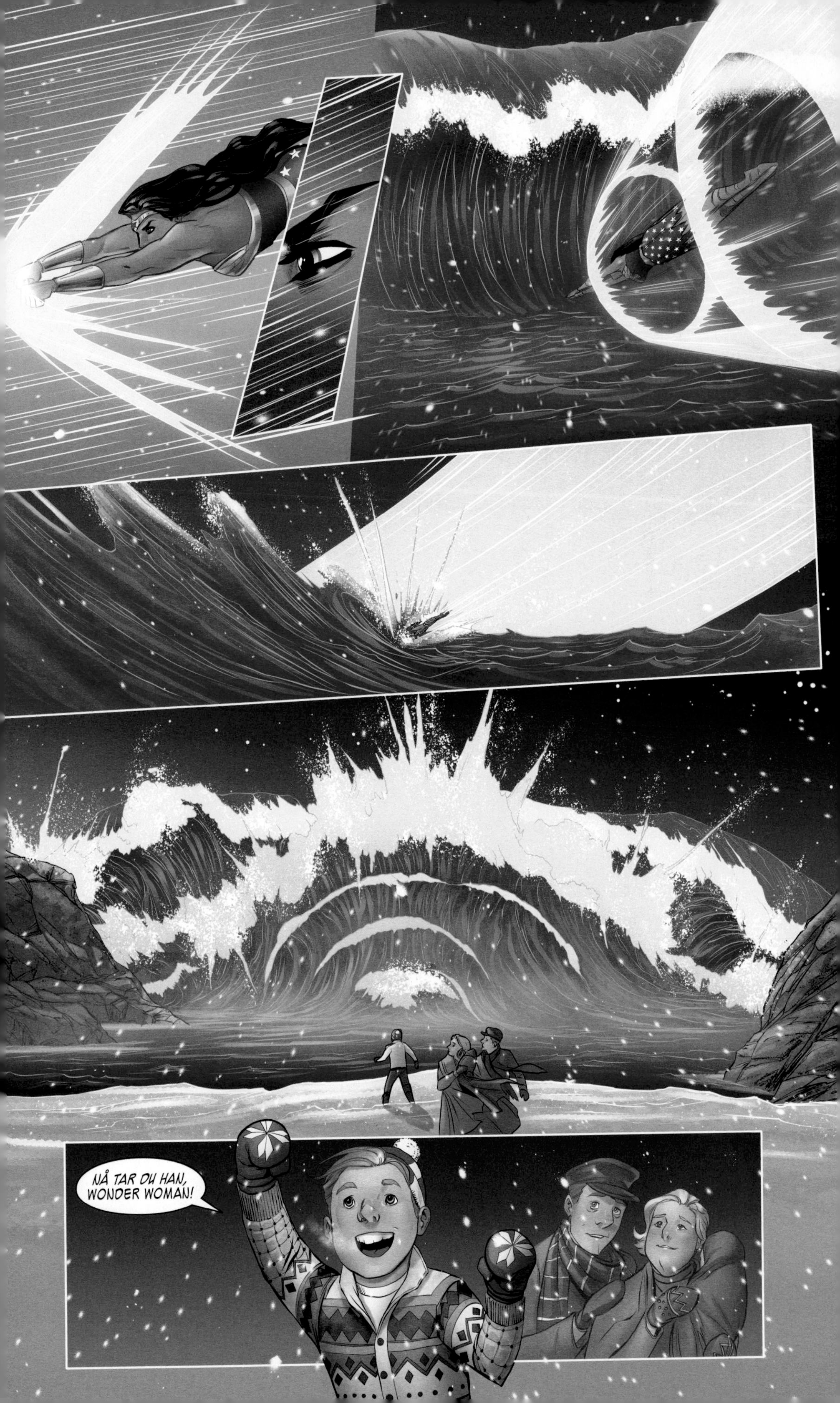
NÅ TAR DU HAN,
WONDER WOMAN!

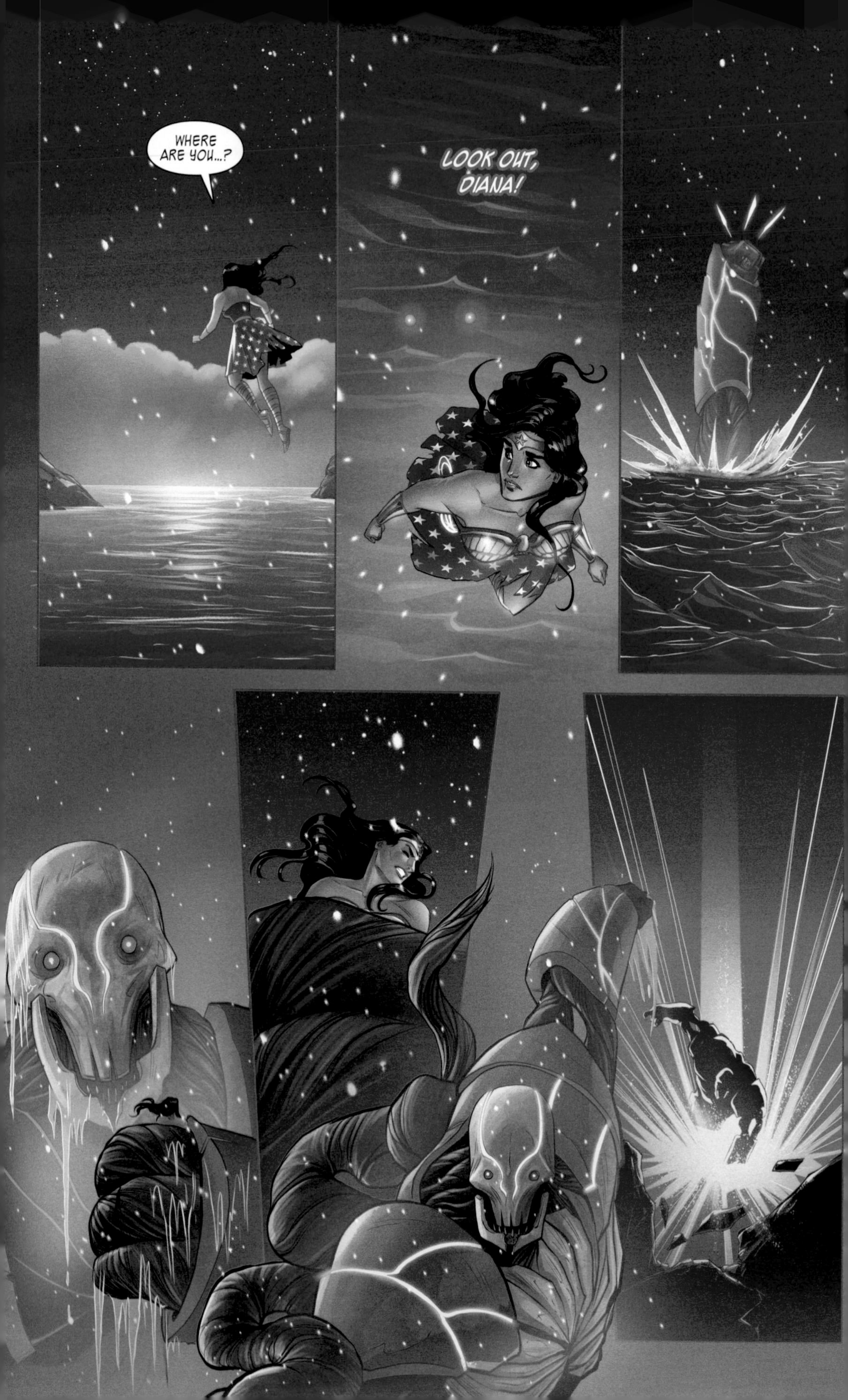
WHERE ARE YOU...?
LOOK OUT, DIANA!

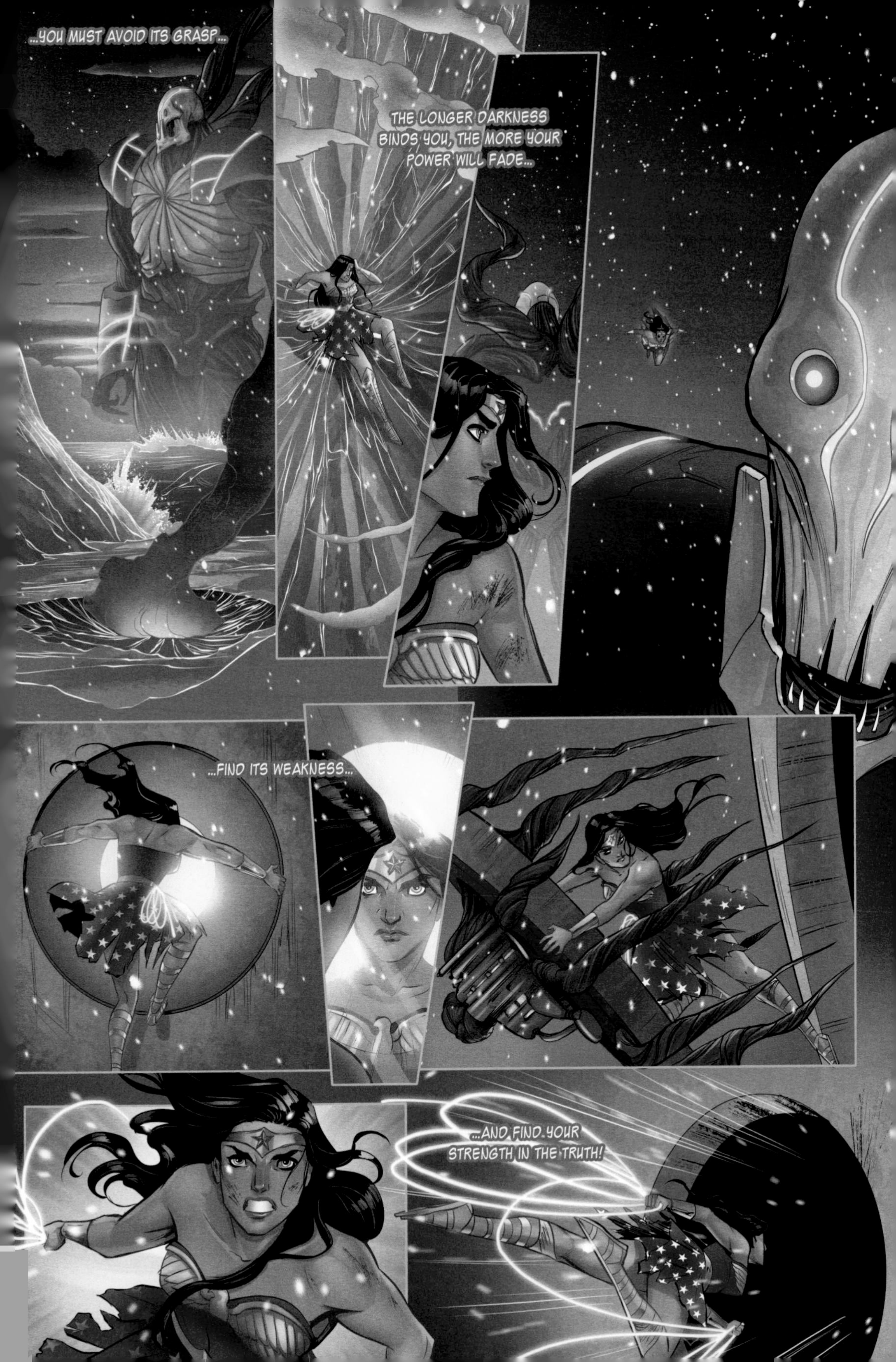
...YOU MUST AVOID ITS GRASP...
THE LONGER DARKNESS BINDS YOU, THE MORE YOUR POWER WILL FADE...
...FIND ITS WEAKNESS...
...AND FIND YOUR STRENGTH IN THE TRUTH!

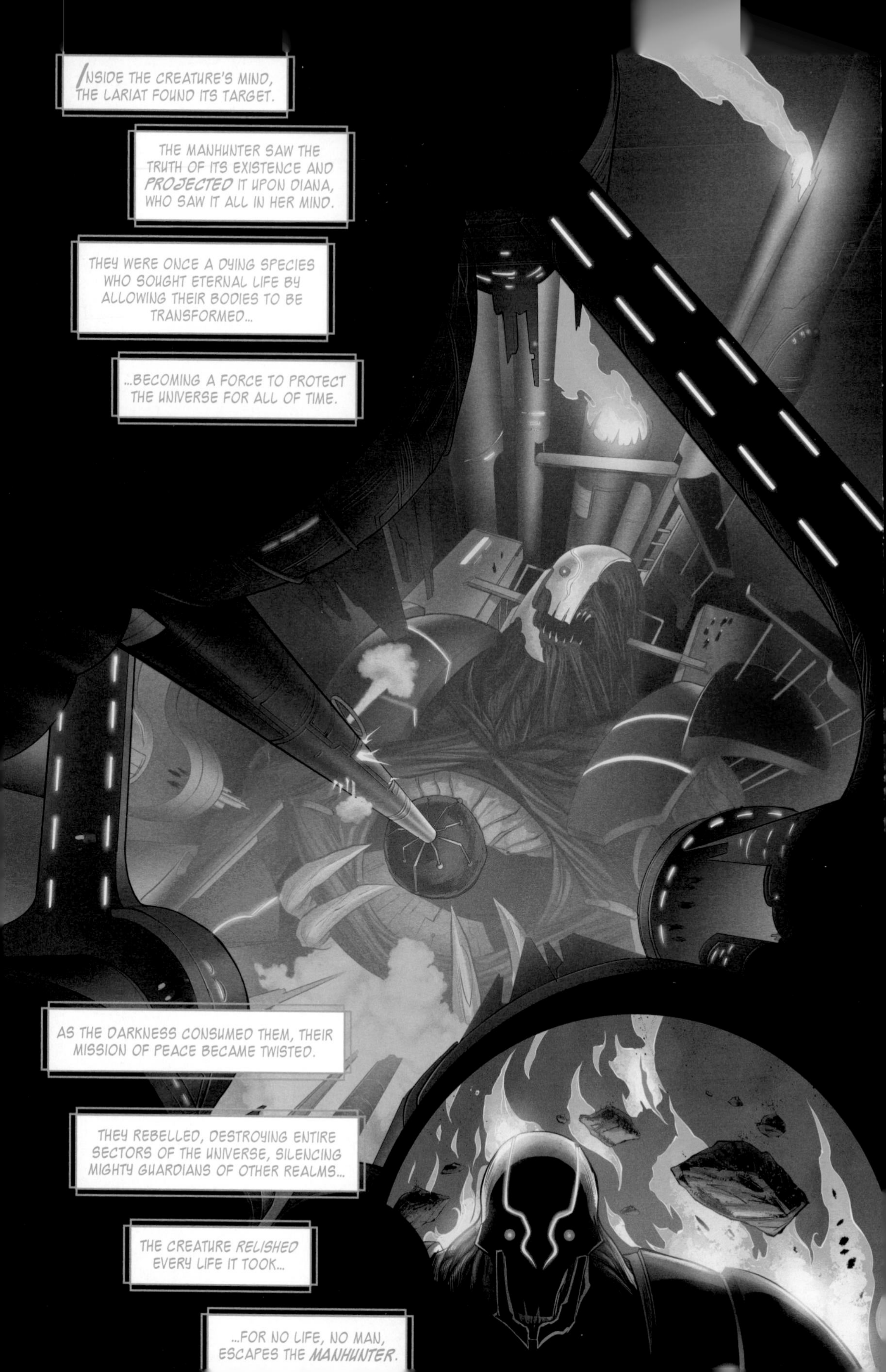
INSIDE THE CREATURE'S MIND, THE LARIAT FOUND ITS TARGET.
THE MANHUNTER SAW THE TRUTH OF ITS EXISTENCE AND *PROJECTED* IT UPON DIANA, WHO SAW IT ALL IN HER MIND.
THEY WERE ONCE A DYING SPECIES WHO SOUGHT ETERNAL LIFE BY ALLOWING THEIR BODIES TO BE TRANSFORMED...
...BECOMING A FORCE TO PROTECT THE UNIVERSE FOR ALL OF TIME.
AS THE DARKNESS CONSUMED THEM, THEIR MISSION OF PEACE BECAME TWISTED.
THEY REBELLED, DESTROYING ENTIRE SECTORS OF THE UNIVERSE, SILENCING MIGHTY GUARDIANS OF OTHER REALMS...
THE CREATURE *RELISHED* EVERY LIFE IT TOOK...
...FOR NO LIFE, NO MAN, ESCAPES THE *MANHUNTER*.

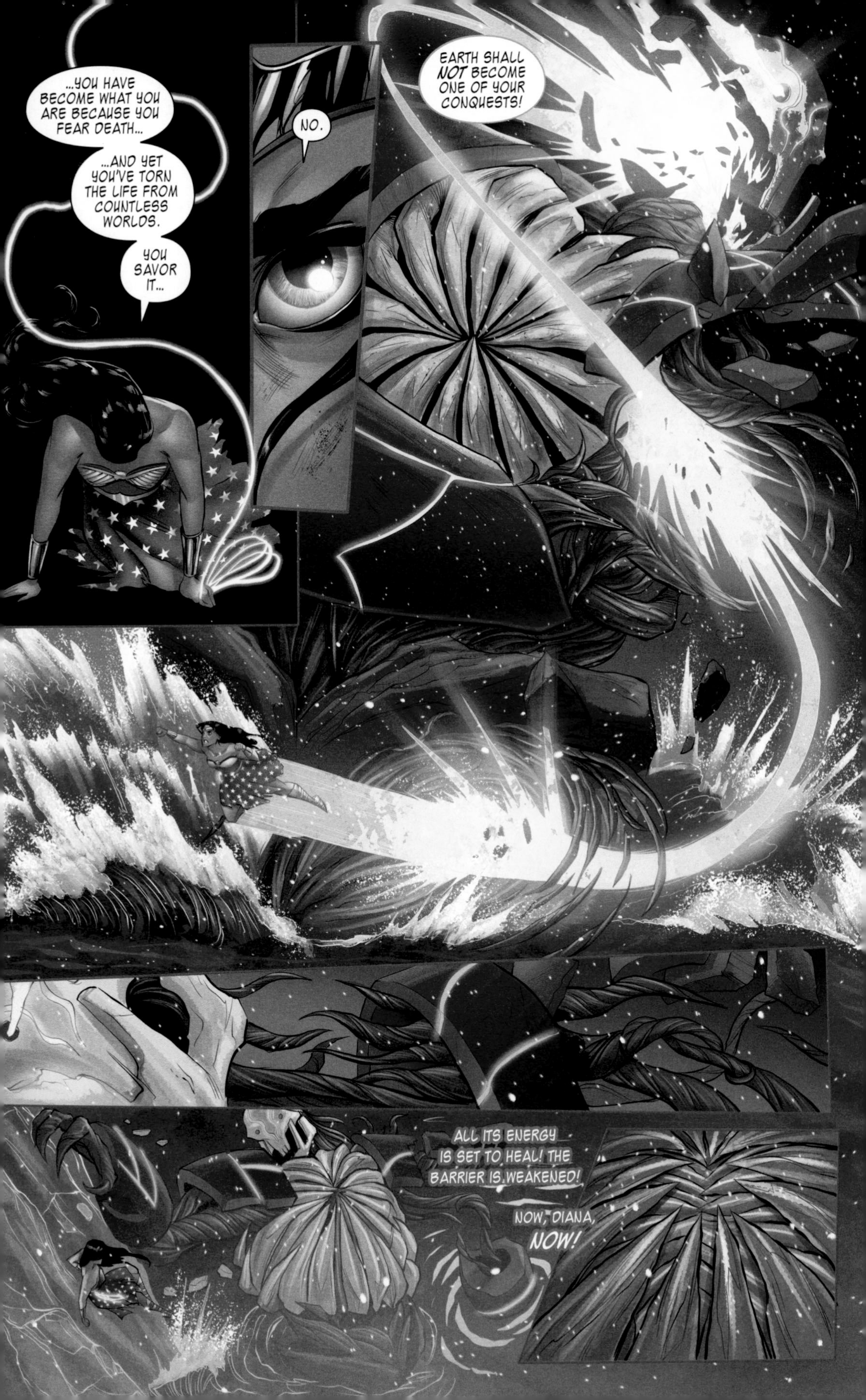
...YOU HAVE BECOME WHAT YOU ARE BECAUSE YOU FEAR DEATH...
...AND YET YOU'VE TORN THE LIFE FROM COUNTLESS WORLDS.
YOU SAVOR IT...
NO.
EARTH SHALL NOT BECOME ONE OF YOUR CONQUESTS!
ALL ITS ENERGY IS SET TO HEAL! THE BARRIER IS WEAKENED!
NOW, DIANA, NOW!

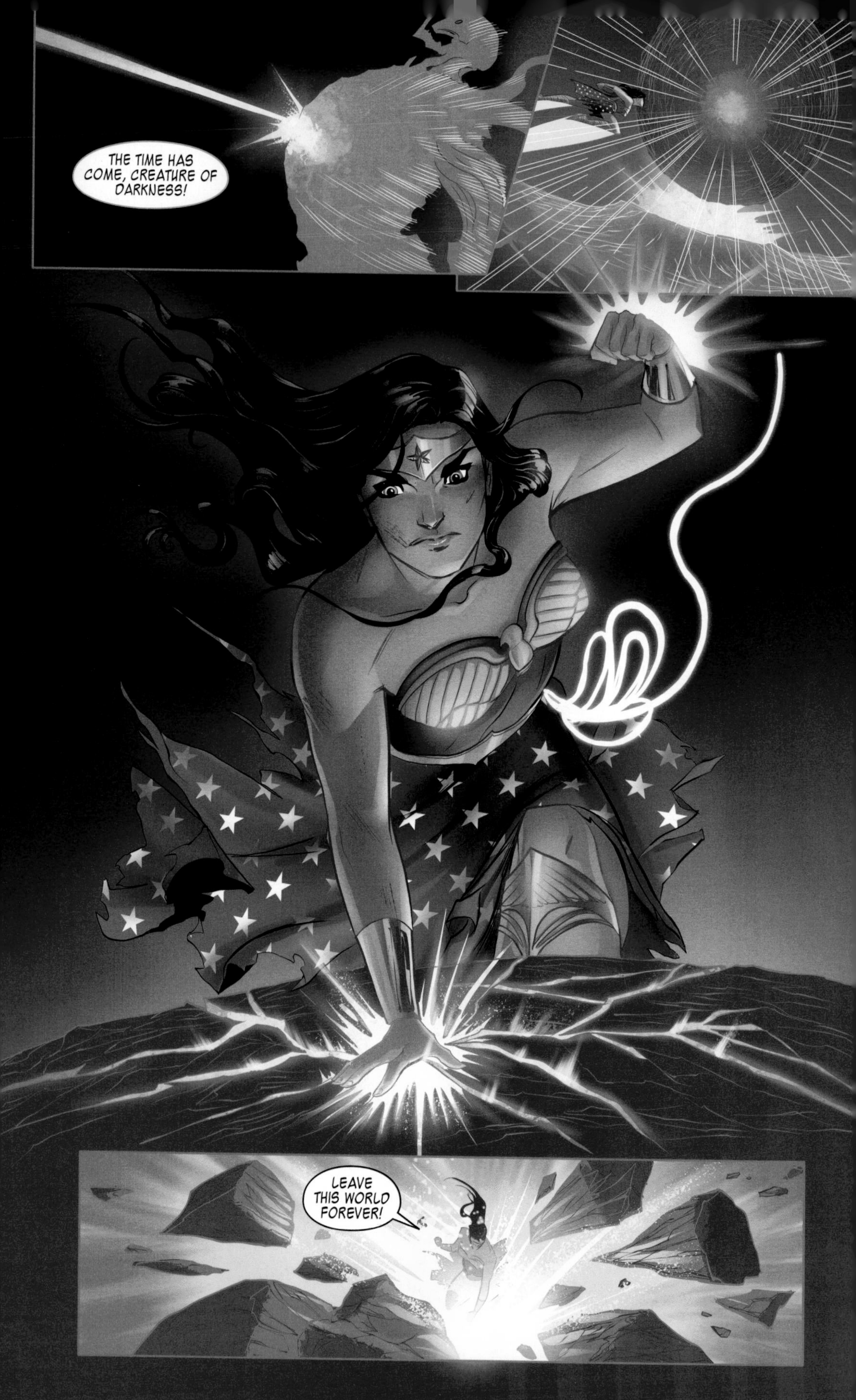
THE TIME HAS COME, CREATURE OF DARKNESS!
LEAVE THIS WORLD FOREVER!

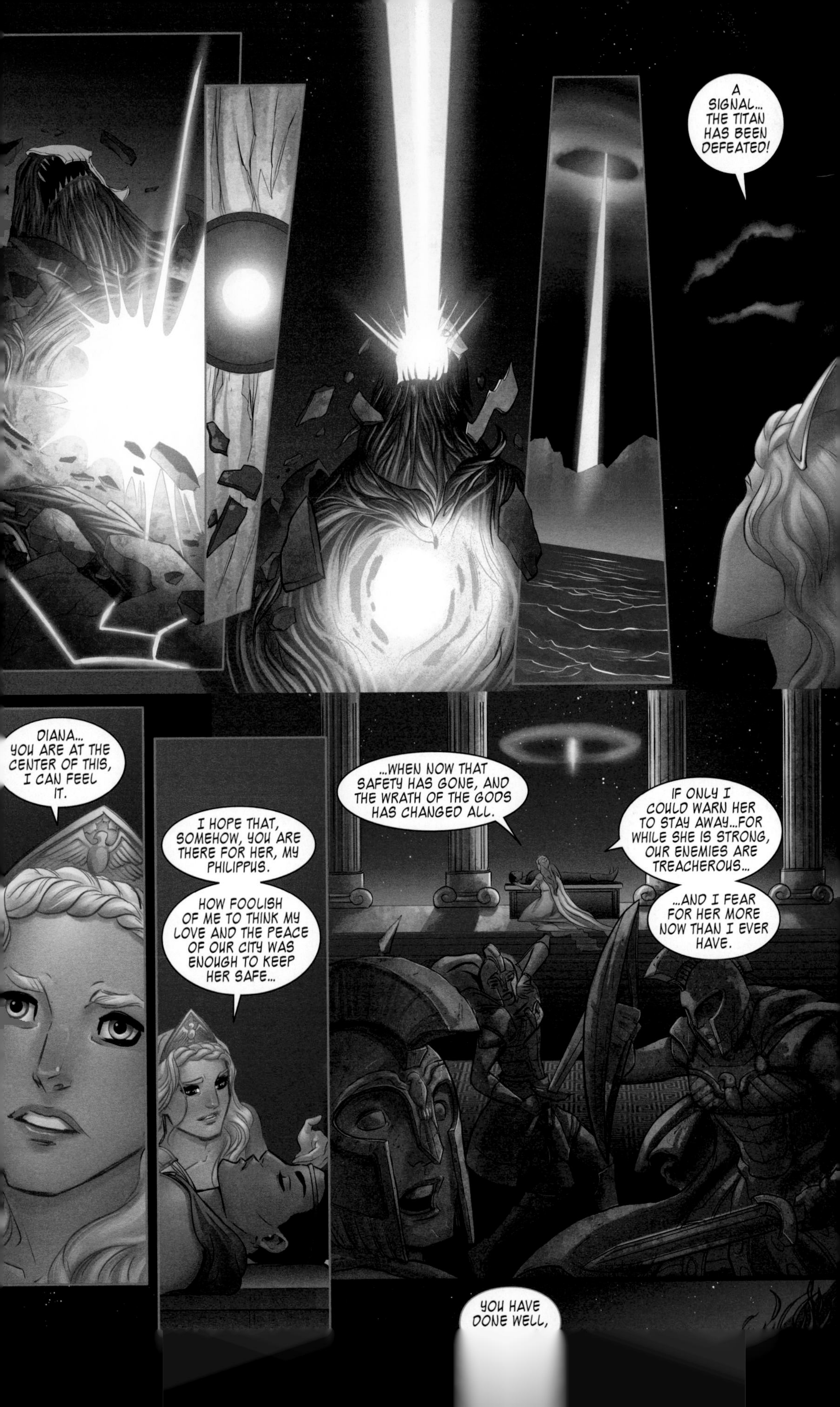
A SIGNAL... THE TITAN HAS BEEN DEFEATED!
DIANA... YOU ARE AT THE CENTER OF THIS, I CAN FEEL IT.
I HOPE THAT, SOMEHOW, YOU ARE THERE FOR HER, MY PHILIPPUS.
HOW FOOLISH OF ME TO THINK MY LOVE AND THE PEACE OF OUR CITY WAS ENOUGH TO KEEP HER SAFE...
...WHEN NOW THAT SAFETY HAS GONE, AND THE WRATH OF THE GODS HAS CHANGED ALL.
IF ONLY I COULD WARN HER TO STAY AWAY...FOR WHILE SHE IS STRONG, OUR ENEMIES ARE TREACHEROUS...
...AND I FEAR FOR HER MORE NOW THAN I EVER HAVE.
YOU HAVE DONE WELL,

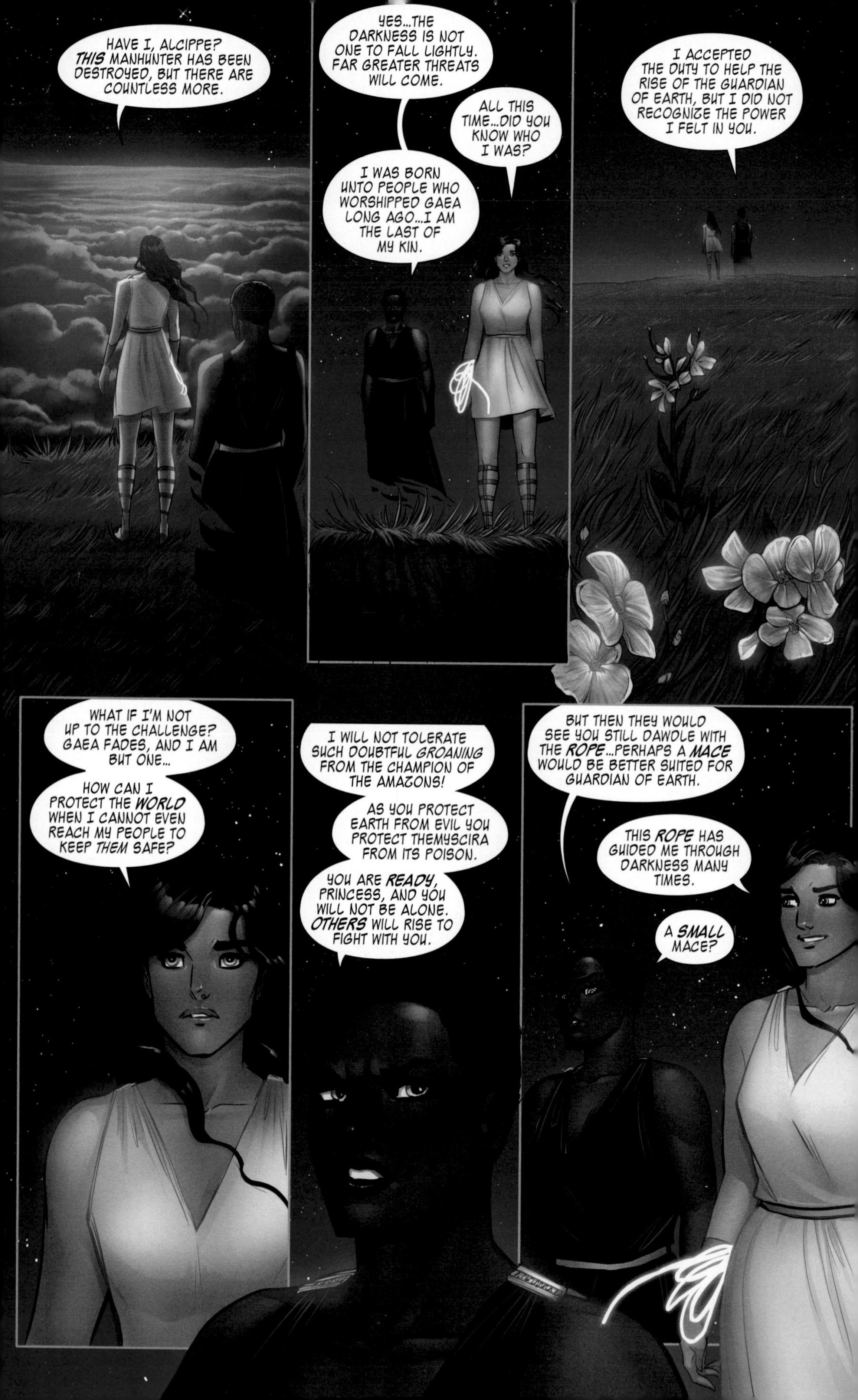

HAVE I, ALCIPPE? THIS MANHUNTER HAS BEEN DESTROYED, BUT THERE ARE COUNTLESS MORE.
YES...THE DARKNESS IS NOT ONE TO FALL LIGHTLY. FAR GREATER THREATS WILL COME.
ALL THIS TIME...DID YOU KNOW WHO I WAS?
I WAS BORN UNTO PEOPLE WHO WORSHIPPED GAEA LONG AGO...I AM THE LAST OF MY KIN.
I ACCEPTED THE DUTY TO HELP THE RISE OF THE GUARDIAN OF EARTH, BUT I DID NOT RECOGNIZE THE POWER I FELT IN YOU.
WHAT IF I'M NOT UP TO THE CHALLENGE? GAEA FADES, AND I AM BUT ONE...
HOW CAN I PROTECT THE WORLD WHEN I CANNOT EVEN REACH MY PEOPLE TO KEEP THEM SAFE?
I WILL NOT TOLERATE SUCH DOUBTFUL GROANING FROM THE CHAMPION OF THE AMAZONS!
AS YOU PROTECT EARTH FROM EVIL YOU PROTECT THEMYSCIRA FROM ITS POISON.
YOU ARE READY, PRINCESS, AND YOU WILL NOT BE ALONE. OTHERS WILL RISE TO FIGHT WITH YOU.
BUT THEN THEY WOULD SEE YOU STILL DAWDLE WITH THE ROPE...PERHAPS A MACE WOULD BE BETTER SUITED FOR GUARDIAN OF EARTH.
THIS ROPE HAS GUIDED ME THROUGH DARKNESS MANY TIMES.
A SMALL MACE?

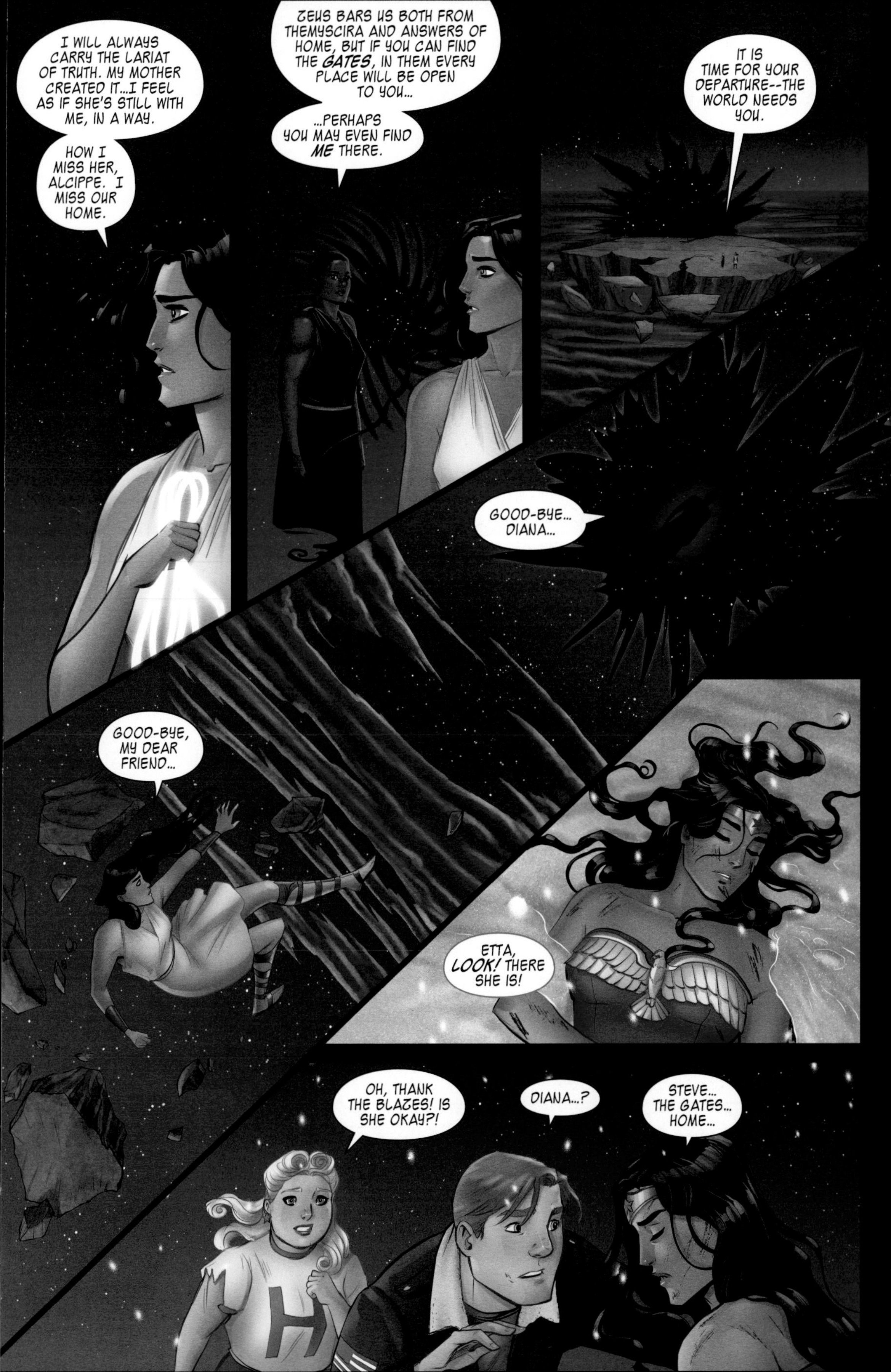
I WILL ALWAYS CARRY THE LARIAT OF TRUTH. MY MOTHER CREATED IT...I FEEL AS IF SHE'S STILL WITH ME, IN A WAY.
HOW I MISS HER, ALCIPPE. I MISS OUR HOME.
ZEUS BARS US BOTH FROM THEMYSCIRA AND ANSWERS OF HOME, BUT IF YOU CAN FIND THE GATES, IN THEM EVERY PLACE WILL BE OPEN TO YOU...
...PERHAPS YOU MAY EVEN FIND ME THERE.
IT IS TIME FOR YOUR DEPARTURE--THE WORLD NEEDS YOU.
GOOD-BYE... DIANA...
GOOD-BYE, MY DEAR FRIEND...
ETTA, LOOK! THERE SHE IS!
OH, THANK THE BLAZES! IS SHE OKAY?!
DIANA...?
STEVE... THE GATES... HOME...

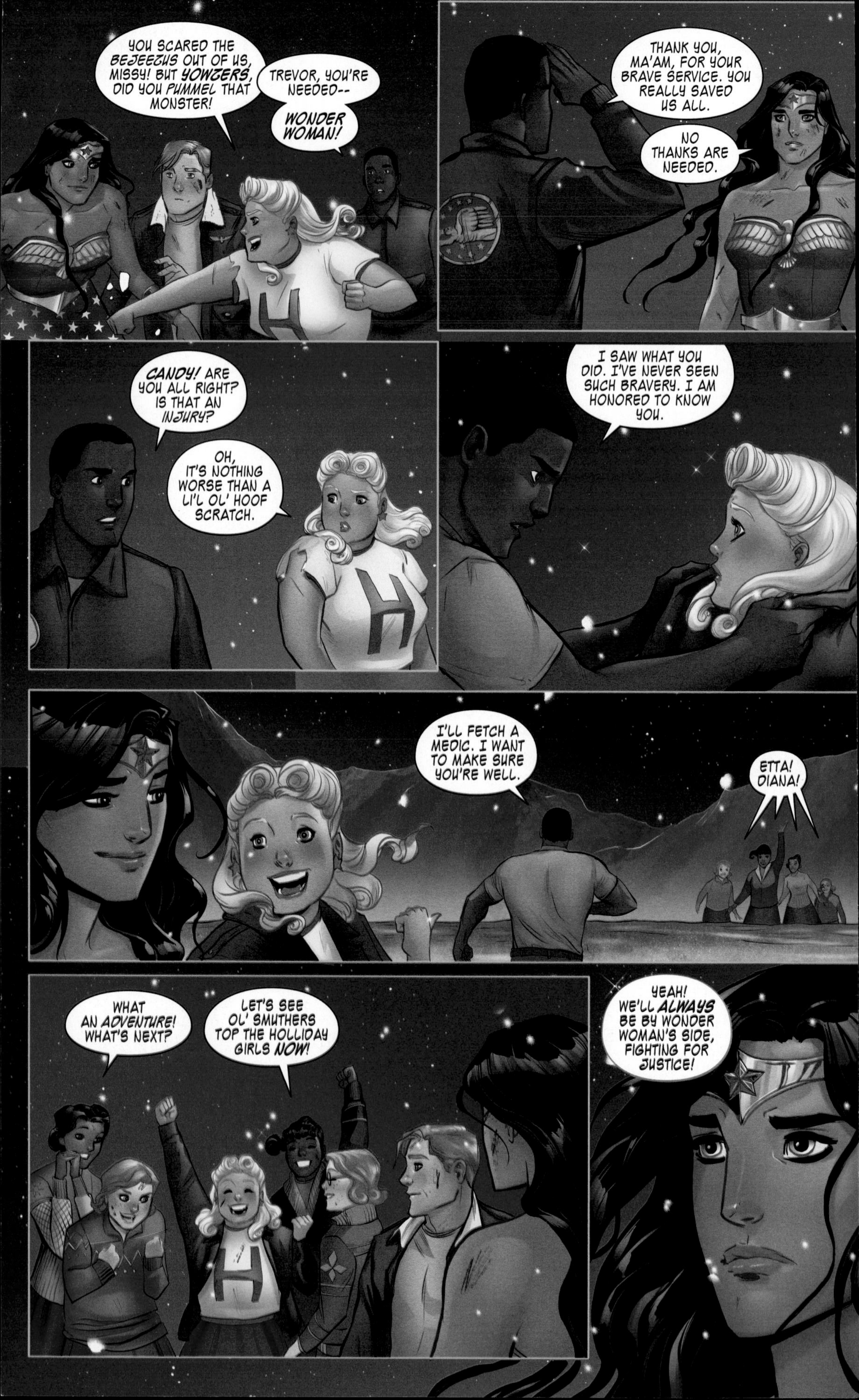
YOU SCARED THE *BEJEEZUS* OUT OF US, MISSY! BUT ***YOWZERS***, DID YOU *PUMMEL* THAT MONSTER!
TREVOR, YOU'RE NEEDED--
WONDER WOMAN!
THANK YOU, MA'AM, FOR YOUR BRAVE SERVICE. YOU REALLY SAVED US ALL.
NO THANKS ARE NEEDED.
CANDY! ARE YOU ALL RIGHT? IS THAT AN *INJURY*?
OH, IT'S NOTHING WORSE THAN A LI'L OL' HOOF SCRATCH.
I SAW WHAT YOU DID. I'VE NEVER SEEN SUCH BRAVERY. I AM HONORED TO KNOW YOU.
I'LL FETCH A MEDIC. I WANT TO MAKE SURE YOU'RE WELL.
ETTA! DIANA!
WHAT AN *ADVENTURE*! WHAT'S NEXT?
LET'S SEE OL' SMUTHERS TOP THE HOLLIDAY GIRLS ***NOW***!
YEAH! WE'LL ***ALWAYS*** BE BY WONDER WOMAN'S SIDE, FIGHTING FOR JUSTICE!

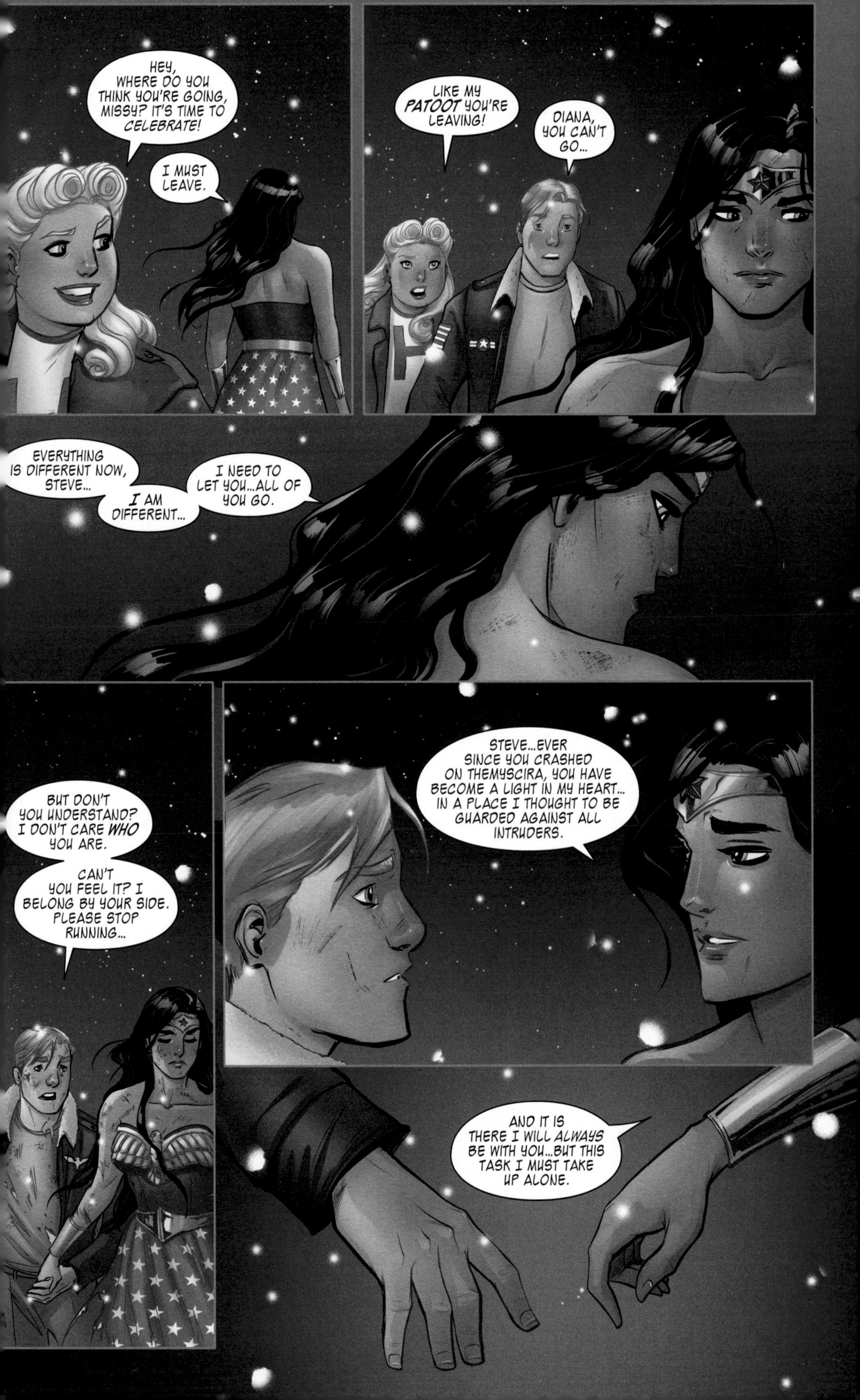
HEY, WHERE DO YOU THINK YOU'RE GOING, MISSY? IT'S TIME TO CELEBRATE!
I MUST LEAVE.
LIKE MY PATOOT YOU'RE LEAVING!
DIANA, YOU CAN'T GO...
EVERYTHING IS DIFFERENT NOW, STEVE...
I AM DIFFERENT...
I NEED TO LET YOU...ALL OF YOU GO.
BUT DON'T YOU UNDERSTAND? I DON'T CARE WHO YOU ARE.
CAN'T YOU FEEL IT? I BELONG BY YOUR SIDE. PLEASE STOP RUNNING...
STEVE...EVER SINCE YOU CRASHED ON THEMYSCIRA, YOU HAVE BECOME A LIGHT IN MY HEART... IN A PLACE I THOUGHT TO BE GUARDED AGAINST ALL INTRUDERS.
AND IT IS THERE I WILL ALWAYS BE WITH YOU...BUT THIS TASK I MUST TAKE UP ALONE.

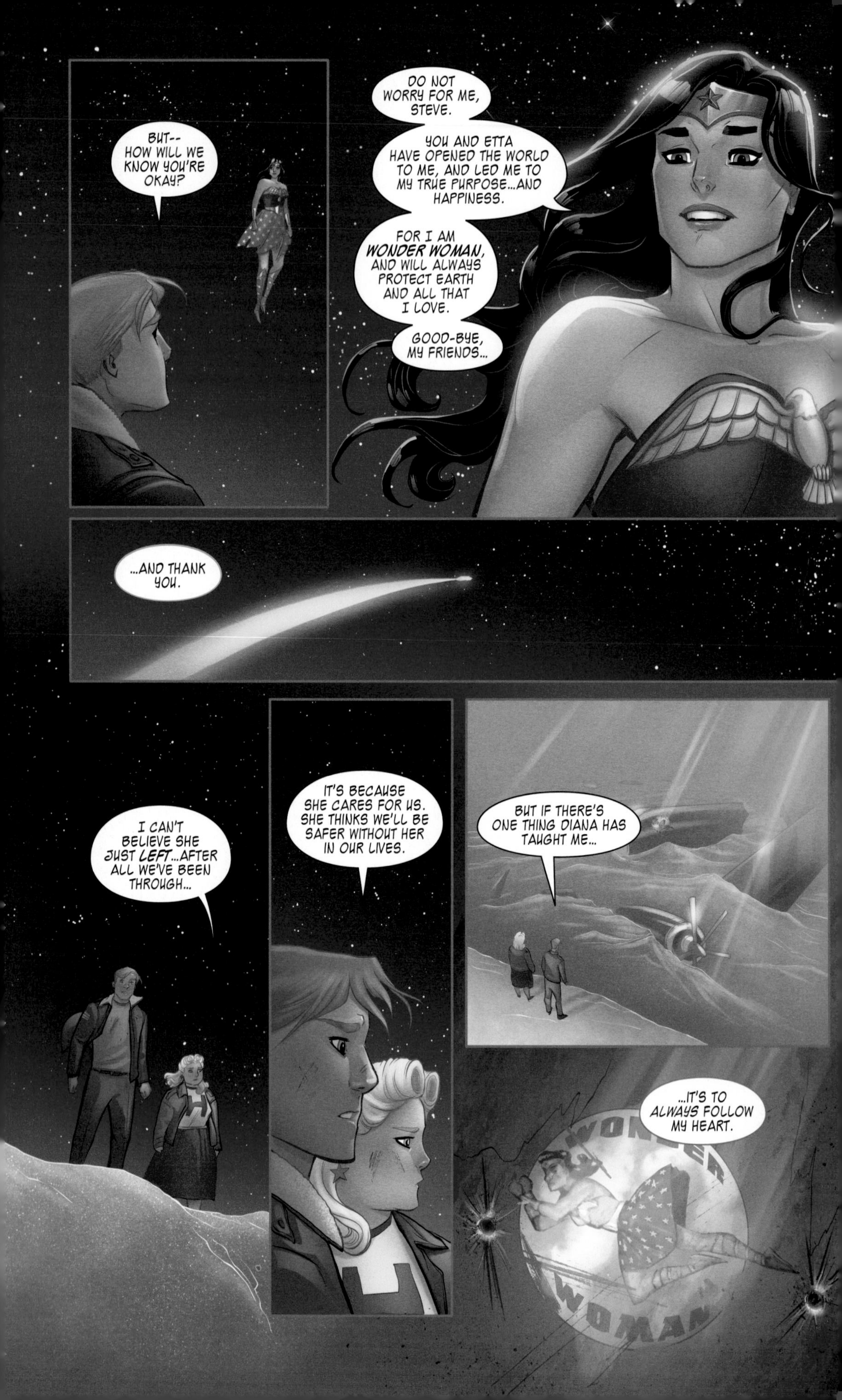
BUT-- HOW WILL WE KNOW YOU'RE OKAY?
DO NOT WORRY FOR ME, STEVE.
YOU AND ETTA HAVE OPENED THE WORLD TO ME, AND LED ME TO MY TRUE PURPOSE...AND HAPPINESS.
FOR I AM WONDER WOMAN, AND WILL ALWAYS PROTECT EARTH AND ALL THAT I LOVE.
GOOD-BYE, MY FRIENDS...
...AND THANK YOU.
I CAN'T BELIEVE SHE JUST LEFT...AFTER ALL WE'VE BEEN THROUGH...
IT'S BECAUSE SHE CARES FOR US. SHE THINKS WE'LL BE SAFER WITHOUT HER IN OUR LIVES.
BUT IF THERE'S ONE THING DIANA HAS TAUGHT ME...
...IT'S TO ALWAYS FOLLOW MY HEART.

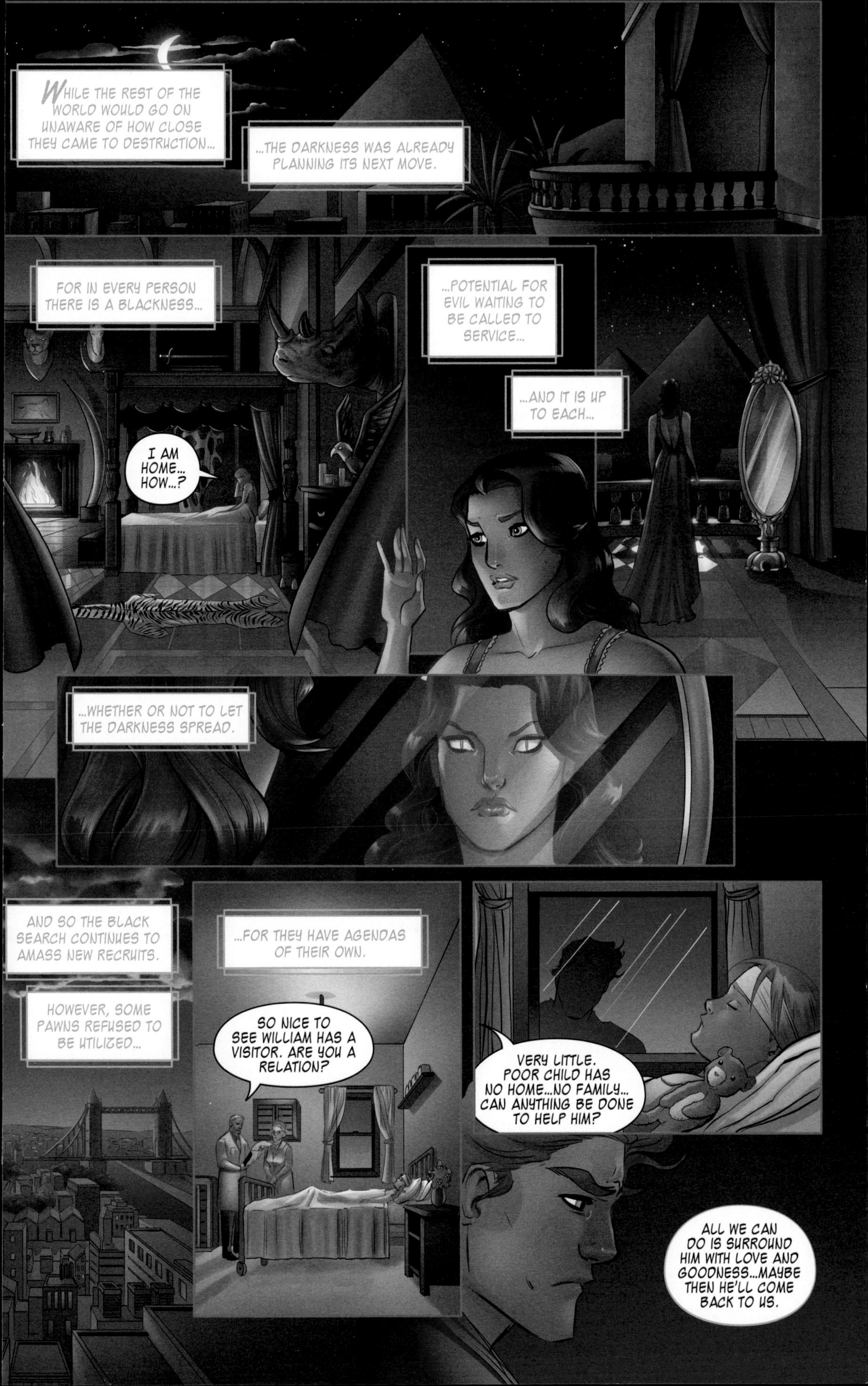
While the rest of the world would go on unaware of how close they came to destruction...
...the darkness was already planning its next move.
For in every person there is a blackness...
...potential for evil waiting to be called to service...
...and it is up to each...
I am home... how...?
...whether or not to let the darkness spread.
And so the Black Search continues to amass new recruits.
However, some pawns refused to be utilized...
...for they have agendas of their own.
So nice to see William has a visitor. Are you a relation?
Very little. Poor child has no home...no family... can anything be done to help him?
All we can do is surround him with love and goodness...maybe then he'll come back to us.

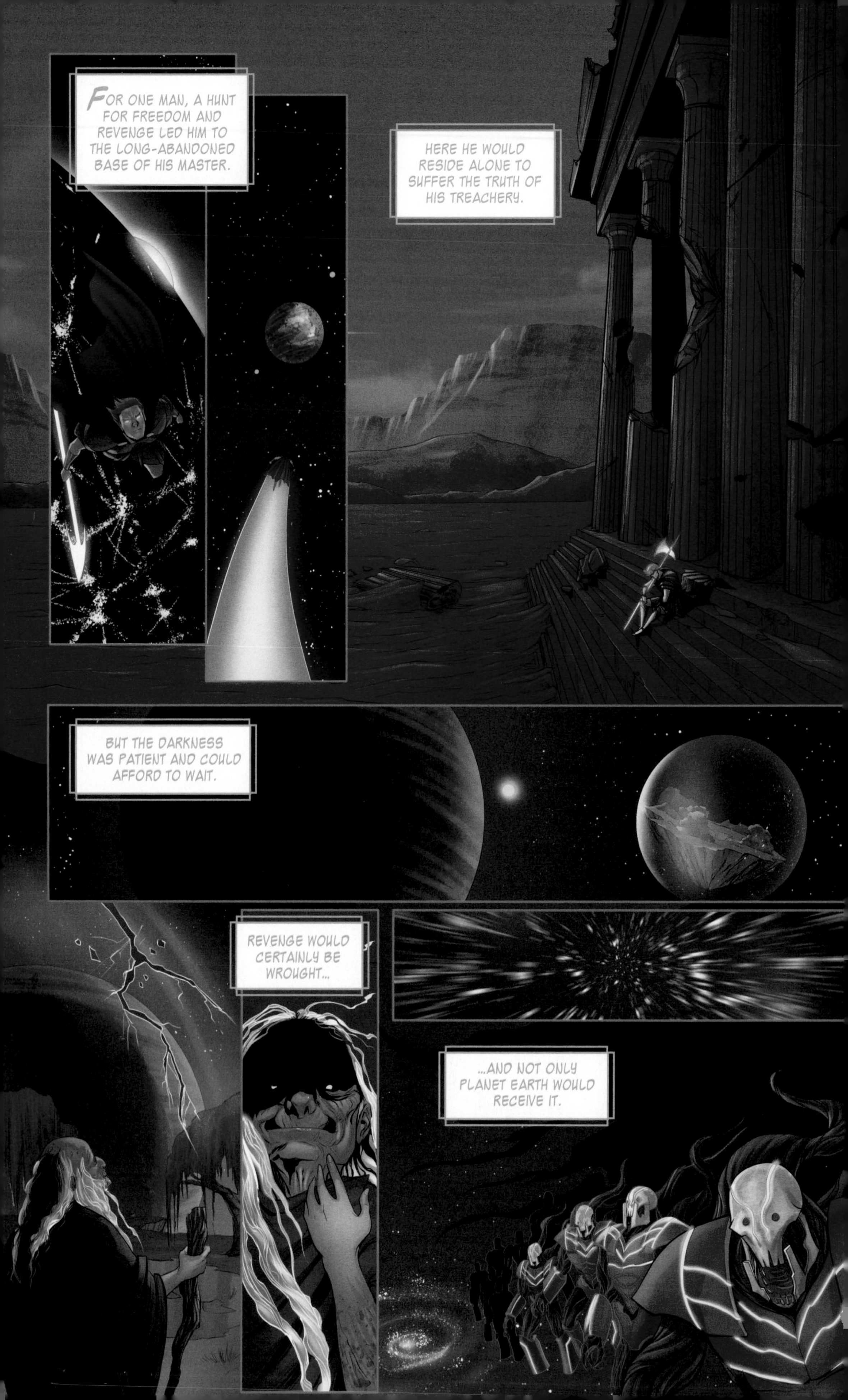
FOR ONE MAN, A HUNT FOR FREEDOM AND REVENGE LED HIM TO THE LONG-ABANDONED BASE OF HIS MASTER.
HERE HE WOULD RESIDE ALONE TO SUFFER THE TRUTH OF HIS TREACHERY.
BUT THE DARKNESS WAS PATIENT AND COULD AFFORD TO WAIT.
REVENGE WOULD CERTAINLY BE WROUGHT...
...AND NOT ONLY PLANET EARTH WOULD RECEIVE IT.

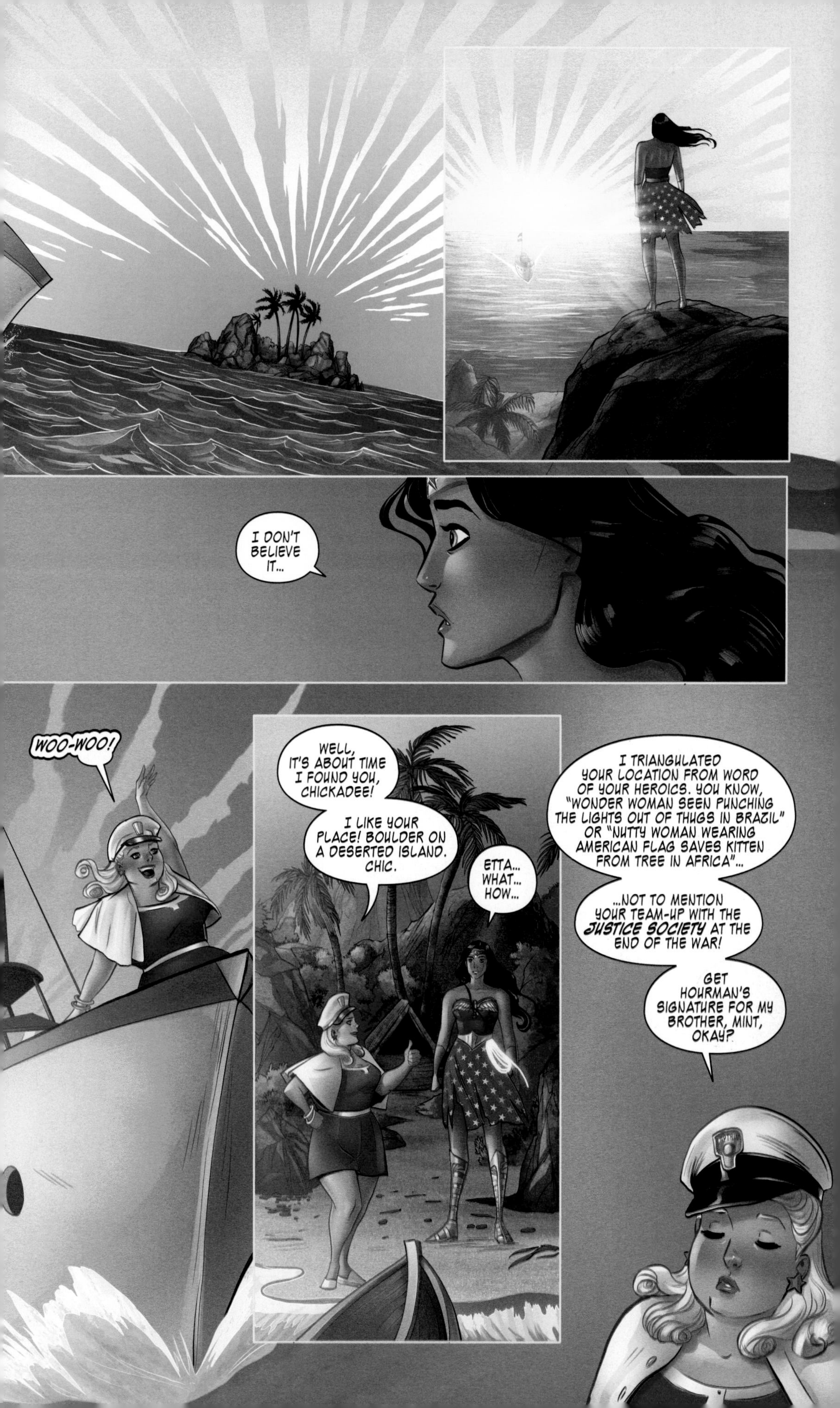

I DON'T BELIEVE IT...
WOO-WOO!
WELL, IT'S ABOUT TIME I FOUND YOU, CHICKADEE!
I LIKE YOUR PLACE! BOULDER ON A DESERTED ISLAND. CHIC.
ETTA... WHAT... HOW...
I TRIANGULATED YOUR LOCATION FROM WORD OF YOUR HEROICS. YOU KNOW, "WONDER WOMAN SEEN PUNCHING THE LIGHTS OUT OF THUGS IN BRAZIL" OR "NUTTY WOMAN WEARING AMERICAN FLAG SAVES KITTEN FROM TREE IN AFRICA"...
...NOT TO MENTION YOUR TEAM-UP WITH THE JUSTICE SOCIETY AT THE END OF THE WAR!
GET HOURMAN'S SIGNATURE FOR MY BROTHER, MINT, OKAY?

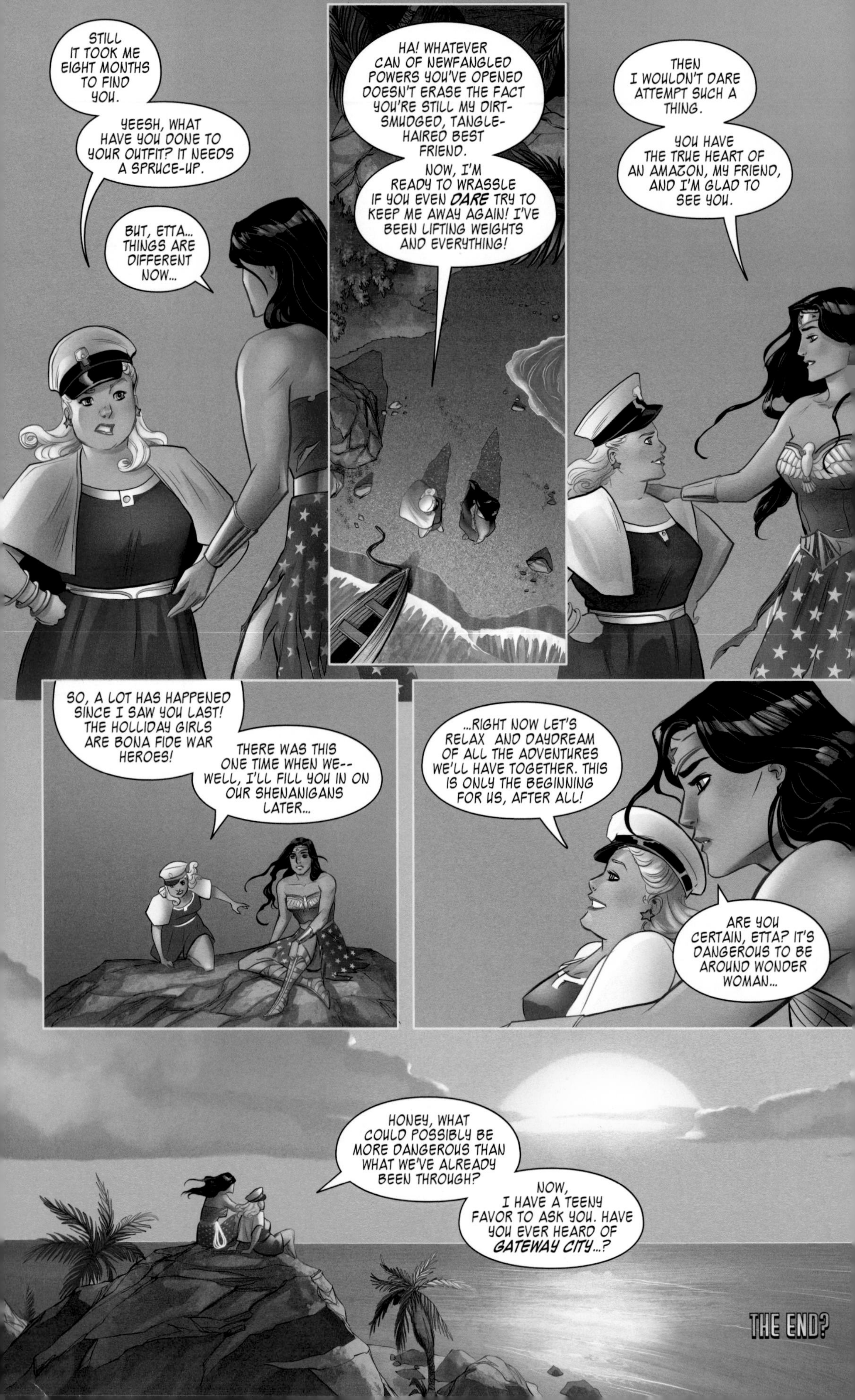
STILL IT TOOK ME EIGHT MONTHS TO FIND YOU.
YEESH, WHAT HAVE YOU DONE TO YOUR OUTFIT? IT NEEDS A SPRUCE-UP.
BUT, ETTA... THINGS ARE DIFFERENT NOW...
HA! WHATEVER CAN OF NEWFANGLED POWERS YOU'VE OPENED DOESN'T ERASE THE FACT YOU'RE STILL MY DIRT-SMUDGED, TANGLE-HAIRED BEST FRIEND.
NOW, I'M READY TO WRASSLE IF YOU EVEN DARE TRY TO KEEP ME AWAY AGAIN! I'VE BEEN LIFTING WEIGHTS AND EVERYTHING!
THEN I WOULDN'T DARE ATTEMPT SUCH A THING.
YOU HAVE THE TRUE HEART OF AN AMAZON, MY FRIEND, AND I'M GLAD TO SEE YOU.
SO, A LOT HAS HAPPENED SINCE I SAW YOU LAST! THE HOLLIDAY GIRLS ARE BONA FIDE WAR HEROES!
THERE WAS THIS ONE TIME WHEN WE-- WELL, I'LL FILL YOU IN ON OUR SHENANIGANS LATER...
...RIGHT NOW LET'S RELAX AND DAYDREAM OF ALL THE ADVENTURES WE'LL HAVE TOGETHER. THIS IS ONLY THE BEGINNING FOR US, AFTER ALL!
ARE YOU CERTAIN, ETTA? IT'S DANGEROUS TO BE AROUND WONDER WOMAN...
HONEY, WHAT COULD POSSIBLY BE MORE DANGEROUS THAN WHAT WE'VE ALREADY BEEN THROUGH?
NOW, I HAVE A TEENY FAVOR TO ASK YOU. HAVE YOU EVER HEARD OF GATEWAY CITY...?
THE END?

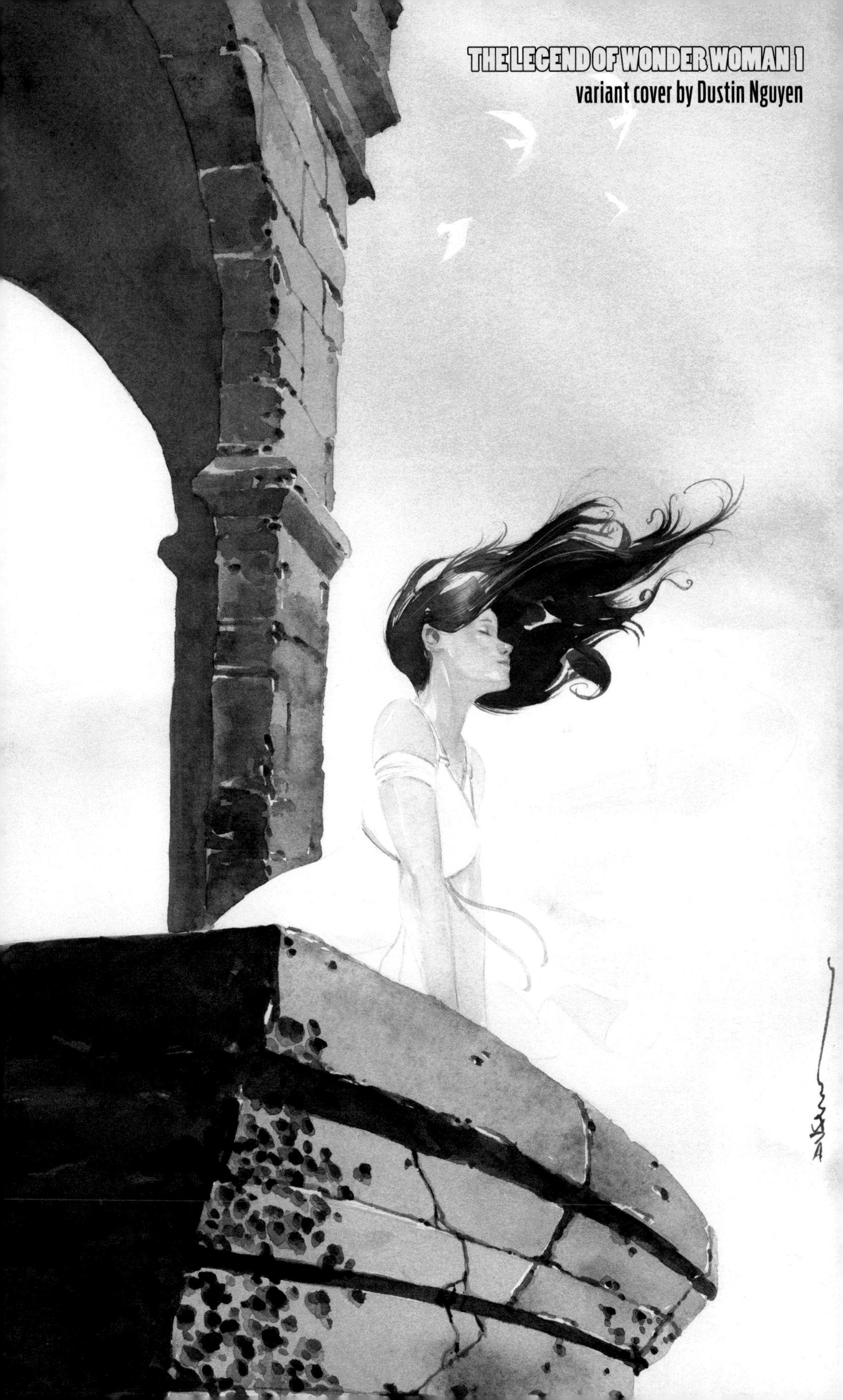

THE LEGEND OF WONDER WOMAN 1
variant cover by Dustin Nguyen

WONDER ★ WOMAN ORIGINS
by RENAE DE LIZ

WONDER WOMAN: ORIGINS

12-issue Series by **Renae De Liz**
(*Womanthology, Peter Pan, The Last Unicorn*)

ACT ONE
CHILD OF THE AMAZON

Through the story of the Immortal Life of Hippolyta, Queen of the Amazons, and her desperate plight to have a child, we discover the Island of Themyscira, the last refuge of mythological creatures and Greek Gods. The Gods finally give her the gift of a baby girl made from clay.

We follow young Princess Diana as she explores the island for adventure, but stumbles upon murderous plots orchestrated by Ares and Hades. Circumstances prevent her from telling her mother, so she ignores her wanderlust to be the best heir to her mother's throne.

As Diana reaches womanhood, she witnesses a mysterious fireball crashing into the island and a man in burned rags in the fiery crater who she then hides to keep him safe. His arrival sets off a chain of events that leads to him and Diana leaving the island forever.

At sea, a supernatural storm created by Ares' sect of Amazons engulfs them, and only with the help of Poseidon does she survive. Lost and alone in the dark, Diana floats towards the lights of the Boston Harbor of 1942.

ACT TWO
THE WORLD WAR

A kind fisherman and his wife pull unconscious Diana to shore and nurse her back to health. Before she departs she is given an American flag that belonged to their son who died in the war. She then takes to the woods surrounding Boston, observing this new land when she crosses paths with a brash, outgoing college girl named Etta Candy, who helps her understand the way of this world and gives her a place to stay in the city at the campus of Holiday College.

Here she learns of the world war going on overseas and is devastated by the scale of suffering. She hears wives' tales of Nazis who can raise the dead and a three-headed monster that kills from the shadows. Diana recognizes the work of Ares and Hades and decides to head to the front lines.

Etta suggests joining the army and accompanies Diana to a recruitment facility, where she is shocked to discover women, considered the weaker sex, are not allowed to be soldiers. She runs into the man who crashed on the island. He has no memory of his time there, but does have a sense of her. Etta recognizes him as Steve Trevor, "The Miracle Soldier," a pilot who went missing during the war, but was found months later on the East Coast shore. He helps Diana and Etta join WASP, a new women's Air Force group.

WONDER WOMAN: ORIGINS
ACT 1: CHILD OF THE AMAZON

WONDER WOMAN: ORIGINS
ACT 2: THE WORLD WAR

Stationed overseas and being trained as pilots, Steve, Etta, and Diana become close. Steve silently falls in love. Diana is not satisfied to sit by him and train. She dons a uniform (made from the flag she was given by the fisherman and his wife to honor their deceased son) and with the magical items her mother, Hippolyta, had given her, she moonlights as "The Wonder Woman," a name given to her by admirers.

She comes face-to-face with a Nazi General, a disciple of Ares and Hades, who was given powers to aid in his plan to create a war so bloody that it will awaken an ancient Titan to destroy the planet. Diana is not strong enough to stop this, but being half immortal, half human, she is given a choice from the Gods either to embrace their power and fight the evil of the war or to live a mortal life filled with human happiness.

She loves the human side of her life and doesn't want to give that up, but can't let those things be destroyed. Conflicted, she runs away...

ACT THREE
THE TITAN

Diana has fled to a secluded island to think. From the shore she sees the explosions of war and makes her decision: she will no longer be Wonder Woman. She will become mortal and fight the war as only a soldier. She tells the Gods they should be responsible for their own mess. She returns to Boston to an ecstatic Etta and finally gives Steve a hopeful smile, which he happily returns.

A critical battle is coming, one that will decide the final tide of the war. Steve, Etta, and Diana are assigned to fly into battle and hold back enemy bombers. Victory is in their sight...until the Disciple General arrives, unleashing mythical monsters and devouring the Allied Forces on ground and in air. Diana watches as Steve's plane is hit and a creature swiftly descends on her own. Her aircraft explodes and she falls to Earth watching as Steve's and Etta's planes plummet, too. Diana begs the Gods for help.

A burst of light brings forth a ghostly image of Pegasus, her childhood friend from Themyscira. It merges with her battered plane and scoops her up as it turns invisible. She's able to help Steve land but discovers that the Disciple's plan worked and the Titan has been awakened.

Diana flies towards the monster but is still not powerful enough. Confronted by the disciple, Diana battles him as Wonder Woman. Nearly beaten, she calls upon the Gods again, this time accepting her fate and her destined godly powers. She quickly overcomes the evil Disciple and moves on to battle the rampaging Titan. Her powers grow and she defeats it. The war is won and Diana stands victorious and alone. She can no longer live the life of a human.

The Gods surround her to congratulate her, but also to let her know the real battle is coming. They inform her that the resurrected Titan was actually one of the many Signal Men hidden inside planets a millennia ago by a horrible intergalactic force in search of a certain planet that holds the key to keeping the universe together...or the key to destroy it.

The Gods tell Diana she must forever protect the Earth and its people, for someday "The One" who will become the key will be discovered. Now that the Gods are weakened, they rely on Wonder Woman.

Diana faces Steve and Etta in a tearful good-bye. The power unleashed by the Gods will also erase their memories. She flies off into her new life as Protector of the Planet.

WONDER WOMAN: ORIGINS
ACT 3: THE TITAN

COVER SKETCHES

by RENAE DE LIZ

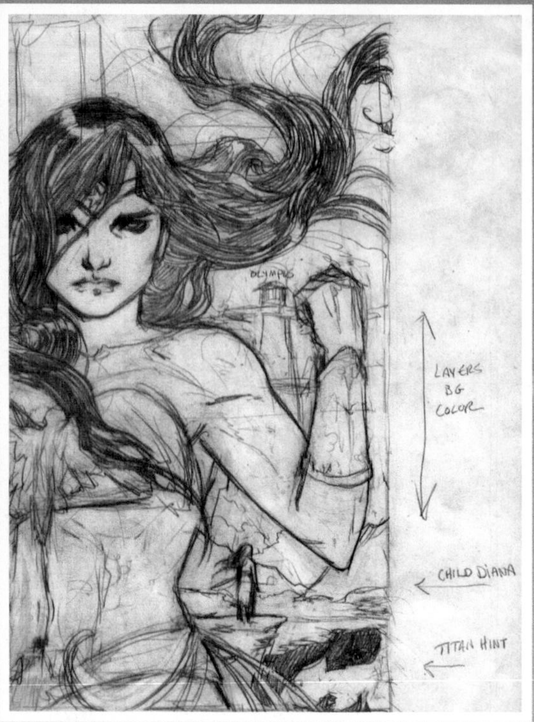

OLYMPUS
LAYERS BG COLOR
CHILD DIANA
TITAN HINT

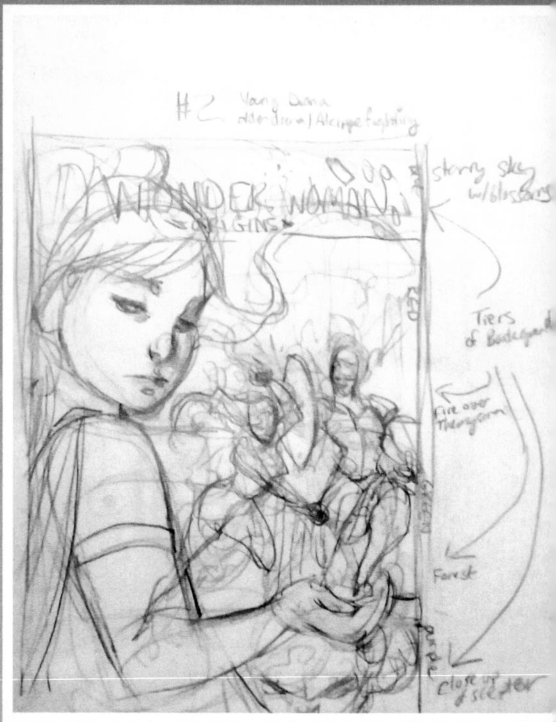

#2 Young Diana
WONDER WOMAN
ORIGINS
Tiers of Bodyguard
Forest

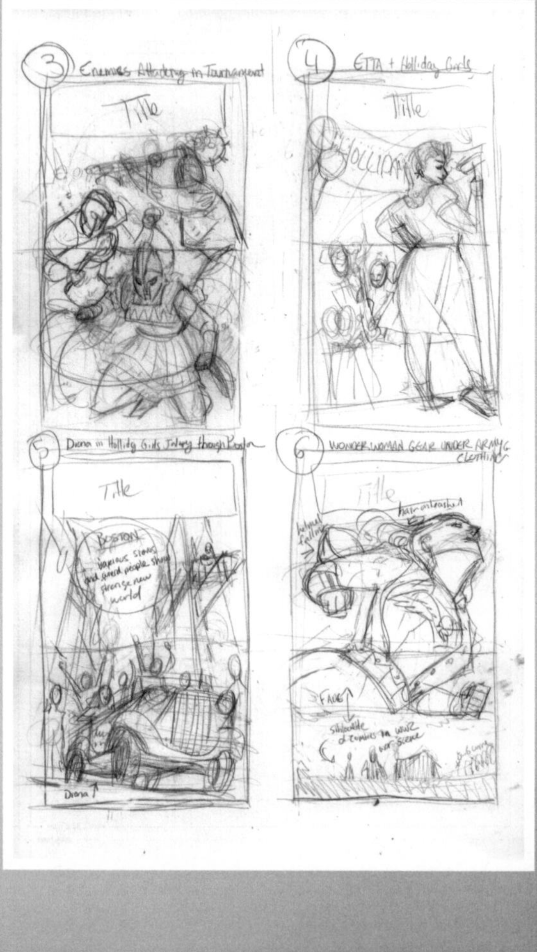

3 Enemies Attacking in Tournament
Title
4 ETTA + Holliday Girls
Title
5 Diana in Holliday Girls Jalopy through Boston
Title
BOSTON
Diana
6 WONDER WOMAN GEAR UNDER ARMY CLOTHING
Title

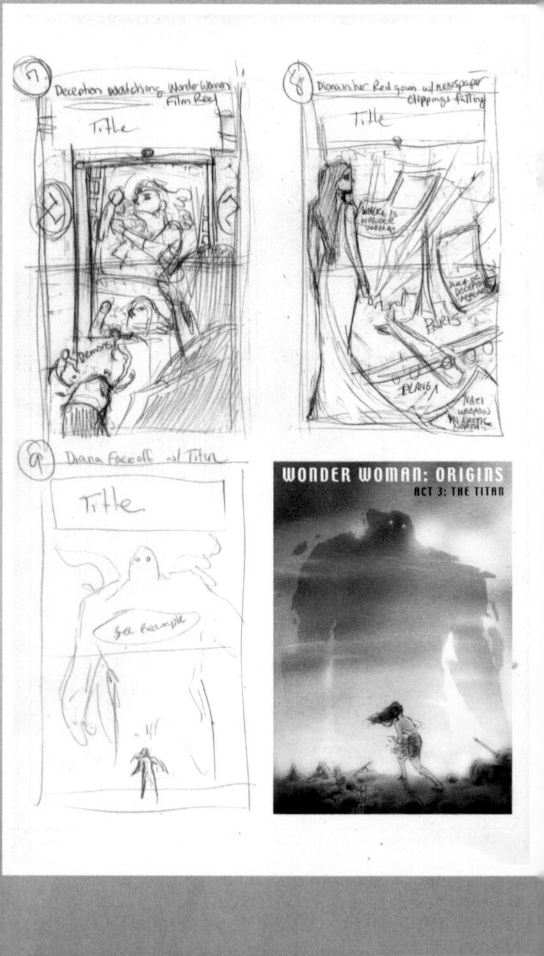

7 Deception watching Wonder Woman Film Reel
Title
8 Diana in her Red gown w/ newspaper clippings falling
Title
WHERE IS WONDER WOMAN
PARIS
9 Diana Faceoff w/ Titan
Title
See Example
WONDER WOMAN: ORIGINS
ACT 3: THE TITAN